Macroeconomics

# Reviews

'Carlin and Soskice have produced a gem of a book. The teaching of macroeconomics after the crisis has changed surprisingly little, limiting itself to incorporating 'frictions' into otherwise standard models that failed during the crisis. The authors embark on a much more ambitious venture. They show how the financial cycle and macroeconomics are inextricably linked, with the risk-taking channel as the linchpin. Their exposition is refreshingly original and yet lucid and accessible. This book will appeal to serious students of economics and to all inquiring minds who have wondered about the role of the financial cycle in macroeconomics.'

– Hyun Song Shin, Economic Adviser and Head of Research, Bank for International Settlements and Hughes-Rogers Professor of Economics, Princeton University

'This is, I believe, the first macroeconomic textbook effectively to incorporate the lessons of the Great Financial Crisis and to describe how financial frictions can impact the macro-economy. The authors weave together the old mainstream, three-equation, model with the newer account of potential financial disturbances in a lucid and efficient manner. As such, it has a major advantage over almost all other extant textbooks, and will be a boon not only for undergraduates, but also for graduates and those wishing to understand the current working of our macroeconomic system, beset as it has been with financial strains.'

– Professor Charles Goodhart, Director of the Financial Regulation Research Programme, The London School of Economics and Political Science

'This illuminating book introduces the reader to macroeconomics in a revolutionary fashion. Namely, by means of very elegant and accessible models based on sound micro foundations and developed against a narrative of the performance and policy regimes of the advanced economies over the post-war period. Unlike most other macro textbooks, this book builds on the most recent research and debates to teach macroeconomics the way it should now be taught: by emphasizing the interplay between macro and finance; by linking growth to innovation, market structure and firm dynamics; and more generally by taking institutions seriously into account when looking at growth, business cycles, and unemployment and the interplay between them. This book is an absolute must-read for students and policy makers, even those with little initial background, who need to be fully acquainted with modern macroeconomics.'

– Philippe Aghion, Robert C. Waggoner Professor of Economics, Harvard

'This is an exciting new textbook. It offers a clear and cogent framework for understanding not only the traditional macroeconomic issues of business cycles, inflation and growth, but also the financial crisis and ensuing Great Recession that have recently shaken the world economy. The paradigm it offers is highly accessible to undergraduates. Yet at the same time it is consistent with what goes on at the frontiers of the field. Overall, the book confirms my belief that macroeconomics is alive and well!'

> – Mark Gertler, Henry and Lucy Moses Professor of Economics, New York University

'To be relevant, economics need to help society understand those phenomena which do it greatest harm—unemployment, inflation and deflation, financial instability, fiscal and banking crisis. Pre-crisis, mainstream economic models failed that societal test and therefore failed society. Wendy Carlin and David Soskice's important new book is the first step towards redemption, providing students and scholars with a rigorous but accessible framework for understanding what troubles society most.'

> – Andrew G Haldane, Chief Economist, Bank of England

'The Carlin and Soskice book does a wonderful job of covering the economics behind macroeconomics and the financial system, alongside presenting the latest research on this and the drivers of the great recession. It also has an impressive array of data and examples woven in with theory explained in a beautifully intuitive way. For any student interested in a refreshingly modern take on the financial crisis and the economics that underlie this, this book is invaluable.'

> – Nicholas Bloom, Professor of Economics, Stanford University

'One of the first macro textbooks to integrate the lessons of the crisis. An elegant bridge between introductory undergraduate and graduate macro texts.'

> – Olivier Blanchard, Chief Economist, IMF, and Professor of Economics, MIT

'In the light of the events of the past decade, it is important that a new macroeconomics text attempts to satisfy the demands of those learning and using macroeconomics to be able to access relatively simple models which reflect the ways in which the financial sector interacts with the real economy. This is by no means an easy task. The new Carlin and Soskice book represents a significant step forward in this regard. Consequently undergraduates, postgraduates and their teachers should be grateful that they can now access teaching materials which have something useful to say about the financial crisis.'

> – Professor Stephen Nickell, CBE, FBA. Honorary Fellow of Nuffield College, Oxford

# Macroeconomics

## Institutions, Instability, and the Financial System

Wendy Carlin

David Soskice

OXFORD

UNIVERSITY PRESS

# OXFORD
## UNIVERSITY PRESS

Great Clarendon Street, Oxford, OX2 6DP,
United Kingdom

Oxford University press is a department of the University of Oxford.
It furthers the University's objective of excellence in research, scholarship,
and education by publishing worldwide. Oxford is a registered trade mark of
Oxford University Press in the UK and in certain other countries

© Wendy Carlin and David Soskice 2015

The moral rights of the authors have been asserted

Impression: 3

Published in the United States of America by Oxford University Press
198 Madison Avenue, New York, NY 10016, United States of America

British Library Cataloguing in Publication Data

Data available

Library of Congress Control Number: 2014953103

ISBN 978-0-19-965579-3

Printed in Italy by L.E.G.O. S.p.A.

*For Niki, and in memory of Andrew*

The chart shows the dramatic events of the past decade and a half in the global economy. Following the Asian crisis in 1998, the emerging market and developing economies grew strongly and became large enough to drive global growth in the 2000s. The financial crisis in the advanced economies plunged the world economy into recession. The Eurozone crisis has depressed global growth from 2010.

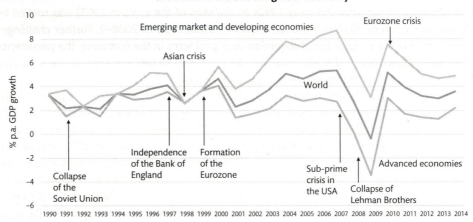

**Growth and crisis in the global economy**

Source: International Monetary Fund, World Economic Outlook Database, April 2014
Series: Gross domestic product, constant prices, percent per annum growth rate

Cover image: Paul Klee, *betroffener Ort* (translated as *Affected Place*), 1922.

# Preface

This is two books in one. It is first a textbook and second the result of our on-going research into building small scale but realistic and comprehensible models of the macro-economy. On both counts it is a response to the challenges facing students, teachers and many pro-fessional economists since the calm of the Great Moderation (the period of low inflation and unemployment from the early 1990s to the start of the crisis in 2007) was rocked by the credit crunch of 2007 and the full-blown financial crisis of 2008–9. Further challenges have followed: the emergence of sovereign debt problems in the Eurozone, the persistence of global imbalances in the aftermath of the crisis and longer term problems regarding sustainable growth in emerging and advanced economies.

Stephen Nickell wrote about our previous book published in 2006 that it 'is based on the mainstream monetary macro model which is now widely used by both academics and policy makers. In a straightforward manner, it shows how this model can be used to address an enormous variety of practical questions without heavy use of mathematical technique. This is modern macroeconomics for undergraduates, post-graduates and business economists alike'. Today there is less of a consensus around a satisfactory 'mainstream model'. During the Great Moderation period of relatively stable growth and low inflation, shocks never pushed economies too far from an equilibrium defined as a zero output gap with inflation at the central bank's target. As a result, what later became serious problems did not arise in the Great Moderation: for instance, sharp rises in the share of debt-constrained households in the economy, 'abnormal' cuts in lending by commercial banks, the freezing up of the inter-bank market or the inability of central banks to set their desired interest rates. As long as the financial system provided continuity of core banking services, there had been an unspoken agreement that there was no need for it to be part of the macro model, and it was not.

Our goal here is to integrate the financial system with the macroeconomic model. In doing this we take account of the gaps in the mainstream model exposed by the financial crisis and the Eurozone crisis. We hope to supply readers with a simple but realistic model which they can use both to analyse the state of the economy and to think systematically about responding to its problems. We integrate the modelling with the presentation of descriptive data, evidence about the empirical testing of the important relationships among variables, and institutional arrangements.

## What this book offers to undergraduates studying economics

It is likely you were attracted to study economics because you wanted to know more about why the world was plunged into a financial crisis and how the policies adopted by central banks and finance ministries in response might work. We aim to equip you with a framework for understanding macroeconomics and the financial system that you will feel comfortable using to explain to your friends what is going on in the global economy.

Just as when studying labour economics, you expect to be able to participate in debates about the minimum wage and the effects of migration, and in industrial economics, about the effects of competition policy and of incentives to boost R&D, so too in macroeconomics you should be able to discuss important real world problems. Some of the questions for which we will provide the tools to address are the following: the role of the global banking system in the upswing to the financial crisis; how a period of economic stability and confidence in macroeconomic management could sow the seeds of a crisis of a scale not seen since the Great Depression; the merits and failings of austerity policies in the Eurozone and the prospects for recovery; why the oil price hike in the mid 2000s did not result in stagflation or high unemployment as had the oil shocks of the 1970s; the consequences for the real exchange rate of the discovery of new natural gas deposits; whether fiscal policy should be delegated to a 'fiscal policy council'; the options for macroeconomic policy in an independent Scotland or Catalonia; how housing bubbles can be explained and why they occur in some economies and not others.

This book gives you a systematic way of thinking through problems like these. You will learn ways of connecting the behaviour of households, firms, governments and central banks to aggregate economic outcomes. We look at how households try to even out fluctuations in their income so that their consumption is fairly stable, but also why they may fail to do this, especially following financial crises when they are debt-constrained. Whereas household behaviour tends to smooth out fluctuations in the economy, the investment decisions of firms are lumpy. We look at how firms set wages and prices, how banks set the lending rate and how the need to maintain the continuity of banking services affects bank risk-taking. Institutions matter to macroeconomic performance and we shall see, for example, that union behaviour or whether households can re-mortgage their house when house prices rise help explain differences across countries in economic outcomes.

In many jobs you may get, whether working in finance or in think tanks, or in management or consultancies, or for governments or central banks, you need to be able to interpret national and international economic trends and policy debates. The confidence to do so comes from learning about how the different actors in the economy behave and how they interact. What are they trying to achieve and what limits their ability to put their intentions into practice? The macroeconomic environment is always changing and we need to be prepared for surprises. Knowing about previous periods of growth, stability and crisis is very helpful in preparing for shocks that might come. It has frequently been said that Federal Reserve President Ben Bernanke's bold response to the crisis in 2008 owed as much to his research on the Great Depression as to his knowledge of economic models. As you work through the chapters, you will build up a picture of how the world economy has evolved since the Great Depression and how economics has affected and been affected by those developments. Chapter 8 provides a longer-run perspective and shows you how to link the analysis of macroeconomic behaviour in the short- and medium-run to long-run growth.

## What this book offers graduate students, professional economists and other interested readers

Our approach is to reduce the complex, mathematically dense models used in frontier research and in central bank and fiscal forecasting exercises to a relatively simple intuitive and unified model—one that can be understood using diagrams and a small number of equations. The model incorporates realistic institutional settings in labour and product markets as well as the financial system, and analyses closed, open and global economies. It is a unified model in that the same tools are used to analyse both stability and crisis.

Long before the crisis, the economist Hyman Minsky had argued that over periods of prolonged prosperity and optimism when both data about macroeconomic volatility and the behaviour of the rating agencies signal declining risk, financial institutions invest in riskier assets. This makes the economic system more vulnerable to a crisis. Minsky's insight suggests that the very tranquillity of the economy in the Great Moderation created the seeds of the crisis by causing banks to take excessive risks. As vividly depicted in the film *The Inside Job*, many macro-economists participated in the general sense of unproblematic well-being.

Nevertheless the mainstream modern monetary framework, captured in the 3-equation model of the real economy (explained below), remains an important foundation of the unified model in this book. But now the link between the financial system and that main-stream real economy model is central to our approach. We also believe that the crisis has shown more clearly how consumer behaviour is affected—and therefore modelled—when the economy is operating with high unemployment and where households have high levels of debt. In addition, we pay more attention to real and financial interactions among global economies than was customary in pre-crisis models, reflecting the importance of global and Eurozone imbalances. It is probably fair to say that in none of these developments is there clear consensus of the kind that had previously characterized the modern monetary framework.

### The modern monetary framework: the 3-equation model

The workhorse model for macroeconomic modelling of economies with an inflation targeting central bank is the 3-equation model. It is often referred to as New Keynesian, the 'Keynesian' drawing attention to the fact that it allows for 'prolonged departures of economic activity from its optimal level as a consequence of instability in aggregate spending' (Woodford, 1999).

The three equations are the IS, which models aggregate demand, the PC, which reflects wage and price-setting behaviour in the economy, and the MR, which represents the best-response behaviour of the inflation-targeting central bank.[1] In the 3-equation model business cycles are driven by shifts in aggregate demand and supply (in contrast to the Real Business Cycle model set out in Chapter 16 where supply side shocks are the drivers of cycles). Output and employment are affected by fluctuations in aggregate demand because of structural features of the economy, often referred to as nominal rigidities, which prevent wages and prices from adjusting rapidly. The central bank is modelled as adjusting interest rates in response to shocks to the economy so as to achieve its inflation target. Aggregate demand fluctuations shift the economy away from the equilibrium rate of unemployment at which inflation is constant. The equilibrium rate of unemployment is the outcome of wage- and price-setting behaviour. Even in the absence of imperfect competition in the labour market, there is involuntary unemployment at equilibrium because employment contracts are incomplete. At the wage chosen by the firm, there are workers who would be willing to

[1] For readers who would like to see the 3–equation model presented in contrast to the old workhorse models of IS/LM and Mundell-Fleming, we refer you to our book published in 2006.

take a job but who are unemployed. Demand shocks shift output and employment away from the equilibrium, and inflation rises when the labour market tightens and falls when it slackens. Supply shocks shift the equilibrium rate of unemployment while institutional and policy differences across countries imply different national rates of unemployment.

The zero lower bound, as well as a deflation trap, can be modelled within the common framework. The best-response function of the policy maker establishes the output gap that will get the economy onto a path back to its constant inflation equilibrium. When interest rate based monetary policy is inoperative, because of the zero lower bound, the best response function is reinterpreted in terms of the stance of discretionary fiscal policy and the extent to which unconventional monetary policy such as quantitative easing can have a direct effect on the lending rate, inflation expectations and asset prices.

### Macroeconomics and the financial system

The widespread adoption of the mainstream monetary macro model of inflation-targeting reflected the tendency in economics teaching and research to separate macroeconomics from finance. The first step to redress this is by integrating a model of the banking system with the 3-equation model, showing how the margin of the lending rate over the policy rate is set in the commercial banking sector, how money is created in a modern banking system and how the central bank can take account of the working of the banking system in order to achieve its desired policy outcome. The basic set-up is one in which money is credit; the money supply is endogenous and the real lending rate is controlled by the central bank through its interest rate policy. Shocks to the banking system can cause macroeconomic shocks unless the central bank makes the appropriate adjustments to the policy rate.

The second step is to highlight characteristics of the financial system that can create vulnerability to a financial crisis, with implications for fiscal balance. This is ignored in the 3-equation macro model. The economy depends on the continuity of core banking services and governments cannot afford to let them fail. This means that systemically important banks do not bear the full cost of their lending decisions. They will have an incentive to take on excessive risk. Schemes of deposit insurance guard against panic-based bank runs but reduce the incentive for small depositors to monitor the risk-taking strategies of banks, even though these strategies can threaten their solvency. In principle banking regulation can impose higher private capital cushions on banks to create a better alignment of private and social costs but the crisis revealed the weakness of pre-existing arrangements.

In the third step, we set out a simple model of the behaviour of highly-leveraged financial institutions as the basis for the development of a leverage or financial cycle in the economy. There is no widely agreed model of this. We use recent research by Shin (2009) and Geanakoplos (2010) as the basis of a model suitable for undergraduate level and for other non-specialist readers. The model explains how risky loans made by retail banks can be transformed into marketable securities by investment banks. By connecting this to Minsky's insight that a period of prolonged macro-economic calm can incubate a crisis, we have the tools to analyse how a leverage cycle can take hold in the economy. The modelling of a financial crisis and the consequences for policy makers of a subsequent balance sheet recession is also set out within the same framework (reflecting the approach of Eggertsson and Krugman, 2012).

**Open economy**

*The extended 3-equation model*

In this new book, we extend the 3-equation model to deal with policy making in the open economy. We show how arbitrage in the forward-looking foreign exchange market interacts with the way that the central bank forecasts the effects of shocks. The interaction between these two forward-looking agents in the economy also determines the mix of exchange rate and interest rate adjustment to shocks.[2]

*Global imbalances*

Although global imbalances were steadily building up during the 2000s, they were not seen as a cause for concern. Inflation targeting was the focus of policy makers' attention and its success in the presence of growing international imbalances in current accounts and real exchange rates prompted the development of models accounting for imbalances as equilibrium phenomena. But once the crisis started it became very apparent that we needed a clearer analysis of the interrelation of open economies in which growing imbalances could signal unsustainable combinations of growth strategies across the world's major economies. We set out a simple 2-bloc version of the 3-equation model to show how the pursuit of different growth strategies in each bloc is nevertheless consistent with the achievement of the inflation targets of the central banks in each bloc.

*Eurozone*

Imbalances among Eurozone economies had also been largely ignored as a source of concern for policy makers. This reflected the presumption in open economy New Keynesian macroeconomic models that real exchange rates would respond in a stabilizing way to the creation of a common currency area. Little attention had been paid either to the current account and associated real exchange rate imbalances in the Eurozone or to the fragile governance structure of the Eurozone itself. All of this came into sharp focus in the Eurozone crisis of 2010.

The case of a common currency area is handled within the core model. Monetary policy making by the ECB at the level of the Eurozone can be understood using the open economy 3-equation model to explain how the Eurozone economy was able to keep close to its inflation target in the first decade of operation. The core model is extended to explore the behaviour of member countries of the Eurozone. It is used to highlight how an attitude of benign neglect by national policy makers towards stabilization policy in their own country contributed to the origins of the sovereign debt crisis of 2010.

**Growth and innovation**

The analysis of long run growth is placed in historical perspective by presenting data from the year 1000 for GDP per capita in several European countries as well as Japan, China and India. This draws attention to the relatively recent experience of steadily rising living standards. We highlight the interconnection of great changes in technology with the emergence of

---

[2] For an initial presentation of this, see Carlin and Soskice, 2010.

capitalism as the dominant economic system in Europe in the 19th century, which marks the beginning of the transformation of the way of life of humans across the globe.

The modelling focuses on capital accumulation and innovation as the proximate sources of growth. The Solow model provides a workhorse to explain the concept of a balanced growth path and to analyse the role of capital accumulation in long run growth. To understand the central role of technological progress in economic performance over the last 250 years, we focus on the dynamism of the capitalist economy and the role of Schumpeterian (or innovation) rents. The Aghion and Howitt model of Schumpeterian growth is used to explain the role of competition in growth and to look at the relationship between fluctuations and growth.

### Understanding microeconomics

*Consumption behaviour: credit-constrained households and balance sheet effects*

In a stable world, the permanent income hypothesis and associated Euler equation appear to be reasonable ways of modelling consumption. Faced with the major disruption of the crisis and recession that followed, however, the importance of credit constraints and of balance sheet effects on the behaviour of indebted households came to the fore. The need for a richer model of consumption following the crisis also made clear the neglect by many economists of financial accelerator effects, which had operated in the household sector in the years of upswing of the financial cycle. In economies where it is possible for households to withdraw equity from their house, house price booms led to a relaxation of credit constraints, prompting households to spend more on housing and on the purchase of other goods and services.

*Imperfect competition and output determination*

In the book we assume that firms operate in imperfectly competitive product markets. This explains why their incentive to change prices immediately in response to demand shocks is limited. The combination of sluggish price adjustment with a sizeable responsiveness of consumption to changes in current income produces demand-driven fluctuations. The multiplier is therefore a useful tool in understanding business cycles.

*Inertial inflation expectations*

In the modelling of inflation in the New Keynesian DSGE (Dynamic Stochastic General Equilibrium) models, which are routinely used in macroeconomic research, wage and price setters use rational expectations to calculate, in a forward-looking way, the expected inflation rate. In the presence of price stickiness, the result is that inflation, like the exchange rate is a jump variable that responds to forecasts of future output gaps. Estimated NK DSGE models used in policy making then include a variety of ad hoc elements to produce sufficient persistence in inflation and output to match the persistence found in the data of actual economies. In the core modelling of this book, we include the persistence of inflation explicitly in the Phillips curve by including lagged inflation. We draw the attention of students to the institutional sources of the differences in the way wages, prices and exchange rates (along with the prices of financial assets) behave. We assume, realistically, that wage setting takes place periodically. In the baseline model, wage setters update their inflation expectations based on past inflation and firms update their prices following the wage round. We show how expectations that are more firmly anchored to the central bank's inflation target reduce the costs of adjusting to shocks.

We explain the importance of the Lucas critique, which highlights problems raised by using a backward-looking Phillips curve when the economic or policy environment changes. These problems are less acute in an environment in which the motivation of policy makers is modelled explicitly as is the case in this book.

*Non-clearing labour markets: incomplete contracts, bargaining and institutions*

When an employer advertises vacancies at a particular wage or salary and hires a worker, she cannot be sure of what she will get in terms of work produced. The wage contract is by its nature incomplete and can be contrasted with a contract to buy a mobile phone, where the purchasers know exactly what they are getting. Because contracts in the labour market are incomplete, there is involuntary unemployment: in order to get the worker to work hard, the firm deliberately sets the wage above the worker's reservation wage, which means there is a cost of job loss. Involuntary unemployment is characteristic of the economy even when wages are flexible and there is no imperfect competition.

In many countries unions play an important role in wage-setting. Even when they don't, there is often bargaining between employer and prospective employee over the wage. This will result in wages being set above the level that the employer would choose. An exception is when unions behave in a coordinated way. This means they take into account the effect of the wage bargain on economy-wide inflation and hence on the response of the policy maker. The precise institutional arrangements for wage setting are important in understanding their implications for equilibrium unemployment.

*Asymmetric information in credit markets*

In credit markets, asymmetric information between lenders and borrowers means that banks will ration credit. Although households are forward-looking, some face constraints in borrowing to smooth their consumption. Other households are impatient and don't save when they could. As a result of credit constraints and impatience, demand shocks are amplified by a multiplier process.

The information asymmetry between banks and the government in turn helps explain why banks take on too much risk—they can lend 'too much'. The problem is exacerbated because of the obligation of governments to maintain the functioning of core banking services in the economy. In the event that excessive risk taking by banks results in bank failures, the government normally bails them out. Banking crises become fiscal crises. The interaction between the institutions in the housing and financial markets creates the basis for a financial accelerator that can drive the upswing of a financial cycle and create vulnerability to a financial crisis.

**Using the book in a variety of courses**

The book is designed to be used in core macroeconomics courses at intermediate and advanced undergraduate level. To increase the flexibility of the book and to make it accessible to a wider audience, non-technical overviews are provided for the main modelling chapters. The overviews encourage students to see the structure of the argument as whole before they get drawn into the details. There are appendices to many chapters in which more technical material is set out; web appendices are used where the technical presentation is lengthier.

There is a macroeconomic simulator on the book's website developed by Javier Lozano, which allows readers to conduct a range of exercises using the closed and open economy versions of the model.

Below are illustrations of the use of different combinations of chapters (chapter numbers are in parenthesis) for a variety of courses.

**Intermediate macroeconomics**

Demand side (1)
Supply side (2)
The 3-equation model and macroeconomic policy (3)
Expectations (4)
Money, banking and the macro economy (5)
The financial sector and crises (selected sections of 6)
The 3-equation model in the open economy (9)
The open economy: demand and supply sides (10)
Growth, fluctuations and innovation (8)
Selected applications from the chapters on Monetary policy (13)
Fiscal policy (14)
The global financial crisis: applying the models (7)

**Advanced macroeconomics**

Microfoundations of the demand and supply sides (1, 2, 4, 15; web appendices)
Money and the financial sector in the macro model (5, 6, 7; web appendices)
Open economy macro (9-12)
Macroeconomic policy (13-15)
Real business cycle and New Keynesian models (16)

**Macroeconomic policy**

Overview sections of Chapters 1–3, 9–11
Expectations (4)
Monetary policy (13)
Fiscal policy (14)
Supply-side policy, institutions and unemployment (15)
The Eurozone economy (12)

**Macroeconomics of money and banking**

The 3-equation model and the macro economy (3; the Overview sections of Chapters 1 and 2 as preparatory reading)
Expectations (4)
Monetary policy (13)
Money, banking and the macro-economy (5)
The financial sector and crises (6)

The global financial crisis: applying the models (7)
Banking and macro-prudential regulation (13, Section 13.6)

### Labour economics: macro

Overview section of Chapter 1
The supply side (2)
The 3-equation model and the macro economy (3)
Supply-side policy, institutions and unemployment (15)

### International monetary economics

Overview sections of Chapters 1 and 2
The 3-equation model and the macro economy (3)
The 3-equation model in the open economy (9)
The open economy: demand and supply sides (10)
Extending the open economy model: oil shocks & imbalances (11)
The Eurozone (12)

# How to use the Online Resource Centre

This textbook is accompanied by a number of online resources available for students and registered lecturers.

Visit the Online Resource Centre at www.oxfordtextbooks.co.uk/orc/carlin_soskice/ to access all of the supporting content.

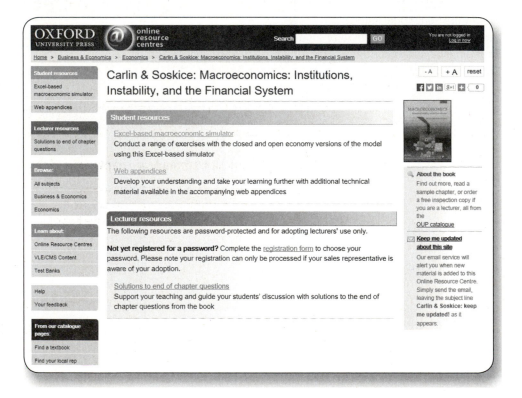

## For students

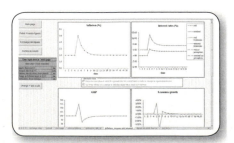

### Excel-based macroeconomic simulator

Conduct a range of exercises with the closed and open economy versions of the model using this Excel-based simulator.

## Web appendices

Develop your understanding and take your learning further with additional technical material available in the accompanying web appendices.

Chapter 16

**Real Business Cycle and New Keynesian models – Web Appendix**

16.1  The equations in a simple RBC model

**Production** The model begins with the production function. This takes the form of the Cobb-Douglas production function:

$$y_t = B_t K_t^\alpha N_t^{1-\alpha} \qquad (16.1)$$

where $y$ is output, $K$ is capital, and $N$ is hours of labour (rather than employment as we usually define it), $\alpha$ is capital's share of income and $1 - \alpha$ is labour's. We assume that next period's capital is equal to the existing capital stock (adjusted for depreciation, $\delta$) plus any new investment:

$$K_{t+1} = I_t + (1 - \delta)K_t.$$

The first step in setting out the model is to take the first order conditions for profit maximization by differentiating the profit function with respect to labour and with respect to capital and setting each equal to zero. For simplicity, we set the price level equal to 1:

$$\text{Max profits} = y_t - w_t N_t - r_t K_t$$

$$\frac{\partial \text{profits}}{\partial N} = (1 - \alpha)B_t K_t^\alpha N_t^{1-\alpha-1} - w_t = 0$$

$$\rightarrow w_t = (1 - \alpha)B_t K_t^\alpha N_t^{-\alpha} = MPL \qquad (16.2)$$

$$\frac{\partial \text{profits}}{\partial K} = \alpha B_t K_t^{\alpha-1} N_t^{1-\alpha} - r_t = 0$$

$$\rightarrow r_t = \alpha B_t K_t^{\alpha-1} N_t^{1-\alpha} = MPK. \qquad (16.3)$$

## For registered lecturers

## Solutions to end-of-chapter questions

Support your teaching and guide your students' discussion with solutions to the end of chapter questions from the book.

6.1  CHECKLIST QUESTIONS                                             5

9. Imagine an investment bank which has equity of 10 and operates in an economy where risk is 0.15, the policy rate is 0, the rate of return on financial assets is 0.05 and the price of financial assets is 1. Use Section 6.5 to answer the following questions:

(a) How many financial assets does the investment bank hold in period 0? What is their leverage?

ANSWER:

(a) From the equation for the investment bank's demand for financial assets, we have:

$$F_0 = \frac{e}{\underset{\text{risk}}{\varsigma} - \underset{\text{return}}{(1 + r - P)}}$$

$$= \frac{10}{0.15 - (1 + 0.05 - 1)} = \frac{10}{0.1} = 100;$$

$$\lambda_0 = \frac{F_0}{e} = \frac{100}{10} = 10.$$

Where $F_0$ is the number of financial assets held by the investment bank in period 0, $\lambda_0$ is its leverage, $e$ is equity.

# Acknowledgements

This book would not have been possible without the contribution of David Hope, who has worked as a researcher – and much more – on the project over a number of years. Marvellously organized, clever, focused and calm, he has subjected our arguments to critical scrutiny and kept the interests of our readers uppermost in our minds.

The development of the simulator for students to use—they can get to know the models by trying out different scenarios—was the brainchild of Javier Lozano. We are deeply grateful to Javier for his imagination and skill in developing the simulator.

A number of people have read and commented on various drafts of the book. We want to single out in particular: Philippe Aghion, Andrea Boltho, Sam Bowles, James Cloyne, Liam Graham, Javier Lozano, Colin Mayer, John Muellbauer, Bob Rowthorn, Hyun Shin, Bob Sutcliffe, David Vines and Stephen Wright. Their reactions and suggestions have immeasurably improved the final product and we are indebted to them for their consistent intellectual support.

Many others have given us comments and ideas for improvement: Chris Allsopp, Hannes Ansorg, Erik Berglof, V. Bhaskar, Richard Blundell, Ciaran Driver, Christian Dustmann, Fabian Eckert, Jonathan Glyn, Ian Goldin, David Goll, Georg von Graevenitz, Peter Hall, Bob Hancke, Soren Harck, Matthew Harding, Frank Harman, David Hendry, Michal Horvath, David Howell, Torben Iversen, Arjun Jayadev, Cloda Jenkins, Simon Johnson, Tom Josephs, Vijay Joshi, Michael Landesmann, Kieran Larkin, Deborah Mabbett, Steve Machin, Andy Martin, Bill Martin, Felix Martin, Massimo di Matteo, Costas Meghir, Jacques Melitz, Thomas Michl, David Miles, Hoang Minh Vu, Jamie Murray, Steve Nickell, Andrew Oswald, Susana Parrago Rodriguez, Tom Pybus, Ming Qiu, Nick Rau, Andy Ross, Mark Schaffer, Waltraud Schelkle, Paul Seabright, Rajiv Sethi, John Sharma, Luigi Spaventa, Andrew Sykes, David Tuckett, John Van Reenen, Charles Vincent and Simon Wren-Lewis. The book has benefited greatly from Wendy's engagement with the Institute for New Economic Thinking at the Oxford Martin School and in New York, and especially from joint work with the members of the CORE project. The reviewers commissioned by OUP provided very helpful guidance.

We had much to learn about the financial system when we began this project. Our 'teachers' have been extraordinarily generous with their time and expertise. We would especially like to thank Claudio Borio, Charles Goodhart, Sujit Kapadia, J.R. (Dick) Sargent, Hyun Shin, and John Vickers.

We have benefited from using teaching notes of Chris Bowdler, David Laibson, Campbell Leith, Sebastien Walker, Karl Whelan, and Simon Wren Lewis.

For help with data and specialist knowledge, we are particularly indebted to Nick Bloom, Nick Crafts, Bishnupriya Gupta, Mathias Drehmann, Kevin O'Rourke and Luigi Pistaferri.

Many thanks to Davide Melcangi who has worked out the answers to the questions and to Kieran Larkin who has done the technical proof-reading, making many improvements.

Wendy's colleagues in the Department of Economics at UCL have very generously supported this project, which has been judged by successive heads of department (Costas Meghir, Steffen Huck and Morten Ravn) a worthwhile use of research time. Fatima Cetin,

John McGlynn and Brian Wallace have provided excellent technical support and Tina Fowler and Nirusha Vigi have helped keep morale high.

Students at UCL in several courses over a number of years have provided feedback on various parts of the book. Their questions and suggestions have pushed us to improve the presentation and fine-tune the coverage. Their enthusiasm has kept us going. Doctoral students in political science at Duke have been a great and critical audience for various parts of the book; and encourage us to believe that it can be used to teach macroeconomics to well-trained social scientists.

We would like to thank the team at OUP led by Kirsten Shankland and Jo Hardern for their cheerful and effective marshalling of the book through the processes of review, revision and production.

Our families and friends have been patient and encouraging. Their probing questions about the crisis and their scepticism about the potential for economists to contribute to dealing with it have provoked us to make the arguments clearer and more accessible to non-specialists. Special thanks from Wendy to Jonathan, Tessa, Lucy and Miles Glyn, to Joan, John, David, and Michael Carlin, and to Mayerlene Engineer, Lizzie Fricker, Liz Harman, Carinna Hockham, Rosemary Joseph, Marion Kozak, Belinda Probert, and Jonathan Rée.

And special thanks for support and close friendship from David to William Soskice, Juliet Soskice-Rosenfeld and Andrew Rosenfeld, to Catherine Soskice and Vikram Gandhi, Oliver, Janet and Izzy Soskice, Ciaran Driver and Anne Phillips, Rebecca Murray and Kevin Prosser, and to Torben Iversen and Charla Rudesill – and in particular, thanks for the probing questions from William and Ciaran. David takes this opportunity to acknowledge the key intellectual relationships he has had during this period with Torben Iversen and with Niki Lacey, which have added greatly to the book from a broader perspective.

We dedicate this book to our two spouses, with deepest love:

Niki Lacey, David's wife and very close friend of Wendy, well-known legal and feminist theorist, has been central in every way to the writing of this book, providing sustenance of all sorts (including on and round the kitchen table), raising occasional eyebrows at the excess of rational choice, and being an inspiration affectively and intellectually for both of us.

Andrew Glyn, Wendy's husband and one of David's closest and oldest friends, died quite unexpectedly just as we had started planning this book. At the peak of his highly influential intellectual career (he already has an entry in the Dictionary of National Biography), he had just finished his prescient book Capitalism Unleashed (OUP 2007). Our other two macroeconomics books (1990 and 2006) had been written with his continuous and unstinting help; his presence and luminosity (and modesty) have remained with us as we wrote this book; but on many occasions we have been keenly aware of his absence.

# Outline contents

# Contents

# List of figures

# List of tables

# Abbreviations

| | |
|---|---|
| ABS | Asset backed securities |
| AD | Aggregate demand |
| APK | Average product of capital |
| BIS | Bank for International Settlements |
| BoE | Bank of England |
| BT | Balance of trade |
| CA | Current account |
| CAGR | Compound annual growth rate |
| CBO | Congressional Budget Office |
| CCA | Common currency area |
| CDO | Collateralized debt obligations |
| CDS | Credit default swap |
| CPB | Central Planning Bureau |
| CPI | Consumer price index |
| CRA | Credit rating agency |
| CRS | Constant returns to scale |
| DSGE | Dynamic stochastic general equilibrium |
| ECB | European central bank |
| ERU | Equilibrium rate of unemployment |
| FOMC | Federal Open Market Committee |
| FPC | Fiscal policy council |
| GDP | Gross domestic product |
| IB | Investment bank |
| ICA | Intertemporal model of the current account |
| ICT | Information and communications technology |
| IMF | International monetary fund |
| LIBOR | London inter bank offered rate |
| LOLR | Lender of last resort |
| LOP | Law of One Price |
| LTV | Loan-to-value |
| MBS | Mortgage backed securities |
| MM | Modigliani-Miller |
| MMF | Money market funds |
| MPC | Monetary Policy Committee |
| MPK | Marginal product of capital |
| MRE | Medium-run equilibrium |
| MRS | Marginal rate of substitution |
| NAIRU | The non accelerating inflation rate of unemployment |
| NBER | National Bureau of Economic Research |
| NFA | Net foreign asset |
| NK | New Keynesian |
| NKPC | New Keynesian Phillips curve |
| OBR | Office for Budget Responsibility |

| | |
|---|---|
| OECD | The Organization for Economic Co-operation and Development |
| PC | Phillips Curve |
| PDE | Price dynamic equation |
| PFPR | Prudent fiscal policy rule |
| PIH | Permanent income hypothesis |
| PPP | Purchasing Power Parity |
| PR | Policy Rule |
| PS | Price setting |
| QE | Quantitative easing |
| RBC | Real Business Cycle |
| REH | Rational expectations hypothesis |
| SGP | Stability and Growth Pact |
| SIV | Structured investment vehicle |
| SOMA | System Open Market Account |
| SRM | Single Resolution Mechanism |
| SME | Small and medium-sized enterprises |
| TARP | Troubled Asset Relief Program |
| TFP | Total factor productivity |
| UIP | Uncovered interest parity |
| VaR | Value at risk |
| VAT | Value added tax |
| WS | Wage setting |
| ZLB | Zero lower bound |

# The demand side

## 1.1 Overview

In the late 2000s, households and firms across the world cut back their spending and the global economy went into recession. There is little disagreement among economists that the dramatic fall in global GDP in 2008–09, which is now known as the global financial crisis, was a negative shock to aggregate demand.

This chapter begins the task of building a macroeconomic model with the demand side of the economy, which concerns the spending decisions of households, firms and government. As we shall see in Chapter 2, the supply side refers to the production activities in the economy. Dramatic changes in aggregate demand—that is, spending in the economy as a whole—as occurred in 2008–09 are unusual. In more normal times, shifts in aggregate spending decisions as well as shifts on the supply side of the economy are sources of the irregular fluctuations from recession to boom that form the business cycle.

If a period of depressed spending is forecast, there is much discussion in the financial press about whether the central bank will intervene and offset the likely recession by cutting the interest rate. The central bank would cut the interest rate because it expects this to encourage spending and help return the economy to stability. Similarly, if a boom in spending were forecast, the central bank would try to dampen it down by raising the interest rate. As well as the central bank, the government also needs to know how spending patterns are likely to evolve and affect output. A recession will depress tax revenue and increase spending on unemployment benefits. Forecasting patterns of spending is therefore a priority, not only for businesses, but also for the monetary and fiscal policy makers.

*Aggregate demand and spending decisions*

In this chapter, we focus on what lies behind the spending decisions in the economy and how they influence the level of economic activity. By the level of activity, we mean output or income. When output changes, employment also changes. For example, when output rises, more workers or longer hours are needed to produce the higher level of output. With more hours worked, the wage bill is larger and with higher sales, total profits are higher. This is why changes in economic activity are thought of as both changes in output and in income (i.e. wages and profits). When we think of a real-world economy, output is normally growing and recessions and booms produce fluctuations around a trend growth rate. However, we will often simplify by working with levels of output rather than its rate of growth.

Spending decisions are complex. For consumers they involve both a static component (what shall I buy today given my current income and the prices of the goods and services that are available?) and an intertemporal one (how do I allocate my spending over time given my expectations about how my income will evolve in the future?). Decision making for firms and the government also involves an intertemporal aspect. Firms make decisions to purchase machinery, equipment and premises based on a business plan that includes forecasts about how input costs and demand for their products will evolve over time. The government must also forecast demographic trends when making plans for building schools and hospitals.

Decisions by the entities that make up the economy—firms, families and government bodies—lie behind the demand side of the economy. However, macroeconomics is concerned with the aggregate sum of spending decisions of these groups, and the consequences of those decisions for economy-wide outcomes such as the rate of unemployment or inflation. Household spending decisions add up to aggregate consumption, $C$; firms' investment decisions add up to aggregate investment, $I$ (note that $I$ refers to spending on machinery, equipment and new houses and other buildings); and government spending on different goods and services adds up to a single number, $G$.

Including the purchase of new housing as part of investment highlights the difference between on the one hand, aggregate demand, which refers to spending on goods and services and on the other hand, the purchase of assets such as company shares or second-hand property. The purchase of a second-hand house does not contribute to aggregate demand. It is the transfer of the ownership of an asset from one household to another. In contrast, the building and selling of a new house uses resources and produces income, hence it influences aggregate demand.

Although the first chapters in the book relate to the closed economy (a single nation without links with others) as noted above, in the fuller model (set out in Chapters 9 and 10) the demand side includes foreign spending on home goods and services, exports ($X$), and domestic spending on foreign goods and services, imports ($M$). Aggregate demand is real expenditure on goods and services produced in the home economy. This can be summarized by an equation relating real expenditure, which is called $y^D$, to its individual components:

$$y^D = C + I + G + (X - M),\qquad\text{(aggregate demand)}$$

where we add to the trio of $C$, $I$ and $G$, the expenditure of foreigners on home output, $X$ and subtract the spending of home agents on output produced abroad, $M$.

### Aggregate demand and government policy

Two of the major tools of macroeconomic policy, monetary and fiscal policy, work by influencing different elements on the demand side. Policy makers worry about fluctuations in aggregate demand because they affect unemployment and inflation.

Monetary policy seeks to stabilize aggregate demand by changing interest rates, which affect the investment decisions of firms and the purchase of durable goods like new cars and houses by households. A rise in the interest rate increases the cost of financing investment projects, and projects that would have gone ahead with lower interest rates are postponed or cancelled. Monetary policy also has indirect effects because the interest rate affects incentives to save and therefore shifts spending decisions over time. For example, by making new borrowing more expensive and increasing the return on saving, a higher interest rate will encourage households to postpone consumption.

Through changes in government spending on goods and services (G), fiscal policy affects aggregate demand directly. Fiscal policy can also be used to affect demand indirectly through its influence on household incomes and through that channel, on household spending. This is how changes in taxation and in the transfers made by the government to households in the form of pensions, disability and unemployment benefits feed through to affect aggregate demand. We will denote taxes minus transfers by T.

An important reason to study the demand side is to construct a model of the transmission mechanism by which monetary and fiscal policy, via the spending decisions of households, firms and the government, affect the economy. Before explaining the first building block of the model, which is the IS curve, we provide some facts about the demand side.

### 1.1.1  Facts about the demand side and business cycles

*Shares of GDP*

Table 1.1 sets out the average composition of gross domestic product (GDP) in five major economies between 2000 and 2005. GDP is the national accounts measure of national output. We discuss the calculation of GDP next subsection. Table 1.1 shows that consumption makes up the largest proportion of GDP in all the five economies. However, the importance of consumption in GDP ranges from 43% in China to nearly 70% in the US. A large part of this cross-country variation can be explained by differences in the contribution of investment. For example, an exceptionally high proportion of Chinese GDP arises from investment spending, which crowds out consumption spending. The table also highlights the variation across countries in the contribution to GDP from net exports. On average, between 2000 and 2005, the UK and the US ran current account deficits with exports in excess of imports, whereas the other three countries were in surplus (see Chapter 10 for further discussion and definitions).

The upper panel of Fig. 1.1 shows how the shares of consumption, investment and government spending in GDP changed over time for the UK from 1948 to 2010. The share of consumption follows a shallow U shape over the period; investment is mildly hump shaped and the share of government spending drifts upward throughout the period. Government spending is dominated by spending on services (e.g. health and education) where

**Table 1.1**  Shares of GDP (in %), current prices, average 2000–2005.

|  | Consumption | Investment | Government spending | Net exports |
|---|---|---|---|---|
| China | 43.0 | 37.5 | 15.1 | 2.9 |
| Germany | 58.6 | 18.7 | 19.0 | 3.5 |
| Japan | 57.1 | 23.7 | 17.7 | 1.4 |
| United Kingdom | 65.3 | 16.7 | 20.0 | −2.5 |
| United States | 69.9 | 19.0 | 15.3 | −4.5 |

*Note:* GDP in current prices is a measure of nominal GDP; shares might not add up to 100% due to stockbuilding and statistical discrepancies.
*Source:* OECD National Accounts (data accessed November 2011).

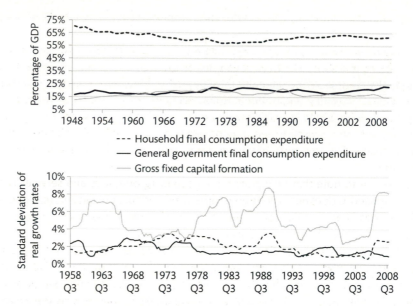

**Figure 1.1** Components of GDP in the UK: as a percentage of GDP between 1948 and 2010 (upper panel) and volatility of growth rates between 1958 Q3 and 2008 Q4 (lower panel).

*Source:* UK Office for National Statistics (data accessed October 2011).

*Note:* Volatility has been calculated as the standard deviation of the GDP growth rate over a rolling 21-quarter period. The upper graph uses data from the series 'Gross Domestic Product by category of expenditure, current prices' and the lower graph uses data from the series 'Gross Domestic Product by category of expenditure, chained volume measures'.

productivity growth is slower than in industry. In sectors with comparatively slow productivity growth, prices rise relative to the rest of the economy. This is an important structural reason for the tendency for government expenditure, when measured in current prices, to rise as a proportion of GDP.

### National accounts

The national accounts are used to measure the output of an economy. The most commonly used measure for calculating national output is gross domestic product, or GDP. GDP can be measured in three different ways. All three equations for calculating GDP are identities, which means that because of the way the variables are defined, the left hand side must always equal the right hand side. This special feature of an identity is signalled by the use of the equals sign with three bars.

Firstly, the *expenditure* method, which is one we use in the model of the demand side. This method measures GDP as the total expenditure on the economy's output of goods and services:

$$y \equiv C + I + G + (X - M),$$   (GDP identity, expenditure method)

where $y \equiv$ output (or GDP), $C \equiv$ consumption, $I \equiv$ investment (including changes in stocks of raw material and finished goods), $G \equiv$ government spending and $(X - M) \equiv$ net exports. This is an identity, as it simply breaks down GDP into its constituent components. A fall in one of the components on the right hand side, for example consumption, will therefore always result in an equivalent reduction in measured GDP on the left hand side.

When a *new* house is bought, just like a new piece of machinery, this is an investment decision—the house provides a flow of services to the household over many years—and is included in the national accounts under *I*. The house and the piece of machinery form part of the economy's capital stock. National accountants have to make many tricky classification decisions: although households buy a variety of durable goods that provide services over many years, by convention it is only housing that is considered as investment in the national accounts. Cars and furniture, for example, are treated in the national accounts as consumption.

It is important to note that only government spending on goods and services is part of aggregate demand. *G* does not include government expenditure on transfers (e.g. pensions or social security payments). When the recipients of transfers spend their income from benefits or pensions, this is then recorded as consumption.

The expenditure method only includes *final* goods. For example, during the production process, firms buy raw materials and *intermediate* goods to make their final goods. The only purchases that are counted in GDP are when the firm sells the finished goods to the consumer. This avoids any double counting. In this way, GDP captures only the *value added* created in the economy. This leads onto the second approach for calculating GDP; the *value added* method. This method measures GDP as the value added created in all sectors of the economy, such that:

$$y \equiv \text{value of output sold} - \text{costs of raw materials and intermediate goods.}$$

(GDP identity, value added method)

The third and final approach for calculating GDP is the *income* method. This method measures GDP as the total income of all agents in the economy, such that:

$$y \equiv \text{salaries of workers} + \text{profits of the owners of capital.}$$

(GDP identity, income method)

The three methods of calculating GDP are all identities and each holds at each point in time. It makes intuitive sense that the total income in the economy is equal to the total expenditure, because for every transaction there is both a buyer and a seller. What is expenditure for the buyer is income to the seller. In practice, however, GDP calculated using the three methods may differ. This is a matter of *measurement error*, which can arise for several reasons. Measurement error may be more serious for one rather than another of the three methods. For example, tax evasion or the existence of a substantial black market are likely to produce a greater problem of underestimation of GDP when measured by incomes than for the other methods. If the underlying components could be measured completely accurately, then each of the three approaches would yield exactly the same estimate of GDP.

### Relative volatility

The lower panel of Fig. 1.1 shows the relative volatility of growth rates for the three components of aggregate demand: a higher standard deviation means higher volatility. We can see that investment is much more volatile than consumption and government spending:

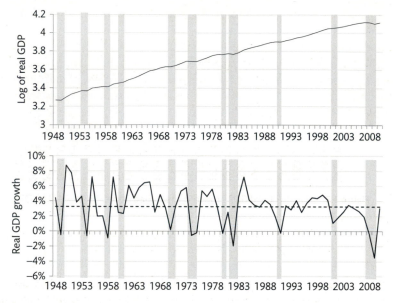

**Figure 1.2** Business cycles in the United States between 1948 and 2010–Log of real GDP (upper panel) and real GDP growth (lower panel).

*Source:* US Bureau of Economic Analysis (data accessed October 2011).

*Note:* The shaded grey areas represent recessions as defined by NBER. Both graphs use data from the series 'Real GDP, chained dollars, billions of chained (2005) dollars'.

the line showing the standard deviation for investment lies above that for consumption and government spending. Investment depends on expected post-tax profits and is very dependent on how optimistic firms are, so it tends to flourish in boom periods and collapse in recessions, making it more volatile than the other components of GDP, or GDP itself. In addition to this, investment can also be postponed in recessions, whereas government spending and consumption cannot be as easily delayed. For example, a household still has to spend money on food and drink in a recession, whereas a firm may choose to wait until the economy has recovered before it undertakes investment. We shall also see—in Section 1.2.6—that fixed investment decisions are often bunched, further accounting for the greater volatility of investment.

### Growth and cycles

The idea that economies fluctuate between phases of boom and recession is confirmed by looking at the data for the USA. Figure 1.2 illustrates the long-run growth and business cycles in the US economy. In the top panel, the log of GDP in constant prices is plotted and shows the rather steady growth rate of GDP over the long run. Using the log scale, a straight line would represent a constant growth rate from 1948 to 2010.[1] In fact, annual growth rates in each decade from 1948 were: 3.3%, 4.8%, 3.2%, 3.0%, 3.1% and 2.5%.

---

[1]  See Section 3 of Chapter 8 for a detailed discussion of growth concepts and the use and interpretation of natural logs.

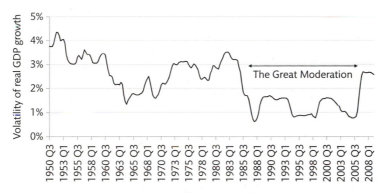

**Figure 1.3** Volatility of real GDP growth in the United States: 1950 Q3–2009 Q1.

*Source:* US Bureau of Economic Analysis (data accessed October 2011).

*Note:* Volatility has been calculated as the standard deviation of the GDP growth rate over a rolling 21-quarter period. Graph uses data from the series 'Real GDP, chained dollars, billions of chained (2005) dollars'.

By plotting the *annual* growth rate of GDP in the lower panel, the fluctuations of the economy around the long-run trend are highlighted. The dotted line represents the average growth rate between 1948 and 2010 of 3.3%. Peaks and troughs of growth occur about twice a decade. In the US, an independent body called the National Bureau of Economic Research (NBER) establishes the dates of US business cycles and states there have been eleven separate contractions (i.e. recessions) over this period, which are represented by the shaded grey areas on the graphs. Recessions start at the peak of a business cycle and end at the trough: during recessions, economic activity is contracting. In the period we are analysing, the recessions range from 6 to 18 months in duration. This is why the *annual* GDP growth rate shown in Fig. 1.2 is not negative in all of the recessions (e.g. the 2001 recession). The longest of these recessions was the 2007–09 global financial crisis (GFC), which spanned a year and a half.

Before the global financial crisis, many macroeconomists claimed that better policy making had produced greater macroeconomic stability. This led to the use of the term 'the Great Moderation' to describe the calmer macroeconomic conditions from the mid-1980s (fewer and shorter recessions as illustrated in Fig. 1.2).

A more precise way to document the Great Moderation is to look at the volatility of GDP growth. Figure 1.3 shows the volatility of US GDP growth since the late 1950s. By plotting the standard deviation of the growth rate over a 21-quarter rolling period, changes in volatility can be seen easily. There is a noticeable fall in the volatility of GDP growth from the mid 1980s. However, the spike in volatility experienced during the recent recession brought the era of the Great Moderation to an end.

### 1.1.2 Introducing the *IS* curve

In this chapter, we begin to build up a way of capturing essential elements of the complex real-world macro-economy in a model. The model is called the 3-equation model because there are three core elements, representing the demand side, the supply side and the policy maker. The *IS* is the curve that represents the demand side. It is called the *IS* curve because it refers to planned investment and savings decisions; hence the *I* and the *S*. It was originally formulated as a simple shorthand version of John Maynard Keynes's description of the demand side in his General Theory.[2]

Models are important for providing a framework in which to think about complex problems more easily and more carefully. By modelling the goods market we can answer interesting questions about the demand side that we might otherwise struggle with, such as:

1. If you give an individual a $100 bonus, how much of it will they spend?
2. How much will output increase following a rise in government spending or a boost in the confidence of households and firms about their future prospects?
3. To what extent will a rise in the interest rate curtail investment in new housing, machinery and equipment?

The *IS* curve is a way of summarizing the way that aggregate output in the economy is affected by changes in the spending decisions of families, firms and government bodies. For example, when firms increase their spending on new equipment, this triggers increased production in the capital goods producing sector of the economy. More people are employed to produce the extra capital goods and as they spend their wages, demand for consumer goods goes up and employment and output expand in those sectors as well. As a result of this process, the economy will move to a higher level of output and employment. We shall see that in response to the initial expansion of spending, output will expand until the extra *Saving* households want to make just balances the extra spending on *Investment*. At that point, the process by which the impact of the initial increase in aggregate demand is multiplied through the economy in subsequent rounds of higher employment, spending by newly employed workers, higher demand for consumer goods, etc. comes to an end.

### Aggregate demand in the private sector

Focusing attention on decisions by the private sector, the level of aggregate demand will be affected by current income and by the following factors.

1. *Expectations about the future*: the plans of firms to invest in new equipment and premises depend on their expectations of *future post-tax profits*. If firms anticipate high levels of capacity utilization and strong order books, they will increase investment in new capacity. Households prefer to have smooth rather than fluctuating consumption, which means they need to save and borrow in order to spread their consumption more evenly over time. To make their saving and borrowing decisions, they must form a view about the future growth of their income. The *life-cycle motive* for saving refers to the planning of saving taking into account the projected pattern of income during a person's working life and retirement. Households will revise upward their estimate of how much they can spend each period if they have new information that leads them to expect their income to grow more strongly.

---

[2] See Keynes (1936). The *IS* curve also underlies the famous *IS/LM* model, which was introduced by John Hicks in 1937 (Hicks, 1937). For a concise and interesting discussion of its origins and impact, see Durlauf and Hester's article entitled *IS-LM* in the New Palgrave Dictionary of Economics: 2nd edition (2008).

Firms and households form their expectations in the face of uncertainty. For example, an increase in the unemployment rate in the economy could be a signal to households that *uncertainty* about their future income has risen, which would trigger an increase in saving for *precautionary* reasons.

2. The extent of *credit constraints*: these arise because of problems faced by banks in assessing the creditworthiness of households and firms. It is impossible for banks to have full information about borrowers' projects and actions. Borrowing by households and by small and medium-sized firms is therefore often restricted by banks. Households and business that cannot borrow as much money as they would like are said to be *credit constrained*. The information problems inherent in bank lending mean that access to credit is often highly dependent on the amount of *collateral* the borrower has with which to secure the loan. The most common form of collateral for households is the value of their house. This means that changes in the value of collateral, which occur for example when house prices change, affect consumption and investment because they either tighten or relax credit constraints.

3. The *interest rate*: there are a number of channels through which the interest rate will affect aggregate demand. When interest rates go up, households find it more expensive to get a mortgage. This reduces the demand for new houses and reduces the demand for furnishings and other consumer durables that go along with moving house. A higher interest rate will lead firms to rein in their spending plans on new capital equipment and buildings. Households will tend to postpone consumption spending because of the improved returns from saving. However, creditor and debtor households would be expected to react differently. For example, a creditor household will find their income has gone up when the interest rate rises and this will boost spending through the income effect. For debtor households, the effect will be the opposite. The first and third effects are normally stronger than the second one and a higher interest rate is associated with lower aggregate demand.

*The IS curve*

The *IS* curve is a way of summarizing in a diagram the demand side in the macroeconomic model. It shows the combinations of the interest rate and output at which aggregate spending in the economy is equal to output.

Figure 1.4 shows the *IS* curve. This is a downward-sloping relationship. To see this, think of the combination of a high interest rate and low output. When the interest rate is high, spending on housing, consumer durables, machinery and equipment will be low. This means aggregate demand is low and a low level of output will satisfy the low demand. Hence, we have the first point on the *IS* curve. Now, take a combination of a low interest rate and high output. Here the situation is the opposite: buoyant spending on new houses, consumer durables and investment goods generates a high level of output and high incomes for households. This is the second point on the downward-sloping *IS* curve.

To show how changes in profit or income growth expectations, uncertainty and the value of collateral can be captured in the diagram, we hold the interest rate constant and look at shifts in the *IS* curve. As an example, in a situation of depressed profit expectations, we would expect firms to postpone new investment. The result is lower investment spending at any interest rate. The *IS* curve shifts to the left (shown by the curve labelled *IS* (pessimistic expectations)).

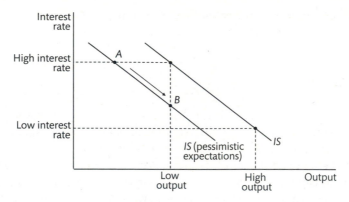

**Figure 1.4** The *IS* curve—the effects of changes in optimism and economic policy.

Using the *IS* diagram, we can show how the central bank or the government can affect the demand side. Following up the situation where the business environment becomes more pessimistic, the central bank could lower the interest rate to stimulate investment. This would be shown as a move *along* the *IS* curve from point *A* to point *B*. As an example, there was much discussion about the decision by the US central bank, the Federal Reserve, to reduce the policy interest rate and keep it low as a way of stimulating investment in the aftermath of the collapse of the Dotcom bubble in 2001. The long period of low interest rates stimulated investment in new house construction, and we shall see in Chapter 7 the role that this played in the background to the global financial crisis of 2008.

Another response to a leftward shift of the *IS* curve due to pessimistic profit expectations could be action by the government rather than central bank. If the government decides to launch a major expenditure programme, such as to improve healthcare provision or to install an information super-highway, this will *shift* the *IS* curve to the right: at a given interest rate, the government purchases a larger amount of goods and services. Under our assumption that suppliers will respond to the higher demand, the economy moves to a higher level of output and employment. In the diagram, this would shift the *IS* curve to the right back towards its initial position.

A much debated issue in macroeconomics is by how much a government expenditure programme would increase output in the economy. Would extra government spending increase output one-for-one, by more or by less? This debate is frequently couched in terms of the size of the 'multiplier': i.e. by how much would expenditure of an extra dollar raise GDP? As we shall see in Section 1.2, in the *IS* diagram, the larger the multiplier,

1. the larger is the rightward shift of the *IS* curve associated with any given amount of additional government spending and

2. the flatter is the *IS* curve, since with a larger multiplier, a given cut in the interest rate has a larger effect on output.

The demand side is only part of the macroeconomic model. To understand how the spending decisions of households, firms and the government fit into the bigger picture, we need to include the supply side and the motivations and behaviour of the policy makers.

Chapter 2 addresses the supply side and Chapter 3 brings in the policy maker. Before moving on, we set out the modelling of the demand side in more detail.

## 1.2 Modelling

The Modelling sections of the chapters in the book provide more details of the models and their components introduced in the Overview sections. Detailed derivations of some of the results are available for download from the book's website.

In order to better understand the demand side of the macro-economy, we build a simple model, which is captured by the *IS* curve. This section focuses on the closed economy *IS* curve and we will come back to the open economy *IS* curve in Chapters 9 and 10. The closed economy *IS* curve splits demand into three components; consumption, investment and government spending.

As a first step in this chapter, we introduce the concept of goods market equilibrium and the definition and mechanics of the multiplier process. Throughout this section, we assume that firms are willing to meet the higher demand for their goods and services, and workers are willing to take the extra jobs or work the extra hours that are offered. In simple terms, we assume that the supply of output adjusts to meet the demand for goods, services and labour. The next step is to bring in additional determinants of aggregate spending listed under points (1) to (3) in the previous section and to modify the *IS* equation to take these into account. Along the way, we refer to empirical evidence to support the richer model.

### 1.2.1 Goods market equilibrium

We begin our discussion and modelling of the goods market by considering each of the components of aggregate demand in the closed economy. The aggregate—or economy-wide—demand for goods and services consists of:

**Consumption demand:**  expenditure by individuals on goods and services. Spending is on both *durable* products such as a car, laptop or sofa and on *non-durable* products such as a theatre show or groceries.

**Investment demand:**  expenditure on capital goods (machinery, equipment, and buildings). Spending is by households on new houses, by firms on new capital goods, including structures, and building up inventories of materials or finished goods, and by government (on public infrastructure projects, such as building a new high speed rail line).

**Demand stemming from government purchases:**  government expenditure on salaries, goods and services. Spending includes public sector wages (e.g. civil servants, doctors), purchases of goods (e.g. educational supplies, ammunition for the army) and purchases of services (e.g. waste disposal and contract cleaning).

*The model of goods market equilibrium*

We now set out a model of the goods market. In the closed economy, aggregate demand, $y^D$, is given by

$$y^D = C + I + G, \tag{1.1}$$

and we ignore imports and exports. All variables are in real terms, which is also referred to as constant price terms. Equilibrium in the goods market requires that planned real expenditure on goods and services (i.e. aggregate demand) is equal to real output

$$y^D = y, \qquad \text{(goods market equilibrium)}$$

where $y$ is output. $y$ is also income: spending on the output of the economy in turn becomes the income of those producing it (wages and profits). This circular flow of income to expenditure and output, and back to the incomes of producers means we can use the terms output, income and expenditure interchangeably. We shall come back to the goods market equilibrium condition after providing some more detail about consumption and investment behaviour.

To start, we assume that aggregate consumption is a simple linear function of after-tax or disposable aggregate income

$$C = c_0 + c_1(y - T), \tag{1.2}$$

where $T$ is total taxes net of transfers.

To get to the consumption function we use as the core of the model of the demand side, we make the additional assumption that taxes are a fixed proportion of income—i.e. $T = ty$, where $0 < t < 1$. The consumption function then becomes

$$C = c_0 + c_1(1 - t)y. \qquad \text{(Keynesian consumption function)}$$

This is referred to as a Keynesian consumption function. It consists of a constant term, $c_0$, which is often referred to as autonomous consumption, and $c_1(1 - t)y$, which shows households spending a fixed proportion of their disposable income. $c_1$ is referred to as the marginal propensity to consume and lies between zero and one ($0 < c_1 < 1$).

Note that the marginal propensity to consume ($MPC$) shows the change in consumption as the result of a change in post-tax or disposable income:

$$MPC \equiv \frac{\Delta C}{\Delta y^{\text{disp}}} = c_1, \qquad \text{(marginal propensity to consume)}$$

where $y^{\text{disp}} = (1 - t)y$.

In this model of consumption, saving is $S = y - C$ and adds to one's assets. Income is the amount that can be consumed without reducing one's assets. The corresponding marginal propensity to save is $s_1$ and $c_1 + s_1 = 1$ (i.e. disposable income can be either saved or spent).

If disposable income is zero, the consumption function predicts consumption equal to $c_0$. For this to be the case, households must have some savings and or they must be able to borrow. A more satisfactory model of consumption must therefore include forward-looking behaviour in order to account for savings, and we build this in to the model of consumption later in the chapter.

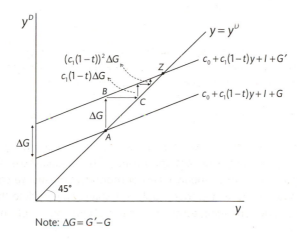

Note: $\Delta G = G' - G$

**Figure 1.5** Keynesian cross—Increase in government spending.

## 1.2.2 The multiplier

We begin with the Keynesian consumption function in order to introduce in the simplest way the concept of how equilibrium in the goods market is determined and how the multiplier process works. If we substitute the consumption function into the equation for aggregate demand, then we get a relation between aggregate demand,

$$y^D = c_0 + c_1(1-t)y + I + G, \qquad\qquad \text{(aggregate demand)}$$

and output, $y$, which we can draw on a diagram with aggregate demand on the $y$-axis and output on the $x$-axis (Fig. 1.5). The intercept of the curve will be $(I + G + c_0)$ and the slope $c_1(1-t)$ which, given the assumptions that both $c_1$ and $t$ are between 0 and 1, will itself be between zero and one. We can also draw the goods market equilibrium condition on the same graph, which will be a 45° line, because in equilibrium

$$y = y^D.$$

The point at which the two curves intersect shows the level of output where planned real expenditure on goods (and services) by firms, households and government is exactly equal to the level of goods being supplied in the economy. To the left of the 45° line, the demand for goods is greater than the supply.

To understand how the model works, we disturb the initial equilibrium at point $A$. Suppose there is an increase in government spending. From the aggregate demand equation, we can see that this shifts the aggregate demand curve upwards by the change in government spending, $\Delta G$. Aggregate demand now exceeds output (Point $B$). As the government increases its purchases of goods (e.g. of office equipment) the stocks of these goods in warehouses decline. The inventory management software records the fall in stocks and triggers an increase in production: output rises. This is the move from $B$ to $C$, where once again $y = y^D$. The higher output in turn raises incomes (in the form of wages of the additional workers employed and the profits of the owners of the firms making higher sales) and according to the consumption function, some proportion of the higher incomes are spent on goods and services in the economy, raising aggregate demand further. The process continues until the new goods market equilibrium is reached at point $Z$, where output and aggregate demand are equal.

Adjustment to shifts in aggregate demand via inventory accumulation and decumulation shows how a purely quantity-based adjustment to a new goods market equilibrium can take place. For the goods market to be in equilibrium it must be the case that $y = y^D$. If we substitute $y$ into the aggregate demand equation we can rearrange to define equilibrium output in terms of the *exogenous variables*. Exogenous variables are those that are determined outside the model. In the model of goods market equilibrium, the exogenous variables are autonomous consumption ($c_0$), investment ($I$) and government spending ($G$), the marginal propensity to consume ($c_1$) and the tax rate ($t$). If we know the value of these five variables, we can work out the level of equilibrium output,

$$y = c_0 + c_1 (1 - t) y + I + G \tag{1.3}$$

$$y - c_1 (1 - t) y = c_0 + I + G$$

$$y = \underbrace{\frac{1}{1 - c_1 (1 - t)}}_{\text{multiplier}} \underbrace{(c_0 + I + G)}_{\text{autonomous demand}}. \tag{1.4}$$

Because $c_1$ and $t$ are between 0 and 1, this simplified model implies that the *multiplier* is greater than 1. This means that a 1% increase in autonomous demand would be predicted to lead to an increase in output of more than 1%. This is referred to as the short-run multiplier as we hold the interest rate and all other policy responses constant—i.e. output is the only variable allowed to change. Note that if consumption was not a function of current income, i.e. if the marginal propensity to consume, $c_1$, is equal to zero, then the aggregate demand line is horizontal and there is no multiplier process amplifying the impact on the economy of the rise in government spending.

In the consumption function, $c_0$ is an exogenous variable, meaning that it is not influenced by any other variables in the equation (i.e. it is determined outside the model). However, the second part of the equation, $c_1 (1 - t) y$, is *endogenous*. In order to calculate the level of aggregate consumption in equilibrium, we therefore need to first work out the equilibrium value of $y$ and then compute the level of consumption.

We now combine algebra and geometry to deepen our understanding of the multiplier process. We return to the previous example shown in Fig. 1.5, where the government uses fiscal policy to increase activity in the economy. Since the aggregate demand curve is flatter than the market-clearing condition, equilibrium output will increase by more than the increase in government expenditure, i.e. the multiplier is greater than one. The initial boost in government spending increases aggregate demand by $\Delta G$. This increases output, and income, and so aggregate consumption increases by $c_1 (1 - t) \Delta G$. Aggregate demand increases by the same amount, and, given that the goods market clears, output and income increase too. Aggregate consumption increases again by $[c_1 (1 - t)]^2 \Delta G$, and so on to infinity. The total increase in output is given by the sum of these changes:

$$\Delta y = \Delta G + [c_1 (1 - t)] \Delta G + [c_1 (1 - t)]^2 \Delta G.... \tag{1.5}$$

$$= \left(1 + [c_1 (1 - t)] + [c_1 (1 - t)]^2 + ...\right) \Delta G. \tag{1.6}$$

This is a geometric progression and its sum to infinity is given by[3]

$$\Delta y = \underbrace{\frac{1}{1 - c_1(1 - t)}}_{\text{multiplier}} \Delta G = k\Delta G,$$ 
(1.7)

where $k$ is the multiplier.

## Application: the paradox of thrift

Imagine the economy is in a recession and the following question is put to an economist: should a policy be introduced to encourage or to discourage saving in order to help the economy recover? On the one hand, the idea of encouraging more saving sounds helpful—if more is saved and invested in new capital stock, that would seem a good recipe for recovery. On the other hand, if more saving means less consumption and there is no increase in investment, won't aggregate demand fall and the recession get worse?

To answer this question requires spelling out how agents are assumed to behave. In an economic model, assumptions about how agents make their decisions are summarized by behavioural equations. In macroeconomics, it is aggregate behaviour that is captured by these equations. In the very simple model we have set out, the behavioural equation for consumption is the Keynesian consumption function. Investment and government spending are assumed to remain constant: in the model so far, they are not affected by other variables (i.e. they are exogenous). The behavioural equations are as follows:

$$C = c_0 + c_1(1 - t)y \ ; G = \overline{G} \ ; \text{ and } I = \overline{I},$$
(behavioural equations)

where we put a bar over the $G$ and the $I$ to emphasize that these are both exogenous. From the behavioural equations, we can write planned real expenditure (aggregate demand) as

$$y^D = c_0 + c_1(1 - t)y + \overline{I} + \overline{G}.$$
(1.8)

As usual, the goods market equilibrium condition is $y^D = y$, and if we substitute Equation 1.8 into this, then in equilibrium, planned savings are equal to planned investment plus government spending:

$$\underbrace{(1 - c_1(1 - t))y - c_0}_{\text{Planned saving}} = \underbrace{\overline{I} + \overline{G}}_{\text{Planned }I\text{ and }G},$$
(equilibrium condition)

---

[3] This is the sum of a geometric series. We want to find an expression for the series $1 + [c_1(1 - t)] + [c_1(1 - t)]^2 + [c_1(1 - t)]^3 + \cdots$, which we call $x$. If we put

$$x = 1 + [c_1(1 - t)] + [c_1(1 - t)]^2 + [c_1(1 - t)]^3 + \cdots,$$

and multiply both sides by the common factor, $[c_1(1 - t)]$, then

$$[c_1(1 - t)] \cdot x = [c_1(1 - t)] + [c_1(1 - t)]^2 + [c_1(1 - t)]^3 + \cdots$$

and if we subtract the bottom equation from the one above, we have

$$x(1 - [c_1(1 - t)]) = 1$$

$$\Rightarrow x = \frac{1}{1 - [c_1(1 - t)]}.$$

We model the proposal to encourage savings by a fall in autonomous consumption from $c_0$ to $c_0'$. Aggregate demand falls initially by $(c_0 - c_0')$ and the multiplier process works in the downwards direction. Using the same logic as illustrated in Fig. 1.5 in reverse, this process continues until we get to the new equilibrium at lower output. At the new lower output level, $y'$, planned savings on the left hand side of Equation 1.9 is equal to planned investment plus government spending on the right hand side, which have not changed:

$$(1 - c_1(1 - t))y' - c_0' = \bar{I} + \overline{G} . \tag{1.9}$$

An important insight emerges from this example. The initial equilibrium was disturbed by a fall in autonomous consumption as households sought to increase their savings. However, the intention to save more did not lead to higher aggregate savings because *income fell* ($\Delta y = k(c_0 - c_0')$). This must be the case for Equation 1.9 to hold.[4] This is called the *paradox of thrift*, because if greater thriftiness is not matched by higher investment in fixed capital, income will fall and there will be no overall increase in savings in the economy.

To summarize, the answer to the question of whether saving should be encouraged in a recession depends on the model of the economy the economist is using—and of course, on how well that model matches the real economy under study. Using the model we have developed so far in this chapter, the answer is clear: encouragement to save more will not help the economy to exit recession. The reason is that there is no mechanism in *this* model through which higher saving is translated into higher investment. Investment remains at $\bar{I}$ throughout. Hence the result of a higher propensity to save is that aggregate demand falls, output falls and the recession is deepened.

By contrast, if the model includes a central bank, then the recession could be averted by the central bank cutting the interest rate and boosting investment to offset the fall in savings. In the next section, we remove the simplifying assumption of exogenous investment to show the impact on the demand side of investment being responsive to changes in the interest rate.

### 1.2.3 The *IS* curve

*Deriving the IS equation*

Throughout this book, we use the *IS* curve to represent the demand side of the economy. In this subsection, we derive the *IS* curve and use it as a starting point to think about how monetary and fiscal policy work. As we discussed in Section 1.1.2, the *IS* curve shows the combinations of output and the real interest rate at which the goods market is in equilibrium.

We first set out the relationship between the real interest rate, $r$, and the nominal interest rate, $i$. This relationship is shown by the Fisher equation:

$$r = i - \pi^E. \tag{Fisher equation}$$

---

[4] We can confirm that the change in aggregate saving is equal to zero. Using Equation 1.7:

$$\Delta y = \frac{1}{1 - c_1(1-t)} \Delta c_0,$$

$$\Delta S = \left[ (1 - c_1(1 - t)) \frac{1}{1 - c_1(1-t)} \Delta c_0 \right] - \Delta c_0 = 0.$$

This equation says that the real interest rate is simply the nominal interest adjusted for expected inflation. It is the real interest rate that is most important for investment and saving decisions, as it represents the true cost of borrowing (and the true return on saving). This interest rate is therefore the one used in the investment equation and in the *IS* curve. When the central bank sets the nominal interest rate, it does this with the intention of achieving a particular real interest rate since it aims to affect interest-sensitive spending. In the Appendix, we show how the Fisher equation is derived.

At this stage, we assume there is just one interest rate in the economy that applies to all borrowing and saving. We make the assumption to keep the maths as simple as possible. In reality, there is a spectrum of interest rates. For example, the interest rate on bank lending will typically be higher than the interest rate set by the central bank. We discuss the banking mark-up in Chapter 5 and the difference between short-term and long-term interest rates in Chapter 7.

Although we shall amend this later in the chapter, in the model to this point, consumption is independent of interest rates. This means that the transmission of monetary policy will work through its effect on investment spending, including on new houses. Up to this point in the chapter, we have assumed that investment is determined by expected future profits, which we have assumed to be exogenous. We now incorporate the interest rate into the investment function as follows:

$$I = a_0 - a_1 r, \qquad\qquad \text{(investment function)}$$

where $r$ is the real interest rate, $a_0$ and $a_1$ are constants and $a_1 > 0$. The main determinant of investment is expected future post-tax profits, which is captured by the term, $a_0$.

We derive the *IS* curve as follows. Substituting the investment function into Equation 1.4 gives us a relationship between the real interest rate and output, which is the *IS* curve. We can then use $k$ to denote the multiplier and simplify to achieve a simple equation for the *IS* curve:

$$y = \underbrace{\frac{1}{1 - c_1(1-t)}}_{\text{multiplier}}[c_0 + (a_0 - a_1 r) + G] \qquad\qquad (1.10)$$

$$= k[c_0 + (a_0 - a_1 r) + G] \qquad\qquad (1.11)$$

$$= k(c_0 + a_0 + G) - ka_1 r \qquad\qquad (1.12)$$

$$= A - ar, \qquad\qquad \text{(IS curve)}$$

where $A \equiv k(c_0 + a_0 + G)$ and $a \equiv ka_1$.

The derivation of the equation for the *IS* curve highlights the fact that given $r$, equilibrium output, $y$, is found by multiplying autonomous consumption and investment, and government spending by the multiplier $k = \frac{1}{1-c_1(1-t)}$. This fixes an $r$–$y$ combination on the *IS* curve. It is clear from Equation 1.12 that a higher multiplier, $k$, or higher interest–sensitivity of investment to the interest rate, $a_1$, increases the effect of a change in the interest rate on output, making the *IS* curve flatter.

The *IS* curve is derived graphically in Fig. 1.6 using the *IS* curve equation shown above. Three curves are shown on the figure: the investment function, the investment function plus autonomous consumption and government spending and the *IS* curve. Two real interest

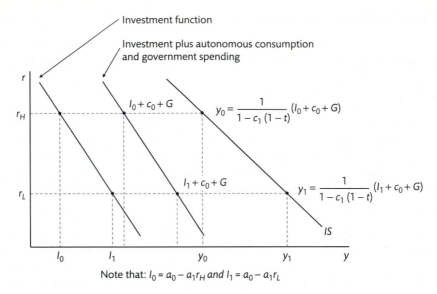

Note that: $I_0 = a_0 - a_1 r_H$ and $I_1 = a_0 - a_1 r_L$

**Figure 1.6** Deriving the IS curve.

rates are shown in the figure: a high real interest rate, $r_H$, and a low real interest rate, $r_L$. At $r_H$, investment is more costly, so the level of planned investment is low, whereas the opposite is true at $r_L$. This leads to a downward-sloping investment function. Autonomous consumption and government spending are unaffected by the interest rate, so when added on, the curve shifts out parallel. The last step to derive the *IS* curve is to multiply $I_0 + c_0 + G$ by the multiplier. This gives output equal to planned expenditure, $y$, on the *IS* curve. The *IS* curve shows all the combinations of output and real interest rate where the goods market is in equilibrium. It is flatter than the other two curves because the multiplier effect of investment is higher when interest rates are low.

Using the *IS* curve equation and the diagram, we can summarize its properties.

1.  The *IS* curve is downward sloping because a low interest rate generates high investment, which will be associated with high output. By contrast, when the interest rate is high, investment and consequently equilibrium output is low.

2.  The slope of the *IS*:

    (a) Any change in the size of the *multiplier* will change the slope of the *IS* curve. For example, a rise in the marginal propensity to consume, $c_1$, or a fall in the tax rate, $t$, will increase the multiplier, making the *IS* flatter: it rotates counter clockwise from the intercept on the vertical axis.

    (b) Any change in the *interest sensitivity of investment* ($a_1$) will lead to a consequential change in the slope of the *IS* curve: a more interest-sensitive investment function (i.e. $\uparrow a_1$) will be reflected in a flatter *IS* curve.

3.  Shifts in the *IS* curve: any change in *autonomous consumption, autonomous investment* or *government expenditure* ($c_0$, $a_0$, $G$) will cause the *IS* curve to shift by the change in autonomous spending times the multiplier.

### 1.2.4 Forward-looking behaviour

The spending decisions of agents in the present are influenced by their expectations of the future. This means there is an intertemporal component to both consumption and investment.

1. Households adjust their current spending based on their expected income in the future. For example, a final year economics undergraduate who secures a lucrative job contract (which is set to commence after university), has low current income, but high expected future income. Having got the job, this individual may borrow in the present, consume more and pay back the money when they start their job. This behaviour is referred to as *consumption smoothing*.

2. Firms make decisions (e.g. purchasing machinery, equipment and premises) based on a business plan that includes forecasts about future demand for their products and input costs. For example, a firm selling cars to China might choose to build a new factory (i.e. undertake investment) based on forecasts that Chinese incomes (and therefore their demand for cars) will continue to rise rapidly over the next 20 years. Investment is intrinsically forward looking, as it incurs a cost today, but the stream of benefits occurs in the future.

*Present value calculation*

We can calculate the present value of a flow of income or profits received in future periods in the following way. We take the example of a firm making an investment decision.

We assume that firms aim to maximize profits, so they undertake investment projects if these offer a return that is higher than costs. The outlay on investment typically precedes the returns, which may be lumpy and spread over a number of years. The way to deal with this is to calculate the 'Present Value' ($V$) of the expected flow of profits $\Pi$, where $\Pi_t$, $\Pi_{t+1}$, ... is the flow of profits in period $t, t + 1$ etc. Suppose the interest rate is 10%. Then if I save €100 today I will have €110 in a year's time ($100 (1 + 10\%)$). Expressed the other way around, we could say that €110 in a year's time has the same value as €100 today—its present value is €100.

More generally, if interest rates are constant at $r$, the value of $X$ in $n$ years' time is the same as that of $X/(1 + r)^n$ today. We can calculate the present value of our stream of expected profits, $\Pi^E$, from an investment project with profits over $T$ years by:

$$V_t^E = \Pi_t^E + \frac{\Pi_{t+1}^E}{(1+r)} + \frac{\Pi_{t+2}^E}{(1+r)^2} + \cdots = \sum_{i=0}^{T} \frac{1}{(1+r)^i} \Pi_{t+i}^E.$$

(expected present value calculation)

We use the superscript $E$ to denote the expected value of a variable.

If the cost of the machine is greater than the present value of the flow of profits from the machine, then it would be more profitable not to buy the machine but instead put the money in the bank or in bonds (which earn interest of $r$). Similarly, if the money to purchase the machine is being borrowed, then if the cost of the machine is greater than the present value, buying the machine will be unprofitable. On the other hand, if the present value is greater than the cost, then this investment is profitable, and a profit-maximizing firm will go ahead with it.

We can also apply the same logic to modelling consumption decisions. We can account for the fact that the future will affect consumption decisions by calculating the present value of the stream of expected income over a person's lifetime. If we assume that individuals live forever, we can use the formula for calculating present value to calculate the expected present value of lifetime wealth ($\Psi^E$, pronounced 'sigh'), which is defined at time $t$ as follows,

$$\Psi^E_t = (1+r)A_{t-1} + \sum_{i=0}^{\infty} \frac{1}{(1+r)^i} y^E_{t+i},$$

(expected present value of lifetime wealth)

where $\sum_{i=0}^{\infty} \frac{1}{(1+r)^i} y^E_{t+i}$ is the present value of expected post-tax lifetime labour income and $(1+r)A_{t-1}$ are the resources available in period $t$ from the assets the individual held at the end of the previous period.[5]

### 1.2.5 Consumption

People's income fluctuates over their life cycle; it also fluctuates when they lose their job, move to a different job or get a promotion. Given that people prefer to smooth out the fluctuations in their income in their spending behaviour, they must take account of the future and they must be able to save and borrow. The modelling of consumption should include how households form expectations about the future and how they borrow and save.

The desire to smooth consumption in the face of fluctuations in income is captured by the assumption of diminishing marginal utility of consumption. A simple way of visualizing this is to consider the choice of consumption in a world of just two periods. If we know income will be higher next period, how does that affect consumption now? Consider the choice between either low consumption equal to income in the first period and high consumption equal to income in the second period, or having the average of the two consumption levels in each period. If there is diminishing marginal utility of consumption, more consumption always increases utility, but successive increases in consumption deliver smaller and smaller benefits. Therefore, households will make the second choice, because consuming the average in both periods offers higher utility than the first choice.

### The permanent income hypothesis (PIH)

The permanent income hypothesis (PIH) states that individuals optimally choose how much to consume by allocating their resources across their lifetimes.[6] Their resources include their

---

[5] The assumption that individuals 'live forever' can be thought of as assuming that households have children or heirs and that they incorporate the utility of their children or heirs into their consumption function. In other words, households behave 'as if' they last forever. The assumption is clearly unrealistic, but it greatly simplifies the mathematical derivation of the permanent income hypothesis (PIH). From this point onward, however, we will refer to lifetime income and earnings in the text, as it is more intuitive to think about forward-looking behaviour in terms of a household maximising utility over their lifetime.

[6] This view of the consumption function was first developed by Modigliani and Brumberg (1954). See also Friedman (1957). For a review of Friedman's theory, its influence on modern economics and the relevant empirical literature, see Meghir (2004).

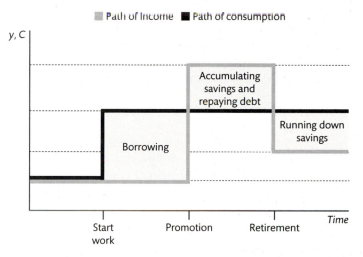

**Figure 1.7** The permanent income hypothesis over the life cycle.

assets and their current and future income. This is a forward looking decision and will depend on interest rates, asset values, expectations of future income and expectations of future taxes. The PIH predicts that optimal consumption is smooth as compared to income. For example, when individuals start work, their income is low and they will borrow to consume more; when income increases, they keep consumption constant and use the excess income to pay off debts and save for retirement; then at retirement, their income falls and they draw down their savings. Figure 1.7 shows how consumption and income change over the life cycle in this simplified example. The important point is that the PIH predicts that households will borrow and save in order to smooth consumption over their lifetimes. Likewise, over the business cycle, if an individual becomes unemployed, the model predicts that they will borrow in order to sustain consumption during the spell of unemployment. As we shall see in Chapter 14 on fiscal policy, the government plays an important role in smoothing consumption through the provision of unemployment benefits.

The PIH model of consumption provides a stark contrast with the Keynesian consumption function where there is no explicit consideration of the future. Aggregate consumption of households is modelled there as the consumption of a fixed amount, $c_0$ and a fixed proportion of the current period's disposable income.

The PIH model is derived in more detail in Section 1.4.2 of the Appendix, but it is useful to set out the intuition and predictions of the model here, as it provides a framework for thinking about forward-looking consumption decisions. Given that income will fluctuate over a person's lifetime, the starting point of the PIH is their desire to smooth out fluctuations in consumption and their ability to save and borrow in order to achieve this.

The next question that arises is whether an individual prefers their smooth consumption path to be one of constant consumption in each period or of rising or falling consumption. This will depend on the relationship between the interest rate on saving and borrowing and the rate at which the individual trades off consumption in the future for consumption in the present. The latter is the subjective discount rate $\rho$, called rho which is a measure of an individual's impatience.

The household chooses a path of consumption to maximize its lifetime utility subject to its lifetime budget constraint, which is

$$\Psi_t^E = (1+r)A_{t-1} + \sum_{i=0}^{\infty} \frac{1}{(1+r)^i} y_{t+i}^E. \qquad \text{(lifetime budget constraint)}$$

Note that when considering the PIH, income, $y$ is defined as post-tax income. The key to solving this problem can be thought about over just two periods, since the same considerations will apply to every subsequent pair of periods.[7] The answer is a simple relationship between consumption this period and next period, which is called an Euler equation (the derivation is in Section 1.4.2 of the Appendix):

$$C_t = \frac{1+\rho}{1+r} C_{t+1}^E. \qquad \text{(Euler equation)}$$

The intuition is clearest if we take the case where the interest rate, $r$, and the subjective discount rate, $\rho$, are the same. This means the household gets the same (objective) return from saving, $r$, as their (subjective) willingness to trade off consumption in the present for consumption in the future, $\rho$. In this case, the agent prefers a constant level of consumption each period, $C_t = C_{t+1}^E$.

We can see that if the discount rate is above the interest rate, $C_t > C_{t+1}^E$ then consumption is falling over time, reflecting the 'impatience' of the household. The opposite is the case if the discount rate is below the interest rate; a patient household will have a path in which consumption rises over time, i.e. $C_t < C_{t+1}^E$. The crucial point to note is that whichever of these consumption patterns is chosen, it is independent of the period by period changes in income.

From now on we focus on the PIH where the subjective discount rate is equal to the real rate of interest, i.e. ($\rho = r$). To implement a life-time consumption plan like this, given each period's income the household must do whatever saving and borrowing is called for in order to deliver the constant level of consumption each period. If current income is above permanent income, individuals save and if it is below, they borrow.

The next step is to use the Euler equation to find out how much individuals consume each period (the derivation is in Section 1.4.2 of the Appendix). When $\rho = r$, consumption is

$$C_t = \frac{r}{1+r} \Psi_t^E. \qquad \text{(PIH consumption function)}$$

The intuition is easy to understand: an individual with this consumption function will borrow and save to deliver a perfectly smooth consumption path (in expectation). The amount they consume each period is equal to the annuity value of expected lifetime wealth and is called 'permanent income'. The individual consumes their permanent income and the formula ensures that in expectation, they will be able to do this forever. Note that consumption remains constant unless $\Psi_t^E$ changes.

---

[7] See Hall (1978) for a full derivation of the PIH and an empirical test of the main implications of the theory.

## Predictions and empirical evidence on the PIH

The predictions of the PIH can be tested. How does consumption react when a change in income occurs? The answer depends on the nature of the change in income.

1. *Anticipated* or foreseen changes in income should have no effect on consumption when they occur. The reason is that anticipated changes will already have been incorporated into consumption through the recalculation of permanent income. Hence, when the change in current income is recorded, the marginal propensity to consume is predicted to be zero (the multiplier is equal to one). A finding of *'excess sensitivity'* to anticipated income changes would contradict the full smoothing behaviour predicted by the PIH.

2. *News or unanticipated* changes in income should affect consumption because they require the recalculation of future lifetime wealth, $\Psi_t^E$.

   (a) News of a temporary increase in income. If current income $y_t$ increases unexpectedly by one unit, consumption increases by the extent to which this raises permanent income. Since the increase in one unit will be spread over the entire future, the PIH consumption function tells us that permanent income and hence consumption rise very little, just by $\frac{r}{1+r}$ times the increase in lifetime wealth. The marginal propensity to consume out of temporary income is $\frac{r}{1+r}$. (For example, if the real interest rate is 4%, the MPC is 3.8%, which implies a multiplier barely above one.)

   (b) News of a permanent increase in income. If there is news that income $y_t$ is higher from now and for every future period by one unit, then permanent income and hence consumption rise by the full one unit. This means the marginal propensity to consume out of post-tax permanent income is one. A finding of *'excess smoothness'* of consumption in response to news of permanent income changes would contradict the simple PIH.

### *Excess sensitivity to* anticipated *changes in income*

The first testable hypothesis suggests that there should be no change in consumption at the time income changes, if the change in income was known in advance. This is because consumption should already have adjusted as soon as the news arrived of the change in future income. An influential study by Campbell and Mankiw (1989) tested this hypothesis econometrically using aggregate data on consumption and income from the G7 countries. The study rejected a model in which all consumers were following the PIH but could not reject a model in which half of all consumers were simply following the 'rule of thumb' of spending their current income. In other words, they found that current consumption was overly sensitive to expected changes in income across the G7.

   A recent study used the 2001 federal income tax rebates in the US as a testing ground: according to the PIH, the one-off (temporary) tax rebate should have very little effect on spending and if there is any effect, it should occur when the announcement was made and not when the cheques arrived. Johnson, Parker and Souleles (2006) were able to identify the causal effect of the tax rebate by using household data and the fact that the timing of the sending of cheques was based on the taxpayer's social security number, which is random. They found that the average household spent 20–40% of the (predictable) tax rebate in the three month period when the cheque was received rather than when the programme was announced. They also found that it was households with low income and wealth that responded most, underlining the likely role of limits on the ability of households to borrow, i.e. credit constraints. This is referred to as the *excess sensitivity* of consumption and is evidence against the strong predictions of the PIH.[8]

Is consumption excessively sensitive to the predictable fall in income at retirement? What is observed is that when income falls in a predictable way on retirement, consumption falls. Although this is a violation of the simple PIH, explanations consistent with consumption smoothing in a more detailed model have been proposed. These include the possibility that consumption falls because spending was related to being at work (i.e. complementary to working, such as the purchase of business suits) and that in the light of the increased leisure of the household, home production substitutes for consumption spending (e.g. cooking replaces the purchase of more expensive ready-made meals). Jappelli and Pistaferri (2010) conclude that evidence on the so-called consumption–retirement puzzle is not clearly in contradiction with the spirit of the PIH. Putting this together with the above discussion, the fact that there is excess sensitivity to anticipated rises in income but not so much to falls in income underlines the important role of credit constraints, which are ignored in the PIH.

*Excess sensitivity to news about temporary income and excess smoothness to news about permanent income*

Turning to the hypotheses that relate to news about income, studies have found that consumption over-responds to temporary income shocks. In the case of positive income shocks, this strongly violates the PIH. An early example of this was the large consumption response of US veterans after the Second World War to an unexpected windfall payout of the National Service Life Insurance. This kind of evidence questions the assumption in the PIH that households make optimizing decisions over a time horizon stretching a long way into the future and use a low discount rate (equal to the interest rate) to compare consumption at near and far horizons. The fact that people respond to a windfall by raising spending suggests that discount rates are higher than assumed in the simple PIH: people appear to be more *impatient* than the hypothesis assumes.

It is also likely that uncertainty about whether observed income changes are temporary or permanent prevents households from acting exactly as PIH would predict. For example, if a household mistakenly thought a temporary change in their current income was permanent, then they would consume more of the income change than would be consistent with PIH behaviour.

Jappelli and Pistaferri (2010) review the recent evidence and suggest that it shows that consistent with the PIH, consumption responds more to permanent than transitory income shocks, but that households do not revise their consumption fully into line with permanent shocks.

---

[8] For a detailed summary of the early literature on excess sensitivity see Deaton (1992). A recent excellent overview of the empirical testing of the excess sensitivity and excess smoothness hypotheses is Jappelli and Pistaferri (2010).

## Credit constraints, impatience and uncertainty

The evidence suggests there are three reasons for the failure of the simple PIH to provide an adequate model of aggregate consumption:

1. The presence of credit constraints, which prevent borrowing by households who lack wealth or collateral.

2. Impatience, which prevents some households from saving as would be indicated by a permanent income view.

3. Uncertainty about future income, which explains precautionary saving over and above the level predicted by the PIH.

### Credit constraints

If people prefer to smooth their consumption, but are prevented from doing so because they cannot borrow to bring forward consumption when their current income is below their expected permanent income, they are said to face credit constraints. The prevalence of credit constraints is an important factor that stops the world from operating as the simple PIH theory would imply. Because of information problems facing banks in assessing creditworthiness, banks are not always willing to lend to households without the wealth or collateral to secure a loan in order that they can smooth their consumption (see Chapter 5). Figure 1.8 shows the consumption response for PIH and credit-constrained households to an anticipated rise in income. The PIH households borrow to raise consumption as soon as the news of the future income increase is received, whereas the credit-constrained households do not have

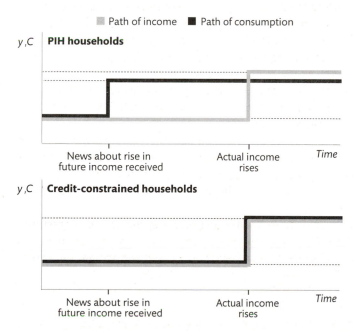

**Figure 1.8** The consumption response of PIH and credit-constrained households to an anticipated rise in income.

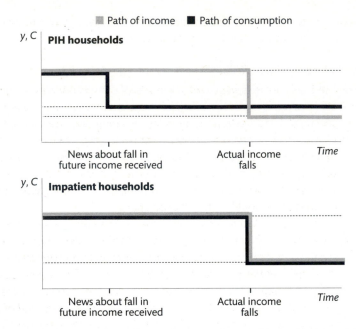

**Figure 1.9** The consumption response of PIH and impatient households to an anticipated fall in income.

this option, so consumption can only rises when income does. Estimates from studies using household data have found that around 20% of the population in the United States is credit constrained.[9] A much higher estimate of closer to two-thirds comes from a study of the way people respond to automatic increases in the limits on their credit cards: if spending responds to such automatic increases, it suggests the card-owner was credit constrained.[10]

### Impatience

The observation that consumption of a substantial fraction of households changes one-for-one with their current income (i.e. no borrowing or saving) reflects two features of the real world. The most important is the presence of credit constraints, which can prevent households from borrowing to smooth their consumption. This seems to especially affect young and low income households. Faced with a spell of unemployment, for example, constraints on borrowing will prevent a household from maintaining its level of consumption.

Whereas credit constraints can explain the inability of households to borrow to smooth consumption, it cannot explain the failure of some households to save, which would allow for some consumption smoothing without relying on bank loans. It seems that there are households who are not only credit constrained, but also impatient. Figure 1.9 shows the consumption response for PIH and impatient households to an anticipated fall in income. The PIH households start saving as soon as the news of the fall in future income is received, which alllows them to smooth consumption over the two periods. In contrast, the impa-

---

[9] See Japelli (1990), Mariger (1986) and Hall and Mishkin (1982).
[10] See Gross and Souleles (2002).

tient households fail to reduce current consumption upon receipt of the news, meaning consumption falls dramatically when income actually falls.

## Experimental evidence on impatience

The impatience of households is represented in a model of consumption by a higher discount rate for the short run than the longer run. A simple illustration of what this means is to consider the following experiment: if you were choosing today for eating *next week*, would you choose fruit or chocolate? About three-quarters of experimental subjects choose fruit. When asked whether they would choose fruit or chocolate to eat *today*, 70% choose chocolate. From this, we can see that preferences are not consistent over time, because if we run time forward to next week, the three quarters who said they would prefer fruit would have shrunk to 30%. When next week comes, they would in fact, choose chocolate.[11]

Impatience is also documented in experiments related to consumption and saving behaviour. For example, subjects have a budget and can choose between two accounts paying the same interest rate: a 'freedom account' with no constraints on withdrawal or a 'commitment account' where there are restrictions on withdrawal before a date chosen by the participant. From a purely economic point of view, the freedom account is preferable because it imposes no constraints on withdrawal. In spite of this, more than half of investment was put in the commitment account (no withdrawal before the goal date), which reveals the desire of the experimental subjects to commit themselves to saving.[12]

## Implications of impatience for consumption and saving

Very large differences between a high short-run and a low long-run discount rate help explain why people simultaneously save in illiquid assets such as housing (where the interest rate is low) and borrow on credit cards, paying a very high interest rate. Households with behaviour of this kind will have a marginal propensity to consume of one. Although a person can agree that their expected well-being is higher if they save more now, they are unable to resist consuming and blowing a hole in their saving plan when they get an unexpected increase in their income. One way of committing to saving is to take out a mortgage. Another is for the government to automatically enrol people in schemes for saving for retirement (from which they can opt out) such as pensions.

## Uncertainty and precautionary saving

If there is uncertainty about future job opportunities or about health, then the household may save as insurance for future contingencies. For example, having a 'buffer stock of savings' could be important to sustain consumption in the event of job loss for a credit-constrained household.[13]

In the face of uncertainty, households would tend to save more early in life than the PIH predicts. Instead of the average propensity to consume falling as income rises over the working life as in the simple PIH, the desire for precautionary savings leads to saving early on with result that consumption rises with income (not by more than income) early in the

---

[11] See Read and van Leeuwen (1998).     [12] See Ashraf et al. (2006).
[13] See Carroll (1997) for an exposition of the buffer-stock savings model.

life cycle and the average propensity to consume rises later on. If saving for a rainy day is important, then the utility provided by having assets to tide the household over if need be outweighs the utility that would have come from higher consumption in the early years.

### An empirical consumption function

To conclude the discussion of consumption, we consider a consumption function estimated on macroeconomic data for the UK, US and Japan.[14] Although the empirical model does not impose the straitjacket of the simple PIH, it nevertheless allows for permanent income considerations to affect consumption; households will have a notion of sustainable consumption constrained by their budget, which includes their income forecasts. They will therefore know that they cannot spend their existing assets now without impairing future consumption and that future income affects their sustainable consumption.

In addition to permanent income considerations based on forecasts, the consumption function that is estimated includes the following factors.

1. Consumption is predicted to respond more strongly to current income than the PIH predicts due to the presence of credit constraints.

2. The effects of income uncertainty on the desire of households to have precautionary savings. Income uncertainty is measured by the change in the unemployment rate and an increase is predicted to reduce consumption.

3. The housing collateral effect through higher house prices is expected to interact with increased credit availability to increase consumption (in the presence of credit constraints). The presence of this effect will depend on the institutional arrangements for mortgage borrowing in the country in question. For example, the availability or otherwise of home equity loans is a crucial distinction. A home equity loan is a loan secured against the equity in an individual's home. Home equity is the difference between the current market value of the house and the remaining mortgage, hence it increases as house prices rise. The collateral channel works through credit constraints being relaxed, but if it is not possible to get a home equity loan, as in France, Germany, Japan and China, this channel does not operate. In fact, if home equity loans are unavailable and high down-payments are required to get a mortgage (as in Japan), then higher house prices can actually dampen consumer spending, as young people have to save more to accumulate the required down-payment.

4. The current real interest rate. There are many interest rate channels, some of which point to a negative and some to a positive effect of a higher real interest rate on consumption.

5. Increases in households' wealth to income ratio are expected to increase consumption.

The consumption function includes the housing and financial variables that are at the centre of the discussion in Chapters 5–7, where the banking system, financial cycles and financial crises are brought into the macro model.

---

[14] See Aron et al. (2012).

For the UK and US, the consumption functions estimated using macroeconomic data suggest that roughly 50% of household consumption is accounted for by permanent income considerations. Current income has an important positive effect on consumption and the real interest rate has a negative effect. The wealth to income ratio has a positive effect but different types of wealth have different effects. For example, cash in a bank or savings account is more spendable than pension wealth. Also, the evidence is that for a given degree of access to new credit, higher debt of $100 reduces consumer spending more than higher pension or stock market wealth of $100 increases spending.

For these two economies, where home equity loans are important, increased credit availability and house prices interact to raise consumption through the collateral effect. A house price boom in conditions where access to credit is easier boosts consumption. We return to look at the implications of the richer analysis of consumption for the *IS* curve in Section 1.2.7.

### 1.2.6 Investment

The decision a firm makes over whether to invest or not will depend on their expectations about future after-tax profits. The role of expectations helps explain the excess volatility of investment over the other components of GDP visible in Fig. 1.1. In developing the *IS* equation, we used a simple linear relation to model investment in Section 1.2, where the amount of investment depended positively on expected future profits (captured by the constant term, $a_0$) and negatively on the real interest rate (a measure of firms' borrowing costs). In this subsection we introduce a more sophisticated forward-looking modelling approach—the *q* theory of investment.

### Tobin's *q* theory of investment

This theory was developed by Nobel Prize winner James Tobin.[15] Like the PIH, Tobin's *q* theory of investment is forward looking. Firms choose the amount of investment to undertake with a view to maximising the expected discounted profits over the lifetime of the project. The *q* theory amounts to comparing the benefits from investment in an increase in the capital stock with the costs of doing so: if the expected benefits exceed the costs, investment should take place.

*Marginal and average q models*

The theory is derived explicitly in the Web Appendix to this chapter, but it is useful to set out the equation for *marginal q* here, as it provides a framework for thinking about forward-looking investment decisions:

$$q = \frac{\text{MB of investment}}{\text{MC of investment}} = \frac{Pf_K}{\delta + r}. \qquad \text{(marginal } q \text{ model of investment)}$$

The model is intrinsically forward looking since the firm is considering the future benefits from investment spending now. Before looking at the expression on the right, we note that the optimal amount of investment occurs when $q = 1$. This is where the expected marginal

---

[15] See Tobin (1969) and Tobin and Brainard (1977).

benefits of investment are equal to the expected marginal cost. Thus, if $q > 1$, the marginal benefit of investment exceeds the marginal cost, so firms should invest to increase the capital stock until $q = 1$. If $q < 1$ the firms should reduce their capital stock.

It is important to note that the $q$ theory of investment is a model in which firms are assumed to make their investment decisions (a flow) by pinning down the optimal capital stock (a stock). Small changes in the desired capital stock can therefore translate into large changes in the flow of investment. This is one reason for the excess sensitivity of investment over GDP (see Fig. 1.1).

The marginal benefits from investment are higher when the price of output is higher and when the investment is more productive. The equation shows that firms should undertake more investment if there is

1. an increase in the price of output, $P$,

2. an increase in the marginal productivity of capital, $f_K$, which indicates the increase in output the new capital equipment will produce,

3. a reduction in the rate of interest, $r$, or

4. a reduction in the rate of depreciation, $\delta$. For example, a rise in the expected rate of depreciation (e.g. as a result of uncertainty about future legislation banning fuel-inefficient cars) would lead to a reduction in the level of current investment because it would reduce the expected benefits to the firm from additional investment in the auto industry.

Is $q$–theory a good way to represent real-world investment behaviour? Marginal $q$ implies firms adjust their level of investment in each period to equate the marginal benefits and marginal costs of investment. This does not fit with the real-world data on investment. When economists looked at very detailed microeconomic data for very large numbers of plants, they found that, contrary to the idea of a smooth investment flow, investment was in fact very bunched.[16] For example, a growing manufacturing firm might build a new factory once every 10 years.

### The share price as indicator of expected profits

Testing $q$ theory directly is difficult because $q$ itself is difficult to measure. This is because it depends on the marginal product of capital and a measure of technology, which cannot be observed. In the real world, firms do not know their production functions and do not think explicitly in terms of marginal products. To operationalize the theory, the market value of the firm as reflected in its stock market valuation is compared with the replacement cost of the capital stock. If the market value is higher then this signals that the firm should increase investment. On the other hand, if the market value is below the replacement cost, then the firm would not want to build a *new* factory because it could buy an existing one more cheaply.

We can define average $Q$ as follows:

$$Q = \frac{\text{Market value of firm}}{\text{Replacement cost of capital}}. \qquad \text{(average } Q \text{ model of investment)}$$

---

[16] See the survey chapter on 'Investment' by Caballero (1999).

This is often called *average Q* to distinguish it from *marginal q*. Whereas *q* is the ratio of the marginal benefit of a unit of investment to its marginal cost, *Q* depends on the total expected return from the firm's capital divided by the total cost. For publicly listed companies, the stock market provides a forward-looking measure of the market value of the firm, which can be used in the numerator of the *Q* equation: when the firm's market value rises relative to the replacement cost of the firm, as reflected in a rise in the price of its shares, the model suggests that investment should go up. A higher interest rate and depreciation rate will raise the replacement cost of capital.

The idea is that the market value incorporates information about how well the firm is expected to be able to implement the investment, whether new competitors will enter the market, whether there are new technological innovations likely to affect the firm's value, the state of the macro-economy and the labour market and the future path of the interest rate. Since investing in a firm is a wager on this uncertain future, investors continuously evaluate these factors and, under certain conditions, the share price and hence the market value of the firm will reflect all the information available.

The stock market is notoriously volatile. For example, in 2008, the UK's leading share index—the FTSE 100—fell 31% and GDP contracted by just 1.1%. The following year, the FTSE 100 rose 22%, whilst GDP continued to contract, but this time by 4.4%.[17] In times of extreme uncertainty, the share price may not reflect the fundamental value of a firm. Large movements in share prices heavily affect market capitalization, which is the measure used to proxy for the market value of the firm in the calculation of average *Q*. As the stock market is volatile and subject to bubbles, fads and herd behaviour, it may not be a good indicator of the firm's prospects.

However, a study using US micro data (over 1,000 firms from 1982 to 1999) shows that a *Q* model of investment can be successfully estimated when analysts' forecasts of a firm's profits are used instead of the stock market price to measure the numerator in the *Q* equation.[18]

## Empirical evidence on investment

The empirical evidence on the *q* theory is that *Q* helps to explain investment but it is not the only influence. In particular, just as was the case for consumption, credit constraints play an important role in explaining investment spending.

### Credit constraints—the role of cash flow

A testable prediction of *q* theory is that current cash flow should have no impact on investment. The reason is that forward-looking firms should take into account any credit constraints that they face: these should already be incorporated into the stock market valuation, *Q*. However, the role of cash flow in empirical studies of investment suggests that *capital market imperfections* are important. The importance of cash flow variables in estimated investment equations is reminiscent of the importance of current income in estimated

[17] GDP data from IMF World Economic Outlook database, April 2012. Stock market data from Bloomberg News articles.
[18] See Bond and Cummins (2001).

consumption functions. As we have seen, the presence of credit-constrained households causes excess sensitivity of consumption to predictable changes in income. Similarly, the presence of cash flow terms in estimated investment functions strongly suggests that firms are credit constrained. Although some firms are able to borrow as much or sell as much equity as they would like in order to finance their investment plans, for others, their investment will be limited by their internal funds.

This is sometimes referred to as the *excess sensitivity of investment to internal funds*. For firms like this, cash flow would be expected to be an important determinant of investment.[19] The reason why firms may be rationed in their access to bank loans is explored in Chapter 5.

A study using UK company data for the period 1975–86 found that company investment was significantly influenced by $Q$ and by credit constraints. However, the impact of $Q$ was found to be very small: a 10% rise in the stock market value of a company was associated with an immediate rise in the investment rate of only 2.5%. Cash flow, on the other hand, was very important. The sample period was divided into two, and it was found that the impact of $Q$ was lower and the impact of cash flow higher in the first part of the sample, during which the UK economy was in a deep recession. This is consistent with the idea of credit constraints biting especially hard in a recession.

### Uncertainty—the option value of waiting

The decision of firms about whether to invest or not is also influenced by uncertainty about the future. Under certain circumstances, there can be a value in waiting to undertake an investment project, since with the passing of time more information arrives, the costs of delay (lost profits from the project) may be outweighed by more secure information on the balance between the costs (including those sunk in the project) and the benefits of undertaking it. The upshot of such considerations is that an expected rate of return considerably higher than the cost of capital will be required to trigger investment. Dixit (1992) gives examples to show that including the so-called 'option value of waiting' can double the hurdle rate (i.e. the return required to trigger investment) for an investment project to proceed.

### 1.2.7 Consumption, investment and the *IS* curve

In the previous subsection, we introduced models of consumption and investment that took account of forward-looking behaviour. Expectations of future income and of future profits play a key role in the spending decisions of households and firms. We also reported empirical evidence on aggregate consumption and investment, which highlighted the role of credit constraints for households and firms. What are the implications for the *IS* curve?

The basic form of the *IS* curve was presented in Section 1.2.3 and we shall see that we can bring together the additional insights about consumption and investment by focusing on the factors that affect the slope of the *IS* curve and which shift it.

---

[19] See, for example, Chirinko (1993).     [20] See Blundell et al. (1992).

The *IS* equation is:

$$y = k(c_0 + a_0 + G) - ka_1r \qquad\qquad (1.13)$$
$$= A - ar, \qquad\qquad \text{(IS curve)}$$

where $A \equiv k(c_0 + a_0 + G)$ and $a \equiv ka_1$; $k$ is the multiplier. A larger multiplier makes the *IS* curve flatter, which increases the impact on output of a change in the interest rate; it also increases the impact on output of a shift in $c_0$, $a_0$ or $G$ for a given interest rate. This makes it clear that the size of the multiplier is important for understanding the effectiveness of both fiscal and monetary policy.

As we shall see in Chapter 14 on Fiscal Policy, there has been a great deal of debate about the empirical size of the multiplier in the context of the use of fiscal stimulus to respond to the Great Recession following the global financial crisis. We shall see that that there is no simple answer to the question: what is the size of the multiplier? It depends on characteristics of the economy and on the context in which, for example, a fiscal stimulus is being applied.

We can summarize the implications of the analyses of consumption and investment from Sections 1.2.5 and 1.2.6 by thinking about how they affect the multiplier and the *IS* curve.

### Factors affecting the multiplier

The PIH predicts that the size of the multiplier is dependent on the permanency of the income shock. The hypothesis suggests the marginal propensity to consume from temporary unanticipated changes in income is close to the size of the interest rate, i.e. only $\left(\frac{r}{1+r}\right)$. The multiplier is therefore predicted to be very close to one for temporary income shocks. On the other hand, permanent income shocks will result in a multiplier larger than one as households update their consumption to reflect their new, higher permanent income.

The presence of credit-constrained and impatient households also impacts the size of the multiplier. For these households, the multiplier effect will be larger than one even for temporary income shocks, as their marginal propensity to consume out of changes in income is equal to one. The larger is the proportion of these 'hand to mouth' or 'rule of thumb' households in the economy, the larger will be the multiplier.

Uncertainty over the permanency of income shocks is another factor that will influence the multiplier. If a substantial proportion of observed income fluctuations are perceived as permanent, then this will result in a multiplier larger than one. In this case, households could be following the PIH, but uncertainty leads their behaviour to be consistent with a Keynesian consumption function.

A change in the multiplier will shift the *IS* curve and change its slope (a higher multiplier makes the *IS* flatter).

### Other factors affecting the slope of the IS curve

In addition to the effect of the size of the multiplier, the slope of the *IS* curve is affected by the interest sensitivity of investment and of consumption. The theoretical prediction of the impact of the interest rate on consumption is ambiguous; a reduction in interest rates boosts consumption through some channels and dampens it through others. The empirical evidence on the consumption function suggests that national institutional structures, particularly in relation to the financial system, are important for determining the strength and direction of the relationship. Aron et al. (2012) find a negative relationship between consumption and the real interest rate in the financially liberalized UK and US economies, but they find a positive relationship in Japan, where households' huge liquid deposits far outweigh household debt.

*Other factors shifting the* IS *curve*

In addition to the effect of the size of the multiplier, the *IS* curve is shifted by a number of other factors. Looking first at consumption, the PIH predicts that anything that changes expected lifetime wealth, $\Psi_t^E$, such as changes in asset prices or news about a future promotion, shifts the *IS*. The empirical findings about consumption highlight three other factors that can shift the *IS* curve:

1. The role of uncertainty: a rise in the rate of unemployment will raise savings for precautionary purposes, shifting the *IS* to the left.

2. A house price boom will boost consumption in a country with home equity loans by loosening credit constraints, shifting the *IS* to the right. However, a house price boom could also shift the *IS* to the left in countries where home equity loans are unobtainable and large down-payments are needed to get a mortgage.

3. A shift in credit market architecture that increases household access to credit, such as financial innovation or deregulation, will shift the *IS* to the right (at least until the accumulation of debt eventualy cancels out some of the shift).

Turning our attention to investment, Tobin's marginal *q* predicts that the following factors will shift the *IS* curve to the right:

1. an increase in the price of output, *P*,

2. an increase in the marginal productivity of capital, $f_K$; and

3. a reduction in the rate of depreciation, $\delta$.

Lastly, the average *Q* equation highlights the role of expectations of future profits as a shift factor for the *IS* curve: a rise in the stock market tends to boost fixed investment as it signals a rise in the value of companies relative to their replacement cost.

## 1.3 Conclusions

This chapter has provided the first building block in the model of the macro-economy. We have set out the *IS* curve, which is used to model the demand side of the economy and is one of the three equations that underpin the 3-equation model that will form the core model of this textbook.

The *IS* curve allows us to think systematically about how changes in the spending behaviour of firms, households and governments can influence output and drive business cycles. The *IS* curve shows the combinations of the real interest rate and output where the goods market is in equilibrium. It slopes downwards to account for the fact that households' consumption and new housing decisions respond negatively to the interest rate; firms will also undertake fewer investment projects as the cost of borrowing increases.

We return to the questions at the start of the modelling section (1.2) and see how the model we have developed helps us work towards an answer. This acts as an exercise to summarize what we have learnt in this chapter.

1.  If you give an individual a $100 bonus, how much of it will they spend? This depends on the model of household spending we are using. If consumer behaviour is well modelled by a Keynesian consumption function (i.e. $C_t = c_0 + c_1(1-t)y_t$) then households will spend a fixed proportion of any extra income they receive. In the case of a $100 bonus, they will spend everything left over once they have paid tax and put some money into savings. However, if consumer behaviour is better modelled by the permanent income hypothesis (PIH), then individuals' current consumption is a function of their expected lifetime wealth (i.e. $C_t = \left(\frac{r}{1+r}\right)\Psi_t^E$). As the bonus is a one-off, it will only increase expected lifetime wealth by a small amount, resulting in a small increase in consumption in this and all future periods. This leads the individual to save the majority of the bonus in the current period. In Section 1.2.7, we showed how the proportions of rule of thumb and forward-looking households in the economy affect the multiplier and the *IS* curve. We also discussed how the extent to which observed changes in income are perceived as permanent can help to reconcile the Keynesian and PIH consumption functions.

2.  How much will output increase following a rise in autonomous demand, such as higher government spending or a boost in the confidence of households and firms? The multiplier will determine the extent to which an €$x$ increase in autonomous demand will increase output. In the simple model presented in Section 1.2.1, the multiplier is always greater than one, as both $c_1$ and $t$ are between zero and one. This means that in the short run, an injection of autonomous demand will always boost output by more than one for one. The extent of the boost of output will depend on the size of the multiplier. The multiplier will be larger if the tax rate ($t$) is low and households have a high marginal propensity to consume ($c_1$). In Section 1.2.7, we saw that if all households are described by the PIH, the permanency of the income change is important for determining the size of the multiplier. When income changes are permanent, the multiplier is greater than one as households update their consumption to reflect the increase in their permanent income. When the income change is temporary, the marginal propensity to consume out of current income is essentially zero as it has a negligible effect on permanent income, and the multiplier is therefore equal to one. Temporary and unanticipated income shocks can, however, result in a multiplier greater than one if some proportion of households are credit constrained or consume according to a rule of thumb. We discuss the multiplier further, with a particular focus on government spending, in Chapters 4, 7 and 14.

3.  To what extent will a rise in the interest rate curtail investment? In the simple model in Section 1.2.3, where $I = a_0 - a_1 r$, a rise in the interest rate of $\Delta r$ will reduce investment by $a_1 \Delta r$. In the marginal $q$ theory of investment (with $q = \frac{PBf_K}{\delta + r}$), an increase in the interest rate will increase the marginal cost of investment. If we assume that $q$ is initially equal to one, (i.e. the marginal cost and marginal benefit of carrying out the investment project are equal) then an increase in $r$ will lead firms to reduce investment. The extent to which investment

will fall depends on how quickly the marginal productivity of capital ($f_K$) rises as investment falls to bring $q$ back toward a value of 1.

This chapter has provided a model of the demand side which can shed light on macro-economic questions. We have discussed how the models of consumption and investment relate to characteristics of the real world. For example, the greater volatility of investment as compared with consumption observed in the data can be partly explained by the factors that influence investment spending decisions and by consumers borrowing and saving to smooth their consumption over the economic cycle. Households vary—some are impatient and find it difficult to save, whereas others are prudent and save for precautionary reasons. The government contributes to consumption smoothing through provision of unemployment benefits. Credit constraints facing both households and firms help better align the models of consumption and investment with the empirical data.

Although the demand side is a major influence on economic activity, it is only part of the story of how the macro-economy works. To develop our understanding of economic fluctuations and longer-run trends, we need to introduce the supply side. This will provide a framework for thinking about how wages and prices are set and what determines the unemployment rate. The supply side is the subject of the next chapter.

## 1.4 Appendix

### 1.4.1 Real and nominal interest rates and the Fisher equation

To clarify why it is the real rather than the nominal interest rate that affects real expenditure decisions in the economy, think about a firm considering an investment project. A higher money or nominal rate of interest will not impose a greater real burden on the firm if it is balanced by correspondingly higher inflation, because the expected profits from the investment project will be higher in money terms and the balance between the real cost and the real return on the project will not have changed.

The real interest rate is defined in terms of *goods* and the nominal interest rate, in terms of *money*. Thinking of a consumer good, the real rate of interest, $r$, is how much extra in terms of units of this good - namely $(1+r)$ units - would have to be paid in the future in order to borrow one unit of the goods today. The nominal rate of interest is how much extra in euros would have to be paid in the future in order to borrow one euro today. If goods prices remain constant then it is clear that the real and nominal interest rates are the same: if you lent one euro today, you would be able to buy $(1 + r)$ goods in the future. In general,

$$1 + r = (1 + i) \cdot \frac{P}{P_{t+1}^E},$$

where it is the expected price level in the future ($P_{t+1}^E$) that comes into play since at time $t$, we do not know what the price level will be at $t + 1$. If we use the following definition of expected inflation:

$$\pi^E = \frac{P^E_{t+1} - P}{P},$$

then

$$\frac{P}{P^E_{t+1}} = \frac{1}{1 + \pi^E}.$$

By rearranging the above expression, it follows that

$$(1 + r) = \frac{(1 + i)}{(1 + \pi^E)},$$

and therefore that

$$r = \frac{i - \pi^E}{1 + \pi^E}.$$

When expected inflation is low, the denominator of this expression is close to one and we have the standard approximation for the relationship between the real and the nominal rate of interest:

$$i \approx r + \pi^E. \hspace{3cm} \text{(Fisher equation)}$$

Inflation expectations will drive the divergence between the real and nominal interest rates. It should be noted that only one of these three terms is observable: the nominal interest rate, $i$. The real interest rate can be estimated from historical data on the nominal interest rate and the rate of inflation: this gives a measure of the so-called *ex post* real rate of interest. Alternatively, an *ex ante* measure can be derived from a model that is able to predict inflation. Finally, if bonds have been issued in the economy that are protected against inflation because the face value is indexed by the rate of inflation, then the yield on such a bond is a real rate of interest and can provide a third measure. But there are only a few countries that have issued index-linked or inflation-proof bonds (UK in 1981, the USA in 1997, France in 1998).

### 1.4.2 Deriving the Euler equation and the PIH consumption function

**Deriving the Euler equation**

The first step in deriving the Euler equation is to set out an expression for the present value of a consumer's utility:

$$V^E_t = U(C_t) + \frac{U(C^E_{t+1})}{1 + \rho} + \frac{U(C^E_{t+2})}{(1 + \rho)^2} + ... \hspace{1.5cm} \text{(expected present value of consumption)}$$

The present value equation uses the expectations operator (i.e. $C^E_{t+i}$ for all $i > 0$) to show that future consumption is uncertain in the present period. In addition, the utility of consumption is discounted to the present period by the consumer's rate of time preference. Future consumption will be worth less in the current period to more impatient consumers.

To derive the Euler equation, we need to assume a specific functional form for the utility function. We choose $U(C_t) = \log C_t$ because it exhibits diminishing marginal returns and is easy to work with. We can take the first derivative of the utility function to find the marginal utility of consumption, which is $U'(C_t) = \frac{1}{C_t}$.

The Euler equation shows the optimal $C_t$ in relation to $C_{t+1}^E$. If we just think about these two periods, then it is easy to derive the Euler equation. In period $t$ the consumer must weigh up the gain from consuming more in this period, against the discounted loss of consuming less in the next period. The gain from consuming one unit more in this period is simply the marginal utility of consumption $\frac{1}{C_t}$. The subjective present value loss of utility in the next period is equal to $\frac{1}{C_{t+1}^E}\frac{1}{1+\rho}(1+r)$. This is because the consumer's income will have fallen by $(1+r)$ next period, multiplied by the marginal utility of consumption next period multiplied by the impatience factor.

The consumer cannot gain any more utility when the gain from consuming one more unit in the current period is exactly the same as the subjective present value loss of consuming one unit less in the next period. This gives us the Euler equation:

$$\frac{1}{C_t} = \frac{1}{C_{t+1}^E}\frac{1}{1+\rho}(1+r)$$

$$C_t = \frac{1+\rho}{1+r}C_{t+1}^E. \qquad \text{(Euler equation)}$$

### Deriving the permanent income hypothesis consumption function

The simplest case of the Euler equation is when the rate of interest is equal to the consumer's subjective discount rate $r = \rho$. This is the case we have focused on throughout this chapter. We can see from the Euler equation that this implies $C_t = C_{t+1}^E$. In other words, it implies that consumption is constant in expectation in all future periods.

In order to derive the permanent income hypothesis, we make the additional assumption that future consumption is known with certainty, so that $C_t = C_{t+1} = \cdots = C_{t+i} = C$. To calculate $C$, we need to set out the expression for the present value of consumption, $\overline{C_t}$:

$$\overline{C_t} = C_t + \frac{C_{t+1}}{1+r} + \dots + \frac{C_{t+i}}{(1+r)^i} + \dots = C\left(1 + \frac{1}{1+r} + \dots + \frac{1}{(1+r)^i} + \dots\right)$$

$$= C\left(\frac{1}{1-\frac{1}{1+r}}\right) = C\left(\frac{1+r}{r}\right). \qquad \text{(present value of consumption)}$$

The permanent income hypothesis implies that the present value of consumption has to be equal to the present value of income, $\Psi_t^E$, so that:

$$\overline{C_t} = C\left(\frac{1+r}{r}\right) = \Psi_t^E$$

$$C_t = C = \left(\frac{r}{1+r}\right)\Psi_t^E, \qquad \text{(PIH consumption function)}$$

where $C_t$ is the amount the consumer consumes in each period. It is their permanent income and is equal to the annuity value of their expected lifetime wealth.

## 1.5 Questions

### 1.5.1 Checklist questions

1. What is the *IS* curve? Why does it slope downwards?

2. Use the equation for the *IS* curve shown in Section 1.2.3 to answer the following questions:

    (a) If we assume that $0 < c_1, t < 1$, then what can we say about the size of multiplier?

    (b) If there is a decrease in government spending of $\Delta G$, by how much does this decrease output?

    (c) Describe the feedback process that means a decrease in government spending can decrease output by more than 1 : 1.

3. Use the Keynesian cross to show the effect of a decrease in autonomous investment on the economy. Discuss the path of the economy as it adjusts to the new medium-run equilibrium. Why does the economy not continue to contract?

4. Use the Keynesian cross to illustrate the paradox of thrift. Model the change in savings behaviour as an increase in the marginal propensity to save, $s_1$ (remember that $c_1 + s_1 = 1$). Show how a rise in investment can counteract the reduction in output associated with the rise in savings.

5. Use the equation for the *IS* curve shown in Section 1.2.3 and Fig. 1.6 to discuss what happens to the *IS* curve in response to the following shocks. In each case provide a real world example of what might cause the shock.

    (a) An increase in autonomous consumption (i.e. $\uparrow c_0$).

    (b) A reduction in the interest sensitivity of investment (i.e. $\downarrow a_1$).

    (c) An increase in the marginal rate of taxation (i.e. $\uparrow t$).

6. According to the permanent income hypothesis, how will the paths of borrowing and consumption change in response to:

    (a) A temporary decrease in income when it occurs.

    (b) A permanent decrease in income when it occurs.

    (c) Are the answers different if the changes in income are unanticipated, i.e. if they are 'news'? Comment on the size of the marginal propensity to consume and the size of the multiplier.

7. Assuming the real interest rate is 4%, calculate how, according to the PIH, consumption and borrowing would change in each of the following cases

    (a) A stock market crash permanently reduces the value of an individual's assets by 1,000.

    (b) Households are told that in a year's time, they will receive a one-off bonus of 1,000. Then in one year's time, it is not paid.

    (c) Comment briefly on your results.

8. Explain the concepts of excess sensitivity and excess smoothness that arise from the empirical literature on the permanent income hypothesis. What could explain these findings?

9. What does Tobin's $q$ tell us firms' investment decisions depend upon? According to Tobin's $q$, when should a firm invest?

10. What is the key problem with measuring marginal $q$? Is there an alternative measurement that can be used instead? Is this alternative measurement likely to be an accurate proxy for marginal $q$?

11. Use Section 1.2.7 to discuss what is expected to happen to the *IS* curve in response to the following shocks:

   (a) A crash in the stock market.

   (b) An increase in the retirement age.

   (c) A decrease in the rate of depreciation.

   (d) An increase in the cost of oil.

   (e) An increase in the rate of technological progress.

## 1.5.2 Problems and questions for discussion

1. This question involves collecting data from national statistics agencies (e.g. the UK Office for National Statistics) and/or international organizations (e.g. the OECD or the IMF). First, select an emerging and a developed economy.

   (a) Collect annual data on real GDP as far back as it is available for both countries. Convert the data to the log scale and plot on a graph. Comment on your findings. Calculate the growth rates of GDP for the two countries over the period and plot them on a graph. How do the business cycles of the two countries compare? To what extent do they appear synchronized?

   (b) Collect current price data on GDP and its components for the two countries. Calculate the percentage of GDP according to each of the four main types of expenditure—i.e. household consumption, government consumption, gross fixed capital formation and net exports (i.e. exports minus imports) and plot the series. How does the composition of GDP and changes over time in the two countries compare? Discuss possible reasons for the differences.

2. We start this question with a simple version of the aggregate demand function, where, to keep the maths simple, we omit taxation and government spending:

$$y^D = c_0 + c_1 y + \bar{I}. \tag{1.14}$$

Now, assume that $c_0 = 200$ and $\bar{I} = 200$. In addition, assume that $c_1 = 0.8$, such that:

$$y^D = 200 + 0.8y + 200. \tag{1.15}$$

   (a) What is the level of output in goods market equilibrium?

   (b) Assume there is a fall in the marginal propensity to consume, $c_1$, to 0.6—i.e. there is a rise in the savings rate, as $s_1 + c_1 = 1$. If we assume that the rise in planned savings leads to the accumulation of unplanned inventories of goods and does not increase planned investment ($\bar{I}$), then what is the level of output that satisfies the new goods market equilibrium?

   (c) Compare the level of savings in the new and old goods market equilibria. Note that in goods market equilibrium; $S = s_1 y - c_0$ and $I = \bar{I}$.

   (d) Comment on your findings in (c) in response to the question of whether it is advisable for the policy maker to encourage households to increase their savings to help escape a recession. Describe in words a mechanism, which is not included in this model, that could provide a connection from a policy encouraging households to save more and exit from a recession.

3. Use Section 1.2.4 and appropriate readings from beyond this book to decide whether the following statements (S1 and S2) are both true or whether one of them is false. Justify your answer.

   S1: According to Tobin's $q$ theory, the path of investment is independent of current cash flow (and profits).

   S2: The empirical evidence shows that current cash flow is an important determinant of investment.

4. Aggregate consumption varies less than GDP and aggregate investment varies more. Can you reconcile these observations with the assumption that consumption and investment decisions are taken by rational, forward-looking agents?

# 2 The supply side

## 2.1 Overview

### 2.1.1 Unemployment

Unemployment is a characteristic feature of a market economy. There are unemployed people looking for work who would be prepared to take a job at the going wage but cannot get a job offer. This is involuntary unemployment and it reflects the fact that the labour market does not clear.

Figure 2.1 illustrates how unemployment varies over time and across countries. We can see that there is a large amount of heterogeneity in unemployment across the developed economies in the figure; following the global financial crisis, average unemployment between 2009 and 2012 ranged from 4.5% in the Netherlands to 21.2% in Spain. In addition, the figure highlights that an individual country can experience large changes in unemployment over time; Irish unemployment fell from 16% in the late 1980s to just above 4% in the early 2000s, before rising again to 14% in the wake of the economic crises of 2009–12.

Unemployment is costly to the economy since it represents a waste of resources, and it is associated with unhappiness and psychological distress to those affected. It is a major source of concern for policy makers.

In this chapter, we develop the supply side of the macroeconomic framework to provide a model of unemployment. Whereas the demand side refers to spending decisions, the supply side refers to production activities in the economy. Although both capital and labour are inputs to the production process, we concentrate on the input of labour. The supply side refers to both the supply of labour by workers and the demand for labour by firms. We return to discuss capital accumulation when we look at long-run growth in Chapter 8. On the supply side, we ask how firms decide how much output to produce, how many workers to employ and what prices to set. We want to know about decisions to work and how wages are set.

### 2.1.2 Why the labour market does not clear

When a market clears, the price is such that there is neither excess supply of, nor demand for, the good. If the market is for 'labour', then the wage would rise in response to excess demand and fall in response to excess supply, with the result that there would be no 'unsold' labour. As we shall see, this is not a good way of thinking about the labour market. The data in Fig. 2.1 covers many countries over more than five decades. It reveals unemployment as

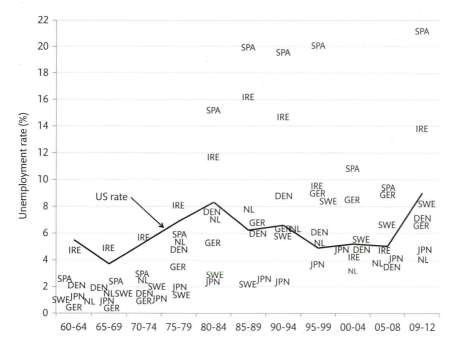

**Figure 2.1** Trends and heterogeneity in unemployment for selected OECD economies, 1960–2012.

*Source:* Howell et al. (2007), Fig. 1.1, p. 10. Updated to 2012 using OECD harmonized unemployment rates.

characteristic of capitalist economies. The general case is one in which there are workers who are willing to work at the going wage but cannot find a job. Consistent with the phenomenon of involuntary unemployment is the large amount of evidence that workers are unhappy when they are unemployed. For example, in an early study, Clark and Oswald (1994) use data for a sample of six thousand British workers in 1991 and find that the unemployed have twice the level of mental distress of the employed.[1]

To understand why the labour market does not clear, we ask the obvious question of why an employer would not offer a job to a worker who is willing to work at a lower wage. One answer is that to be useful to an employer, a worker has to exert effort on the job and when the employer hires the worker at an hourly wage or a monthly or annual salary, she cannot pin down the supply of labour effort. Moreover, she cannot easily observe the effort the worker is making. The way the employer creates an incentive for the worker to work conscientiously is to create a cost to the worker of losing his job. When the employer chooses to set the wage above the level at which a worker would be prepared to take a job, the employee knows that if he loses his job he runs the risk of being unemployed. This makes him work effectively enough to keep his job. The term *efficiency wage setting* is used to describe this aspect of the supply side of the economy.

Thinking of the labour market in this way highlights two key factors that will influence the wage the employer sets.

---

[1] For a review of the literature on unemployment and happiness, see Oswald (1997).

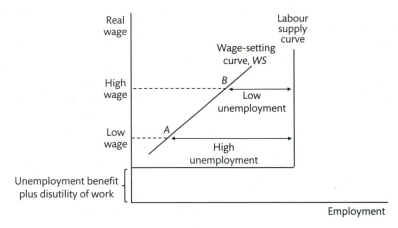

**Figure 2.2** The wage-setting curve, WS.

1. First, is the income available to the worker if he is unemployed. If the alternative to working is claiming unemployment benefit and assuming there is a disutility associated with working, the utility the worker gets from working and receiving the wage must be higher than the utility from the alternative of not working and receiving unemployment benefit.

2. Second, the employer will have to offer a higher wage when the probability of the worker getting another job is higher: the wage she sets will rise as the economy-wide unemployment rate falls.

Figure 2.2 is a diagram with employment on the horizontal axis and the real wage on the vertical axis. The wage-setting curve is upward sloping. To get the worker to work hard, the wage is set above what the worker gets if he is not working (the unemployment benefit) plus the disutility of turning up to work, and it rises as unemployment falls. At point *A*, unemployment is high and a low wage is set: the cost of job loss is relatively high. At point *B*, unemployment is low. Given the relatively low cost of job loss, a higher wage is set.

A rise in the unemployment benefit will shift the wage-setting curve upwards and vice versa.

The labour supply curve is inverse-L shaped. The wage has to be above the unemployment benefit plus the disutility of work for workers to be willing to work effectively. The vertical portion of the labour supply curve is a simplification. Two factors lie behind a steep or 'inelastic' labour supply curve at the level of the economy as a whole. For workers who are already working, a rise in the wage has both an income and a substitution effect. The substitution effect suggests that labour supply rises with the wage because working becomes more worthwhile. The income effect suggests the opposite: since it is assumed that there is a disutility of working, if the same income can be earned from fewer hours of work, labour supply will fall. It is even possible for the labour supply curve to be backward bending if the income effect outweighs the substitution effect. The second factor concerns the decision to participate in the labour market. As the wage increases, participation goes up. There will be a steep labour supply curve if the tendency of workers to enter the labour force when the wage goes up is offset by a fall in hours of work by those who are working.

A point on the wage-setting curve is an answer to the question: what wage has to be paid to secure adequate worker effort (effective labour input) at a given level of unemployment (and associated level of employment)?

A point on the labour supply curve is an answer to the question: if a given wage were to be offered, how much labour would workers be willing to supply?

The horizontal gap between the wage curve and the labour supply curve is therefore involuntary unemployment, because it shows the extra supply of labour that would be offered at that wage but is not employed when wages are set on the wage-setting curve. The vertical gap between the wage-setting curve and the horizontal part of the labour supply curve is inversely related to the cost of job loss at the relevant level of employment: a higher efficiency wage has to be paid when the labour market is tight and it is relatively easy to get another job.

The efficiency wage explanation of why the labour market does not clear is based on the nature of the relationship between employer and worker.[2] Using the language of micro-economics, the special features of labour make it impossible to write a complete contract for the supply of labour in the same way that a contract can be written for the supply of energy or other inputs to the production process. The employer cannot specify in a contract every aspect of the work she requires of the worker and she is unable to perfectly monitor his output. Since worker effort is essential to the employer, it is the wage-setting curve and not the labour supply curve that is relevant for how wages in the economy are set, and, as we shall see, for pinning down the unemployment rate consistent with constant inflation. The outcome is that involuntary unemployment is characteristic of the economy.

It might be suggested that the employer use piece rates rather than an hourly wage to pay workers. By paying for the worker's output rather than the worker's time, the problem of not being able to observe effort is solved. But taking a look at any economy quickly reveals that very little economic activity is organized around piece rates for labour. This is particularly true of modern service-based economies, where output is less easily quantifiable. In addition, much of the production activity in the economy is based on team production, where the contribution of an individual worker is hard to determine.

### 2.1.3 Supply side effects on unemployment

The supply side effects on unemployment relate to both the labour supply and labour demand parts of the economy. The wage-setting curve relates to the *supply of labour* and shows that the real wage that has to be paid to workers rises as employment rises and lies above the labour supply curve. This curve shows the *wage-setting real wage*. This is positively sloped for the efficiency wage reasons explained in the previous subsection. In the modelling section, we discuss a number of other explanations for the wage-setting curve. One of these relates to the case where workers have market power. If the wage is set by a union, then the union can set wages above the efficiency wage. In this case, the wage-setting curve would be above the one that applies in the absence of unions.

---

[2] The efficiency wage model was first formalized in Shapiro and Stiglitz' landmark 1984 paper *Equilibrium Unemployment as a Worker Discipline Device.*

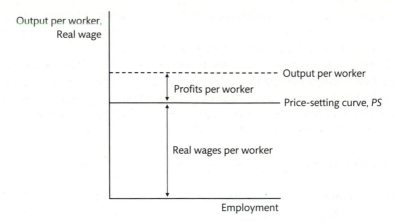

**Figure 2.3** The price-setting curve, PS.

The other side of the labour market reflects the *demand for labour* by imperfectly compet-itive firms. This defines a second real wage: this is the real wage that makes production (and hence, the employment of workers) profitable for the price-setting firm. This curve shows the *price-setting real wage*.

As our baseline case, we use a simple model of labour demand where there is a constant real wage at which price-setting firms find it profitable to employ workers. In the modelling section, we derive the price-setting real wage from the firm's pricing decision. Here we focus on the outcome. We assume that the firm's production function is very simple: labour is the only input, and productivity, which is output per worker, is constant. In order to produce, the firm requires a fixed profit margin and this implies the real wage at which it finds it profitable to employ workers. Given these assumptions, the price setting real wage curve is flat (see Fig. 2.3). As shown in the diagram, output per worker is divided into two chunks: profit per worker and the real wage.

Figure 2.4 shows the wage-setting and price-setting curves. The intersection of the price-setting (PS) curve and the upward-sloping wage-setting (WS) curve determines the real wage, employment and unemployment when the supply side is in equilibrium. The intersection of

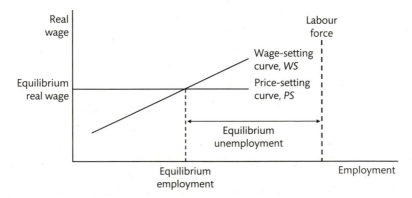

**Figure 2.4** Supply-side equilibrium: the intersection of the wage-setting and price-setting curves.

the wage- and price-setting curves fixes the equilibrium real wage and employment level. At the equilibrium, the real wage is consistent with what is needed to secure sufficient labour (on the *WS* curve) and for production to be profitable (on the *PS* curve).

We can use Fig. 2.4 to show how the unemployment rate is defined. The labour force is shown by a vertical line. This is the total number of people reported by the statistical agency who are working or looking for work. The unemployment rate is defined as unemployment divided by the sum of employment and unemployment, that is, the numbers unemployed divided by the labour force:

$$\text{Unemployment rate} \equiv \frac{\text{unemployed}}{\text{employed} + \text{unemployed}} \equiv \frac{\text{unemployed}}{\text{labour force}}.$$

Equilibrium unemployment is the difference between employment at the *WS* − *PS* intersection and the labour force. From Fig. 2.5, it is clear that equilibrium unemployment will rise if the wage-setting curve shifts up or if the price-setting curve shifts down. Taking the case of a higher unemployment benefit first, we have already seen that a higher unemployment benefit will shift the *WS* curve up. In Fig. 2.5a, this shifts the *WS* curve up to *WS'*. The new *WS* − *PS* intersection is at a lower level of employment. The economics behind this can be explained as follows. For equilibrium, the real wage has to be on the *PS* curve; otherwise firms will not be prepared to produce output. An increase in unemployment benefits reduces the cost of job loss, which shifts the *WS* curve upwards. In order that the real wage on the wage-setting curve is brought down into line with the *PS* curve, it is necessary for unemployment to be higher. Given the higher out-of-work benefits, a higher risk of job loss (which is associated with higher unemployment) is necessary to make an unchanged real wage consistent with wage setters' behaviour.

Equilibrium unemployment will also be higher if the *PS* curve shifts down (from *PS* to *PS'* in Fig. 2.5b). If there is a reduction in the extent of competition in the goods market, which allows the mark-up of price over unit labour costs to rise, the price-setting real wage will be reduced: under the new conditions, firms will only produce if the real wage is lower. In terms of Fig. 2.3, a higher mark-up increases the share of output per worker that goes to profits

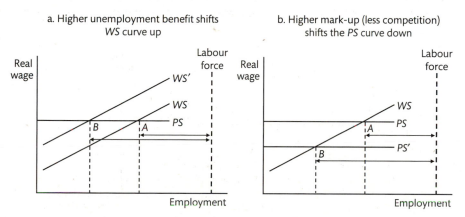

**Figure 2.5** The impact on equilibrium unemployment of shifts in the *WS* and *PS* curves.

*Note*: the double-headed arrows show equilibrium unemployment for each case.

and reduces the share to wages, and hence, the real wage. The new equilibrium is at a lower real wage and higher unemployment. For the wage-setting real wage to be reduced to the new equilibrium level, there must be higher unemployment in the economy. With a higher cost of job loss, the efficiency real wage is lower.

The concept of equilibrium unemployment is a medium to long-run concept. It tells us the unemployment rate at which both wage and price setters are content with the prevailing real wage. The kinds of policies that can be implemented to affect equilibrium unemployment are those that shift the *WS* or the *PS* curve. These are *supply-side policies*.

In the modelling section and in Chapter 15 on supply-side policies, we enrich the model of the supply side by introducing additional institutions and policies that shift the wage- and price-setting curves. A more detailed examination of both institutions and policies is presented in Chapter 15. These include the role of unions, taxes, workplace policies that affect the disutility of exerting effort, labour and product market regulations, and competition policy. These factors help explain both the cross-country variation and the changes over time in the 5-year average unemployment rates shown in Fig. 2.1.

### 2.1.4  Nominal rigidities and demand-side policy

When discussing equilibrium unemployment, the focus is on the medium run when the economy is at a $WS - PS$ intersection, and hence on the effect of supply-side policies and institutions on unemployment. In this subsection, we introduce *nominal rigidities* and the role of *demand-side* policies. The term nominal rigidity refers to the fact that nominal wages (in dollars or euros) and prices do not adjust immediately to fluctuations in aggregate demand to keep the economy at equilibrium unemployment.

In Chapter 1, we assumed an extreme form of this rigidity, namely that prices and wages don't change at all in response to shifts in demand. This meant that when aggregate de- mand shifted, as a result, for example of an investment boom, output and employment in the economy responded fully to bring supply into line with the higher demand. We used the multiplier process to model the response of output and employment based on the as- sumption that wages and prices remained unchanged. An alternative extreme assumption is that the economy is always at the medium-run equilibrium, i.e. at a *WS/PS* intersection, and therefore that fluctuations in aggregate demand do not affect output and employment. The terms 'fixed price' and 'flex price' are sometimes used to label these two extreme cases.

In building a model suitable for analysing real-world economies, we need a model that is neither 'fixed price' nor 'flex price'. The model we set out includes nominal rigidities but wages and prices are not completely fixed. Wages are changed at intervals, for example, at an annual wage review. Nominal rigidities characterize both wage and price setting. More detailed arguments and evidence are provided in the modelling section. Here we summarize the main points. Before doing so, it is important to distinguish between real and nominal wages.

*Nominal wages, real wages and inflation*

To this point, all of the discussion about the supply side has been in terms of the *real* wage. This is because it is the real wage that workers care about (i.e. how much their dollar or euro wage buys in goods and services) and therefore, that the employer has to be concerned with when setting the wage to secure the worker's effort. From the labour demand side, it is the cost of labour in terms of the price they get for their output that firms care about. However, workers are paid a wage in money terms: this is the *nominal* wage and firms set prices.

We can see how real and nominal wages are related in the model as follows. Given the unemployment rate, employers (or unions if they are setting wages) set the nominal wage so as to achieve their desired real wage on the wage setting curve. This means they must make an assumption about the *consumer price level* when they set the nominal wage. Similarly, firms set their *product price* making an assumption about the nominal wage to achieve the price-setting real wage on the *PS* curve. The consumer price level is the outcome of price-setting by firms across the economy.

Note that when wages are set by the employer, it would be the firm's human resources division that sets the nominal wage taking account of the consumer price level to ensure workers supply adequate effort for the firm's operations. Given the nominal wage, the marketing and strategy divisions set the price for the firm's product.

Modern economies are typically characterized by a positive rate of inflation. Central banks often target an inflation rate of 2%. If nominal wages rise by 2% per annum and prices rise by 2% per annum, the real wage is unchanged. At a $WS - PS$ intersection, the real wage is constant, which means nominal wages and prices are rising at the same rate. This is a constant inflation equilibrium.

### Rigidities in wage setting

Nominal wages are set periodically, usually at an annual wage round or review. They are not continuously adjusted by the wage setter. Barattieri et al. (2010) analyse US survey data and find that wages are indeed very 'sticky'; they are most likely to be adjusted just once every year. The authors also find that there is little variation in the frequency of wage changes across different industries and occupations.

An important reason for the stickiness of wages relates to the interactions between employers and workers, where considerations of fairness and morale play an important role. Campbell and Kamlani (1997) surveyed 184 firms and find strong support for two explanations of wage rigidity (in this case, why wages are not cut as much as possible in a recession). First, firms were concerned that wage cuts would lead their most productive workers to quit, whereas layoffs could target the least productive workers. Second, respondents linked wage cuts to reduced worker effort, particularly when wage cuts were viewed as being 'unfair'. Bewley (2007) reviews the empirical literature on fairness and wage rigidity and finds that fairness is one of the primary determinants of company morale. He also finds that wage cuts are only viewed as being fair when they are seen as saving a large number of jobs.

### Rigidities in price setting

The frequency of price changes varies a great deal across industries. However, for large parts of the economy, firms are cautious about frequent price adjustments in response to fluctuations in demand because of their concern about their competitors' and customers' reactions.

A detailed survey of how firms set prices using a structured questionnaire of a random sample of 330 US firms found that almost half of all prices were changed no more than

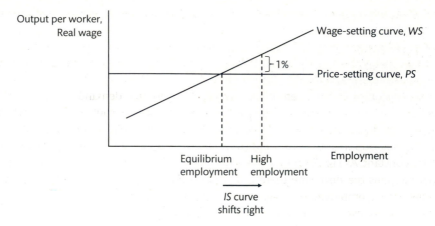

**Figure 2.6** The response of wages and prices to a cyclical upswing.

annually. The survey identified the following major reasons for price stickiness: firms are deterred from raising prices because of concerns their competitors will not follow suit; cost increases are generally industry-wide and can serve as convenient signals that other firms are probably under pressure to raise prices; implicit contracts with customers deter price hikes when demand rises but permit them when costs rise; and firms hold prices steady until the next regularly scheduled price review.[3]

*Aggregate demand shocks and the role of nominal rigidities*

In the macroeconomic model, we make simplifying assumptions about how wage and price rigidities operate. The simplifying assumptions reflect the arguments presented about why wages and prices are adjusted infrequently. We assume that wage contracts are reviewed annually at the 'wage round'. This means that if an aggregate demand shock occurs in the interval between wage rounds, the wage is not adjusted. We assume that prices are not adjusted in response to shifts in aggregate demand; however, prices are adjusted immediately following the wage round. Since the adjustment in wages will reflect changes in aggregate demand, prices respond to changes in aggregate demand with a lag.

The timeline for wage and price setting, shocks and changes in output and employment can be summarized as follows:

Aggregate demand shock  → output and employment change

Next wage round  → nominal wages change

Immediately after the wage round  → prices change

Before looking at an aggregate demand shock, we look at what happens when the economy is at supply-side equilibrium in an environment of constant inflation. The equilibrium is where the WS and PS curves intersect in Fig. 2.6. Inflation in the previous year was 2%.

At the next annual wage round, wage setters observe that prices have risen 2% over the previous year and they will set a 2% nominal wage increase to keep the real wage constant.

---

[3] See Blinder et al. (1998).

After the wage round, firms will observe that the 2% increase in wages has increased their costs by 2%. If they raise their prices by 2%, this will keep their profit margin constant (the real wage will remain on the *PS* curve). As long as the economy remains at the equilibrium level of employment, wage and price inflation will remain unchanged at 2% per year and the real wage will remain constant.

We now look at what happens when there is an aggregate demand shock of the kind discussed in Chapter 1: for example, an investment boom raises output. Since the investment boom does not affect the *WS* or the *PS* curve, it has no effect on equilibrium unemployment. The investment boom raises output and employment in the short run: we assume output per worker is constant. As Fig. 2.6 shows, the economy is no longer in medium-run equilibrium.

What happens the next time there is an opportunity for wages to be adjusted? At the next wage round, employment is higher and wage setters will respond by setting a nominal wage increase to take the real wage up to the point on the *WS* curve at the higher level of employment. They will need a 2% nominal wage increase as usual, plus an additional increase. In the example shown in Fig. 2.6, this is an extra 1%. Nominal wages go up by 3%. How do price setters respond to the higher wages? Their costs have risen by 3% (rather than the usual 2%), so they mark up this cost increase in their prices and price inflation goes up from 2% to 3%. Firms are likely to feel comfortable about raising their prices at this point, because they can observe that wages have gone up during the annual wage round for their competitors as well. We have the result that an expansion of aggregate demand that pushes output and employment above the equilibrium level is followed by a rise in wage and price inflation.

To summarize, when the economy is at equilibrium unemployment, inflation is constant. A demand shock will shift the economy away from equilibrium because wages and prices do not adjust instantly to keep the economy at equilibrium. Instead, output and employment respond to the change in aggregate demand. In the example of an investment boom, this leads to a fall in unemployment and a rise in inflation. More generally, a positive demand shock leads to a movement away from equilibrium with higher employment and a rise in inflation; a negative demand shock leads to lower employment and lower inflation.

This behaviour of the economy, which is called an upswing or downswing of the *business cycle*, creates a role for a policy maker who aims to improve welfare by keeping the economy close to the medium-run equilibrium unemployment rate. The involuntary unemployment characteristic of the economy when it is at the constant inflation equilibrium (i.e. *WS − PS* intersection) is raised in a business cycle downswing and lowered in an upswing. A policy maker who focuses on stabilization and uses demand side policy is introduced in Chapter 3.

### 2.1.5 Facts about the supply side

*Efficiency wage setting*

There is a large body of empirical evidence documenting the existence of a 'wage curve', which is represented in the model by the *WS* curve.[4] Microeconomic data on local labour

---

[4] For an introduction to the empirical literature on using microeconomic evidence to estimate wage curves, see Blanchflower and Oswald (1995).

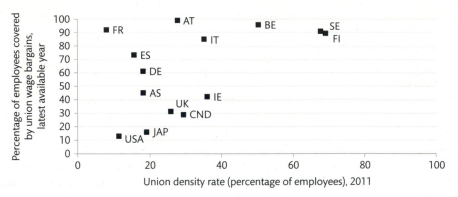

**Figure 2.7** The importance of unions in wage setting: selected OECD countries.

*Source:* Jelle Visser, Amsterdam Institute for Advanced Labour Studies AIAS, ICTWSS Database Version 4 (April 2013). AS Australia, AT Austria, BE Belgium, CND Canada, DE Germany, ES Spain, FI Finland, FR France, IE Ireland, IT Italy, JA Japan, SE Sweden. See footnote 8.

markets is used to uncover the relationship between a change in the unemployment rate at the local level and the wage that is paid. A comprehensive meta-study of more than 200 estimates from a large number of countries points toward the existence of a wage curve with an elasticity of –0.07. This means that a 10% rise in the unemployment rate (for example, an increase in the rate of unemployment from 10% to 11%) would, holding everything else constant, lead to a fall in the real wage of 0.7%.[5]

A vivid example of efficiency wage setting from the early years of mass manufacturing in the US is documented by Raff and Summers (1987): this is Henry Ford's introduction of a $5 day for his production workers in 1914. This represented a 240% pay increase for workers at his plant. Worker turnover fell from 370% in 1913 to only 16% in 1915 and absenteeism was reduced from 10% to 2.5% in just one year.[6] The authors conclude that in this case, wage increases resulted in significant productivity benefits and higher profits.

It is important to understand that the increase in pay was not a response to labour shortage. On the contrary, there were queues of workers wanting to work in the factory and yet instead of allowing the wage to fall to 'clear the market', Ford did the opposite, raising wages substantially.[7] This is taken as a famous illustration of the payment of efficiency wages. As will be discussed further in Chapter 15, efficiency wages appear to be intrinsic to the labour market, even in emerging economies that rely on cheap labour, such as China.

*Union wage setting*

In many economies, unions play a central role in wage setting, as shown by Fig. 2.7. In some European countries, wages set by unions cover virtually the entire workforce (e.g. 99% in Austria). In the US, by contrast, only 13% of workers are covered. In general, we can think of

---

[5] See Nijkamp and Poot (2005).

[6] Turnover is measured as the total amount of workers hired in a year divided by the average workforce for that year. For example, Ford had to hire 50,448 workers in 1913 to maintain an average workforce of just 13,623. This equates to annual turnover of 370%. All figures from Raff and Summers (1987).

[7] See Raff and Summers (1987).

the labour market comprising two parts: a unionized sector and a non-unonized sector. In the latter, wages are not covered by union agreements and employers set efficiency wages; in the unionized sector, wages are set by unions. When unions set wages, they can use their bargaining power to set the wage above the efficiency wage. In the model, this implies a higher *WS* curve.

The variation in the presence and organization of unions across countries is interesting because it gives a hint at one of the reasons unemployment rates may differ across countries for lengthy periods of time. In some countries, labour markets are highly unionized, in others they are not. Types of union bargaining vary widely. In some countries with very high coverage of the workforce by union wage bargains, unemployment is lower than the OECD average (e.g. in Austria and the Nordic countries) whereas in others, such as France or Italy, unemployment rates are relatively high.

This suggests that the answer to the question of the role of unions in unemployment is more complex than we might think at first. It turns out that in institutional situations where unions are powerful and recognize their influence on the whole economy, they tend to exercise bargaining restraint, which is compatible with low unemployment (a downward shift in the *WS* curve in the model). In other settings, powerful unions take a narrower perspective and do not exercise restraint. Their bargaining power allows them to set higher wages and the economy ends up with higher unemployment.

The importance of unions and collective bargaining in wage setting in OECD countries is demonstrated in Fig. 2.7.[8] The scatterplot shows union density, which is the proportion of wage and salary earners in employment who are union members, and bargaining (or union) coverage, which is the proportion of wage and salary earners who are covered by wage bargaining agreements. The latter measure accounts for the fact that wage bargaining agreements might implicitly stretch wider than those workers who are in unions. For example, the latest available data for France shows union density of just 8% but bargaining coverage of 92%.

### The constant inflation rate of unemployment

Actual unemployment will deviate from the equilibrium rate of unemployment over the economic cycle as a result of fluctuations in aggregate demand, for example due to shifts in the *IS* curve as discussed in Chapter 1. In Fig. 2.8, we show actual unemployment rates and estimates made by the OECD of constant inflation unemployment rates in four advanced economies.

The constant inflation or equilibrium rate of unemployment is sometimes called the NAIRU—the Non-Accelerating Inflation Rate of Unemployment. This is an estimate of the unemployment rate at which inflation would be constant. The figures show, as expected, that the NAIRU is much less volatile than actual unemployment in all four countries. Actual unemployment is measured in a comparable way across countries using labour market surveys (the so-called harmonized rate of unemployment published by the OECD).

---

[8] The variables used from database were UD and UD_s for union density and AdjCov for bargaining coverage. See AIAS website for detailed definitions. Union density data is for 2011 for all countries except France and Spain, where it is for 2010. Bargaining coverage is for the latest available year, which ranges between 2007 and 2011.

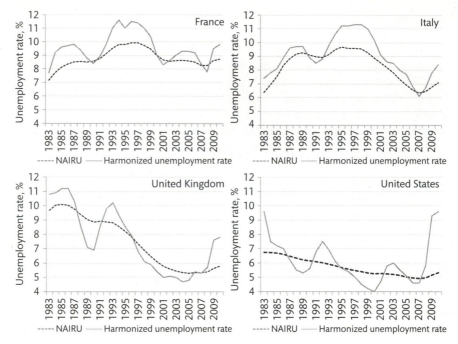

**Figure 2.8** Non-Accelerating Inflation Rate of Unemployment (NAIRU) and harmonized unemployment rates in France, Italy, the United Kingdom and the United States: 1983–2010.

*Source:* OECD Economic Outlook (accessed December 2011).

Patterns of unemployment differed between the continental European economies (France and Italy) and the UK and US over this period. Unemployment rates in France and Italy were consistently above equilibrium, whereas there were periods when unemployment was both above and below equilibrium in the UK and the US.

Figure 2.8 also shows that actual and equilibrium unemployment were on average higher in these continental European economies than in the Anglo-Saxon ones over the period, with all countries excluding France experiencing a sustained drop in the equilibrium rate of unemployment from the mid nineties to the onset of the global financial crisis in 2008. In all four countries, actual unemployment rose dramatically during the global economic downturn and was slow to fall thereafter.

In Fig. 2.8, we saw that unemployment differs from equilibrium unemployment over the economic cycle. In the *WS − PS* model, when output is above equilibrium (i.e. when unemployment is below equilibrium), this creates upward inflationary pressure and vice versa.

Figure 2.9 displays the inflation rates in selected OECD countries from the 1960s to the present: whilst inflation in the past decade has been low at 2% to 3% in many of the OECD countries, it was much higher, and often at rates between 10% and 20% in the 1970s. By comparing Fig. 2.8 and Fig. 2.9, we can see that the decline in inflation in France and Italy from high rates at the end of the 1970s to very low rates in the mid 2000s is consistent with the persistence of unemployment above the estimated constant inflation rate during this period.

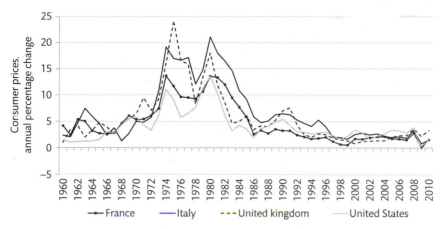

**Figure 2.9** Consumer price inflation rates in France, Italy, the United Kingdom and the United States: 1960–2010.

*Source:* OECD Monthly Economic Indicators (accessed January 2012).

In Chapter 3, we look at the costs of getting inflation down from its high levels in the 1970s in terms of prolonged high unemployment. The years of so-called 'stagflation'—a combination of high unemployment and high inflation—imposed heavy costs on economies. As a consequence, policy makers sought to find better ways of managing the economy. One outcome was a move to inflation targeting and central bank independence.

## 2.2 Modelling

Following the distinction between the role played by real and nominal rigidities introduced in Section 2.1, we break down the modelling of the supply side in this section into two parts, each of which is focused on an important question.

1. Supply-side effects on unemployment. In Section 2.2.1, we shall look in more detail at the structural features of the economy that determine the medium-run equilibrium level of output and unemployment around which the economy fluctuates over the course of the business cycle.

2. Nominal rigidities, inflation and the business cycle. What happens when the economy is away from equilibrium—e.g. as a consequence of fluctuations in aggregate demand? In particular, what is the response of inflation? Answering this question in Section 2.2.2 involves extending the discussion of inflation from Section 2.1 and introducing Phillips curves.

In the applications section (2.3) at the end of the chapter, we show how we can combine the demand and supply sides to model the business cycle. Shocks to aggregate demand and to the supply side move the economy away from equilibrium. This leads us into Chapter 3, where we introduce the policy maker and show how policy intervention can stabilize the economy following a shock.

### 2.2.1 Supply side effects on unemployment

In Section 2.1, we begin with the fact that the employer cannot write and enforce a complete contract specifying work effort. Faced with this problem, the employer will *choose* to pay a wage that is higher than the wage at which the worker would be prepared to work. The implication is that there is involuntary unemployment in equilibrium. In the Appendix, we set out the textbook model of a perfectly competitive labour market where the labour market clears in equilibrium (we call this the hiring hall case). Some readers may find it is a useful reference point because it shows how the textbook model differs from the model of the supply side that we use in this book.

### Incomplete employment contracts and price-setting firms

Since involuntary unemployment is a ubiquitous characteristic of market economies, this is a defining feature of the supply-side equilibrium in the macro model we are building. As we discuss in Section 2.1, wages will be set above the level at which a worker would supply labour. This defines the wage-setting curve. Facing downward-sloping demand curves for their products, firms set prices as a mark-up over their costs. This defines the price-setting curve. The real wage and equilibrium employment are the outcome of these wage- and price-setting decisions across the economy.

### The labour supply side and wage setting

Efficiency wage setting means there must be a cost of job loss. At the prevailing real wage, say, $w_0$, additional workers would be prepared to work. However, they cannot bid down the wage because the employer knows that given the state of the labour market, unless $w_0$ is paid, the cost of job loss will not be high enough for workers to stay and work diligently.

The economics and management literatures stress a broad range of incentive problems faced by employers because of information problems in the labour market. In addition to the role of motivation that we have discussed, employers face problems of retention and recruitment.

Worker turnover is costly to employers. Workers move from job to job, from employment to unemployment (and vice versa) and also leave and enter the labour force. In the simple explanation of efficiency wages set out above, the worker either worked hard enough to be valuable to the employer or not. A richer model would include the employer's need to pay a wage that takes account of the costs she incurs due to turnover. The employer's optimal response to this is to raise the wage—it pays the employer to pay a higher wage in order to reduce turnover. Moreover, when unemployment is lower, it is easier for a worker to find another job and turnover will go up. This provides another explanation for the positively sloped wage-setting curve that is above the labour supply curve.

Similar arguments apply to recruitment. Recruitment in the real world is normally a difficult process, in which the firm has to compete against other firms to get the new hires it wants, and having unfilled vacancies is costly to the firm. In this case, it pays the employer to pay a higher wage in order to reduce the incidence of unfilled vacancies. A realistic assumption is that the proportion of its vacancies that it can fill depends positively on the wage it offers relative to its competitors and negatively on the tightness of the labour market.

Taking account of all of these considerations, the unemployment rate is therefore a key determinant of the 'wage-setting real wage', which lies above the labour supply curve.

In terms of nominal wages, and writing the wage setting equation in terms of employment, it is

$$W = P^E \cdot B(N, \mathbf{z}_w),$$

where $P^E$ is the expected price level and $B$ is a positive function of the level of employment, $N$, and a set of wage-push variables, $\mathbf{z}_w$. Whether wages are set by unions, employers, or through bargaining, it is the *nominal* (i.e. money) wage that is fixed. However, workers will evaluate wage offers in terms of the *real* wage it is expected to deliver—i.e. it is the nominal wage relative to the expected consumer price level that affects workers' standard of living and hence their utility.

The wage equation can be written in terms of real wages to define the upward-sloping wage-setting curve:

$$w^{WS} = \frac{W}{P^E} = B(N, \mathbf{z}_w). \qquad \text{(wage-setting real wage equation, } WS\text{)}$$

We set out a simple formal model of efficiency wage setting in Chapter 15. The basic diagram is shown in Fig. 2.10. The opportunity cost of taking a job consists of two elements: the unemployment benefit and the disutility of exerting effort when working. The wage on the wage-setting curve is above the opportunity cost of working and increases as the unemployment rate falls. As we shall see in Chapter 15, the equation for the wage-setting curve is non-linear: this is because as involuntary unemployment approaches zero, the cost of job loss goes toward zero and the wage that has to be paid to elicit effort goes toward infinity. Similarly, as the wage approaches the opportunity cost of working, it will not be possible to recruit labour. The figure highlights the presence of both voluntary and involuntary unemployment when the economy is at a medium-run equilibrium on the WS curve.

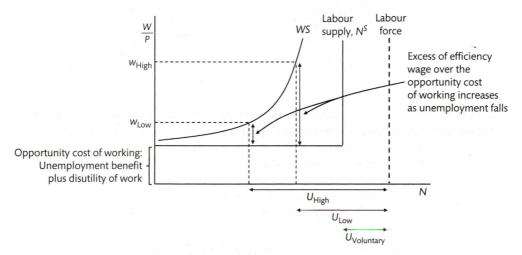

**Figure 2.10** Efficiency wage setting.

To simplify the diagrams, we normally draw the *WS* curve as linear: it will be shifted by the unemployment benefit (Fig. 2.5a) and by the other wage push factors, $z_w$, including the effects of unions.

When workers have market power in the labour market, then the gap between the wage on the *WS* curve and the opportunity cost of working consists of:

1. the mark-up per worker (in real terms) that has to be paid in order to get the worker to exert effort and

2. any additional mark-up associated with worker bargaining power.

Workers can have bargaining power in the labour market because they have particular skills or because they are organized into unions. In unionized workplaces, wages are set through negotiations between the employer and the union. A simplified model of union wage-setting takes the case of the so-called monopoly union, where the union can unilaterally set the wage. The union sets the wage in the interests of its members, who are concerned with both the real wage and employment. It aims to strike a balance between (i) too high a wage, which will push up the price of the firm's product and decrease demand for the firm's output and hence reduce employment; and (ii) too low a wage, which will fail to use the union's monopoly power to secure better living standards over and above the efficiency wage. A model of union wage-setting is developed in Chapter 15.

*Shifts in the* WS *curve*

The wage-push factors in the wage-setting curve (the $z_w$'s) include institutional, policy, structural and shock variables.

The *WS* curve shifts down, which reduces equilibrium unemployment, when:

1. There is a fall in the level of unemployment benefits or their duration. This raises the cost of job loss.

2. There is a fall in the disutility of effort. Improvements in working conditions shift the *WS* curve downwards because they increase the cost of job loss, reducing the wage that has to be paid to get workers to work effectively.

3. Unions are given less legal protection. This reduces the union mark-up.

4. Unions are weaker, for example as measured by a lower proportion of trade union members amongst employees (lower trade union density) or when a lower proportion of employees are covered by collective bargaining agreements (lower collective bargaining coverage). (We discuss the evolution of trade union density and coverage for OECD countries over the last 50 years in Chapter 15.)

5. Unions agree to exercise bargaining restraint in the context, for example, of a wage accord, because this lowers the real wage that is acceptable to unions at a given unemployment rate.

## The labour demand side and price setting

In a textbook, perfectly competitive goods market, firms are price and wage-takers: they maximize profits by taking the market price, *P*, and setting it equal to their marginal cost:

$$P = MC$$
$$= \frac{W}{MPL}$$
$$\Rightarrow \frac{W}{P} = MPL.$$

The marginal product of labour (or labour demand) curve therefore shows the employment level a competitive firm will choose at a given real wage.

By contrast, firms facing downward-sloping demand curves *set a price* to maximize profits. The mark-up on marginal cost will depend on the elasticity of demand, which is the responsiveness of output demanded to a change in price. As the elasticity of demand rises, the mark-up falls until we get to the special case of perfect competition, where the elasticity of demand is infinite and the price is the one that clears the market.

When a firm faces a downward-sloping demand curve (and assuming for simplicity it does not behave strategically towards other firms), it maximizes profits when marginal revenue is equal to marginal cost. If the (absolute value of the) elasticity of demand ($\eta$, called eta) is constant, then there is a constant mark-up of ($\frac{1}{\eta-1} = \mu$) and we have the price-setting formula (derived in the Appendix):

$$P = \left(1 + \frac{1}{\eta - 1}\right)\left(\frac{W}{MPL}\right) \equiv (1 + \mu)\left(\frac{W}{MPL}\right). \qquad \text{(price-setting (mark-up) equation)}$$

For example, if the elasticity of demand is 8, $\mu = 0.14$, and the price is set at 14% above marginal cost. The Greek letter $\mu$, mu, is pronounced 'mew'.

The next step is to derive the price-setting real wage from the price-setting equation:

$$\frac{W}{P} = \frac{1}{(1 + \mu)}MPL \qquad (2.1)$$
$$= (1 - \mu)MPL, \qquad \text{(price-setting real wage)}$$

where to simplify the equations, we use the approximation $\frac{1}{(1+\mu)} \approx (1 - \mu)$, which holds for low values of the mark-up, $\mu$.[9]

Figure 2.11 illustrates the *PS* curve: the price-setting real wage is a fraction of the marginal product of labour. For the example of the elasticity of demand of 8, the price-setting real wage is 86% of the level of the marginal product of labour.

The excess of the real wage on the labour demand curve above that on the *PS* curve at any level of employment is the supernormal profits per worker (in real terms) associated with imperfect competition in the product market.

For simplicity in working with the macro model, we normally use a horizontal rather than a downward-sloping *PS* curve. As we have seen, switching from perfect to imperfect competition does not in itself lead to a horizontal *PS* curve. Additional assumptions are required.

---

[9] For the (absolute value of the) elasticity of demand above 5, the approximation is close. For other values of the elasticity, it is necessary to use the exact definition of the mark-up.

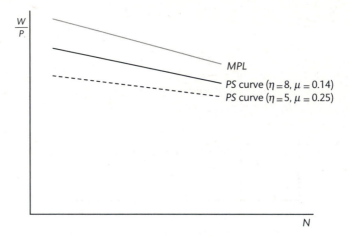

**Figure 2.11** Relationship between the *MPL*, the price elasticity of demand ($\eta$), and the *PS* curve.

Two alternatives are:

1. If the marginal product of labour is constant (which implies that it is equal to the average product) and the mark-up is constant, the price-setting real wage is equal to a constant fraction of labour productivity.

2. If firms set their prices using a rule of thumb, basing their price on their average costs over the business cycle (i.e. as the economy moves from recession to boom and vice versa) the *PS* curve would also flatten. Such a 'normal cost pricing' rule might result from firms wishing to limit the extent to which they modify their prices in response to changes in costs associated with changes in demand.

When looking explicitly at different patterns of how the real wage moves over the course of the business cycle or at the implications of supply-side policies for real wages, we should consider the more general downward-sloping *PS* curve. In other cases, it is more straightforward to use a flat *PS* curve.

Taking the simplest case, to derive a flat *PS* curve, we assume constant productivity and a constant mark-up. Given these assumptions, if firms set prices to deliver a specific profit margin, then the fixed amount of output per worker is split into two parts: profits per worker and real wages per worker. The real wage implied by pricing behaviour is therefore constant and the *PS* curve is flat. Price setting can then be summarized as the marking up of unit labour costs by a fixed percentage, $\mu$,

$$P = (1 + \mu)\left(\frac{W}{\lambda}\right),\tag{2.2}$$

where unit labour costs are the cost of labour per unit of output; i.e. $W \times N$ divided by $y$. We define $\frac{y}{N}$ (output per worker) as $\lambda$ (lambda, labour productivity) and using the same approximation as above, we have:

$$\frac{W}{P} = \frac{1}{(1 + \mu)}\lambda\tag{2.3}$$

$$= (1 - \mu)\lambda.\tag{2.4}$$

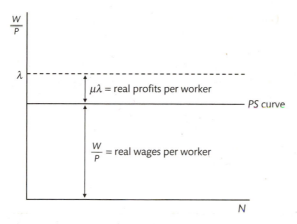

**Figure 2.12** The price-setting real wage curve: *PS*.

We write the price setting real wage equation:

$$w^{PS} = \frac{W}{P} = \lambda(1 - \mu). \qquad \text{(PS, price-setting real wage equation)}$$

In other words, given the mark-up, the level of labour productivity, and the nominal wage, the price level set by firms implies a specific value of the real wage.

A simple rearrangement of the *PS* equation shows how output per worker is decomposed into real profits per worker and the real wage as a result of the firm's price-setting decision and this is illustrated in Fig. 2.12:

$$\lambda = \mu\lambda + \frac{W}{P} \qquad (2.5)$$

output per worker = real profits per worker + real wages per worker.

### Shifts in the *PS* curve

*The tax wedge: how are W and P measured?*

Before providing examples of the price-shift variables, one clarification is needed. Once income taxes, labour taxes such as social security contributions and indirect taxes such as VAT are introduced, we have to be clear about what $W$ and $P$ measure and which measure we show on the axis in the labour market diagram. This is a matter of choosing a convention, and we find it convenient to show the real consumption wage in the labour market diagram. This entails measuring $W$ as the post-tax money wage paid to the employee and to measure $P_c$ as the consumer price index, i.e. inclusive of indirect taxes, $t_v$.

$$P_c = P(1 + t_v).$$

This means that when we show $w = W/P_c$ on the axis of the labour market diagram, this is the real consumption wage—the concept relevant from the perspective of the utility of the worker.

By contrast, the real wage that is of relevance to the employer is the real product wage, which is the full cost of labour to firms—inclusive of income tax and non-wage labour costs such as social security contributions paid by employers and employees—divided by the price the firm gets for its product (i.e. excluding indirect taxes). This is called the producer price. The difference between the real consumption wage and the real product wage is called the *tax wedge*. Given the way we have defined the labour market diagram in terms of $W$ and $P_c$, the wedge shows up as a price-push factor. Any increase in either direct or indirect taxation reduces the price-setting real wage and therefore shifts the *PS* curve downwards. The derivation of the *PS* curve including the tax wedge is shown in the Appendix.

### Price-push factors

We incorporate the tax wedge as one of the price-push factors and write the *PS* curve compactly as:

$$w^{PS} = \lambda F(\mu, \mathbf{z}_p),$$    (*PS* curve including price-push factors)

where $\mathbf{z}_p$ is a set of price push variables including the tax wedge.

The *PS* curve shifts up, reducing equilibrium unemployment, when there is

1. a fall in the tax wedge, which is included in $\mathbf{z}_p$,
2. a fall in the mark-up, $\mu$, due, for example, to a change in competitive conditions such as tougher competition policy rules or enforcement, or
3. a rise in productivity, $\lambda$.

It is important to note that what matters for shifting the *PS* curve and therefore for affecting equilibrium unemployment is the tax wedge as a whole: a rise in income tax or in indirect tax will push equilibrium unemployment up. There is nothing special about the effect of the so-called payroll taxes, i.e. the employer and employee social security contributions. In Chapter 15, we look at the evidence about how much the equilibrium rate of unemployment is expected to increase if the tax wedge increases by ten percentage points.

Other factors included in $\mathbf{z}_p$ may be regulations that increase the cost of employment, such as business registration and some employment regulations. However, such regulations do not necessarily have the effect of increasing price push and therefore raising the equilibrium rate of unemployment. For example, although regulations enforcing health and safety standards impose costs on firms, they may have a compensating positive effect on productivity.

### Equilibrium in the labour market

The labour market is characterized by an upward-sloping *WS* curve and a flat or downward-sloping *PS* curve. The labour market is in equilibrium where the curves cross (see Fig. 2.13):

$$w^{WS} = w^{PS}$$
$$B(N, \mathbf{z}_w) = \lambda F(\mu, \mathbf{z}_p),$$    (labour market equilibrium)

and this defines the unique equilibrium level of employment $N_e$. The associated equilibrium rate of unemployment is $U_e/L$, where $L$ is the labour force.

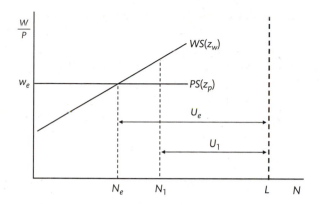

**Figure 2.13** Equilibrium employment and unemployment: $N_e$ and $U_e$.

## Unemployment in equilibrium

The equilibrium rate of unemployment is the outcome of the structural or supply-side features of the economy that lie behind the wage-setting and price-setting curves. It can therefore in principle be changed by supply-side policies or structural changes that affect either the wage-push or price-push factors.

An increase in the degree of product market competition—as a result, say, of changes in the application of competition policy or because the internet makes it easier to compare prices—would produce a lower profit margin ($\mu$) and a higher real wage at each level of employment (the $PS$ curve would shift up). Similarly, any government policy change that affects wage- and price-setting outcomes will shift equilibrium unemployment. Policies related to the cost of job loss such as unemployment benefits, changes in taxation, labour, and product market regulation and incomes accords are all relevant. It is thus easy to imagine that international differences in policy and in institutional structures produce differences in equilibrium unemployment. We return to analyse supply-side shifts and the evidence regarding their role in explaining cross-country unemployment trends in Chapter 15.

## 2.2.2 Nominal rigidities, inflation and the business cycle

### Demand-driven cycles

In Section 2.1 we explained that the economy will be shifted away from the medium-run equilibrium (where the $WS$ and $PS$ curves intersect) by fluctuations in aggregate demand. Wages and prices do not adjust spontaneously to keep the economy at equilibrium unemployment. We reported the survey evidence that wages are set periodically and that employers do not cut nominal wages when unemployment goes up.

What about prices? Fluctuations in aggregate demand lead to business cycle upswings and downswings if firms respond to changes in demand by altering output and employment. If prices and wages change but output does not change, then we would not observe demand-driven business cycles. One explanation for demand-driven cycles is that imperfectly competitive firms find it profitable to respond to shifts in demand by changing their output.[10] Price stickiness refers to the reluctance of firms to change prices in the face of changes in aggregate demand.

The demand curve faced by an imperfectly competitive firm is shifted by shocks to aggregate demand in the economy of the kind introduced in Chapter 1. It is clear from the mark-up equation (price-setting (mark-up) equation) that when profits are maximized, the price will be above marginal cost: the firm will make supernormal profits.

In general, a shift in the firm's demand curve will change the profit maximizing price and quantity. However, since its price exceeds its marginal cost, the firm can afford not to change its price, and its decision comes down to a trade-off between the costs and benefits of doing so. It seems there are costs associated with changing prices. One type of cost is the so-called menu cost. The term comes from the idea that there are costs involved in changing the prices on menus in restaurants. This is a relevant consideration for those firms that operate with posted prices like restaurants, or firms with printed price catalogues. However, these costs seem much less relevant for firms where prices can be changed at the touch of a button. However, even when the technology is available to adjust prices at low cost, a firm may worry that it will lose customers if it changes its price when other firms producing similar products do not. Given that the benefits of changing price are likely to be modest under imperfect competition, the costs do not have to be large to outweigh the benefits.

In the model of pricing we use in defining the price-setting curve, the price is set as a mark up on unit labour costs:

$$P = (1 + \mu)\left(\frac{W}{\lambda}\right). \tag{2.6}$$

This means that the price responds only to changes in labour costs and since productivity, $\lambda$, is constant, the price responds only to changes in nominal wages. In this model, firms do not change their prices at all in response to changes in aggregate demand. We can summarize by saying that in the model, prices are sticky in response to shifts in demand and flexible in response to changes in costs, that is, to changes in wages.

A large study has used firm level (i.e. micro) data sources and surveys to investigate price stickiness in the euro area.[11] The authors find that firms in the euro area change their prices infrequently, on average once a year. They also found that the main sources of price stickiness are strategic interactions between competing firms and implicit or explicit contracts with their customers, with menu costs being judged less important. The older survey evidence reported in the overview section noted that firms coordinate their price increases around industry-wide wage rounds.

*Business cycles and inflation: the Phillips curve*

As we saw in the previous subsection, there is a unique unemployment rate at which the labour market is in equilibrium. At this equilibrium, the WS and PS curves intersect, which means both wage and price setters are content with the prevailing real wage and have no incentive to alter their behaviour. In this section, we focus on nominal rigidities and how

---

[10] See Solow (1998) for further discussion of this point.          [11] See Álvarez et al. (2005).

fluctuations in aggregate demand produce business cycle upswings and downswings around the equilibrium rate of unemployment.

To simplify the modelling, we have assumed that labour productivity is constant. This implies that changes in output are reflected by one-for-one in changes in employment. When drawing diagrams, it means that the horizontal shift in output is the same as in employment. In the real world, there is not a one-for-one relationship between changes in output and employment. Okun's law refers to the empirical relationship between a change in aggregate demand, output and the unemployment rate.

### Box 2.1 Okun's Law

When output rises, workers who have been kept on the pay-roll but have not been fully employed (e.g. those working shorter than normal hours) may be fully utilized, with the result that higher output does not—at least initially—entail a rise in employment. This is called labour hoarding. Also even if employment rises, unemployment does not necessarily fall if the new jobs are taken by those who were not previously in the labour force. People of working age who are neither employed nor unemployed are called economically inactive and the decision of whether or not to participate in the labour market is dependent on economic conditions.

The combination of labour hoarding and changes in the labour force mean that a 1% change in output growth above or below its trend tends to be associated with respectively a fall or rise in the unemployment rate of less than 0.5 percentage points. This empirical relationship between changes in the growth rate relative to its trend and changes in the unemployment rate is called Okun's Law (an Okun coefficient of −0.5). The responsiveness of unemployment to changes in growth is lower in countries with tighter regulations on hiring and firing (as observed in many continental European countries) and with stronger traditions of lifetime employment (as observed in Japan).

Ball, Leigh and Loungani (2012) find that Okun's Law has been a 'strong and stable relationship' in the major advanced economies since the Second World War. They argue that this relationship did not change substantially in the financial crisis of 2008-09, but that there is a large variation across countries in the coefficient in the relationship (i.e. the degree of responsiveness of the unemployment rate to output). They find an Okun's coefficient of −0.45 for the US, −0.15 for Japan and a much higher coefficient of –0.85 for Spain, where temporary employment contracts are prevalent.

A positive aggregate demand shock increases employment above the equilibrium level, and inflation rises. The timing of events is summarized as before:

Aggregate demand shock → output and employment change

Next wage round → nominal wages change

Immediately after the wage round → prices change

This behaviour is modelled by the Phillips curve. We now need to formalize that relationship to develop the model of inflation and unemployment.

The WS curve says that the real wage increases with employment. It simplifies the modelling to express this in terms of the *output gap*, $(y_t - y_e)$, and to write the WS curve in linear form:

$$w^{ws}(y_t) = (W/P)^{ws} = B + \alpha(y_t - y_e) + z_w,$$ (WS curve; linear form)

where $B$ is a constant reflecting the unemployment benefit and the disutility of work, and $z_w$ is the set of wage-push factors. As a result of price setting always restoring the real wage to the equilibrium real wage which is equal to $w_e = B + z_w$, wage setters will attempt to increase the expected real wage by $w^{WS}(y_t) - w_{-1} = w^{WS}(y_t) - w_e = (B + \alpha(y_t - y_e) + z_w) - (B + z_w) = \alpha(y_t - y_e)$. If wage-setters expect prices to increase by $(\Delta P/P)_{t-1}$, we use the approximation $(\Delta W/W)_t - (\Delta P/P)_{t-1} \approx w^{WS}(y_t) - w_{-1}$. Thus we have $(\Delta W/W)_t - (\Delta P/P)_{t-1} = \alpha(y_t - y_e)$ or

$$(\Delta W/W)_t \approx (\Delta P/P)_{t-1} + \alpha(y_t - y_e). \qquad \text{(wage inflation)}$$

This says that wage setters set the percentage increase in the nominal wage to cover the previous period's price increase and to reflect any positive or negative output gap at the time of the wage round.

Turning to price setters, we use the price-setting rule, and noting from the timeline that firms set prices immediately after wages have been set, we have:[12]

$$P = (1 + \mu)\frac{W}{\lambda}, \text{ and}$$

$$(\Delta P/P)_t = (\Delta W/W)_t - (\Delta \lambda/\lambda)_t. \qquad \text{(price inflation)}$$

Substituting the expression for wage inflation into the equation for price inflation gives the following equation for inflation in the simple case where productivity is constant. This is called the Phillips curve:

$$(\Delta P/P)_t = (\Delta P/P)_{t-1} + \alpha(y_t - y_e) \qquad (2.7)$$

$$\underbrace{\pi_t}_{\text{current inflation}} = \underbrace{\pi_{t-1}}_{\text{lagged inflation}} + \underbrace{\alpha(y_t - y_e)}_{\text{output gap}}, \qquad \text{(Phillips curve, PC)}$$

where $\pi_t$ is the rate of inflation. If $P_t$ is today's price level and $P_{t-1}$ is last period's price level, then the rate of inflation over the past year is $\pi_t$:

$$\pi_t \equiv \frac{P_t - P_{t-1}}{P_{t-1}} = \Delta P/P.$$

[12] The conversion of the price-setting equation into the price inflation equation is carried out as follows. If you are unfamiliar with logs and their properties, see Section 8.3 in Chapter 8. We assume that $\mu$ remains constant over time. In continuous time, we find an expression for the growth rate of $P = (1 + \mu)W/\lambda$ by first taking logs, then differentiating with respect to time and using the fact that $\frac{d\log x}{dx} = \frac{1}{x}$:

$$\log P = \log(1 + \mu) + \log W - \log \lambda$$
$$\frac{d\log P}{dt} = \frac{d\log(1+\mu)}{dt} + \frac{d\log W}{dt} - \frac{d\log \lambda}{dt}.$$

By assumption, $d\log(1 + \mu)/dt = 0$.

Multiply each term by $\frac{dx}{dt}$ and use $d\log x/dx = 1/x$

$$\frac{d\log P}{dP}\frac{dP}{dt} = \frac{d\log W}{dW}\frac{dW}{dt} - \frac{d\log \lambda}{d\lambda}\frac{d\lambda}{dt}$$
$$\frac{dP/dt}{P} = \frac{dW/dt}{W} - \frac{d\lambda/dt}{\lambda}$$
$$\pi = \frac{dW/dt}{W} - \frac{d\lambda/dt}{\lambda}.$$

Writing this in discrete time, gives the expression in the text.

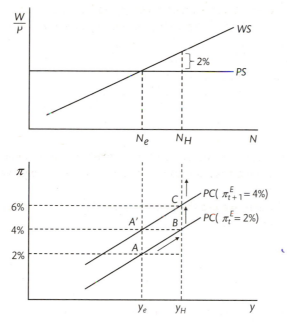

**Figure 2.14** The derivation of the Phillips curve.

## Graphical derivation of the Phillips curve

In Fig. 2.14, an investment boom because of more optimistic business expectations shifts the *IS* curve to the right. Output and employment rise. The fall in unemployment shifts the balance of power in the labour market towards workers as reflected in the positively sloped *WS* curve. At the next wage round, wage setters respond to the positive output gap: they will need a 2% nominal wage increase to cover last period's inflation plus an additional increase equal to $\alpha$ times the output gap (see the wage inflation equation). In the example shown in Fig. 2.6, this is an extra 2%. Nominal wages go up by 4%.

How do price setters respond to the higher wages? Their labour costs have risen by 4%, so they mark up this cost increase in their prices, and price inflation goes up from 2% to 4% (see the price inflation equation). We have the result that an expansion of aggregate demand that pushes output and employment above the equilibrium level is followed by a rise in wage and price inflation. By joining together points *A* and *B*, we have an upward sloping line in the inflation–output diagram. This is a Phillips curve.

Will inflation stay at 4%? Let us assume that employment remains at its high level until the next wage round. How do wage setters respond? The first thing to notice is that employees will be disappointed with their real wage over the past year: they had expected a high real wage in line with the tighter labour market. This did not eventuate because firms passed on the labour cost increase immediately in higher prices. With this behaviour generalized across the economy, the consumer price index will have risen by 4%. Wage setters will now negotiate a wage increase to make good the erosion of their expected real wage over the past year (an increase of 4%) and they will secure another 2% to take the expected real wage to its high level on the *WS* curve. Firms will follow by putting prices up by 6%. A new Phillips curve

**Table 2.1** Constant, rising, and falling inflation.

| Period | Output | Inflation (% per year) and employment | | | |
| | | Lagged inflation | 'Gap' | Wage inflation | Price inflation |
| --- | --- | --- | --- | --- | --- |
| −1 | $y_e$ | 2 | 0 | 2 | 2 |
| | | Case 1: constant inflation | | | |
| 0 | $y_e$ | 2 | 0 | 2 | 2 |
| 1 | $y_e$ | 2 | 0 | 2 | 2 |
| 2 | $y_e$ | 2 | 0 | 2 | 2 |
| | | Case 2: rising inflation | | | |
| 0 | $y_H$ | 2 | 2 | 4 | 4 |
| 1 | $y_H$ | 4 | 2 | 6 | 6 |
| 2 | $y_H$ | 6 | 2 | 8 | 8 |
| | | Case 3: falling inflation | | | |
| 0 | $y_L$ | 2 | −2 | 0 | 0 |
| 1 | $y_L$ | 0 | −2 | −2 | −2 |
| 2 | $y_L$ | −2 | −2 | −4 | −4 |

is defined by joining up point $A'$ and C. Each Phillips curve is labelled by lagged inflation. Case 2 in Table 2.1 shows the output and inflation outcomes following a positive demand shock in period 0.

If we take the converse case of an equal size negative demand shock that moves unemployment above the equilibrium rate and reduces output to $y_L < y_e$, the same reasoning gives the result that inflation is falling. The process will be the exact reverse of that set out above for the positive demand shock. The summary of the output and inflation outcomes for this example is shown as Case 3 in Table 2.1. This example shows that unemployment above the equilibrium is accompanied by falling inflation.

### Summary of the Phillips curve (PC)

We have shown that the Phillips curve (PC) is derived from the wage-setting and price-setting curves. In the formulation of the PC that underlies the core 3-equation model, each Phillips curve shows a feasible set of output and inflation pairs for a given rate of lagged inflation. The Phillips curves are pinned down by lagged inflation because of the presence of lagged inflation in the wage inflation equation. Wage setters are interested in the real wage. When setting the nominal wage increase, they take a view about the way the consumer price index is likely to evolve over the course of the wage contract. A simple rule for doing this uses consumer price inflation over the previous period.

In modelling inflation and Phillips curves, it is usual to express the role of lagged inflation in terms of inflation expectations. We use this language and return in Chapter 4 to a detailed investigation of how expectations are formed. Thus, we can write:

$$\pi_t^E = \pi_{t-1}, \qquad \text{(adaptive inflation expectations)}$$

where $\pi_t^E$ is expected inflation in period $t$ and $\pi_{t-1}$ is actual inflation in period $t-1$. When we model wage setters' behaviour in wage negotiations in this manner, then we say that they have *adaptive expectations*. This is because they update their expectations every period based on the out-turn for inflation in the last period. As shown in Fig. 2.14, we pin down the vertical height of the Phillips curve by expected inflation. Throughout this book, we will denote the Phillips curve by $PC(\pi_t^E = x\%)$. In the adaptive expectations case, $x$ is simply last period's inflation rate.

The Phillips curves are upward sloping, reflecting the effect of the output gap, $(y_t - y_e)$, on wages and prices through the wage- and price-setting curves, and hence on inflation. As we saw in the previous subsection, if output is above equilibrium, then inflation will be higher than last period's inflation and vice versa. In the model, workers get a base wage increase equal to lagged inflation, and they also get an additional wage change to reflect the position of the economy relative to equilibrium. A positive output gap will result in a positive additional wage change and a negative output gap the opposite. This reflects the positively sloped wage-setting curve.

We can see from Fig. 2.14 that each adaptive expectations Phillips curve is defined by two characteristics:

(1) the lagged inflation rate ($\pi_{t-1}$), which fixes the height of the Phillips curve on a vertical line above the level of output associated with the equilibrium rate of unemployment; and

(2) the slope of the *WS* curve, which fixes its slope.[13] The Phillips curves will be steeper if the *WS* curve is steeper and vice versa.

In equation form, the Phillips curve is:

$$\pi_t = \pi_t^E + \alpha(y_t - y_e)$$

$$\underset{\text{current inflation}}{\pi_t} = \underset{\text{lagged inflation}}{\pi_{t-1}} + \underset{\text{output gap}}{\alpha(y_t - y_e)}. \qquad \text{(adaptive expectations Phillips curve)}$$

We can see from this expression that the Phillips curve shifts up or down whenever lagged inflation changes and that its slope depends on $\alpha$, which in turn reflects the slope of the *WS* curve.

Evidence on inflation dynamics in many countries over the past few decades suggests that changes in output (and employment) are followed by changes in inflation, which is summarized by saying that output leads inflation; and that inflation is persistent.[14] Consistent with this evidence, the Phillips curve states that inflation depends on past inflation, $\pi_{t-1}$ and the output gap, which reflects the difference between current unemployment and the equilibrium rate of unemployment.

The assumption that prices are adjusted immediately to cost increases means that the real wage remains on the *PS* curve and is constant over the business cycle. Empirically, at the

[13] Note that if the *PS* curve was downward sloping, the slope of the Phillips curve would be steeper, reflecting the slope of both the *WS* and the *PS* curves. At output above equilibrium, for example, there would not only be the 'gap' due to the slope of the *WS* curve but there would be a second 'gap' between the existing real wage and that on the *PS* curve. Firms would push up prices further to reduce the real wage down to the lower real wage on the *PS* curve.

[14] For evidence, see Christiano et al. (2005); also Estrella and Fuhrer (2002) and Muellbauer and Nunziata (2004).

aggregate level, real wages are mildly pro-cyclical. In the model, if lags in price setting are introduced (in addition to the lag in wage-setting due to the annual wage round), then the real wage would lie in between the WS and PS curves. Real wages would then be pro-cyclical reflecting the upward-sloping wage-setting curve. Real wages would rise in business cycle upswings and fall in downswings.

## 2.3 Applications

### Shocks in the absence of a stabilizing policy maker

We shall see in Chapter 3 that an inflation-targeting central bank will diagnose the nature of a shock and then respond by adjusting the interest rate. To motivate the introduction of a policy maker who seeks to stabilize the economy, we show what happens to the economy when it is disturbed by a demand or supply shock in the absence of such a policy maker. We look in turn at demand shocks, represented in the model by a shift of the IS curve or a shift along it due to a change in the interest rate, and at supply shocks, represented by shifts in the WS and or the PS curves.

### An aggregate demand shock

By drawing the IS diagram above the labour market diagram we show the positive aggregate demand shock explicitly in Fig. 2.15a (i.e. the left hand panel of Fig. 2.15). Our assumption that there is no stabilizing policy maker is reflected in the fact that the IS curve remains at $IS'$ following the shock and the real interest rate is kept constant at its initial level, $r_e$.

We assume the economy begins at equilibrium output $y_e$ with lagged inflation of 2%. A positive aggregate demand shock shifts the IS curve to $IS'$. An example of such a shock would be the US economic boom associated with higher government spending (on military and non-military goods and services) that coincided with the start of the Vietnam war in 1965. US GDP growth was 6.4% in 1965 and 6.5% in 1966, compared to an average of just 3.9% for the other years in that decade.[15]

As shown in Fig. 2.15a, the shock is accompanied by ever-increasing inflation: with output above equilibrium at $y_H$, there is a gap between the WS and the PS every period, wages and prices are adjusted first as wage setters try to achieve the real wage $w_H$ and second as firms push up prices to restore their profit margin (which implies the real wage is kept at $w_e$). The process is exactly the same as in the example used to derive the Phillips curve in the last section (see Fig. 2.14 and Case 2 in Table 2.1).

With the real interest rate kept constant at $r_e$, a positive demand shock is associated with higher employment and rising inflation. In Chapter 3, we address the question of why the policy maker will not be happy with a situation of ever-increasing inflation and what they could do to stabilize the demand shock and get inflation back to the initial level of 2%.

---

[15] Figures calculated using data on real GDP from the US Bureau of Economic Analysis.

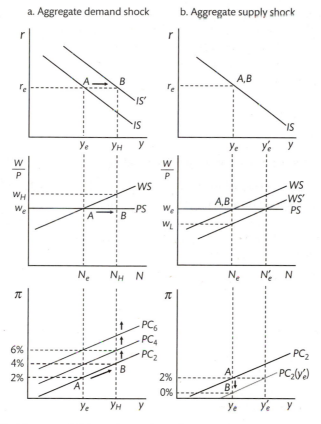

**Figure 2.15** World without a stabilizing policy maker: inflationary implications of aggregate demand and supply shocks.

*Note: $PC_x$ is used as short form for $PC(\pi_t^E = x\%)$, where $x$ is the level of lagged inflation and $t$ is the time period.*

## An aggregate supply shock

We now turn to the implications of an aggregate supply shock. We can model an aggregate supply shock as a shift in

1. the production function, i.e. a technology or productivity shock (change in $\lambda$)

2. the WS curve, e.g. a shift in bargaining power from workers to employers or in any of the other wage-push factors (i.e. $z_w$)

3. the PS curve, e.g. more intense competition in the product market (i.e. $\downarrow \mu$) or a shift in any of the price-push factors, (i.e. $z_p$).

To illustrate the implications for output, employment and inflation, we take the example of a downward shift in the WS curve. An example of such a shock would be the Dutch supply-side reforms of the 1980s. The Netherlands was seen as one of Europe's 'employment miracles'. In 1983, unemployment stood at 8.3%, whereas the average for the 1990–2008 period was just 4.6%. The Dutch reforms included reduced unemployment benefit generosity, increased expenditure on active labour market policies to make workers more employable and closer coordination in the wage bargaining process.[16]

To illustrate the key differences in the response of the labour market to supply and demand shocks, we analyse the adjustment of the economy to the supply shock using Fig. 2.15b. We assume the economy begins at equilibrium output $y_e$ with lagged inflation of 2%. A positive supply shock shifts the WS curve downward to WS'. This raises the equilibrium level of employment from $N_e$ to $N'_e$ and the equilibrium level of output from $y_e$ to $y'_e$. Again, we assume there is no stabilizing policy maker, so the real interest rate is kept constant at its initial level of $r_e$ following the shock.

At the original output level, $y_e$, there is now a negative gap between the WS and PS curves. Wage setters respond to the gap by reducing their real wage claim to $w_L$. They do this because there is now increased competition for jobs (as a result of the active labour market policies) and a higher cost of job loss (as a result of lower benefit generosity). Wages therefore rise by 0% and in order to keep their profit margins constant firms do not change their prices. Inflation falls from 2% to 0% and the Phillips curve shifts down.

In the following periods, the adjustment of the economy is similar to that of a negative demand shock (see Case 3 in Table 2.1). Inflation falls in each period. This process will carry on indefinitely, as long as output is kept below the new equilibrium—i.e. unemployment cannot be kept at a level above equilibrium without falling inflation.

A positive supply shock is defined as one that raises equilibrium output and employment. We have shown that a positive supply shock is associated with falling inflation *at the initial output level* $y = y_e$. If the supply shock is permanent, then the economy is capable of operating with lower unemployment and constant inflation. As we shall see in Chapter 3, the policy maker is likely to respond to the shock by reducing the interest rate to allow the economy to operate at the new equilibrium output level of $y'_e$ with constant inflation.

## 2.4 Conclusions

This chapter has provided the second building block for the model of the macro-economy. We have set out the $WS - PS$ model, which is used to determine the equilibrium level of output in the economy. From the $WS - PS$ model, we derived the Phillips curve, or PC, which is used to model wage and price inflation and is one of three equations that underpins the 3-equation model of the macro-economy that will be set out in the next chapter.

The $WS - PS$ model shows that wages at equilibrium unemployment are higher than workers would be willing to accept; this means there is involuntary unemployment. With monopolistic (or equivalently imperfect) competition in goods markets, firms charge a mark-up on their goods and make supernormal profits. At the supply-side equilibrium, the rate of unemployment is such that both wage and price setters are content with the prevailing real wage. The real wage is constant, which implies that wages and prices are rising at the same rate: inflation is constant. Inflation could be constant at a rate of zero, in which case nominal

---

[16] See Nickell and Van Ours (2000a).

wages and prices would remain unchanged. Modern economies are typically characterized by positive inflation.

By combining the analysis of aggregate demand summarized in the *IS* curve with the supply side (*WS* and *PS* curves), we can analyse current and historical episodes of unemployment. For example, we can model both the rapid growth of unemployment following the global financial crisis and the gradual increases in equilibrium unemployment that characterized many European economies from the 1970s. In the first case, there was a large negative aggregate demand shock, which pushed economies away from their constant inflation equilibrium unemployment rates and increased involuntary unemployment. In the second case, negative supply shocks pushed up equilibrium unemployment, leaving it higher, even when stable inflation was restored.

Given the economy's supply side characteristics, the Phillips curve shows the feasible set of inflation and output pairs for a given rate of lagged inflation. We can interpret the lagged inflation term either as agents forming expectations about how prices will evolve in a backward-looking manner or as agents negotiating wage increases to compensate them for the erosion of their real wages associated with last period's inflation. We shall show in the next chapter that the Phillips curve acts as a constraint on the policy maker, limiting their choice of viable inflation–output combinations in each period.

The modelling undertaken in Sections 2.2 and 2.3 has provided a framework with which we can shed light on important questions concerning the supply side of the economy. As a summary of the chapter, we return to each of the key questions posed in these sections:

1. **Supply side effects on equilibrium unemployment**. What determines the medium-run equilibrium level of output and unemployment around which the economy fluctuates? The equilibrium rate of unemployment is pinned down by the intersection of the *WS* and *PS* curves. Structural features of the economy, such as unionization, along with policy choices, such as the generosity of unemployment benefits and the stringency of competition policy, will affect equilibrium unemployment. Swings in demand will move the economy away from equilibrium, resulting in actual unemployment deviating from equilibrium (see Fig. 2.8). Unemployment below equilibrium is associated with output above equilibrium, i.e. a positive output gap ($y > y_e$). In Chapter 15, we shall consider possible feedback from actual to equilibrium unemployment, which is referred to as 'hysteresis'.

2. **Nominal rigidities, inflation and the business cycle.** What happens to inflation when the economy is away from equilibrium? When output is above equilibrium, the increased tightness of the labour market is reflected in a higher wage-setting wage. There is a lower cost of job loss and workers will need to expect higher real wages in order to exert effort. These are expected real wages because the real wage outturn depends on what happens to inflation in the economy as a whole over the period of the wage contract. In this case *WS* > *PS*, and workers will get a wage increase that more than compensates them for the erosion in real wage due to last period's inflation. However, firms protect their profit margins and will immediately raise prices following the wage round. This means that workers' real wage expectations are constantly frustrated when output is above equilibrium. The only way in which output can remain above equilibrium is with rising inflation, as shown in Fig. 2.14. The opposite is true for output below equilibrium. The relationship between output and inflation can be summed up by the Phillips curve: $\pi_t = \pi_{t-1} + \alpha(y_t - y_e)$. This equation shows that

the current period's inflation ($\pi_t$) depends positively on both last period's inflation ($\pi_{t-1}$) and the output gap ($y_t - y_e$).

3. **Demand shocks, supply shocks and the Phillips curve.** How does the economy respond to demand or supply shocks in a world without a policy maker who aims to stabilize the economy? The economy reacts differently to supply and demand shocks. We can highlight these differences by seeing how they are captured by different parts of the model. Demand shocks affect the *IS* curve and supply shocks affect the *WS* or *PS* curves and consequently the Phillips curve, *PC*. A positive demand shock leads to ever-increasing inflation as long as demand is kept at a level where there is a positive output gap. In contrast, a positive supply shock increases equilibrium output and is associated with falling inflation as long as output is kept at the initial equilibrium rate of output. Falling inflation signals that the economy is capable of operating at a higher equilibrium level of output.

Having a framework of the kind set out in Chapters 1 and 2 is essential in understanding how policy makers assess the state of the economy and whether intervention is required. This sets the stage for the introduction of the policy maker with stabilization objectives in the next chapter. In Chapter 3, we show why governments introduced inflation-targeting central banks in a bid to improve economic performance.

## 2.5 Appendix

### 2.5.1 The textbook model: competitive markets and complete contracts

To help bring out the way the labour market works and to clarify the notion of involuntary unemployment, it is useful to provide a comparison with a simple textbook model. In the textbook model, the intrinsic feature of the labour market of variable effort is neglected. It is assumed that the wage buys a specific amount of work.

What would a market for labour mean when employment contracts are complete? The image to have in mind is not of the labour market in a real economy but of a hiring hall where employers and workers gather. In the hall, employers shout out job offers and workers respond. Since the textbook model assumes that what the employer gets in exchange for a particular hourly wage offered is unambiguous, he will be happy to hire labour on this basis. In the hiring hall, a wage is posted and workers respond by accepting or declining to work.

As discussed in Section 2.1, we assume the labour supply curve to be quite inelastic. This reflects the offsetting income and substitution effects of a wage change, as well as the effects of changes in labour force participation. Imagine the wage offers are being broadcast outside the hiring hall and people are drawn in to participate in the labour market by higher wage offers.

Turning to the labour demand side, in the textbook model, there is a downward-sloping labour demand curve, which shows the labour demanded at a given real wage. Assuming for simplicity that the capital stock ($K$) is fixed, output is a positive function of the level of employment ($N$), i.e.

$$y = f(N; K),$$

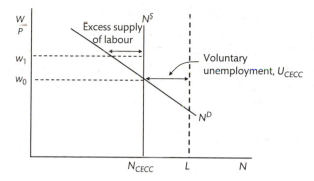

**Figure 2.16** Market clearing equilibrium in a textbook labour market with complete employment contracts.

where $f$ is the production function. It is assumed that the production function is characterized by diminishing returns, which means that as more workers are employed—holding capital constant—the extra output produced by each additional worker declines. Another way of putting this is that the marginal product of labour, which can be written as $\frac{\partial y}{\partial N}$ or MPL, declines as employment rises. The labour demand curve ($N^D$) is often referred to as the MPL curve since under perfect competition, firms take the real wage as given and employ labour up to the point at which the marginal product of labour is equal to the exogenously given real wage (the wage shouted out in the hiring hall).

The market clears at the real wage where the labour demand curve intersects the labour supply curve. Bringing together the labour demand and labour supply schedules as in Fig. 2.16, the labour market clears with the real wage $w_0$ and employment, $N_{CECC}$ (for Competitive Equilibrium Complete Contracts).

Any temporary displacement of the economy from equilibrium is assumed to be eliminated by a movement in real wages. For example, if the real wage rises above the market-clearing level (due say, to an unexpected fall in the price level), then labour supply exceeds labour demand at that real wage ($w_1$). The excess supply of labour will result in falling nominal wages until the unique competitive equilibrium is re-established with the real wage at $w_0$ and employment at $N_{CECC}$. In this model, the only people who will be unemployed will be those *voluntarily* unemployed in the sense that at the going real wage, they prefer searching for a job or leisure over the goods and services obtainable through working.

In Fig. 2.16, the rate of unemployment in the market-clearing equilibrium is $U_{CECC}/L$, where $L$ is the labour force, i.e. the sum of the employed and the unemployed. It is important to remember that in the textbook model, the economy is at a welfare optimum in the market-clearing equilibrium, so the voluntary unemployment that exists does not signify a problem. Rather, it reflects the choice by workers about whether and how much to work at the existing real wage. It is difficult to motivate the study of supply-side institutions and policies and of demand-side (that is, stabilization) policy in this model.

### 2.5.2 The mark-up and the elasticity of demand

A firm maximises profits when marginal revenue (MR) = marginal cost (MC). With labour as the single factor of production this means that

$$MC = \frac{W}{MPL},$$    (marginal cost)

where $W$ is the nominal wage and $MPL$ the marginal product of labour.

Total revenue is

$$R = Py,$$    (total revenue)

where $P$ is the price for which the firm sells their output, and $y$ is the quantity of output they sell. The firm faces a standard downward-sloping demand curve. The elasticity of this demand curve, $\eta$, measures the responsiveness of output demanded to a change in the price. If there is perfect competition, the demand curve is flat and $\eta = \infty$, since under perfect competition, a marginal increase in the price will mean the firm loses all of its sales. The less elastic demand (in absolute value) is the demand curve, the less demand the firm loses by increasing its price.

Marginal revenue is

$$MR = \frac{dR}{dy} = P + y\frac{dP}{dy}.$$    (marginal revenue)

If we divide each side of the equation for marginal revenue by $P$ and substitute in the definition of $\eta$, where

$$\eta = -\frac{dy}{dP}\frac{P}{y},$$    (elasticity of demand)

we get

$$MR = P + y\frac{dP}{dy}$$

$$\frac{MR}{P} = 1 - \frac{1}{\eta}$$

$$\rightarrow MR = P\left(1 - \frac{1}{\eta}\right).$$

Then at the profit-maximizing optimum, where $MR = MC$, we have

$$P\left(1 - \frac{1}{\eta}\right) = \frac{W}{MPL}$$

or

$$P = \left(\frac{\eta}{\eta - 1}\right)\frac{W}{MPL}.$$    (pricing formula, in terms of elasticity, $\eta$)

This can be written in terms of a mark-up $\mu$ on marginal labour costs

$$P = (1 + \mu)\frac{W}{MPL},$$    (pricing formula, in terms of the markup, $\mu$)

where $\mu = \frac{1}{\eta - 1}$.

In the case of perfect competition $\eta = \infty$ and $\mu = 0$. As the demand curve becomes more inelastic, the mark-up, $\mu$, rises. If, for example, $\eta = 6$, the firm will mark up marginal costs by 20%; $\mu = \frac{1}{\eta - 1} = \frac{1}{6 - 1} = 0.2$.

### 2.5.3 Deriving the *PS* curve including the tax wedge

The wage element of costs for firms is the full cost of labour to firms—i.e. the gross wage paid to the worker (which includes the income tax and social security payments that have to be made by the worker) plus the employer's social security contributions. All direct taxes are summarized in the tax rate, $t_d$. This is shown in the pricing equation, where $P$ is the producer price:

$$P = (1 + \mu) \frac{W^{\text{gross}}}{\lambda} = (1 + \mu) \frac{W(1 + t_d)}{\lambda}. \qquad \text{(price equation)}$$

But to get the *PS* curve we need the price-setting equation in term of the consumption price, $P_c = (1 + t_v) P$, so that:

$$P_c = (1 + t_v) P = (1 + t_v)(1 + \mu) \frac{W(1 + t_d)}{\lambda},$$

which implies

$$\frac{W}{P_c} = \frac{1}{(1 + \mu)} \frac{\lambda}{(1 + t_d)(1 + t_v)}$$

and using our approximation that $\frac{1}{1+\mu} \approx 1 - \mu$, we have:

$$w^{PS} = \frac{W}{P_c} = \frac{\lambda(1 - \mu)}{(1 + t_d)(1 + t_v)}. \qquad \text{(PS equation including tax wedge)}$$

An approximation to the tax wedge is given by: $\frac{1}{(1+t_d)(1+t_v)} \approx (1 - t_d - t_v)$. We can see that:

1. Any fall in the wedge, for example, a fall in income tax, implies an upward shift in the *PS* curve, indicating that the real wage is higher at any level of employment since the tax take is smaller.

2. The smaller wedge means that *WS* and *PS* curves cross at higher employment: there is a lower equilibrium rate of unemployment because a higher real consumption wage on the *WS* curve is consistent with equilibrium for price setters (on the new higher *PS* curve).

## 2.6 Questions

### 2.6.1 Checklist questions

1. Explain in words and using a diagram what is meant by labour market clearing (refer to Appendix 2.5.1). Why is labour market clearing not observed in real-world labour markets?

2. Why is the wage-setting curve upward sloping? If there is a disutility of working, why are workers unhappy when they are unemployed?

3. Derive the price-setting curve. What does the equation for the *PS* curve tell us about the ability of firms to make supernormal profits? Explain in words why the decisions of firms about what price to set has implications for the real wage in the economy. Provide two different explanations for why the *PS* curve might be flat.

4. What is being assumed about the timing of wage setting and price setting that enables us to say that the economy is always on the *PS* curve but only on the *WS* curve in a medium-run

equilibrium? What timing assumptions would deliver the result that the economy is always on the *WS* curve but only on the *PS* curve in a medium-run equilibrium?

5. Explain in words the inflationary consequences of an upswing in aggregate demand. Assume the economy is initially at equilibrium and make sure you adequately explain the transmission mechanisms as well as the final result.

6. Evaluate the following statement:

   'When the economy is in equilibrium in the *WS* − *PS* model, there is only voluntary unemployment, because no agent has an incentive to change their behaviour.'

7. Equation 2.2 in Section 2.2.1 shows that firms set prices as a mark up over unit labour costs. Use this equation to show the relationship between wage growth and price growth in the economy. What assumptions do we have to make for wage changes to translate one-for-one into price changes? In this case, how will a rise in wages impact on a firm's profit margin?

8. Assess the following statements S1 and S2. Are they both true, both false or is only one true? Justify your answer.

   S1. When output is above equilibrium, wage setters will secure wage increases that reflect the tightness of the labour market.

   S2. If output is consistently above equilibrium, then wage-setters' real wage expectations are constantly frustrated.

9. Use the *WS* − *PS* model to graphically derive a set of Phillips curves. Explain the intuition behind the diagram. Provide an explanation of how a situation of deflation could occur (deflation is a situation in which inflation is negative so that prices are falling). What are you assuming about the real interest rate?

10. Giving in each case an example of what could have caused it, explain how unemployment can be above equilibrium due to the following. Use diagrams, such as those in Fig. 2.15, to show the inflationary implications of each shock (assume there is no stabilizing policy maker).

    (a) Aggregate demand being too low

    (b) A wage-setting shock

## 2.6.2 Problems and questions for discussion

1. Collect an inflation report from the central bank website of an OECD economy (e.g. the Bank of England, the ECB, the Federal Reserve etc.) and answer the following questions:

   (a) What factors do they view as important drivers of inflation (or the outlook for inflation)?

   (b) Divide these factors into supply-side and demand-side factors.

   (c) For each factor, provide a plausible explanation for which curve of the model they affect (e.g. *IS*, *WS* or *PS*).

   (d) For each factor, in which direction would you expect the affected curve to shift?

2. Read the following statement and then answer the questions below: 'Just by looking at real-world labour markets, it is obvious they are far too complex to be accurately modelled by either the efficiency wage model or the textbook model with complete contracts'. [Hint: the textbook model is set out in the Appendix.]

   (a) Does the statement provide a good justification for not using a model when thinking about the supply side of the economy?

(b) What are the key predictions of the efficiency wage model and the textbook model with complete contracts?

(c) The predictions of which model more closely match what we observe by analysing real-world data? Provide examples to justify your answer.

3. Consider two key events in recent economic history; the credit crunch that plunged the world into recession in 2008 and the Fukushima nuclear disaster that struck Japan in 2011. Find data on the path of the monthly harmonized unemployment rate from the start of 2007 onwards for both the US and Japan using OECD.Stat. Answer the following questions:

(a) Describe (i) how US unemployment reacted to the credit crunch; and (ii) how Japanese unemployment reacted to the Fukushima nuclear disaster.

(b) Using the material in this chapter and the previous chapter, make an assessment of which curves were likely to have been affected by these economic shocks—i.e. was it the *IS*, *WS* or *PS* curve that were affected (or some combination of them)? Make sure you justify your answer.

(c) Given your answer to part (b), do you predict that the equilibrium level of unemployment shifted in response to these shocks? Justify your answers.

4. Collect data for GDP and the unemployment rate for OECD economies between 2007 and 2010 from OECD.Stat. Produce a scatterplot of percentage point changes in GDP and the unemployment rate (from peak to trough) over the course of the Great Recession. Answer the following questions:

(a) Describe briefly what the graph shows.

(b) Does the data support Okun's Law (i.e. an Okun coefficient of –0.5)?

(c) If not, then suggest some factors that might account for the differences in Okun coefficients observed across the OECD economies.

# The 3-equation model and macroeconomic policy

## 3.1 Overview

In Chapter 1, we focused on the way shocks to aggregate demand produce fluctuations in output and employment. In Chapter 2, we looked at how supply-side features of the economy determine the constant inflation equilibrium. Then, at the end of Chapter 2, we put these supply- and demand-side elements together. This produced a picture of an economy affected by both demand and supply-side shocks, which are amplified by the multiplier process and dampened by households' and firms' ability to tide themselves over through borrowing when their current income falls. In contrast to the generally slow-moving shifts in equilibrium unemployment, actual unemployment rises and falls in accordance with business cycles largely driven by fluctuations in aggregate demand.

In the model as laid out in Chapter 2, there was no policy intervention to prevent the gap between the real wage workers expect to secure (on the WS curve) and the real wage firms are prepared to pay (on the PS curve) from producing ever-increasing inflation when unemployment is lower than the equilibrium rate. This incompatibility between the claims of workers and firms—and hence the inflationary pressure in the economy—could in principle be resolved in two ways:

1. First, by supply-side institutional change or policies to raise equilibrium output by either shifting the WS curve downwards or shifting the PS curve upwards. Examples of this include policies to weaken the bargaining power of workers by worsening the living conditions they would face if they lost their jobs (brought about, for instance, by lowering unemployment benefits). Another example is an institutional change which increases bargaining restraint by unions. One policy which might shift the PS curve upwards would be the promotion of more competition, thus reducing the mark-up on product prices.

2. Second, by the use of demand management policy to reduce employment and output to the level consistent with a WS − PS equilibrium, where inflation will be constant. This policy lever takes supply-side institutions and policies as given.

In this chapter, the focus is on the second set of policies mentioned above. This means that we do not deal here with supply-side policies that aim to influence equilibrium unemployment (that is postponed to Chapter 15, which can be read immediately after this chapter). Here, we begin with unemployment at its equilibrium rate (the *WS* − *PS* intersection), where the output gap is zero and inflation is constant. If, at this point, the economy suffers a shock, how would the policy maker respond so as to stabilize it at its constant-inflation level?

Shortly, we will look in more detail at how demand management policy is implemented to stabilize the economy (for example by raising aggregate demand in the face of a negative demand shock or dampening it in the face of a positive demand shock). But, before that, we need a little more background information about the policy regime and its recent history. During the 1990s, many countries around the world adopted a new macroeconomic policy regime known as inflation targeting. It means that the government gives responsibility to the central bank to stabilize the economy by adopting a specific target for the annual rate of inflation, the most commonly adopted rate being 2%. To help clarify the reasons why these changes in regime and policy have taken place it would be useful to answer three related background questions:

1. Why do governments often define the central bank's responsibility as the control of inflation?

2. Why, in any case do governments regard inflation as a problem which needs to be controlled?

3. Why do governments hand over the problem of keeping inflation low and stable to the makers of monetary policy (the central banks) rather than controlling inflation themselves?

Regarding the first of these questions, we have already seen that the rate of unemployment at which inflation is constant depends on structural features of the labour market and the goods market. It is these structural features which determine the positions of the *WS* and *PS* curves in the supply-side model. But, since the central bank does not have policy instruments with which it can change these supply-side economic features, it is clearly not the right policy maker to be charged with reducing equilibrium unemployment. The government will have to do this, in ways which are discussed in Chapter 15.

We shall see, however, that there is one important way in which the central bank's behaviour does affect unemployment. A central bank that is given responsibility for maintaining high employment as well as keeping inflation close to its target level would be less inclined to support policies of rapidly cutting inflation through pushing unemployment up sharply. In Chapter 13, we return to the question of how variation in the behaviour of different central banks around the world can be represented in the model.

The second preliminary question is why policy makers are concerned about inflation at all. One reason why governments might pursue low inflation is that the level of inflation is a key priority for voters. Governments might have to pay a large electoral price if they fail to control inflation. The importance the US general public gives to inflation is highlighted in a 1997 paper by Shiller, who surveys both economists and members of the public in the US about their views on inflation. Table 3.1 shows that the general public (more than economists) see controlling inflation as a national priority. We shall look in more detail at the factors that lie behind voters' concerns with inflation in the next subsection.

**Table 3.1**   Public attitudes on the importance of preventing high inflation.

Do you agree that preventing high inflation is an important national priority, as important as preventing drug abuse or deterioration in the quality of our schools?

| | Fully agree | | Undecided | | Completely disagree | |
|---|---|---|---|---|---|---|
| US all | 52% | 32% | 4% | 8% | 4% | n = 117 |
| Economists | 18% | 28% | 11% | 26% | 18% | n = 80 |

*Source:* Survey data from Shiller (1997).

This leaves the third preliminary question: why, in the inflation-targeting regime, is stabilization policy placed in the hands of the central bank rather than the government? This question is best broken down into two separate parts.

The first part is: why is monetary policy chosen over fiscal policy as the primary tool for stabilization policy? There are both practical and political economy reasons why monetary policy is the preferred stabilizer even when both monetary and fiscal policy are available. Firstly, changing public expenditure or taxation normally involve lengthy parliamentary processes, and there is no equivalent to the gradual adjustment possible through quarter-point changes in the interest rate at monthly intervals. Secondly, fiscal policy is inherently political since it involves the use of tax revenue, a fact which is captured by the classic refrain of struggles for democracy: 'No taxation without representation'. Monetary policy is viewed as more neutral and does not so obviously create winners and losers, making it a less contentious policy instrument for use in short-run demand management.

The second part is: why does the government cede control of monetary policy to an independent central bank? The government can potentially gain an electoral advantage by controlling monetary policy. For example, they could raise output above the equilibrium or change politically sensitive mortgage interest rates in the run-up to an election. In light of this, why have governments around the world chosen to delegate control of monetary policy to a committee of independent experts? It is because governments lack low inflation credibility, which translates into higher inflation. The political pressures to manipulate interest rates for electoral gain are the source of this credibility deficit. Independent central banks are free from these pressures so are more likely to deliver low and stable inflation. To the extent that voters care about inflation and sound macroeconomic management, this provides the incentive for the government to relinquish control of this policy lever. These arguments have been persuasive among both left- and right-wing policy makers, as illustrated by the fact that one of the very first acts of the British Labour Party when it came to power in 1997 was to make the Bank of England independent.

The discussion in Chapter 1 brought out the extent to which households are able to limit the costs to them of fluctuations in income that arise from shocks to the economy through smoothing their consumption. Nevertheless volatility remains and the policy maker aims to provide additional stabilization. We shall see in the course of this chapter how the central bank responds to a range of shocks: its interest rate decisions affect aggregate demand and the output gap, guiding the economy back to the medium-run equilibrium with low steady inflation as its objective.

### 3.1.1  The role of the central bank in stabilization

Since the early 1990s a growing number of central banks have been assigned the task of stabilizing the macro-economy around a low target rate of inflation. This is known as an inflation-targeting monetary policy regime. In response to a surge in inflation, we would expect to see the central bank raise the interest rate; this would lower interest-sensitive spending, such as spending on housing, machinery and equipment, due to the increase in the interest rate (in other words, in the cost of borrowing). The cut back in investment would lead in turn to lower aggregate demand and a fall in output. Unemployment would go up and inflationary pressure would diminish.

In 1997, the year in which the Bank of England was made independent, the Bank's Chief Economist, Mervyn King, who later became Governor, explained:[1]

> [M]onetary policy can be described in terms of two policy variables—a medium-term inflation target and a response of interest rates to shocks that create fluctuations in inflation and output. The overriding objective of monetary policy is to ensure that on average inflation is equal to the target. But such a target is not sufficient to define policy. There is a subordinate decision on how to respond to shocks as they occur.

Figure 3.1 provides a schematic overview of the macro model, including the policy maker. On the left hand side, the role of the demand and supply sides are summarized. The

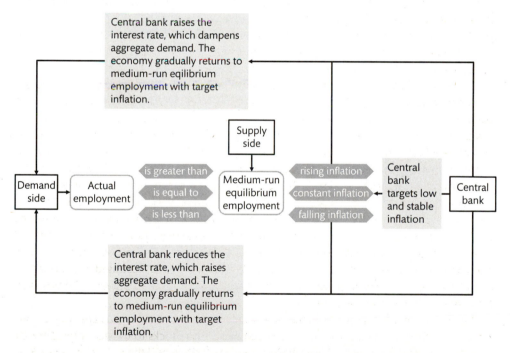

**Figure 3.1**  Schematic overview of the macro model.

[1] Excerpt taken from: Mervyn King, 29th October 1997, *The Inflation Target 5 Years On*, speech delivered at the LSE. He became the Governor of the Bank of England in 2003.

components of aggregate demand determine the level of output and employment in the goods market equilibrium. The structural features of the economy on the supply side determine the equilibrium rate of unemployment at which inflation is constant. The third panel shows the implications for inflation: if unemployment is at the equilibrium rate, then inflation will remain constant and the central bank will do nothing. If unemployment is below the equilibrium rate, inflation is rising and vice versa for unemployment above it. An increase in inflation above the central bank's target will trigger intervention by the central bank: it will raise the interest rate. Equivalently, a fall in inflation below target will trigger an easing of monetary policy with a lower interest rate.

The outside arrows depict the feedback from the central bank's monetary policy rule to aggregate demand. This illustrates how a central bank uses a monetary policy rule to hold inflation close to a low target value.

Figure 3.2 shows the course of inflation in a selection of developed economies since 1980. The chart shows that a period of high and volatile inflation was followed by one where inflation was lower and more stable. The introduction of inflation targeting regimes was part of the evolution of the policy framework, where from the end of the 1970s, governments used macroeconomic policy to squeeze inflation out of the economy by depressing aggregate demand.

The shift from high to low inflation shown in the chart began before the large fall in the oil price in 1986 and the gradual emergence of low-cost (especially Chinese) manufacturers into world markets, which subsequently also had a significant effect on inflation. Although formal inflation targeting was not adopted by the US Federal Reserve until very recently,

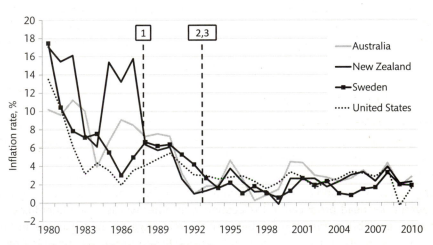

**Dates inflation targeting was first adopted:**
1. Reserve Bank of New Zealand—April 1988
2. Sveriges Riksbank (the Swedish central bank)—January 1993
3. Reserve Bank of Australia—March 1993
Note: The US had no formal inflation target over this period, but did adopt a target of 2% in January 2012.

**Figure 3.2** Inflation rates—before and after the adoption of inflation targeting: 1980–2010.

*Source:* IMF World Economic Outlook, September 2011.

its inflation behaviour was similar to the other countries shown in Figure 3.2, where its date of introduction in New Zealand, Australia and Sweden is shown. The move towards formal or informal inflation targeting is frequently identified with the beginning of the 'Great Moderation' (the period of unprecedented macroeconomic stability shown in Figure 1.3 in Chapter 1).

There are, however, two very important situations in which the central bank cannot be relied on to stabilize shocks by changing the interest rate as described above. The first of these situations is when the economy experiences such a large negative demand shock that even when the central bank cuts the nominal interest rate all the way to zero this is not low enough to stimulate a revival of aggregate demand. With a nominal interest rate of zero, the real interest rate, which is the one relevant to the investment decisions of firms, is not low enough to stimulate interest-sensitive spending. This problem of the *zero lower bound* is closely related to the possibility that the economy can become caught in a *deflation trap*, where it enters a vicious cycle of falling output and inflation. Once the usual channel of monetary stabilization is shut down, the central bank can try to stimulate the economy using other policies, such as quantitative easing, or it can share responsibility for stabilization with fiscal policy. The cases of the zero lower bound and the role of fiscal policy as stabilizer are addressed later in this chapter. We leave a discussion of quantitative easing until Chapter 7.

The second case in which monetary policy cannot be used to achieve stabilization is when the economy has a fixed exchange rate. This is easy to see in the setting of a common currency area such as the Eurozone: member countries of the Eurozone all use the euro as their currency and they share a single central bank, the European Central Bank (ECB). As a result, these countries do not have their own monetary policy maker which could stabilize shocks that are specific to their country. Because all Eurozone countries have the same monetary policy, any stabilization of shocks to a particular country would have to be achieved by the use of fiscal policy (a case explained in Chapter 12).

### 3.1.2 Inflation and deflation

*Rising inflation and distributional conflict*

Rising inflation reflects distributional conflict as different social groups (wage set-ters/employees and price setters/employers) seek to protect their interests. In an economy in which groups such as unions can influence nominal wages and where firms have price-setting power, a situation of rising inflation reflects inconsistent claims by these groups on the output per head produced in the economy. In other words, when unemployment is below the equilibrium rate, the gap between the real wage on the WS curve and on the PS curve reflects distributional conflict and causes inflation to rise. As shown in Chapter 2, as unemployment falls, workers become more powerful in the labour market and are able to secure a higher expected real wage: this is the reason the WS curve is upward-sloping. But firms will seek to secure their profit margin by setting prices accordingly—leaving a gap between the higher real wage workers expect on the WS curve and the unchanged real wage on the PS curve.

A similar logic applies with efficiency wage-setting: the conflict of interest between the two sides of the labour market means that the wage employers need to pay to get workers

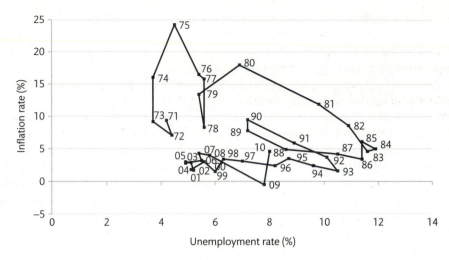

**Figure 3.3** UK inflation and unemployment: 1971–2010.

*Source:* UK Office for National Statistics (data accessed February 2012).

to work sufficiently hard (given the state of the labour market) may differ from the wage that is consistent with the profit margin firms seek. Lower unemployment reduces the cost of job loss and raises the efficiency wage. This pushes inflation up.

Rising inflation produces social tension as frustration mounts. As we shall see, inflationary episodes of this kind have frequently been followed by painful periods of disinflation, where a period of output below equilibrium (accompanied by high unemployment) is required to bring inflation down.[2]

The empirical evidence suggests that periods of disinflation to bring down inflation from moderate rates (up to double digit rates per annum) have involved significant costs in OECD economies where this has occurred. Figure 3.3 shows the path of inflation and unemployment in the UK between the early 1970s and 2010. The high level of inflation in the 1970s was tackled by tight monetary policy from 1979. The process of getting inflation down from a higher level to the targeted one is known as disinflation. It is likely to be a costly process, involving a period of high unemployment to squeeze inflation out of the system. The costs of high unemployment include the direct waste of resources, the erosion of skills and increased vulnerability to mental illness that comes with long spells of unemployment, and the damage to the functioning of families and communities. Figure 3.3 shows that reducing inflation from rates above 20 to below 5% was associated in the British economy with a rise in unemployment from 4 to 12% during the disinflationary episode.

### The benefits of low and stable inflation

The survey on public attitudes to inflation summarized in Table 3.2 shows that the main reason the US public dislike inflation is due to the erosion of living standards that are believed

---

[2] An early formal model of equilibrium unemployment and of the inflation process as one of conflicting distributional claims is in Rowthorn (1977).

to accompany high inflation. We can relate this to an aspect of the dynamics of the WS–PS model. The US public's biggest complaint about inflation accords with the outcome of the WS–PS model in an inflationary environment, in the sense that rising inflation leads to the persistent frustration of workers' real wage expectations.

In the model in Chapter 2, we used the simplest case regarding the timing of wage and price setting. If firms are able to adjust prices immediately after wages have been set, rising inflation reflects a situation in which the real wage wage setters require is systematically frustrated (in other words, the expected real wage of workers as indicated by the WS curve is above the real wage on the PS curve). In this simple case, the real wage outcome is on the PS curve, not on the WS curve. If there are lags in price setting as well as in wage setting, then the real wage lies between the PS and WS curves and neither wage nor price setters are fully satisfied. This case is more realistic because the empirical evidence suggests that real wages are mildly pro-cyclical, which means that when there is a positive output gap the real wage ends up between the WS curve and the PS curve (that is, higher than at the constant inflation equilibrium) and vice versa for a negative output gap.

Table 3.2 reveals a divergence between what the public and the economists view as the most significant costs of inflation. Whereas the public appear to worry about their real incomes being eroded by inflation, economists do not see this as much of a concern and place more stress on the interference that high inflation creates for the ability of prices to convey information. Periods of high inflation are also often ones with volatile inflation. To see why this matters, consider an economy with technical progress in which innovation takes place unevenly across sectors. In sectors with rapid innovation, prices will be falling relative to prices in other sectors where technology is more stagnant (think of the falling prices of computing power). These are economically significant changes in *relative prices* and should lead to a reallocation of resources in the economy. Volatile inflation can therefore distort resource allocation to the extent that it masks these relative price changes. In short, volatile inflation has adverse real effects on the economy that are hard to avoid.

When inflation is high, people also want to hold less money. This is because inflation acts as a tax on holding money balances, eroding their real value over time. The so-called inflation tax imposes inefficiencies because it distorts behaviour: people spend more time managing their financial assets incurring what are referred to as 'shoe-leather costs'. Other

**Table 3.2**  What is peoples' biggest gripe with inflation?

Which of the following comes closest to your biggest gripe about inflation:
1. Inflation causes a lot of inconveniences: I find it harder to comparison shop, I feel I have to avoid holding too much cash, etc.
2. Inflation hurts my real buying power, it makes me poorer.
3. Other.

|  | 1 | 2 | 3 | |
|---|---|---|---|---|
| US all | 7% | 77% | 15% | n = 110 |
| Economists | 49% | 12% | 40% | n = 78 |

*Source:* Survey data from Shiller (1997).

firms incur costs as a consequence of the need for frequent price changes costs ('menu costs').

### The optimal rate of inflation

Given the costs associated with high inflation can we infer that the optimal rate of inflation is zero or even negative? In thinking about the optimal inflation rate, think about the following: the return on holding notes and coins is zero so with any positive inflation rate, the return in real terms, i.e. after controlling for inflation, is negative. The negative real return leads people to waste effort economizing on their money holdings (shoe leather costs again) and this is inefficient given that it is virtually costless to produce money.

If we follow the logic of this argument, then with a positive real rate of interest, for the *nominal* interest rate to be zero, inflation would have to be negative (i.e. prices falling, which is called deflation). This was Milton Friedman's view of the optimal rate of inflation: the rate of deflation should equal the real rate of interest, leaving the nominal interest rate equal to zero.[3] Friedman's rule ensures that people avoid shoe leather costs, but is this sufficient to say that deflation is optimal?

### The danger of deflation

An important reason why central banks target a low but positive inflation rate—most commonly 2%—is that they wish to prevent the economy from falling into a deflation trap, a problem which can emerge when weak aggregate demand leads inflation to fall and eventually become negative. When aggregate demand is very weak, the central bank will want to reduce interest rates in order to stimulate interest-sensitive spending like investment. This can push the nominal interest rate close to its lower bound of zero. But when a nominal interest rate close to zero is combined with falling prices (deflation), this implies a positive real interest rate which may be too high to stimulate private sector demand and get the economy back to equilibrium. Continued weak demand will make inflation more negative, thereby pushing the real interest rate up. This is exactly the opposite of what the central bank wants, which is to reduce the interest rate sufficiently to escape the deflation trap.

In addition, deflation increases real debt burdens. Debts are typically denominated in nominal terms, with borrowers having to pay back a fixed amount each period. If wages (and prices) are falling every period then the burden of the debt increases as a proportion of income. This will lower households' disposable income and squeeze firm's profits, exerting a drag on economic growth and slowing down recovery.

Deflation poses a third problem related to the apparent difficulty in cutting nominal wages. If workers are particularly resistant to nominal wage cuts, then a positive rate of inflation creates the flexibility needed to achieve changes in *relative* wages. For example, if, due to a fall in demand for one kind of labour, a real wage cut is required it can be achieved with an inflation rate of, say, 2% p.a. with the nominal wage left unchanged in the sector where the real wage cut is necessary. This argument is referred to as inflation's role in 'oiling the wheels of the labour market'.

---

[3] See Friedman (1969).

Central bank independence and inflation targeting coincided with the achievement of a low and stable inflation environment as reflected in Fig. 3.2. This helped to reinforce the virtues of a 2% inflation target and central banks have not seriously considered changing to a higher target. In fact, the US Federal Reserve, which has historically avoided having an official inflation target, announced at the start of 2012 that it was joining other developed economies in targeting 2% inflation.[4]

### 3.1.3  Introduction to the 3-equation model

Figure 3.1 puts together the demand and supply sides of the economy and shows the role an inflation–targeting central bank can play in responding to a shock that takes the economy away from equilibrium. What the inflation-targeting central bank does is to raise the interest rate in response to inflation which is above the target rate in order to dampen aggregate demand and to lower the interest rate when inflation falls below the target rate.

A crucial characteristic of a modern monetary policy regime is that the central bank is forward looking. The central bank forecasts inflation by analysing what is going on in the economy and it must take into account the lags between changes in the interest rate it uses for policy purposes and the impact of that rate on economic activity. The importance of forecasting and lags for the work of central banks is highlighted in the monetary policy strategy document of the Sveriges Riksbank (the Swedish central bank):[5]

> It takes time before monetary policy has a full impact on inflation and the real economy. Monetary policy is therefore guided by forecasts for economic developments.

When three things are known—what the central bank is trying to achieve, how it thinks about the constraints it faces arising from the behaviour of the private sector, and how it implements its policy—this information will provide a skeletal model enabling an analysis of how the bank will respond to a variety of shocks to the economy. These responses to shocks can then be summarized in the form of a simple monetary policy rule. This rule sits at the heart of the 3-equation model, which is produced by adding the Monetary Rule (MR), curve to the *IS* curve from the demand side and the Phillips curve (*PC*) from the supply side.

We now turn to each of the three questions in turn to pin down how monetary policy is conducted within the 3-equation framework:

1. What is the central bank trying to achieve? It is assumed that its aim is to use monetary policy to stabilize the economy, which means keeping the economy close to equilibrium output and keeping inflation close to its targeted rate. The central bank may be penalized if it fails to meet its inflation target. In the UK, for example, if the inflation rate diverges more than one percentage point above or below the 2% target then the Governor of the Bank of England is obliged to write an open letter to the Chancellor of the Exchequer explaining the reasons for the bank's failure and a plan for returning inflation to target. This is, at the least, embarrassing for the Governor and costly in terms of the central bank's

---

[4]  Federal Reserve FOMC statement of longer-run goals and policy strategy, January 25th 2012.
[5]  Excerpt taken from: Sveriges Riksbank, 2010, *Monetary policy in Sweden.*

reputation. The closer is the economy to having output at equilibrium and inflation on its target, the lower is the reputational cost to the bank.

2. What forces prevent the central bank from achieving its target? This is essential information in order to assess the prospects of economic stabilization. As seen in Chapters 1 and 2, the economy is affected by shocks to demand and supply, which affect output and inflation. An unforeseen boom, for example, which takes output above equilibrium, will increase inflation above the target as the position of workers in the labour market strengthens. This aspect of wage behaviour is captured in the Phillips curve (PC). The central bank has to take into account behaviour, including the persistence of inflation, when it designs its response to the initial shock to the economy.

3. How does the central bank translate its objectives into monetary policy? It uses a monetary policy rule. This can be represented in the same diagram as the Phillips curves, that is, in a diagram with output on the horizontal axis and inflation on the vertical axis. This will demonstrate how the central bank will choose its preferred policy response given the constraint it faces from the behaviour of wage and price setters, which is captured by a particular Phillips curve.

To implement its preferred policy response in practice, the central bank diagnoses the shock and its forecast effect on inflation and output. It uses this, together with its preferences for stabilization, to estimate the output gap it is trying to achieve. The MR curve illustrates the central bank's best response to the shock. It then uses the relationship between the interest rate and output in the IS curve to implement that choice.

*An example—a consumption boom*

The example of a consumption boom is used to show how the model works. Figure 3.4 shows how the central bank analyses a shock of this kind.

The shock has its initial positive impact on output and employment (shown by the rightward shift of the IS curve and the movement from A to B in the IS diagram). By following the diagrams in Fig. 3.4 from top to bottom, we can see that the labour market impact of the consumption boom is reflected in a disturbance of the initial constant-inflation equilibrium. At the first wage-setting round following the fall in unemployment, wage and price inflation will rise from the target inflation rate of 2%. As illustrated in the wage-setting and price-setting diagram, the shock has opened up a gap of 1% between the prevailing (low) real wage and the (high) real wage consistent with the tighter labour market following the consumption boom. This means that workers will get a 2% wage rise to compensate them for the erosion of their real wages due to last period's inflation and an additional 1% increase to bring their real wage up to the level indicated by the wage-setting curve. In this case, wages rise by 3% and firms automatically raise their prices by 3% to protect their profit margins; in other words, inflation rises to 3%.

The increase in inflation from 2% to 3% is shown by the movement along the Phillips curve from A to B. Here, we need to take into account the fact that the higher inflation of 3% will become embedded in the expectations of wage setters. For the next wage-setting round—the one the central bank must anticipate in taking its stabilization decision—expected inflation of 3% will mean that the relevant Phillips curve facing the central bank is the one labelled 'PC (expected inflation = 3%)'. Given this forecast of inflationary behaviour, the central bank

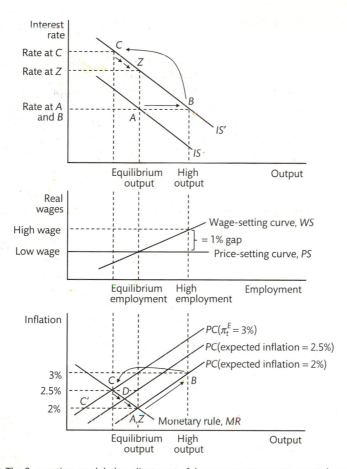

**Figure 3.4** The 3-equation model: the adjustment of the economy to a permanent demand shock.

chooses its best response to the situation—the place on the new *PC* where it would like to locate. Its preference is likely to be for a balanced response—making progress in getting inflation back toward target but not imposing a harsh recession—such as at point *C*. This is a point on the *MR*, which shows the central bank's optimal output–inflation pair for any Phillips curve it faces.

In the top panel of the diagram is the *IS* curve. If the central bank takes the view that in the absence of any response on its part the consumption boom would persist, it will need to choose the interest rate shown by point *C* in order to dampen aggregate demand sufficiently to move the economy onto the path which leads to the inflation target. Once the economy is on the *MR* curve at point *C*, inflation will come down as forecast. Lower inflation will then shift expected inflation down. We can see this in the shift of the Phillips curve downwards to '*PC*(expected inflation = 2.5%)'. The central bank will choose point *D* as its best response to the new inflation environment it faces and will adjust the interest rate down from its peak. In the subsequent periods, the central bank will continue to guide the economy along the *MR* curve by reducing the interest rate as inflation returns to the target rate. The adjustment process finishes when the economy is back at equilibrium output and target inflation (point *Z*.).

There will, however, be a higher interest rate at the new equilibrium, as shown in the *IS* diagram (the top panel of Fig. 3.4). A reduced level of investment is needed to offset the persistent consumption boom.

*A summary of modern inflation-targeting central banking*

Central bank thinking on monetary policy in the era of inflation targeting was succinctly summarized by Glenn Stevens, the Assistant Governor of the Reserve Bank of Australia in a speech in 1999, in which he lists the six key things that have been learnt about monetary policy after 200 years of thought by economists and others:[6]

1. monetary policy affects principally, or only, prices [and not economic activity] in the medium term;

2. it affects activity in the short term;

3. because of lags, policy has to look forward;

4. but the future is uncertain, as is the impact of policy changes on the economy;

5. expectations matter, so giving people some idea of what you are trying to do, and acting consistently, is useful;

6. and an adequate degree of operational independence for the central bank [from the government] in the conduct of monetary policy is important.

## 3.2 Modelling

In the previous two chapters, we have built simple models of the demand and supply sides of the economy. The primary aim of this chapter is to add the policy maker to the model of the macro-economy. This gives the three curves in the graphical model based on the three equations that give the model its name:

1. *IS* curve.

2. *PC* curve.

3. *MR* curve.

   This section extends the introduction to the 3-equation model by setting out in more detail how the central bank goes about achieving its objective of keeping inflation at target. This gives the *monetary rule*, or *MR* curve, which determines the output gap the central bank should set in order to stabilize the economy following an economic shock. We go on to use the 3-equation model to analyse a range of shocks in Section 3.3.

### 3.2.1 The 3-equation model

The first task of this section is to derive the *MR* curve, which shows the chosen output gap of the central bank in response to any economic shock. The *MR* curve shows the path along

---

[6] Source: Mr G.R. Stevens, Assistant Governor of the Reserve Bank of Australia, 20 April 1999, *Six Years of Inflation Targeting*, speech to the Economic Society of Australia, Sydney. Square brackets indicate additions to the text made by the authors.

which the central bank seeks to guide the economy back to target inflation (and equilibrium output). The mathematical derivation of the model is shown in the Appendix.

The basic method for deriving a monetary policy rule involves the following steps:

1. Define the central bank's preferences in terms of a utility (or loss) function to capture the costs it incurs of being away from the inflation target and from equilibrium output. This produces the policy maker's indifference curves in output-inflation space and shows what the policy maker would like to do—i.e. to be close to the inflation target at equilibrium output.

2. Define the constraints faced by the policy maker from the supply side of the economy: these are the Phillips curves, which are also shown in output-inflation space. These show the 'objective' trade-off between inflation and unemployment in the short run and pin down what it is feasible for the central bank to achieve.

3. Derive the best response *monetary rule* in output-inflation space: this is the *MR* curve. For a given Phillips curve that it faces, the *MR* shows the central bank's desired output-inflation combination.

4. Once the central bank knows where it wants to be by using the *MR* curve, it uses the *IS* curve to implement that choice, since the *IS* curve shows the interest rate that will deliver the central bank's chosen level of output. The interest rate is the central bank's policy lever for influencing aggregate demand.

## The central bank's preferences

Where do the central bank's preferences come from? A pragmatic way of thinking about how to model this is to infer their preferences from their behaviour. From the empirical analysis of the behaviour of the US central bank, the Federal Reserve, the economist John Taylor inferred a monetary policy rule. The famous Taylor Rule can be derived from a model in which the central bank minimizes fluctuations from the inflation target and the size of the output gap. Since our aim is to throw light on the way central banks behave, we use this loss function.

In this subsection, we use the central bank's loss function (i.e their utility function) to derive indifference curves representing the trade-off in its preferences between inflation being away from its target and output being away from equilibrium. Looking first at inflation, we assume that it wants to minimize fluctuations around the inflation target $\pi^T$:

$(\pi_t - \pi^T)^2.$

A loss function is just like a utility function except that the higher the loss, the worse it is for the central bank. This loss function has two implications. First, the central bank is as concerned to avoid inflation below its target as it is inflation above its target. If $\pi^T = 2\%$ the loss from $\pi_t = 4\%$ is the same as the loss from $\pi_t = 0\%$. In both cases $(\pi_t - \pi^T)^2 = 4$. Second, it attaches increased importance to bringing inflation back to its target the further it is away from $\pi^T$; the loss from $\pi_t = 6\%$ is 16, compared to the loss of 4 from $\pi_t = 4\%$.

We turn now to the central bank's second concern of keeping output close to equilibrium. We assume the central bank seeks to minimize the gap between $y_t$ and $y_e$—remembering that it has no way of controlling $y_e$ itself—in order to aid it in achieving its inflation target.

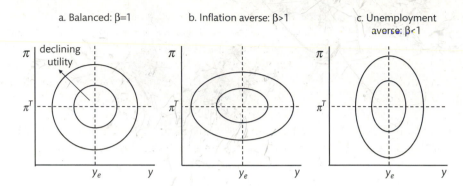

**Figure 3.5** Central bank loss functions: utility declines with distance from the 'bliss point'.

The central bank's loss as a result of output being different from its target of $y_e$ is

$$(y_t - y_e)^2.$$

Note that this loss function also assumes a symmetrical attitude to positive and negative deviations—in this case, from the equilibrium level of output. The most straightforward way of thinking about this is that the central bank understands the model and realizes that inflation is only constant at $y_t = y_e$. If $y_t < y_e$ then this represents unnecessary unemployment that should be eliminated. If $y_t > y_e$, this is unsustainable and will require costly increases in unemployment to bring the associated inflation back down. Whenever the economy is disturbed, the central bank sees its task as steering the economy back to this constant-inflation output level.

Adding the two loss functions together, the central bank's loss function is:

$$L = (y_t - y_e)^2 + \beta(\pi_t - \pi^T)^2, \qquad \text{(central bank loss function)}$$

where $\beta$ is the relative weight attached to the loss from inflation. This is a critical parameter: a $\beta > 1$ will characterize a central bank that places less weight on deviations in employment from its target than on deviations in inflation, and vice versa. A more inflation-averse central bank is characterized by a higher $\beta$.[7]

With $\beta = 1$, the central bank is equally concerned about inflation and output deviations from its targets. The loss function is simple to draw: each indifference curve is a circle with $(y_e, \pi^T)$ at its centre (see Fig. 3.5a). The loss declines as the circle gets smaller. When $\pi_t = \pi^T$ and $y_t = y_e$, the circle shrinks to a single point (called the 'bliss point') and the loss is at a minimum, which is zero. With $\beta = 1$, the central bank is indifferent between inflation 1% above (or below) $\pi^T$ and output 1% below (or above) $y_e$. They are on the same loss circle.

If $\beta > 1$, the central bank is called inflation–averse: it is indifferent between (say) inflation 1% above (or below) $\pi^T$ and output 2% above (or below) $y_e$. They are on the same loss curve. This makes the indifference curves ellipsoid as in Fig. 3.5b. They are flat because the central bank is willing to trade off a small fall in inflation for a large rise in unemployment above equilibrium. A central bank with less aversion to inflation ($\beta < 1$) will have ellipsoid indiffer-

---

[7] The central bank's preferences can be presented in this simple way if we assume that the central bank's discount rate is infinite. This means that it only considers one period at a time when making its decision.

ence curves with a vertical rather than a horizontal orientation (Fig. 3.5c). In that case, the indifference curves are steep, reflecting that the central bank is only willing to trade off a given fall in inflation for a smaller fall in output than in the other two cases. If the central bank cares only about inflation then the loss ellipses become one dimensional along the line at $\pi_t = \pi^T$.

The value of $\beta$ does not reflect whether the central bank focuses on achieving an inflation target or an output target. Rather, a central bank with lower $\beta$ is willing to trade off a longer period during which inflation is away from target to reduce the impact on unemployment of the adjustment path back to equilibrium than would a more inflation–averse central bank with a higher $\beta$. Central bank preferences are discussed in more detail in Chapter 13.

## The Phillips curve constraint

As discussed in Chapter 2, output affects inflation via the (adaptive expectations) Phillips curve:

$$\pi_t = \pi_t^E + \alpha(y_t - y_e) \tag{3.1}$$
$$= \pi_{t-1} + \alpha(y_t - y_e), \qquad \text{(Phillips curve, } PC\text{)}$$

where $\pi_t^E = \pi_{t-1}$.

The Phillips curve is a constraint for the central bank because it shows all the output and inflation combinations from which the central bank can choose for a given level of expected inflation. In other words, in any period, the central bank can only choose to locate the economy at a point on the Phillips curve it faces. In the Phillips curve used in this chapter, expected inflation is simply lagged inflation—other methods of forming inflation expectations will be discussed in Chapter 4.

This is shown in Fig. 3.6, where the upward sloping lines are the Phillips curves we worked with in Chapter 2. In the diagram, it is assumed that $\alpha = 1$, so that each Phillips curve has a slope of 45°. Each Phillips curve is labelled by a given level of expected inflation, which in the adaptive expectations Phillips curve is equal to lagged inflation. Assume that $\pi_t^E = \pi_{t-1} = \pi^T = 2$ (remember that this $PC$ must go through point A at which $y = y_e$ and $\pi = 2$). The central bank is in the happy position of being able to choose bliss point A or $(\pi^T, y_e)$ at which its loss is zero.

What happens if there has been a shock to inflation and it is not equal to the inflation target? Suppose, for example, that lagged inflation was 4%. The central bank is faced with the constraint of the Phillips curve shown by $PC(\pi_t^E = 4)$ and can only choose among points along it. The bliss point is no longer obtainable. The central bank faces a trade-off: if it wants a level of output of $y_e$ next period, then it has to accept an inflation rate above its target, i.e. $\pi_t = 4 \neq \pi^T$ (i.e. point B). On the other hand, if it wishes to hit the inflation target next period, it must accept a much lower level of output next period (point C). Point B corresponds to a fully accommodating monetary policy in which the objective is purely to hit the output target ($\beta = 0$), and point C corresponds to a completely non-accommodating policy, in which the objective is purely to hit the inflation target.

It is clear from Fig. 3.6 that given its preferences, if the central bank is faced by $PC(\pi_t^E = 4)$, then it can do better (achieve a loss circle closer to A) than either point B or point C. It minimizes its loss function by choosing point D, where the $PC(\pi_t^E = 4)$ line is tangential to

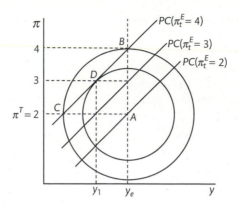

**Figure 3.6** Loss circles and Phillips curves.

the indifference curve of the loss function closest to the bliss point. Thus if is it on $PC(\pi_t^E = 4)$ it will choose an output level $y_1$ which will in turn imply an inflation rate of 3% and a Phillips curve the following period of $PC(\pi_t^E = 3)$.

### Deriving the monetary rule (MR) curve graphically

The MR curve shows the central bank's preferred output-inflation combination for any Phillips curve it faces. It can be derived graphically by finding the points of tangency between the Phillips curves and the loss circles. As shown in Fig. 3.7a, points A, B and C all minimize the loss function of the central bank for their given Phillips curve. For example, take point B, which is on $PC(\pi_t^E = 3)$. If the central bank were to choose any other point on that Phillips curve, then the economy would be on a loss circle further from the bliss point and hence at a lower level of utility.

If we join up the points of tangency as shown in Fig. 3.7b, this gives us the MR curve. This shows the output and inflation combination that the central bank will choose to minimize its loss function for any given Phillips curve it is faced with.

In the Appendix, we derive the monetary rule using the equations for the central bank's loss function and the Phillips curve. The equation for the MR curve shown in Fig. 3.7 is:

$$(y_t - y_e) = -\alpha\beta(\pi_t - \pi^T).$$ (Monetary rule, MR)

The MR tells the central bank what output gap it should choose when it observes that inflation is away from its target. The monetary policy rules used by central banks are often described as Taylor Rules. The difference between the MR and a Taylor Rule is that the latter is expressed in terms of the interest rate the central bank should choose to implement its chosen output gap. Taylor Rules used by central banks are discussed in Chapter 13. To find out the interest rate the central bank should choose once it has decided on its preferred output gap using the MR, for example, to achieve point C at an output level of $y_1$ in Fig. 3.7, we need to introduce the IS curve. In addition to the Phillips curve (PC) and the monetary rule (MR), the IS is the third equation in the 3-equation model.

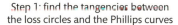

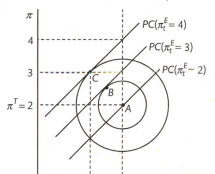

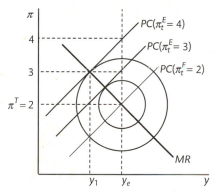

**Figure 3.7** Deriving the *MR* curve.

### Implementing central bank policy—the *IS* curve

In the previous subsection, we set out the process by which the central bank pins down its preferred output gap in response to an economic shock. The instrument the central bank uses to implement its policy is the real interest rate, $r$. The fact that the central bank must adjust the *nominal* interest rate that it sets in order to achieve a particular *real* interest rate on the *IS* curve is called the Taylor Principle.

The real interest rate is chosen to secure the appropriate level of aggregate demand and hence output. The central bank chooses the best point along the Phillips curve that it faces and in order to deliver the right level of aggregate demand, it must set the interest rate at the level shown by the *IS* curve. The *IS* curve shows the effect of changes in the interest rate on aggregate demand and was introduced in the following form in Chapter 1:

$$y = k(c_0 + a_0 + G) - ka_1 r \tag{3.2}$$
$$= A - ar, \tag{IS curve}$$

where $A \equiv k(c_0 + a_0 + G)$, $a \equiv ka_1$ and $k$ is the multiplier. The term $A$ includes the multiplier and the demand shift variables such as government spending and both the autonomous and forward-looking components of consumption and investment.

In the 3-equation model, we will use a 'dynamic' *IS* curve to represent the demand side, which captures the fact that aggregate demand responds negatively to the real interest rate ($r$) with a one period lag. This is in line with the Bank of England's estimates that the impact of interest rates on output takes up to (a maximum of) one year.[8]

The dynamic *IS* curve is defined as follows,

$$y_t = A_t - ar_{t-1}. \tag{dynamic IS curve}$$

[8] Compare the *How Monetary Policy Works* section of the Bank of England's website.

### 3.2.2 **Using the 3-equation model**

This section shows how the 3-equation model can be used to explain the response of the central bank to a shock. The economy is initially at the central bank's 'bliss point'—output is at equilibrium and inflation is at target. This is the medium-run equilibrium, $y_e$, where the WS and PS curves intersect and there is therefore no pressure on inflation to change. The interest rate that is associated with equilibrium is known as the *stabilizing rate of interest*, or $r_S$.

*Inflation shock*

An inflation shock is the simplest to analyse and serves to highlight the dynamic behaviour of the model. The term inflation shock is used to refer to an exogenous shift in the Phillips curve. This could be caused, for example, by a natural disaster such as a drought that reduces agricultural output and raises food prices, or by a temporary burst of union militancy, which pushes up wages.

In the 3-equation model framework, the central bank follows two main steps to stabilize the economy after an inflation shock:

1. The inflation shock shifts the Phillips curve upwards. The central bank must choose the position on the new Phillips curve that minimizes their loss function. This will be where the MR curve intersects the new Phillips curve. As inflation is above target, the central bank will have to reduce output below equilibrium to squeeze inflation out of the system.

2. The central bank uses the IS curve to find the increase in the real interest rate required to get the economy back onto the MR curve. The higher interest rate dampens output and inflation starts to fall. The central bank then gradually reduces the interest rate until output rises back to equilibrium and inflation falls back at target.

Figure 3.8 provides a summary of the dynamic adjustment of the economy to an inflation shock (start at the top and follow round). Figure 3.9a shows the typical fashion in which shocks can be modelled graphically in the 3-equation model, with the IS diagram at the top and the PC − MR diagram directly below it. This allows the position of the economy to be shown simultaneously on both diagrams. As shown in Fig. 3.9a, the adjustment of the economy to the inflation shock is as follows:

**Period 0** The economy starts at A, where the central bank's utility is highest. The economy is then hit by an inflation shock which shifts the PC to PC(inflation shock) in the lower panel and the economy moves from A to B. Point B is not on the central bank's MR curve. The central bank forecasts the PC in the next period. In this case, the PC will stay in its post shock position, as output has not deviated from equilibrium as a result of the shock. We denote next period's PC as $PC(\pi_1^E = \pi_0)$. Faced with this PC, the central bank would like to locate at point C, back on the MR curve. They therefore set the interest rate at $r_0$. The interest rate can only affect economic output with a one period lag, however, so the economy ends period 0 with inflation at $\pi_0$, output at $y_e$ and the interest rate at $r_0$.

**Period 1** The new interest rate has had time to reduce aggregate demand by dampening investment. The economy moves to point C, with output below equilibrium at $y_1$ and inflation at $\pi_1$. The central bank forecasts the PC in the next period. The Phillips curve shifts when

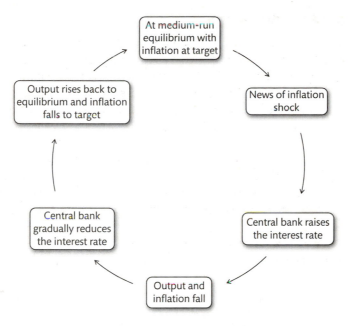

**Figure 3.8** Dynamic adjustment to an inflation shock.

inflation expectations are updated: hence the *PC* will change in the next period, moving to $PC(\pi_2^E = \pi_1)$. Faced with this *PC*, the central bank would like to locate at point *D*, back on their *MR* curve. They therefore reduce the interest rate to $r_1$. The interest rate can only affect economic output with a one period lag, however, so the economy ends period 1 with inflation at $\pi_1$, output at $y_1$ and the interest rate at $r_1$.

**Period 2 onwards**   In period 2, the economy moves to point *D*, as the lower interest rate stimulates demand. This increases output to $y_2$ and inflation falls to $\pi_2$. The same process now repeats itself until the economy is back at equilibrium at *Z*. This involves the central bank forecasting next period's *PC* and setting the interest rate in the current period to ensure they stay on the *MR* curve in the following period. The adjustment from *D* to *Z* will take a number of periods. The economy will move gradually down the *MR* curve, as the central bank slowly adjusts the interest rate down from $r_1$ to $r_S$. This causes output to rise slowly from $y_2$ to $y_e$ and inflation to fall slowly from $\pi_2$ to $\pi^T$. The economic adjustment to the inflation shock ends when the economy is back at point *Z*, with output at $y_e$, inflation at $\pi^T$ and the interest rate at $r_S$.

Figure 3.9b shows the path of the key macroeconomic variables over time following the inflation shock. These types of graphs are called *impulse response functions* and are useful for visualizing the adjustment path of the economy following an economic shock. In this case, we can see that inflation has risen after the shock and is then slowly brought back to target. The interest rate follows a similar path, rising as soon as the shock takes place and then slowly being reduced to target. The path of output is slightly different, in that it does not change until one period after the shock. This is because the higher interest rate takes one period to affect output, as shown by the *IS* relation underlying the model, $y_t = A - ar_{t-1}$.

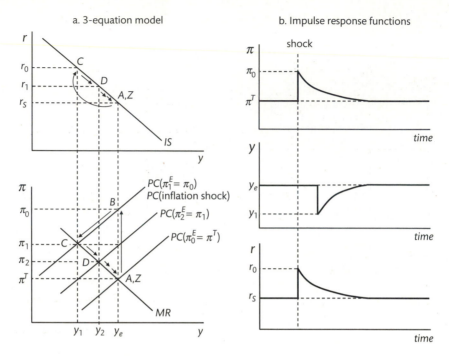

**Figure 3.9** Inflation shock and the monetary rule.

The 3-equation model can be used to analyse a wide range of situations faced by the central bank. In Section 3.3, it is used to analyse demand and supply shocks and to examine the special case of a deflation trap.

## 3.3 Applications

In this section, we show more examples of the 3-equation model at work, focusing on demand- and supply-side shocks. We highlight the integral role played by central bank forecasting in identifying the best response interest rate to ensure medium-run economic stability. We go on to analyse the special case of a deflation trap, where a sizeable negative demand shock pushes the economy into a vicious cycle of falling inflation and output. We provide some escape routes from a deflation trap, whilst noting their potential pitfalls. We end this section by looking at a supply shock, which is a shift in either the wage- or price–setting curve. In this case, the central bank acts to stabilize the economy at the new equilibrium level of output fixed by the new intersecton of the *WS* and *PS* curves.

### 3.3.1 A temporary demand shock

We assume that the economy starts off in equilibrium with output at the equilibrium and inflation at the target rate of $\pi^T$ (see Fig. 3.10). The economy is then disturbed by a temporary positive aggregate demand shock. By a temporary aggregate demand shock, we mean that the shock shifts the *IS* curve to *IS'*, but it only remains at *IS'* for one period. The economy is

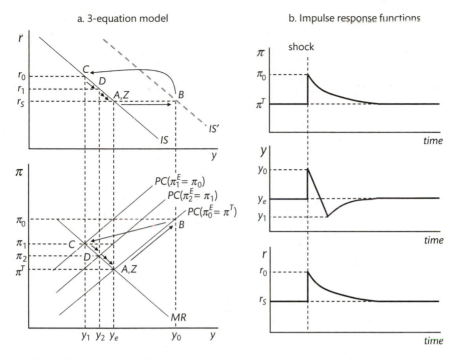

**Figure 3.10** Adjustment of the economy to a temporary positive aggregate demand shock.

shifted from A to B in Fig. 3.10 as a result of the aggregate demand shock. This rise in output builds a rise in inflation above target into the system. Because of inflation inertia, this can only be eliminated by pushing output below and (unemployment above) the equilibrium. The central bank therefore raises the interest rate in response to the aggregate demand shock because it can work out the consequences for inflation. It must raise the interest rate in order to depress interest-sensitive demand and reduce output. The central bank is forward looking and takes all available information into account.

The adjustment to the shock is shown in Fig. 3.10.

**Period 0** The economy starts at A—the central bank's bliss point. Following the demand shock, the economy moves from A to B. The shock has increased both output ($y_0 > y_e$) and inflation ($\pi_0 > \pi^T$). Point B is not on the central bank's MR curve. The central bank forecasts the PC in the next period. The Phillips curve shifts when inflation expectations are updated: hence the PC will change in the next period, moving to $PC(\pi_1^E = \pi_0)$. Faced with this PC, the central bank would like to locate at point C, back on their MR curve. They therefore set the interest rate at $r_0$. The central bank expects the demand shock to be temporary, so that the IS curve will shift back in the next period. This is the reason they use the original IS curve to set the interest rate. The interest rate can only affect economic output with a one period lag, however, so the economy ends period 0 with inflation at $\pi_0$, output at $y_0$ and the interest rate at $r_0$.

**Period 1** The new interest rate has had time to affect aggregate demand. The higher rate of interest dampens investment. This reduces output and the economy moves to point C, with output below equilibrium at $y_1$ and inflation at $\pi_1$. The central bank forecasts the PC in the next period: the PC will move to $PC(\pi_2^E = \pi_1)$. Faced with this PC, the central bank would like to locate at point D, on their MR curve. They therefore reduce the interest rate to $r_1$. The interest rate can only affect economic output with a one period lag, however, so the economy ends period 1 with inflation at $\pi_1$, output at $y_1$ and the interest rate at $r_1$.

**Period 2 onwards** In period 2, the economy moves to point D, as the lower interest rate stimulates demand. This increases output to $y_2$ and inflation falls to $\pi_2$. The same process now repeats itself until the economy is back at equilibrium at Z. The economic adjustment to the temporary demand shock ends when the economy is back at point Z, with output at $y_e$, inflation at $\pi^T$ and the interest rate at $r_S$.

We can use a Reserve Bank of Australia press release from March 2005 to provide an example of a case where an inflation-targeting central bank increased interest rates by 25 basis points to 5.5% in response to rising demand pressures:[9]

> In Australia, there are high levels of confidence in both the business and household sectors, credit growth is providing ample support for spending, employment is growing strongly and national income and spending will continue to be boosted this year by the rising terms of trade.

### 3.3.2 Forecasting and lags

The example of the central bank's reaction to a demand shock can be used to highlight the role played by forecasting and lags in the effect of monetary policy on aggregate demand and output. In the previous subsection, we discussed the adjustment of the economy to a temporary positive demand shock (Fig. 3.10). We now use Fig. 3.11 to compare this to the case of a permanent demand shock. It is left as an exercise for the reader to set out the detailed period by period adjustment for the permanent case.

The examples highlight two important points about the central bank's reaction to an aggregate demand shock:

1. The central bank has to forecast both the PC and IS curves. The forecasting of the IS curve means predicting the length of the shock—is it temporary or permanent?

2. The reason that the central bank must forecast the IS is that the persistence of the shock affects the central bank's preferred reaction. In Fig. 3.11, where the shock is permanent, the IS curve remains at IS'. The initial increase in the interest rate (i.e. from $r_S$ to $r_0$) is much greater in the case of a permanent shock. In addition, a permanent shock leads to a higher stabilizing rate of interest in the new equilibrium—$r_S'$. This is because the higher autonomous aggregate demand (for example, due to improved consumer confidence) needs to be offset by lower interest-sensitive aggregate demand (i.e. investment) if output is to return to its equilibrium level $y_e$.

What happens if the central bank is uncertain about whether the shock is temporary or permanent? In this case, the central bank would be likely to set an interest rate somewhere in

---

[9] Excerpt taken from: Mr Ian Macfarlane, 2nd March 2005, *Statement by the Governor, Mr Ian Macfarlane: Monetary Policy.*

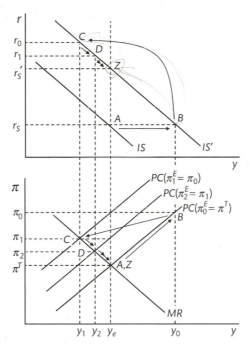

**Figure 3.11** Adjustment of the economy to a permanent positive aggregate demand shock.

between the interest rates it would set in the cases presented in Figs. 3.10 and 3.11. In reality, central banks are unlikely to be able to tell (in the period of the shock) whether shocks will be temporary or permanent, so use their best judgement to respond to shocks and often have to adjust interest rates as new information arrives.

In the benchmark 3-equation model, the interest rate affects output with a one period lag: $y_t = A - ar_{t-1}$. However, it is interesting to see what happens if the central bank could affect output immediately, i.e. if $y_t = A - ar_t$. In this case, as soon as the IS shock is diagnosed, the central bank would raise the interest rate to $r'_s$. The economy then goes directly from A to Z in the IS diagram (in Fig. 3.11) and it remains at A in the PC−MR diagram, i.e. points A and Z coincide. Since the aggregate demand shock is fully and immediately offset by the change in the interest rate, there is no chance for inflation to rise.

This underlines the crucial role of lags and hence of forecasting for the central bank: the more timely and accurate are forecasts of shifts in aggregate demand (and of other kinds of shock), the greater is the chance that the central bank can offset them and limit their impact on inflation. Once inflation has been affected, the presence of inflation inertia means that the central bank must change the interest rate and get the economy onto the MR curve in order to steer it back to the inflation target.

The Bank of England's first strategic priority for 2012/13 was to 'keep inflation on track to meet the Government's 2% target'. One of the key actions the Bank committed to take to achieve this objective was to 'exploit the new suite of models in forecasting and analysis'.[10]

---

[10] These excerpts are taken from *The Bank's Strategy* section of the Bank of England's website.

This shows the focus and resources modern central banks apply to forecasting and modelling to make better informed monetary policy decisions.

### 3.3.3 The deflation trap

Problems arise for using monetary policy along the lines of the 3-equation model when the real rate of interest needed to stabilize demand cannot be achieved because the nominal interest rate cannot be reduced further.

**The zero lower bound on nominal interest rates**

In Chapter 1, we set out the Fisher equation, which shows the relationship between the real and nominal interest rates and the expected rate of inflation:

$$i = r + \pi^E. \hspace{4cm} \text{(Fisher equation)}$$

When responding to an economic shock, the central bank adjusts the nominal interest rate ($i$), in order to affect the real interest rate ($r$) which in turn affects aggregate demand through the *IS* relation. To do this, it must take into account expected inflation as shown by the Fisher equation. In this regard, we can model the central bank as setting the real interest rate.

We saw in Fig. 3.1, that the central bank will respond to falling inflation by reducing the interest rate to stimulate aggregate demand. There is, however, a limit to the extent to which the central bank can reduce the nominal interest rate. The lowest nominal interest rate the central bank can set is zero (see the box below). From the Fisher equation, we can see that if the real interest rate that is needed to achieve the central bank's chosen output gap on the *MR* curve is, for example, 0.75%, and expected inflation is −1%, then a nominal interest rate of −0.25% would be required. With a *zero lower bound (or ZLB)* on the nominal interest rate, the minimum real interest rate that can be achieved is set by:

$$\min r \geq -\pi^E. \hspace{4cm} (3.3)$$

This means that in our example, the minimum real interest rate achievable is 1%, which is not low enough get the economy on to the *MR* and on the path back to equilibrium. This condition is shown in Fig. 3.12 where the stabilizing real interest rate is below the minimum feasible rate of 1%. Given the depressed state of aggregate demand depicted by the position of the *IS* curve, if inflation has fallen to −1%, then it will be impossible to achieve the equilibrium level of output using conventional monetary policy. The economy is stuck at point *A* on the *IS* curve.

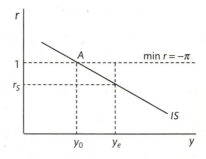

**Figure 3.12** The zero lower bound on the nominal interest rate.

## Box 3.1  Why can't nominal interest rates fall below zero?

There is no technical reason why nominal interest rates cannot be negative. The central bank could, for example, set the interest rate at –5%. In this environment, an individual who put $100 in the bank at the start of the year could withdraw $95 at the end of the year. This is not beneficial for savers, but this could be the interest rate required to get the economy onto the $MR$ curve and back to equilibrium. It would certainly be expected to stimulate borrowing, by making the cost of obtaining credit cheaper.

There is, however, a major practical implication to negative interest rates; the presence of currency. When nominal interest rates are negative, there is nothing to stop people simply holding their savings in cash, which has a nominal interest rate of zero.

The existence of high denomination notes, such as the $100 bill and the €500 note, reduces the cost associated with carrying large sums of money in cash. If only very small denomination notes were left in circulation then this cost of carrying cash might become so large that accepting negative interest rates would be preferable. However, monetary authorities have shown no intention of moving towards this system so currency still acts as the limiting factor on setting nominal interest rates.[a]

[a] For a more thorough discussion on negative interest rates see Willem Buiter's Maverecon blog column for the Financial Times entitled 'Negative interest rates: when are they coming to a central bank near you?' (May, 2009).

### The deflation trap and the 3-equation model

We can use the 3-equation model to provide a period by period explanation of how a negative aggregate demand shock can lead to the economy becoming stuck in a deflation trap, where output and inflation are falling without limit. We assume that the economy starts off with output at equilibrium and inflation at the target rate of $\pi^T$ as shown in Fig. 3.13. The economic adjustment to the shock is as follows:

**Period 0**  The economy starts at $A$—the central bank's bliss point. The economy is hit by a large permanent negative aggregate demand shock which shifts the $IS$ curve to $IS'$ and the economy moves from $A$ to $B$. The shock has reduced both output ($y_0 < y_e$) and inflation ($\pi_0 < \pi^T$). In fact, inflation has become negative—i.e. there is deflation. Point $B$ is not on the central bank's $MR$ curve. The central bank forecasts the $PC$ in the next period. Inflation is currently below equilibrium at $\pi_0$, which means the $PC$ will shift in the next period, moving to $PC(\pi_1^E = \pi_0)$. Faced with this $PC$, the central bank would like to locate at point $C'$, back on their $MR$ curve. This would require setting an interest rate of $r_0'$. However, this is below the minimum real interest rate the central bank can achieve (by setting nominal interest rates to zero). The lowest interest rate they can achieve is $r_0 = -\pi_0$. The central bank expects the demand shock to be permanent, so that the $IS$ curve will stay at $IS'$ in the next period. This is the reason they use the new $IS$ curve to set the interest rate. The interest rate can only

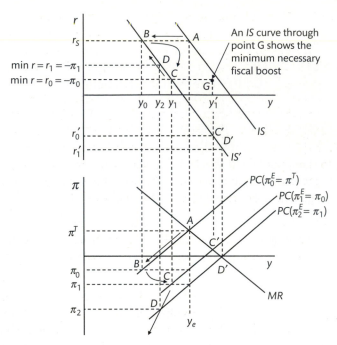

**Figure 3.13** How a large negative permanent aggregate demand shock can lead to the economy entering a deflation trap.

affect economic output with a one period lag, however, so the economy ends period 0 with inflation at $\pi_0$, output at $y_0$ and the interest rate at $r_0$.

**Period 1**  The new interest rate has had time to affect aggregate demand. The lower rate of interest boosts investment. This increases output and the economy moves to point C, with output still below equilibrium at $y_1$. This level of output is far below the the central bank's best response level of $y_1'$, which causes inflation to fall further to $\pi_1$. The central bank forecasts the PC in the next period. The PC will move to $PC(\pi_2^E = \pi_1)$. Faced with this PC, the central bank would like to locate at point D', back on their MR curve. This would require setting an interest rate of $r_1'$. However, this is below the minimum real interest rate the central bank can achieve (by setting nominal interest rates to zero). The lowest interest rate they can achieve is $r_1 = -\pi_1$. The interest rate can only affect economic output with a one period lag, however, so the economy ends period 1 with inflation at $\pi_1$, output at $y_1$ and the interest rate at $r_1$.

**Period 2 onwards**  In period 2, the economy moves to point D, as the higher interest rate dampens demand. This reduces output to $y_2$ and inflation falls further to $\pi_2$. The economy has entered a deflation trap—both output and inflation are falling every period and conventional monetary policy is powerless to stop them. In each future period, inflation becomes more negative, which increases the minimum real interest rate the central bank can achieve. The higher interest rate dampens demand, which further reduces inflation. In other words, the economy is caught in a vicious cycle. The arrows on Fig. 3.13 show that the economy will not revert to medium-run equilibrium in this case, but rather it will diverge, with ever-falling inflation and output.

The downward spiral of the economy in a deflation trap explains why policy makers are so keen to avoid this situation. We have shown in Fig. 3.13 that conventional monetary policy (e.g. adjusting interest rates) is insufficient to escape a deflation trap. There are, however, two policies which could be initiated to pull the economy out of this downward spiral:

1. The *IS* curve could be shifted to the right (to go through point *G*) in the period after the initial demand shock. This would allow the central bank to achieve their desired output level of $y_1'$ by setting the minimum achievable interest rate of $r_0$. This positive demand shock could take place via a spontaneous recovery of autonomous investment or a recovery of autonomous consumption. Alternatively, the government can step in and implement the desired output gap shown by the *MR* curve by using fiscal policy. In this case, the *MR* becomes a more general policy rule and would be labelled *PR*, for policy rule.

2. The creation of more positive inflation expectations. If expected inflation becomes less negative, the min *r* line shifts down and the *PC* curve shifts up. This may allow the central bank to use the interest rate based monetary rule in the usual way to move the economy to the south–east along the *IS* curve.

However, the idea of escaping from the deflation trap by creating positive inflation expectations may not work in practice. The way to create expectations of inflation in the future is to create expectations of future higher aggregate demand: if the authorities do not take measures to create the demand, there is no reason to think that people will expect higher inflation.

Another potential option for central banks stuck at the zero lower bound is to introduce unconventional monetary policies, such as quantitative easing. We leave a discussion of this policy option until Chapter 7, however, as it is easier to explain once we have introduced the banking system into the model.

### 3.3.4  A supply shock

At the end of Chapter 2, we looked at the implications for inflation of a positive aggregate supply shock. This was modelled as a downward shift of the *WS* curve, which could be the result of a number of factors, such as a decrease in union bargaining power or a reduction in unemployment benefits. The initial effect of this supply shock is a downward shift of the Phillips curve. We will now go on to explain how the central bank stabilizes the economy in the event of a supply shock and the characteristics of the new medium-run equilibrium (see Fig. 3.14).

The stabilizing interest rate is lower (at $r_s'$) in the new medium-run equilibrium. Since equilibrium output is higher as a consequence of the supply-side shift, a lower real interest rate is required to provide the appropriate level of aggregate demand. This example highlights that supply shocks differ from inflation and demand shocks in two key ways:

1. Firstly, a supply shock changes the equilibrium level of output (i.e. $y_e'$ in Fig. 3.14).
2. Secondly, a supply shock shifts the *MR* schedule so that it goes through the point where inflation is at target and output at the new equilibrium (i.e. *MR′* in Fig. 3.14)

The period by period adjustment of the economy to a positive supply shock and the central bank's intervention is illustrated in Fig. 3.14 and described below.

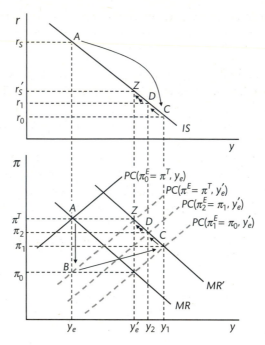

**Figure 3.14** The adjustment of the economy to a positive permanent aggregate supply shock.

**Period 0**  The economy starts at A—the central bank's bliss point. The economy is hit by a permanent positive aggregate supply shock. This fundamentally changes the equilibrium level of output in the economy, increasing it from $y_e$ to $y'_e$. At A, the economy is now below equilibrium output and there is pressure on inflation to fall (as $WS < PS$, see Chapter 2). The Phillips curve shifts down from $PC(\pi_0^E = \pi^T, y_e)$ to $PC(\pi_0^E = \pi^T, y'_e)$, reflecting the change in the equilibrium level of output. The economy moves from A to B, where output is still at its original level, but inflation has fallen to $\pi_0$.

The central bank predicts that the shock is a permanent supply shock, so they shift the MR curve outwards to ensure their bliss point is now where output is equal to $y'_e$ and inflation is equal to $\pi^T$. Point B is not on the central bank's new MR curve, MR'. The central bank forecasts the PC in the next period. Output is currently below the new equilibrium level of $y'_e$, which means the PC will shift in the next period, moving to $PC(\pi_1^E = \pi_0, y'_e)$. Faced with this PC, the central bank would like to locate at point C, on their new MR curve, MR'. They therefore set the interest rate at $r_0$. The interest rate can only affect economic output with a one period lag, however, so the economy ends period 0 at with inflation at $\pi_0$, output at $y_e$ and interest rates at $r_0$.

**Period 1**  The new interest rate has had time to affect aggregate demand. The lower rate of interest boosts investment. This increases output and the economy moves to point C, with output above the new equilibrium at $y_1$ and inflation at $\pi_1$. The central bank forecasts the PC in the following period. Output is still away from the new equilibrium, so the PC will change again in the next period, moving to $PC(\pi_2^E = \pi_1, y'_e)$. Faced with this PC, the central bank would like to locate at point D, on the MR' curve. They therefore increase the interest rate to $r_1$. The interest rate can only affect economic output with a one period lag, however, so the economy ends period 1 with inflation at $\pi_1$, output at $y_1$ and interest rates at $r_1$.

**Period 2 onwards** In period 2, the economy moves to point $D$, as the higher interest rate dampens demand. This reduces output to $y_2$ and inflation rises to $\pi_2$. The same process now repeats itself in the usual way until the economy is back at equilibrium at $Z$. Adjustment to the supply shock ends when the economy is back at point $Z$, with output at $y'_e$, inflation at $\pi^T$ and the interest rate at $r'_s$.[11]

A positive supply shock can be the result of a shift in the WS or PS curves. We have shown the example of a downward shift in the WS curve above, but equally a positive supply shock could reflect an upward shift of the PS curve, due to increased product market competition or productivity gains. This latter case applies to the United States in the late 1990s, where the ICT revolution spurred productivity increases. The Federal Reserve correctly identified this as a positive supply shock and took into account its role in moderating inflation:[12]

> Responding to the availability of new technologies at increasingly attractive prices, firms have been investing heavily in new capital equipment; this investment has boosted productivity and living standards while holding down the rise in costs and prices.

## 3.4 Conclusions

This chapter has provided the final building block for the 3-equation model of the macro-economy by setting out the monetary rule, or MR curve, which shows the central bank's chosen combination of output gap and inflation rate relative to target for any given Phillips curve they face. The equations of the 3-equation model are:

1. IS curve: $y_t = A - ar_{t-1}$.
2. PC curve: $\pi_t = \pi_{t-1} + \alpha(y_t - y_e)$.
3. MR curve: $(y_t - y_e) = -\alpha\beta(\pi_t - \pi^T)$.

The policy maker is modelled as an inflation-targeting central bank not because this is necessarily the best policy-making arrangement, but because it most closely resembles how modern stabilization policy is undertaken. We noted the economic and political reasons that have been used to explain why, in the more than two decades running up to the global financial crisis, stabilization policy was put in the hands of the monetary policy maker.

In Chapter 1, we introduced the IS curve to model the demand side of the economy. In Chapter 2, we introduced the Phillips curve (PC) to model the supply side of the economy.

---

[11] Note that, the Phillips curve in the new equilibrium is denoted by $PC(\pi^E = \pi^T, y'_e)$. This does not include a time subscript because the Phillips curve is in this position in two periods—in period 0 straight after the supply shock and then in the period when the economy completes its adjustment to the new equilibrium at point $Z$.
[12] Excerpt taken from: The Federal Reserve Board, July 22nd, 1999, *Monetary Policy Report submitted to the Congress.*

In this chapter, we have introduced the *MR* curve to model the policy maker. These are the three components of the 3-equation model. The modelling section of this chapter set out the 3-equation model in full; the Appendix shows the mathematical derivation. Putting them together provides a framework in which to answer a variety of questions about the macro-economy and stabilization policy in particular:

1. Why target low and stable inflation? Central banks target low and stable inflation to minimize the negative effects of inflation on the economy—such as price distortions, shoe leather costs, menu costs—and to avoid high and rising (or volatile) inflation. Does that mean it is optimal to target 0% inflation? No, because central banks also want to guard against the threat of deflation (i.e. falling prices). Deflation is particularly problematic for the economy due to the possibility of entering a deflation trap. In light of this, the majority of developed economy modern central banks have chosen to target 2% inflation.

2. How do modern central banks go about achieving their inflation target? How do they react to economic shocks? The central bank's best response position—their 'bliss point'—is to be in medium-run equilibrium, with inflation equal to target ($\pi^T$) and output equal to equilibrium ($y_e$). The *monetary rule* (or *MR*) curve of a central bank shows the output and inflation combinations that minimize their *loss function* (i.e. maximize their utility) for any given Phillips curve they face. In response to an economic shock, the central bank finds the relevant Phillips curve and uses the *MR* curve to find their preferred output gap. The real interest rate ($r$) is the policy lever they use to achieve their desired output gap. It affects aggregate demand via the *IS* relation. The central bank then continues to adjust the interest rate to guide the economy to the new medium-run equilibrium. The use of the interest rate to implement monetary policy is sometimes called a Taylor rule based monetary policy. Demand shocks will cause the economy to diverge from its initial equilibrium level of output for a number of periods, whereas permanent supply shocks will cause the economy to move to a new equilibrium level of output.

3. What role do lags and forecasting play in monetary policy? The model reflects the real-world phenomenon that it takes time for the real interest rate to affect aggregate demand. This means that forecasting plays a large role in the central bank's setting of interest rates. For a shock in period zero, the central bank has to forecast where the Phillips curve will be next period and then set the appropriate interest rate (using the *MR* curve) to minimize their loss function. The Phillips curve also contains a backward-looking component, which means that if inflation is above target, a period of output below equilibrium (i.e. high unemployment) is required to reduce inflation back to target (and vice versa).

An important component of the core 3-equation model is the equilibrium rate of unemployment: it is possible to go straight from here to the analysis of the supply side institutions and policies that determine unemployment in Chapter 15. In this part of the book, we go on to consider a number of extensions to the model. In Chapter 4, we look in more depth at the way in which expectations about the future are formed. The role played by the banking system and how this can lead to instability and financial crises is integrated in the model in Chapters 5 and 6. The 3-equation model is extended to the open economy in Chapter 9.

# 3.5 Appendix

### 3.5.1 The 3-equation model in more detail

In the chapter, graphical analysis was used to provide a simple and intuitive explanation of the 3-equation model. In this section, we set out more carefully how the model works, focusing on the mathematical derivation of the $MR$ curve. We start by deriving a more general form of the central bank's monetary rule. In setting out the equations that form the basis of the 3-equation model, we need to make explicit the timing structure. By choosing the interest rate in period zero, the central bank affects output and inflation in period 1. We assume it is only concerned with what happens in period 1. This is the reason that its loss function is defined in terms of $y_1$ and $\pi_1$. If we let $\beta$ and $\alpha$ take any positive values, the central bank chooses $y$ to minimize

$$L = (y_1 - y_e)^2 + \beta(\pi_1 - \pi^T)^2, \qquad \text{(central bank loss function)}$$

subject to

$$\pi_1 = \pi_0 + \alpha(y_1 - y_e). \qquad \text{(Phillips curve)}$$

By substituting the equation for the Phillips curve into the central bank loss function we can rewrite the loss function as:

$$L = (y_1 - y_e)^2 + \beta((\pi_0 + \alpha(y_1 - y_e)) - \pi^T)^2.$$

If we now differentiate this with respect to $y_1$ (since this is the variable the central bank can control via its choice of the interest rate), we have:

$$\frac{\partial L}{\partial y_1} = (y_1 - y_e) + \alpha\beta(\pi_0 + \alpha(y_1 - y_e) - \pi^T) = 0. \qquad (3.4)$$

Rearranging the Phillips curve to find $\pi_0$ and substituting this back into equation 3.4 gives:

$$(y_1 - y_e) = -\alpha\beta(\pi_1 - \pi^T). \qquad \text{(monetary rule, } MR)$$

The *monetary rule* shows the central bank's best response to a shock; it is the relationship between the inflation rate chosen indirectly and the level of output chosen directly by the central bank to maximize its utility (minimize its loss) given its preferences and the constraints it faces. The monetary rule is an inverse relation between $\pi$ and $y$ with a negative slope, which shows that the central bank must reduce aggregate demand and output, $y$, below $y_e$ so as to reduce $\pi$ below $\pi^T$.

In the general form of the $MR$ curve shown above, it can be seen directly that the larger is $\alpha$ (i.e. the more responsive are wages to employment) or the larger is $\beta$ (i.e. the more inflation averse is the central bank), the flatter will be the slope of the monetary rule.

In the first case this is because any reduction in aggregate demand achieves a bigger cut in inflation, i.e. whatever its preferences, the central bank gets a 'bigger bang (i.e. fall in inflation) for its buck (i.e. fall in aggregate demand)'.

In the second case, this is because, whatever the labour market it faces, a more inflation-averse central bank will wish to reduce inflation by more than a less 'hard-nosed' one.

## Box 3.2   Summary of the 3-equation model

In formally deriving the *MR* curve, we now have all the components to set out the central bank's decision-making process:

1. The central bank minimizes its loss function, which expresses its objective of keeping inflation close to target, $\pi^T$

$$L = (y_t - y_e)^2 + \beta(\pi_t - \pi^T)^2,$$     central bank loss function

2. subject to the constraint from the supply side, which is the Phillips curve (*PC*).

$$\pi_t = \pi_{t-1} + \alpha(y_t - y_e).$$     Phillips curve, *PC*

3. This produces the monetary rule function (*MR*), which fixes the best response output gap $(y_t - y_e)$,

$$(y_t - y_e) = -\alpha\beta(\pi_t - \pi^T).$$     monetary rule, *MR*

4. which is implemented through the central bank's choice of *r* using the dynamic *IS* equation, incorporating the lag from the interest rate to output

$$y_t = A - ar_{t-1}.$$     dynamic *IS* curve

Figure 3.15 shows the 3-equation model when the economy is in medium-run equilibrium—i.e. output is at equilibrium and inflation is constant at target. In the $PC - MR$ diagram, the economy is at the central bank's 'bliss point'—the levels of output and inflation that minimize the loss function (i.e. $y_e$ and $\pi^T$). In the *IS* diagram, we can use the *IS* curve to read off the interest rate the central bank must set to keep inflation constant and output at $y_e$. This is the *stabilizing rate of interest*, $r_S$.

In the case when output is at equilibrium (i.e. $y_e$) and the interest rate is at its stabilizing level (i.e. $r_S$), we can rewrite the dynamic *IS* curve as:

$$y_e = A - ar_S.$$     (*IS* curve, in medium-run equilibrium)

We can use the two versions of the *IS* equation to find a relationship between deviations of output from equilibrium and the interest rate from its stabilizing level. We do this by subtracting one from the other, such that:

$$y_t - y_e = -a(r_{t-1} - r_S).$$     (*IS* equation, in deviations)

In period zero, this becomes,

$$y_1 - y_e = -a(r_0 - r_S),$$     (*IS* equation, in deviations, in period zero)

which takes into account the fact that interest rate changes in period zero do not affect output until period one (i.e. the lag structure of the model). It can be useful to think of the *IS* equation in deviations form in the 3-equation model and particularly for deriving interest rate rules, which will be discussed in detail in Chapter 13.

Figure 3.15 can also give us an insight into how varying the underlying targets or parameters will affect the 3-equation model. There are six key parameters that affect the

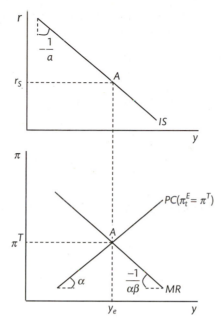

**Figure 3.15** The 3-equation model in medium-run equilibrium.

underlying curves in the 3-equation model and the central bank's best response to economic shocks:[13]

1. the central bank's inflation target, $\pi^T$: this affects the position of the MR line;

2. the central bank's preferences, $\beta$: this determines the shape of the loss ellipses and affects the slope of the MR line;

3. the slope of the Phillips curve, $\alpha$: this also affects the slope of the MR line;

4. the interest sensitivity of aggregate demand, $a$: this determines the slope of the IS curve;

5. the equilibrium level of output, $y_e$: this determines the level of output at which there is no pressure on inflation to change and affects the position of the MR line;

6. the stabilizing interest rate, $r_S$: the central bank adjusts the interest rate relative to $r_S$ so it must always analyse whether this has shifted, e.g. as a result of a shift in the IS or due to a change in the equilibrium level of output, $y_e$.

## 3.6 Questions

### 3.6.1 Checklist questions

1. Why is monetary policy chosen over fiscal policy as the preferred tool for stabilization policy? What does the government gain from controlling monetary policy? Why would they choose to delegate responsibility for monetary policy to an independent central bank?

[13] The Macroeconomic Simulator available from the Carlin and Soskice website can be used to test the effects of varying key parameters on the adjustment path of the economy following an economic shock. See Questions 3 and 4 in Section 3.6.2.

2. 'If the economy has high but stable inflation, the government has much to lose and little to gain by reducing inflation to a low rate.' Explain and assess this statement.

3. What are the advantages and disadvantages of a target inflation rate of 4% as compared with one of 0% per annum?

4. Explain what is meant by the central bank's loss function. How are the central bank's preferences reflected in the loss function? Draw the loss 'circles' for the cases where

   (a) $\beta = 1$;

   (b) $\beta < 1$;

   (c) $\beta > 1$.

   In which of the three cases will the central bank reduce inflation back to target quickest after an inflation shock? Is there any downside to adopting this policy stance?

5. Assume that $\alpha = \beta = 1$, derive the $MR$ curve graphically using the tangencies between the loss circles and the Phillips curves. With reference to the diagrams, explain the effect of the following (in each case, assume all other parameters are held constant):

   (a) An increase in the slope of the Phillips curve, $\alpha$

   (b) An increase in central bank's inflation aversion, $\beta$.

6. Following an inflation shock, explain why unemployment goes up before the economy returns to medium-run equilibrium.

7. Draw the 3-equation model and give a detailed period by period description of the adjustment process for the case where the economy is hit by a permanent negative aggregate demand shock.

8. With reference to the scenario in Question 7, explain the behaviour of the central bank and the economy in a situation where there is no lag in the $IS$ curve.

9. Draw the impulse response functions for output, inflation and the real interest rate after a permanent positive aggregate demand shock and a permanent positive supply shock. [Hint: the 3-equation model diagrams for these two cases are shown in Figs. 3.11 and 3.14 respectively.]

10. Use the 3-equation model diagrams to show how the economy can fall into a deflation trap. Explain, with reference to the diagram, how the central bank/government can intervene to escape the trap. Show the relevant $IS$ curve and re-label the $MR$ as the $PR$ to indicate that fiscal policy is being used. Are there any reasons why these policies might not work?

### 3.6.2 Problems and questions for discussion

1. Pick one developed economy and one emerging or developing economy. Use the latest version of the IMF World Economic Outlook Database to download inflation data for each of the countries from 1980 to the latest available data. Plot the data in a graph. Answer the following:

   (a) Describe the evolution of inflation in each country.

   (b) Do the countries have independent central banks?

   (c) If the country does have an independent central bank, did inflation fall when the central bank gained independence? Propose some reasons why.

   (d) If the country does not have an independent central bank, have they managed to find other mechanisms to establish a low inflation monetary policy regime? Propose some reasons why.

2. Select two out of the following central banks: Bank of England, Reserve Bank of New Zealand, Bank of Canada, and the Swedish Riksbank. Each of these central banks has adopted explicit 'inflation targeting'. For each of your chosen banks, answer the following questions:

   (a) What is their target level of inflation and how do they justify choosing that level?

   (b) What actions did it take following the collapse of Lehman Brothers in September 2008 and how did it explain these actions?

   (c) Did they hit the zero lower bound on nominal interest rates during the global financial crisis? If so, how could they adjust their inflation target to reduce the likelihood of this happening again in the future? Check for evidence of a public debate about this issue.

3. This question uses the Macroeconomic Simulator available from the Carlin and Soskice website http://www.oup.com/uk/orc/carlin_soskice to model a negative temporary aggregate demand shock. Start by opening the simulator and choosing the closed economy version. Then reset all shocks by clicking the appropriate button on the left hand side of the main page. Use the simulator and the content of this chapter to work through the following:

   (a) Apply a temporary 5% negative demand shock. Save your data.

   (b) Use the impulse response functions from the simulator to help explain the path of the economy following the shock.

   (c) Draw the $IS - PC - MR$ diagrams for this scenario.

   (d) Adjust the central bank preferences (i.e. $\beta$) to 0.5 and save your data. Now, adjust the central bank preferences to 1.5 and save your data again.

   (e) How has varying $\beta$ affected the impulse response functions? Relate this to the effect that changing $\beta$ has on the $MR$ curve.

4. This question uses the Macroeconomic Simulator available from the Carlin and Soskice website http://www.oup.com/uk/orc/carlin_soskice to show how the economy can get stuck in a deflation trap and what it can do to escape it. Start by opening the simulator and choosing the closed economy version. Then reset all shocks by clicking the appropriate button on the left hand side of the main page. Use the simulator and the content of this chapter to work through the following:

   (a) Apply a temporary 8% negative demand shock. Save your data.

   (b) Use the impulse response functions to help explain the path of the economy following the shock.

   (c) Apply a temporary increase in public expenditure of 7% alongside the original demand shock. Save your data.

   (d) Comment on the changes to the impulse response functions. [Hint: it might be necessary to view the second case in isolation to accurately view the movements in the impulse response functions]

   (e) Has fiscal policy been effective at stabilizing the economy? If so, explain why using the 3-equation model framework.

# 4 Expectations

## 4.1 Introduction

In this chapter, we focus on how households, firms and policy makers form expectations about the future and how this is modelled by economists. In Chapters 1–3, we touched on the importance of uncertainty and expectations in the macro-economy. We introduced forward-looking theories of consumption and investment in Chapter 1, where expectations about the future influence decision making in the current period. In Chapter 2, we saw that wage setters need to form expectations about inflation when setting nominal wage increases.

In the last chapter, we introduced the dynamic macroeconomic model, which showed how a forward-looking central bank seeks to keep the economy close to its inflation target. The 3-equation model of the macro-economy emphasizes the importance of forecasting: in order to stabilize the economy the central bank must diagnose the shocks affecting the economy and forecast their effects on the output gap and inflation. In the light of these forecasts, the central bank judges how best to set the interest rate. It continuously updates its forecasts and adjusts its policy as new information is received.

We begin this chapter by highlighting the role of expectations in the core elements of the macro model we have developed by considering in turn the three elements: the *IS* curve, the Phillips curve, and the monetary rule.

*The IS curve*

In the models of consumption and investment in Chapter 1, expectations about the future influence the spending decisions of households and firms. Tobin's Q theory is a very clear example of a model of investment in which there is an institutional mechanism—the stock market—that aggregates information about the views of those outside the firm about the firm's expected future profits. When Tobin's Q is greater than one, the model predicts positive investment. The stock market is signalling 'build' not 'buy' because the expected value of the firm based on expected future profits from expanding the capital stock is greater than its replacement cost.

For the household, the permanent income hypothesis encapsulates the idea that consumption decisions today reflect all the available information about expected future income: the household prefers a smooth path of consumption so it is in its interest to aggregate the available information and—if it can—consume close to its permanent income.

The economist Nick Bloom suggests that periods of very high stock market volatility occur when economic agents are very unclear about the future. There is evidence that the effects of this type of uncertainty on fixed investment decisions can be so severe that they can actually cause the economy to go into recession (as occurred for example, after the 9/11 terrorist attacks). Another example was the extreme *policy uncertainty* in late 2012, when the USA was described as coming to the edge of a fiscal cliff. It was unclear whether the Republican-dominated Congress and the re-elected Democrat president would be able to agree on fiscal measures that would prevent tax rises and spending cuts from automatically coming into force. As a result, private agents faced serious policy uncertainty.

Bloom (2011) finds that when agents are very unclear about the future they wait and do nothing. For example, firms uncertain about future demand do not invest or hire. Similarly, consumers do not make large purchases of consumer durables if they are uncertain about their next paycheck. In times of acute uncertainty the economy therefore comes to a standstill as agents 'wait and see'. As we shall see in the next section, where we look at the concepts of risk and uncertainty, John Maynard Keynes suggested that overcoming the paralysis caused by uncertainty can come down to 'whim, sentiment, or chance'.

### The Phillips curve

In the modelling of wage- and price-setting behaviour to this point, we have used backward- rather than forward-looking expectations. Wage setters use past inflation as a guide to how they expect prices to evolve over the year ahead. As in the case of those who make spending decisions, it is highly likely that wage setters think about the future. After all they are interested in setting a particular *real* wage, which means that the future movement of the prices of goods in the consumption basket is of concern. To this point, however, we have assumed that the best that wage setters can do in their wage negotiations is to get nominal wage increases that compensate them for any erosion of the real wage that occurred due to unanticipated inflation over the previous period. They use a rule of thumb that says the best forecast for the change in the consumer price index in the year ahead is last year's inflation.[1]

We can model the behaviour of wage setters as that of rational forward-looking agents who are prevented from implementing their forecast of inflation in their wage bargain because of institutional arrangements such as wage indexation or because the costs of coming to an agreement over how inflation will evolve over the coming year are too high. Alternatively, we can model the behaviour as rule of thumb where last period's inflation outturn is the 'expected inflation' agreed on by the wage setters and built into the wage bargain. Note that the Bank of England's fan chart in Fig. 4.1 suggests that, even for one year ahead, the Bank's Monetary Policy Committee sees a very wide range of possible outcomes for inflation.

Inflation forecasts by central banks and private sector forecasters have become a common feature of developed economies and can provide insight into how individuals form inflation expectations. The macroeconomic implications of inflation forecasts are limited, however, unless we know whether agents incorporate inflation forecasts into their expectations for- mation and the extent to which agents act on their expectations.

Armantier et al. (2011) attempt to answer this question in a particular context by carrying out a financially incentivized investment experiment to see if agents' forecasts of inflation feed into their behaviour. The experimental subjects stand to win money if they use forecast

---

[1] Du Caju et al. (2008) provide detailed evidence on how price increases (past, past unforeseen and expected) are incorporated through formal indexation and informal practices in the wage bargains of 23 European countries, the US and Japan.

inflation when choosing between two kinds of financial investment. The authors find that most individuals tend to act on their expectations, but that the less financially and numerically literate respondents had most trouble doing so.

### The MR curve

The policy maker in the 3-equation model (the inflation-targeting central bank from Chapter 3) is a forward-looking agent. As we have seen, the central bank makes a forecast about inflation in the next period and, based on this, decides the interest rate to set. This is an example of rational expectations behaviour: we have assumed that the central bank knows the model of the macro-economy and that having diagnosed the nature of any shock, it chooses its best response interest rate.

However, as we have seen, forecasting inflation is by no means easy for the central bank, due to the inherent uncertainty surrounding macroeconomic developments (and their effects on inflation). This point was echoed by Charles Bean of the UK Monetary Policy Committee (MPC) in a speech in 2005:[2]

> Uncertainty is an ever-present feature of the economic landscape that monetary policy makers cannot escape. Broadly speaking, there are three types of uncertainty that confront us on the MPC: uncertainty about the data; uncertainty about the nature and persistence of shocks; and uncertainty about the structure of the economy [in other words, uncertainty about what is the correct model].

In the next section, we look more closely at the concept of uncertainty and contrast it with the concept of risk. We provide examples of how expectations are formed in real-world situations under conditions of risk and uncertainty and introduce the rational expectations hypothesis. Section 4.3 focuses on how different hypotheses about inflation expectations are reflected in the Phillips curve. Section 4.4 contrasts adaptive and rational expectations in the 3-equation model and discusses the influence of central bank communication on the formation of inflation expectations. In Section 4.5, we explain the Lucas critique and why poor economic outcomes can result if policy makers fail to anticipate how the private sector will respond to changes in policy. This discussion is extended in Section 4.6 where the concept of inflation bias is introduced.

## 4.2 Risk, uncertainty and expectations

### 4.2.1 Risk and uncertainty

Forming expectations about the future is a vital part of economic life. People form expectations about what they think will happen in the future when they decide how much to spend or to save, whether or not to stay a further year in higher education, whether to rent or buy an apartment, whether this is the right time to have a child, to retire and so on. A business pays a lot of attention to how it believes the market for its products will develop and how its competitors will respond when it decides on the price to set. When deciding whether to accept a

---

[2] This is an excerpt from Charles Bean's speech to Oxonia on 22nd of February 2005 entitled *Monetary Policy in an Uncertain World*.

job offer, we take a view about how we think wages and conditions, including prospects for getting promotion, will evolve in this job compared with those in an accessible alternative. Our ability to think about the future, combined with the fact we do not know exactly what will happen in the future, makes the study of expectations of central importance to economics.

While we can never know exactly what will happen in the future, in some cases we can make a much more informed prediction than in others. This matters when thinking about how households, firms and policy makers form expectations. It is therefore necessary to define some precise terminology before we can properly discuss expectations. The essential distinction we need to make is that between *risk* and *uncertainty*.

Risk exists when individuals make decisions about the future based on *known* probabilities. In such conditions agents can work out an expected outcome. For example, a group of ten people all put $10 into a pot and a winner is randomly selected to receive the total contents of $100. Before the random selection is made, the expected payoff to each participant is 0.1 (their probability of winning) multiplied by $100 (the prize for winning), which is equal to $10. In this example there is risk, given that each individual will receive either $0 or $100 after the random selection is made. But they know beforehand the probability with which each possible outcome (winning or not winning) will occur.

Uncertainty differs from risk in two important ways: first, uncertainty exists where it is impossible to assign probabilities to known outcomes and, second, where there are some outcomes which may be unknown.

John Maynard Keynes, one of the most influential economists of the twentieth century, believed some things were inherently uncertain and that we could not attach any meaningful probabilities to them.[3] He summed up uncertainty in this widely cited excerpt from a journal article that he wrote in 1937:[4]

> the prospect of a European war is uncertain, or the price of copper and the rate of interest twenty years hence, or the obsolescence of a new invention, or the position of private wealth owners in the social system of 1970. About these matters there is no scientific basis on which to form any calculable probabilities whatever. We simply do not know.

Whether we are considering risk or uncertainty matters greatly for the way we analyse how expectations are formed. Households facing risk can accurately attach probabilities to different future states of the world, which makes it much easier for them to evaluate in the present, decisions which affect the future. But in the case of uncertainty, this is not possible, because totally unforeseen events, such as the Arab Spring of 2010–11 or a major natural disaster, may occur.[5]

## Risk

Even in the case of risk, decision models are far from perfect and might attach inaccurate probabilities to the occurrence of a given event. A recent example is the risk management

---

[3] This view was first emphasized by Frank Knight (1921) and John M. Keynes (1921).

[4] Excerpt from page 214 of Keynes (1937).

[5] See Peter P. Wakker's article on *Uncertainty* in The New Palgrave Dictionary of Economics: 2nd Edition (2008) for a summary of the evolution of economic thinking on risk and uncertainty. It contains a discussion of a number of decision models that can be used under unknown probabilities.

models used by investment banks just prior to the global financial crisis. The models grossly underestimated the probability of a nationwide fall in house prices in the US. When house prices did fall, this triggered the worst financial crisis since the Great Depression (see Chapter 7).

Up to a point risk can be understood and compensated for. The academic discipline of economics has become more sophisticated and mathematical over time. Econometrics, particularly regression analysis, can shed light on relationships between economic variables. The results of regression analyses are frequently represented in regression tables showing the standard errors associated with the estimates of the constant term and the coefficients.

Soyer and Hogarth (2012) report the results of a survey of 257 academic economists. The survey was conducted to find out how well economists can make probabilistic inferences given different presentations of data from a linear regression analysis. The authors find that when results are presented in a regression table, economists view outcomes as more predictable than can be justified by the model due to a failure to take adequately into account the error term. Respondents place 'too much' weight on the precision of the estimated coefficients. The bias is only removed when scatter plots of the data are shown to respondents without regression tables. The example shows that when faced with known probabilities (i.e. risk), individuals are not going to be capable of making fully informed decisions unless they are able to accurately interpret probability distributions. If even professional economists are guilty of misinterpreting probability distributions, then it is likely that such misinterpretion is a regular occurrence in the macro-economy in general.

## Uncertainty

There are few aspects of the macroeconomic future that can truly be reduced to known probabilities. In some scenarios, however, meaningful reduction to probabilities seems more possible than in others; we are not operating in a world of total uncertainty. Economic fore-casters and policy makers frequently have to straddle the divide between risk and uncertainty. They cannot accurately attach probabilities to future outcomes, but can attach subjective probabilities (that is, their own opinions) to different scenarios.

This approach is exemplified by the Bank of England's behaviour in relation to its target, which is to achieve an annual rate of inflation of 2% two years in the future. Figure 4.1 is a fan chart for the annual change in the Consumer Price Index (CPI), the Bank's chosen measure of inflation. It is taken from the Bank of England Inflation Report, which is published four times a year. The fan chart shows the (subjective) probability of various outcomes for inflation in the future. The dotted vertical line on the chart marks two years from the date of publication, which is the inflation rate the Monetary Policy Committee (MPC) is mandated to target. The shaded bands refer to the likelihood of observing inflation of that level if the economic conditions at the time of publication were to prevail on 100 different occasions. The Bank of England MPC's best collective prediction is that inflation will fall within the darkest central band of the fan on 10 out of 100 occasions.

The probability mass of each identically shaded pair of bands on either side of the central band sum to 10%. In any given quarter, inflation over the forecast period is expected to lie within the fan on 90 out of 100 occasions and anywhere outside the fan on 10 out of 100 occasions. The 10% probability that inflation will fall outside the fan reflects uncertainty. In

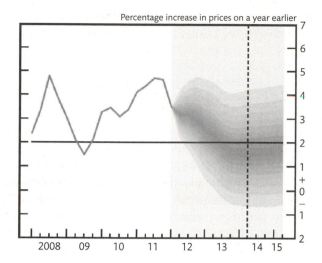

**Figure 4.1** Bank of England's CPI inflation projection based on market interest rate expectations and £325 billion asset purchases.

*Source:* Bank of England *Inflation Report*, May 2012.

other words, there is a 10% chance that something unexpected will happen—e.g. a dramatic spike in world oil prices due to a war in the Middle East—that will move inflation outside the forecast fan. The problem of grappling with risk and uncertainty is highlighted in the way the Bank of England handled the Eurozone crisis when creating its fan charts. It stated in its August 2012 Inflation Report (p.39):

> the MPC's fan charts exclude the most extreme outcomes associated with developments in the euro area, but the possibility of such outcomes crystallizing is expected to continue to weigh on asset markets and confidence, and these influences are included in the fan charts.

The global financial crisis was not foreseen by the majority of economists, central bankers or investment bankers. In this respect, it was an uncertain event; before the crisis, virtually no probability was being attached to a future state of the world which included a near collapse of the global financial system and a global recession.

The unexpected behaviour of the British economy is reflected in the poor quality of macroeconomic forecasts during this period. For example, in the 12 quarterly inflation reports between August 2007 and May 2010, the Bank of England's average forecast for inflation a year ahead was 1.9%, and outturn inflation was 3.2% per annum. This represents an average error of +1.3 percentage points. This compares with an average error of just +0.1 percentage points between August 2001 and May 2004 (which can be considered 'normal times').[6]

A second example of increasing uncertainty in the wake of the financial crisis is the activity of the the Office for Budget Responsibility (OBR), a fiscal policy council set up by the UK government. The OBR is responsible for providing independent macroeconomic and fiscal forecasts to underpin the government's annual budget. The OBR forecasts are also used to

---

[6] See Bourne (2011).

determine whether the government is on target to meet its fiscal objectives; they rely on the OBR's estimate of potential output (that is, in our notation, $y_e$). Potential output cannot be observed, even for historical periods, so is inherently uncertain and subjective. Nevertheless, an estimate of potential output is crucial to whether the government will meet its fiscal objectives. An incorrect estimate of the output gap could contribute to the pursuit of an entirely different path of government spending over the following five years. The estimate clearly has large consequences for the real macro-economy. The example highlights that important policy decisions, with significant economic consequences, are based on forecasts that are deeply uncertain in turbulent times.

Examples of the pervasiveness of uncertainty in the macro-economy do not mean that households and firms fail to benefit from forming expectations about the future. Decisions have to be made in the present and it is integral to such decision making that people invest time and effort in forming expectations. They do this as well as they can, taking into account that unanticipated events are bound to occur. The complicated nature of forming expectations in the face of uncertainty is well articulated by Keynes:[7]

> We are merely reminding ourselves that human decisions affecting the future, whether personal or political or economic, cannot depend on strict mathematical expectation, since the basis for making such calculations does not exist; and that it is our innate urge to activity which makes the wheels go round, our rational selves choosing between the alternatives as best we are able, calculating where we can, but often falling back for our motive on whim or sentiment or chance.

### 4.2.2 Expectations formation in real-world situations

This section looks at some examples of how agents form expectations in real-world situations. The examples highlight that expectations are a key input into economic decision making in a wide range of contexts, and that in the real world, even the same agents may not form expectations in the same way when making decisions in different situations.

For instance, students use textbooks. Some will buy them new, some will buy them second-hand and some will not buy them at all, preferring to use a copy from the library. We might not always think of expectations playing a major role in the decision to purchase something as commonplace as a textbook, but the evidence suggests that they do. Chevalier and Goolsbee (2009) investigated the textbook market in the US for the ten semesters between 1997 and 2001. They find that students are less willing to pay for (or buy at all) books which have a short projected life. The reason for this is that when a new edition is released, older editions cannot be resold to the campus bookstore or online. The study suggests that publishers cannot consistently raise revenue by shortening revision cycles and that the market for textbooks in the US is characterized by forward-looking, rational behaviour.

Chevalier and Goolsbee's research illustrates one situation in which students' behaviour was shown to be consistent with what is called rational expectations behaviour: they were using all the information available about the costs and benefits of different courses of action to make a reasoned decision about whether to purchase a textbook, including a model of

7 See Chapter 12: *The State of Long-Term Expectation* in Keynes (1936).

publishers' behaviour. But in other contexts students have been shown to form expectations in a biased manner. Foster and Frijters (2012) analyse how students form expectations concerning their own final course grade. The authors examined a large cross section of students at two Australian universities, collecting data on students' expectations at mid-semester of their final grade and their actual final grade. The results show that students typically overestimate their final grade, even though it should be fairly predictable based on the information available to them, such as past performance, ability and effort levels. The authors find statistical evidence that this bias arises from the direct utility students gain from holding high expectations. The high self-esteem is associated with higher expectations.

In financial markets, profits and ultimately livelihoods can depend on having accurate expectations. The trader who accurately picks the stock which outperforms the general index is likely to reap a financial reward from that decision. But how do money managers form expectations? Psychoanalyst David Tuckett does not believe that the behaviour of money managers can be described as rational since they operate in a world of 'radical uncertainty' and ambiguous information. He conducted a detailed survey of money managers and found that they are able to commit to making decisions under conditions of radical uncertainty by creating narratives, or trading stories, about the fundamental facts thought likely to influence the price of financial assets.[8] In this world, it is not that agents do not expend effort and take into account all available information when forming expectations. Rather, because future asset prices are extremely unpredictable in the buying and selling of stocks, they do not behave completely rationally.

### 4.2.3 The rational expectations hypothesis (REH)

The previous section showed that in some circumstances, agents make decisions in a rational forward-looking manner (e.g. the US textbook market). In order to formalize this approach to forming expectations, we set out the *rational expectations hypothesis (REH)*:

> The rational expectations hypothesis refers to a choice by the economist about how to model behaviour. A rational expectations model is one where the *agents in the model* use the model and all available information to forecast and therefore do not make systematic errors. The term model-consistent expectations can be used instead of rational expectations.

How does this compare to the approach taken in the 3-equation model in Chapter 3? Up to this point, we have assumed that wage setters form inflation expectations in a backward-looking manner (i.e. adaptively). In a period of rising inflation, agents using adaptive expectations make systematic errors, because inflation turns out every period to be higher than had been expected.

This is illustrated graphically in a situation of ever-increasing inflation when output is above equilibrium (see Table 2.1 and Fig. 2.15a in Chapter 2). As inflation increased from 2% to 4% to 6%, wage setters were repeatedly wrong in their anticipation of a higher real wage (on the *WS* curve) when the output gap was positive. By maintaining the assumption that expectations were formed adaptively, we did not allow agents to learn from their mistakes

---

[8] See Tuckett (2012).

and *change the rule* they used. Their expectations formation behaviour is therefore not model consistent.

No one can know the correct model of the real world so no one can be fully rational in the way that agents in a model can be. We use models to help us understand the world. In the world, forming expectations rationally as agents can do in a model is not possible. Apart from the presence of uncertainty, and the fact that unlike agents in a model, those in the world do not know the model, forecasting involves time and cognitive effort. These considerations mean that the usefulness of a rational expectations-based model for understanding particular situations depends on the setting.

In our example of students and the textbook market, the evidence suggests that students were able to figure out the model that was being used for the frequency with which new editions were being introduced, and they responded by only buying in the cases where a longer edition cycle was in place. In this case, the behaviour of the students fitted the prediction of a model with agents forming rational expectations. In the case of students forecasting their grades, however, their ability to make rational judgements was impaired because of the utility they (irrationally) derived from forming over-optimistic expectations.

In the world, we can observe that some agents devote considerable resources to forecasting. For example, central banks build, test and refine their models of the economy. Their models and forecasts are subject to extensive external scrutiny and it is unlikely that the central bank would make systematic mistakes without being forced to reconsider its methods. But making systematic mistakes is quite different from being repeatedly wrong in its forecasts.

The earlier quote from Charles Bean of the Bank of England highlights the difficulties that the central bank faces in spite of all of the resources it has available to understand the nature of the shocks and the structure of the economy. Households face larger obstacles. Economics students spend years trying the understand the 'predictions of the relevant economic theory'. Rules of thumb (such as adaptive expectations) may provide a better description than rational expectations of the behaviour of a range of private sector agents.

As we shall see, models with rational expectations provide powerful insights about the dangers of neglecting how individuals and households respond to changes in the economic or policy environment. No rule of thumb is of much use if the environment changes in such a way as to render it obsolete from the point of view of the agent.

## 4.3 Phillips curves, expectations and inflation

This section investigates in more detail how economists have modelled the way agents in the macro-economy form inflation expectations. In the 3-equation model of Chapter 3, we used a specific assumption about inflation expectations, which produced the Phillips curve that we used in that model. As we shall see, the Phillips curve will take different forms depending on the way inflation expectations are modelled.

### Notation and timing

We start by setting out the notation that will be used throughout the remainder of this chapter. We are primarily concerned with how agents at the beginning of period *t* form expectations of the current period's inflation. The current period is denoted by a $t$ subscript. These expectations will be formed on the basis of the information available at the beginning of period $t$—we say expected inflation in period $t$, conditional on the information set (denoted by $\Omega$) dated $t-1$, is therefore:

$$E_t(\pi_t \mid \Omega_{t-1}) \equiv \pi_t^E.$$

We use $\pi_t^E$ to denote expected inflation in period $t$ (conditional on the information set in period $t-1$) throughout the rest of the chapter as it makes the notation simpler. The information set in period $t$ includes the outturn of all the macroeconomic variables up to and including period $t-1$. This means that, in period $t$, agents know the actual rate of inflation for every period up to and including period $t-1$ (i.e. the last period). As we shall see, when agents have rational expectations, then apart from a random shock that occurs in period $t$ itself, they also know inflation in period $t$ because they can work out the implications for inflation of the shocks that have occurred up to and including period $t-1$. The only thing that could make inflation in period $t$ different from what they calculate is an unpredictable shock to inflation within period $t$ itself.

### Phillips curves

The term Phillips curve is used for the relationship between inflation and output arising from the supply side of the economy. There is no single form for the Phillips curve, but rather, it depends on the way we model inflation expectations. To allow us to discuss different hypotheses about expectations, we write the Phillips curve like this:

$$\pi_t = \pi_t^E + \alpha(y_t - y_e). \qquad \text{(standard Phillips curve)}$$

We shall call this a standard Phillips curve.

In this section, we set out two ways in which inflation expectations are modelled.

1. *Adaptive* expectations—agents expect inflation to be what it was in the previous period. This is a simple form of what is called error correction behaviour. Agents set aside their forecast of inflation last period and take last period's outturn as their best guess of inflation this period. This is the model we use most of the time in this book.

2. *Rational* expectations—agents in the model use the model to form their forecasts. This implies expectations are forward looking, all available information is used and systematic errors are avoided.

The rest of the section is divided into two parts. First, we look at inflation in the UK since the end of the Second World War and relate this to the modelling framework. Second, we set out the adaptive and rational expectations Phillips curves and discuss their implications for the trade-off between output and inflation.[9]

---

[9] We do not discuss the New Keynesian Phillips curve in this chapter. It is based on the assumption that firms are fully forward-looking with rational expectations but are constrained from flexibly adjusting their prices. This case is examined in Chapter 16.

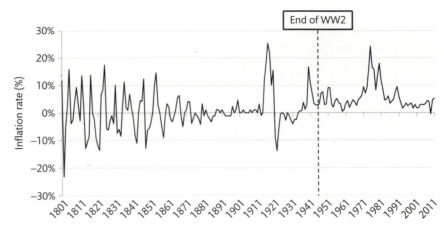

**Figure 4.2** UK inflation: 1801–2011.

*Source:* UK Office for National Statistics (accessed June 2012).

*Note:* Variable shown is the annual percentage change of the long term indicator of prices of consumer goods and services.

## Inflation in the post-war period

We can see from Fig. 4.2, that inflation in the UK fluctuated around zero between 1801 and the end of World War II (WWII). In the 1950s and 1960s, however, inflation was positive in almost every year but there was no trend. This was followed by a period of high inflation from the end of the 1960s through to the early 1980s. Disinflation followed.

One interpretation of the period of stable but positive inflation in the 1950s and 1960s is that governments were pursuing activist demand management policies and were happy to achieve low rates of unemployment even if there was some positive inflation. This can be understood against the background of the Great Depression in the 1930s and the awareness of policy makers of the dangers of deflation. At the time, policy makers feared unemployment and deflation more than inflation. Their policies reflected this, yielding consistently positive, although fairly stable, inflation.

However, toward the end of the 1960s, inflation began to rise year after year. One part of the explanation is that important developments on the supply side of the economy in the late 1960s and the 1970s led to a rise in equilibrium unemployment, which meant that conventional measures of 'high employment' implied more inflationary pressure. In this period there was a shift in bargaining power toward workers reflected in a wave of strikes across Europe referred to as the 'hot autumn' of 1968 (an upward shift in the *WS* curve) and a fall in the rate of productivity growth (which implies a downward shift in the *PS* curve, assuming wage-setting behaviour does not adjust quickly to the slower productivity growth).[10] As well as this, there was a series of commodity price shocks (which imply downward shifts

[10] Productivity growth slowed for two reasons. First because the gains from the widespread adoption of so-called Fordist mass production methods in the catching up countries of Western Europe and Japan were becoming exhausted. And second, the limits to further productivity gains based on Fordism were being reached even in the technology leader, the USA.

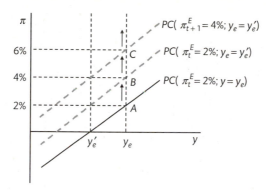

**Figure 4.3** The government attempts to maintain low unemployment after a negative supply-side shock.

in *PS* curve) preceding the first oil shock of 1973. The oil shocks are discussed in detail in Chapter 11.

We can interpret the new inflationary behaviour using the model of Chapter 2. As an example, we take an economy initially at point *A* in Fig. 4.3 with inflation stable at 2% and output at equilibrium, $y_e$. The supply–side shocks reduce equilibrium output to $y_e'$. If the government continues to pursue an unchanged level of output, inflation will rise continuously.

Inflation expectations are updated to correct for the erosion of the expected real wage.[11] Under this hypothesis, wage setters update their expectations based on the outturn of inflation. Workers do this to safeguard their real wages, which are otherwise eroded in every period where inflation is above its expected level. The *PC* therefore shifts upwards as a result of agents updating their expectations (Fig. 4.3).

As long as the government keeps $y > y_e'$, inflation expectations will adjust upwards as wage setters see the expected real wage eroded. With $y = y_e$, the shifted *PC* results in inflation of 4%. The only outcome of the government continuing to pursue an output target above equilibrium will be ever-increasing inflation, as shown by the movement from *B* to *C* (and onwards) in Fig. 4.3. A government policy of this kind is referred to as an accommodating policy, effectively, there is a vertical *MR* curve through points *A*, *B* and *C*. It contrasts sharply with the behaviour of an inflation–targeting central bank as set out in the 3–equation model.

## Expectations and the output–inflation trade-off

In the adaptive expectations framework, workers respond to their forecasting errors—i.e. they update their expectations based on the outturn for inflation last period. We modify the standard Phillips curve to get the adaptive expectations Phillips curve as follows:

$$\pi_t = \pi_t^E + \alpha(y_t - y_e)$$
$$= \pi_{t-1} + \alpha(y_t - y_e), \qquad \text{(adaptive expectations Phillips curve)}$$

where $\pi_t^E = \pi_{t-1}$.

---

[11] The pioneering work on adaptive expectations was carried out by Nobel Prize winners Edmund Phelps and Milton Friedman in the late 1960s and early 1970s. See, for example, Phelps (1967) and Friedman (1968).

The equation can be rearranged to show how inflation changes over time:

$$\pi_t - \pi_{t-1} = \Delta\pi_t = \alpha(y_t - y_e). \tag{4.1}$$

Equation 4.1 shows that inflation will continue to increase as long as output remains above equilibrium, which matches the outcome shown in Fig. 4.3.

The model predicts there is no long-run trade-off between inflation and unemployment. The presence of a trade-off would mean that policy makers could choose to operate the economy at a level of output above equilibrium if they were willing to accept a higher level of inflation. In other words, they could choose their preferred point on a single Phillips curve. In the model, this is not possible, because there is always pressure on inflation to rise (and the *PC* to shift upwards) if output is above equilibrium.

Using this model, we could say that the low and stable inflation of the 1950s and 1960s shown in Fig. 4.2 only held as long as the government did not systematically try to run the economy at a level of activity higher than the equilibrium. The supply shocks of the late 1960s and the 1970s led to governments running the economy with levels of aggregate demand that produced levels of output above equilibrium.

Nobel prize winner Milton Friedman described the prevailing postwar policy stance in his famous 1968 Presidential Address:[12]

> Today, primacy is assigned to the promotion of full employment, with the prevention of inflation a continuing but definitely secondary objective.

He then neatly sums up the inflationary consequences of pursuing this policy and acknowledges that there is no long-run trade-off between unemployment and inflation:[13]

> In order to keep unemployment at its target level of three per cent [which in this hypothetical example is below the 'natural' rate], the monetary authority would have to raise monetary growth still more.... the 'market' rate [of unemployment] can be kept below the 'natural' rate only by inflation...
> To state this conclusion differently, there is always a temporary trade-off between inflation and unemployment; there is no permanent trade-off.

Figure 4.4a uses US data to illustrate the reasonably stable relationship between inflation and output in the 1950s and 1960s. The relationship completely fell apart during the following 15 years (see Fig. 4.4b).

In many developed economies, the 1970s were characterized by 'stagflation'—a combination of high unemployment and high inflation—which destroyed any notion of a long-run trade-off between inflation and output. The experiences of this decade marked the end of a period where macroeconomic policy had been guided by the principles of Keynesian demand management which accorded priority to avoiding deflation. In macroeconomics, it ushered in the era where models were built based on agents using rational expectations to form their forecasts and guide their actions.

---

[12] These excerpts are from Friedman (1968).

[13] Friedman uses slightly different terminology than we have so far in this chapter. The 'natural rate' of unemployment is equivalent to the equilibrium rate of unemployment. The 'market' rate is equivalent to the actual unemployment rate.

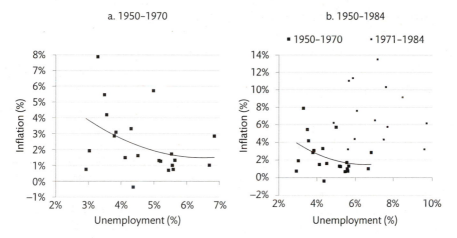

**Figure 4.4** US empirical Phillips curves:
a. 1950–1970
b. 1950–1970 and 1971–1984.

*Source:* US Bureau of Labor Statistics (accessed June 2012).

*Note:* The black curves on the graphs are quadratic regression lines.

The adaptive expectations hypothesis states that wage setters respond to their forecasting errors but they do this in a purely mechanical way. This involves them making *systematic errors* because as long as $y > y_e$, the real wage outcome is below what had been expected since the inflation outturn is higher than expected (see Fig. 4.3). This suggests we investigate the implications of wage setters not just updating their *expectations* but changing their *forecasting rule*. This is the basis of the next expectations hypothesis, rational expectations.

In the rational expectations framework, it is only unanticipated shocks to inflation and the output gap that result in inflation being different from its expected value. If we apply the rational expectations hypothesis (REH) to the standard Phillips curve it becomes:

$$\pi_t = \pi_t^E + \alpha(y_t - y_e) + \epsilon_t, \tag{4.2}$$

where

$$\pi_t^E = \pi_t$$
$$\rightarrow y_t = y_e - \frac{\epsilon_t}{\alpha} \qquad \text{(rational expectations Phillips curve)}$$

and $\epsilon_t$ is a random shock term. In this model of behaviour, expectations are correct apart from the random shock term. It is crucial that the error process is of a particular kind, namely 'mean zero white noise' in order to rule out systematic errors. A mean zero white noise shock is sometimes positive and sometimes negative, but on average it is zero. We can see that applying rational expectations to the standard Phillips curve produces the result that there is no longer a trade-off at all between inflation and the output gap.

## 4.4 Expectations and the 3-equation model

In this section, we look at how inflation expectations influence the 3-equation model. We contrast the 3-equation model with backward-looking inflation expectations introduced in the last chapter with the 3-equation model with rational inflation expectations. This allows us to show how the key predictions of the 3-equation model are altered by the use of rational inflation expectations. We end the section with a discussion of how modern central banks use their communication strategies to try to anchor inflation expectations close to the inflation target.

### 4.4.1  A graphical example

To see the implications of rational expectations in the 3-equation model, we take a simple example in which the central bank adopts a new lower inflation target, $\pi^T$. In Fig. 4.5a (i.e. the left-hand panel of Fig. 4.5), the economy is initially at point $A$, with output at equilibrium, but inflation above the new target. To minimize their loss function the central bank would like to reduce inflation to $\pi^T$, moving the economy from $A$ to $Z$. This implies a new $MR$ curve, labelled $MR'$. We assume they announce this policy change at the start of period $t + 1$. Under rational expectations, and assuming the announcement is credible, the economy will jump immediately (i.e. within period $t + 1$) from $A$ to $Z$. We can see this using the rational expectations $PC$ in Equation 4.2. The disinflation is *costless*, in the sense that it has not involved any rise in unemployment.

As we have seen in Chapter 3, if expectations are formed adaptively, then the disinflation would not be costless. In this case, the policy announcement would be coupled with action by the central bank to tighten monetary policy by raising the interest rate so as to move the economy to point $B$ in Fig. 4.5b. It would then take a further $x - 1$ periods of active adjustment of the interest rate before the economy reached point $Z$ and the Phillips curve had shifted to the new equilibrium at $PC(\pi_{t+x}^E = \pi^T)$. This process would result in unemployment being above equilibrium for some time—i.e. it would be costly.

### 4.4.2  Comparison of adaptive and rational inflation expectations

To help make the difference between the adaptive and rational expectations assumptions clear, it is useful to apply rational expectations to the 3-equation model and compare the results with the familiar behaviour of the model with adaptive expectations. In the 3-equation model set out in Chapter 3, we assumed wage setters set the nominal wage increase according to the $WS$ curve and price setters followed immediately by marking up their prices. To summarize:

$$(\Delta W/W)_t = \pi_t^E + \alpha(y_t - y_e),$$

where

$$\pi_t^E = \pi_{t-1}, \tag{4.3}$$
$$\pi_t = (\Delta W/W)_t , \tag{4.4}$$
$$= \pi_{t-1} + \alpha(y_t - y_e). \qquad \text{(PC in adaptive expectations 3-equation model)}$$

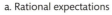

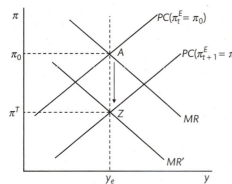
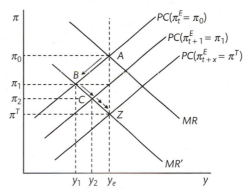

**Figure 4.5** The effect on output and inflation of the central bank reducing the inflation target from $\pi_0$ to $\pi^T$.
a. Rational expectations.
b. Adaptive expectations.

If instead of the adaptive expectations assumption, $(\pi_t^E = \pi_{t-1})$, wage and price setters use rational expectations, then for expectations of inflation to be fulfilled, i.e.

$$\pi_t = \pi_t^E,$$

output must be at equilibrium, i.e. $(y_t = y_e)$. The implication when $y_t \neq y_e$ is that there is no value of inflation that satisfies the equation for fulfilled expectations, $\pi_t = \pi_t^E$; hence inflation will be infinite.

$$\pi_t = \pi_t^E + \alpha(y_t - y_e) + \epsilon_t$$
$$\implies \pi_t^E < \infty \text{ if and only if } y_t = y_e \text{ and } \pi_t^E = \infty \text{ if and only if } y_t \neq y_e.$$

To see why inflation must be infinite when $y_t \neq y_e$, we take the case where output is slightly above equilibrium output, so that the term $\alpha(y_t - y_e) = \varepsilon$, a small positive number. Under the rational expectations hypothesis, both sides of the Phillips curve have to be equal in expectation, hence $\pi_t = \pi_t^E + \varepsilon$. The only value of inflation that satisfies this equation and where inflation expectations are fulfilled (i.e. $\pi_t = \pi_t^E$) is when $\pi_t = \pi_t^E = \infty$.

By assuming rational expectations behaviour of wage and price setters in the 3-equation model, it is clear that the central bank must set the real interest rate at the start of period $t$ to deliver $y_t = y_e$ in expectation. Otherwise inflation is expected to be infinite. This in turn implies that the *IS* curve must take the form:

$$y_t = A - ar_t, \qquad \text{(IS curve in the REH 3-equation model; no lag)}$$

where there is no lag between interest rate setting and output. Households and firms are assumed to know the model and to behave as such: this eliminates the lags in the *IS* equation because they know that output must be at equilibrium for inflation to be other than infinite.

The next step is to pin down the level of inflation expected by wage and price setters. The core idea is that rational expectations behaviour on the part of wage and price setters means that they understand how the model works. Hence, they know that the central bank chooses $y_t$ where the *MR* curve intersects the Phillips curve, $PC\left(\pi_t^E\right)$. They choose their inflation expectations, $\pi_t^E$ at the start of period $t$ so those expectations are consistent with the outcome for inflation, $\pi_t$. They do not make systematic mistakes. Random shocks will occur and mean that the outturn for inflation can differ from what was expected, but the key is that these deviations of outturns from expectations are unsystematic. To save notation, we do not show the error term $\epsilon_t$ in the Phillips curve equation.

Wage and price setters know that $\pi_t$ is generated by the following two equations, $PC\left(\pi_t^E\right)$ and *MR*:

$$\pi_t = \pi_t^E + \alpha(y_t - y_e) \qquad\qquad \text{(PC in REH 3-equation model)}$$
$$y_t - y_e = -\alpha\beta(\pi_t - \pi^T), \qquad\qquad \text{(MR in REH 3-equation model)}$$

where $\pi^T$ is the inflation target of the central bank. In a diagram, this implies that the Phillips curve goes through the *MR* at $\pi = \pi^T$. In terms of equations, the wage and price setters know that

$$\pi_t = \pi_t^E - \alpha^2\beta(\pi_t - \pi^T)$$

and that for their inflation expectations to be fulfilled, i.e. $\pi_t = \pi_t^E$, they have to choose

$$\pi_t^E = \pi^T.$$

The rational agents in the economy know that the central bank is targeting inflation of $\pi^T$, so this is the level of inflation that they expect. The central bank knows that this is how inflation expectations are formed and hence that the relevant Phillips curve it faces is

$$\pi_t = \pi^T + \alpha(y_t - y_e).$$

Putting this together with the *MR*, the central bank knows that the output gap it wishes to set is

$$y_t = y_e.$$

Graphically, as noted above, this is the intersection of the $PC(\pi_t^E = \pi^T)$ and the *MR*.

Given all of this information and the fact that if there is a random shock in period $t$ that none of the actors can know about when they make their decisions at the beginning of period $t$, the central bank simply uses the *IS* curve (with no lags) to set (or maintain) the interest rate, $r_t$, as follows:

$$y_t = A - ar_t = y_e.$$

The central bank sets the interest rate at its stabilizing rate.

The assumption of rational expectations on the part of all of the actors in the model (and the associated assumption of no lags in the *IS* curve) produces important changes in the 3-equation model:

1. The economy is—apart from random shocks—at equilibrium output with inflation at target. The dynamic behaviour of the economy in response to different kinds of shocks analysed in Chapter 3 disappears. Inflation does not get 'built into the system' and, therefore,

there is no costly process of disinflation to return the economy to target inflation and equilibrium output.

2. The job of the central bank is much simpler. It does not have to take account of the lags in the response of aggregate demand to its interest rate decisions (in the *IS* equation) to work out its interest rate response. In contrast to the 3-equation model with adaptive expectations, there is no role for a stabilizing central bank that guides the economy along the *MR* curve to equilibrium.

3. Since wage and price setters are forward looking, the central bank can influence expectations directly. By contrast, with adaptive expectations, actual inflation has to fall before it influences expected inflation.

### 4.4.3 Central bank communication and anchoring inflation expectations

The modern, inflation-targeting central bank spends a large amount of time and effort on communication. It is hard to explain this if the world is well-explained by the rational expectations model of the previous section. Central banks do not limit their communication to informing the public and the financial markets of their interest rate decisions. They will typically also provide: macroeconomic commentary and forecasts, a monthly or quarterly inflation/monetary policy report, which sets out the detailed reasoning behind interest rate decisions, minutes from committee meetings, transcripts of speeches by prominent members of the central bank, a statistics hub containing data on historic interest rates and exchange rates and the financial sector, in-house economic research on monetary economics and financial markets; and games (e.g. ECB) and competitions (e.g. Bank of England) involving monetary policy.

The aim is to keep inflation expectations anchored at the inflation target. If the central bank's commitment to the inflation target is perfectly credible and inflation expectations are firmly anchored, then an inflation shock would just be a one-period shock to inflation—i.e. there would be no need for a painful increase in unemployment to bring inflation back to target. In this case, in the period following the shock, the Phillips curve would revert to the one indexed by $\pi^T$ and as a result, the central bank has to do nothing.

We can capture this idea in a simple way by modifying the adaptive expectations Phillips curve to model expected inflation as a weighted average of the inflation target and lagged inflation, where the weight on the inflation target is called $\chi$ (chi, for credibility):

$$\pi_t = \left[\chi\pi^T + (1-\chi)\pi_{t-1}\right] + \alpha(y_t - y_e) \tag{4.5}$$

where

$$\pi_t^E = \chi\pi^T + (1-\chi)\pi_{t-1}. \qquad \text{(partially anchored expectations)}$$

For a fully credible central bank, $\chi = 1$ and the Phillips curve is anchored to $\pi^T$. For $\chi = 0$, inflation expectations are entirely backward looking. In Fig. 3.9 in Chapter 3, we set out the case when $\chi = 0$, as inflation inertia is a key assumption of the standard 3-equation model. We can use the same kind of diagram to set out two other cases (see Fig. 4.6), firstly where expectations are firmly anchored to the inflation target (i.e. $\chi = 1$) and secondly where expectations are only partially backward looking (i.e. $\chi = 0.5$).

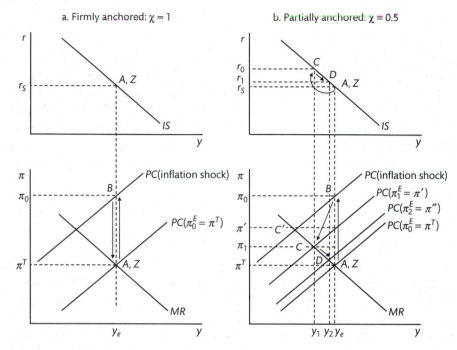

**Figure 4.6** Varying the level of central bank credibility, using the example of an inflation shock:
a. Firmly anchored: $\chi = 1$
b. Partially anchored: $\chi = 0.5$.

Figure 3.9 in Chapter 3 and Fig. 4.6 show the three benchmark cases following an inflation shock and allow us to compare the adjustment of the economy back to medium-run equilibrium:

### $\chi = 0$ : fully backward-looking

After the inflation shock, the central bank must raise interest rates to squeeze inflation out of the system. It requires a number of periods where output is below equilibrium (and unemployment is above equilibrium) to get the economy back to the initial equilibrium (i.e. the central bank's bliss point). This case is shown in Fig. 3.9 in Chapter 3.

### $\chi = 1$ : firmly anchored at $\pi^T$

After the inflation shock, there is just one period of high inflation. In the second period, the Phillips curve reverts to its original position (i.e. $PC(\pi_0^E = \pi^T)$), as inflation expectations are firmly anchored to the target. This means that the central bank does not have to change interest rates and hence output does not deviate from equilibrium—the disinflation is costless.

### $\chi = 0.5$ : partially anchored at $\pi^T$

After the inflation shock, the central bank has to raise interest rates, but to a lesser extent than when expectations are fully backward looking. The fall in output is lower, and adjustment back to the initial equilibrium is quicker than when $\chi = 0$. If $\chi = 0.5$, then in the period following the shock, the Phillips curve moves down to intersect the $y_e$ line at a level of inflation which is an average of inflation last period (i.e. $\pi_0$) and target inflation (i.e. $\pi^T$). In Fig. 4.6b this is shown as the inflation level $\pi'$, and on this new Phillips curve the central bank chooses a level of inflation $\pi_1$ at point C. In contrast, point $C'$ in the lower panel of Fig. 4.6b marks the inflation–output combination associated with $\chi = 0$.

This modification of the 3-equation model highlights the role played by ability of the central bank to affect inflation expectations, which is referred to as its credibility in inflation targeting. More firmly anchored inflation expectations will reduce the negative impact of stabilization policy on the economy by restoring output and inflation to target more rapidly. The more credibility a central bank has, the lower the costs associated with disinflationary policies, thus central banks place a lot of emphasis on transparency and communication.

Two interrelated elements of credibility are important:

1. Will the central bank stick to its policy objective?
2. Can the central bank help shape expectations of inflation?

The communications strategies of central banks appear to address both. In relation to the first, they emphasize the independence of monetary policy decisions from political pressure and seek to explain that the bank's work will not be affected, for example, by the pressures on the government from an upcoming election. In terms of the second element, the central bank knows that if by helping the public to believe in the inflation target, it can keep the Phillips curves close to the inflation target, it will incur lower losses.

Independence is not the only driver of central bank credibility, transparency also plays a role. A transparent central bank is one that lets the public and financial markets into their decision-making process. The more the central bank communicates what they are doing and why, and their view of the future path of the economy and interest rates, the more easily the general public and the private sector can form inflation expectations. These concerns are illustrated by the Monetary Policy Framework of the Bank of Canada:

> The inflation-control target has helped to make the Bank's monetary policy actions more readily understandable to financial markets and the public. The target also provides a clear measure of the effectiveness of monetary policy. One of the most important benefits of a clear inflation target is its role in anchoring expectations of future inflation. This, in turn, leads to the kind of economic decision making—by individuals, businesses, and governments—that brings about non-inflationary growth in the economy.

The understanding of how monetary policy should be operated evolved rapidly in the wake of the failure of attempts to use money supply targets to bring inflation down in the late 1970s and early 1980s. By the end of the 1990s, central banks across the developed world had realized the importance of independence, transparency and credibility for successfully maintaining low and stable inflation. Figure 4.7 shows the relative levels of transparency and independence of global central banks in the 2000s.

*Evidence*

The academic literature on central bank communication has two distinct strands. The first strand uses constructed indices of transparency to test the empirical relationships between transparency and macroeconomic variables, such as inflation and output. The second strand

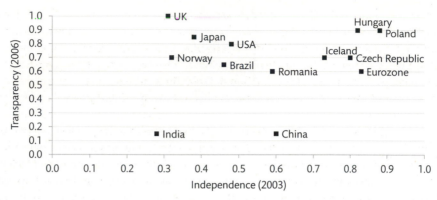

**Figure 4.7** Central bank independence (in 2003) and transparency (in 2006).

*Source:* Crowe and Meade (2008).

focuses more explicitly on communication, trying to assess whether communication leads to better predictions of central bank behaviour and therefore has a desirable effect on economic stability.

Demertzis and Hughes Hallett (2007) and Dincer and Eichengreen (2009) are two papers from the first strand. They both find that central bank transparency reduces inflation variability, but has no statistically significant effect on the level of inflation.

Sturm and De Haan (2011) is a paper in the second strand, which identifies five indicators of European Central Bank communication that are based on the ECB President's introductory statement at the press conference following the ECB policy meetings. The authors find that although the indicators are often quite different from one another, they add information that helps predict the next policy decision of the ECB. This finding is backed up by Blinder et al. (2008), which provides a review of the available literature on central bank communication. The paper comes to the conclusion that more and better central bank communication improves the predictability of monetary policy decisions.

## 4.5 The Lucas critique

Macroeconomic policy throughout the post-war period has been heavily influenced by innovations in academic macroeconomics. Equally, macroeconomic theory and modelling has evolved partly in response to developments in the real economy. For example, the Keynesian doctrine was strongly shaped by the policy mistakes of the Great Depression and came to dominate policy making in the three decades after WWII.

In a similar fashion, the stagflation of the 1970s coincided with the development of *New Classical Macroeconomics*. This school of economics has not only been very influential in policy-making circles since the 1980s, but has also fundamentally changed the course of macroeconomic modelling. The underlying principle of New Classical Economics is that macroeconomic models should be based on rigorous microeconomic foundations, and in particular, on forward-looking optimizing agents with model-consistent expectations. The real business cycle model was developed in this tradition. It is set out in Chapter 16.

Such models were thought necessary to address the so-called *Lucas critique*, which highlighted the dangers of forecasting by using models that rely on the relationships found in historical data. Such forecasting methods will be unreliable if those relationships are conditional on the policy regime that was in place during the historical period being analysed. If the policy regime is different in the future, then the relationships found in historical data could well break down. Why? Because economic agents will change their behaviour in response to the new policy regime.[14]

The Lucas critique was directed at the use of the large econometric models that had been developed for forecasting. Such models dominated governments and central banks from the 1950s to the mid-1970s. A well-known example was the MPS model designed by Modigliani and his collaborators in the late 1960s. This model was used for quantitative forecasting and macroeconomic analysis by the Federal Reserve Board.[15] Lucas was very sceptical that these models, which were based on relationships from historical data, could provide any meaningful forecasts. He made a powerful critique of the policy mistakes that can be arise if wage and price setters use rational expectations, and policy makers interpret data as though they are not using rational expectations.

To explain this, we use the 3-equation model with rational expectations. To begin, we take an example where the government uses fiscal policy (tax or spending giveaways) to get a pre-election boost in its popularity. It may be tempted to allow a small increase in inflation before the election in order to let output and employment increase.

Suppose the government sneaks in such a spending increase after the central bank has set the interest rate for the period. Hence from the central bank's point of view there has been an unexpected permanent increase in aggregate demand, engineered by fiscal policy so that $y_t > y_e$. However, the central bank cannot do anything about it until next period.

What now happens to inflation during the current period? Assume that wage and price setters set prices with the same information as the central bank, that is before the government had increased expenditure. Since wage and price setters have rational expectations, they continue to assume that $\pi_t^E = \pi^T$ and they believe that $y_t = y_e$, so inflation remains at target. The next period the central bank reacts to the higher level of government spending and sets $r$ so $y_{t+1} = A - ar_{t+1} = y_e$. Inflation is therefore at $\pi^T$ in the next period and output falls back to equilibrium.

Hence if wage and price setters have rational expectations, the best that the government can do is to get a one-period gain in output. Nevertheless *in the data*, one would observe a one period rise in output without a rise in inflation above target.

The next step is to introduce a government that is suspicious of independent central banks. It believes, for example, that central banks are 'conservative' and are simply concerned to keep output and employment low. The central bank defends its behaviour and, using the Phillips curve with rational expectations, explains that increased government expenditure raises inflation if output is above equilibrium; and if wage and price setters have rational expectations and output is maintained above equilibrium, there will be great increases in inflation.

---

[14] See Lucas (1976). For a definition of the *Lucas critique* see Lars Ljungqvist's definition in The New Palgrave Dictionary of Economics: 2nd Edition (2008).

[15] See Brayton et al. (1997).

In spite of the advice of the central bank, the evidence the new government uses is that the old government increased government expenditure and output increased, without any change in inflation. Hence the new government thinks the central bank is simply conservative. It therefore takes away the independence of the central bank and says that the central bank must not raise interest rates when it increases government expenditure. The new government then increases government expenditure. Since the central bank is forbidden from reacting by raising interest rates, inflation will jump upward in the period after the shock and will remain elevated thereafter if the government continues to pursue the policy. If wage setters have rational expectations, they can only be 'fooled' by the government for one period, after which they will build the higher level output into their wage requests. Hence, if the higher output is not offset by the central bank in the period after the surprise shock, then the boost in government spending will result in higher inflation. As we saw above, with rational expectations, inflation would be expected to be infinite.

This example illustrates how the use of historical data showing the association of a fiscal expansion, higher output and no increase in inflation to forecast the outcome of a fiscal policy intervention can produce a poor economic outcome. In this example, the correct model of behaviour is one with rational expectations of wage and price setters: this can account both for the data observed from the pre-election episode and for the failure of the new government's policy of abolishing central bank independence and pursuing fiscal expansion.

Note also however, that a poor economic outcome can also result if a policy maker assumes that wage setters have rational expectations when they do not. Assuming the REH, a policy maker would expect that the announcement of a lower inflation target would produce a costless shift to lower inflation at equilibrium output. As Fig. 4.5 illustrated, if behaviour is better captured by adaptive expectations, then the anticipated costless disinflation would not take place. An inflation-targeting central bank would have to raise the interest rate and depress output below equilibrium in order to bring inflation down to the new target.

## 4.6 Expectations hypotheses, inflation bias and time inconsistency

In this section, we return to the 3-equation model where the policy maker engages in inflation targeting. The focus is on the problems that can arise when the *government* is able to exert control over monetary policy. What happens if the government has an inflation target but also an output target, which is a lower unemployment rate than is consistent with a zero output gap? The result of this policy stance is that the economy ends up at equilibrium output but with a higher rate of inflation. This outcome is called 'inflation bias'. Since inflation is above target and output is at equilibrium, the outcome is unambiguously worse than the case where the monetary authority targets a zero output gap. Inflation bias highlights the danger of government control of monetary policy and provides a justification for tying the government's hands through the delegation of monetary policy to an independent central bank.

The speed with which inflation reaches its higher equilibrium level after the new output target is announced depends on whether inflation expectations are adaptive or rational. We use the 3-equation model and begin with adaptive expectations where the economy adjusts over time to the new equilibrium.

We shall see in this section why inflation 'goes to infinity' under rational expectations in the case discussed under the Lucas critique and why there is a *finite* inflation bias in the case discussed here. Inflation only goes to infinity if the government or the central bank continue to pursue a level of output above equilibrium regardless of the consequences for inflation. The reason this does not happen in the inflation bias case analysed in this section is that although the government has an output target above $y_e$, it also has an inflation target. Hence there is a downward-sloping *MR* curve. We shall see that at the medium-run equilibrium with inflation bias, the economy is on the *MR* curve: the policy maker does not raise output because it would move them off their *MR* curve, which shows their optimal position given the Phillips curve they face.

### 4.6.1 Adaptive expectations and inflation bias

A myopic government or one with an upcoming election may prefer to use monetary policy to target a level of output above equilibrium—i.e. $y_H > y_e$. We illustrate this case in Fig. 4.8, where the central bank's *MR* curve has shifted out as a result of their more expansionary policy stance. Now, the *MR* goes through the new output target, $y_H$, where the new loss circles are centred. The central bank's bliss point is now at $A'$, where output is at $y_H$ and inflation is at target.

The adjustment of the economy after the change in policy stance is as follows:

1. The central bank forecasts that the Phillips curve will not move next period, because actual inflation has not changed as a result of the change in output target and agents form expectations in a backward-looking manner (e.g. $\pi_t = \pi_{t-1}$). The central bank therefore minimizes their loss function by lowering the interest rate, which stimulates aggregate demand and moves the economy to point *B*. Given the new *MR* curve, point *B* is the central bank's optimal point on the original Phillips curve. At point *B*, the government is closer to their new bliss point than they were at point *A*; they are willing to accept the rise in inflation, because output is closer to their new output target.

2. At point *B*, however, output is above equilibrium, so there is pressure on inflation to change. Inflation rises, the Phillips curve shifts upward and the central bank reoptimizes by raising the interest rate and moving the economy to point *C*.

3. At point *C*, output is still above equilibrium, so there is still pressure on inflation to change. Again, inflation rises, the Phillips curve shifts upward and the central bank reoptimizes by raising the interest rate. This adjustment process continues over a number of periods until the economy reaches the new medium-run equilibrium at point *Z*.

Figure 4.8 shows the inflation bias result. When the government tries to target a level of output above equilibrium the only result of the policy is that inflation is higher than its target. Output in the medium-run always has to be at the equilibrium level of output, as this is the only output level at which there is no pressure on inflation to change. On the new *MR* curve in Fig. 4.8, the medium run equilibrium has to be at point *Z*. At point *Z*, the government is further from its bliss point than if it had stuck with the original output target of $y_e$ and

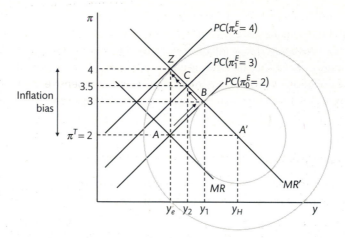

**Figure 4.8** The inflation bias.

remained at point A. The example highlights the futility of governments targeting a level of output above equilibrium.

We can quantify the inflation bias by taking the difference between the equilibrium rate of inflation and target inflation: the inflation bias is equal to 4% − 2% = 2%.

The next step is to derive the same result mathematically and pin down the determinants of the size of the inflation bias. The loss function the central bank now wants to minimize is

$$L = (y_t - y_H)^2 + \beta(\pi_t - \pi^T)^2,$$    (4.6)

where $y^H > y_e$. This is subject as before to the Phillips curve,

$$\pi_t = \pi_{t-1} + \alpha(y_t - y_e).$$    (4.7)

Minimizing the central bank's loss function—Equation 4.6—subject to the Phillips curve—Equation 4.7—implies the first order condition:

$$y_t - y_H + \alpha\beta(\pi_{t-1} + \alpha(y_t - y_e) - \pi^T) = 0$$
$$y_t - y_H + \alpha\beta(\pi_t - \pi^T) = 0.$$

So the new monetary rule is:

$$y_t - y_H = -\alpha\beta(\pi_t - \pi^T).$$

This equation indeed goes through $(\pi^T, y_H)$. Since equilibrium requires that there is no pressure on inflation to change, it must be the case that $y_t = y_e$ and that $\pi_t = \pi_{t-1}$. If we substitute this back into the monetary rule we have:

$$y_e = y_H - \alpha\beta(\pi_{t-1} - \pi^T)$$
$$\Rightarrow \pi_t = \pi_{t-1} = \pi^T + \underbrace{\frac{(y_H - y_e)}{\alpha\beta}}_{\text{inflation bias}}.$$    (inflation bias)

In equilibrium, inflation will exceed the target by $\frac{(y_H - y_e)}{\alpha\beta}$. This is called the inflation bias and it will be positive whenever $y_H > y_e$.[16] The steeper is the central bank's monetary rule (i.e. the less inflation averse it is, lower $\beta$), the greater will be the inflation bias. A lower $\alpha$ also raises the inflation bias. A lower $\alpha$ implies that inflation is less responsive to changes in output. Therefore, any given reduction in inflation is more expensive in lost output; so, in cost-benefit terms for the central bank, it pays to allow a little more inflation and a little less output loss.

### 4.6.2 Rational expectations, inflation bias and time inconsistency

When wage and price setters have rational expectations, inflation bias also arises. Unlike adaptive expectations, however, the adjustment process is instantaneous. We can use Fig. 4.8 to illustrate the adjustment process under rational expectations. When the policy is announced, the economy jumps straight from point $A$ to point $Z$. This is because the forward-looking, rational agents in the economy can see that given the new $MR$ curve, the new medium-run equilibrium will be at point $Z$.

We can also derive the mathematical equation for the size of the inflation bias under rational expectations. Suppose that the goal of the government is to minimize the loss function:

$$L = (y_t - y_H)^2 + \beta(\pi_t - \pi^T)^2,$$

where $y_H > y_e$. All the actors can work out that if the central bank minimizes this loss function subject to the rational expectations Phillips curve, $\pi_t = \pi_t^E + \alpha(y_t - y_e)$, this leads to the new $MR$ curve:

$$y_t - y_H = -\alpha\beta(\pi_t - \pi^T).$$

When the central bank chooses its optimal $y_t$, it has got to be on both the new $MR$ and the $PC$. But if the wage and price setters use rational expectations so that $\pi_t = \pi_t^E$, then the central bank has to set $y_t = y_e$ because, as we have seen above, if it did not, inflation would soar (to infinity) and even a pro-employment policy maker would want inflation to be finite. Hence it has no alternative but to set $y_t = y_e$.

In that case the left hand side of the $MR$ equation can be written

$$y_t - y_H = y_t - y_e + y_e - y_H = y_e - y_H = -(y_H - y_e) \text{ so that the } MR \text{ equation is now:}$$
$$y_H - y_e = \alpha\beta(\pi_t - \pi^T)$$
$$\Rightarrow \pi_t = \pi_t^E = \pi^T + \frac{(y_H - y_e)}{\alpha\beta}.$$
Inflation bias

The determinants of inflation bias are the same as before.

The situation described is an odd one for a rational central bank or government to find themselves in. Behaving rationally, but with an output target of $y_H$, they end up with

---

[16] For an early model of inflation bias with backward-looking inflation expectations, see Phelps (1967).

$$\pi_t = \pi^T + \frac{(y_H - y_e)}{\alpha\beta}$$

$$y_t = y_e$$

whilst if they targeted $y_e$, they would have ended up with

$$\pi_t = \pi^T$$

$$y_t = y_e.$$

Paradoxically, they would have been better off aiming for the *lower* output level $y_e$ as the output target—a target they did not want.

Given the inflation bias result, can government that chooses the monetary policy stance commit to an output target of $y_e$? No, because of the problem of time inconsistency. A government that prefers $y_H > y_e$ always has an incentive to use monetary policy to boost output after rational wage and price setters have set prices. Using this approach, the government can achieve a one period boost in output without a rise in inflation (exactly as in the Lucas critique example), which moves them closer to their bliss point. In this scenario, rational wage and price setters can foresee that the government will adjust its policy stance after they have set prices, so will preempt the government and set prices consistent with the government pursuing an output target of $y_H$. The economy jumps to point $Z$ in Fig. 4.8.

In other words, a government with a preference for output above equilibrium cannot credibly commit to targeting output of $y_e$. The government therefore ends up with inflation bias built into the system; output remains at equilibrium but inflation is persistently above target.

### 4.6.3 Approaches to mitigate inflation bias

**Delegation**

The problem of inflation bias can be solved by the monetary policy maker giving up their over-ambitious output target. This logic lies behind the idea of delegating monetary policy to an independent central bank, which has no incentive to target output above equilibrium. Put another way, the independent central bank can credibly commit to targeting output of $y_e$. Delegation is socially beneficial; welfare is higher if a body with different preferences from the government (and the private sector who elect them) has control over monetary policy.

In the standard central bank loss function, the policy maker cares only about minimizing the loss in the current period, i.e. there is extreme myopia. Whereas governments are likely to be characterized by myopia as a consequence of the electoral cycle, an independent monetary policy committee will take account of the consequences of inflation this period for next period's inflation (and their chances of meeting the inflation target). In order to encourage independent central bankers to take a medium-term view of policy, chairmen and committee members typically have long tenures that extend over multiple electoral cycles. The simplest way of representing this in the one-period loss function is to place a greater weight on the inflation deviation, i.e. to use a higher value of $\beta$. In other words, the longer term view of independent central bankers makes them more inflation averse than the government.

The empirical evidence supports the argument that delegation reduces inflation bias. Klomp and Haan (2010) use 59 previous studies that examine the relationship between inflation and central bank independence to carry out a meta-regression analysis. The authors find that the overall body of empirical evidence shows that central bank independence exerts a statistically significant negative effect on inflation (i.e. reduces it). They find a significant 'true effect' of central bank independence on inflation, even once they control for a significant publication bias, which makes it harder to publish results that do not show a statistically significant effect. The literature also suggests that adopting an inflation-targeting regime with an *explicit* inflation target improves macroeconomic performance in terms of both inflation and output stability by anchoring the public's inflation expectations to the central bank's objectives.[17]

In many OECD economies, inflation bias is no longer a significant problem, because control of monetary policy has been delegated to an independent central bank that is run by officials who are motivated by concern about their professional reputations. This point is summarized neatly by the economist Peter Howitt, who highlights the role of foreign exchange market operators in containing any tendency of domestic policy makers to try to boost output above equilibrium. We return to the role of the foreign exchange market in Chapter 9:[18]

> The 'temptation' to raise the level of economic activity with some surprise inflation might exist if society were indeed locked into expectations. In reality, however, the temptation just doesn't arise, as practitioners of central banking have long maintained. Central bankers are keenly aware that although there are long and variable lags between monetary stimulus and any resulting rise in the level of economic activity, there are no lags at all between such stimulus and the currency depreciation and capital flight that will occur if the stimulus is taken by investors as a signal of future weakness in the currency. Because of this, there is no reason for believing that discretionary central banks have the inflationary bias that the game-theoretic [time-inconsistency] view attributes to them. . . .

> Responsible people entrusted with such important and delicate jobs as the management of a country's central bank are typically motivated by the desire to be seen as having done a good job, to have acquitted themselves well. They pursue this objective by doing everything possible to avoid major inflations, financial panics and runs on the currency, while carrying out the day-to-day job of making available the base money needed for the financial system to function.

## Reputation building

Another solution to the problem of inflation bias lies with the government or central bank building a reputation for being tough on inflation. Suppose that the government has delegated monetary policy to the central bank but wage setters remain unsure of just how independent the central bank is. They only know that there is a probability $p$ that the central bank is independent and a probability $(1 - p)$ that it is a puppet of the government. The only

[17] For example, Orphanides and Williams (2005).
[18] Howitt (2001). Howitt refers to the useful paper by Mervyn King, then Deputy Governor of the Bank of England; from 2003, Governor of the Bank of England: King (1997). Another useful source is the short book of three lectures by Alan Blinder reflecting on how he used academic research when he was Vice-Chairman of the Federal Reserve Board: Blinder (1999).

way that they can find out is by observing the decisions taken by the central bank. If this is the case, how should the central bank behave? This problem can be analysed in detail using game theory.[19] Here we convey the flavour of the solution.

The situation is one in which the central bank interacts with wage setters more than once. Will a 'weak' central bank with an output target above the equilibrium find it rational to behave as if it were tough—i.e. with an output target closer to the equilibrium? If so, then we can say that it is possible to build a reputation for toughness as a method of solving the inflation bias problem.

Let us begin with the case in which the interaction between the central bank and wage setters occurs twice: in period one, wage setters choose $\pi_1^E$ with no knowledge of whether the central bank is weak or tough (but they know there is a probability of $p$ that it is tough); the central bank then chooses output in period one, $y_1$ knowing $\pi_1^E$. In period two, the wage setters choose $\pi_2^E$ knowing $y_1$; the central bank then chooses $y_2$ knowing $\pi_2^E$.

The result is that a weak central bank will choose to act like a tough one in the first period, which will establish a low expected inflation rate in the second period, thereby providing bigger gains from boosting output in the second period. The central bank gains because in the first period, the outcome is inflation at its target (no inflation bias) and output at the equilibrium (instead of the time inconsistency outcome of inflation above the target and output at equilibrium) whilst in the second period, it can gain by setting output above the equilibrium (i.e. by exploiting the short-run trade-off between inflation and unemployment by a surprise increase in inflation).

When the game is extended from two to many periods, the benefits to the central bank from behaving as if it were tough increase. This is because the situation in period one (where inflation bias is avoided) is repeated again and again until the last period. This type of model provides an explanation for the process by which a reputation for toughness can be built in the face of public scepticism.

## 4.7 Conclusions

This chapter has taken a closer look at the role of risk, uncertainty and expectations in the macro-economy. We have shown that *risk* (known probabilities) and *uncertainty* (unknown probabilities and unknown events) are pervasive in the economy, which means that economic agents (e.g. households, firms, the government, etc.) must form *expectations* about the future if they are to make the best decisions possible.

For example, workers form expectations about inflation, which they use as part of the wage setting process to ensure their real wage expectations are met. We set out the two ways in which inflation expectations are commonly modelled: *adaptive* expectations, where expected inflation is equal to last period's inflation; and *rational* expectations, where agents form their forecasts using the model and taking into account all available information.

---

[19] See Vickers (1986). For a simplified version of the central bank signalling game presented in Vickers' paper see Carlin and Soskice (2006), Chapter 16.

We also looked at the impact on the 3-equation model and its predictions when inflation expectations are modelled in different ways. This allows us to answer some interesting questions about the part played by expectations in the macro-economy:

1. When inflation expectations are formed rationally, how does this change the role of the central bank in the economy? The central bank's job is easier under rational expectations. They can directly influence the public's inflation expectations, so do not need to incur the employment cost of pushing down inflation before inflation expectations can be lowered. Disinflation is therefore costless. The introduction of rational expectations removes the lag between interest rate changes and output changes, meaning the central bank no longer has to gradually adjust the interest rate to guide the economy along the *MR* curve. After a rate change, the economy immediately jumps to the new equilibrium. Central banking is simpler if inflation expectations are formed rationally and consequently the economy is at equilibrium apart from random (i.e. unanticipated) shocks.

2. Why do modern central banks communicate to the public and financial markets about monetary policy? Central bank communication is directly related to transparency and credibility. In the absence of rational expectations, it is more likely that inflation expectations will stay close to target if the public are better informed about monetary policy. This was one of the key reasons for central banks introducing explicit inflation targets in the first place.

3. What is the Lucas critique? What dangers does it highlight for economic policy making? The Lucas critique concerns the problems of basing policy decisions on forecasting models that rely on relationships found in historical data. If the relationships in the models are conditional on the historical policy regime, then the models are rendered obsolete when the policy regime changes. There is a danger that constructing policy using these models will fail to produce the intended policy response due to the fact that economic agents change their behaviour when the new policy regime is introduced.

4. What happens when the monetary policy maker with an inflation target, targets output above equilibrium? How do expectations affect this process? When a monetary policy maker targets output above equilibrium, an inflation bias is built into the system; output is at equilibrium but inflation is persistently above target. The economy ends up at equilibrium output because there is always pressure on inflation to rise when output is above equilibrium. Whether expectations are adaptive or rational does not influence the eventual equilibrium, only the pace of adjustment. Under adaptive expectations the process of adjustment takes time, under rational expectations the economy jumps straight to the new medium-run equilibrium. Inflation bias is most likely to occur when the government exerts control over monetary policy. A government with an over-ambitious output target would actually be better off targeting $y_e$, but cannot credibly commit to that output target. The problem can be alleviated by delegating control of monetary policy to an independent central bank.

The modelling in this chapter has built on the core 3-equation model introduced in the last chapter. We have shown the impact on the macro-model of assuming the private sector as well as the central bank has rational expectations. It is very useful to understand the rational expectations hypothesis and its implication for the 3-equation model, because of the large impact the hypothesis has had on the development of academic macroeconomics and economic policy making.

Until the last chapter of the book, which introduces the real business cycle model and the New Keynesian DSGE model, we use as the base case a hybrid model where the central bank is forward-looking and has model-consistent expectations. The behaviour of wage setters is modelled by a Phillips curve with lagged inflation (where fully anchored expectations is a special case) and there is a lag in the *IS* curve. These choices reflect features of real-world economies (disinflations are costly in terms of unemployment and there are lags in monetary transmission) and provide a reasonable match to the way central banks describe their decision–making. Nevertheless, the Lucas critique needs to be kept in mind when designing and evaluating economic policy.

## 4.8 Questions

### 4.8.1 Checklist questions

1. What role do expectations play in the *IS* curve that underpins the 3-equation model? Provide an example of a situation where a change in expectations of the future can influence households' behaviour in the current period and shift the *IS* curve.

2. Describe the difference between risk and uncertainty. Provide an example of each case.

3. This question focuses on the discussion of Chevalier and Goolsbee (2009) in Section 4.2.2. Make sure you re-read this discussion before answering the following questions. Chevalier and Goolsbee (2009) suggests that the market for textbooks in the United States is rational and students are forward looking. If expectations were not rational and forward looking, how would you expect the example to differ? Would publishers be able to raise revenue by speeding up revision cycles?

4. Assess the following statements S1 and S2. Are they both true, both false or is only one true? Justify your answer.

    S1. Rational expectations means agents do not to make systematic errors.

    S2. Rational, forward-looking central banks' forecasts are often wrong.

5. When we add rational expectations to the 3-equation model, how does that change the predictions of the model?

6. Explain what is meant by the following statement: 'disinflation can be costless if the central bank is perfectly credible'. Draw the impulse response functions for output, inflation and the real interest rate following an inflation shock and interpret your results, when:

    (a) inflation expectations are fully backward looking

    (b) inflation expectations are firmly anchored to the inflation target.

7. Assess the following statements S1 and S2. Are they both true, both false or is only one true? Justify your answer.

    S1. Better communication by central banks can influence the path the economy takes after an economic shock.

52. Better communication by central banks does not affect how economic agents react to interest rate changes (which is the main tool used by monetary policy makers to achieve their inflation target).

8. Provide a definition of the Lucas critique. What is the relevance of the critique to the stagflation of the 1970s?

9. Imagine the government is able to exert control over monetary policy. What happens under adaptive expectations when the government targets a level of output above equilibrium? Is there a short-run trade-off between inflation and unemployment? How about under rational expectations?

10. Can a government with an overly ambitious output target credibly commit to targeting equilibrium output? If not, then how can they solve the inflation bias problem?

### 4.8.2 Problems and questions for discussion

1. Use this chapter and your own knowledge and further research to answer the following questions:

   (a) Is Keynes' treatment of expectations consistent with the rational expectations hypothesis?

   (b) What is meant by agents making 'systematic errors' under adaptive expectations?

2. Collect data on inflation and unemployment for the UK and the US during the 1970s and 1980s using OECD.Stat. The 1980s was a period of significant disinflation for the two economies. Use the data gathered and the content of this chapter to answer the following questions:

   (a) Was the disinflation costly (in terms of rising unemployment)?

   (b) Does the data provide evidence that inflation expectations were being formed rationally during this period?

   (c) How can the concept of anchored expectations be used to suggest what the UK and US governments could have done to reduce the costs associated with disinflation.

3. Assume that inflation expectations are formed rationally. Use the 3-equation model to show the adjustment of the economy to a permanent demand and a permanent supply shock. Provide a period by period explanation of the adjustment process (as done in Chapter 3). How does the central bank reaction differ from the cases where we assumed adaptive inflation expectations (as shown in the last chapter)?

4. This question uses the Macroeconomic Simulator available from the Carlin and Soskice website http://www.oup.com/uk/orc/carlin_soskice to show how central bank credibility affects the adjustment of the economy following an inflation shock. Start by opening the simulator and choosing the closed economy version. Then reset all shocks by clicking the appropriate button on the left hand side of the main page. Use the simulator and the content of this chapter to work through the following:

   (a) Apply a 2% positive inflation shock. Save your data.

   (b) Adjust the degree of inflation inertia/credibility of the central bank to zero (i.e. full credibility, which is equivalent to setting $\chi = 1$ in Equation 4.5). Save your data.

   (c) Use the impulse response function and Section 4.4.3 to compare the adjustment path of the economy following the shock in each case. Use the 3-equation model to explain any differences in the adjustment paths.

(d) Set the degree of inflation inertia/credibility of the central bank to 0.5 (i.e. partial credibility). Save your data.

(e) What do our answers to parts a. to d. tell us about the benefit to a central bank of increasing their credibility?

(f) How might a central bank go about increasing their credibility?

# 5 Money, banking and the macro-economy

## 5.1 Introduction

If the banking system is working well its presence is hardly noticed. It is treated as part of the background infrastructure of the economy much like the electricity grid. When the financial crisis erupted in 2008, economists and the public were suddenly aware of the financial system and realized it was poorly understood and poorly regulated.

This chapter is the first of three that focus on the interaction of the financial system and the macro-economy. The financial crisis highlighted the lack of attention this branch of macroeconomics has received in recent decades. To make the chapters easier to navigate, we start by briefly setting out the content we will cover in each chapter:

**Chapter 5** We set out the role that the banking system plays in the 3-equation model of the macro-economy. We look more closely at the functioning of the banking sector, focusing on the provision of loans to the private sector and showing how central bank interest rate decisions affect banks' lending rates. The chapter opens by highlighting the difference between the policy rate and the lending rate, taking the example of how a shock to the banking system can have macroeconomic effects. It ends by taking a macroeconomic shock—the example of an investment boom—to highlight how the banking system fits into the central bank's policy-making process.

**Chapter 6** Chapter 5 focuses on the banking system under an inflation-targeting regime in 'normal times'. In Chapter 6, we reevaluate the usual assumption in macroeconomics that the financial system runs smoothly by looking at potentially destabilizing features, such as the financial accelerator and asset price bubbles. We also look at how financial regulation affects bank risk-taking behaviour. These features can both amplify and propagate shocks through the economy, which can lead to financial cycles and banking crises. We show how financial upswings can occur alongside successful inflation targeting, leaving modern economies vulnerable to financial crises.

**Chapter 7** We apply the framework developed in the previous two chapters to the global financial crisis of 2008–09 and its aftermath. This allows the financial crisis and the macroeconomic policy and banking regulation responses it provoked to be explained and analysed within a coherent macroeconomic framework.

As stated above, the aim of this chapter is to clarify the role played by money and banking in the macro-economy. We do this by incorporating banks Into the core 3-equation model introduced in Chapter 3. This extension to the core model highlights the vital importance of banks in facilitating borrowing and lending in the economy and in the transmission of monetary policy. The continuity of the flow of core banking services lies behind the *IS* curve. Whenever we use the *IS* curve, we assume households and firms can implement their planned spending decisions by using money, credit and the payments system.

In the 3-equation model up to this point, we have assumed that the central bank is able to achieve the output gap it desires in order to stabilize the economy by setting the *policy* interest rate. Once we introduce the banking system, we need to distinguish between the policy rate set by the central bank and the *lending* rate, which is the rate relevant for the spending decisions of households and firms represented by the *IS* curve. For the central bank to implement its policy decisions, there needs to be a predictable relationship between the policy and lending rates.

We shall see that the lending rate is a mark-up on the policy rate, which reflects the optimizing behaviour of banks. The costs of providing bank account facilities and of assessing credit-worthiness, and the banks' profits, are met from the margin between their lending rate and the cost of their borrowing.

We can represent this in the 3-equation model by explicitly labelling the vertical axis in the *IS* diagram 'Lending interest rate, r', since this is the one relevant for *IS* decisions. Figure 5.1a (the left hand panel) shows the decision-making of the central bank in the usual way in the lower panel. Once it has decided on its optimal output gap (here, a zero output gap), it figures out from the *IS* curve the associated lending rate, labelled 'Desired lending interest

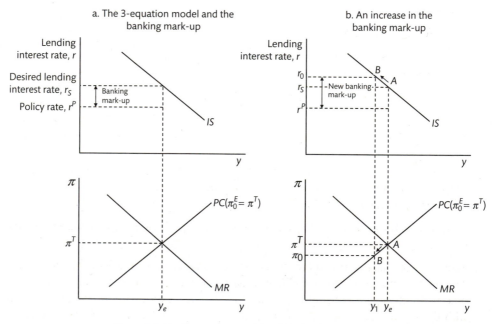

**Figure 5.1** The 3-equation model and the banking mark-up.

rate, $r_S'$. Given its knowledge of the banking system, which means the size of the mark up of the lending rate above the policy rate, the central bank sets the policy rate to deliver its desired lending rate, which in this case is the stabilizing interest rate, $r_S$. The policy rate that delivers $r_S$ is labelled 'Policy rate, $r^{P'}$. The banking mark-up (also referred to using the terms margin, spread or wedge) is indicated as the gap between the two.

By extending the 3-equation model in this way, we can look at the implications for the economy of a shock to the banking system. Let us use as an example a situation where banks suddenly take the view that the loans they have made are riskier. As we shall see, this leads them to increase the margin of the lending rate above the policy rate. In the example, the increase in the lending rate is a shock unanticipated by the central bank so the policy rate is unchanged. Figure 5.1b shows the macroeconomic consequences: the unexpected rise in the lending rate for an unchanged policy rate leads to a contraction of aggregate demand to the north-west along the *IS*. The economy is plunged into recession.

From our analysis in Chapter 3, an inflation-targeting central bank would react to the fall in output as a consequence of the negative shock to aggregate demand (the move along the *IS* curve to point *B*) by forecasting a reduction in inflation below target. It would then find its desired position on the *MR* curve, work out the lending rate that would deliver this positive output gap and lower the policy rate accordingly to get the economy on the path back to medium-run equilibrium.

We can summarize the causal chain of central bank decision-making as follows:

bad shock to banks

→ rise in interest rate margin

→ fall in output

→ fall in forecast inflation

→ CB finds desired output gap on MR

→ CB calculates lending rate on IS

→ CB sets new lower policy rate to get economy on MR.

The important point to take away from this example is that shocks to the banking system that change the interest rate margin influence aggregate demand—i.e. they have real economic effects.

In this chapter we shall set out a simple way of representing a modern financial system that captures its essential role in the macro-economy.

The new elements we introduce are:

1. A distinction between the policy interest rate, which is set by the central bank, and the lending rate, which is the cost of borrowing to the private sector, and is set by

2. Banks, which make loans to the private sector, take deposits from them, borrow and lend in the money market, and keep reserve accounts at the central bank. In addition to setting the lending rate, we shall see why banks impose credit rationing with the result that some households (and small and medium-sized firms) face credit constraints.

3. The money market, which is where borrowing and lending among commercial banks takes place and also where saver households can buy and sell government bonds.

4. The governance structure of the financial system, which describes the relationships between government (and taxpayers), central bank and banks. The governance structure establishes responsibility for maintaining confidence in the financial system and for responding to liquidity and solvency (bankruptcy) problems of banks.

The structure of the chapter is as follows: we begin with money and the role it plays in the macro-economy. We then set out the elements of a modern banking system in Section 5.3, explaining how the mark-up of the lending rate over the policy rate is determined and exploring the reasons why banks impose credit rationing and give rise to the presence of credit-constrained households.

In Chapter 1 we saw how the presence of credit-constrained households affects the *IS* curve through its effect on the size of the multiplier: a higher proportion of credit-constrained households means a higher multiplier. In this chapter, we look at why households are credit-constrained and in Chapter 6, we shall see that credit-constrained households play an important role in explaining financial fluctuations and crises.

As well as introducing the useful role banks play in the economy, Section 5.3 introduces the problems of liquidity and solvency of banks. This leads on to a description of the governance of the financial system in terms of relationships between government, central bank and banks. Section 5.4 explains how balance sheets work and how they help to illuminate the relationships among savers, borrowers, banks (and the central bank) in the economy.

In the last section of this chapter, we bring all the elements together to extend the 3-equation model to include banks. We use an example to illustrate how the model works: an investment boom, which shifts the *IS* curve.

## 5.2 Money and the macro-economy

### 5.2.1 Money

In a decentralized economy with many different kinds of goods, money allows transactions to occur without requiring the 'double coincidence of wants'. The double coincidence of wants is where two parties each have a good or service that the other party wants. This requirement of a 'barter' or 'moneyless' economy is very restrictive and drastically cuts down the amount of viable trades each person can make. Money allows us to compare the value of all goods and services in terms of a common standard—the unit of account.

This enables specialization and promotes efficiency. Money cuts down enormously on the time spent obtaining information about the relative costs and profitability of different ventures, and on finding people with whom one can trade. Managing money so as to maintain confidence that it will serve these functions effectively is potentially of great value in terms of real output.[1]

---

[1] For an interesting discussion of barter, money and trust, see the two short chapters (6 and 7) in Seabright (2010).

## 5.2.2 Money supply and money demand

There are many different ways to measure the money supply, which vary depending on the liquidity of the form the money is held in. The central role of money in facilitating transactions can explain why people are willing to hold money in its narrowest form such as notes and coins or in a current account, even though in terms of return they are dominated by other safe assets that pay interest, such as a term account.

The difference between narrow money and the term account is liquidity, which measures the ease with which money can be used for transactions. Whilst current accounts sometimes pay interest, it is at a very low rate. Other safe assets pay higher interest rates but they offer less liquidity. Periods of notice are required to withdraw money from higher interest accounts and it is often necessary to keep a minimum balance in such an account, reducing the flexibility with which it can be used for transactions.

In our treatment of money in the macro model, it is not necessary to get into the technicalities of how central banks define the different measures of the money supply. The precise definitions can be found on the central banks' websites.[2]

In the discussion that follows, we concentrate on:

1. Narrow money, also called central bank money or high-powered money, which is notes and coins and the reserve balances of banks held at the central bank. These are the most liquid forms of money. This is referred to as M0.

2. Broad money, which is central bank money plus commercial bank money. The measure used by the Bank of England that is closest to the broad money measure used in this chapter is M2, which is also called retail M4. This only includes holdings of sterling notes and coins and sterling denominated 'retail' deposits with UK monetary financial institutions.

Money is created directly by both banks and the central bank and can be used to buy goods and services, buy assets or repay debts. By contrast, government bonds, for example, are not money because they cannot be used to pay for goods or services, or to service or pay down debts. In normal times, money created by the central bank and by commercial banks are perfect substitutes for fulfilling the functions of money described above. In a financial crisis, however, this equivalence breaks down because doubts arise about the *liquidity* of commercial bank money. The money issued by the central bank in the form of notes and coins is legal tender, which means it cannot legally be refused in settlement of debt. The money created by commercial banks in the form of deposits is not legal tender. We explore this further in Chapter 7 in the context of the credit crunch associated with the global financial crisis.

Households decide on the amount of *cash* they wish to hold. Desired cash holdings will respond to changes in means of payment such as the introduction of payment via mobile phones and contactless payment.

The amount of *reserves* reflects the decisions by *banks* about their prudent ratio of reserves to deposits. Reserves provide banks with the liquidity they need in order to settle balances with other banks and to pay customers who want to withdraw deposits. They will not hold more reserves than prudent because they get a lower return on reserves than on making loans.

---

[2] Information taken from the Bank of England's website: http://www.bankofengland.co.uk/Pages/home.aspx.

Given the choice by banks of their liquidity ratios (the ratio of reserves to deposits), the amount of central bank money is pinned down by the size of bank deposits and cash the public wish to hold. Subject to the constraints of their liquidity, commercial banks will create money by extending loans when it is profitable for them to do so. This will depend on the demand for loans, given by the *IS* curve, and on the funding costs they face, which will be determined by the policy rate set by the central bank.

In a modern economy, cash is less than 3% of the money supply. Commercial banks create money by granting credit, which shows up in the bank accounts of households and firms. The type of bank account chosen for depositing the money (e.g. current account, term account etc.) will affect which of the broad measures of the money supply reported by central banks such newly created money is counted in.

To simplify the modelling in our discussion of money and banking in the macro model, we shall assume that current accounts are non-interest bearing. We assume households can choose to hold their financial assets as money (either in cash or in a current account) or as government bonds. Later we introduce a further choice, of holding bank equity, or shares in banks. In the real-world economy, households also hold bonds issued by companies and shares in non-financial companies as well as in banks but we do not introduce these into the model.

## Box 5.1   What is a bond?

A bond is a financial instrument sold by an institution wishing to borrow, such as a government or a company, to an investor wishing to lend. The key difference between a bond and a bank loan is that the bond can be bought by any willing investor in the bond market, and the initial buyer can sell the bond to another investor through the same market at the prevailing price. Bank loans cannot be sold along in the same way.

In the simple case of a perpetual bond, the nominal interest rate, $i$, on a bond, often known as the 'yield', is given by

$$i = \frac{\text{coupon}}{\text{price}},$$   bond yield

where 'coupon' is a fixed payment made to the bondholder every period forever, unless the bond issuer defaults. The word coupon is used to refer to the fixed payment on the bond because this used to be a physical paper coupon which bondholders would detach and present to claim their periodic payment. The 'price' is the price at which the bond *currently trades* on the bond market. This price generally differs from the price at which the bond was initially sold, but gives an indication of the price at which new bonds would sell. Consider the following numerical example. If the price of the bond is $100, and the coupon is $5, then the interest rate is 5%. If the price of the bond rises to $200, the interest rate falls to 2.5%, since the coupon remains $5. Since the coupon is fixed, it is the price of the bond which determines the interest rate paid on such bonds, and the price of the bond and the interest rate are inversely related.

Given the assumptions we have made, the stock of commercial bank money in the economy is measured by the size of current accounts. Ultimately this depends on the *decisions of households* and *firms* about the deposits they wish to hold, i.e. on the demand for money. Households' and firms' choice of how much money to hold will depend on their level of income and the interest rate:

1. As their income increases, households will want to carry out more transactions, so will hold more money (deposits).

2. A higher interest rate will make buying bonds more attractive and will reduce the proportion of income households and firms wish to hold in deposits.

This is called the demand for money function and is written:

$$\frac{M^D}{P} = f(y, i; \Phi)$$

where $y$ is output and $i$ is the nominal interest rate. The nominal interest rate, $i$, affects the demand for money. When deciding whether to hold money balances as money or bonds, the opportunity cost of holding money is the interest rate on bonds, $i$. Using the Fisher equation, $i = r + \pi^E$, we can think of the nominal interest rate having two components, the real interest rate and expected inflation. If inflation goes up, this adds to the opportunity cost of holding money and the demand for money will fall.

The demand for money depends positively on output and negatively on the nominal interest rate and is shifted by structural changes in the financial sector, which are captured by the variable, $\Phi$ (phi). It is these private sector decisions, which, when combined with the central bank's choice of the policy rate, fix the amount of money in the economy.

There is a range of structural factors that can shift the money demand function and which we refer to by $\Phi$. An important one is confidence. All over the world, the demand for money went up in 2008–09 in the face of the fear associated with the global financial crisis and credit crunch. The fear that the financial system might malfunction led households and firms to want to hold more money. And looking across the spectrum of money from cash to the broadest definition, people wanted to hold more of the narrower forms of money like cash.

Another factor that shifts the demand for money is innovation in payments technology. This includes the diffusion of mobile phones with the capability of making payments and transferring money between types of accounts. Over the past decade banks introduced 'sweep' options, which would automatically transfer balances from the current account to a higher interest earning account when the balance was above a certain level—or vice versa. This led to a fall in the demand for more narrowly defined money.

The demand for money is also affected when new financial instruments are introduced or when they become accessible to a wider range of households and firms. During the 2000s it was observed that the demand for money became less predictable as a consequence of the growth in mortgage refinancing activity. On the firm side, there have been changes in cash management policies as well, which shifted the demand for money.

Figure 5.2 illustrates how equilibrium in the money market comes about. If we hold constant the structural shift and confidence factors summarized in $\Phi$, then at a given level of output, the demand for money is determined as shown in the diagram. When the central bank sets the policy rate, it allows the supply of money to adjust to whatever is the level of demand. If the demand for money function were to shift to the right—as a consequence, for example, of a loss of confidence in the financial system—then at the central bank's policy

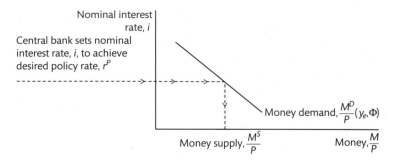

**Figure 5.2** The central bank policy rate and the demand for money.

rate, and holding the level of output constant, the supply of money will increase to meet the additional demand. An example of this case is shown in the next section (see Fig. 5.5).

### 5.2.3 **Money, banks and the 3-equation model**

In the real world, there are many different interest rates ranging from the policy rate set by the central bank, to the two-week lending rate in the interbank market, to the yield on short term and longer term government bonds, to the lending rate on mortgages and the interest rate on credit card debt and pay-day loans. There are also many different financial markets. To understand the role of the financial system in the macro-economy, it is necessary to simplify drastically. We will work with two interest rates and one financial market, the 'money market'.

In the model, we refer to households buying government bonds from the money market. In reality, they buy these bonds from the capital markets, which are markets that house financial securities with longer maturities than the money markets. Money markets are typically restricted to securities with maturities of under one year. The left hand side of Fig. 5.3 shows the assumptions made about interest rates in the model. The key assumption is that all short- and medium-term interbank loans and government bonds are assumed to have an interest rate of $r^P$, the policy rate. We collectively term these interest rates 'the money market rate'. We make this assumption to keep the modelling as simple as possible.

Note also that we shall refer to real interest rates in the modelling, although it is nominal interest rates that are observed in the world. The reason is that the central bank's aim is to affect output and employment in the economy (output and employment) by affecting spending that is sensitive to the real interest rate.

The right hand side of Fig. 5.3 provides some data on UK interest rates in 2006. We can see that there is a spectrum of interest rates in the money and capital markets. Money market rates are closer to the Official Bank Rate, which is the policy rate at which banks can borrow from the central bank, than to the five-year mortgage rate, which is the rate at which banks lend to households. This is the important distinction in this chapter. In Chapter 7, we introduce another important characteristic of interest rates: the term structure and the associated yield curve.

Figure 5.4 shows that the spread between Bank of England policy rate and the mortgage rate being charged by UK banks. The chart suggests a stable relationship in 'normal times', which was disrupted by the financial crisis. This highlights that the key transmission

| The model | | | The UK in 2006 (annual average rates) | | |
|---|---|---|---|---|---|
| The lending rate | | $r$ | Rate on 5 year fixed rate mortgages | | 5.25 |
| Money market rate | Short- and medium-term interbank lending rates | $r^P$ | Capital and money market rates | Sterling 6 month mean interbank lending rate | 4.87 |
| | | | | Sterling 2 month mean interbank lending rate | 4.71 |
| | Short- and medium-term government bond yields | $r^P$ | | 5 year government bond yield | 4.63 |
| The policy rate | | $r^P$ | Official Bank Rate | | 4.64 |

**Figure 5.3** The assumptions made in the model about real interest rates and the associated nominal interest rates from the UK in 2006.

*Source:* Bank of England (data accessed October 2013).

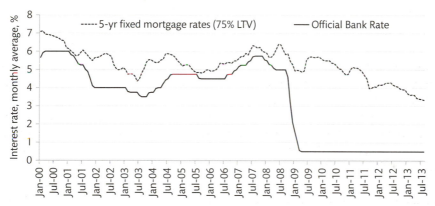

**Figure 5.4** UK Official Bank Rates and 5-yr fixed mortgages rates (75% LTV): Jan 2000–Aug 2013.

*Source:* Bank of England (data accessed October 2013).

mechanism of monetary policy (i.e. that changes in $r^P$ by the central bank alter the long-term borrowing costs for households and firms) broke down in the post-crisis world.

We can summarize the important causal relationships by bringing together Figs. 5.1 and 5.2. The modern monetary framework set out in Chapter 3 works in the following way. The starting point is the central bank's forward looking diagnosis of the state of the economy and forecast inflation. This fixes its desired output gap in the usual way in the lower panel of Fig. 5.5. We take the example where the central bank wishes to keep the economy at equilibrium output, i.e. at $y = y_e$. Given the mark-up of the lending rate over the policy rate, the central bank sets the policy rate at $r^P$ such that $r = r_S$, the stabilizing interest rate.

We can now trace through the implications for the banks: a policy rate of $r^P$ as shown in Fig. 5.5 is chosen by the central bank so that the banking system provides credit to the private sector to implement their spending plans shown by the *IS* curve at $r = r_S$ and $y = y_e$.

The outcome for the demand and supply of money is shown in the right-hand panel. With output at equilibrium, private sector demand for money given the policy rate set by the

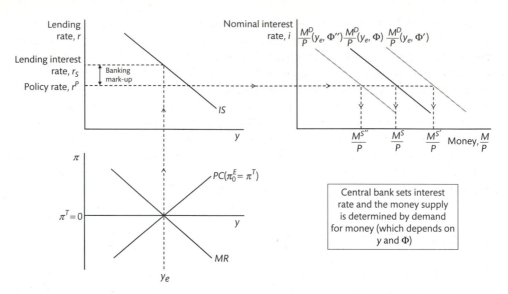

**Figure 5.5** The 3-equation model and the demand for money with inflation set to zero.

central bank is shown by $\frac{M^D}{P}(y_e; \Phi)$. For the interest rate to remain unchanged at the central bank's desired rate, there must be equilibrium between the demand and supply of money.[3] Hence the supply of money is given by the intersection of the dashed line indicating the chosen interest rate and the money demand curve. In this framework, the amount of money in the economy is the *outcome* of the responses of banks and the private sector to the central bank's interest rate decision. To emphasize this, we show three demand for money functions with different values of $\Phi$ and the associated levels of the money supply.

One of the very important features of a modern monetary economy is that there is, in fact, no well-defined and stable downward sloping money demand function. As the different definitions of the money supply suggest, people and firms are likely to shift their choice of bank account type and the amount of bonds they want to hold in response to financial innovation. This is one reason monetary policy in the modern monetary framework is defined as *interest rate* policy.

For a central bank using interest rate policy, innovations in the payments system, or other structural changes in the economy that shift the private sector's demand for money, do not alter the central bank's ability to achieve its desired output gap. By keeping the policy rate unchanged, any shift in the money demand function affects the money supply but does not feed back to influence real economic activity (see Fig. 5.5). This means we do not need to keep track of the money supply or be concerned about shifts in the demand for money when we work with the simple macro model.

---

[3] Remember that it is the real interest rate that affects behaviour in the *IS* curve and the nominal interest rate that affects money demand. Figure 5.5 has been drawn with an inflation target of zero and expected inflation of zero to allow the simplest diagram. We know from the Fisher equation that when $\pi^E = 0$, then $r = i$.

In this model, the commercial banks create money whenever they make a loan and this is sometimes referred to as 'endogenous' money. However, this does not give the banks the ability to control the amount of economic activity in the economy: this depends on the interest rate. The interest rate is controlled by the central bank as long as it is able accurately to predict the mark-up applied by the commercial banks. The new element introduced by including the banking system in the model is that in addition to the factors we have discussed in Chapter 3, the central bank's ability to steer the economy depends on there being a reliable relationship between the policy interest rate and the lending rate. Assuming the central bank can predict the mark-up of the lending rate over the policy rate, it is able to achieve its stabilization goals. We illustrated how a shock to the mark-up because of a sudden increase in banks' perception of the riskiness of their loans can cause a recession in Fig. 5.1b.

## 5.3 A modern financial system

In this section, we provide a stylized account of the elements of a modern banking system. We begin with the way the central bank sets the policy interest rate in an inflation-targeting regime. We then look at bank behaviour and how the lending rate is set. The next step is to explain why information problems inherent in the economy mean that banks impose credit rationing. This ties up a loose end by providing an explanation for the presence in the economy of credit-constrained households. We next note both the useful things banks do and the trouble they can cause through liquidity and solvency problems. This leads on to a discussion of the governance relationships in the economy between the banking system, government and the central bank.

### 5.3.1 The central bank sets the policy interest rate

In this subsection, we set out and answer some key questions about how modern, inflation-targeting central banks operate monetary policy through interest rate setting. The discussion of Quantitative Easing, which dominated monetary policy making during the Great Recession, is postponed to Chapter 13 on Monetary Policy.

1. How does the central bank set the policy rate? An independent, inflation-targeting central bank has direct control over the policy rate of interest. It is typically chosen by committee in monthly meetings, such as the Monetary Policy Committee at the Bank of England.

2. How does the central bank go about ensuring that other short-term interest rates are kept close to the policy rate? We concentrate here on the economic principles rather than the technicalities.[4] Although institutional structures vary slightly across countries, the policy rate is commonly the rate at which the central bank both lends to financial institutions and pays on reserves. The opportunity for arbitrage between short-term interbank lending rates (money market rates) and the rate paid on reserves means that money market rates stay close

[4] For a detailed description of how a modern inflation-targeting central bank sets interest rates see Part 1 of *The Sterling Monetary Framework* available on the Bank of England website: http://www.bankofengland.co.uk/markets/Pages/sterlingoperations/redbook.aspx.

to the policy rate. For example, if money market rates were above the policy rate then banks will be willing to supply more loans to other banks, but less willing to borrow from other banks. As a result of these shifts in supply and demand, the price of loans in the market would therefore adjust downwards toward the policy rate. The short-term interbank lending rates will never fall below the policy rate, however, as no bank has an incentive to lend money to another bank at a rate lower than the one they would receive by putting the money on reserve at the central bank.

3. How is the money supply affected by monetary policy? The money supply is not directly targeted. It is determined by the demand for money at the policy interest rate set by the central bank. Paul Tucker, Deputy Governor of the Bank of England, describes how this process works in the UK: 'We are able to implement monetary policy because the economy has a demand for central bank money and, as monopoly suppliers, we can set the terms on which we provide it [i.e. the policy interest rate]. The demand for our money is manifested in two ways– holdings of notes, and bankers' balances with us'.[5] This is consistent with the process shown in Fig. 5.5; given the banking system's demand for central bank money, central bankers 'set the price of this money and then supply the quantity demanded consistent with that price'.[6]

4. How does the policy rate affect the lending rate in the economy? The central bank knows that there is a mark-up between the policy rate and the rate at which banks lend to households and firms. They use their knowledge of the mark-up to set the policy rate so as to achieve their desired lending rate (from the *MR* curve). It is the lending rate that influences the level of aggregate demand in the economy. We turn next to the factors that influence the size of the banking mark-up.

### 5.3.2 The mark-up of the lending rate over the policy rate

We begin by asking how an individual bank behaves. Banks face a demand for new loans from the private sector. They also face a cost of funding when their new deposits are insufficient to fund their desired lending. They will therefore borrow from the money market at the policy rate to fill the gap between deposits and desired lending.

In this subsection, we look at what determines the lending rate in the economy. Most banks in the OECD economies are privately owned and it is reasonable to model them as maximizing profits like other private sector firms. To model the mark-up of the lending rate over the policy rate, we simplify on a number of counts. In particular, we ignore the administration costs to banks of providing loans, such as bank salaries and expertise for assessing loans and certain external costs such as advertizing and renting and maintaining a network of branches.

A simple formal model is set out in the Appendix to this chapter. In the model, the profits of banks depend on:

---

[5] This excerpt is taken from the Bank of England Quarterly Bulletin: Autumn 2004 and is available online from: http://www.bankofengland.co.uk/publications.

[6] Excerpt taken from: Paul Fisher (MPC member), 19th November 2009, *The Bank of England's Balance Sheet: Monetary Policy and Liquidity Provision during the Financial Crisis,* speech at the Professional Pensions Show, Excel Centre, London.

1. the expected return on the loans they make;
2. the rate they pay for borrowing in the money market;
3. and what they lose (i.e. the opportunity cost) of holding bank capital, or equity.

What is meant by the expected return on bank loans? It is the return that banks can expect on the loans they provide to customers, taking into account that not all customers will repay their loans. What factors determine the expected return on bank loans? Bank lending is necessarily risky. There is no guarantee that interest payments on a loan will be repaid or that the principal will be paid back in full when repayment is due. In maximizing their expected rate of return, banks must take this risk, which is called *credit risk*, into account.

It is important to realize that even bank lending that is backed by collateral, called secured lending, carries credit risk. For example, when you sign a mortgage agreement with a bank, the bank has a charge over your house. This is called a collateralized loan. Should you fail to keep up your payments, the bank can repossess the house.

However, as has become very clear in the aftermath of the global financial crisis, foreclosure is very costly in terms of transactions and legal costs, and the house falls into disrepair when foreclosure is anticipated. Recovery is normally a fraction of the value of well-maintained properties. Losses on loans can therefore occur even if the house price has not fallen. Collateral reduces but it does not eliminate credit risk because its value depends on the state of the market when the asset has to be sold.

Given that lending is risky, even in a competitive banking market, banks will charge a mark-up or margin above the rate at which they can borrow money. Banks borrow money in the money market at the policy rate, $r^P$. The more risky are the loans it makes, the higher will be the margin of $r$ above $r^P$. In addition to the riskiness of the loans, it is also possible that the willingness of banks to take on risk varies. We will call this the bank's risk tolerance. A bank with a lower risk tolerance will require a higher margin of $r$ above $r^P$ to compensate it for a given riskiness of loans.

Finally, the ability of the bank to bear risk depends on how much capital or equity it has. The bank's equity or capital cushion is the difference between the value of its assets and its liabilities. A smaller capital cushion means it is less able to bear risk because a smaller fall in the value of its assets (holding liabilities constant) would wipe out its equity and it would be insolvent. A bank with a lower capital cushion (less equity) is less able to bear credit risk and it will therefore choose a higher interest rate margin and choose to make fewer loans. For an explanation of the way assets, liabilities and equity (net worth) are recorded in bank balance sheets, see Section 5.4.

These three elements: risk, risk tolerance and bank equity, explain the gap between the interest rate set by banks, $r$, and the policy rate, $r^P$. An increase in the riskiness of projects or a fall in risk tolerance or in the equity cushion will increase the lending rate for a given policy rate. In fact, the profit-maximizing bank chooses to respond to these changes by both raising the price they charge for loans (i.e. the interest rate) and by making fewer loans.

We add one more equation to the 3-equation model:

$$r = (1 + \mu^B)r^P, \qquad \text{(interest rate margin; banking mark-up equation)}$$

where $\mu^B$ is the banking mark-up that depends positively on risk, and negatively on risk tolerance and the capital cushion.

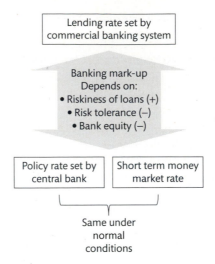

**Figure 5.6** The relationship between the policy interest rate, the short term money market rate and the lending interest rate.

Figure 5.6 shows the relationship between the key interest rates in the model. As discussed in Section 5.3.1, under normal conditions, the policy interest rate and the short-term money market rate are equal. The lending rate is higher than the policy and money market rate. The size of the gap between the lending and other rates (i.e. the margin or mark-up) is determined by the factors in the double-headed arrow.

If the banking sector is not competitive, a further factor will affect the mark-up of the lending rate over the policy rate. In a parallel fashion to the goods market in Chapter 2, in which the mark-up of the price above unit labour costs rises with the extent of market power, a bank with market power will set a higher margin of the lending rate above the policy rate.

### 5.3.3 Banks, credit constraints and collateral

In this subsection, we explain why when modelling bank behaviour, we need not only to understand the determinants of the margin of the lending rate over the policy rate but also to understand why banks ration credit. This involves the concepts of credit risk, along with two kinds of information problem: moral hazard and adverse selection.

Managing credit risk is a major part of a bank's business and we showed in the previous section that the mark-up of the lending rate over the policy rate varies positively with credit risk. We now explain why banks will not only adjust their mark-up to reflect the average credit risk of their loan portfolio but will also impose credit rationing.

Credit rationing and the associated credit constraints faced by households play an important role in the macroeconomic model. In analysing household behaviour in Chapter 1, the size of the multiplier and the slope of the *IS* curve were shown to depend on the weight of credit-constrained households and firms in the economy. In Chapter 6, we shall extend the model further to show how changes in asset prices relax the borrowing constraint for credit-constrained households and the role this plays in financial booms and busts.

## Credit risk, information problems and credit constraints

Credit risk is ever-present: will the investment project be the success it is forecast to be in the firm's business plan? Will household members remain in employment and will their salaries grow in the way that was expected when they took out a mortgage to allow them to buy their house?

Even more important than the fact that the future is unknown, however, is the way information problems can affect behaviour. If I want to borrow money from you to launch a new venture and it turns out that I am unable to repay, you don't know if that is because I was unlucky or because, given that you lent me the money, I exerted less effort than I would have done if all the funding had been my own. It may be difficult for you to find this out and to find out the returns generated by the project.

The problem of possible default by the borrower for reasons other than bad luck is an example of *moral hazard* and it affects the willingness of banks to lend and why that is affected by the wealth of the borrower. As the example above suggests, the more of your own wealth you are able (and prepared) to invest in your project, the easier it is to borrow. When your own funds are at stake, your incentives are better aligned with those of the lender. Borrowers with insufficient wealth to invest in their project may be denied credit.

In addition to the problem of moral hazard, there is another pervasive information problem. In the permanent income hypothesis of Chapter 1, it is assumed that households are able to borrow to carry out their consumption plans in line with their expected permanent income. However, to make you a loan so that you can consume your permanent income implies the lender can observe your expected future earning capacity.

Given it does not have this information, it might seem obvious for the bank to simply charge a higher interest rate to cover the risk that your self-reported future earning plans fail to materialize. However, because you have better information about your expected future earnings than the bank, this is a situation of *asymmetric information*. It means that if the bank were to charge a higher interest rate, individuals with stronger prospects (known to themselves but difficult to signal credibly to the bank) would self-select away from bank credit; the cost of borrowing is viewed as too high by individuals with a high probability of success. The self-selection leaves the weaker applicants dominating the pool seeking bank credit. Since banks will not want to be left with the lower quality applicants as a consequence of their choice of a higher lending rate, they will respond by refusing or rationing credit. This is a problem of *adverse selection* and provides a second explanation for credit rationing by banks.

The pervasiveness of information problems and the response of banks to them explains why the macroeconomic model includes credit-constrained households. Figure 5.7 provides a visual representation of the causal chain in the bank's decision making process in regard to making loans. It highlights the importance of borrower wealth in both aligning the incentives of banks and borrowers and in signalling to the bank the quality of the project. An unfortunate effect of the problems of moral hazard and adverse selection is that borrowers who do not possess the wealth to provide an equity stake in their project will be denied credit, even if they have a high quality project.

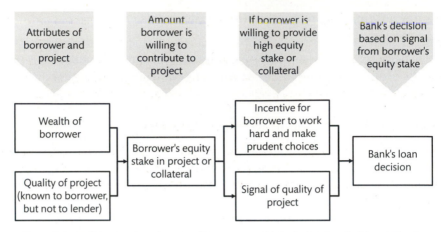

**Figure 5.7** Credit constraints: the role of borrower wealth in the lending decisions of banks.

### Collateral

Collateral plays a key role in the banking system. It refers to the use of an asset as a guarantee for a loan: if the loan is not repaid then the creditor has a claim on the collateral. This is why loans backed by collateral are called secured loans (see the balance sheet in Fig. 5.9)—they are secured because an asset is pledged as collateral in case the borrower defaults on the loan.

For most households, their biggest investment is in a house. As we shall see in more detail below, banks are prepared to lend the large amounts of money needed to buy a house because of (a) collateral and (b) the down payment by the purchaser. The down payment plays the role explained above of ensuring that the borrower has some of their own 'skin in the game'.

Collateral means the loan is secured against the value of the house: if the borrower fails to meet his loan repayments, the bank can repossess the house and sell it. As noted above, this still means the bank bears credit risk on the loan. This was a serious issue for banks in the United States, Spain and Ireland during the global financial crisis, where severe recessions and falling house prices led to many banks taking heavy losses on collateralized real estate loans.

### 5.3.4 The role of banks in a fractional reserve system

Banks fulfill a number of useful functions in the economy. We summarize those roles and then turn to the more problematic issues of liquidity risk and solvency.

1. Maturity transformation. On the bank lending side, savers want access to their savings at short notice, but borrowers want to finance long-term projects including mortgages. Banks assist in this maturity transformation in the economy. However, maturity mismatch creates *liquidity risk* for banks, which we analyse below. Banks hold only a fraction of deposits in liquid form in their reserve accounts at the central bank, which means it is called a *fractional reserve banking system*.

2. Aggregation. Typical savings quantities (e.g. regular savings by households) are much smaller than typical loan requirements (e.g. for lumpy investment projects such as house

purchase or building a new production facility) and banks provide the service of aggregating the small savings and making larger loans.

3.  Risk pooling. Some borrowers will default, which reflects the *credit risk* discussed above. Whereas this might bankrupt individual lenders, larger institutions, such as banks, can withstand a certain proportion of defaulting, and hence offer little or no risk to savers.

### Liquidity risk, lender of last resort and deposit insurance

Liquidity risk is the risk that a bank in a fractional reserve system has inadequate reserves to meet the demand by depositors to withdraw money from their accounts. The decision by banks about their reserve holdings reflects their desire to protect themselves against liquidity risk.

Even well-run banks can suffer from an unexpected shortage of liquidity. A 'banking panic' arises when throughout the banking system, bank deposit holders suddenly demand that banks convert their debt claims into cash to such an extent that banks suspend convertibility of deposits into cash. In a fractional reserve system, a bank will be unable to pay out to everyone if all its depositors try to withdraw their funds at once.

One way of explaining a banking panic is using a 'coordination problem' model: if there is a panic trigger, it can create a self-fulfilling belief that banks will fail. The argument is simple: because the depositor at the front of the queue will certainly get back all his funds, there is an incentive to be the first to withdraw if there is a danger that everyone might withdraw (even if the bank is essentially sound) and produce a *bank run*.

This explains why central banks provide insurance in the form of a back-stop provision of central bank money through the Lender of Last Resort facility (LOLR). The lender of last resort steps in to provide liquidity normally at a penalty interest rate to (otherwise solvent) banks who do not have the cash to meet their short-term liabilities. This was implemented in a big way in 2008 by central banks in many countries, as will be discussed in Chapter 7.

Government guarantee schemes are designed to prevent liquidity problems, both at an individual bank level and at the level of the banking system (e.g. stopping problems at one bank from spreading fear across the banking sector as a whole). Systems of deposit insurance (for which banks pay) mean that bank deposits below a certain level (e.g. $250,000 in the US and £ 85,000 in the UK) will be honoured in full in the event the bank is unable to do so.[7]

The classic scenario involving banking panics is the USA in the early 1930s.[8] During the Great Depression, about 20% of US banks failed. To get a sense of the scale of what occurred, in the 1920s there were about 600 bank failures per year. Then, between 1930 and 1933 there were about 2,000 failures per year. When mergers and liquidations are taken into account,

---

[7] More information on deposit insurance limits and conditions can be found on the websites of the state-backed organizations responsible for deposit insurance; the Federal Deposit Insurance Corporation in the US (http://www.fdic.gov/deposit/deposits/dis/index.html) and the Financial Services Compensation Scheme in the UK (http://www.fscs.org.uk/what-we-cover/eligibility-rules/compensation-limits/).

[8] However, one should not get the idea that this was a problem specific to that time or place. There were many serious banking panics in the UK in the past (e.g. in the 1820s), and there were severe banking panics in Argentina in 2002. There were also other US banking crises in 1819, 1837, 1857, 1873, 1884, 1893, 1907 and in the 1980s, but these were all less severe than that of the early 1930s. We discuss the banking panic in the UK bank Northern Rock in Chapter 7.

of the 25,000 US banks in operation at the peak of business in mid-1929, there were only 15,000 left by mid-1933.[9]

Both liquidity back-stops and deposit guarantee schemes have to be well-designed to tread the fine line between:

1. protecting the public from spillovers and coordination failures arising from 'bad luck' affecting the banking system, which by its nature is very interconnected, and

2. avoiding moral hazard.

The moral hazard problem in this case is that such schemes create incentives for *banks* to avoid taking due care in their loan decisions and more broadly, in their prudential behaviour. They also reduce the incentives for *households* to be prudent. If a household knows their deposits are guaranteed up to a certain amount, they will, for example, be less sceptical of the business model of banks offering very attractive deposit rates. Bad management of banks will escape the attention of depositors.

This subsection has focused on maturity mismatch on the lending side. In addition to this, banks also take on liquidity risk on the funding side. This most commonly occurs when banks borrow short-term in the money market to fund their longer term lending (e.g. mortgages). Problems with maturity mismatch on the funding side arose in the credit crunch in 2008–09 and will be discussed in Chapter 7.

### Solvency and bail-out

Another potential danger for banks is insolvency. A bank is insolvent or bankrupt when the value of its assets (i.e. what it owns) is less than the value of what it owes (its debts or liabilities). At this point, the bank will go out of business if it is not bailed out by the government. Insolvency has immediate and direct negative effects for the bank's depositors, creditors, shareholders and bondholders.

When insolvency threatens a bank that is interconnected through chains of lending and borrowing, the functioning of the money market comes under pressure and the flow of credit freezes up. A solvency problem for a small number of banks can quickly become a widespread liquidity problem in a modern banking system, because no bank can be sure whether it is safe to borrow from another. The spillover effect from the failure of a systemically important bank to the functioning of the banking system and its supply of core banking services lies behind the behaviour of governments in stepping in to save or 'bail out' insolvent banks.

The response of the Japanese central bank to the financial crisis of the 1990s was to avoid banking failures. The approach of the US Federal Reserve in the early 1930s was passive or even encouraging, as witnessed by the famous suggestion that the US banking crisis of the early 1930s was good because it would 'purge the rottenness out of the system'.[10] As we shall see in Chapter 7, in the global financial crisis many banks in a range of different countries

---

[9] The crisis led to the establishment of the Federal Deposit Insurance Corporation (FDIC) in 1934. Between 1934 and 1981 on average there were fewer than 15 bank failures per year.

[10] Andrew Mellon, the US Secretary of the Treasury at the time, urged the market to 'liquidate labour, liquidate stocks, liquidate the farmers and liquidate real estate . . . It will purge the rottenness out of the system.' (Quoted in *The Economist*, 28 Sept.–4 Oct. 2002.)

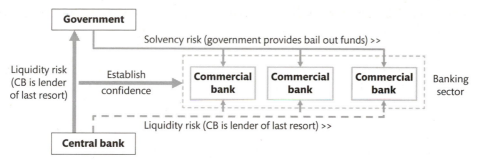

**Figure 5.8** Governance arrangements between the government, the central bank and the banking system.

*Source:* adapted from Winckler (2011).

were bailed out. But a systemically important bank—Lehman Brothers—was allowed to fail with drastic effects on the world economy. Both responses—governments saving banks and governments letting banks fail—carry dangers.

### 5.3.5 Governance arrangements: banks, central bank and government

Figure 5.8 shows the division of responsibility between the government and the central bank when it comes to dealing with liquidity and solvency problems in the banking system.

1. The central bank is the lender of last resort to the banking system and provides liquidity in times of market distress.

2. The government (i.e. the taxpayer) is responsible for the solvency of the banking system. If banks are to be bailed out, this is done by the government ultimately backed up by their tax-raising powers.

3. The central bank is lender of last resort to the government. This is easiest to understand if we take the case where the government steps in to bail out failing banks. This leads to a rise in its debt, which is called *sovereign debt*. When there is a large increase in government debt, private sector holders of government bonds may lose confidence in the government's ability to service their debt and to repay the principal. As a consequence, they sell the bonds. This leads to a drop in the price of the bond and a rise in the interest rate. The higher interest rate signals the market perception of elevated sovereign default risk. It makes government borrowing more costly, further increasing the risk of default. This is the point at which the central bank's role of lender of last resort to the government plays a part. In a country with its own central bank, this is the lender of last resort to the government. It can always step in to buy government bonds should the need arise. This action would support the price of bonds and prevent interest rates from rising to reflect sovereign debt risk.

4. A well-functioning governance system is characterized by mutual confidence between the government and the central bank, which in countries with their own central bank, is ultimately a part of government. From the previous point, we can see that the central bank can always buy government bonds. This is important in circumstances in which the government has to rescue the banking system through bail-outs, leading its own debt to rise. The

confidence that the central bank will support the government in extremis helps to stabilize expectations in the economy. In a closed economy, the central bank can create all the money it wants, subject to the proviso that the private sector is willing to accept payment in the currency it issues. The pathological situation of hyperinflation arises when this ceases to be the case. Under less extreme conditions, the system of mutual confidence helps the economy to cope with the threat of a combined banking and public debt crisis: if the financial markets see the system as credible, a sovereign default risk premium will not arise and interest rates on government bonds will remain low.

The different elements of the governance arrangements came into sharp focus during the global financial crisis and the associated Eurozone crisis. In relation to (1), central banks provided liquidity to the banking system in the early part of the financial crisis when markets were not functioning smoothly. Governments had to step in to rescue banks through recapitalization and nationalization once they became insolvent (2). The consequence was a sharp rise in government (i.e. sovereign) debt.

The risk of sovereign default and its connection to the function of the central bank as the lender of last resort to government (3) was brought into the spotlight by the Eurozone crisis of 2010. In the context of a common currency area, there are multiple governments but only one central bank: the European Central Bank is not the lender of last resort to the Eurozone member governments. When confidence in the ability of some Eurozone governments to service their debts fell, the default risk rose and interest rates on the bonds issued by these governments spiked, in contrast to the situation for countries with similar levels of government debt outside the Eurozone and hence, with their own central bank (4). See Chapter 12 for further analysis of the Eurozone crisis and a diagram similar to Fig. 5.8 depicting the governance arrangements in the Eurozone.

## 5.4 The financial system and balance sheets

To extend the macro model to include banks we need to introduce balance sheets. Balance sheets allow us to keep track of changes in the assets and liabilities of banks and households that take place through lending and borrowing, and through changes in asset prices. They are a neat device for viewing solvency.

Figure 5.9 provides a simplified illustration of the balance sheet of a commercial bank designed to bring out the important elements for economic analysis. The figure records the balance sheet identity of a commercial bank. The identity also holds for all other economic agents, such as the entire banking system, households, the central bank, etc.

The balance sheet identity is

Net worth (equity)
    ≡ Assets − Liabilities
    ≡ what you own or is owed to you − what you owe others outside the bank.

Another way of saying this is that the net worth of an entity is equal to what is owed to the shareholders. This explains why net worth is on the liabilities side of the balance sheet.

| Assets | % of balance sheet | Liabilities | % of balance sheet |
|---|---|---|---|
| 1. Cash and reserve balances at the central bank | 2 | 1. Deposits | 50 |
| 2. Government bonds, which can be used as collateral for repo borrowing | 10 | 2. Wholesale repo borrowing secured with collateral | 30 |
| 3. Asset-backed securities, which can be used as collateral for repo borrowing | 20 | 3. Unsecured borrowing | 16 |
| 4. Wholesale reverse repo lending | 11 | | |
| 5. Loans (e.g. mortgages) | 55 | | |
| 6. Fixed assets (e.g. buildings, equipment) | 2 | | |
| Total Assets | 100 | Total liabilities | 96 |
| | | **Net worth** | |
| | | Equity | 4 |

| Memorandum item: Leverage (Total Assets/Net worth) | 100/4 = 25 |
|---|---|

**Figure 5.9** The balance sheet of a typical commercial bank before the financial crisis.

Of course, if the value of your assets is less than the value of what you owe others, then your net worth is negative. In the case of a bank, because of the maturity mismatch between its liabilities and its assets, it could become insolvent if either the assets drop in value, or there is a run on liabilities, which forces asset sales at discounted prices; so-called 'fire sales'.

The balance sheet identity can be reorganized as follows:

Assets ≡ Liabilities + Net worth (equity).

The second way of writing the identity highlights the funding of the bank: it funds its assets through a combination of debt (liabilities) and equity (net worth).

On the asset side of the simplified bank balance sheet in Fig. 5.9 are six main items, which are things owned by or owed to the bank:

1. *Cash and reserves at the central bank*: These are the bank's highly liquid assets. Cash and central bank reserves provide the liquidity the bank needs to operate. Although central banks now typically pay the policy rate of interest on bank reserves, these do not earn as much as bonds or loans, so a bank will not want to hold higher reserves than it considers prudent to meet its liquidity needs.

2. *Government bonds*: Banks hold these assets as they are interest-earning and relatively safe. Note that the price of bonds varies inversely with the interest rate so they are not 'capital-safe'—although this risk is small for very short-dated bonds. Government bonds in advanced economies are normally considered to be free of sovereign default risk. Because they are low risk, they can be used as high-quality collateral when the bank borrows from the money market. As noted above, loans backed by collateral are called secured loans.

3. *Asset-backed securities (ABS):* Privately issued securities that are backed by a bundle of loans, such as car or credit card loans. The interest paid depends on the riskiness of the loans underpinning the security. These securities can also be backed by mortgages

(i.e. MBS). High-quality ABS or MBS (i.e. those given a high rating by credit ratings agencies) can be used as collateral for money market borrowing.

4. *Wholesale reverse repo lending*: This makes more sense to explain in the context of the related item on the liabilities side, wholesale repo borrowing. See item 2 in the following text.

5. *Loans:* This is the largest item on the balance sheet and includes all loans made by the bank, such as mortgages and car loans. This is the bank's core activity and is why the banking system is so crucial to the functioning of the economy.

6. *Fixed assets:* The physical assets of the bank, such as its buildings and equipment.

To the right of the assets column, we have indicated the approximate proportions of the different assets in a typical bank balance sheet in the pre-crisis period (or 'normal times'). The bank holds very low amounts of cash and reserves. Government bonds make up about 10% of its balance sheet and about the same proportion is wholesale loans. The bank holds 20% of its assets in asset-backed securites, as they typically offer a higher rate of return than government bonds or money market lending. By far the largest part of the bank's balance sheet is made up of loans to households and firms: this is the bank's core business. It makes profits by lending at a higher interest rate than the cost of its funds.

Turning to the liability side there are three main items:

1. *Deposits:* The largest item on the liabilities side are deposits by households and firms. In our example, they comprise over half of the bank's liabilities.

2. *Wholesale repo borrowing secured with collateral*: The term 'repo' is unfamiliar to most people. It is shorthand for sale and repurchase agreement and is a very common form of short-term secured borrowing by banks. This is the way banks fund their everyday activities—they borrow from the money market by selling assets to another bank (the lending bank) and promising to buy them back in a few weeks or months. The repurchase price is always higher than the sale price, providing interest for the lending bank. The loans are secured (or collateralized), which means that if the bank selling the assets is not able to buy them back, then the lender will keep the assets. High-quality assets are typically required for repo transactions, such as government bonds or highly-rated privately issued securities (e.g. ABS or MBS).[11] Item 4 on the asset side shows the reverse repos held by the bank. These are loans made by the bank in the money market. Large banks typically engage in both lending and borrowing in the repo market. This function is sometimes referred to as the *market maker* function. The important point is that large volumes of short-term borrowing and lending take place among banks.

3. *Unsecured borrowing*: Banks may sell bonds as a way of raising funds. Unlike repo borrowing, this is not normally secured with collateral. This means that the bank bond holders would not be repaid if the bank were to become insolvent, which we explain next. Banks can also borrow unsecured in the money market (interbank market).

---

[11] In the financial crisis, the quality of the so-called private label securities (ABS and MBS) was called into question when their price fell sharply. This was an important factor in the credit crunch of 2009, which is explained in Chapter 7.

Below the solid line in the right hand side of the balance sheet is the *bank's net worth*. This is also referred to as the bank's equity; what it is worth once its liabilities are subtracted from its assets. A bank is *insolvent* (bankrupt) if the value of its liabilities exceeds the value of its assets; its net worth is negative.

An important characteristic of a bank is its *leverage*: this is the ratio of its assets to its equity. In the example shown in Fig. 5.9, the bank has a leverage ratio of $100/4 = 25$. As we shall see in Chapters 6 and 7, leverage played a central role in the build-up to the financial crisis of 2008.

Figure 5.10 shows the balance sheet of the British bank Barclays just before the financial crisis. It is more complicated than the simple balance sheet in Fig. 5.9, because Barclays combines the activities of a retail bank and an investment bank.

On the asset side of the Barclays balance sheet we can see entries for cash and reserves, loans, reverse repos, and fixed assets (e.g. buildings, equipment) just as in Fig. 5.9. The remaining assets in Fig. 5.10 (which do not appear in our simple model and are shown in italics) relate to Barclays' investment banking activities. Barclays' holdings of government bonds are contained within the trading portfolio assets and other assets categories. On the liabilities side of the Barclays balance sheet, we can see entries for deposits, repos and unsecured lending, exactly as in Fig. 5.9. The other items on the liabilities side of Barclays' balance sheet (in italics) refer to items that mainly relate to investment banking. Lastly, Barclays' equity was around $27.4bn in 2006 and their leverage ratio, calculated as the value of assets divided by equity, was 36.4.

### Banks, the central bank and the money market

As discusssed in relation to Fig. 5.8, the central bank is ultimately a branch of the government, even in the age of independent central banking. This means that the assets and liabilities of the central bank always balance and the central bank has no net worth. It is not necessary to

| Assets | | Liabilities | |
|---|---|---|---|
| 1. Cash and reserve balances at the central bank | 7,345 | 1. Deposits | 336,316 |
| 2. Wholesale reverse repo lending | 174,090 | 2. Wholesale repo borrowing secured with collateral | 136,956 |
| 3. Loans (e.g. mortgages) | 313,226 | 3. Unsecured borrowing | 111,137 |
| 4. Fixed assets (e .g. buildings, equipment) | 2,492 | 4. *Trading portfolio liabilities* | 71,874 |
| 5. *Trading portfolio assets* | 177,867 | 5. *Derivative financial instruments* | 140,697 |
| 6. *Derivative financial instruments* | 138,353 | 6. *Other liabilities* | 172,417 |
| 7. *Other assets* | 183,414 | | |
| Total Assets | 996,787 | Total liabilities | 969,397 |
| | | **Net worth** | |
| | | Equity | 27,390 |

| Memorandum item: Leverage (Total Assets/Net Worth) | $996,787/27,390 = 36.4$ |
|---|---|

**Figure 5.10** The consolidated balance sheet of Barclays PLC in 2006, £m.

*Source:* Barclays PLC Annual Report 2006.

discuss the central bank balance sheet in detail in order to understand its interactions with the commercial banks and the role it plays in macroeconomic stabilization. In light of this, we choose to focus only on those balance sheet entries that are at the heart of our modelling framework.

The key entry on the asset side of the central banks balance sheet is *reverse repos*. This is where the central bank's lending to the commercial banks through the repo system is recorded. The central bank charges the policy rate on these loans and requires high quality collateral to back up these transactions. It is these loans that set the interest rate floor on all other loans in the economy, which are set as a mark-up on the rate at which commercial banks can borrow from the central bank (that is, the policy rate).

The key entry on the liabilities side of the central bank balance sheet is *reserve balances*, which record the reserve accounts of the commercial banks at the central bank. Parallel to the way households can withdraw money from their current accounts in a commercial bank, banks can withdraw money from their reserve account at the central bank to settle claims. These accounts can be interest-bearing (sometimes only above a minimum reserve requirement), in which case they will yield the policy rate of interest.

Before we move to show how the private sector, banks and the central bank interact by working through an example, it is important to stress that when the banking system is operating normally, large volumes of transactions take place between banks in the money market. These transactions depend on the confidence that the counterparty bank is solvent. In Chapter 7 we see how these operations are disrupted when such confidence collapses.

## 5.5 Banks and macro stabilization

A good way of understanding the extended 3-equation model incorporating the banking system is to work through an example. The example focuses on a macroeconomic shock—an investment boom that shifts the *IS* curve. We have looked at this type of shock before; it is another example of the positive aggregate demand shock discussed in Chapter 3. In this chapter, however, we lift the curtain on the part played by the financial system. We look at how the new investment is financed through the banking system, the role played by the new deposits generated by the higher household incomes due to the expansion of output and how the central bank responds to the macroeconomic shock.

The key elements in the causal story from the investment boom to the return of the economy to equilibrium are as follows:

1. Banks make new loans to households and firms and as a consequence, need to replenish their reserves at the central bank.

2. The higher incomes generated by the investment boom lead households to increase their deposits and their purchases of bonds.

3. Because of the purchase of bonds, the increase in deposits is insufficient to fund the new loans to firms and households. Banks therefore borrow from the money market, which allows them to replenish their reserves and to fund their lending.

4. However, since the central bank wishes to bring inflation back to target following the investment boom, it raises the policy rate so as to get the economy onto the *MR* curve.

5. The higher policy rate raises the cost of funding to banks and, in line with the central bank's intentions, the banks pass this on in a higher lending rate, which reduces desired spending. Interest-sensitive spending falls and the economy begins the process of adjustment back to equilibrium output and target inflation.

### 5.5.1  Example: an investment boom shifts the *IS* curve

In this example, the economy is initially at the constant inflation equilibrium. We assume that the equilibrium is disturbed by an improvement in business sentiment, which boosts investment and shifts the *IS* curve to the right. In this example, we assume that firms borrow from the banking system to finance *all* of the extra investment.

At this point, it is important to reiterate that we are presenting a simplified model of the financial system in this section and not a description of the real world. The model displays the key elements of the financial system's role in macro stabilization without adding all the layers of complexity that exist in the global financial system. We clearly state the simplifying assumptions we are making as we work through the example.

*How is new investment financed? Where does the money come from?*

In response to the change in sentiment, firms wish to undertake new investment projects. We make the assumption that firms have to borrow from a bank to implement their plans and we shall see that the banking system has to raise funds to finance the new investment.

Figure 5.11 shows how the banking system facilitates the transformation of new savings into new investment.

In more detail, when output and income go up as a result of the higher investment spending, savings also go up. On the assumptions we have made, households must decide how to allocate their new savings between (a) deposits in the banking system, (b) the purchase of financial assets (i.e. government bonds in the money market) and (c) shares in banks

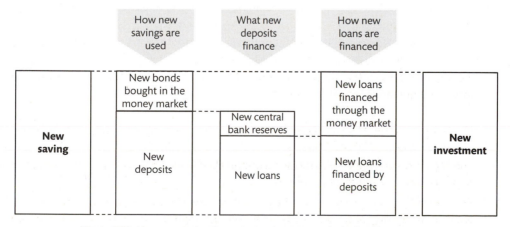

**Figure 5.11** How new saving finances new investment via the banking system.

(i.e. bank equity). For simplicity, we abstract from the possibility that savers buy shares in firms. As discussed earlier in the chapter, savers choose between these three different ways of holding their new savings—each has its own advantages and they can be placed on a risk–return spectrum.

1. Deposits are the safest way of holding financial assets, but do not earn interest.[12] They are safe in nominal terms and accessible because they can be withdrawn without notice. They are therefore ideal for transactions purposes. The amount of deposits households and firms want to hold depends positively on income and inversely on the interest rate.

2. Government bonds can be bought by savers in the money market. They pay an interest rate. However, bonds can gain or lose value. When the interest rate goes up, the price of bonds falls and the holder makes a capital loss. This does not happen with deposits. Bonds cannot be used as a means of payment and although we assume there is no default risk on government bonds, they are less liquid and more risky than deposits.

3. Finally, bank shares are the riskiest of the three assets. They offer the possibility of dividends and of an increase in the value of the shares. Bank shares are the least liquid of the three assets.

For the remainder of this example, we assume that the amount of bank shares that the private sector wishes to hold remains constant each period. This means that we also assume that new savings that arise as a result of higher incomes are distributed solely between deposits and government bonds bought in the money market and are not used to buy additional bank shares.

### How will the central bank respond to the investment boom?

Figure 5.12 shows the flows of funds that are triggered by the investment boom. The figure shows how the economic agents in the macro-economy interact and the determinants of the key variables that feed in to the central bank's response to the boom. Working around the figure clockwise beginning with the private sector on the left hand side, as we have seen in previous chapters, it is the private sector that determines equilibrium output, $y_e$. Output, $y_t$, reflects aggregate demand and in the example, the boom shifts the $IS$ curve to the right and boosts $y_t$.

The lending rate, $r$, is determined by the banking system. As we have seen in Section 5.3.2, because loans made by banks are risky, the lending rate is above the policy rate, which is the safe interest rate at which the banking system can borrow from the money market. Given the mark-up of the lending rate over the policy rate, the inflation-targeting central bank fixes the policy rate $r^P$ to achieve its desired output gap, so as to achieve its inflation target.

Returning to our example, we shall see that:

1. since new deposits in banks will not be enough to fully fund the new lending, banks will borrow the balance from the money market; and

[12] In reality there are a huge variety of bank accounts, some of which allow instant access and pay interest. We simplify by assuming bank deposits pay no interest, but this simplification does not change the conclusions of the model.

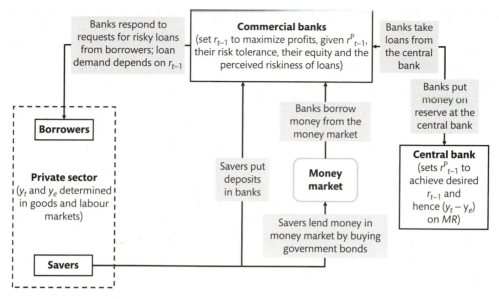

**Figure 5.12** The flows of funds in the economy as the result of a boom in investment.

2. the total amount that is lent for the new investment will be equal to the amount of additional savings.

Referring to Fig. 5.11, point 1 follows from the fact that only part of the additional savings are put on deposit, with the remainder used to buy bonds. After making the new loans, the banks will have to replenish their reserves at the central bank. The banks therefore borrow the balance of new savings from the money market. The logic of how the equilibrium between new savings and new investment arises is shown in Fig. 5.11.

Point 2 follows because in our simplified set-up we assume that all of the new investment is funded by borrowing from the banking system. In practice, firms can fund investment by using retained profits, by issuing bonds of their own (corporate bonds) or issuing new equity. Since we want to understand the role of banks, we concentrate here exclusively on the commercial banks as the source of funding. In goods market equilibrium, savings are equal to investment, so new investment will be funded by borrowing, which will be equal to total new savings.

The central bank figures out that firms will borrow and invest and that output will go up. The central bank will not be content with the expansion of output associated with the investment boom. It will be concerned with the higher inflation caused by the rise in output and fall in unemployment. It will seek to get inflation back to the target rate.

The central bank will announce a new higher policy rate. The higher policy interest rate in the money market increases the cost to the banks of borrowing funds. They will therefore increase their lending rate according to the mark-up equation. In turn, the higher lending rate will choke off the demand for loans from the private sector because even with the buoyant sentiment, some investment projects that were expected to be profitable at the original lending rate will no longer be profitable at the higher rate.

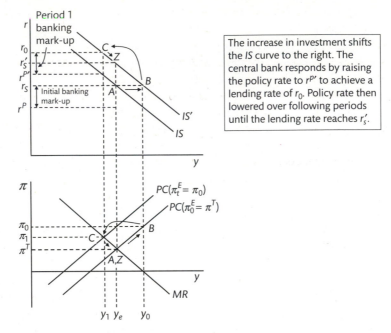

The increase in investment shifts the *IS* curve to the right. The central bank responds by raising the policy rate to $r^{P'}$ to achieve a lending rate of $r_0$. Policy rate then lowered over following periods until the lending rate reaches $r_s'$.

**Figure 5.13** An investment boom in the 3-equation model with the banking system.

In terms of the model, the central bank uses its control over the *policy interest rate* to affect the *funding costs of banks*, inducing them to raise their *lending rate* so as to dampen investment plans and get the economy on to the *MR* curve to the left of equilibrium output. In each subsequent period, the central bank adjusts its policy rate and the economy gradually returns to the inflation target.

Figure 5.13 uses the 3-equation model to trace the impact of the investment boom on the economy. The adjustment of the economy is similar to the case of a positive aggregate demand shock in Chapter 3. The only difference is that in Chapter 3 we made the simplification that the central bank directly set the lending rate, whereas in this chapter the central bank sets the policy rate to achieve their desired lending rate (taking into account the banking mark-up). We can see that the initial reaction of the central bank to the investment boom is to raise $r^P$ to $r^{P'}$ so as to achieve their desired lending rate of $r_0$—the period one mark-up is shown on the figure. The increase in the lending rate dampens aggregate demand and pushes down inflation. The central bank then gradually reduces the policy rate over the following periods until the lending rate reaches its new stabilizing rate at $r_s'$.

## 5.6 Conclusions

In this chapter, we have provided a simple way of representing a modern financial system, which highlights its essential role in the macro-economy. The financial system facilitates economic transactions, allows households and firms to implement their planned spending decisions and is the transmission mechanism for inflation-targeting monetary policy.

We have also introduced the concept of a balance sheet, which documents what an economic agent owes against what it is owed and shows their net worth. This is a useful framework for discussing the two major problems in the banking sector; liquidity and solvency. In a modern banking system, these problems are the joint responsibility of the central bank and the government (i.e. taxpayers).

The main focus of the chapter has been to extend the core 3-equation model set out in Chapter 3 to include the banking system. We have added more flesh to the bones of monetary policy transmission by making the distinction between the *policy rate of interest* (the rate set by the central bank) and the *lending rate of interest* (the rate that influences the spending and investment decisions of households and firms). The lending rate is determined by the profit-maximizing decisions of banks and is set as a mark-up on the policy rate of interest.

The 3-equation model including the banking system provides a framework in which we can answer interesting questions about the role of the banking system and money in the macro-economy, such as:

1. What factors affect the banking mark-up? There are three key factors that influence the mark-up of the lending rate ($r$) over the policy rate ($r^P$) in the model. The mark-up will increase as banks' loans are perceived to be riskier, and will fall the more risk tolerant are the banks and the larger the capital cushion they have with which to absorb losses.

2. Does an inflation-targeting central bank manage the money supply? The central bank does not actively manage the money supply. The amount of money in the economy is determined by the demand for money at the policy rate set by the central bank. The demand for money can change for a number of reasons other than alterations in interest rates, such as changes in the structure of the financial system or in households' confidence in financial markets. In the modern monetary framework, a change in the demand for money will alter the money supply, but will not alter real economic activity unless the central bank chooses to change the policy rate. This is why modern monetary policy is defined as *interest rate policy*.

3. How does the central bank react to economic shocks? The central bank reacts in exactly the same way as it does in the core 3-equation model, by adjusting the interest rate to stabilize the economy at equilibrium output and target inflation. The mechanism through which this takes place is more thoroughly explained once we include the banking system. The central bank sets the policy interest rate. The lending rate is then determined as a mark-up on the policy rate. Following an economic shock, the central bank must use the *MR* curve to determine its desired output gap, then set the policy rate that will deliver that output gap next period (taking into account the banking mark-up). Unlike the simple 3-equation model, the extended model can address the question of the implications for the economy of shocks to the banking system itself.

This chapter has provided a theoretical framework for thinking about the interaction between the banking system and the macro-economy. The next chapter will move away from the case where the system functions smoothly to analyse the darker side of financial markets: financial cycles and banking crises.

## 5.7 Appendix

### 5.7.1 Modelling the banking mark-up ($r$–$r^P$)

This appendix formally sets out a simple model of the banking mark-up. We assume a competitive banking system throughout for simplicity. The main conclusions of the model would be unchanged if we moved to a monopolistic banking system. The only substantial difference between the two models is the assumptions around pricing. Banks are 'price takers' in the competitive case—they take the lending rate as given and maximize profits based on the amount of loans they provide. In contrast, the monopoly bank is a 'price setter'—it chooses the lending rate in order to maximize its profits.

In reality, banking systems are usually more oligopolistic, an intermediate case between monopolistic and competitive. For example, the UK banking system has a handful of firms that dominate the market. The important point to note is that for all types of market structure, the factors influencing the banking mark-up are the same and work in the same direction. The market structure simply affects the size of the mark-up. When banks have market power they are able to charge a higher lending rate, holding everything else constant.

### The supply of loans by banks

The first step in setting out the banking model is to define the key variables: $r$ = the lending rate, $r^P$ = the policy rate, $L$ = the amount of bank loans, $D$ = customer deposits at the bank, $e$ = bank equity, $\tau$ = bank risk tolerance, $v$ = the uncertain part of the bank's return on loans and $\text{var}(v)$ = the riskiness of loans = the variance of the uncertain part of the return on loans.

A competitive bank is a 'price taker', so will choose the amount of loans it provides in order to maximize its profits. The lending rate is decided by the interaction of the supply and demand for loans. We can derive the supply of loans by solving the bank's maximization problem. The bank's profit function is:

$$V_B = \underbrace{\frac{rL - r^P(L - D - e)}{e}}_{\text{expected return}} - \underbrace{\frac{1}{2\tau}\text{var}(v)\left(\frac{L}{e}\right)^2}_{\text{total risk}}. \qquad \text{(bank profit function)}$$

The top line of the expected return function shows the return that the bank makes on their loans ($rL$) minus their total funding costs ($r^P(L - D - e)$). The funding costs reflect the fact that the bank has to borrow from the money market at a rate of $r^P$ to finance the loans not financed by deposits or equity. The total risk of the bank includes a measure of the riskiness of loans ($\text{var}(v)$) and a measure of the banks leverage ($\left(\frac{L}{e}\right)^2$). The negative impact of total risk on the bank's profits then reduces the more risk tolerant (i.e. ↑ $\tau$) the bank is. The specific functional form of the negative part of the profit function was chosen for computational ease.

To find the supply of bank loans, we simply need to differentiate the profit function with respect to $L$, then set it equal to zero and rearrange for optimal $L$:

$$\frac{\partial V_B}{\partial L} = \frac{r - r^P}{e} - \tau^{-1}\text{var}(v)\frac{L}{e^2} = 0$$

$$r - r^P = \tau^{-1}\text{var}(v)\frac{L}{e}$$

$$\rightarrow L^S = \left(\frac{e\tau}{\text{var}(v)}\right)(r - r^P). \qquad \text{(the optimal supply of bank loans)}$$

The optimal supply of banks loans increases with the banking mark-up, the equity of the bank and its risk tolerance, and falls with the riskiness of loans. We can also rewrite this equation to give the bank's desired leverage:

$$\lambda^S = \frac{L^S}{e} = \left(\frac{\tau}{\text{var}(v)}\right)(r - r^P). \qquad \text{(optimal bank leverage)}$$

### The demand for loans by households

The next stage in the model of the banking mark-up is to set out an equation for the demand for loans. Recall this form of the *IS* curve introduced in Chapter 3:

$$y = A - ar. \qquad \text{(IS curve)}$$

In using this equation here, we radically simplify by assuming that $A$ is the non-interest sensitive demand for loans. We can see from the *IS* equation that aggregate demand depends inversely on the lending rate. We can therefore write the aggregate demand for loans as:

$$L^D = \bar{L} - ar. \qquad \text{(demand for loans by households)}$$

We can break this equation down further by splitting the autonomous loan demand, $\bar{L}$, into demand from credit constrained households ($A_C$) and from unconstrained households ($A_U$), such that,

$$\bar{L} = A_C + A_U = A$$
$$\rightarrow L^D = A_C + A_U - ar.$$

(demand for loans by credit constrained and unconstrained households)

The credit constrained households are able to borrow $A_C \leq lW$, where $W$ is a measure of their wealth and $l$ is the fraction of wealth that banks are willing to lend to households. These households are credit constrained if they wish to borrow $A_C > lW$. The unconstrained households demand $A_U - ar$ of loans; their demand for loans falls as the interest rate rises. This is in contrast to the credit constrained households who are completely insensitive to changes in the lending rate.

### Equilibrium in the loan market

We now have all the components to derive the lending rate. It is simply determined by equating supply and demand in the loan market:

$$L^S = L^D$$
$$\rightarrow \left(\frac{e\tau}{\text{var}(v)}\right)(r - r^P) = \bar{L} - ar. \qquad \text{(equilibrium in the loan market)}$$

To simplify the equilibrium equation we define $\omega \equiv \frac{var(v)}{e\tau}$. We now rearrange to find the equilibrium lending rate:

$$\left(\frac{e\tau}{var(v)}\right)(r - r^P) = \bar{L} - ar$$

$$\frac{1}{\omega}(r - r^P) = \bar{L} - ar$$

$$r(1 + a\omega) = r^P + \omega\bar{L}$$

$$r = \frac{r^P + \omega\bar{L}}{1 + a\omega}. \qquad\qquad \text{(equilibrium lending rate)}$$

We can see that, holding the policy rate constant, the banking mark-up increases when:

1. the demand for loans, $\bar{L}$, increases;
2. the riskiness of loans, $var(v)$, increases;
3. the risk tolerance of banks, $\tau$, falls;
4. equity, $e$, falls.[13]

We can also rewrite the equilibrium lending rate to show the impact of credit constraints on the mark-up. We know that $\bar{L} = A_C + A_U$ and that $A_C$ is a positive function of the wealth of credit constrained households. If we assume that credit constrained households borrow up to their maximum (i.e. $A_C = lW$), then the equilibrium lending rate becomes

$$r = \frac{r^P + \omega(A_C + A_U)}{1 + a\omega}$$

$$r = \frac{r^P + \omega(lW + A_U)}{1 + a\omega}.$$

(equilibrium lending rate for credit constrained and unconstrained households)

This equation shows that the higher the wealth of credit constrained households, the higher the banking mark-up.

## Central bank's choice of $r^P$ in equilibrium

In equilibrium, the central bank will set $r^P$ such that the lending rate is at the stabilizing rate of interest, $r_S$. This is the lending rate at which output is at equilibrium, $y_e$. We can substitute $r_S$ into the lending rate equation and $y_e$ into the demand for loans equation and rearrange

---

[13] We can take the composite risk term, $\omega$, and show that unless $r$ is so high that $L^D$ is negative, the three final results hold. They follow from:

$$r = \frac{r^P + \omega\bar{L}}{1 + a\omega}.$$

$$\frac{\partial r}{\partial \omega} = \frac{\bar{L}}{1 + a\omega} - \frac{r^P + \omega\bar{L}}{(1 + a\omega)^2}a.$$

$$\frac{\partial r}{\partial \omega} > 0 \rightarrow \frac{1}{1 + a\omega}\left(\bar{L} - a\left(\frac{r^P + \omega\bar{L}}{1 + a\omega}\right)\right) > 0$$

$$\rightarrow \bar{L} - ar > 0.$$

to find an equation for the policy rate:

$$r_S = \frac{r^P + \omega \bar{L}}{1 + a\omega}.$$

$$r^P = r_S(1 + a\omega) - \omega \bar{L}$$

$$L = \bar{L} - ar_S$$

$$r^P = r_S - \omega(\bar{L} - ar_S)$$

$$r^P = r_S - \omega y_e. \qquad \text{(the policy rate in equilibrium)}$$

The equation shows that the central bank first needs to know the lending rate that will stabilize output at equilibrium. The next step is to take account of all the factors that influence the mark-up. Lastly, they subtract the mark-up from the stabilizing lending rate to find the equilibrium policy rate.

# 5.8 Questions

## 5.8.1 Checklist questions

1. Why do saver households not lend directly to borrower households? How can banks help solve this problem?

2. What happens to the money supply and to aggregate demand when confidence in financial markets is boosted? Assume the policy interest rate stays the same throughout. Illustrate your answer using a 3-equation model diagram (as in Fig. 5.5).

3. Why are loans to households and firms considered risky? Make sure you refer to and explain the following terms in your answer:

    a. Uncertainty.

    b. Moral hazard.

    c. Asymmetric information.

4. Are the following two statements both true or is only one of them true? Justify your answer.

    S1. The bank lending rate will increase the riskier loans are perceived to be.

    S2. Given S1, the more risk that banks can tolerate, the higher the bank lending rate will be.

5. The following four borrowers are categorized according to their level of wealth and the quality of their proposed investment project. Which of the borrowers will receive a loan from the bank for their project and why?

    a. Low wealth, low quality project.

    b. Low wealth, high quality project.

    c. High wealth, low quality project.

    d. High wealth, high quality project.

6. Is deposit insurance always a 'good thing'?

7. Set out a simple balance sheet for a single commercial bank (as in Fig. 5.9). Define each item in turn and discuss why that item has been labelled as an asset or a liability. Why is net worth on the liabilities side of the balance sheet?

8. What are the channels through which banks can fund their lending? In the model presented in this chapter, can banks influence the level of aggregate demand in the economy?

9. What are the key differences between the way that monetary policy is conducted in the 3-equation model (from Chapter 3) and in the 3-equation model with the banking system? Does this change the policy implemented by the central bank following economic shocks?

10. Use the 3-equation model to show the impact of a reduction in consumer confidence on the economy. Make sure you show the period 1 mark-up on your diagram and discuss what happens to both the policy rate and the lending rate (as in Fig. 5.13). How would you expect a reduction in competition in the banking sector due to mergers between banks to affect the macro-economy?

## 5.8.2 Problems and questions for discussion

1. Collect the annual report of a US commercial bank from 2006. Find the consolidated balance sheet and condense it into a form similar to the Barclays' balance sheet shown in Fig. 5.10. Answer the following questions:

    a. What proportion of customer deposits does the bank hold with the central bank as reserves?

    b. How much of the bank's loans are funded through customer deposits?

    c. What is the bank's leverage?

2. Use central bank websites to collect data on monthly policy rates and mortgage rates in two developed economies between 2000 and 2012. Plot the data on graphs, as per Fig. 5.4. Answer the following:

    a. How do the banking mark-ups compare in the two countries?

    b. Do the banking mark-ups change over time?

    c. Use the chapter and the Appendix to discuss possible reasons for any differences observed over time and between countries.

3. In the wake of the global financial crisis, there has been a lot of discussion about whether banking is 'socially useful'. Use the simple model of the macro-economy and the financial system to explain the benefits to the economy of the banking system and its role in stabilization policy. What factors are not considered in the basic model which could lead to the banking system destabilizing the economy? Could these activities be considered socially useful?

4. The UK government introduced lending targets for the five major UK banks after the global financial crisis. Use the simple model of the macro-economy and the financial system to discuss this policy. Make sure you refer to:

    a. Whether you think the policy makes economic sense.

    b. Are there any potential pitfalls with the policy?

    c. How could it affect stabilization policy?

# 6 The financial sector and crises

## 6.1 Introduction

The central role of banks in the macroeconomy arises because they provide credit to households and small and medium sized firms. The financial system is like the beating heart of the economy; a systemic banking crisis is akin to a cardiac arrest and puts the economy as a whole in serious danger. Up to this point, we have assumed that the financial system functions smoothly and that households and firms can optimize their spending decisions by using the credit facilities and payment services provided by banks. In this chapter we reassess this assumption and lift the lid on the potentially destabilizing features of the financial system, such as the financial accelerator and asset price bubbles, which can amplify and propagate shocks through the economy.

We introduce the concept of a financial cycle to provide a framework for better understanding the relationship between key financial variables, such as house prices and private credit, and the macro-economy. Figure 6.1 illustrates the upswing and downswing of a financial cycle centred on borrowing by households from banks to finance housing. In the upswing phase, there is a house price boom. This increases the market value of houses, which means households can borrow more from banks based on the increased value of their housing collateral. This step is shown in the top box, which says 'Household borrowing increases'. The extra borrowing by households, which is based on the higher house prices, in turn allows households to buy more housing, which feeds back into higher house prices and the upswing of the financial cycle continues. For example, when house prices rise, a family can sell their house and use the capital gain they have made to borrow more and fund the purchase of a yet higher priced house.

The upswing does not continue forever. At a certain point, house prices begin to fall. The right hand side of Fig. 6.1 shows the downswing of the cycle. Lower house prices reduce the collateral of households, forcing them to reduce their indebtedness. As a result of lower borrowing, the demand for housing falls and this triggers a further round of falling house prices.

If the downswing of a housing based financial cycle illustrated in Fig. 6.1 is severe enough, it can turn into a banking crisis. Some households become insolvent (or 'under water') because the value of their house falls below the value of the mortgage they owe on it. The knock-on effect is that the banks that have extended the mortgage do not get repaid. The banks are

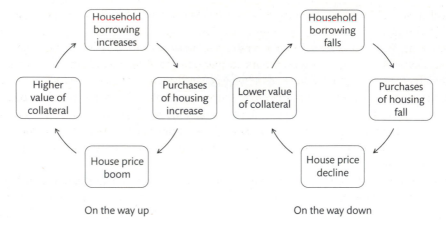

**Figure 6.1** Upswing and downswing of the house-price cycle.

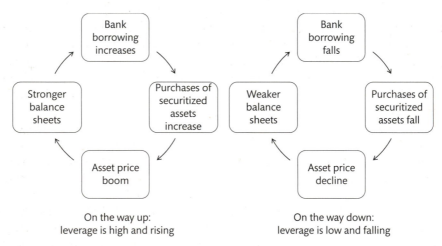

**Figure 6.2** The upswing and the downswing of the bank-based financial cycle.

*Source:* adapted from Shin (2009a).

then unable to service their own borrowing. Once the value of a bank's assets falls below the value of its liabilities, it is insolvent. The insolvency of a bank can quickly turn into a full blown banking crisis if the government does not step in to prevent the fear of the collapse of core banking services from spreading.

A banking crisis based on a house price boom and bust—but without the role of new financial instruments, to which we turn next—is sometimes called a 'plain vanilla' banking crisis. In the recent global financial crisis, the banking crises in Ireland and Spain were of the plain vanilla variety.

Figure 6.2 looks very similar to Fig. 6.1 and introduces a different driving force, which was important in the global financial crisis of 2008–09, especially in the USA. In this case, the focus of attention is not on the borrowing by households to finance the purchase of houses but on the *borrowing by banks to buy financial assets*. The financial assets in question are called *securitized assets* and include assets based on mortgages. The name for this class of risky assets is asset-backed securities (ABS). The cycle begins with a rise in the price of these assets. This strengthens the balance sheet of banks through a process called mark-to-market accounting. A bank that uses mark-to-market accounting records the price of assets on their balance sheet at their current market value and not at the value they were bought at. This means that when asset prices increase, the bank's assets rise in value and their balance sheet strengthens. As a consequence—and parallel to the role played by collateral in allowing households to borrow more when the price of their house goes up—banks borrow more. The additional assets they buy increase the size of their balance sheet and push the asset price up further.

The downswing of the financial cycle for banks has the same form as the house price one for households. When the price of asset-backed securities falls, the balance sheets of banks weaken and they have to reduce their indebtedness. Their demand for the securitized assets falls and the downswing continues. A banking crisis occurs when the fall in the value of bank assets is sufficient to wipe out their equity: with debts (or liabilities) in excess of the value of their assets, their net worth is negative and the bank is insolvent.

The collapse of a house price cycle brings misery to families as houses are repossessed. A banking crisis—either of the plain vanilla kind or of the kind illustrated in Fig. 6.2 based on increased risk-taking by banks—can bring down the financial system as a whole and threaten the livelihoods of people throughout the economy. The danger of spillover from a banking crisis makes the banking industry special and poses particular problems for the design of economic policy.

Upswings and downswings of house prices and financial cycles typically last longer than the familiar business cycle. The financial variables related to these longer run fluctuations like house prices and bank credit were not targeted by central bankers and we will show the way in which potentially dangerous upswings can develop alongside successful inflation targeting.

Recessions that stem from financial crises are especially severe. They are also typically followed by weak recoveries as households and firms pay off debt accumulated during the boom years. It should therefore be a priority for policy makers to formulate policy such that it safeguards the economy from financial crises. The first step in this process is to understand the economic mechanisms that lie behind the upswings and downswings of the financial cycles illustrated in Figures 6.1 and 6.2. That is the aim of this chapter. In Chapter 13, we return to the design of a safer financial system.

## 6.2 Bank behaviour, cycles and crises

### 6.2.1 Bank behaviour and the macro-economy

*Banks and the IS curve*

The economy relies on the continuous functioning of core banking services. The standard modelling in macroeconomics of the *IS* curve focuses on the spending decisions of households and firms. When we work with the *IS* curve, we assume households and firms can implement their spending plans by borrowing from the banking system. The assumption that the financial system functions smoothly and can therefore be ignored in macroeconomic modelling is brought into question by experience of financial crises, and most recently, by the global financial crisis.

*Banks are a special case for policy makers*

The special treatment of the banking industry by policy makers arises for two reasons. The first is that the economy depends on the continuous provision of core banking services (which includes running the payments system). The second is that problems in one bank spill over to fears about the functioning of the system as a whole. This is referred to as contagion. The dramatic and largely unanticipated effects of the collapse of Lehman Brothers in 2008—an investment bank with no depositors—described in Chapter 7 highlight this. Lehman Brothers was allowed to fail and there were catastrophic effects across the world. The consequences of the bankruptcy of what turned out to be a systemically important bank highlights why the exit of a failing bank is difficult for governments to allow.

As explained in Chapter 5 and summarized in Fig. 5.8, when a bank faces a problem of liquidity or solvency, this threatens the provision of core banking services in the economy because of the danger of spillovers and contagion to other banks.

Liquidity risk is a characteristic of fractional reserve banking systems like the one described in Chapter 5. Banks extend credit on a long term basis and if there is an unusual surge of depositors wishing to withdraw their deposits, the bank can find itself unable to meet this demand. The central bank acts as lender of last resort (LOLR) who can step in to provide liquidity normally at a penalty interest rate to (otherwise solvent) banks who do not have the cash to meet their short-term liabilities. Systems of deposit insurance (for which banks pay) are designed to prevent a liquidity problem in one bank from spreading fear across the banking sector as a whole. We return to the problem of liquidity risk that arose in the global financial crisis in Chapter 7. The problem lay in bank funding and not in a classic bank run by retail depositors, and hence was not alleviated by deposit insurance schemes.

Bankruptcy of a bank—as opposed to the liquidity problems discussed above—is a problem for public policy in a way that it is not for a company in another industry. The reason is the expectation that governments are likely to step in to bail out a failing bank in order to prevent the disruptive effects on the economy of bank failure.

Policy makers therefore face a difficult trade-off between:

1. On the one hand, the need to maintain the continuity of core banking services—otherwise the spending decisions represented by the *IS* curve in the macro model are interrupted, and the economy experiences a potentially catastrophic negative demand shock, and

2. On the other, the need to avoid moral hazard. For example, if schemes like deposit insurance affect the behaviour both of households and firms, who, confident in the belief that any liquidity problem will not affect their savings, feel less incentive to monitor the activities of banks, then the arrangement is said to produce moral hazard. Deposit insurance will also lessen the attention of banks to their prudential behaviour.

The positive probability that an insolvent bank would be bailed out creates a wedge between the private and social cost-benefit calculus of the bank's decisions. The downside risk is partly 'socialized' in the sense that taxpayers normally bear the risk in the case of a bail-out were it to occur. This would be predicted to affect behaviour and make banks less sensitive to extra risk than would be the case if the bank (owners, managers, bond-holders, depositors) had to face the full cost of bankruptcy.

In addition to these two reasons for special treatment of the financial sector, policy makers must take into account an important market failure in bank behaviour. When an individual bank makes commercial decisions, it does not take into account the effect of its decisions on *overall risk* in the financial system, and of the costs to the economy of a financial crisis that might ensue.

This is an example of the problem of externalities that is well-studied in economics, in which the social costs of an individual's actions diverge from the private costs. In the case of pollution, a tax can be levied or bans imposed on emissions of a certain type or scale to bring private and social costs into alignment. Externalities of excessive risk-taking by a bank that is systemically important threaten the continuity of the supply of economy-wide core banking services because of the likelihood of contagion. Governments are afraid to let this happen.

Lying behind the policy problems is an information problem: for example, if the regulator could accurately observe the risks that are being taken on by a bank, it could intervene to keep it at the socially optimal level. One way that a policy maker could mitigate this market failure is to impose capital regulation as a method of inducing the bank to take on less risk (and thereby to operate closer to the socially optimal level of risk taking). This means the policy maker sets the size of the private capital cushion, which is there to absorb losses in the event the bank's assets fall in value. In the wake of the global financial crisis, there has been a widespread policy debate about how to make the financial system safer, to which we return in Chapter 13.

### The activities of banks

The activities of banks in modern economies are not confined to providing core banking services. They also trade in financial assets. To understand the role of the financial sector in the macroeconomy, and in particular, in financial upswings, downswings and crises, we focus on two types of activity. These are (a) the provision of core banking services including mortgage lending and (b) engagement in the creation and trading of financial assets and of contracts based on assets, called derivatives.

In this chapter, we abstract from the complexity of the institutions and the details of the assets and derivatives that were at the centre of the upswing to the global financial crisis. To provide a framework for understanding the fluctuations in the economy in which the banking system plays a central role, we use the term *retail banking* to refer to the provision of core banking services including mortgage lending, and the term *investment banking* to refer to the creation and trading of securitized financial assets and derivatives.[1]

1. A retail bank engages in traditional banking activity and behaves as it did in Chapter 5. Its key characteristics are that its core business is principally deposit taking, payment services and lending—to individuals and SMEs (i.e. small and medium-sized enterprises).

2. An investment bank (IB) trades in a variety of financial products (such as derivatives, fixed income instruments, currencies and commodities). In the real world, the principal activities

---

[1] The definitions of retail and investment banks that follow are similar to those in the UK's Independent Banking Commission's report, IBC (2011).

of investment banks include the provision of assistance to institutions such as governments and corporations in raising equity and debt finance, giving advice in relation to mergers and acquisitions, acting as counterparty to client trades and market-making. Not all investment banks accept deposits. From a macroeconomic stability point of view, the important activity of IBs is trading in financial products. When we model investment banks, we shall focus entirely on trading in securitized assets and derivatives based on them.

Many large international banks are universal banks, which means they combine the activities of retail and investment banks. In addition, a substantial part of banking activity in the years before the global financial crisis took place in the so-called *shadow banking system*. Shadow banks engage in credit intermediation and although they are often related to banks, they are not covered by banking regulation. It was in the shadow banking system that much of the activity creating securitized financial assets and derivative contracts based on assets took place in the 2000s. For example, Countrywide Financial, a US non-bank mortgage lender, became the largest mortgage lender in the country in the years prior to the crisis. The company achieved this rapid growth by aggressively expanding its subprime lending business.[2]

As we shall see in Chapter 7, many large banks engage in both retail and investment banking activities, and operate related entities that are part of the shadow banking complex. However, when they do this, they separate their accounts into the so-called *banking book*, in which the retail bank assets (like mortgage loans) are reported and the *trading book*, in which the investment bank assets and derivatives are reported.

In this chapter, we set up a simple model of investment banks, which can be taken to include the trading book activities of other banks, including the related activities of the shadow banking complex. An important feature of investment banks is that the assets are 'marked-to-market' as illustrated in the financial cycle shown in Fig. 6.2. This means that asset values in the balance sheet reflect market prices. We shall see that mark-to-market valuation of financial assets plays an important role in financial fluctuations. We shall also assume that investment banks are risk–neutral and characterized by a business model called Value at Risk (VaR), which we explain below.

Just as we represent household and firm behaviour in a very stylized way in the *IS* curve in the 3-equation model, we shall do the same for the financial system by setting out simple models to characterize important features of bank behaviour. In Chapter 7, we return to the banks of the real world and apply the models developed here to shed light on the part they played in the global financial crisis.

### 6.2.2 Financial crises and their cost to the economy

Ben Bernanke defines financial crises as extreme disruptions to the normal functioning of financial markets, which often have a significant effect on the real economy.[3] As the book by Reinhart and Rogoff (2009a) reports, financial crises are nothing new. In fact, the authors find that relatively frequent financial crises have characterized developing and advanced

---

[2] See the Reuters article from the 15th of October 2010 entitled, *Factbox: Countrywide's subprime lending*.
[3] See Ben Bernanke's speech on June 15th 2007, entitled *The Financial Accelerator and the Credit Channel*. The speech is available on the Federal Reserve website.

economies for at least the last 800 years. The authors focus their more detailed empirical analysis on the period since 1800 (due to data availability) and produce a dataset of all the financial crises in this period. This includes 66 economies, covering a range of levels of development and geographical regions.

The authors find evidence of four broad varieties of crisis; inflation crises, currency crises, sovereign debt crises (domestic and external) and banking crises. This chapter focuses on *systemic banking crises*, which are crises that 'lead to the closure, merging or takeover by the public sector of one or more financial institutions'. These crises are typically associated with the bursting of house price and credit bubbles and the collapse of highly-indebted borrowers (e.g. banks and households). We use the terms 'financial crisis' and (systemic) 'banking crisis' interchangeably.

What impact do systemic banking crises of this nature have on the real economy? In a study focusing primarily on the financial crises in the post-WWII period (but excluding the 2008–09 crisis), Reinhart and Rogoff (2009b) find that financial crises are drawn out affairs and (although they vary considerably) they typically have three key characteristics:

1. Deep and prolonged asset price collapses: declines in real house prices average 35% over a period of six years and declines in equity prices average 55% over a period of three to four years.

2. Large and lasting adverse impacts on output and employment: on average, real GDP per capita contracts 9% (from peak to trough) over two years and unemployment rises seven percentage points over four years.

3. Government debt explodes: in real terms, the government debt stock rises 86% on average in the three years following a banking crisis.[4] This is primarily due to the collapse in tax revenues associated with the deep output contraction and the implementation of counter-cyclical fiscal policy. Bank bailout costs are usually second order.[5]

These characteristics highlight the sheer magnitude of the impact financial crises typically have on the real economy. The IMF (2009) report provides further evidence; analysing 122 recessions in 21 advanced economies they found that recessions associated with financial crises are more severe and long-lasting than those recessions associated with other shocks.

The global recession of 2008–09 was extremely damaging, as it was not only associated with a financial crisis, but was highly synchronized across the major advanced economies. The GDP of the advanced economies contracted by 3.5% in 2009 alone and the cumulative cost of lost output over the crisis was even larger.[6] For example, by the first quarter of 2013, UK GDP was still 4% below its pre-crisis peak in Q1 of 2008 and was a full 17% below the level

---

[4] The authors use the percentage increase in the government debt stock instead of the debt-to-GDP ratio to avoid steep output drops complicating the interpretation of the debt-to-GDP ratios. The authors index pre-banking crisis government debt at 100 and find that the average government debt stock rises to 186 (i.e. an increase of 86%) in the three years following a banking crisis.

[5] Bank bailout costs in the global financial crisis (which are not considered in the Reinhart and Rogoff data) were, however, very large compared to government tax revenue in some countries (e.g. Ireland). We discuss the case of the Irish bank bail-out in more detail in Chapter 12.

[6] Source: IMF World Economic Outlook database, October 2012.

it would have been had the pre-crisis trend not been interrupted by the crisis and extended recession.[7] We analyse the global financial crisis in more detail in the following chapter.

### 6.2.3 Financial cycles and business cycles

Chapters 1–5 were all about the business cycle—the fluctuations of the economy from recession to boom to recession. In the earlier chapters we set out a model in which business cycles can be driven by demand and supply shocks and by policy changes. In business cycle recessions, unemployment goes up and well-being goes down—for people who lose their jobs, for those who find it more difficult to find a job and for those in employment who are more anxious about keeping the job they have. In business cycle booms, although unemployment goes down and real wages tend to rise, both of which raise well-being, inflation goes up and there is normally a cost to be paid in terms of a subsequent recession for squeezing inflation out of the economy. For these reasons, the policy maker tries to keep the economy close to the medium-run equilibrium.

Where the business cycle is based on fluctuations in GDP, upswings and downswings of financial cycles refer to fluctuations in key financial variables, such as credit and house prices. Unlike the business cycle, there is no widely accepted methodology for measuring the financial cycle. However, we can summarize the key features of financial fluctuations and crises using the work of economists and economic historians (see, for example, Reinhart and Rogoff (2009a and 2009b) and Schularick and Taylor (2012)):

1. In the upswing of a financial cycle, house prices rise more rapidly than over the long run and banks extend more credit. Positive feedback processes amplify rising house prices and rising levels of debt in the banking sector. The upswing of a financial cycle is often associated with both households and banks increasing their borrowing.

2. The upswing often ends with a collapse in house prices and a banking crisis.

3. In the downswing of a financial cycle, households and banks reduce their levels of indebtedness. This *deleveraging* is referred to as a process of 'repairing their balance sheets'. The need for banks to rebuild their capacity to absorb losses following the reversal of the boom phase (where they have experienced large losses on their loans) means they set a higher interest rate spread above the policy rate and are less willing to make loans.

4. When a housing boom reverses, borrower households need to increase their savings. Some need to recover from negative equity or 'being under-water' due to the collapse of house prices (these are the banks' bad loans).

5. Both aspects of the aftermath of the downturn in the financial cycle imply a deeper recession than is the case in the absence of these balance sheet (or wealth) effects.

6. Public sector debt increases sharply when there is a financial crisis because of the depth and length of the recession that follows and because of government support for failing banks.

---

[7] The pre-crisis trend level of growth was calculated as the average quarterly growth rate for the 15 years prior to the recession (i.e. 1993 Q1 and 2007 Q4). Source: UK Office for National Statistics (data accessed June 2013) and authors' calculations.

Two mechanisms play an important role in the dynamics of a financial cycle: asset price bubbles and financial accelerators. The latter are based on the effect of asset price changes on the balance sheets of households and banks. Before explaining these mechanisms, we provide some empirical information about financial cycles.

### Stylized facts about the financial cycle

In this subsection, we present some stylized facts about the financial cycle and contrast them with the characteristics of the more familiar business cycle. We use the research of economists at the Bank for International Settlements (BIS) in Basel led by Claudio Borio in our presentation of the financial cycle. This group was one of the few that had done systematic research on the interaction of macroeconomic policy and financial instability before the global financial crisis, and the BIS economists have been credited with having warned about the dangers of the build-up of leverage (i.e. the shrinkage of capital cushions) in the financial sector ahead of the crisis.[8]

The BIS financial cycle measure reflects fluctuations in three financial variables; private credit, the private credit-to-GDP ratio and residential property prices. The choice of these variables was informed by the historical evidence on financial fluctuations described above and by their behaviour. These variables follow very similar patterns over time and their peaks are often associated with banking crises. By contrast, stock market prices are not included in the financial cycle measure as they exhibit much more short term volatility than the chosen variables and their peaks are less frequently associated with crises.

The fluctuations in the financial cycle variables are typically longer than the business cycle fluctuations in output. The gap between business cycle peaks is typically five to six years in advanced countries, whereas financial cycles in the major advanced economies can be more than twice or even three times as long.[9]

Three stylized facts about the financial cycle are:

1. Banks play a key role in the cycle through both their lending and their borrowing behaviour (i.e. both the asset and the liability sides of their balance sheets).

2. The housing sector is procyclical and the purchase of new and second-hand housing is often financed by borrowing from banks.

3. The inter-relationship between banks and housing is central to the financial cycle, and the peak of the financial cycle is often followed by a banking crisis.

Figure 6.3 shows the business and financial cycles for the United States from the 1970s to the middle of 2011.[10] The curve labelled financial cycle reflects the behaviour of bank credit and house prices. The more prolonged upswings and downswings of the financial cycle as compared with those of the business cycle are evident in the chart. Note that although the

---

[8] For an example of the BIS research on financial instability (carried out prior to the crisis), see Borio and White (2004). The two papers we use as the basis for our discussion of the financial cycle are Borio (2012) and Drehmann et al. (2012).

[9] See Borio (2012).

[10] The data for the financial cycle graphs is presented in Drehmann et al. (2012) and has been kindly provided by the authors.

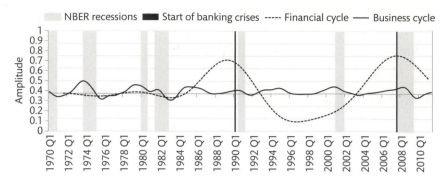

**Figure 6.3** The financial and business cycles in the United States: 1970 Q1–2011 Q2.

*Source:* Drehmann, Borio and Tsatsaronis (2012).

financial cycles are not derived from data on banking crises, the peaks of the financial cycle in the USA coincide almost exactly with the onset of the last two banking crises.

The underlying series for the private credit (as a percentage of GDP) and real house prices are shown in Fig. 6.4. The cyclical components of these variables (and of private credit volume) form the financial cycle shown in Fig. 6.3. The cyclical components are estimated relative to trend (i.e. they are the fluctuations in the series around the long-run trend). The trend in both variables was upward sloping until the financial crisis of the late-2000s.[11]

Reinhart and Rogoff (2009a) provide further evidence for choosing these indicators for measuring financial fluctuations. They use the so-called 'signals approach' to test the relative importance of different indicators as early warning signs for banking crises. They find that real house price growth is close to the top of the list of reliable indicators, whereas real stock price growth is relatively less successful at predicting future banking crises. This is because stock price growth produces more false alarms (i.e. peaks of stock price cycles are less often associated with crises).

The data in Fig. 6.4 shows that US house prices rose steadily from the early 1970s to the late 1990s, boomed in the early to mid-2000s and then fell dramatically between 2006 and 2011. House prices peaked in 2006 Q1 at almost 2.5 times their 1970 value. Figure 6.4 also shows that (with the exception of a brief fall in the early 1990s) US households and firms continually increased their borrowing in the four decades preceding the financial crisis of the late 2000s. The peak of the housing and credit cycles were closely associated with both the onset of a banking crisis and a prolonged recession in the late 2000s.

Looking at business cycles and financial cycles together in Fig. 6.3 suggests that if policy makers are preoccupied with stabilizing the business cycle, they may overlook the fact that a financial cycle upswing can continue during a recession such as that of the early 2000s.

Figure 6.5 shows the financial and business cycles for the UK, Germany, Sweden and Japan, which are constructed in the same way as for the USA. The picture for the UK looks fairly similar to that of the USA, with the upswing in the financial cycle prior to the recent crisis beginning in the mid 1990s and really taking off in the mid-2000s. However, the other three

---

[11] The details about how the cycles are extracted from the underlying data are provided in Drehmann et al. (2012).

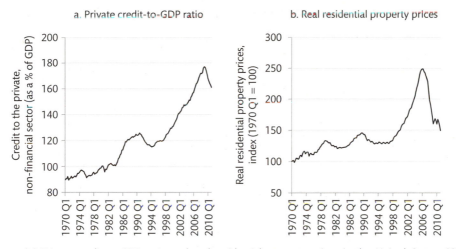

**Figure 6.4** Private credit-to-GDP ratio and real residential property prices in the United States: 1970 Q1–2011 Q1.

*Source:* Drehmann, Borio and Tsatsaronis (2012).

countries display much more variety. Note that the amplitude of financial cycles can be compared over time and across countries but there is no meaningful comparison between the amplitude of business cycles and financial cycles. However, the relative length of business cycles and financial cycles can be compared.

In neither Sweden nor Japan did the financial cycle move above trend in the 2000s. Both had experienced large banking sector crashes in the late-80s to early-90s, which adversely affected financial variables in those economies throughout the Great Moderation period.

Germany presents a different case altogether. The amplitude of its financial cycle is substantially smaller than that of the other three countries and the 2008–09 financial crisis actually came at the trough of their financial cycle. The long-term absence of substantial financial cycles in Germany reflects its different housing market (where home ownership rates are low, and where neither high loan-to-value mortgages nor home equity loans are available). In other words, in Germany it is not possible to re-mortgage your apartment or house based on its market value. The German case highlights the impact that the institutions a society adopts can have on the amplitude of financial cycles as well as on business cycles through their effect on aggregate consumption behaviour, as discussed in Chapter 1.

From the mid-1990s, Germany's growth was weak. This is reflected in Fig. 6.5 by the frequency of recessions in Germany, which stands in sharp contrast to the UK in the same period, which was recession-free and where a financial cycle built up. Demand for and supply of credit to domestic households by German banks was muted. Germany's banking crisis in 2007 was imported from the US subprime crash through the overseas activities of its banks.

By looking at the country experiences, and noting the variability of the financial cycle over time, it is clear that economic policy and particular innovations in the financial sector are important for understanding why a financial cycle takes hold and its amplitude. The focus of this chapter is on the mechanisms that led to housing and credit booms in a number of financially liberalized developed economies in the 2000s (e.g. the UK and the US). These

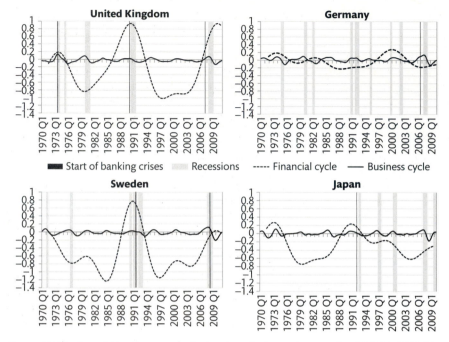

**Figure 6.5** The financial and business cycles in selected advanced economies: 1970 Q1–2011 Q2.

*Note:* We have added recessions onto these graphs based on defining a recession as a period of two or more consecutive quarters of negative growth (i.e. contraction) in real GDP.

*Source:* Drehmann, Borio and Tsatsaronis (2012); OECD (data accessed March 2013).

countries were at the core of the global financial crisis. We analyse the crisis in detail in the next chapter and discuss the important role played by banks headquartered in countries where financial cycles did not take hold such as Germany.

## 6.3  Basic mechanisms

We discuss two mechanisms that play an important role in the analysis of financial crises. The first is the asset price bubble and the second is the financial accelerator. The latter is a mechanism through which changes in asset prices (such as for houses or financial assets) affect the balance sheet of an agent, which in turn leads to a change in borrowing and spending. As a result of asset price bubbles and financial accelerator processes, the financial sector can amplify and propagate shocks as illustrated in Figs. 6.1 and 6.2. A famous example of a pure bubble is the tulip bulb bubble of the 17th century. Both processes were at play when the house price bubble in Sweden in 1990 was amplified and propagated through the economy by financial accelerator effects as households borrowed more against the rising value of their housing.

### 6.3.1  Asset price bubbles

Figure 6.6 shows three cases, each of which illustrate price dynamic processes in different kinds of markets. In the diagrams in the upper panels, the price of the good at time *t* is on

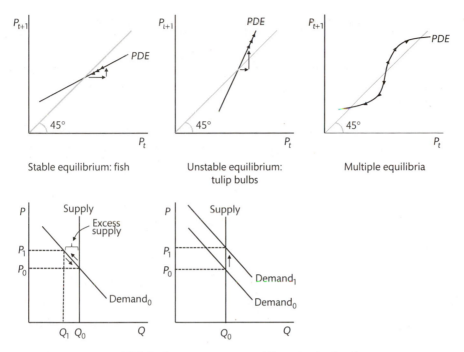

**Figure 6.6** Price dynamic processes in different kinds of markets.

the horizontal axis and the price at time $t+1$ is on the vertical axis. There is a 45 degree line, which shows a situation of price stability, i.e. where $P_t = P_{t+1}$. The diagrams in the lower panels show the associated supply and demand diagrams for each case (excluding the multiple equilibrium case).

The market on the left hand side is the market for a non-durable good, such as fish. The line labelled *PDE*, which stands for price dynamic equation, shows the relationship between the price this period and next period and is flatter than the 45 degree line. When there is a positive shock to the price in time $t$, the *PDE* shows that the price in the next period begins to fall back to the initial equilibrium. This is just what we would expect in an ordinary market. We show the supply and demand diagram for this case in the lower left-hand panel. When the price rises, demand falls and there is a gap between the unchanged supply and the lower demand (i.e. there is excess supply) that depresses the price, with adjustment taking place until demand and supply are once again equal at the initial price (i.e. $P_0$).

In the second diagram, the *PDE* line is steeper than the 45 degree line. Here, a positive price shock in time $t$ is followed by a higher price in period $t+1$. How can this happen? It can only happen in the market for a durable good or asset that can be stored and we will take the example of the market for tulip bulbs. If the conviction takes hold that the price of tulip bulbs will increase further, then this leads the demand curve to shift up in the supply and demand diagram (shown in the lower middle panel). The reason for the upward shift in the demand curve is that agents believe the price of tulip bulbs will go up further. If this happens, then holding more tulip bulbs is a good strategy: there will be a capital gain from holding them because they can be sold later at a higher price than the price paid to acquire them.

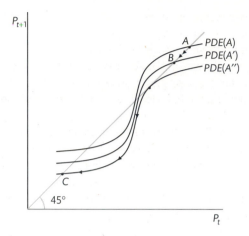

**Figure 6.7** The impact of changes in price expectations in a market with an S-shaped *PDE* curve.

The normal response to a price increase in a situation of excess supply is a fall in price, as was the case for fish in the first example. In the tulip bulb case, however, the initial price rise leads the demand curve to shift upwards. In a self-fulfilling bubble, this process can continue indefinitely—at least until something happens to change the expectation of continuously rising prices (and of a growing deviation of the price from its initial 'fundamental' value).[12]

The third diagram combines the features of the other two to produce an S-shaped *PDE* curve. In this case there are three intersections with the 45 degree line: the one in the middle resembles the unstable tulip bulb case; the other two resemble the stable fish case. In a market with an S-shaped *PDE* curve, the economy will be pulled to the stable high or low price equilibrium.

In order to assess the role that expectations play in markets characterized by an S-shaped *PDE* curve, we can write the *PDE* process as $P_{t+1} = f(P_t; A_t)$, where $A_t$ is a variable that shifts the curve. One simple way of thinking about this is for $A_t$ to represent the proportion of the population with a given expectation about next period's price, and the proportion responds to what has happened to the price in the previous period. We show this case in Fig. 6.7.

Let us assume the housing market is at the high price equilibrium at *A*. A shock occurs that leads a small fraction of agents to expect a lower price next period (i.e. *A* falls to *A'*). The S-shaped *PDE* curve shifts downward to *PDE(A')*, those whose expectations have changed sell houses, and the price falls. The new equilibrium is at *B*. In the following period the notion of falling house prices is adopted by more people, which shifts the *PDE* down. As more and more people come to believe the price will fall, the *PDE* curve shifts down. Eventually, a tipping point is reached at which the *PDE* has shifted down to *PDE(A'')*, such that it is tangent to the 45 degree line. This is a tipping point because in the following period, the middle equilibrium has disappeared and the economy is pulled toward the low price equilibrium at *C*.

---

[12] For a deeper analysis of bubbles, see the paper by Blanchard and Watson (1982). They have a nice solution to the problem of the tulip case: a bubble requires an increasing price sequence and at some point, this is going to be unsustainable. Their idea is that the bubble can burst at any date with some probability, which means everyone knows it is going to burst eventually, but still find it optimal to go along with the burgeoning bubble.

By looking at these three cases, we can see how a process of self-fulfilling price expectations can operate in the market for a durable good. There is no point buying more fish in the hope of making a capital gain on them because the fish will rot. Hence, a process of self-fulfilling expectations cannot get underway in the fish market. In the market for tulip bulbs in the seventeenth century or for office space in Tokyo in the late 1980s, however, there is a rationale for paying a higher price in order to get hold of more of the asset so as to benefit from the expected capital gain.

In the left-hand diagram of Fig. 6.6 there is a stable equilibrium price, in the middle diagram, there is no stable equilibrium price and in the right-hand one, there are two stable and one unstable equilibria. The diagram with multiple equilibria captures the possible dynamics of a housing or other asset market where there are repeated booms and busts. The economy will tend to move through a process of self-fulfilling price expectations toward either the upper or the lower equilibrium: a housing boom or a housing bust.

---

### Box 6.1   The big ten financial bubbles

As we have seen, financial crises are not a new phenomenon. Historically, crises have frequently, but not always, been preceded by asset price bubbles. Kindleberger and Aliber (2011, p. 11) set out the ten most significant financial bubbles of the last 400 years. Notice that asset price bubbles have occured across a wide variety of countries and time periods. The bubbles of the last 100 years have predominantly been focused on real estate, stocks and foreign investment.

  1636: The Dutch Tulip Bulb Bubble

  1720: The South Sea Bubble

  1720: The Mississippi Bubble

  1927–29: The late 1920s stock price bubble

  1970s: The surge in loans to Mexico and other developing economies

  1985–89: The bubble in real estate and stocks in Japan

  1985–89: The bubble in real estate and stocks in Finland, Norway and Sweden

  1990s: The bubble in real estate and stocks in Thailand, Malaysia, Indonesia and several other Asian countries between 1992 and 1997; and the surge in foreign investment in Mexico 1990–99

  1995–2000: The bubble in over-the-counter stocks in the United States

  2002–07: The bubble in real estate in the United States, Britain, Spain, Ireland and Iceland; and the debt of the government of Greece

---

### 6.3.2   The financial accelerator

A central element of the macroeconomic model we have been studying in this book is the presence of credit-constrained households. For these households, an increase in their wealth provides them with more collateral and relaxes the credit constraint by allowing them to borrow more. We assume that home equity loans are available, such that a household can use the equity in their house as collateral to obtain a loan.[13]

---

[13] Home equity loans were available in the UK and the US prior to the crisis. They were not available in France, Germany or Italy.

By definition, a credit-constrained household will spend more when the credit constraint is relaxed. This provides a connection between a change in asset price, the extent of credit constraints and household spending, that is, between a change in asset price and the *IS* curve.

The financial accelerator is a positive feedback process through which a change in the price of an asset affects the macroeconomy.[14] The asset could be a financial asset such as company stocks (shares) or bonds. We illustrate the mechanics of the financial accelerator using the case of housing because this is where the financial accelerator mainly operates for the household sector.[15] Its operation can be summarized in the following five steps:

1. The credit constraints facing a household depend on the value of the collateral it has. The value of its collateral is its net worth, which as we saw in Chapter 5, is the difference between the value of the house and the size of the mortgage. It is important to highlight that the financial accelerator works because it is the *market* price of the house that establishes its value. When the household's net worth increases, it is able to borrow more. This is referred to as a relaxation of the credit constraints it faces.

2. A positive shock to house prices relaxes credit constraints.

3. Households borrow more. This step rests on the assumption that there is a set of borrower households who have borrowed up to the limit set by the credit constraints. Hence, when the constraint is relaxed by a rise in the value of their housing collateral, they will borrow more.

4. Some of this borrowing is used for consumption and some is used to buy more housing, both existing houses and newly constructed ones. This has a direct effect in shifting the *IS* curve.

5. The increased demand for housing, pushes the price up further and the financial accelerator process begins again at step 1.

The financial accelerator is a positive feedback process because on the basis of an initial exogenous rise in the price of the asset (in this case, the house), a key constraint limiting the household's desired spending—including on housing—is relaxed. This has two important effects. It *amplifies* the business cycle because it stimulates spending by previously credit-constrained people. This shifts the *IS* curve to the right. The shift will be reinforced by the increase in construction (e.g. new house building) that accompanies the rise in demand for housing (e.g. USA, Ireland and Spain in the 2000s). Second, it feeds back to push house prices up further. The second effect *propagates* the shock because it relaxes the credit constraints by increasing the value of the collateral, and allows the positive feedback process to continue.

We can highlight the central role of credit constraints in this process by comparing it to the special case where there are no credit-constrained households. In this case, an exogenous

---

[14] See Bernanke et al. (1999) for a detailed discussion of the financial accelerator. Alternatively, for a high level discussion see Ben Bernanke's speech on June 15th 2007, entitled *The Financial Accelerator and the Credit Channel*. The speech is available on the Federal Reserve website.

[15] Muellbauer (2010) provides an excellent explanation of these processes. The paper also assesses the different modelling approaches and looks into their consistency with the data. Aron et al. (2012) provide empirical evidence on the financial accelerator. The authors find that the housing collateral channel on consumption (i.e. the financial accelerator) operates in the UK and US household sectors but is absent in Japan.

rise in house prices is simply a temporary shock to permanent income. There will be hardly any effect on aggregate demand and there will be no positive feedback process driving house prices up further.

The financial accelerator does not have to rest on bubble behaviour. It is driven by the combination of credit constraints and collateral effects. In the financial accelerator, the demand for the asset is shifted by a change in wealth caused by the change in the asset's price. A rise in price relaxes the credit constraint and drives demand higher because of increased wealth. By contrast, in the case of the bubble based on self-fulfilling expectations, it is the *expectation* of a capital gain (i.e. an expected increase in the price of the asset) that leads the demand curve for housing to shift.

Although these are distinct mechanisms, they can interact with each other. For example, the bursting of a bubble can be the source of a price shock, which will lead the financial accelerator to amplify and propagate the shock further through the economy. The example of a bubble bursting highlights that the financial accelerator operates in both the upswing and downswing stages of the financial cycle.

## 6.4 The housing feedback process and the 3-equation model

In this section, we draw together the insights from the two mechanisms (asset price bubble and financial accelerator) to describe a housing positive feedback process, which can drive a financial cycle. We re-introduce the 3-equation model to show the relationship between the house-price driven financial cycle, the business cycle and the inflation-targeting central bank. A simple formal model of the housing positive feedback process is set out in the Appendix. The specific features of the housing positive feedback process as they played out in the run-up to the global financial crisis are set out in Chapter 7.

The large volume of evidence presented in Reinhart and Rogoff (2009a) suggests that rising house prices (in real terms) and the expansion of private credit go together in the upswing phase of a financial cycle. Reinhart and Rogoff show that house price booms have typically preceded systemic banking crises in both emerging and advanced economies in the post-WWII period. The literature also provides strong evidence that pre-crisis asset price booms are associated with substantial expansions in credit (both domestic and external).[16]

### 6.4.1 Credit constrained households, housing collateral and house prices

In Step 3 above, credit-constrained households are up against their borrowing constraint. The house-price feedback can be set in motion by, for example, an exogenous rise in the price of housing, or by a change in regulation (or in self-imposed guidelines) of banks related to the loan-to-value ratio they use when making mortgage decisions or collateral rules.

A rise in the loan-to-value (*LTV*) ratio banks are allowed to use in making mortgages leads to a rise in the demand for mortgages. For an individual borrowing to buy a house,

---

[16] See Mendoza and Terrones (2008) and Schularick and Taylor (2012).

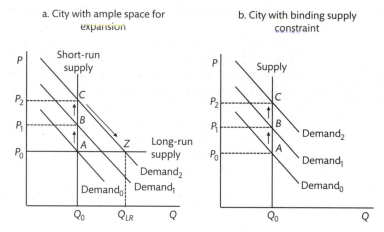

**Figure 6.8** The impact of long-run supply constraints on the formation of house price bubbles.

the *LTV* ratio is calculated as the value of the loan received divided by the value of the property purchased. For example, if a borrower took out a loan of $160,000 to buy a house worth $200,000, then the *LTV* ratio would be 80%. In the USA, mortgages with *LTV* ratios in excess of 100% became widely available in the mid-2000s.[17] This meant that borrowers could receive a loan larger than the value of the property they were buying without providing any down-payment. These looser lending standards made it possible for lower income groups to purchase residential property and consequently boosted mortgage demand.

Bank collateral rules can also influence mortgage demand. They specify how a change in the market value of a house affects the ability of a household to borrow. If these rules for home equity loans are loosened it becomes easier for households to borrow against their housing assets. As a result, credit constrained households increase their borrowing for both consumption and housing.

When the price of houses goes up, a bubble may develop as explained in the previous section. The rise in demand for mortgages pushes up house prices ($\Delta P_H > 0$), which may in turn trigger the expectation that house prices will rise further ($\Delta P_H^E > 0$). When a bubble is formed, the economy is characterized by a price dynamic equation (*PDE*) line with a slope of more than 45 degrees (Fig. 6.6 central panel).

However, rising house prices do not necessarily reflect a bubble. Instead they could reflect changes to the fundamental determinants of price (i.e. supply and demand). We illustrate this by comparing two cases, as shown in Fig. 6.8. In the first (shown in the left-hand panel), the supply curve for housing, although inelastic in the short-run, is perfectly elastic in the long run; in the second (shown in the right-hand panel), supply is inelastic in the long-run as well.

Figure 6.8a could describe a situation in a city surrounded by plenty of space for expansion and where there are no planning impediments to further house building. In this case, we see demand for housing rising in two consecutive periods, which cause prices to rise from $P_0$ to $P_1$, and then from $P_1$ to $P_2$. This is due to supply being perfectly inelastic in the short-run;

---

[17] See IMF (2011). For evidence on the role of housing in the financial accelerator in the UK and the US see Aron et al. (2012).

new houses cannot be built instantaneously. However, after the initial price rises, supply responds, more houses are built and this reduces the price back down to the long-run price ($P_0$). In the new equilbrium, the price has returned to its long-run level, but new house building has increased the supply of housing to $Q_{LR}$. In other words, new supply has mopped up the additional demand.

If one observed steeply rising house prices where these fundamentals were in place, it would be reasonable to infer that a bubble is underway. The reason is that if the long-run supply curve is flat, house prices must eventually fall to the level consistent with that supply curve. In this setting, ever-increasing house prices must be explained by extrapolative expectations driving a bubble process.

By contrast, take a situation where the long-run supply curve is vertical, as shown in Fig. 6.8b. This could arise because of binding constraints on building more housing due to a combination of physical and planning reasons. In this case, the initial increases in housing demand cause prices to shift upwards (from $P_0$ to $P_1$ and then to $P_2$) exactly as in the first example, but as there is no supply response, there is no pressure for prices to fall in the long-run.

When these fundamentals are in place, it is possible for house prices to rise persistently without a bubble. The demand curve is shifted, for example by population inflows or in the case of London property after 2010, by wealthy citizens of Eurozone crisis countries looking for a safe place to put their money. This shifts the demand curve for housing upwards. As long as the demand curve is shifting upwards, the price of housing rises without a bubble and fuels the financial accelerator. When the supply curve is inelastic, it is harder to distinguish a bubble from price movements based on the fundamentals.

When a housing bubble bursts, we would predict there to be lots of empty houses because of the expansion in supply triggered by the high and rising prices. This was the case in the USA, Ireland and Spain in the episodes of rising house prices before the global financial crisis. The problem of over-supply is often exacerbated by the fact that new houses take time to build. New supply may continue to come on to the market even after house prices have started to fall. By contrast, when house prices fell in the UK, there were not lots of empty houses—because of planning constraints, supply had responded weakly to rising demand.

### 6.4.2 A plain vanilla financial crisis

We can summarize how a house-price based boom can turn into a financial crisis as follows.

1.  When a property bubble bursts and house prices fall, the net worth of households falls. Some households are unable to service their mortgage.
2.  Houses are repossessed by the bank (this is called foreclosure) and sold at a loss, i.e. at a price below the balance of the remaining mortgage.
3.  The net worth of banks falls due to the losses they incur on mortgage loans.
4.  If a bank is sufficiently exposed to falling property prices, it can become insolvent: the shrinkage of the value of its assets wipes out its capital cushion.

This is an example sometimes referred to as a 'plain vanilla' banking crisis. Plain vanilla is a standard kind of ice-cream—only one flavour and without sprinkles. A plain vanilla crisis does not rely on the more sophisticated behaviour of banks involving novel financial instruments or the investment and shadow banking activities described in the bank-centred positive feedback process in the next section.

Plain vanilla banking crises have occurred frequently in many countries over the years, and governments have been forced to intervene to save and restructure banks so as to prevent contagion and a broader break-down of the supply of core banking services. Examples are the banking crisis known as the secondary banking crisis in the UK of 1973–77 and the US Savings and Loans crisis of the 1980s. Housing–banking booms and busts of this kind have not gone out of fashion—this is what happened in Ireland and Spain in the 2000s.

### 6.4.3 Housing feedback process and the 3-equation model

If home equity loans are available, households enjoying a relaxation of their credit constraints due to the higher market value of their house borrow more in order to spend more on housing, and on consumption of goods and services. This can lead to the construction of new houses, which boosts aggregate demand. In the 3-equation model these effects produce a rightward shift of the *IS* curve and, holding everything else constant, this will push up inflation and lead to a tightening of monetary policy in the usual way by the central bank. Note, however, that the link to the central bank is *only* via the effect of the increased loans on aggregate demand and the forecast effect on CPI inflation: there is no direct link from the behaviour of house prices per se.[18]

Suppose the central bank successfully shifts the economy on to the *MR* curve and CPI inflation begins to fall. The response of the central bank to the associated forecast rise in inflation will not necessarily prevent the continuation of the upswing of the financial cycle. This is because there is no mechanism in the model that directly links the stabilizing action of the central bank to the *sources* of the house price feedback process. Higher interest rates would be expected to dampen demand for mortgages, but an interest rate increase designed to get CPI inflation back to target will not necessarily cut off an asset price bubble and the financial accelerator mechanism. This is illustrated by the continuous upswing in US house prices between the 1970s and the mid-2000s shown in Fig. 6.4.

Figure 6.9 summarizes the housing-related financial cycle and its interaction with the business cycle. The top section of the diagram shows how changes in regulation or collateral rules in the retail banking system can lead to a house price boom. The bottom section shows the link between the housing market and the 3-equation model. The increased loans for consumption and for investment in new housing increase aggregate demand, which in turn creates inflationary pressure. In the normal way, the central bank policy maker reacts by tightening monetary policy to bring forecast inflation back to target. The diagram highlights the fact that house price increases do not affect either aggregate demand or inflation (i.e. there is no direct link between house prices and the 3-equation model).

---

[18] The measures of inflation targeted by central banks do not typically include house prices directly, but do account for changes in the price of rental accommodation or the imputed costs of owner-occupied accommodation. This includes only the consumption component of owner occupied housing and ignores the volatile investment component. The elements of housing costs included do not influence the overall price indices that enter the inflation target to a high degree. To see this, plot the US Consumer Price Index against the US Consumer Price Index less Shelter (data available from the US Bureau of Labor Statistics website).

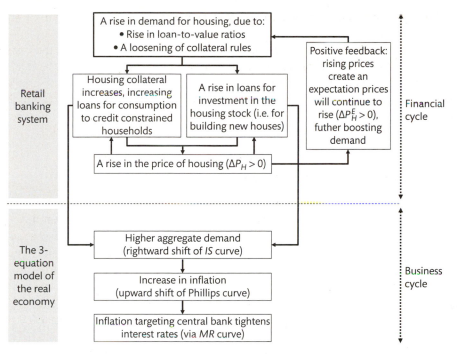

**Figure 6.9** The 3-equation model of the macro-economy and the financial cycle: the house price positive feedback process.

## 6.5  The bank leverage-centred feedback process

In Section 6.2.1, we explained the reasons why, from the perspective of society at large, banks will take on too much risk. In this section, we focus not on the level but on changes in the amount of risk taken on by banks. To do this we introduce a second positive feedback process. This relates to *bank behaviour* and *financial assets*. It involves a different kind of behaviour by banks from the *retail* banks making housing and consumer loans that we modelled in Chapter 5 and discussed in the previous section. We introduce investment banks and as explained in Section 6.2.1, we focus entirely on their asset trading activities.

The model we present is highly stylized. We refer to the main actor as an investment bank. However, it is clear from the experience in the 2000s, discussed further in Chapter 7, that the sort of behaviour captured in the model was observed not only in some investment banks but also in some retail banks, universal banks and bank-like institutions known as shadow banks. We assume that an investment bank buys mortgages from the retail bank and uses a large number of mortgages as the raw material from which to produce financial assets. These are known as securitized assets. In Chapter 7, we explain the characteristics and origins of the two main types of financial asset (MBS, mortgage-backed securities and CDO, collateralized debt obligations) that were central to the upswing of the financial cycle in the 2000s.

Once mortgages are converted into securitized assets, the forces of demand and supply for the financial asset come into play. These forces are quite separate from the ones in the

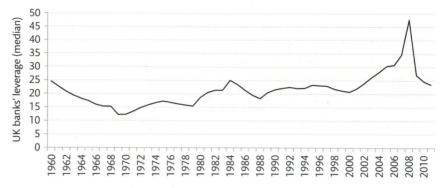

**Figure 6.10** UK banks' leverage: 1960–2011.

*Source:* Bank of England Financial Stability Report, June 2012.

real economy that underlie the initial demand for loans by households to fund the purchase of a house.

Unlike the plain vanilla banking crises described in the previous section, a financial cycle upswing and banking crisis in which a major role is played by investment banks and asset-backed securities appears to be new (although securitized assets themselves are not new). The details of how the upswing developed in the 2000s combining elements of a familiar plain-vanilla housing-centred cycle with the newer role played by banks borrowing to buy financial assets are described in the following chapter. Here we concentrate on the mechanisms at work in a bank leverage-centred upswing and downswing.

The key stylized fact that lies behind the model of investment bank behaviour presented here is the dramatic increase in the leverage of banks, (i.e. the ratio of their assets to their equity) and especially investment banks during the 2000s. Figure 6.10 highlights the dramatic increase in leverage in the UK banking system prior to the global financial crisis; leverage rose from 20 to 48 between 2000 and 2008.

### 6.5.1 Investment bank behaviour and leverage

In this section, we provide the details of a financial cycle generated by bank behaviour illustrated schematically in Fig. 6.2. In the bank leverage-centred case, mechanisms similar to those in the housing case are at work in the upswing of the financial cycle, which creates vulnerability to a financial crisis. The main elements of the cycle are as follows.[19]

1. Both investment banks and savers invest in financial assets. The assets are also referred to as risky securities or securitized assets. These two groups of investors differ in an important respect: savers are risk averse and investment banks are risk neutral. It may help to imagine the savers are pension funds although in our simple model, they are the saver households. The upswing begins with the widespread belief that risk has fallen significantly. As demand for the financial asset goes up, the price rises. Risk averse savers reduce their

---

[19] The analysis in this section is based on a number of papers by Hyun Song Shin (see Shin 2009, Shin 2010, Adrian & Shin 2011) as well as on Geanakoplos (2010).

demand in response but risk neutral investment banks do not. Investment banks will want to hold more of the risky asset as long as the expected return is positive. Hence the financial assets are transferred from savers to investment banks. As long as there is a positive expected return, the demand by investment banks to hold the risky security is only limited by their ability to borrow the money from savers (in the money market). Savers are prepared to lend as long as their loans to the investment banks are risk free; and that requires that investment bank equity is big enough to cover the worst case scenario. As a result of this process, the leverage of the investment banks can increase substantially as a result of the fall in risk.

2. The second 'upswing' period of reaction to the fall in risk comes about because the rise in the price of the financial asset leads to a capital gain for the investment banks on their initial holdings of securities. This increases the equity of IBs because they use the mark-to-market valuation of their assets. This means that the investment banks have more equity available to cover the worst case risk; so savers are now prepared to lend more and the investment banks are happy to borrow to buy more assets so long as there is a positive expected return, however low. The increase in investment bank holdings of securitized assets will be equal to the rise in equity multiplied by the high leverage level.

3. Given the volume of securitized assets now held by IBs, a completely unexpected reversal of the previous optimistic beliefs about risk (validated, for example, by rating agencies on the basis of their historical data) and a consequent fall in asset prices leads to major capital losses which can wipe out much IB equity, and put the solvency of some IBs at risk.

## The simple model

### Assumptions

To make the arguments about the behaviour of IBs as transparent as possible, we make a number of additional simplifying assumptions.

1. In the two upswing periods of the financial cycle we hold conditions in the real economy unchanged. In other words, the dynamics of the upswing of the financial cycle do not depend on spillovers to the real economy. In the modelling, this means we keep the number of financial assets, which we call $F$, constant. As in the case of the housing cycle, holding the supply of the asset constant focuses attention on the interaction between the price and demand. Moreover, since the repayment schedule of the households with mortgages is based on the loan they took out, it is not affected by the fluctuations in asset prices that take place in the financial sector.

2. We assume investment banks are not deposit–taking so they cannot fund their asset purchases through deposits.

3. We assume that the riskiness of assets is known to everyone.

### Value at Risk behaviour of the investment bank

Setting out a model using equations and a numerical example helps to clarify the behaviour of a stylized investment bank, which is otherwise unfamiliar. We go through the steps that were summarized above.

The price of an $F$ asset is $P$. The expected return from the asset is $(1 + r)$ per $F$ asset (note that in the VaR model, $r$ refers to the rate of return on the asset; not to the lending rate). Thus as long as the expected return is greater than the price they have to pay, i.e. $(1 + r) > P$, their expected profit is positive $(1 + r - P > 0)$, which means the investment bank spends $PF$ buying as many of the $F$ assets it can.

The maximum an investment bank can spend on the $F$ assets is equal to their equity, $e$, plus the amount they can borrow from savers, $B$. Hence, $PF = B + e$. This tells us the amount they want to borrow.

The next step is to figure out how much the investment banks can borrow. This depends on the behaviour of savers. We assume that savers are prepared to lend to investment banks at the money market rate, $r^P$, as long as they run strictly no risk. We assume further that savers who are considering lending to investment banks make the assumption that the maximum possible loss per $F$ asset is $\check{z}$. We can think of the ratings agencies (see Chapter 7, Section 7.2.3) being responsible for assessing the degree of risk and assigning a rating (such as AAB), from which savers can infer $\check{z}$.

Given that the maximum loss per $F$ asset is $\check{z}$, the lowest possible total return to the investment bank is $(1 + r - \check{z})F$. On that basis, savers are prepared to lend an amount $B$ as long as even in the worst case, the investment bank can pay savers back $(1 + r^P)B$. In the worst case, the investment bank gets its lowest total return minus the cost of borrowing, $r^P$, i.e. $(1 + r - r^P - \check{z})F$, We can make the notation simpler without altering the logic, by assuming $r^P = 0$.

The maximum the investment bank can borrow is

$$\max B = (1 + r - \check{z})F.$$

As we have seen above, as long as the expected return from buying an $F$ asset is positive, i.e. $(1 + r) > P$, the risk–neutral investment bank will buy as many as they can. The maximum they can fund is equal to the maximum they can borrow plus their equity:

$$PF = \max B + e = (1 + r - \check{z})F + e.$$

As an example, suppose $r = 0.07$, and $\check{z} = 0.04$, then the worst possible outcome is that each securitized asset yields only $1 + 0.07 - 0.04 = 1.03$. If the investment bank held $F$ of these assets, then the most it would have available to pay back the lenders (savers) at the end of the period would be $1.03F$. So the most that the investment bank would be able to borrow from the savers would be $B = 1.03F$ –since the savers would be sure to get that back even in the very worst case scenario. If the investment bank also had equity of 10, it would then have $1.03F + 10$ available to buy the assets. If the price of an asset was 1.05, and it spent all it had available to spend, then it would spend $1.05F = 1.03F + 10$. (And you can solve that equation, as we will do in a more general way below, to see that $F = 10/0.02 = 500$.)

Thus, investment banks spend all they can by borrowing 'up to the hilt' and using their own capital (i.e. equity) for buying $F$ assets as long as $(1 + r) > P$ by however small an amount.

From this equation, we can work out how many F assets the investment bank buys.

$$PF = (1 + r - \bar{z})F + e$$
$$\rightarrow (P - (1 + r - \bar{z}))F = e$$
$$\rightarrow F = \frac{e}{(P - (1 + r - \bar{z}))} = \frac{e}{\underset{\text{risk}}{\bar{z}} - \underset{\text{return}}{(1 + r - P)}}. \qquad \text{(investment bank demand for } F\text{)}$$

If you fill in the values for $r$, $\bar{z}$, $P$ and $e$ from above, you will see that $F = 500$.

This equation highlights that the investment bank's demand for the $F$ asset rises with its equity and rises as risk falls relative to return. Recalling the definition of leverage,

$$\text{leverage} = \lambda = \frac{\text{assets}}{\text{equity}} = \frac{F_0}{e} = \frac{1}{\text{risk} - \text{return to investment bank}},$$

(leverage of investment bank)

it is clear that leverage will rise when risk falls relative to the return to the investment bank. (As noted earlier, the value of assets is in fact $PF$, but for simplicity we assume that $P = 1$; it does not much affect the leverage level.)

Note that the fact that the investment bank's leverage depends on the gap between risk and return does not reflect its attitude to risk. We assume all along that the investment bank is risk-neutral. The role that risk is playing is via the savers: a fall in risk makes savers willing to lend more to the investment bank. Since the worst possible outcome has become less bad, the investment bank can borrow more whilst respecting the value at risk constraint. Respecting the value at risk constraint means the investment bank can repay the lenders in the worst case. The vital role played by the credit ratings agency in establishing maximum risk is evident from the leverage equation. It is clearly possible for leverage to go very high if risk falls—as long as the return to the investment bank remains positive.

### Numerical example of upswing and crash

This subsection sets out a simple numerical example of an upswing and a subsequent crash. The formal model behind the example is set out in Section 6.8.2 of the Appendix.

The economy begins with equity of 10, a rate of return on the financial asset of 0.07, initial price of 1 and risk level of 0.12. The second column of Table 6.1 summarizes the initial conditions. The policy rate is assumed to be zero (and constant). From the equation for the

**Table 6.1** Numerical example of upswing in the financial cycle and crash.

|  | Period 0 | Period 1 | Period 2 | Period 3 |
|---|---|---|---|---|
| Policy rate, $r^P$ | 0 | 0 | 0 | 0 |
| Rate of return on financial assets, $r$ | 0.07 | 0.07 | 0.07 | 0.07 |
| Equity, $e$ | 10 | 10 | 20 | wiped out |
| Risk level, $\bar{z}$ | 0.12 | 0.04 | 0.04 | 0.12 |
| Price of financial assets, $P$ | 1 | 1.05 | 1.05 | 1 |

investment bank's demand for the $F$ asset, we have:

$$F_0 = \frac{e_0}{\underset{\text{risk}}{z_0} - \underset{\text{return}}{(1+r-P_0)}}$$

$$= \frac{10}{0.12 - (1+0.07-1)} = \frac{10}{0.05} = 200;$$

$$\lambda_0 = \frac{F_0}{e_0} = \frac{200}{10} = 20.$$

*Upswing*

The upswing begins as a result of a fall in risk. The conditions under which a dangerous upswing can develop centre on the key equation for the demand for the financial asset by the investment bank:

$$F = \frac{\text{equity}}{\text{risk} - \text{return}} = \frac{e}{\bar{z} - (1+r-P)}.$$

Investment bank holdings of $F$ will rise sharply (pushing leverage up high) in an upswing if:

1. the return on the asset, $(1+r-P)$, is quite high relative to risk;

2. the initial risk is rather low;

3. prices rise less than risk falls, which means that return does not fall as much as risk does.

Using the numbers in Table 6.1, we look at what happens if risk falls to 0.04. We assume that everyone in the model economy agrees that risk has fallen because, for example, of the credibility of the credit ratings agencies who have given higher credit ratings to the $F$ asset. The fall in risk leads both IBs and saver households to demand more financial assets, pushing up their price. We assume that as the price increases, reducing the expected return on the assets, the demand from risk-neutral investment banks remains undiminished, while that of the risk-averse holders of assets is sharply reduced, thus transferring assets to the investment banks.

We divide the upswing into two periods, 1 and 2. In period 1 we look at the effect of the fall in risk and consequent price increase in increasing investment bank holdings of F from $F_0$ to $F_1$, which results from an increase in leverage. In period 1 we assume that investment bank capital does not change. In period 2, we look at the additional effect on the investment bank's demand for assets as a result of the capital gains made in period 1 (i.e. the increase in price in period 1 on the assets held at the start of period 1), namely $F_0$. This increases investment bank capital via mark-to-market valuation of assets, and the demand for assets now rises because of the higher level of IB capital multiplied by the higher leverage reached in period 1. We assume artificially but not wholly unrealistically that this new increased demand for assets does not lead to a further increase in price because the expected return at $P_1$ (while positive and therefore attractive to risk-neutral investment banks) is so low that other risk averse holders of these financial assets require virtually no incentive in the form of higher prices to part with them.

In this case, we assume that price rises from 1 to 1.05, or by 5%.

We can now use our simple model and the data from the table to find the leverage and asset holdings of the IB after the fall in risk:

Period 0: risk = 0.12; return = $1 + r - P = 1 + 0.07 - 1 = 7\%$; so leverage is $\lambda_0 = \frac{1}{(0.12-(1+0.07-1))} = \frac{1}{0.05} = 20$ and investment bank holdings of $F$ are $F_0 = \lambda_0 e_0 = 200$.

Period 1: risk = 0.04; return = $1 + r - P = 1 + 0.07 - 1.05 = 2\%$; so leverage is $\lambda_1 = \frac{1}{(0.04-(1+0.07-1.05))} = \frac{1}{0.02} = 50$ and investment bank holdings of $F$ are $F_1 = \lambda_1 e_0 = 500$.

Now we turn to period 2, the second part of the upswing. In this part, the capital gains made in period 1 increase investment bank capital from $e_0 = 10$ to $e_2 = 20$. And this leads to a further dramatic increase in $F$ from $F_1 = 500$ to $F_2 = 1000$.

The equity of the IB in period 2, $e_2$, is calculated by looking at the capital gain they made on their $F$ assets following the rise in price. The price rose from 1 to 1.05 between periods 0 and 1. This implies that on their pre-existing assets of 200, there is a capital gain of $1.05 \times 200 - 200 = 10$. Hence, equity has doubled from $e_0 = 10$ to $e_2 = 20$.

Periods 1 and 2 provide a picture of a world in which everyone feels safe—the credit rating agencies have shifted the assessment of risk down—yet it has all the hallmarks of a dangerous situation. As discussed in Chapter 7, it may describe the world Lehman Brothers and the other investment banks were operating in during the 2000s. Investment banks were making very small profits on huge holdings of assets, reflected in very high leverage, and the belief that the assets were almost completely safe. Chapter 7 explains the concentration of the 'very safe' super-senior tranches of securitized assets in the hands of the investment banks.

In spite of the low expected return of 2%, investment banks are prepared to increase their leverage. Although the return has gone down from 7% to 2%, risk has gone down by more (from 0.12 to 0.04). With the return still positive, investment banks increase their holdings. Savers are prepared to expand their lending because they too believe risk is so low. The outcome is a new equilibrium in period 1 (as shown in the third column of Table 6.1), the first period of the upswing, in which leverage rises from 20 to 50, and $F$ rises from 200 to 500. In period 2, the second period of the upswing, shown in Table 6.1, investment bank equity rises by 10 from 10 to 20 as a result of the capital gains made by the IB in period 1—a price rise of 5% on the investment bank's initial holdings of $F_0 = 200$. And this sharply increases investment bank holdings since the increase in capital is multiplied by the leverage reached in period 1 of $\lambda_1 = 50$. Thus in period 2, $F$ rises from $F_1 = 500$ to $F_2 = 1000$.

To check the funding split between equity and borrowing, we note that equity increased to 20 as a result of marking-to-market the financial assets. This implies that 980 of the investment bank's assets were funded by borrowing, i.e. $B_2 = 980$. Figure 6.11 shows the expansion of the IB's balance sheet in response to the fall in risk. The figure is drawn to scale and highlights just how small the IB's capital cushion is compared to the size of their balance sheet in the upswing period. We shall see how this high leverage makes IBs more vulnerable to bankruptcy in the next subsection.

The important point to take away from this simple example is that investment banks will always buy as many assets as they can if the expected profit is positive (as they are risk-neutral). The amount they can buy is constrained by their equity and the amount that savers are willing to lend to them. The fall in risk boosts the IB's asset holdings because it loosens their funding constraint by increasing both their equity and the amount they can borrow from savers.

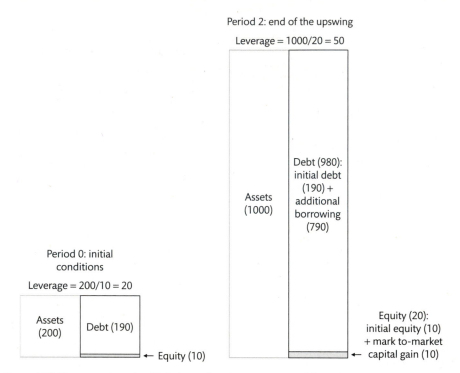

**Figure 6.11** The expansion of an IBs balance sheet in response to a fall in risk. Leverage = Assets/Equity.

## Crash

Suppose that in period 3, some 'scary bad news' arrives in the economy and shifts beliefs about risk back to its initial higher level.[20] This could be the result, for example, of a fall in house prices that underlie the securitized assets. If risk is reassessed upwards from 0.04 to 0.12, the demand for securitized assets will fall. If we look at the implications of a fall in price back from 1.05 to 1, then the capital loss on the investment bank's assets is $0.05 \times 1000 = 50$. The investment bank's equity is 20 in period 2 and it will be wiped out by the capital loss, as shown by the fifth column in Table 6.1. The investment bank will be bankrupt.[21]

### Overview

To summarize, there are a fixed number of financial assets that have been created from the mortgage loans and are traded. There are two kinds of investors interested in holding the F assets: the investment bank which is risk–neutral and uses the VaR business model and the

---

[20] The term has been used by Fostel and Geanakoplos (2012), who define 'scary bad news' as news that increases uncertainty and the volatility of asset prices.

[21] Note that although this numerical example shows a case where IB goes bankrupt, this need not always be the case. Whether an IB goes bankrupt or not will depend on the size of changes in risk and the degree of responsiveness of price to changes in risk. For example, had risk risen only a small amount in period 3, resulting in a price fall of 0.1, then equity would have fallen by $0.01 \times 1000 = 10$ and the IB would have avoided bankruptcy.

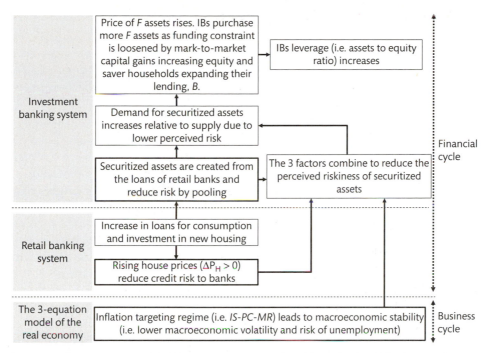

**Figure 6.12** The 3-equation model of the macro-economy and the financial cycle: the bank-centred positive feedback process.

saver households. The behaviour of the investment bank in which it reacts positively to an increase in the price of the securitized asset is a form of financial accelerator, which triggers a process of rising asset prices similar to the tulip bulb case in Fig. 6.6. In this way the assets will become more concentrated in the hands of the IBs, who will borrow from the savers in order to buy more of the assets.

### The upswing of the financial cycle

Figure 6.12 illustrates how an upswing of a financial cycle based on bank behaviour and securitized assets can begin. Three pathways are shown that can lead to a reduction in the perceived riskiness of the securitized assets. Lower risk in turn increases the demand for the securitized asset by both investment banks and savers relative to the fixed supply, which leads to a rise in its price.

The perception on the part of an individual investor (such as an investment bank or a saver household) that securitized assets are less risky can arise from developments in the macro-economy, in the housing market or in the financial sector itself as a result of financial innovation. These beliefs are influenced by the ratings given by the credit rating agencies. As we shall see in Chapter 7, each of these appears to have played a role in setting in motion the long upswing of the financial cycle prior to the global financial crisis.

Starting from the bottom of the diagram:

1. The more successful is macro-economic stabilization policy such as inflation-targeting, and hence the less volatile is the macro-economy, the lower is the risk of unemployment

that would make the repayment of mortgage debt less likely. This makes the securitized asset based on mortgages safer.

2. The second source of lower risk is due to rising house prices: higher house prices reduce the credit risk to the bank since the market value of the asset (i.e. the bank's collateral) rises relative to the associated debt, which is fixed by the historical or purchase price of the house.

3. The third is financial innovation. Financial innovations include a procedure called tranching in which individual mortgages are divided into segments and combined into new financial assets with different levels of risk. Another innovation is the invention of credit default swaps, which are financial contracts called derivatives that offer protection (i.e. insurance) against the default of securities issued by a borrower (e.g. mortgage based assets).

Each of these channels can lower the risk perceived by the investor. As perceived risk falls demand from all investor types rises and pushes up the price. Because of their risk–neutrality, investment banks respond to the rise in the price of the financial asset, $F$, by increasing their demand further. The ability to fund increased purchases of assets through (a) the higher equity associated with mark–to–market valuation of their assets and (b) by borrowing from savers based on the easing of the Value-at-Risk constraint can lead to a very large increase in the number of assets held by investment banks and in their leverage.

### The downswing of the financial cycle and financial crisis

Figure 6.13 shows how the upswing can go into reverse. In the diagram, the trigger is a reversal in the upward trend of house prices (see the middle panel). Risk goes up. This puts the $F$-feedback process into reverse. The demand for securitized assets falls relative to the supply and the price of the financial asset falls. Given the extent of borrowing by the investment banks, a sufficient fall in the price of the $F$ asset would cause the IB to become insolvent. Through its effect on the functioning of the banking system, where retail and investment banks are interconnected, the crash reduces the willingness and ability of banks to make new loans. Banks will sell assets and call in loans in order to strengthen their weakened balance sheets. These actions will dampen aggregate demand through the $IS$ relation as shown by the arrows into the bottom panel in Fig. 6.13. Just as the financial accelerator process fuelled the upswing, it amplifies and propagates the downswing.

The financial cycle can turn down *without* a full-blown financial crisis and insolvent banks—but nevertheless with important effects on the real economy. The reversal of the $F$-feedback process will impose capital losses on the asset side of the investment bank's balance sheet even if the capital cushion is not eroded entirely.

The lower demand for the financial asset will reinforce the weakness in the financial and real estate sectors. Retail banks, IBs and borrower households will all seek to reduce their leverage, i.e. to reduce their debts. This will reduce aggregate demand. As we shall see in Section 6.6, saver households will have no reason to increase aggregate demand to offset this. We also use Section 6.6 to explore whether the policy maker can counteract the impact of the downturn in the financial cycle on the real economy.

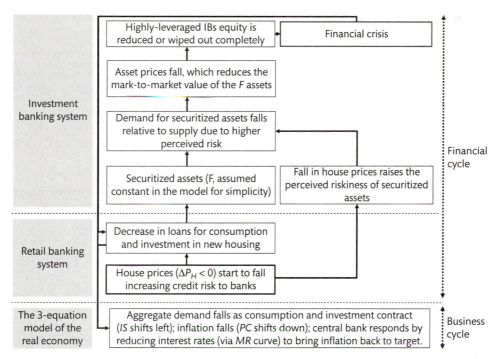

**Figure 6.13** The 3-equation model of the macro-economy and the financial cycle: a fall in house prices leading to increased perceptions of risk and a financial crisis.

### The paradox of credibility

In his explanation of financial crises, the economist Hyman Minsky (1982) highlighted the way in which a benign period in the economy could sow the seeds for a subsequent crisis. When everyone believes risk has gone down, they behave in such a way that makes the system riskier. This logic has been referred to as a paradox of credibility (Borio and Lowe, 2002, Borio and White, 2004).

A question that may spring to mind is whether it is satisfactory to model the economy in such a way that in the upswing of the financial cycle everyone is swept up in the belief that risk has fallen—permanently. Economists do not generally like models based on 'false beliefs'. Nevertheless, as Minsky argued, the model appears to provide a useful way of thinking about how a paradox of credibility can create the conditions for a financial crisis. For example, it appears to provide insight to the circumstances that led to the upswing of the financial cycle in the 2000s, which was followed by falling house prices and the bankruptcy of Lehman Brothers, leading to the banking crisis and downswing.

In the 2000s, 'false beliefs' seems to be a reasonable way of describing the mindset of decision makers—policy makers, managers of banks and individuals—about the lower macroeconomic risk due to the implementation of the modern macroeconomic framework, the ever-upward trajectory of house prices and improvements in risk management by more sophisticated financial institutions.

As an example, British chancellor Gordon Brown famously claimed that the new macroeconomic framework would produce stability and put an end to 'boom and bust':

Every time in recent decades when the British economy has started to grow, governments of both parties have taken short-term decisions which too often have created unsustainable consumer booms, let the economy get out of control and sacrificed monetary and fiscal prudence. And everyone here will remember how quickly and easily boom turned to bust in the early nineties.

So Britain did need a wholly new monetary and fiscal framework that went beyond the crude Keynesian fine tuning of the fifties and sixties and the crude monetarism of the seventies and eighties and, instead, offered a modern British route to stability.[22]

With Bank of England independence, tough decisions on inflation, new fiscal rules and hard public spending controls, we today in our country have economic stability not boom and bust, the lowest inflation in Europe, and long term interest rates—essential for businesses planning to borrow and invest—lower than for thirty five years.[23]

## 6.6  A balance sheet recession and the financial accelerator

Balance sheet recessions are those that follow the bursting of large, credit-fuelled, asset price bubbles, such as Japan in the 1990s or the USA and many countries in Europe following the global financial crisis. Recessions of this type are different from the usual business cycle downturn because of the effect of the collapse in asset prices on the balance sheets of households and firms. This brings the financial accelerator process into play, which amplifies and propagates the downturn. Households and firms deleverage, that is, they reduce their debt so as to repair their balance sheets. This means they increase their savings. This reduces aggregate demand and unless there is a balancing source of increased aggregate demand, it slows down recovery.[24]

In this section we provide an overview of how a balance sheet recession can be modelled using the tools we have developed in this chapter along with the familiar 3-equation model. We follow the logic of Eggertsson and Krugman (2012), in which the forced repayment of bank loans plays a major part.

We continue to assume that households are of two types—saver and borrower households. Saver households are not credit constrained. They are able to borrow freely and can be modelled using the permanent income hypothesis (PIH) as set out in Chapter 1. They are able to smooth their consumption by lending and borrowing. This also allows them to take advantage of changes in the interest rate to save more when the interest rate is high and vice versa, so as to maximize their utility. In addition to the PIH motivation, we assume saver households save for precautionary reasons. We model this in a simple way by assuming they adjust their savings to achieve a target level of wealth.

Borrower households are credit constrained. This means that their spending depends on the credit they can get from the banks. According to the financial accelerator, the collateral

[22] Excerpt taken from a speech by (then British chancellor) Gordon Brown at the Lord Mayor's Dinner for Bankers and Merchants of the City of London, Mansion House, City of London, June 20th 2001.
[23] Excerpt taken from a speech by (then British chancellor) Gordon Brown at the TGWU 'Manufacturing Matters' conference, March 28th 2002.
[24] See Koo (2003 and 2011) for a more detailed discussion of balance sheet recessions. For a formal model, see Eggertsson and Krugman (2012).

value of housing plays a very important role in the lending decisions of retail banks to households. We assume banks apply a maximum loan-to-value (*LTV*) ratio (i.e. loan value divided by property value) when they extend loans to households. In addition, we assume that the initial value is $LTV_{High}$, which reflects the loose credit conditions that typically prevail in the years preceding a financial crisis.

We assume that borrower households are fully 'borrowed up' each period, which means that they borrow up to the limit of the prevailing *LTV* ratio. The maximum amount borrower households can borrow for new housing and consumption is pinned down by the loan-to-value ratio and this period's change in the value of the existing housing stock. However, borrower households may want to save if their net worth in houses is less than their target wealth. As we shall see, this plays a role in a balance sheet recession. Borrower households' aggregate demand consists of their income minus the interest payments they owe to the saver households plus spending on new housing and consumption minus the saving needed to achieve their target wealth.

The *IS* curve in this model economy is the sum of the aggregate demand of saver and borrower households, weighted by the proportion of households in the economy that are credit constrained (i.e. borrower households).

*Pre-crash equilibrium*

We assume that in the period before the crash, the economy is in equilibrium. This means:

1. both savers and borrowers are exactly achieving their wealth targets;
2. borrowers have borrowed the maximum possible, which is the loan to value ratio multiplied by the capital gain on their housing in the previous period;
3. the central bank has set $r^P$, such that output is at the constant inflation equilibrium, i.e. $y^D = y_e$.

*The crash and a balance sheet recession*

Given this framework, we are now able to explore the channels through which a collapse in the price of securitized assets and housing affects aggregate demand and shifts the *IS* curve to the left. We distinguish between (1) a loan-to-value effect and (2) a collateral effect. There are two other effects: (3) the consequence of banks calling in housing loans when borrowers go 'under water', in the sense that the market value of their house is less than the mortgage outstanding; and (4) the increase in savings as both borrower and saver households seek to rebuild target wealth following the fall in the value of houses and financial assets.

*(1) Retail banks reduce their loan-to-value ratio*

The banks respond to the fall in the value of their assets due to the fall in prices of housing and securitized assets by reducing their loan-to-value ratio: $LTV_{High} \rightarrow LTV_{Low}$. This implies a fall in aggregate demand.

*(2) Fall in value of housing collateral*

When we move from a situation of rising to falling house prices, i.e. from $\Delta P_H > 0$ to $\Delta P_H < 0$, this reduces the value of potential collateral. This has the effect of reducing loans for consumption with a straightforward multiplier effect on aggregate demand.

### (3) Balance sheet effect

A potentially much more important effect is that banks may try and call in loans because the value of the collateral, i.e. the market price of the house, has, for example, fallen below the value of the loan, so that the value of the house is worth less than the mortgage. We shall see why when loans are called in (i.e. repaid) this may have significant deflationary effects. The argument centres on the fact that if borrowers are credit-constrained they have to pay the full amount of the loan repayment out of consumption—so aggregate demand from borrower households falls by the *full amount* of the repayment, call it $-\Delta \tilde{L}$. The wealth of saver households rises by this cash transfer, that is by $\Delta \tilde{L}$. But because saver households decide consumption on the basis of permanent income (which determines the expected value of future consumption and via the desire for smoothing, of present consumption), their present consumption only rises by the contribution which the repayment makes to permanent income. If the saver households reinvest the $\Delta \tilde{L}$ in the money market, then permanent income and therefore saver households' consumption rises by $r^P \Delta \tilde{L}$, which is a small fraction of the amount by which the aggregate demand of borrower households falls. In this case, aggregate demand falls as the increase in spending by saver households is not sufficient to offset the reduction in spending by borrower households.

### (4) Rebuilding target wealth after a fall in house and financial asset prices

In addition to the effects operating through the constraints placed on aggregate demand as a consequence of falling asset prices as banks reduce loan-to-value ratios and call in loans, households themselves will respond to the fall in the prices of housing and financial assets. The main channel is the desire of borrower households to rebuild their wealth back toward the target level in response to the fall in wealth due to falling house prices. Saver households, which have seen a reduction in the value of their financial assets ($F$), will also seek to rebuild their wealth. In both cases, aggregate demand will be depressed. In practice this may be the most important longer run effect.

The deleveraging shock forces the borrowers to drastically reduce their spending and pay down a proportion of their existing debts, which adversely affects aggregate demand unless savers can be induced to increase their spending to compensate (e.g. by a lower interest rate). However, the ability of monetary policy to stabilize the economy is limited by the zero lower bound, as we discussed in Chapter 3. In the case of a large enough deleveraging shock, the economy can fall into a deflation trap with the twin evils of falling output and prices (see Chapters 3 and 7) in which the paradox of thrift applies so that higher intended savings by households reduce aggregate savings because of the fall in output caused by the lower aggregate demand (see Chapter 1).

The model of a balance sheet recession highlights the following policy implications.

1. In the context of a balance sheet recession, fiscal stimulus can be effective by boosting aggregate demand in order to give the private sector time to repair their balance sheets.
2. The increase in government debt can then be repaid once the 'deleveraging process' is over.
3. Although fiscal stimulus is called for in a balance sheet recession when the private sector is trying to save more, the very same balance sheet problems dampen the size of the

multiplier. This increases the burden on fiscal policy, which makes the government's stabilization task more difficult in both economic and political terms.

## 6.7 Conclusions

This chapter has focused on financial cycles and financial crises, and their impact on the macro-economy. A well-functioning banking system allows firms and households to implement their spending plans through borrowing. Banks can, however, take on more risk than is socially optimal because they don't take into account the impact of their actions on system-wide risk. Moreover, the possibility of government bailout reduces the costs to them of downside risk. The financial sector is also an amplifier and propagator of shocks through the economy, due to mechanisms such as the financial accelerator and asset price bubbles. These shocks often spill over into the real economy and can have devastating effects (as we saw during the recent financial crisis).

In order to better understand the financial sector and its relationship with the real economy, we introduced the concept of the financial cycle, which tracks fluctuations in key financial variables, such as credit and house prices. Upswings and downswings of the financial cycle typically last longer than is the case for the business cycle, and peaks in the cycle are commonly associated with the onset of financial crises. In the inflation-targeting monetary policy framework, financial variables are only considered to the extent that they influence headline inflation. This means potentially dangerous financial imbalances can emerge even in the face of successful inflation targeting.

At the centre of the models presented in this chapter are two feedback processes similar in structure: the house price and financial asset price feedback processes. The two can also interact with the result that in a (perceived) low risk environment there are both housing and financial asset price bubbles and rapid increases in leverage of IBs. The model also shows that any shocks that subsequently increase the perceived level of risk can leave IBs vulnerable to large losses and even bankruptcy. This sort of shock and the associated balance sheet recession can have serious implications for the real economy, reducing aggregate demand through several channels.

This framework allows us to answer a number of questions about financial cycles and financial crises and their effect on the economy:

1.  What factors can account for a reduction in the perceived level of risk in the economy? Three candidates are: (1) a reduction in macroeconomic volatility increasing the likelihood that households will be able to service their mortgages, (2) rising house prices, which increase the value of housing collateral compared to mortgage loan values, and (3) financial innovation aimed at reducing credit risk. All three were present in the Great Moderation that preceded the global finanical crisis.

2.  Why does a fall in risk typically lead to a rise in the leverage of IBs? Risk-neutral IBs using a Value-at-Risk business model want to buy as many financial assets as possible as long as they offer a positive expected return. They are restricted in the amount they can purchase by the size of their equity and their ability to borrow from saver households. It is the saver households' response to the fall in risk that enables the IBs to borrow more and 'lever up' by

expanding their balance sheets. Savers are willing to lend more to the IBs after the fall in risk as they believe there is a lower chance of the bad state of the world occuring.

3.  Why do rising housing and financial asset prices not dampen the upswing of the financial cycle? This is due to the positive feedback effects when these assets rise in price. When house prices rise, households can take out more loans for consumption (using housing wealth as collateral) and have more incentive to invest in housing (due to the expectation of future house price increases). In terms of financial assets, a rise in price will lead to a capital gain for the IBs as they mark-to-market the value of their assets. They then use this additional equity to fund the purchase of more financial assets (as long as their expected profit is still positive), further pushing up asset prices.

4.  What does the term 'balance sheet recession' refer to and what does this mean for the recovery phase of the business cycle? The term refers to recessions that follow the bursting of large credit-fuelled asset price bubbles. Recovery from a balance sheet recession is typically slower than from other recessions as households, firms and banks are 'deleveraging' (i.e. paying down debt). This reduces aggregate demand and drags on the recovery.

This chapter has provided a theoretical framework for thinking about the financial cycle and financial crises. The following chapter applies the framework to the global financial crisis of 2008–09 to shed light on the mechanisms that caused the crisis.

# 6.8 Appendix

## 6.8.1 Modelling the housing-centred positive feedback process

In this subsection, we set out a simple mathematical model of the housing-centred feedback process. We collapse the model to just two periods and show how a reduction in risk increases house prices and can fuel a house price cycle as set out earlier in the left-hand panel of Fig. 6.1. The key components of the housing cycle model are: $\Delta P_{H,1}$ = the change in house prices between period 0 and period 1; $\Delta H_1^D$ = the change in the demand for housing between period 0 and period 1; $\Delta P_H^E$ = the change in expected house prices; $L_1$ = the amount of loans provided by retail banks in period 1; $\bar{l}$ = the loan-to-value ratio; $H_0$ = the housing stock in period 0; and $z_t$ = the perceived riskiness of loans in period $t$.

The model has four main equations. The first shows that house price changes are proportional to the change in demand for housing and the change in expected house prices,

$$\Delta P_{H,1} = \alpha \Delta H_1^D + \beta \Delta P_H^E. \tag{6.1}$$

The second shows that the change in expected house prices is proportional to the change in actual house prices,

$$\Delta P_H^E = \gamma \Delta P_{H,1}. \tag{6.2}$$

The third shows that the change in demand for housing is proportional to the new loans that have become available during the upswing,

$$\Delta H_1^D = \delta L_1. \tag{6.3}$$

The final equation shows that retail bank loans in period 1 depend on the loan-to-value ratio, the change in the value of the housing stock and the change in risk perceptions between period 0 and period 1,

$$L_1 = \bar{l}\Delta P_{H,1}H_0 - a(z_1 - z_0). \tag{6.4}$$

We can immediately see from these equations how a bubble could arise in house prices following a fall in risk. The reduction in risk boosts the amount banks are willing to lend, and credit-constrained borrowers take out additional loans to expand their purchases of housing. This increases house prices and also expectations of future house price rises, which feeds back into loan supply (as the extra collateral allows households to borrow more). Put another way, the fall in risk and the positive feedbacks produce an upswing in house prices.

We can now substitute Equations 6.2, 6.3 and 6.4 back into Equation 6.1 and rearrange to find the impact of a change in risk on house prices:

$$\Delta P_{H,1} = \alpha\delta(\bar{l}\Delta P_{H,1}H_0 - a\Delta z_1) + \beta\gamma\Delta P_{H,1}$$

$$\rightarrow \Delta P_{H,1} = -\frac{\alpha\delta}{1 - \alpha\delta\bar{l}H_0 - \beta\gamma}a\Delta z_1. \tag{6.5}$$

Equation 6.5 shows that a reduction in risk ($\Delta z_1 < 0$) leads to an increase in the price of housing. This is due to the positive feedback mechanisms outlined above. The equation also shows that if the market perception of risk suddenly increased, then house prices would collapse, potentially leading to a financial crisis.

### 6.8.2 A positive feedback model of investment bank behaviour

This model formalizes the numerical example in the chapter, and it is important to read the example to understand the intuition and underlying assumptions, including periodization, in this Appendix. As in the numerical example, a fall in risk causes the upswing in the market for securitized assets, and an equivalent rise in risk causes the downswing and possible bankruptcy. Again as there, the problem arises because capital gains due to the increase in price during the upswing are based on a relatively low level of pre-existing assets in period 0, while the capital losses from an equivalent fall in price in the downturn are based on the much larger amount of assets held at the top of the upswing.

We assume that the upswing (initiated by a fall in z from $z_0$ to $z_1$) consists of two periods. In period 1, we look at the effects of the fall in the risk (holding IB equity constant): the fall in risk boosts demand for securities by both IBs and passive savers; this pushes up the price of the securities; we assume that (risk-averse) savers are more sensitive to the price increase than IBs, so the rise in price implies the transfer of some securities from savers to IBs. During period 1, leverage increases while equity remains constant.

In period 2 of the upswing, we calculate the effect of the price increase on mark-to-market increase in equity and the effect of the increase in equity on further increasing the demand for securities by IBs (with no such effect on savers). In period 2, we make the simplifying assumption that there is no further increase in prices—the intuition here is that at price $P_1$ risk-averse savers are making a very low average return so that their supply of securities is now perfectly elastic at that price; this reflects risk-neutral IB demand 'up to the hilt' so long as there is *any* positive expected return, up to the limits of what IBs can borrow. In the model, $F$ is demand for securities by IBs (we don't explicitly model saver behaviour).

## Period 1

$$F_1 - F_0 = \Delta F_1 = \frac{e_0}{z_1 - (1 + r - P_1)} - \frac{e_0}{z_0 - (1 + r - P_0)} \approx -b(\Delta z_1 + \Delta P_1), \tag{6.6}$$

where $-b(\Delta z_1 + \Delta P_1)$ is a first order linear approximation. Specifically,

$$F_1 = \frac{e_0}{(z_1 - (1 + r - P_1))} = F(z_1, P_1) \approx F(z_0, P_0) + F_z(z_0, P_0)\Delta z_1 + F_P(z_0, P_0)\Delta P_1.$$

It is easy to see that $F_z = F_P = -\frac{e_0}{(z_0 - (1 + r - P_0))^2}$.

We define leverage in period 0 as $\lambda_0 \equiv \frac{F_0}{e_0} \rightarrow \lambda_0 = \frac{1}{(z_0 - (1 + r - P_0))}$, so that $b = F_0 \lambda_0$.

Thus, $\Delta F_1 > 0$ is the *net* result of the initial fall in risk ($\Delta z_1 < 0$) and the subsequent rise in price ($\Delta P_1 > 0$) because of the initial rise in demand.

We next assume the effect of a change in demand on price is given by,

$$\Delta P_1 = \alpha \Delta F_1, \tag{6.7}$$

where the effect on price of the smaller increase in demand by savers is implicitly included on the right hand side, as being some proportion of $\Delta F_1$.

Substituting Equation 6.7 into Equation 6.6, we can see that the net effect of the fall in risk on demand for securities by IBs (before taking account of mark-to-market rise in equity) is:

$$\Delta F_1 = -\frac{b}{1 + b\alpha} \Delta z_1 \equiv -\gamma \Delta z_1 \text{ with } \gamma > 0. \tag{6.8}$$

Hence, Equations 6.7 and 6.8 imply:

$$\Delta P_1 = -\alpha \gamma \Delta z_1, \tag{6.9}$$

if we assume that $P_0 = 1$, $P_1 = 1 - \alpha \gamma \Delta z_1 > 1$.

We may worry that for large changes in $z$ the approximation in Equation 6.6 is not highly accurate, so in practical terms it may be better to use Equations 6.6 to 6.9 to work out the increase in price, and then given $P_1$ to use the exact formula to work out both the increase in leverage and the increase in assets held by IBs:

$$\Delta \lambda_1 = \frac{1}{(z_1 - (1 + r - P_1))} - \frac{1}{(z_0 - (1 + r - P_0))} > 0 \text{ if } \Delta F_1 > 0 \tag{6.10}$$

$$\text{and } \Delta F_1 = \frac{e_0}{(z_1 - (1 + r - P_1))} - \frac{e_0}{(z_0 - (1 + r - P_0))} = e_0 \Delta \lambda_1. \tag{6.11}$$

## Period 2

In this period, we look at the effect of the increase in capital as a result of the capital gains in period 1:

$$\Delta e_2 = F_0 \Delta P_1. \tag{6.12}$$

The increase in securities demanded as result of $e$ increasing is given by

$$\Delta F_2 = \lambda_1 \Delta e_2, \tag{6.13}$$

so the bigger the increase in leverage in period 1 the bigger will be $\Delta F_2$.

The total holdings in securities at the end of the upswing are

$$F_2 = \Delta F_2 + \Delta F_1 + F_0 = \lambda_1 \Delta e_2 + e_0 \Delta \lambda_1 + F_0. \tag{6.14}$$

### Period 3: the downswing

If we assume an equivalent fall in prices during a downswing caused by $\Delta z_2 = -\Delta z_1$, so that $\Delta P_2 = -\Delta P_1$, this causes a capital loss on $F_2$ and this is much greater than the earlier capital gain on $F_0$. The capital gain in the upswing was $\Delta e_2 = F_0 \Delta P_1$ and the capital loss on the downswing is $\Delta e_3 = F_2 \Delta P_2 = -F_2 \Delta P_1$. Hence, the net loss over the whole cycle is:

$$e_3 - e_0 = \Delta e_2 + \Delta e_3 = F_0 \Delta P_1 - F_2 \Delta P_1 = -(F_2 - F_0) \Delta P_1 = (F_2 - F_0) \alpha \gamma \Delta z_1. \tag{6.15}$$

This implies insolvency, i.e. $e_3 \leq 0$, when $e_0 + (F_2 - F_0) \alpha \gamma \Delta z_1 \leq 0$, which is true for large enough $\Delta z_1$.

## 6.9 Questions

### 6.9.1 Checklist questions

1. Does the problem of moral hazard indicate that insolvent banks should not be rescued? Justify your answer.

2. What are the three key characteristics of systemic banking crises? How would you expect these characteristics to influence the *IS* curve?

3. Compare and contrast the business and financial cycles on the following measures:

   (a) the components of the series;

   (b) the length of the cycle.

   Why are equity prices not incorporated into the measure of the financial cycle set out in Section 6.2.3?

4. To what extent is the financial cycle taken into account when inflation-targeting central banks are setting monetary policy?

5. Imagine a city with abundant space for expansion. Are the following statements true, false or uncertain? [Hint: use Fig. 6.6 and accompanying text for guidance.]

   (a) A spike in demand for housing will see house prices rise in the short-run.

   (b) An extended period of high demand for housing will lead to a house price bubble.

6. Using the housing market as an example, explain the following concepts:

   (a) loan-to-value ratio;

   (b) asset price bubble;

   (c) financial accelerator.

7. In the financial asset feedback process, which factors can contribute to a reduced perception of risk? How does the perceived reduction in risk lead to IBs becoming more highly leveraged? Make sure your answer refers to the Value-at-Risk model.

8. Imagine an investment bank which has equity of 10 and operates in an economy where risk is 0.15, the policy rate is 0, the rate of return on financial assets is 0.05 and the price of financial assets is 1. Use Section 6.5 to answer the following questions:

   (a) How many financial assets does the investment bank hold in period 0? What is their leverage?

   (b) In period 1, risk falls to 0.04 and price of financial assets rises to 1.03. What happens to the IB's leverage and holdings of financial assets?

   (c) In period 2, the IB marks to market its financial assets. How much does this increase their equity? How many financial assets do they hold at the end of this period?

   (d) In the next period risk rises back towards its initial level. Calculate how much asset prices need to fall to bankrupt the IB. What does this tell us about the dangers of leverage in the banking system?

9. What is a balance sheet recession? What factors make these recessions more difficult to recover from than normal recessions? Illustrate a balance sheet recession in the 3-equation model.

10. Discuss the following statement: 'central banks can offset the fall in borrower demand in a balance sheet recession by reducing interest rates and inducing savers to spend more'. Illustrate your answer using the 3-equation model.

### 6.9.2 Problems and questions for discussion

1. Pick a developed economy with an inflation-targeting central bank. Use their national statistical office or other international (e.g. the OECD) sources to find a historical data series for real house price growth, inflation and GDP growth. Did a house price boom precede the most recent recession? Does the central bank in the country you have chosen include house prices (or equivalent) in the measure of inflation which underpins their inflation-targeting regime? If not, then what is their justification? Does the data you have collected suggest their choice (of whether to include house prices or not) has impacted their ability to fulfil their mandate (i.e. keep the economy at target)?

2. Do arguments presented in Chapter 5 and Chapter 6 explain how information problems lead banks to lend too little to some customers and too much to others? Justify your answer.

3. Adapt Fig. 6.9 to show how the economy can experience a plain vanilla financial crisis following a collapse in house prices. [Hint: use Fig. 6.13 to see how the equivalent flow diagram was constructed for the bank-centred financial crisis.]

4. Evaluate the following statement: 'credit ratings agencies and saver households are just as much to blame as investment banks when investment banks go bankrupt during the downswing phase of a financial cycle based on securitized assets'.

# 7 The global financial crisis: applying the models

## 7.1 Introduction

The recession that swept across the world in 2008–09 was the most severe contraction the global economy has experienced since the Great Depression. The Global Financial Crisis seemed to come out of nowhere. At the time, economists were pleased with how well the new macroeconomic policy regime based on inflation-targeting was working. High and volatile inflation of the 1970s and 1980s had been defeated and the calmer macroeconomic environment was sufficiently marked to be called the Great Moderation. Many countries had successfully brought unemployment back to levels that had prevailed before the big increases of the 1970s.

However, under the conditions of tranquility of the Great Moderation, levels of debt in households and banks increased dramatically. This did not set off alarm bells among macroeconomists in universities or central banks. The film *The Inside Job* gives a sense of the prevailing complacency among economists.

To understand the global financial crisis it is necessary to understand what preceded it, which can be described using the model developed in Chapter 6 as the upswing of a financial cycle. The model helps us to understand the reasons for the huge expansion of credit and debt in both the financial and the household sectors of many advanced economies during the 2000s, and to understand why inflation-targeting central banks did not see compelling reasons to intervene in the face of these developments in the financial sector.

Figure 7.1 highlights the increase in debt seen in the US economy. The accumulation of debt was concentrated in the household and financial sectors. Household debt as a percentage of US GDP rose by 8 percentage points between 1988 and 1998 and 29 percentage points between 1998 and 2008. The equivalent figures for financial sector debt were 30 percentage points and 48 percentage points. Similar patterns were observed in other countries that experienced credit-fuelled booms during the Great Moderation, such as the UK, Spain and Ireland. Household debt as percentage of GDP was 44% in Spain and 69% in the UK in 1999 but rose rapidly to 88% and 105% (respectively) by 2008.[1]

---

[1] Source: Oxford Economics.

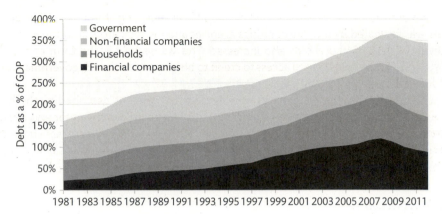

**Figure 7.1** Credit market debt outstanding by sector (as a percentage of GDP) in the United States: 1981–2012.
*Source:* Federal Reserve Flows of Funds Accounts, March 2013.

The sharp rise in indebtedness in the 2000s ran alongside booms in asset prices. For example, US house prices rose by 90% between the first quarter of 2000 and the first quarter of 2006.[2] Central banks predominantly chose not to react to the build up of debt and rising asset prices in the run-up to the crisis. Alan Greenspan, the Chairman of the Federal Reserve from 1987–2006, was a key proponent of the view that central banks should not lean against asset price bubbles by raising interest rates, but instead should 'focus on policies to mitigate the fallout when it occurs and, hopefully, ease the transition to the next expansion'.[3]

The commonly held view in the pre-crisis period was that central banks should only react to financial developments to the extent that they influenced forecast CPI inflation over the central bank's planning horizon.[4] Well before the crisis, economists at the Bank for International Settlements in Basel pointed out, however, that there have frequently been periods in history where low and stable inflation has coincided with the build up of private sector debt that sowed the seeds for future banking crises.[5] This also appears to have been the case during the Great Moderation.

At the core of the financial crisis in 2008–09 was the behaviour of the financial sector. We start the chapter by introducing the incentives, financial instruments and actors that figured prominently in the global financial crisis (Section 7.2). The remainder of the chapter is organized as follows.

### Upswing of the financial cycle (Section 7.3)

The deregulation of banks from the 1980s onwards resulted in them becoming more highly leveraged. This means that they had higher levels of debt. There was a proliferation of new

---

[2] Source: The S&P/Case-Shiller Home Price Index, Composite US SA.

[3] Excerpt taken from Alan Greenspan's Opening Remarks to: *Rethinking Stabilization Policy*: A symposium sponsored by the Federal Reserve Bank of Kansas City, Jackson Hole, Wyoming, August 29–31, 2002.

[4] See, for example, Bernanke and Gertler (2001).

[5] See, for example, Borio and White (2004).

financial products created through securitization and tranching. The mis-pricing of these assets was facilitated by the role of ratings agencies and the regulatory authorities.

Levels of debt of households also increased. This was mainly in the form of mortgage debt. Poorer households gained access to credit to buy houses. In the US, government policy encouraged the supply of 'sub-prime mortgages'.

Rising house prices fuelled more borrowing by households, as described by the house-price positive feedback process set out in Chapter 6. The financial accelerator also operated in banks and in the rapidly growing *shadow banking sector,* leading to increased demand for the assets and further price rises. This formed the basis of the upswing of the financial cycle, in which, as we shall see in this chapter, global banks played a central role.

### The crisis (Section 7.4)

The collapse of house prices in the US sub-prime housing market revealed the liquidity risk associated with the new ways banks were funding their operations by borrowing short-term in the money market. Fear spread through money markets and stock markets and willing buyers for risky assets of all kinds vanished. This episode, which began in the summer of 2007, was called the *credit crunch*.

In September 2008, US investment bank Lehman Brothers filed for bankruptcy triggering the *global financial crisis*. Fear and uncertainty led to orders for goods and services being cancelled. International trade, investment and consumption spending slumped. This can be represented in the macroeconomic model as a large shift of the *IS* curve to the left.

### Policy intervention in the crisis (Section 7.5)

As suggested by the governance structure of the financial system illustrated in Fig. 5.8, central banks stepped in to provide liquidity so that money markets could function. They slashed policy interest rates to close to zero to try to stimulate spending. Central banks used the unconventional technique of 'quantitative easing' in an attempt to provide stimulus to the economy.

Governments stepped in to save banks from failing and spreading contagion across the financial sector. They could not allow the continuity of core banking services to break down. In addition, they sought to counterbalance the collapse of private sector demand by increasing spending and cutting taxes.

Policy makers in central banks and government acted fast because they were very aware of the need to prevent a deflation trap from developing. As set out in Chapter 3, a deflation trap is dangerous because falling prices increase the burden of nominal debt and raise real interest rates. This depresses demand further and makes stabilization more difficult.

As we saw in Chapter 6, recessions that are preceded by housing booms and are associated with banking crises make rapid recovery difficult. A major reason is that high levels of *private* sector debt take a long time to whittle down. Recession itself worsens the government's fiscal position. A related reason is that the role of governments in saving banks and in supporting aggregate demand in the heat of a financial crisis leaves them with a higher level of debt. When households, banks and government are all trying to reduce their levels of debt, demand in the economy will remain depressed.

## 7.2 Pre-crisis financial system: incentives, instruments and actors

### 7.2.1 Incentives

In Chapter 6, we saw that the special characteristics of the banking industry have important economic consequences. An individual bank takes no account of the implications of its decision of how much risk to take on for the aggregate risk of contagion. By neglecting the social costs of spillovers from its own bankruptcy to the rest of the economy, it will take on higher risk than is socially optimal. Moreover, the fact that for a systemically important bank there is a probability of bail-out by the government means that the individual bank may take on more risk than would be privately optimal in the absence of a possible bail-out.

The phrase 'banking on the state' has been used to describe the way banks took advantage of the fact that banking sector gains are privatized (i.e. accrue to bank shareholders, managers and employees), but the losses are (at least partly) socialized (i.e. the banking system is insured by the state).[6]

In addition to the prediction that banks will choose *too low* a capital cushion (that is, choose leverage that is too high) because they ignore the external effects of their decision and they place too little weight on the downside risk because of the possibility of state bail-out, the financial accelerator behaviour sketched in Figs. 6.1 and 6.2 can lead to a process of *rising* leverage. High and rising leverage of systemically important banks raises aggregate risk in the economy and creates vulnerability to a financial crisis as we have seen in Chapter 6—both in the form of a 'plain vanilla' financial crisis and a financial crisis centred on risk-taking by banks in their purchase of financial assets.

In the period before the global financial crisis:

1.  The incentives of banks encouraged them to adopt strategies that added to aggregate risk in the economy.

2.  The regulators indirectly encouraged this by allowing banks to use their own models to calculate the riskiness of their portfolios and report their risk-weighted assets.

3.  There was a widespread lack of concern for the possibility that the financial system was becoming a risk to the economy as a whole. Small investors such as households no doubt believed regulators and professional investors were managing risk. Deposit insurance schemes encouraged these beliefs.

4.  The benign macroeconomic environment and the widely held view that macroeconomic policy making had improved with the implementation of inflation targeting had the effect of encouraging households and banks to believe that aggregate risk in the economy had fallen.

### 7.2.2 Instruments

There were three financial instruments at the centre of the financial crisis; the mortgage-backed security (MBS), the collateralized debt obligation (CDO) and the credit default swap

---

[6] See Alessandri and Haldane (2009).

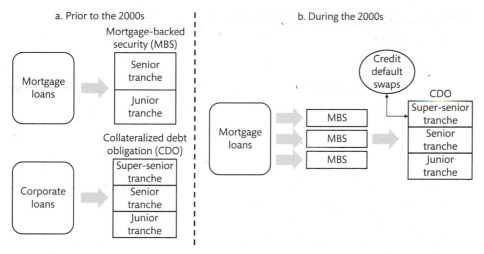

**Figure 7.2** A stylized picture of the relationship between three key financial innovations (CDOs, MBSs and CDSs) prior to the 2000s and during the 2000s.

(CDS). The instruments were typically constructed using complex mathematical computer models and ushered in an era in which global finance became all but incomprehensible to those outside the industry. This section aims to cut through the complexity by providing a brief overview of these instruments that helps to illuminate the part they came to play in the pre-crisis global financial system.[7] Figure 7.2 sets out a simplified version of the relationship between the three key financial instruments (MBSs, CDOs, and CDSs) prior to the year 2000 and then in the upswing phase of the financial cycle after the year 2000.[8]

1. **Mortgage-backed securities (MBSs).** A mortgage-backed security is a financial product secured by a collection of mortgages and referred to as a securitized financial asset. The investor buying the security receives a coupon on their investment that is generated by homeowners paying the interest on their mortgages. The risk of the MBS is the credit risk associated with homeowners not being able to repay their mortgages. The MBS mitigates this risk through two channels. The first is diversification; the mortgages underlying the securities were taken from different geographical regions of the United States. The second involved dividing the securities into 'tranches'; investors in the lower or 'junior' tranche received a higher return, but were the first investors to lose money if some of the underlying mortgages defaulted. The investors' 'senior' tranche received much lower interest, but also bore less risk. They would only take losses should enough mortgages default to wipe out the entire junior tranche (see Fig. 7.2). MBSs predated the crisis by around 20 years. It was thanks to their good track record and lack of defaults prior to the 2000s that they were not commonly talked about.

---

[7] This section is based on MacKenzie (2009). For a detailed account of the role financial instruments played in the global financial crisis, see Tett (2009).

[8] The diagram is a simplified version of the extremely complex relationship between the three financial innovations. For example, CDOs in the 2000s often also contained corporate and other types of loans. The important thing to take away from the diagram is that CDOs made up of MBSs were not widespread before the 2000s.

2. **Collateralized debt obligations (CDOs).** A collateralized debt obligation is similar to a MBS in that it is based on a bundle of underlying loans and is tranched to offer investors a range of products with different risk–return profiles. When CDOs were invented, they were focused on corporate rather than housing loans. In repackaging and tranching these loans, a key precaution taken to avoid credit risk was to make sure the loans were well diversified across industries. The risk of a CDO comes down to the extent of 'correlation' in the bundle of loans. When correlation is low, defaults are isolated events and only the junior tranche is at risk. In contrast, when correlation is high, defaults are subject to clustering, which can endanger the safer tranches of the CDO.

3. **Credit rating agencies (CRAs).** The risk of financial products is assessed by the credit ratings agencies (CRAs) using computer models and data on past correlations of asset performance (including default). The safest securities are given a rating of Triple A, which means the CRA attaches almost zero probability to default. Only a handful of corporations and governments have a triple A rating. The CRAs rated CDOs by analysing the correlations between the companies underpinning the products. They could do this relatively accurately due to the wealth of available data, such as stock prices and historical default data. When correlation was perceived to be low, the CRAs decided that is was so unlikely that the senior tranche would suffer losses that they awarded the CDO in question a triple A rating.

4. **CDOs based on MBSs.** It was when banks began to create CDOs formed from MBSs (see Fig. 7.2) in the 2000s that they became so dangerous. Evaluating the correlation of the underlying MBSs was intrinsically difficult because there was little historical default data. The CRAs set the correlation at very low levels in their models and senior tranches were awarded triple A ratings. The impeccable credit rating and the high return (relative to other 'safe' assets) on the senior tranches meant they were very attractive to institutional investors (e.g. pension funds, hedge funds, global banks) and were sold all across the globe, with Europe being a particularly strong source of demand. The CRAs, banks and investors, however, failed to take into account the similarity of the MBSs within the CDOs. Paradoxically, it was the geographical diversification of individual MBSs that led to CDOs based on MBSs becoming homogenized and therefore highly correlated. If house prices were to fall across the US, then it was not just some of those MBSs that would suffer losses, they all would. The banks originating the CDOs did not totally eliminate their credit risk, however, as upon generation of a CDO, there was a large tranche left over: the so-called 'super-senior tranche'. This tranche only took losses after the senior tranche was wiped out, and it was viewed as completely inconceivable that the super-senior tranche would take losses. In light of this, the tranche offered such low interest rates that it was difficult to sell to outside investors. Banks therefore largely kept this tranche and bought insurance on it in the form of a credit default swap (CDS)

5. **Credit Default Swaps (CDSs).** The US insurance giant AIG sold insurance in the form of credit default swaps (CDSs) on the super-senior tranches of CDOs held by banks and pledged to repay them in full should the super-senior tranche default. The very small insurance premiums paid by the banks provided AIG with a steady income stream and large profits in good times, but generated staggering losses when the value of CDOs collapsed, leading to a $180bn government-funded bailout. The AIG bail-out dwarfed the size of the bail-out for any individual bank in the US.

### 7.2.3 **Actors**

In the wake of widespread financial deregulation, the global financial landscape had changed dramatically from the 1970s. Banks across the developed world increased their return on equity, reduced their capital buffers and moved into higher risk activities, although as we shall see, as reported to regulators, risk had gone down. The state safety net for the banking system widened and deepened.

In the upswing prior to the global financial crisis, this process accelerated, with banks aggressively pursuing strategies to increase their return on equity, also referred to as the 'search for yield'. The search for yield was much encouraged by the behaviour of the yield curve between 2003 and 2006; short term interest rates rose sharply but long rates were virtually stable. The yield curve is explained in Section 7.5. Different parts of the interconnected global financial system went about the search for yield in different ways. The strategies that were followed were influenced by the regulatory framework in which the banks were operating. For example, while retail banks in the US and the government-sponsored housing enterprises such as the Federal Home Loan Mortgage Corporation (known as Freddie Mac) and the Federal National Mortgage Association (FNMA, known as Fannie Mae) entered the sub-prime mortgage market, the US investment banks and European banks were taking advantage of the lighter regulation of their leverage to shift their activities to the 'trading book' (see Chapter 6).

*The US retail banks and government sponsored housing agencies*

The first half of the 2000s was associated with a rapid expansion of sub-prime mortgages in the United States. The US retail banks were at the heart of this process. Their regulatory framework made it difficult to pursue a strategy of high leverage to boost the return on equity, so they increased the riskiness of their asset pools instead. The banks making sub-prime mortgage loans were effectively removing a proportion of the credit risk from their balance sheets when they sold the mortgages on (via MBSs and CDOs), hence they had less incentive to properly assess the creditworthiness of the individuals to whom they were lending.

This strategy was also followed by government-sponsored enterprises Fannie Mae and Freddie Mac and insurance giant AIG, who sold insurance in the form of credit default swaps (CDSs) on the super-senior tranches of CDOs held by banks.

*Global banks, the ratings agencies and the financial regulators*

Many of the large continental European banks are *universal banks* that engage in a combination of retail, commercial, wholesale and investment banking activities. The pre-crisis period also saw the rise in the UK and the US of universal banks. In the US, this was formalized with the repeal in 1999 of the Glass-Steagall Act, which had been introduced in 1933 to improve the safety of the banking system by separating retail from investment banking activities following the experience of the banking crises in the Great Depression. Prominent examples of universal banks include Barclays in the UK and Citigroup in the US.

The global banking data further support the divergence in strategies between US retail and European global banks in the pre-crisis period. The data show that US retail banks' balance

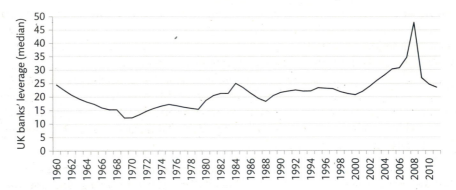

**Figure 7.3** UK banks' leverage: 1960–2011.

*Source:* Bank of England Financial Stability Report, June 2012.

sheets had a higher risk per unit of assets than those of the European banks in the run-up to the crisis, but that European banks had much higher leverage.[9]

The lack of regulatory restrictions on simple leverage in Europe meant that the banks could 'lever up' (i.e. expand their assets relative to their equity). Figure 7.3, which is repeated from Chapter 6, shows the dramatic increase in the leverage of UK banks in the years preceding the financial crisis. In terms of the modelling in Chapter 6, the European banks shifted more of their activities onto the trading book in the years before the crisis, where mark-to-market gains on these assets lifted short-term profits and the return to equity. The lax treatment of 'risk-weighted assets' by the regulators played a part in this.

The Basel II regulatory regime under which the European banks operated from 2004 required banks to put a given amount of capital aside (i.e. a minimum capital cushion) for each asset they held, depending on its risk weight. A risk weight is a measure of the riskiness of an asset.

The higher the rating of the asset (i.e. the safer it was perceived to be by the CRAs), the less capital is needed to be held against it (i.e. it received a low risk weight). For example, triple A sovereign debt received a risk weight of 0%, meaning that no capital had to be held against it.[10] Assets are rated by CRAs, and three of them—Fitch, Moody's and Standard and Poor's—cover around 95% of the world market.[11] They rate both government bonds and privately created assets on a scale from triple A downwards. Under the Basel II regulatory framework, banks were allowed to use their own models to calculate their risk-weighted assets.

In the instruments section, we discussed the creation of financial assets with a range of risk profiles from an underlying pool of risky assets (including sub-prime mortgages). The European banks avidly consumed the (supposedly) safest of these assets (i.e. those rated triple A) during the 2000s. In the run-up to the crisis, there were fewer than ten companies

[9] See Alessandri and Haldane (2009). For cross country data on leverage by type and size of bank using micro data, see Kalemli-Ozcan et al. (2012).

[10] For more information on risk-weights in the Basel II Accord see: http://www.bis.org/publ/bcbs128b.pdf.

[11] See the European Commission website on CRAs (accessed March 2013): http://europa.eu/rapid/press-release_MEMO-13-13_en.htm.

in the world deemed creditworthy enough to warrant a triple A credit rating. In contrast, over 50,000 CDOs were assigned a triple A rating. Banks could use triple A-rated CDOs to increase their total assets without requiring much additional equity to be held. Borrowing to purchase these assets increased the leverage of the European banks.

From the perspective of the economy as a whole, the problem was that risk weights were *falling* due to the proliferation of triple A-rated assets whilst aggregate risk in the system was *rising*. Purchasers of these assets were often ill-informed about the quality of the assets they were buying and relied too heavily on the ratings of the ratings agencies, as this quote from Gillian Tett attests:[12]

> The Germans, and the other continental Europeans 'were like the Japanese a decade earlier—the joke [on the trading desks] was that you could stuff them almost anything', one American banker later recalled.

### The shadow banking system

In the model presented in Chapter 6, we simplified by assuming that only investment banks borrowed to buy securitized assets. This was in order to keep the model as simple as possible and to draw a conceptual line between the activities of retail and investment banks. As we have seen, universal banks include both retail and investment banking activities. Along with investment banks, they were involved in the creation of the so-called shadow banking system.

The *shadow banking system* is defined by the Financial Stability Board (2012) as 'credit intermediation involving entities and activities outside of the regular banking system'. Shadow banking is the global capital-market based credit system: banks moved activities into associated bank-like entities such as structured investment vehicles (SIVs) to keep these banking activities off their balance sheets and outside the scope of bank regulation. The shadow banking entities became heavily involved in both the demand and supply of securitized assets, as described in the stylized model in Section 7.5 and in the previous section.[13]

The global shadow banking system grew rapidly in the years preceding the financial crisis; it accounted for $65 trillion in 2011, up from $26 trillion in 2002. Put another way, the system was equivalent to 25% of global financial assets in 2011.[14] At the same time as aggregate risk was increasing in the regulated banking sector for the reasons discussed above, it was being further boosted by the rapid growth of shadow banking.

### Bank concentration and interconnectedness

The increases in *concentration* and *interconnectedness* were two key trends in financial systems prior to the financial crisis. The first trend saw the consolidation of national banking systems into the hands of a small number of 'too-big-to-fail' financial giants.[15] For example,

---

[12] Excerpt from Tett (2009), pp. 116–117.

[13] See Claessens et al. (2012).

[14] These figures are taken from Claessens et al. (2012). This paper provides an excellent overview of shadow banking and the relevant economics and policy.

[15] For a powerful analysis of the problem of 'too-big-to-fail' banks, see Johnson and Kwak (2010) *13 Bankers: The Wall Street Takeover and the Next Financial Meltdown*.

the assets of the three largest UK banks exceeded 70% of total UK banking assets just prior to the crisis.[16] The second trend saw banks across the globe become more intertwined and dependent upon one another. For example, up to two-thirds of the huge expansion in banks' balance sheets in the run-up to the crisis was a result of increased claims within the financial system, rather than with non-financial agents.[17]

The nature of modern financial systems has led researchers to model them as networks, much in the same way epidemiologists or statistical physicists model their subject matter. Gai et al. (2011) provide an example of this technique, using a network model of interbank relations to mimic the key structural features of the financial system. The authors use this model to show how higher levels of concentration and interconnectedness in the financial system can increase the chances of systemic liquidity crises when key institutions become distressed.

In the wake of the economic crisis, some economists drew comparisons between ecological food webs and the spread of infectious diseases, and financial networks. This body of work criticizes banks' risk management processes for failing to take account of systemic risk. Haldane and May (2011) use a simple model to show that increasing homogeneity in the financial system—all the banks doing the same thing—increases system-wide risk. If all banks hold a similar set of assets this might minimize their own risk of failure (when considered in isolation) but can potentially make the system much more liable to collapse.

This research has led central banks around the world to begin to concentrate on how to design a regulatory framework that minimizes the risk of the system as a whole (referred to as macro-prudential regulation), as opposed to each bank individually (micro-prudential regulation).

## 7.3 The upswing of the financial cycle

In this section, we use the concept of the financial cycle, the model of bubbles and of the two types of financial accelerator developed in Chapter 6 to help explain the upswing of the financial cycle prior to the global financial crisis. We focus on the United States where the crisis had its roots.

### Sub-prime lending in the US

The US government has been involved in promoting home ownership since the 1930s, when the first housing Government-Sponsored Enterprises such as the FNMA (Fannie Mae) were established. The enterprises were aimed at supporting existing homeowners and keeping credit flowing for new mortgages in the wake of the Great Depression.[18]

These early government policies were focused on boosting home ownership amongst the general population. The mid-1990s saw the government change tack, however, and more aggressively pursue policies aimed at increasing home ownership rates amongst low income

---

[16] See Gai et al. (2011).

[17] See Gai et al. (2011).

[18] For an overview of the history of the housing Government-Sponsored Enterprises, see: http://fhfaoig.gov/LearnMore/History.

earners, particularly those families that were unable to obtain mortgages through traditional channels. The stated aim of the Clinton Administration's *National Homeownership Strategy* was to ensure that 'working families can once again discover the joys of owning a home' and to 'add as many as eight million new families to America's homeownership rolls by the year 2000'.[19]

This legislation coincided with the beginning of the rapid expansion of sub-prime lending. It is estimated that at the onset of the global financial crisis in mid-2007, sub-prime mortgages accounted for 14% of all first-lien mortgages in the US and that 69% of all US households owned their own homes.[20]

The role of US government policy in encouraging home ownership among low income earners in the run-up to the global financial crisis can be linked to rising income inequality, macroeconomic stability and financial fragility (Rajan, 2010).[21] Real wages for median workers had stagnated in the US from the 1970s. One way of interpreting the macroeconomic importance of the policy of encouraging higher worker indebtedness (and aspirations for home ownership) is that it helped to sustain aggregate demand following the bursting of the dotcom bubble in 2000 in an economy where real wage growth for the majority of workers had ceased.

In terms of the 3-equation model, weak business investment post 2000 and the longer run weakness in consumption demand threatened to lead to deflation in the recession of 2001. This encouraged policy makers to support the sub-prime housing market as a source of aggregate demand (i.e. to prevent the *IS* curve from shifting to the left). Little attention was given to the potential risks of financial fragility arising from rising household indebtedness.

There is a lot of evidence that securitization and structured finance had the effect of reducing the cost of funding for banks and reducing the surveillance by banks of their housing loans. Brunnermeier (2009, p.82) summarizes the expansion of this sub-prime lending:

> Mortgage brokers offered teaser rates, no-documentation mortgages, piggyback mortgages (a combination of two mortgages that eliminates the need for a down payment), and NINJA ('no income, no job or assets') loans.

It is left to the student to investigate each of the methods of sub-prime lending, but what they all had in common is that they extended housing loans to sections of society that were previously credit constrained. Sub-prime lending allowed less creditworthy individuals, such as those without savings for down payments, those without stable employment and those with poor credit ratings, to obtain mortgages for the first time.

Consistent with the financial accelerator mechanism of Chapter 6, more lending fuelled rising house prices, and rising house prices in turn increased the willingness of banks to lend without making checks on the ability of borrowers to repay from income because the rising prices increased the value of the banks' collateral. In line with the model of extrapolative price expectations, the expectations of rising house prices also increased the incentive for households to borrow more, which means that their leverage increased.

---

[19] The document is available online here: http://www.globalurban.org/National_Homeownership_Strategy.pdf.
[20] See Ben Bernanke's speech on May 17th 2007 entitled *The Subprime Mortgage Market*.
[21] And, for a formal model of shifts in bargaining power and financial instability, see Kumhof and Ranciere (2010).

Leverage is defined as the ratio of an agent's assets to their equity. For example for a borrower household, its asset is the house it owns, its liability is the mortgage taken out to buy the house and its equity is the difference between the two. At the time the house is purchased, the household's equity is the downpayment they made. In this case, the household's leverage is the ratio of the value of their house to their equity. The more debt (i.e. the bigger the mortgage) the household has relative to its equity, the higher is its leverage.

When asset prices are rising, higher leverage makes the return on equity higher. If the house price is $200,000 and the household makes a downpayment of 10%, i.e. $20,000, it borrows $180,000. Its initial leverage ratio is $\frac{200}{20} = 10$. Suppose the house price rises to $220,000, i.e. a rise of 10%. The return to the equity the household invested is 100% (from $20k to $40k). Households who are convinced house prices are going to rise will want to increase their leverage—that's how they get a high return. To see this, calculate the return on equity if the downpayment had been only 5%, i.e. an initial leverage ratio of $\frac{200}{10} = 20$.

As discussed in Chapters 1 and 6, the role of a financial accelerator effect in the consumption function is confirmed in empirical research by Aron et al. (2012), who find that growth in housing wealth (i.e. rising house prices) positively affects consumption in the UK and the US. The authors also find that the strength of this relationship increased as these economies became more financially liberalized during the Great Moderation.

Figure 6.1 showed how the house price feedback process can produce the upswing of a leverage cycle, whereby rising house prices improve household balance sheets and encourage them to 'lever up' further. This increases returns to households when house prices are rising, but as we shall see, if the house price falls, then all of the equity of the household can be wiped out. In our example with a leverage ratio of 10, a fall in the house price by 10% wipes out the equity; if the leverage ratio is 20, a fall of only 5% eliminates the household's equity. Any greater fall in the house price means that they own an asset worth less than the amount they owe on it.

The combination of a long period of rising house prices and easy access to cheap credit increased the incentive for households to become more highly leveraged. Under these circumstances, in addition to the operation of the financial accelerator, a bubble in house prices can arise.

In Chapter 6, we saw that a bubble occurs when the price of an asset rises beyond what is consistent with the fundamentals (in terms of long-run forces of demand and supply). The idea of a house price bubble is well illustrated by the construction boom in the US in the 2000s. In cities like Phoenix or Las Vegas, Arizona, house prices increased by between 75 and 100% from 2003 until their peak in 2006. A look at Phoenix on Google Earth shows that there is virtually unlimited scope for house-building. This suggests that the long-run supply curve for housing is flat and that the higher prices were not sustained by fundamentals (see Fig. 6.8).[22]

## The global financial upswing

The financial upswing of the 2000s was different from those that came before it. The size of cross-border banking flows meant this upswing affected more countries across the globe and was of a larger magnitude than previous upswings. The financial boom had its roots in

[22] David Laibson Frank Hahn Lecture, Royal Economic Society 2009 *Bubble economics* http://res. fileburst.com/video/2009/slides/davidlaibson.pdf.

the US sub-prime mortgage market, but was transmitted around the world due to a number of different factors. Some of the factors predated the 2000s such as: (a) European regulatory regimes allowing for high leverage because of low risk weighting, and (b) the incentives for risk taking provided by the implicit state guarantee for the banking system.

The preexisting factors became salient when they were combined with important developments in the financial system that occured during the 2000s such as:

1. financial innovations creating assets from US mortgages and consumer loans that could easily be traded around the world,

2. the growing dominance of 'too big to fail' banks,

3. the rise in importance of and trust in the ratings of ratings agencies for bank portfolio decisions, and

4. the prevalence of incentives in banks for 'search for yield' behaviour, which was rewarded with high bonuses.

The global banking system, including the shadow banking complex, became involved in a bank-centred financial accelerator process of the kind set out in Chapter 6. An important component of the steep upswing in the financial cycle between 2000 and the global financial crisis arose because European global banks became heavily involved in borrowing from the US money markets and in using these funds to buy the securitized financial assets from the shadow banking complex. The European banks therefore played an important role in helping

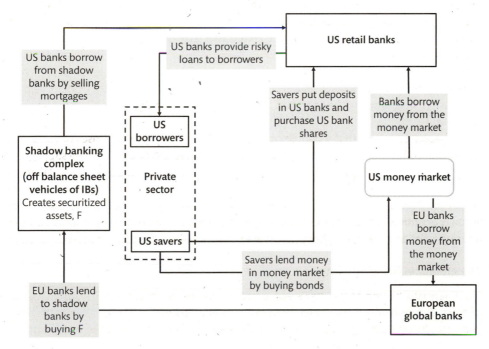

**Figure 7.4** The banking system in the upswing of the financial cycle including cross-border banking activities.

Note: F are the securitized assets introduced in Chapter 5.

to inflate the US sub-prime bubble by indirectly providing credit to US borrowers. The role of cross-border activities is illustrated in a schematic way in Fig. 7.4.

The sheer size of the European lending to the US in the pre-crisis period was staggering. The data reported in Shin (2012) from the Bank of International Settlements shows that European BIS reporting banks lent to US counterparties around $5 trillion dollars in 2007. The research highlights the large presence of European banks in the market for securitized assets prior to the crisis:[23]

> [T]he picture that emerges is of a substantial amount of credit being extended to US borrowers by the European banks, albeit indirectly through the shadow banking system in the United States through the purchase of mortgage-backed securities and structured products generated by securitization.

In addition, Shin (2012) finds that a high proportion of the money used to purchase these assets came from US prime money market funds (MMFs). In 2008, the short-term liabilities of European banks accounted for roughly half the total assets of US prime MMFs, highlighting the importance of US money markets as a source of funding for global European banks.

## 7.4 The crisis

### 7.4.1 The scale of the crisis and nature of the post-crisis recession

The global financial crisis produced the worst recession since the Great Depression of the 1930s (setting aside the effect on global output of the economic collapse in the defeated countries at the end of the Second World War). The upper panel of Fig. 7.5 shows the GDP growth performance of 19 developed economies (including Japan and the biggest economies from Western Europe, North America and Australasia) over the last 140 years.

The behaviour of GDP was not uniform across different countries–this was a recession that started in developed economies and took its largest toll there. This is illustrated in the lower panel of Fig. 7.5, which shows that emerging and developing economies managed to avoid a recession. The large, fast growing, emerging economies were also the driving force behind the economic recovery, with India and China expanding by over 10% in 2010 and continuing to markedly outperform the advanced economies in both 2011 and 2012.[24]

The failure of US investment bank Lehman Brothers in the third quarter of 2008 is frequently cited as the pivotal event for the global economic downturn. Figure 7.6 shows the dramatic deterioration of macroeconomic indicators across the G7 that followed this event. The charts separate the United States from the remainder of the G7 (referred to as the G6). To make comparisons easier, in each chart, the index for each measure (except the unemployment rate) is set at 1 for the fourth quarter of 2007 and a vertical line marks the collapse of Lehmans in September 2008.

In April 2009, the IMF pointed out that two features of the recession—its association with deep financial crisis and its highly synchronized nature—suggest that it was likely to be unusually severe and followed by a slow recovery.

---

[23] See Shin (2012), p. 167.        [24] Source: IMF World Economic Outlook database, April 2013.

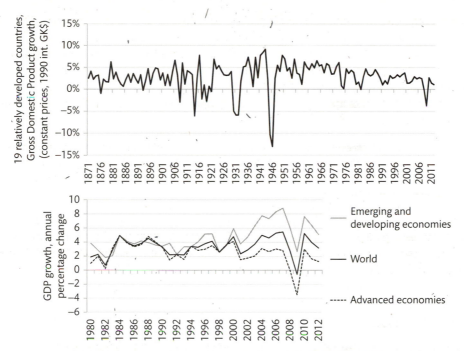

**Figure 7.5** Major developed economies GDP growth 1871–2012 (upper panel) and GDP growth by country group 1980–2012 (lower panel).

*Source:* Angus Maddison (GGDC); The Conference Board *Total Economy Database*™, January 2013; IMF *World Economic Outlook*, April 2013.

The data in Fig. 7.6 show that in line with the IMF forecast:

1. The recovery in GDP was not V-shaped: growth in the recovery was not faster than the previous trend growth rate and did not take economies rapidly back to their previous trend growth path. Instead, growth was at best similar to the trend growth rate (i.e. the post-trough path is roughly parallel with the pre-crisis path). In some countries such as the UK, however, growth did not return to the pre-crisis trend. The post-crisis period was characterized by an L-shaped response. As noted in Chapter 6, by the first quarter of 2013, UK GDP was still 4% below its pre-crisis peak in Q1 of 2008 and was a full 17% below the level it would have been had the pre-crisis trend not been interrupted by the crisis and extended recession.[25] Elsewhere in Europe, the situation was worse, as the Eurozone crisis compounded the effects of the financial crisis (see Chapter 12).

2. As the models of consumption and investment in Chapter 1 would predict, the response of consumption to the crisis was smoother than that of investment.

[25] The pre-crisis trend level of growth was calculated as the average quarterly growth rate for the 15 years prior to the recession (i.e. 1993 Q1 and 2007 Q4). Source: UK Office for National Statistics (data accessed June 2013) and authors' calculations.

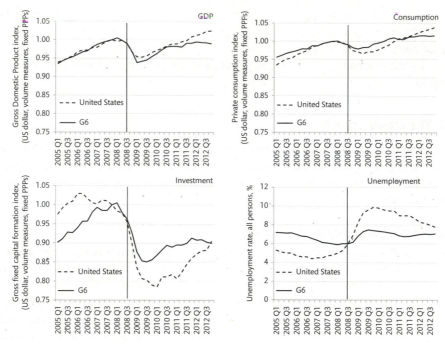

**Figure 7.6** Key macroeconomic indicators for the G7 economies between 2005 Q1 and 2012 Q4.

*Note:* GDP, consumption and investment have been normalized so that 2007 Q4 = 1. The unemployment rate refers to the harmonized unemployment rate for all persons and is seasonally adjusted. The vertical line at 2008 Q3 is to mark the collapse of Lehman Brothers.

*Source:* OECD (data accessed June 2013).

3.  Whereas the behaviour of GDP, consumption and investment were similar in the US and the G6, unemployment was not. For the G6, unemployment was falling prior to the crisis whilst it was rising in the US. The post-crisis rise in unemployment in the US was much greater than in the G6, with the unemployment rate doubling in the US. (We discuss cross-country unemployment patterns in the crisis in Chapter 15.)

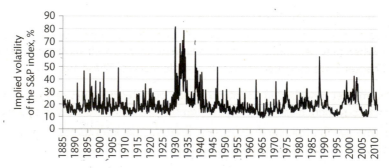

**Figure 7.7** The implied volatility of the S&P index between 1885 and 2011.

*Source:* Nicholas Bloom (2008, 2009).

The volatility of the S&P stock index is often used to proxy for 'fear' in financial markets. Figure 7.7 shows that fear reached its highest level since the Great Depression in the autumn of 2008. This was clearly a crisis that emanated in financial markets, but did not end there. It quickly spread to affect real economic activity, plunging the world economy into recession.

### 7.4.2 The credit crunch

The credit crunch of 2007–09 was at first largely confined to financial markets. It had three key stages, beginning with the fall in house prices in the US. The second stage was the seizing up of money markets and the third, the collapse and bankruptcy of Lehman Brothers in September 2008.

*The collapse of the sub-prime housing market*

The Federal Reserve embarked on a cycle of tightening monetary policy from late 2004 onwards in response to mounting inflationary pressures arising from the increase in oil and commodity prices. After a time this started to depress the housing market, as it made it more expensive to borrow, and pushed up the repayments of existing borrowers. The associated fall in house prices meant sub-prime borrowers started to struggle to make their repayments. They could no longer rely on using the rising values of their properties to obtain more loans (to keep up with mortgage repayments) and the financial accelerator mechanism propagated the effects across the economy. Households began to go into negative equity and to default on their housing loans.

The first sign in the financial markets of the growing default rate on home loans came in February 2007 when the index of the value of mortgage credit default swaps (a type of CDS) dropped sharply.[26] In early August 2007, the problems in the US housing market hit the money markets. Consistent with the arguments above about the role of European banks, the announcement by the French bank BNP Paribas that it could not value its structured financial products, and was therefore stopping redemptions from some of its investment funds signalled that the crisis was going global. BNP Paribas' investment funds (and others across the world) had bought tranches of the CDOs containing sub-prime mortgages and suddenly the value of these assets was in doubt.

*The seizing up of the money markets*

In the course of their normal activities, banks rely on two important money markets to fund themselves when they need short-term liquidity to re-finance their short-term loans. (In the model of Chapter 5, we collapsed these into a single market.) These are:

1. The repo market described in Chapter 5, which operates by banks selling securities and agreeing to buy them back as the loan matures. These loans are secured by collateral.

2. The commercial interbank money market where banks lend to each other short term (from overnight up to three months) unsecured.

---

[26] See Fig. 1 in Brunnermeier (2009).

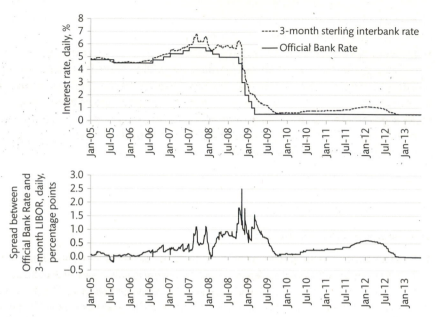

**Figure 7.8** UK Official Bank Rates and three month sterling interbank rates (upper panel) and their spread (lower panel): Jan 2005–May 2013.

*Source:* Bank of England (data accessed June 2013).

Banks had become increasingly dependent on short-term funding, especially the type that used mortgage-backed securities (such as asset backed commercial paper) as collateral. Short-term funding has to be rolled over frequently. When sub-prime borrowers started defaulting and house prices fell, these securities became hard to value, and hence lenders were reluctant to continue accepting them as collateral for loans. Other collateral was used in repo transactions in the money market but as solvency questions arose for some banks, bigger haircuts were called for and these markets began to seize up from the autumn of 2007.[27]

An important indicator of the seizing up of the money markets in the credit crunch was the behaviour of interest rates on the interbank market. Before the crisis, the difference between the Bank of England official bank rate and the three-month interbank rate (which is unsecured) was very low, reflecting the prevailing mood of low risk. Once fears developed about liquidity risk, this reduced the supply of interbank loans (which suddenly seemed risky), pushing the interest rate on them up.

Figure 7.8 shows what happened to the three month interbank rate relative to the Bank of England official bank rates between January 2005 and May 2013. The spread between these two interest rates shows the risk premium attached to interbank lending and is displayed in

---

[27] A bigger haircut means that the loan that can be taken out against a given market value of an asset, which is being used as collateral is smaller. For example, in the case of a safe asset, the haircut might be 5%, which means a $1000 US Treasury Bill will be accepted as collateral for a $950 loan.

the lower panel: the jump in August 2007 is clear. Liquidity risk emerged as an important phenomenon in the short-term money market.

Although banks appeared to have shifted all three forms of risk (see the box on types of risk) through the creation of special purpose investment vehicles, which were part of the shadow banking complex, the banks themselves were ultimately subject to liquidity risk. When demand for short-term asset-backed commercial paper dried up because households, firms, local government finance offices, pension funds etc. did not know how to value them, then the bank's structured investment vehicle (SIV) was not able to fund itself and the parent bank had to provide the required liquidity.

---

### Box 7.1 Types of risk

Banks are exposed to the following risks.

1. *Liquidity risk*. As we have explained in Chapter 5, the service offered by the bank to instant access savers is that they can withdraw their deposits at will. An unexpected withdrawal of deposits by savers exposes the bank to liquidity risk and will require the bank to get hold of liquidity (i.e. before loans are due to mature): it has to borrow or sell some assets. Banks can also be exposed to liquidity risk if lenders refuse to roll over short-term debt on maturity (i.e. provide another identical loan).

2. *Credit (or default) risk*. If the borrower fails to meet their mortgage interest payments, this is a default and it means a loss for the bank. A bank is itself subject to credit risk and ultimately to insolvency when the value of its assets falls.

3. *Interest rate risk*. If the bank makes a mortgage loan at a fixed interest rate and pays savers a variable interest rate linked to the central bank's policy rate, then if the central bank increases the policy rate, the spread falls and the bank suffers a fall in its profit margin.

---

The bank run on the British bank Northern Rock in September 2007 illustrates the role of short-term funding. With Northern Rock, the UK (where, at the time, there was only limited deposit insurance) experienced its first bank run in over 140 years, when depositors nationwide queued to retrieve their savings. The queues started to form in response to the announcement in the media of the Bank of England's emergency liquidity support for the bank.

In this case, the bank run was not a panic-based coordination failure—it was based on the insolvency of the bank arising from its liquidity problems. The bank eventually had to be nationalized. The underlying cause of its failure pre-dates the depositor bank run and reflected a shift in bank funding from deposits to money market funding. In the summer of 2007, only 23% of Northern Rock's liabilities were in the form of retail deposits, by far the largest component was short-term borrowing from money markets.

This case shows how banks that had not been involved in sub-prime lending directly were nevertheless pulled into the sub-prime crisis through being over leveraged and relying too much on short-term debt to finance their operations (Shin, 2009b). When fear hit the money markets, it became impossible for Northern Rock to fund its loans as they came due to be rolled over: its excessive level of liquidity risk was revealed and depositors rationally sought to withdraw their deposits.

### Lehman Brothers—the pivotal event

In Figs. 7.7 and 7.8 showing respectively the 'fear index' of stock market volatility and the spread in the interbank market, there is a large spike on 15th September 2008. This marks the day that Lehman Brothers declared bankruptcy. This highly leveraged institution became insolvent, as short-term funding dried up and the value of its assets collapsed. Unlike the US investment bank Bear Stearns that was rescued in March 2008, Lehmans was not rescued. The ramifications for the financial markets of letting Lehman's fail were bigger than the US government had expected. The S&P 500 fell nearly 5% that day and the VIX index (which measures the volatility of the S&P 500 and is shown in Fig. 7.7) jumped from 25.6 to 31.7. This was not just a one off shock however, but had wide ranging consequences for financial markets and for the real economy. It was the catalyst that plunged the majority of the world economy into the recession illustrated in Figs. 7.5 and 7.6.

### 7.4.3 The crisis, macroeconomic policy and the 3-equation model

The credit crunch and recession following the global financial crisis revealed two shortcomings in the widely adopted inflation-targeting monetary policy regime.

1. The first is that the policy interest rate may only weakly affect the lending rate faced by firms and households; and

2. The second is that in a crisis, conventional monetary policy loses its effectiveness if the central bank needs to achieve a real interest rate that is unattainable because the nominal rate cannot be lowered below zero (the ZLB described in Chapter 3).

#### The policy rate and the lending rate

In Chapter 5, we saw that (a) the policy rate and the money market rate are virtually identical and (b) the spread between the policy rate, $r^P$, and the lending rate, $r$, depends on the riskiness of loans, the risk appetite of the banks and the capital cushion, all of which are stable in normal times. It is the combination of (a) and (b) along with the interest-sensitivity of aggregate demand that under normal circumstances gives monetary policy its power.

#### Spread of money market above policy rate

Figure 7.8 shows that the spread between market and policy interest rates rose during the crisis. Providers of funding to banks (e.g. money markets with cash to invest) required a risk premium on loans to take into account the probability that the bank they were lending to would go out of business and be unable to repay. In the wake of the unexpected bankruptcy of Lehman Brothers, this risk premium was substantial, as shown by the jump in the series in mid-September 2008.

#### Spread of mortgage rate above policy rate

Figure 7.9 relates to (b) and shows that the spread between Bank of England base rate and the mortgage rates being charged by UK banks also increased dramatically after the collapse

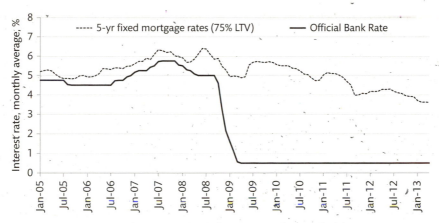

**Figure 7.9** UK Official Bank Rates and five-year fixed mortgages rates (75% LTV): Jan 2005–Apr 2013.

*Source:* Bank of England (data accessed June 2013).

of Lehman Brothers. The figure (repeated from Chapter 5) shows that UK mortgage rates remained at a high level even after the threat of financial collapse receded and in the face of severe cuts in central bank interest rates. This reflects a rise in funding costs for the banks due to the rise in money market rates, reflecting both increased liquidity risk and increased credit risk of banks and of borrowers. The model of Chapter 5 would predict a rise in the mark-up of the lending rate above the cost of funding to reflect the higher credit risk on their loan book. Compared with the benevolent conditions of the Great Moderation, which are likely to have raised the tolerance of risk by banks, the shift to a post-Lehman's world would have been expected to reduce risk tolerance and push the mark up over funding costs higher. The risk tolerance term can be interpreted as reflecting the credit risk of banks themselves.

To summarize, a double spread in lending rates emerged in the crisis due to the higher credit risk of the bank itself as well as of the borrower. The disconnect between the policy rate and the lending rate in the crisis represented a breakdown of a key transmission mechanism of monetary policy in the modern monetary framework of inflation targeting, which relies on changes in the policy rate ($r^P$) by the central bank to alter the lending rate ($r$) for households and firms.

## The zero lower bound on nominal interest rates

The first step to understanding what happened after the credit crunch requires reintroducing the concept of the zero lower bound (ZLB) on nominal interest rates, which was covered in detail in Chapter 3. We need to rewrite the Fisher equation to reflect the distinction between $r$ and $r^P$. To reiterate briefly, when we combine the Fisher equation, $i = r^P + \pi^E$, with the fact that nominal interest rates cannot fall below zero, we find the minimum real interest rate that the central bank can set in any period is:

$$\text{Min } r^P = -\pi^E. \tag{7.1}$$

## The negative demand shock

According to the S&P/Case-Shiller US National Home Price Index, US house prices began falling in mid-2006. One contributory factor was the rise in interest rates as the Federal Reserve responded to the inflation shock caused by the hike in oil prices in 2005. The smooth return of the economy to target inflation that would normally be expected did not take place. Instead, falling house prices triggered the sub-prime crisis with the national and international ramifications we have described.

We can map the consequences of the sub-prime crisis in the 3-equation model (see Fig. 7.10). To make the diagram as clear as possible, we assume the economy begins in equilibrium with inflation at target. In the autumn of 2007, the credit crunch began. We can model this as follows:

1. The fall in house prices caused a marked reduction in consumption and housing investment. In addition, investment fell due to the increase in uncertainty. These effects combined

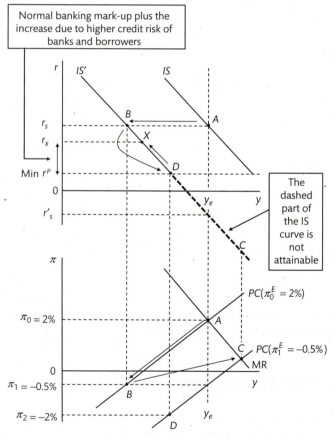

**Figure 7.10** The sub-prime crisis and the limits to conventional monetary policy.

to cause a severe reduction in aggregate demand and the *IS* curve shifts a long way to the left to *IS'*.

2. The central bank forecasts inflation in the usual way and identifies its target output gap to get the economy on to the *MR* curve. The desired real interest rate is low (point *C*), due to the size of the negative demand shock (note that the new stabilizing real interest rate is at $r'_s$). Since the *nominal* interest rate cannot be negative, we use Min $r^P$, as defined by Equation 7.1, to check whether the desired real interest rate is attainable.

3. From Fig. 7.10, we can see that even when the nominal interest rate is cut to zero, monetary policy is unable to get the economy on to the *MR* line at point *C*. The dashed section of the *IS* curve to the right of its intersection with the Min $r^P$ line indicates the points on the schedule that are unattainable: the Min $r^P$ line is pinned down by the fact that expected inflation is −0.5%: this means that the lowest possible real interest rate, given that the nominal interest rate cannot go below zero, is 0.5%. The highest attainable level of output is shown by point *D*.

4. In fact, in 2008, the situation was worse than shown by point *D*. Unusually large interest rate spreads above the policy rate emerged, so that borrowers were faced with the higher lending rate shown by point *X*, even further away from the central bank's desired output level at point *C*.

*The deflation trap*

In the analysis of the credit crunch in the 3-equation model, the limits to the effectiveness of monetary policy are clear. As interest rates in the major advanced economies were slashed to near zero during the crisis, policy makers feared the economy would enter a deflation trap with a vicious circle of falling prices, rising real interest rates and contracting output. The case of the economy falling into a deflation trap is shown using the 3-equation model in Chapter 3 (see Fig. 3.13).

Once a deflation trap is entered, another channel can depress aggregate demand further. If asset prices in the economy (e.g. property prices) are falling as well as goods prices, then debtors in the economy will not only find that the real burden of their debt is rising (the debt is fixed in nominal terms but prices are falling), but also that the assets that they have used as security or collateral for the debt are shrinking in value. This is the financial accelerator process described in Chapter 6. It will amplify the downward spiral of economic activity. The financial accelerator mechanism shifts the *IS* curve further to the left. Heightened uncertainty in economy is likely to make investment less sensitive to the interest rate, thereby steepening the *IS* and weakening the investment response even if positive inflation expectations and a sufficiently low real interest rate could be generated.

## 7.5 Policy intervention in the crisis

In this section we look first at the lessons that were drawn by policy makers from the Great Depression as to how they should respond to the global financial crisis. Second, we look at the policies that were implemented in the teeth of the crisis in 2008–09. Third, we turn to the policies adopted in the Great Recession that followed the global financial crisis. We shall see that the policies implemented in the crisis phase in 2008–09 were strongly influenced by the economic analysis of the Depression that had accumulated over the years since the 1930s. However, although monetary and fiscal policy were used aggressively to support economic activity, the fiscal stimulus used in the crisis phase was rapidly replaced by fiscal austerity in Europe whilst economies were still in recession. The special circumstances of the members of the Eurozone, where a sovereign debt crisis emerged in 2010 is discussed in Chapter 12.

### 7.5.1 **What went wrong in the Great Depression?**

The policy response to the Great Depression exacerbated the world's economic woes.[28] There were two key mistakes made by the US authorities, which crippled their economy and reverberated around the world.

1. Contractionary monetary and fiscal policy: the slump in economic output was met with a tightening of policy. The money supply contracted by a third between 1929 and 1933, largely as a result of poor policy from the Federal Reserve and a slew of bank failures. The government also increased tax rates on individuals and businesses. These contractionary policies reinforced the downwards spiral of demand in the economy.

2. A rise in protectionism: in the early stages of the depression, President Hoover introduced the infamous Tariff Act of 1930, which raised import tariffs on over 20,000 products to record levels. This was met with retaliatory measures from the US's main trading partners and world trade plummeted.

The Great Depression was a painful and prolonged period of economic contraction, which saw global stock markets crash, industrial production collapse and globalization retreat. Figure 7.11 shows the path of key macroeconomic variables during the Great Depression and the financial crisis of 2008–09 and the monetary and fiscal policy responses. The beginning of the two downturns looked ominously similar, but the bounceback was a lot more rapid following 2008–09.

In contrast to the Great Depression, as the financial crisis hit, governments stepped in to support domestic demand by introducing fiscal stimulus packages. Alongside this, central banks slashed interest rates and kept them at historic lows for an extended period of time. In 2008-9, expansionary monetary and fiscal policies were adopted more decisively and applied more consistently, which helped to avoid a repeat of the Great Depression. Economic historians Crafts and Fearon (2010, p. 288) commented on the policy response to the recent global financial crisis:

> [M]onetary and fiscal policies were pursued on a scale that would have been unacceptable during the 1930s but, crucially, these bold initiatives prevented financial meltdown. ... the 'experiment' of the 1930s shows only too clearly the likely outcome in the absence of an aggressive policy response.

---

[28] For an excellent overview of the Great Depression and its lessons for policy makers and economists, see Crafts and Fearon (2010).

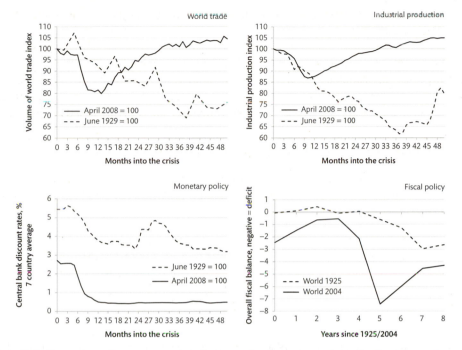

**Figure 7.11** Comparison of macroeconomic indicators and policy response during the Great Depression and the Global Financial Crisis.

*Source:* Eichengreen and O'Rourke (2010); CPB—Netherlands Bureau for Economic Policy Analysis—World Trade Monitor, May 2013; Bank of England, St Louis Federal Reserve, Bank of Japan, ECB, Riksbank and National Bank of Poland (accessed June 2013); IMF World Economic Outlook, Jan 2009; IMF Fiscal Monitor, April 2013.

## 7.5.2 Monetary and fiscal policy in the crisis phase

The lessons from the policy errors of the Great Depression had a marked influence on policy makers in 2008. Ben Bernanke—one of the world experts on the economic analysis of the Great Depression and chairman of the US Federal Reserve during the financial crisis—was acutely aware of the dangers of a deflation trap and took advantage of the numerous policy tools at his disposal to ensure the US economy escaped this fate.

The policy response to the recent global economic downturn addressed several problems:[29]

1. *the liquidity problem*: central banks took action to deal with the seizing up of the money markets and associated liquidity problems of banks;

2. *the bank solvency problem*: central banks and governments took action to save failing banks and prevent contagion;

---

[29] This subsection was compiled using news reports and press releases from banks and central banks (e.g. the Federal Reserve, the Bank of England and the ECB). For a high level overview of the monetary and fiscal response to the crisis see Mishkin (2011).

3. *the stabilization of aggregate demand and expectations*: central banks used conventional and unconventional monetary policy, and governments used expansionary fiscal policy.

### The liquidity problem: central bank response

Following the seizing up of the money markets in the credit crunch, the central banks of major developed countries were quick to act to provide liquidity to the banks. The Bank of England (BoE) made $10bn of reserves available for three-month loans to banks and widened the list of acceptable collateral. The ECB injected €95bn in overnight credit into the interbank market and the Federal Reserve injected $24bn. These actions provided some respite in the interbank markets, but the spread between LIBOR and base rates remained high (see Fig. 7.8).

The Federal Reserve introduced the Commercial Paper Funding Facility, which bought three-month unsecured and asset backed commercial paper from eligible issuers with money from the New York Federal Reserve. There was also a coordinated response from the ECB, BoE and the Swiss National Bank to provide short-term US dollar funding where requested. These are just a selection of the numerous initiatives central banks employed to ensure that financial institutions could meet their short-term funding needs during these turbulent times.

### The solvency problem: central bank and government responses

The bankruptcy of Lehman Brothers crystallized one fact; this was not just a liquidity crisis, but also a solvency crisis. The write-down of the value of a range of financial assets on banks' books shrank their asset bases. Due to their high leverage ratios, this was particularly damaging to banks' equity (or net worth). The banks needed capital urgently if they were to plug the gaps in their balance sheets and avoid failure.

The private capital markets and sovereign wealth funds were not willing to provide this additional investment on a sufficient scale, so banks had no choice but to turn to their governments. The US Treasury announced a $700bn bailout plan in October 2008, and similar bailouts took place across Europe.

The support for the financial system over the duration of the crisis came in three main forms:

1. Taking *ownership stakes* in lenders/banks: governments took equity stakes in financial institutions in exchange for providing capital. The US government took preferred equity stakes in eight major US financial institutions in exchange for $166bn of bailout money, with Bank of America and Citigroup collecting $45bn each. The sturdier of these banks repaid some or all of this money in 2009, freeing them from the federal restrictions that accompanied the funds (e.g. curbs on executive pay).

2. Nationalization: in certain cases, the government took *control* of financial institutions by taking very high equity stakes. This happened with some banks in the UK (e.g. Northern Rock and RBS), Ireland and Iceland, as well as mortgage providers Freddie Mac and Fannie Mae and insurance giant AIG in the US. In some of these cases, the government

became heavily involved in the day-to-day running and strategic decision making of these organizations.

3. Toxic asset purchases: this removed some of the toxic assets from banks' balance sheets. This was most widely used in the US and took place through the Federal Reserve, which set aside $600bn to buy up mortgage backed securities.

## Stabilization policy: preventing a deflation trap

Conventional monetary policy was used decisively. In November 2008, the Bank of England's Monetary Policy Committee (MPC) cut the policy rate by 150 basis points (from 4.5% to 3%) in one step. This was a much bigger cut than predicted by market commentators. Similar monetary policy responses came in the US, the Eurozone and other industrialized economies. See Fig. 7.11 for the comparison with the response of monetary policy in the Great Depression. The MPC's concern was that inflation would undershoot the target and that the economy would be forced into a deflation trap. The aim was to stimulate aggregate demand, and to keep inflation expectations anchored at 2% in order to prevent a process of deflation becoming entrenched.

### Quantitative easing: unconventional monetary policy

From the 3-equation model (in Chapter 3), the importance of avoiding a deflation trap is clear. In the financial crisis, conventional monetary policy was restricted by the zero lower bound on nominal interest rates, which meant that monetary policy makers had to turn to unconventional policies to stimulate demand and prop up inflation expectations. The main policy used was quantitative easing (often referred to as QE). When the policy interest rate is as low as it can be, central banks use asset purchases to try to boost asset prices and lower yields.

QE is described as *unconventional* because the policy lever it uses is different to that used in modern inflation-targeting monetary regimes, which adjust short-term interest rates to influence aggregate demand.

QE can take a number of forms, but in essence, it involves the central bank creating new central bank (or high-powered) money as discussed in Chapter 5 to buy financial assets (e.g. government bonds or the financial assets discussed in Chapter 6). The aim of this policy is to support asset prices and bring down long-term interest rates. If successful, this should help to boost aggregate demand by encouraging consumption and investment.

By buying government bonds, the central bank raises demand for them, which pushes up their price and lowers the interest rate. The price will not respond much to increased demand by the central bank if the private sector has very strong preference for liquidity, which may be the case following a financial crisis. Nevertheless, in circumstances where the banking system is failing to do its job in lending to the real economy, it is hoped, for example, that by the central bank boosting demand for financial assets, it will make it easier for firms to sell corporate bonds to finance their investment.

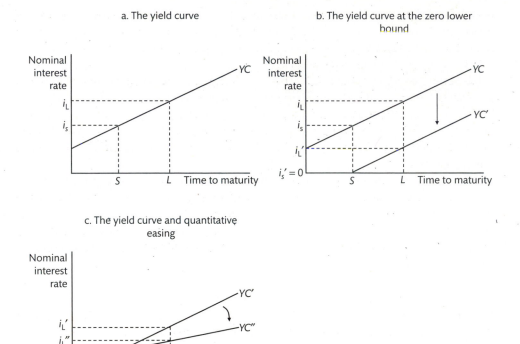

**Figure 7.12** Monetary policy and the yield curve.

## Monetary policy and the yield curve

The yield curve shows the relationship between the nominal interest rate of a bond and its time to maturity (i.e. the time remaining before the full value of the bond must be repaid to the seller). In this subsection, we set out a simplified yield curve and show how it is affected by both conventional and unconventional monetary policies. This is useful for highlighting the key differences between the two types of monetary policy and why QE is used when conventional monetary policy is restricted by the ZLB.

Figure 7.12a (the top left-hand panel of Fig. 7.12) shows a simplified yield curve. In this example, there are just two kinds of bonds: short-term ($S$) and long-term ($L$) and their nominal interest rates are $i_S$ and $i_L$. The curve slopes upwards because investors demand a premium over short-term interest rates to hold long-term bonds. This is due to the higher level of uncertainty associated with the long term. For example, an investor might be fairly certain whether or not there will be a recession in the next two years, but is likely to be much less certain whether there will be one in the next twenty years. There is also more inflation uncertainty in the long term and because inflation impacts the real return on bonds, investors will require a premium to hold long-term bonds.

Next we consider the central bank's response to a negative demand shock. We know from the 3-equation model that the central bank will reduce the short-term interest rate. If the demand shock is sufficiently large it will reduce it to zero. Figure 7.12b shows this case. If we assume that the interest rate spread between long-term and short-term bonds stays the same, then the reduction in short-term rates shifts the yield curve downward from $YC$ to $YC'$. The long-term interest rate falls to $i'_L$.

In a severe recession it could be that even reducing the short-term interest rate to zero is insufficient to stabilize the economy. The central bank could undertake QE in this scenario: buying government bonds in secondary markets, increasing their price and reducing their interest rate. This policy can be thought of as pivoting the yield curve, as shown in the movement of the yield curve from $YC'$ to $YC''$ in Fig. 7.12c. This reduces long-term interest rates further to $i''_L$.

Quantitative easing therefore operates by reducing interest rates at the long end of the yield curve. To the extent that higher bond prices and lower long-term interest rates influence the level of consumption and investment in the economy, QE can help to stimulate the economy when conventional monetary policy is stuck at the ZLB. Chapter 13 includes a more detailed discussion of QE, including its transmission mechanisms and the impact it has on the central bank's balance sheet.

## Fiscal policy: automatic stabilizers and fiscal stimulus

The limits of traditional monetary policy were reached in the recession of 2008-09, so to further support the global economy, governments turned to fiscal policy.

The 3-equation model can be used to illustrate the issues facing policy makers. The $MR$ line in Fig. 7.10 needs to be reinterpreted as the policy rule, and labelled $PR$, so as to include fiscal policy as an instrument. Since the best response to the shock is to achieve the positive output gap marked by point C in Fig. 7.10, the government would need to introduce a fiscal stimulus to shift the $IS$ curve to the right. To achieve the desired output gap, fiscal policy would need to take account of the effect on aggregate demand of the real interest rate, $r_x$ arising from expected deflation combined with the increase in the margin of the lending rate over the policy rate due to increased credit risk of banks and borrowers.

This analysis fits well with the policy response of major governments in the wake of the global financial crisis. We can see from Fig. 7.11 that fiscal policy was eased much more aggressively during the recent crisis than in the Great Depression.

Discretionary fiscal policy can be defined by the gap between the current budget deficit and the impact of the automatic stabilizers. This is shown in Equation 7.2,

discret. fiscal impulse at time $t \equiv$ budget deficit $-$ impact of aut. stabilizers

$$\equiv [G(y_t) - T(y_t)] - a(y_e - y_t) \tag{7.2}$$

where $a$ is a constant and the term $a(y_e - y_t)$ captures the impact on the budget deficit of the automatic stabilizers. When output is at equilibrium (i.e. $y_e = y_t$), the automatic stabilizer term is zero. A budget deficit that persists when output is at equilibrium is therefore discretionary and is referred to as the structural or cyclically adjusted budget deficit.

The first channel of fiscal policy was to allow the *automatic stabilizers*[30] to operate and to accept the associated increase in the deficit. In a recession, without any explicit change of policy, government transfers tend to increase (e.g. more people collect unemployment benefits) and taxes tend to fall as a percentage of income (e.g. if the income tax system is progressive). The greatly increased size of government, including the welfare state, between the 1930s and 2009 meant the automatic stabilizers operated to limit the leftward shift of the *IS* curve in response to the negative aggregate demand shock following the collapse of Lehman Brothers.

In response to the severity of the fall in aggregate demand, governments in both emerging and developed economies also chose to use *discretionary fiscal policy*—referred to during the crisis as 'fiscal stimulus'.

The stimulus packages came in many forms, as illustrated by these examples:

1. the UK cut its headline rate of VAT (i.e. sales tax) temporarily from 17.5% to 15%,

2. many European countries introduced car scrappage schemes, which paid consumers to scrap their existing vehicle upon the purchase of a new one; and

3. the Australian government sent out 'tax bonuses' to middle and low income individuals and families (i.e. the government gave cash handouts to the population).

There was considerable variation in the size of the stimulus packages relative to GDP. The state of the public finances in the run up to the recession and the cost of bailing out the banks meant the UK's fiscal stimulus was much smaller than those in North America, Australia and Germany for example. Figure 7.13 shows the size of the stimulus packages (announced prior to March 2009) relative to GDP and splits them between tax cuts and spending increases in a selection of OECD countries.

Unlike the 1930s, the fiscal policy response to the crisis was coordinated across countries. If countries were left to themselves they would not internalize the positive externalities of a stimulus package and the amount of stimulus would be suboptimal. The reason for this is that a proportion of any stimulus will leak abroad through imports, benefiting your trading partners, but without them having to incur any fiscal cost themselves. Without a credible commitment mechanism, every country would attempt to 'free-ride' on the fiscal expansions of others and the stimulus would be suboptimal. This was avoided in 2008–09 by world leaders meeting at global summits and committing to each other and their electorates that they would introduce stimulus packages (e.g. the G20 summits in Washington D.C. in late 2008 and London in April 2009). This made backing out politically costly at the domestic and international level.

The working of automatic stabilizers and the implementation of fiscal stimulus measures led to large deteriorations in fiscal balances. The IMF estimated that relative to 2007, fiscal balances as a percentage of GDP worsened by 5.9% across the G20 in 2009 (this does not include any support measures for the banking sector). The crisis-related discretionary measures (i.e. the stimulus packages) were predicted to account for 2% of this change in fiscal balances and other factors (including automatic stabilizers) accounted for the remaining

---

[30] See Chapter 14 for a more detailed explanation of automatic stabilizers.

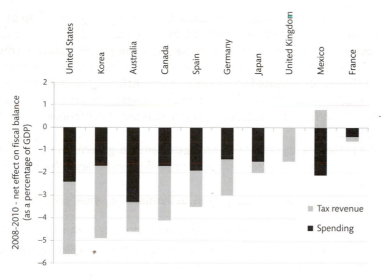

**Figure 7.13** The size and mix of the fiscal stimulus packages of selected OECD countries in relation to GDP, 2008–2010.

*Source:* OECD Economic Outlook Interim Report, March 2009.

3.9%. It is a testament to the depth of the recession that automatic stabilizers played such a significant role.

A country that has a high level of government debt may face constraints on its borrowing. In the financial crisis, Ireland's deficit and debt ballooned because it had to rescue banks, which were very large relative to the size of the economy. Its ability to implement stabilization through fiscal policy was severely constrained. This was also affected by the particular problems faced by a country that needs to borrow to finance fiscal stimulus when it does not have its own currency. Countries in the Eurozone, like Ireland, faced this problem, which is discussed further in Chapters 12 and 14.

Economic theory provides guidance on the conditions under which fiscal stimulus is likely to be effective in boosting aggregate demand and output. The arguments are set out in Chapter 14, where it is clear that there is no general answer to the question: fiscal policy effectiveness depends on the state of the economy, the stance of monetary policy and the design of the policy measures. We focus here on the specific case relevant to the aftermath of the financial crisis, that is, following a large negative aggregate demand shock that results in spare capacity in the economy. Fiscal stimulus is more effective:

1. When monetary policy supports expansionary fiscal policy by preventing interest rates from rising. This is the case when the economy is at the zero lower bound and also when QE is being used to lower long term interest rates. In the 3-equation model, this keeps the interest rate from rising to choke off demand.

2. When it takes the form of a temporary rise in government spending. The higher government spending raises demand for goods and services directly. Even when this is accompanied by higher *taxation* to pay for it (a so-called *balanced budget spending increase*)

aggregate demand will go up. This is seen most easily by noting that the increase in taxation only affects the second and subsequent rounds of the multiplier process once the higher incomes from the extra government spending have been received (see Chapter 1). This does not dampen the direct (first round) effect of higher government spending on aggregate demand and, in an economy with spare capacity and low interest rates, on output.

3. Similar logic applies to the possibility that if the government *borrows* to fund its extra spending, households may anticipate future higher taxation to pay for this. Although any increase in private saving for this purpose will dampen the *multiplier process*, it does not extinguish the positive effect on aggregate demand of the first round effect (see Chapter 14).

4. When it takes the form of temporary tax cuts and there are credit-constrained households in the economy. If such households would have borrowed more to smooth their consumption had they had access to credit, then a tax cut will lead to higher spending.

Fiscal expansion is likely to be most effective in a financial crisis when it is timely, temporary and targeted—and as noted above, when it is coordinated across countries. Temporary fiscal measures shift the timing of spending decisions (not only for households, but also for the public sector by, for example, bringing forward infrastructure spending), which is the objective, and help reduce concerns that fiscal intervention will lead to long-run commitments with implications for public debt.

### Did expansionary monetary and fiscal policy responses work?

Researchers will investigate this question for many years to come. At this stage, we note that the initial stages of the financial crisis of 2008–09 bore a close resemblance to the Great Depression. The world economy, however, managed to turn itself around much quicker this time than it did in the 1930s. Part of the reason for this is likely to have been the direct and expectational effects of the coordinated policy response of the world's central banks and fiscal authorities. The highly accommodative policy employed during the global financial crisis prevented a collapse of the global financial system and helped to support demand during a time of particularly low activity and high uncertainty.

A second very important reason was the coordinated commitment to trade openness (instead of the resort to protectionism that had occurred in the Great Depression). The rapid resumption of strong growth in the increasingly important emerging economies supported growth in the global economy during the lengthy recession in the advanced countries (see the lower panel of Fig. 7.5).

### 7.5.3 Austerity policies in the post-crisis recession

Fiscal stimulus policies introduced in response to the global financial crisis appear to have helped to prevent countries from experiencing a deeper output contraction and deflation. Fiscal stimulus was followed, however, by discretionary *contractionary* fiscal policy in many of these economies *before* they had exited from recession. The adoption of tighter fiscal policy with the express aim of reducing the debt to GDP ratio (rather, for example, than to stabilize aggregate demand) is referred to as fiscal consolidation or austerity.

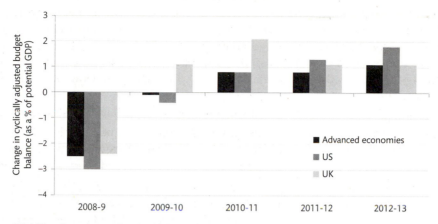

**Figure 7.14** The discretionary fiscal policy stance measured by the change in the cyclically adjusted budget balance: 2008–9 to 2012–13.

*Source:* IMF Fiscal Monitor, April 2013.

Figure 7.14 shows the discretionary fiscal policy stance of the advanced countries as a whole and the US and UK separately from 2008–2009 until 2013. The indicator is the change in the cyclically adjusted budget balance: a negative value, as is shown for 2008–2009, indicates a rise in the cyclically adjusted budget deficit, that is, a loosening of fiscal policy. Although in the advanced countries as a group and in the US, there was still some fiscal stimulus in 2009–2010, this was not the case in the UK, where austerity policies were introduced as early as 2009–10. The relative harshness of fiscal consolidation in the UK shows up clearly in 2010–2011 with the discretionary withdrawal of demand of more than 2% of GDP. Note that this measure of the discretionary fiscal policy stance shows fiscal policy as tighter if the change is positive (represented by positive bars in Fig. 7.14) even if a cyclically adjusted deficit remains.

Chapter 14 on fiscal policy provides a detailed analysis of many of the issues relevant to the austerity debate such as debt dynamics, the possibility of 'expansionary fiscal consolidation' and the relevance of Ricardian equivalence. It also provides a summary of the debate about empirical estimates of the size of the multiplier. The aim in this section is narrower: to pursue the question of the likely consequences of adopting fiscal austerity in the form of early fiscal tightening during a post-financial crisis recession. In Box 7.2, we present the historical experience of the UK in the 1930s to shed light on the policy mix that allowed the economy to recover from the Depression by offsetting the depressing effect of the fiscal austerity imposed at that time.

As we showed in Chapter 6, in a balance sheet recession following a financial crisis there are strong headwinds dragging on aggregate demand because of the legacy of the collapse of the upswing of a financial cycle. Banks, borrower households and governments experience levels of debt above their desired or target levels. Moreover, when many countries are in the same position, demand is reduced not only by the attempt of each of these parties to save more but also by the spillovers through trade links of similar contractionary policies abroad. There is a domestic coordination failure as well as an international coordination failure. Although both failures were avoided in the intense phase of the financial crisis, they characterized the Great Recession that followed.

Experience during the Great Recession led the IMF to revise upwards its estimates of the size of multipliers to a range between 0.9 and 1.7.[31] The factors they list as raising the multiplier under the conditions prevailing in 2012 were the ZLB, the extent of slack (i.e. underutilized resources) remaining in the affected economies and the synchronized fiscal consolidation across countries. However, the modelling in Chapter 6 of the balance sheet recession highlights the need to set against the factors boosting the size of the multiplier in a deep recession, the dampening effect that accompanies a balance sheet recession caused by households increasing their saving to get back to their target wealth.

The historical example from the UK in the box below and the examples from OECD countries in the 1980s and 1990s discussed in Chapter 14 suggest that the negative effects of fiscal austerity can be offset, but only under very special conditions.

De Long and Summers (2012) set out a model that analyses the macroeconomic impact of fiscal stimulus when the economy is depressed—i.e. nominal interest rates are at the ZLB and unemployment is above equilibrium. They argue that fiscal stimulus is likely to be self-financing (in the sense that the benefits for future growth outweigh the upfront fiscal cost) when even a small amount of hysteresis takes place in the downturn. Hysteresis is where high cyclical unemployment has permanent negative effects and raises equilibrium unemployment (as a result, for example, of workers becoming de-skilled whilst unemployed). Hysteresis is discussed in Chapter 15. De Long and Summers (2012) therefore suggest a strong need for caution when considering premature fiscal consolidation in a depressed (e.g. post-crisis) economy.

The pressure on policy makers to shift from fiscal stimulus to austerity comes from the deterioration in government finances. But the evidence that has accrued suggests that the appropriate response to this is not to attempt to deal with the accumulation of public sector debt by an early tightening of fiscal policy. Unlike an individual household where debt is reduced by saving more, the paradox of thrift explained in Chapter 1 shows that in an economy with some spare resources (i.e. with a negative output gap), the attempt by the government as well as the private sector to save more can reduce aggregate demand and output, leaving aggregate saving unchanged but output lower.

The experience of the Great Recession shows that the effect of austerity policies is dependent on the state of the economy and on circumstances such as whether other countries are also in recession and on the policies being pursued there. Economists use the term 'state and time' dependence to characterize such a situation.

This suggests we can learn about the effect of austerity policies not only from economic models, by estimating the size of multipliers, and from running simulations with single or multi-country econometric models but also from historical episodes. An interesting case is the British economy in the 1930s, in which growth was restored at the same time as fiscal austerity was implemented (see Box 7.2). In the UK, unlike the situation

---

[31]  See IMF (2012a).

post-2008, the Depression of the 1930s did not follow a financial boom and there was no debt hangover.

---

### Box 7.2  Depression policy mix in the UK

The Depression of the 1930s was far less traumatic in the UK than in the US or Germany.[a] There were no bank failures. Growth resumed and GDP recovered to its pre-crisis level within five years (unlike the longer recession following the global financial crisis in 2008–09). High unemployment was the big problem for the UK in the 1930s: the unemployment rate doubled from 8% in 1929 to peak at 17% in 1932 and was still above 10% in 1938, the year before the start of the second world war.

British experience in the Depression is interesting because it was a unique episode in the UK, where a policy of fiscal austerity was implemented in a recession when the interest rate was close to the zero lower bound. How did strong growth return?

The extent of fiscal austerity was considerable: via a combination of spending cuts and tax increases, demand was removed from the economy and the structural budget deficit was reduced by 4% of GDP between 1929–30 and 1933–34 and yet the economy grew reasonably strongly from 1932 onwards. Economic historians agree that fiscal austerity depressed growth during this period. The explanation of why growth resumed depends on the strength of the countervailing policies. The economic historian, Nicholas Crafts argues that an important part of the explanation lies with the shift of the control of monetary policy away from the Bank of England to the Treasury, where an explicit policy announced by the Chancellor of targeting an increase in the price level was pursued.

The aim was to end deflation by generating expectations of higher inflation so as to reduce the real interest rate (remember the Fisher equation introduced in Chapter 1).

The mechanism was to be through devaluation of the exchange rate. We explain the relationship between changes in the exchange rate and inflation in detail in Chapter 10. At this stage, all that is needed is an intuitive understanding that a 'cheaper pound', which was possible because the UK had left the Gold Standard, would push up the prices of imported goods. Following a devaluation of about 30%, the Treasury intervened in the foreign exchange market to sell pounds and keep the exchange rate from appreciating. The combination of higher expected prices and high unemployment depressed real wages and the improvement in business profits led to a recovery of investment. There was also a major contribution of house building to aggregate demand stimulated by the low interest rates, an unimpaired banking system and the expectation that construction costs would rise. Unlike the current situation in the UK, there were few planning restrictions on house building in the 1930s.

[a]  See Crafts and Fearon (2010) and Crafts (2013).

---

### 7.5.4  Fixing banks first may mean less government debt later

Experience from previous financial crises suggests that there is a case for governments to be pro-active as owner of a bank it has bailed out and focus on cleaning up the bank's balance sheet (see the box below). If the economy quickly gets back well-functioning banks, the length of the recession following a financial crisis is likely to be shortened with a faster return to normal economic activity and the normal functioning of macroeconomic policy. The fiscal hit to the government finances would be front-loaded if this strategy was adopted. Initially government debt would rise by more than in the case where the government does not move decisively to restore the banking system to health. However, the subsequent sequence of fiscal deficits is likely to be smaller (Borio, 2012).

The presence of bad loans (i.e. loans that are unlikely to be serviced or repaid) on the balance sheet of a bank makes it reluctant to extend new loans. Banks are also reluctant to identify bad loans, because this reduces the perceived value of their assets. A policy of ignoring the failure of customers to service and repay their loans is referred to as forebearance.

If non-performing loans are not identified and removed from the bank, the bank's ability to make new loans is impaired. Moreover, if firms that have no realistic prospect of servicing their loans are allowed to survive, this depresses productivity growth in the economy. Poorly functioning banks can lead to a failure of a key mechanism of the capitalist economic system referred to by Joseph Schumpeter as 'creative destruction'. Firms with poor prospects should exit from the economy and firms with promising prospects should be able to enter and have access to finance to expand. In Chapter 8 we set out a Schumpeterian model of endogenous growth, which highlights the role of entry and exit for overall productivity growth in the economy.

The expression zombie bank is used to refer to banks burdened by bad loans, and zombie firms are those kept alive by bank forebearance. Box 7.3 compares the delayed approach in Japan to writing off bad debt and the recapitalization of the banking system with the rapid response in Nordic economies. In Japan, the delay of nearly a decade produced zombie banks and firms.

---

### Box 7.3  Cleaning up banks after a financial crisis—Japan and the Nordic countries

The importance of bank restructuring and its implications for public debt is illustrated by comparing the strategies pursued by countries that experienced major banking crises in the late 1980s/early 1990s.[a] Japan provides a prime example of what not to do. It is no coincidence that their 'lost decades' began with a severe downswing in the financial cycle. The government chose not to intervene to recapitalize banks with the result that Japanese banks were weighed down with non-performing assets for years to come. The failure to swiftly clean up the banks meant that they went through an extended period of deleveraging at exactly the same time as households and non-financial firms, causing aggregate demand to stagnate. This approach was extremely costly for the real economy, with Japanese GDP growth averaging just 0.7% per annum between 1992 and 1999.[b]

The Nordic approach on the other hand is widely viewed as a benchmark for dealing with the mess left over after financial crises. The Nordic governments moved quickly to repair bank balance sheets in the immediate post-crisis phase, using measures such as recapitalization, disposing of toxic assets and reducing excess capacity in the financial system. The upfront cost of this approach is obviously larger than the laissez-faire approach, but recovery is typically much quicker. For example, GDP growth in Sweden between 1992 and 1999 was 2.4% per annum.[c] The quick restructuring of the banking system after a crisis means that banks have the ability to extend new loans to households and firms and support aggregate demand. Of course the difference between Japanese and Nordic economic performance following their financial crises is not fully explained by the way failing banks were treated. One important difference is that the Nordic countries benefited from substantial exchange rate depreciations and export-led growth through the 1990s.

One step taken by the Swedish government to resolve the banking crisis of the early 1990s was to separate failing banks' assets into two different institutions, which are referred to as a 'bad bank' and a 'good bank'.[d] Following the collapse of Sweden's credit boom (see Fig. 6.5 in Chapter 6 for Sweden's financial cycle) five of its seven largest banks needed government bail-outs or huge capital injections from their own shareholders. Two were nationalized and eventually merged. The non-performing loans from the nationalized banks were dumped into a 'bad bank' called Securum. Rather than simply liquidating them, Securum took an activist approach to disposing of its assets so as to maximize their value to the taxpayer. The assets ranged from the exotic like the British Embassy building in Burma to the more routine, such as property in Europe and Swedish industrial firms. Securum was wound up after five rather than the planned 15 years. The cost to the Swedish taxpayer of the banking crisis turned out to be small.

[a] This box is based on the discussion in Borio (2012).
[b] Source: IMF World Economic Outlook Database, April 2013.
[c] Source: IMF World Economic Outlook Database, April 2013.
[d] See Christopher Brown-Humes article in the Financial Times entitled *Swedish model points the way* (22/9/2008).

The historical experience documented in Reinhart and Rogoff (2009a) suggests that the 'clean up the banks first' policy has rarely been adopted. An interesting question is why, from the point of view of policy makers, it is more difficult to implement this policy than the alternative of incurring many years of fiscal deficits, accumulating government debt and slow growth as bank balance sheets are slowly repaired.

## 7.6 Conclusions

This chapter has applied the models of the financial system and macroeconomy from the previous two chapters to the global financial crisis of 2008–09. The pre-crisis period saw the interaction of the housing and bank-centred financial accelerator processes cause a substantial upswing in the financial cycle in developed economies. This period was associated with the accumulation of private debt in many of these economies, as banks levered-up to increase their returns and households borrowed to consume beyond their means.

The housing-feedback process was driven by the US banks aggressively extending mortgages to people less and less able to repay them. The interlinked financial asset-based feedback process involved the US banks, the global European banks and the shadow banking complex. They turned mortgages into tradeable assets (through securitization and tranching) and sold them to financial institutions round the world, which borrowed against the mark-to-market value of their assets to purchase them. The safety nets for institutions that had become 'too-big-to-fail' and the regulatory environment that allowed banks to calculate their own risk-weighted assets made possible these strategies, which added to the riskiness of the system as a whole.

These approaches were highly profitable in the upswing, but ruinous when the sun stopped shining. A downturn in the US housing market and the bankruptcy of systemically important US investment bank Lehman Brothers triggered a set of events that led to the worst recession since the Great Depression. A slump on the scale of the Great Depression was avoided because aggregate demand was stabilized with fiscal and monetary stimulus and governments and central banks acted quickly to shore up the battered financial system. Whilst the lessons of the Great Depression were learned, many governments implemented fiscal austerity policies before private sector indebtedness had been reduced. Lengthy recessions followed.

The crisis highlighted the inadequecies of the pre-crisis policy framework that combined inflation-targeting central banks with light touch financial regulation. A major theme in the post-crisis policy debate is that measures should be put in place to prevent the upswing of a financial cycle with its pro-cyclical build up of debt and leverage, which creates the basis for the upswing of a financial cycle, and the vulnerability of the economy to financial crisis. In other words, policy should be designed to prevent a financial cycle from taking hold. As we have seen, the root of the problem is that banks take excessive risks when measured from society's point of view. This arises because banks do not internalize the impact of their actions on systemic risk and because they are implicitly subsidized by the prospect of a bailout. The post-crisis policy debate, which is centred around better protecting modern economies from costly financial crises, is taken up in Chapter 13.

## 7.7 Questions

### 7.7.1 Checklist questions

1. Explain the role of the following factors in the upswing in the financial cycle that preceded the global financial crisis:

    (a) The implicit state guarantee for 'too-big-to-fail' institutions.

    (b) The assumption that MBSs bundled together in CDOs were not highly correlated.

    (c) Capital regulation based on risk-weighted assets.

2. Why did rising house prices make US retail banks more willing to provide mortgages for low-income earners with poor credit histories?

3. Assess the following statements S1 and S2. Are they both true, both false or is only one true? Justify your answer.

    S1. The European global banks did not dramatically increase the risk in their loan portfolios in the upswing before the financial crisis.

    S2. The European global banks followed a riskier strategy (than previously) in the upswing before the financial crisis.

4. Assume that an investment bank is at its maximum desired leverage of 20: it has $10 million of its own equity (net worth) and has borrowed $190 million to buy assets of $200 million. The price of the bank's assets falls and reduces their mark-to-market value to $195 million. What has happened to the bank's equity and leverage? How much must the bank reduce their assets to restore leverage to its desired level? How will it affect the bank's efforts to return to their desired leverage if other financial institutions are attempting to de-lever at the same time?

5. The following quote about the financial system is taken from Alessandri and Haldane (2009): 'Although *diversification* may purge *idiosyncratic risk*, it simultaneously reduces *diversity* and

thereby increases *systematic risk*'. Explain the quote and how it relates to the vulnerability of the financial system to crises. Make sure your answer fully explains the terms in italics in the quote.

6. Explain the difference between a bank having a liquidity problem and a solvency problem. How does each problem affect a bank's balance sheet?

7. Use yield curve diagrams to explain how conventional (i.e. adjusting short-term interest rates) and unconventional (i.e. quantitative easing) monetary policies aim to influence the level of aggregate demand in the economy.

8. Evaluate the following statement: 'Discretionary expansionary fiscal policy should not be used in an economic downturn, because this will lead to tax rises and spending cuts in the future that will damage economic growth'.

9. What policy mistakes were made in the Great Depression? How can these mistakes be shown using the 3-equation model? Show in a diagram how fiscal stimulus could have averted a deflation trap.

10. Discuss the following statement: 'Balance sheet recessions involve a debt overhang, hence the government should impose austerity to reduce the debt burden'.

## 7.7.2 Problems and questions for discussion

1. Pick three financial institutions, one from the US, one from the UK and one from Continental Europe. Download their annual reports for a pre-crisis year (i.e. before 2008). Use their balance sheets to ascertain whether these banks are best described as retail, investment or universal banks. How do the banks you have chosen vary in regard to the key concepts discussed in this chapter (refer to Chapters 5 and 6)? Your comparison should refer to:

   (a) The leverage of each bank.
   (b) The level of interconnectedness of each bank with governments and foreign banks.
   (c) The holdings of mortgage-backed securities of each bank.
   (d) The funding structure of each bank (e.g. debt vs. equity, short- vs. long-term).

2. Select two economies (outside of the G7 and the Eurozone). Use OECD. stat and the IMF World Economic Outlook database to gather data on key macroeconomic variables and policy responses of these two countries during the recent financial crisis. Plot this data graphically (as shown for the G7 in Fig. 7.6) and compare the path of these series before and after the fall of Lehman Brothers in September 2008. Which economy fared better? Use the data collected and your own knowledge to suggest some reasons why.

3. 'One way of reducing the likelihood of encountering the Zero Lower Bound problem is to have a higher inflation target.' Discuss. In your answer, refer to the role of inflation expectations in the performance of the British economy in the Depression of the 1930s (see Crafts, 2013).

4. Making reference to historical precedent, propose and defend a combination of monetary, fiscal and supply-side policies that would have speeded up the exit of the British economy from the Great Recession.

5. Why might it take longer for an economy to bounce back from a 'balance sheet recession' (i.e. a recession that is preceded by the bursting of an asset price bubble which damages private-sector balance sheets) than from a normal recession? What role is played by the policy toward the restructuring of insolvent banks?

# 8 Growth, fluctuations and innovation

## 8.1 Introduction

In this chapter, we bring together the short- and medium-run modelling of the macroeconomy developed in the earlier parts of the book with the analysis of long-run growth. The theme of this chapter is to understand how the more or less continuous process of rising living standards experienced in some parts of the world for more than 200 years depends on the process of accumulation of physical and human capital and technological progress.

   As we shall see, continuously rising living standards have not always been characteristic of human societies and they have been experienced very unevenly across the countries of the world. Continuous technological dynamism is not inherent to human societies. Where it is observed, we see a subtle mixture of competitive pressure and some protection for innovators that allows them to reap rewards of their costly investment in new products or processes.

### Capitalism transforms the world

Figure 8.1 plots estimates of global GDP per capita since the year 1000 for five countries in different regions of the world. Taking such a long-run view brings into focus the extraordinary

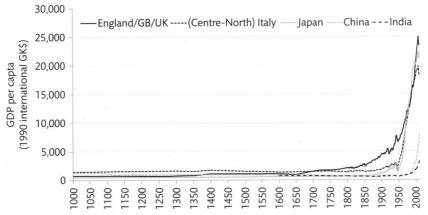

**Figure 8.1** GDP per capita (1990 international Geary-Khamis dollars): 1000–2010.

*Source:* New Maddison Project Database - Bolt and Van Zanden (2013); Broadberry (2013).

*Note:* All data from the New Maddison Project Database apart from data for China pre-1850, which is from Broadberry. All series have been linearly interpolated to create annual series.

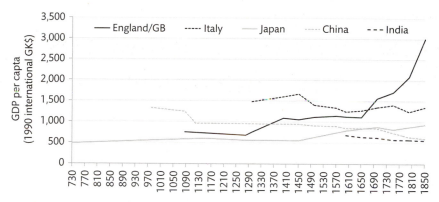

**Figure 8.2** GDP per capita (1990 international Geary-Khamis dollars): 730–1850.

*Source:* Broadberry (2013).

*Note:* All series have been linearly interpolated to create annual series.

character of economic development in the last 250 years. The figure is shaped like an ice hockey stick. Average living standards in these different parts of the world were fairly stagnant for a very long sweep of human history. The UK, where the Industrial Revolution began around 1750, was the first place where a long period of sustained and rapid growth of living standards occurred. Other countries followed at different times.

With growth of more than 2% per annum, living standards were doubling every generation in the countries where capitalism came to be firmly established. The result of this uneven development was that entire countries fell behind, and the world came to be made up of the rich nations and poor ones. Figure 8.1 reveals a rapidly widening gap between the UK and China until late in the twentieth century.

The world economy has not always been characterized by vast differences in living standards across countries. Recent research results in Fig. 8.2 show estimates of GDP per capita for England, Italy (the centre and north of the country), Japan, China and India for the period from the year 1000 until 1850.[1] The data are in real terms and are comparable across countries. The research shows that from the middle of the seventeenth century, England and the Low Countries (not shown in the figure) diverged from the Asian countries. Japan, China and India had living standards between 60 and 70% of those of England in 1600, but by 1850, they were between 20 and 30% as high. Strikingly, in this period, North West Europe pulled away from Southern Europe. In 1600, living standards in the north and centre of Italy were comparable with those in England, but by 1850, the average Italian was only half as well off as the average English person.

The interconnection of great changes in technology with the emergence of capitalism as the dominant economic system in Europe in the nineteenth century marked the beginning of the transformation of the way of life of humans across the globe.

---

[1] Note that the Broadberry data differs slightly from the data shown in Fig. 8.1 for the pre-1850 period. The pre-1850 data (for all countries except China) in Fig. 8.1 is taken from the New Maddison Project Database because this is the only source that covers the whole 1000–2010 period. We show the Broadberry data when zooming in on the early period in Fig. 8.2, as we believe these are the best estimates available for pre-1850 GDP per capita in these economies.

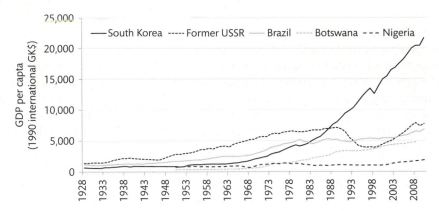

**Figure 8.3** GDP per capita (1990 international Geary-Khamis dollars): 1928–2010.

*Source:* New Maddison Project Database—Bolt and Van Zanden (2013).

*Note:* Where data are missing, series have been linearly interpolated to create annual series.

Capitalism is an economic system in which the capital stock is privately owned and where employers hire workers to produce goods and services with the aim of making a profit. Figure 8.1 vividly captures the uniquely productive character of this economic system. The hallmark of capitalism is that individuals who are wealthy or are creditworthy and are therefore able to borrow can take big risks in introducing new products and organizational methods. The combination of individuals reaping the rewards of successful risk-taking in large-scale ventures but bearing the costs of failure distinguishes capitalism from other economic systems; as summarized by Bowles (2006):[2]

> For the first time in history, competition among members of the economic elite depended on one's success in introducing unprecedented ways of organizing production and sales, new technologies, and novel products.

A large-scale experiment with a different economic system—that of the planned economy—was implemented by communist regimes in the Soviet Union and Eastern Europe, China and in a number of other countries. The Soviet Union introduced its first five-year plan in 1928. A second wave of countries operated planned economies from the late 1940s. Under central planning, production takes place in state-owned enterprises, and resources are allocated to different sectors according to the decisions of planning bureaucrats. There was no incentive for people to take the risk of introducing new products, services or methods of production since they would not reap the rewards if the venture was successful. The potential for large gains from innovation in a capitalist economy was absent in a planned economy. There was also no penalty for failure. Enterprises operated with what has been described by the Hungarian economist Janos Kornai as *soft budget constraints*, which means that running at a loss did not lead an enterprise to cease operation.

Figure 8.3 shows the evolution of living standards across a selection of emerging and developing economies between 1928 and 2010. The former USSR (i.e. the Soviet Union) could not match the growth in living standards observed in capitalist South Korea in the

---

[2] This excerpt is taken from p. 335 of Bowles (2006).

post-WWII period. Planning was abandoned in Eastern Europe and the Soviet Union in the early 1990s, and a major factor in its collapse was the failure of the planning system to deliver parity in living standards with peer market economies. Figure 8.3 also shows that the collapse of planning and the embrace of the market in the former Soviet bloc was followed by a lengthy transitional recession. Living standards fell, and in many countries it was over a decade before they were restored to their pre-transition levels. This experience was a surprise to many observers and highlighted the need to understand the pre-conditions for the successful operation of a market economic system. As we shall see later in this chapter, rapidly rising living standards and a process of catching up to the world technology frontier has been the exception rather than the rule for most countries for most of the period since capitalism took root, first in north-west Europe and soon after in the countries where European migrants settled. Figure 8.3 provides examples of market economies in Africa and South America where growth in living standards across the twentieth century was weaker than in the planned Soviet Union.

Looking back at the experience of the planned economies in the former Soviet Union and Eastern Europe and comparing them with the rest of the countries in the world suggests that planning allowed poor countries to industrialize by introducing large-scale electrification and widespread education. For poor countries, the benefits of planning in these important dimensions of modernization appear to have outweighed its weakness in dampening market incentives. For countries that had already industrialized and introduced schooling for their populations before planning was introduced, the costs of planning in hampering innovation outweighed the benefits, and these economies lagged further and further behind the world technology frontier.[3] The weakness of the planned economies in innovation is highlighted by their absence from the top 100 innovations made in the world after the experiment with planning began.[4]

Once planning was abandoned, the potential of a capitalist system to generate dynamism through accelerated diffusion of innovations was apparent. A good example is the very fast transformation that took place in the availability of telephone services, which had been accorded low priority by the planners. Kornai (2013) states that:

> The clear causal relationship between capitalism and the abundant supply of the phone service is present on several levels. The transition to private ownership based on the liberalized market economy put an end to the shortage economy. Phone services are supplied because domestic or foreign entrepreneurs profit from this business. Because of the close substitutability of the cable connected telephone by mobile phones the former cannot remain a monopoly. On the contrary, we witness a fierce rivalry between phone companies. Thirty years ago in the Soviet Union or in Eastern Europe, the would-be customer begged the bureaucracy for the great favor of getting a phone line. Nowadays phone companies are bidding for the favour of the customer.

### Proximate and fundamental sources of growth

The discussion of the successes and failures of the planned and the capitalist economic systems suggests that the *proximate* or immediate sources of the growth of living standards are

---

[3] For more detail, see Carlin, Schaffer and Seabright (2013).
[4] See Table 1 in Kornai (2013).

first, the accumulation of capital—both physical and human—and second, the development and diffusion of new technology. Unlike previous economic systems, both planning and capitalist systems succeeded in mobilizing resources to raise the human and physical capital intensity of production required for industrialization. With more equipment, including infrastructure such as electrification, and with better skills, more output per worker could be produced. However, the capitalist system proved superior to planning in generating continuous technological progress in the form of new methods of production and new products that raised living standards.

The *fundamental* causes of growth are those that explain what lay behind the accumulation of capital and the development of technology that have transformed human lives. What explains why capitalism emerged in one part of the world—north–west Europe—and not elsewhere (for example, in the Yangzi Delta in China or in southern Europe) and what explains why some countries and regions have benefited from the accumulation of capital and dynamism capitalism offers and some have not? Three broad explanations have been proposed: the role of geography (for example, location in tropical or temperate climate zones), culture (for example, protestant or catholic Christianity, or Islam) and institutions (such as property rights).[5]

There is not scope in this book to investigate the fundamental causes of growth. Rather, we focus on the proximate causes of growth: factor accumulation and technological progress. We begin, in the next section, by showing the connection between short- and medium-run models of the business cycle and a very widely used model of economic growth based on factor accumulation; the Solow–Swan model. The model was independently developed by Robert Solow (in the USA) and Trevor Swan (in Australia) in 1956.[6] For brevity, we will refer to the Solow model from now on. It shows how, if we abstract from the fluctuations in demand and supply that produce business cycles, the willingness of a society to save and invest more of annual output (and consume a smaller share) will lead it to adopt a more capital-intensive method of production with higher output per head. We show the connection between this result and the predictions of the models studied earlier in the book.

In the third section, we introduce the basic concepts and tools that are essential for studying growth theory, such as calculating growth rates and using log and exponential functions.

The fourth section sets out the Solow model in more detail and introduces the concept of a balanced growth path. As well as describing the role of capital accumulation in growth in a single economy, the Solow model also provides a set of predictions about the convergence of poor economies to the living standards of rich ones. In Section 8.5, we use data from the real world to weigh up the empirical support for these predictions.

Section 8.6 shows how technological progress is introduced in the Solow model. In a purely mechanical way this can account for the growth in living standards observed in developed economies since the industrial revolution. We show how growth accounting can be used as part of the description of the role of technological progress in long-run economic performance, and investigate how well the Solow model can explain the cross-country distribution of living standards observed in the world.

---

[5] See Acemoglu, Johnson and Robinson (2005), Acemoglu and Robinson (2012), North (1991) and Sokoloff and Engerman (2000).
[6] See Solow (1956) and Swan (1956).

The Solow model with technological progress does not, however, address the structural role of innovation in the economic system. The centrality of innovation to the market economy relies on the pursuit of temporary profits by the entrepreneur who is the first mover bringing a new product or service to the market. The economist Joseph Schumpeter, who wrote in the first half of the twentieth century, explained that the creative role of the entrepreneur brought with it the destruction of methods and products rendered unprofitable by the innovation. The term 'creative destruction' is identified with this feature of a market economy.[7]

To pursue these ideas, we introduce endogenous technological progress and the way endogenous growth models work in Section 8.7, and in Section 8.8 we present insights from the Schumpeterian growth model developed by Aghion and Howitt. This model has proved very rich in providing insights about growth that can be tested using cross-country and industry data. Questions that are addressed include the role of competition in growth and whether macroeconomic stabilization policy is good for long-run growth.

## 8.2 Short- and medium-run macro models and growth theory

The short- and medium-run macroeconomic model developed in this book is organized around the concept of the output gap $(y_t - y_e)$. We have looked at how shocks to aggregate demand or supply shift current output and/or equilibrium output, the implications for unemployment, and how the policy maker responds to the forecast inflation or deflation that arises.

One way of thinking about a growth model is that it pins down the growth rate of equilibrium output—it abstracts from deviations of output from trends caused by shocks to either aggregate demand or supply. Growth models ignore inflation by conducting all of the analysis in real terms. Problems of aggregate demand are ignored as well by assuming that all savings are automatically invested. This means that attention is focused on the determinants of the growth of equilibrium output.

A simple way to highlight the different assumptions of the short- and medium-run models and of the Solow growth model is to look at the implications in each case of a rise in the savings rate. In the short-run model with sticky prices and no policy intervention, a rise in the savings rate leads to a fall in aggregate demand and in output. This is the famous paradox of thrift case explained in Chapter 1.

In this chapter, $Y$ denotes real output and $y$ output per capita, $y \equiv Y/N$. The same convention also holds for capital, where $K$ is the real capital stock and $k$ is the per capita equivalent, $K/N$.

### The short- and medium-run macro model

The short-run model with a Keynesian consumption function and an investment function where investment depends inversely on the real interest rate (see Chapter 1) is illustrated in

---

[7] Creative destruction and the role of the entrepreneur were central to Schumpeter's 1934 work; in his later writings (1942), he focused on coordination of research in large corporations.

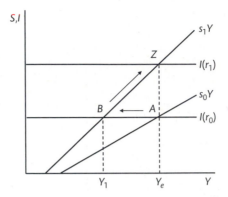

**Figure 8.4** Paradox of thrift.

Fig. 8.4. For simplicity, the government is ignored. Hence, goods market equilibrium is fixed by the equation of planned savings with planned investment, and the economy is initially at point $A$. The equilibrium is disturbed by a rise in the savings ratio to $s_1$ (i.e. by a fall in the marginal propensity to consume). This shifts the saving function to $s_1 Y$ and there is a new short-run equilibrium at lower output shown by point $B$.

The reason the economy moves to a lower level of output in the short-run model is that higher planned saving means lower aggregate demand, because in that model there is no mechanism through which the higher savings translate into higher investment spending. Lower aggregate demand in turn depresses output, and the intention to save more is thwarted as the economy settles at a lower level of output, leaving total savings unchanged and equal to the initial level of investment—hence, the paradox of thrift. This is shown by the movement from $A$ to $B$ in Fig. 8.4.

Note, however, that in the medium-run model with an inflation-targeting central bank, if the economy was initially at equilibrium output (i.e. $Y_e$ at point $A$), the rise in saving would have led to a negative output gap and lower forecast inflation (at point $B$). According to the 3-equation model, the central bank would cut the interest rate to $r_1$ thereby shifting the investment function up and the economy would have returned to its medium-run equilibrium (point $Z$).

### Introducing the Solow model

Let us now introduce a very simple version of the Solow growth model. It will be so simple that there is no long-run growth: we shall assume there is no population growth and no technological progress in the economy. This set-up helps to bring out the essential characteristics of the Solow model and how it differs from the short- and medium-run model.

The heart of the Solow model is a production function with diminishing returns to capital. This is shown in Fig. 8.5a (the left-hand panel), where capital is on the horizontal axis and output on the vertical axis. The shape of the production function, $F(K)$, is concave, which reflects the fact that as more capital is made available to each worker, the marginal product of capital is positive but declining. The other feature of the production technology that plays a role in the model is depreciation. Depreciation is the reduction in the value of capital stock over time due to age or wear and tear. In the model, it is assumed that a proportion, $\delta$, of

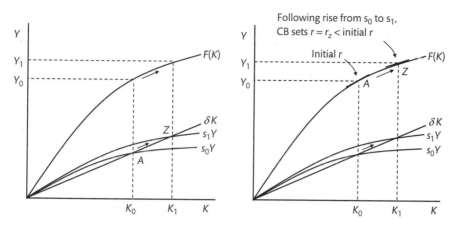

Figure 8.5 A rise in the savings rate in the Solow model.

the capital stock depreciates each period so that an amount $\delta K$ of savings has to be invested each period to keep the level of the capital stock constant.

In Fig. 8.5a, the rate at which the capital stock is used up each period through depreciation is shown by the line labelled $\delta K$. The saving rate in the economy is $s$, and the curve labelled $s_0Y$ shows the amount of output that is saved in each period. Since the saving rate lies between zero and one, the $s_0Y$ curve is the same shape but a fraction the size of the production function. Where the savings curve intersects the depreciation curve shows the equilibrium capital stock: the capital stock will stay unchanged at this level because the amount of saving and investment in each period are exactly what is required to replace the depreciated capital stock. Since savings are automatically invested, there is no problem of inadequate aggregate demand. The economy is always at equilibrium output and employment.

Given this set-up, we can now ask what happens when the saving rate goes up. With more saving and investment than is required to keep the capital stock fixed at its initial level, $K_0$, the capital stock will increase. With more capital stock in the economy and a given amount of labour, there is a more capital-intensive method of production, output per worker will be higher and total output in the economy will go up. Labour will remain fully employed.

This is illustrated in Fig. 8.5a. Because of diminishing returns, eventually all investment (shown by the $s_1Y$ curve) is used to replace the depreciated capital stock (shown by the $\delta K$ line) and at that new point of intersection, point $Z$, the capital stock ceases to grow. This defines the new equilibrium capital stock and associated output level ($K_1$, $Y_1$).

### The Solow model meets the 3-equation model

We can connect the Solow model to the 3-equation model in the following way. To see this, we need to drop the Solow assumption that savings are automatically invested. This allows us to introduce the possibility of inadequate aggregate demand and a role for the central bank as policy maker.

Now, assume there is an increase in the saving rate from $s_0$ to $s_1$ as in the previous experiments. We assume that the central bank understands both the paradox of thrift and the Solow model. The central bank will see that a new higher level of output is possible at a higher capital/labour ratio (from its understanding of the Solow model). However, from the paradox of thrift and 3-equation model, it knows it must reduce the interest rate in order to stimulate investment: this will both prevent output from declining as predicted by the paradox of thrift, and stimulate investment (and capital accumulation) to make use of the additional savings in the economy, taking the economy along the production function to point Z in Fig. 8.5b (the right-hand panel).

The slope of the production function is equal to the marginal product of capital since it shows the change in output associated with a change in capital. The central bank therefore uses the production function to identify the lower marginal product of capital associated with the new equilibrium: in this simple model, the marginal product of capital is equal to the real interest rate plus the rate of depreciation. Hence it sets the interest rate at the lower rate $r_Z$, so that $r_Z + \delta = MPK_Z$ shown by the slope of the production function at point Z in Fig. 8.5b. Because of the intervention of the central bank, investment rises in response to the lower interest rate and the economy moves to the new equilibrium at higher output and a more capital intensive method of production.

## 8.3 Growth concepts and useful tools

In order to set out the main concepts and tools used in growth theory, we consider the path of GDP per capita in the United States in the post-war period. Table 8.1 shows the real GDP per capita of the US for selected years between 1950 and 2011.

We use these statistics to calculate a number of different growth rates. Mastering these simple techniques is essential for getting a handle on growth theory and will also come in handy when examining any economic time series data.

### Annual growth rates

The annual growth rate is calculated in discrete time using the following formula:

$$\gamma_y = \frac{y_{t+1} - y_t}{y_t} = \frac{\Delta y}{y}.$$

We can now calculate the annual growth rate of US GDP per capita between 2010 and 2011 by inserting the relevant figures from Table 8.1 into the formula:

**Table 8.1**   Real GDP per capita for the United States, 1950–2011.

|  | Real GDP per capita (2005 US$) | Log of real GDP per capita |
|---|---|---|
| 1950 | 12,802 | 9.457 |
| 2010 | 42,287 | 10.652 |
| 2011 | 42,646 | 10.661 |

*Source:* Penn World Table 8.0, July 2013.

$$\frac{y_{t+1} - y_t}{y_t} = \frac{42,646 - 42,287}{42,287} = \frac{359}{42,287} = 0.0085 = 0.85\%.$$

It is useful to note that when national statistics agencies (e.g. the US BEA) release national accounts data on GDP or GDP per capita and they quote a headline figure for annual growth, this is the calculation they are making. For example, the growth rate of US real GDP per capita in 2011 was 0.85%.

The annual growth rate can also be calculated a slightly different way. It gives exactly the same result, but is often easier to use in computer programmes such as Microsoft Excel:

$$\frac{y_{t+1} - y_t}{y_t} = \frac{y_{t+1}}{y_t} - 1 = \frac{42,646}{42,287} - 1 = 0.0085 = 0.85\%.$$

### The log difference method for computing annual growth rates

Economic statistics can often be easier to manipulate using logs. Transforming a time series into logs can seem like an unnecessary complication, but once you get to grips with the basic mathematical properties of logs it opens up a range of useful tools. A prime example of this is using the log difference method to approximate annual growth rates, as shown by the following formula:

$$\gamma_y \approx \log(y_{t+1}) - \log(y_t).$$

We can now once again use the figures from Table 8.1 to calculate the annual growth rate:

$$\gamma_y \approx \log(42,646) - \log(42,287) = 10.661 - 10.652 = 0.0085 = 0.85\%.$$

The growth rate exactly matches that calculated in the previous subsection. The log difference method gives a good approximation of the annual growth rate when growth rates are relatively small (i.e. when $\log(1 + \gamma_y) \approx \gamma_y$).

### Compound annual growth rates

The compound annual growth rate (or CAGR) provides the trend rate of growth over multiple periods. It is necessary to have a formula that takes into account the fact that $y_0$ (i.e. the base year for calculating the annual growth rate) is rising in each period. If we ignored 'compounding' and just calculated the percentage growth for the whole period and divided it by the number of years in the sample, then this would overstate the annual growth rate. We will give an example of this shortly.

The formula for the compound annual growth rate for discrete time periods is

$$\bar{\gamma}_y = \left(\frac{y_t}{y_0}\right)^{1/t} - 1,$$

where $y_0$ is GDP per capita in the first year of the time series, $y_t$ is GDP per capita in the last year of the time series and $t$ is the number of periods in the time series.

We can now use the figures from Table 8.1 to calculate the trend rate of growth for US GDP per capita between 1950 and 2011:

$$\bar{\gamma}_y = \left(\frac{42,646}{12,802}\right)^{1/51} - 1 = (3.33)^{1/51} - 1 = 2.4\%.$$

On average, between 1950 and 2011, US real GDP per capita grew by 2.4%. This implies that the growth in 2011 of 0.85% was well below the post-war trend rate. The US economy was still in the midst of recovering from the global financial crisis of 2008–09 at this point. Unusually, for a post-recession period, growth was *slower* than the trend.

It is easy to use the US data to illustrate the inaccuracy of calculating the trend rate of growth without taking compounding into account. The percentage change in GDP per capita between 1950 and 2011 was $(42,646/12,802) - 1 = 233\%$. If we divide this by the number of periods in the sample then we get a trend rate of growth of $233\%/51 = 4.6\%$. The 'naive' method of computing the trend rate of growth gives an answer nearly twice as high as the correct answer, which shows the dangers associated with using a formula that is wrong because it neglects compounding.

### The exponential method of calculating compound growth rates

There is another method of calculating compound growth rates that involves using exponentials and logs. This method is particularly useful when we are dealing with continuous time and not discrete time as in the previous subsection. The formula for calculating the compound growth rate in continuous time, $\bar{g}_y$, is derived from the following relationship:

$$y_t = y_0 e^{\bar{g}_y t} \quad \text{or alternatively,}$$
$$y_t = y_0 \exp(\bar{g}_y t).$$

We can use the figures from Table 8.1 to show that this formula produces the same trend rate of growth for the US economy as does the CAGR. We first need to take logs of the equation shown above and then rearrange to get $\bar{g}_y$ in terms of the other variables.

$$\log y_t = \log(y_0 \exp(\bar{g}_y t))$$
$$\log y_t = \log y_0 + \bar{g}_y t$$
$$\bar{g}_y = \frac{\log(y_t/y_0)}{t}$$
$$\bar{g}_y = \frac{\log(42,646/12,802)}{51} = 2.4\%.$$

### The relationship between exponential growth and logs

We have shown that logs and exponentials possess properties that can be useful when manipulating economic data, but how do economic time series relate to their log series (i.e. the time series created when we take logs of the original series)? We answer this question by looking at a time series of US GDP per capita growth from 1870 through to 2012.

Figure 8.6a (the left-hand panel) shows the raw data and Fig. 8.6b shows the log series. It is immediately noticeable that the underlying series shows exponential growth, whereas the log series shows an upwards linear trend. This is no coincidence. It has to do with the relationship between series that exhibit exponential growth and their log series, which was set out in the previous subsection. If we go back to the equation that shows how $\log y_t$ relates to time, then we can see that it is a linear relationship with an intercept of $\log y_0$ and a slope

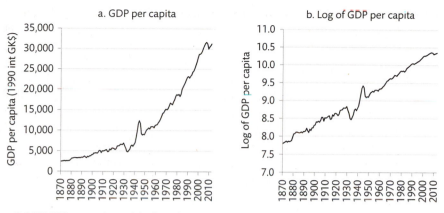

**Figure 8.6** US GDP per capita and the log of US GDP per capita: 1870–2012.

*Source:* Statistics on World Population, GDP and Per Capita GDP, 1-2008 AD (copyright Angus Maddison, University of Groningen. Last updated March 2010. Available from http://www.ggdc.net/maddison/oriindex.htm; The Conference Board Total Economy Database™, January 2013.

of $\bar{g}_y$ (or the trend rate of growth):

$$\log y_t = \log y_0 + \bar{g}_y t.$$

In general, any economic time series which has a constant rate of growth over many years will appear to increase exponentially. This is due to the effect of compounding. When the log of the series is taken then it will become a linear series with a slope equal to the trend rate of growth.

## The rule of 70

The relationship between GDP per capita and time that is shown in the exponential growth model leads us to a neat rule. The rule allows us to calculate approximately how long it takes for GDP per capita to double if an economy is growing at a constant rate of growth.[8]

$$\text{doubling time} = \frac{70}{\text{percentage growth rate}}.$$

In the previous subsections, we saw that the trend rate of US GDP per capita growth was 2.4% in the post-war period. This leads to a doubling time of 70/2.4% = 29 years. If the rate of GDP per capita growth was faster than this, say 5%, then it would double roughly every 14 years. In contrast, a rate of growth at 1% would see GDP per capita taking 70 years to double.

---

[8] The rule of 70 comes from the fact that $\log 2 \approx 0.7$. If we take $y_0$ to be the GDP per capita in period 0 and $t_d$ to be the time it takes to double, then using the exponential growth formula, we have:

$$2y_0 = y_0 \exp \bar{g}_y t_d.$$

We can then take logs of both sides and rearrange to derive the rule of 70:

$$t_d = \frac{\log 2}{\bar{g}_y}.$$

### The use of continuous time in growth models

In the book thus far we have worked mainly in discrete time, where there are set time periods that are usually assumed to be equally spaced—i.e. period $t$, period $t+1$ etc. In growth theory, however, it is easier and requires less cumbersome notation to derive the results in continuous time. Continuous time is not split into discrete periods of a year or a quarter, but instead runs along a continuum. In our GDP per capita example, this would mean that the difference in GDP per capita could be observed at any two points in time and not solely between set time periods.

Throughout this chapter we will therefore use the so-called dot notation to refer to the rate of change of key variables. $\dot{y}$ or 'y dot' is the rate of change of GDP per capita and is closely related to the familiar concept of the change in GDP per capita between period $t$ and period $t+1$, $y_{t+1} - y_t$, which is often abbreviated to $\Delta y$. $\dot{y}$ is the continuous time equivalent of $\Delta y$ and is defined as the time derivative of $y$, that is $dy/dt$. To summarize:

$$\Delta y \equiv y_{t+1} - y_t \qquad \text{(rate of change, discrete time)}$$
$$\dot{y} \equiv dy/dt. \qquad \text{(rate of change, continuous time)}$$

In addition, we can divide each rate of change equation by $y$ to find the proportional growth rate of GDP per capita:

$$\gamma_y = \frac{y_{t+1} - y_t}{y_t} = \frac{\Delta y}{y} \qquad \text{(proportional growth rate, discrete time)}$$
$$g_y = \frac{\dot{y}}{y} = \frac{dy/dt}{y}. \qquad \text{(proportional growth rate, continuous time)}$$

In each case, the growth rate, e.g. 0.02, is multiplied by 100 to produce a *percentage* growth rate.

## 8.4 The Solow model

As we shall see later in the chapter, the Solow model is limited in its ambition to uncover the dynamics of the growth and innovation process. Nevertheless, it has proved to be a reliable workhorse model of the role of capital accumulation in growth. Much more detailed expositions of the Solow model are set out in specialized growth textbooks, such as Weil (2012) and Jones and Vollrath (2013). Here we select the aspects of the model that are essential to understanding why the Solow model has played such a central role in empirical studies of growth.

### 8.4.1 The model

*The production function*

We begin with production in a one-good economy. The single good is something like corn or wheat, which can be consumed or can be invested, i.e. used as a capital input, so as to produce more goods next period. Labour is also used in production, which takes place according to the *production function* $Y = AF(K, N)$, where the production function is smooth and where the marginal products of capital and labour are positive and diminishing. All variables are in real terms.

Additionally we shall assume that the production function exhibits *constant returns to scale* (CRS). This refers to the idea that duplicating production facilities doubles output. It allows us to define output and capital in *intensive form* (i.e. per worker) as $y = Y/N$ and $k = K/N$.

In practice economists often use a particular production function for the Solow model. It is the Cobb–Douglas production function given by

$$Y = AK^{\alpha}N^{1-\alpha} \tag{8.1}$$

$$\frac{Y}{N} = A\frac{K^{\alpha}}{N}\frac{N}{N^{\alpha}} \tag{8.2}$$

$$y = Ak^{\alpha}, \qquad \text{(Intensive production function)}$$

where we divide through by $N$ to get it in the intensive form shown in the final equation. $A$ is referred to as total factor productivity, or *TFP*. The parameter $\alpha$ is between 0 and 1 and is capital's share of income. Labour's share is $(1 - \alpha)$.

Writing the production function in intensive form highlights the meaning of *TFP*: it says that output per worker (that is, labour productivity) will depend on capital per worker, $k$, and *TFP*. *TFP* captures all the reasons apart from the amount of capital the worker has to work with that affect their productivity. This will include the technology in use, the efficiency with which technology and capital are used, and management quality.

The intensive form of the production function is shown in Fig. 8.7. The function is concave, which reflects the assumption of diminishing returns to capital. As production becomes more capital intensive (i.e. a movement to the right along the $x$-axis), output per capita increases, but by a smaller amount with each additional increase in capital intensity. The figure also shows how the average product of capital (*APK*) and the marginal product of capital (*MPK*) are calculated. At any point on the production function, the *APK* is simply calculated as $y/k = (Y/N)(N/K) = Y/K$, and the *MPK* is derived as the slope of the tangent to the production function at a given level of capital per worker. When using a Cobb–Douglas production function of $Ak^{\alpha}$, $MPK = \frac{d[Ak^{\alpha}]}{dk} = A\alpha k^{\alpha-1}$. It is plain to see from Fig. 8.7 that $APK > MPK$ for any point on the production function. This is always the case when the production function exhibits diminishing returns.

### How do labour and capital inputs change over time?

*How does the labour input grow?*

We shall assume that the labour force grows at a constant rate $n$. If we work in continuous time it is natural to define this growth rate as:

$$n = \frac{\dot{N}}{N} = \frac{dN/dt}{N}, \qquad \text{(growth rate of labour)}$$

which implies that the labour force grows exponentially and for any initial level $N_0$, at some point $t$ in the future the level of the labour force is $N_t = N_0 \exp(nt)$.

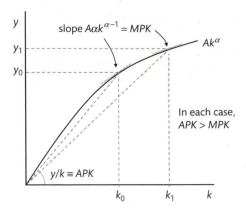

**Figure 8.7** The production function.

*How does the capital input grow?*

To see how the capital stock changes, i.e. $dK/dt$ (or $\dot{K}$), we need to deduct depreciation from gross investment, i.e.

$$\dot{K} = I - \delta K, \qquad \text{(change in capital stock)}$$

where $I$ is gross investment and $\delta$ is the rate at which capital depreciates.

We assume that we are dealing with a closed economy, which means that no borrowing from abroad is possible and hence, assuming there is no government sector, savings are equal to investment. In addition, the economy has a constant exogenously given savings rate $s$ out of current income $Y$. Together, these imply that

$$I = sY.$$

Next, we incorporate the condition that savings is equal to investment and substitute in the production function to get:

$$\dot{K} = I - \delta K = sY - \delta K = sAK^{\alpha}N^{1-\alpha} - \delta K. \qquad (8.3)$$

By dividing through by $K$, we have

$$g_K = \frac{\dot{K}}{K} = s\frac{Y}{K} - \delta = s \cdot APK - \delta, \qquad \text{(Growth rate of capital stock)}$$

which says that the growth of the capital stock depends on the average product of capital, $APK$, and is therefore a declining function of the capital–labour ratio ($k$) (see Fig. 8.8).

### 8.4.2 Steady state or balanced growth

Steady state or balanced growth is defined by a situation in which output and capital grow at the same rate, i.e. the capital to output ratio is constant. In the model without technological progress, capital and output grow at the rate given by the rate of population growth:

$$g_Y = g_K = n. \qquad \text{(Steady state growth)}$$

In steady state growth, since output and labour are growing at the same rate, the capital–labour ratio will be constant. This is called the steady state capital–labour ratio $k^*$. The capital–output ratio is often called $v$ and the steady state value of $v$ is $v^*$. From the equation for the growth rate of the capital stock, steady state growth requires

$$g_K = s\frac{Y}{K} - \delta = n$$

which implies:

$$v^* = \left(\frac{K}{Y}\right)^* = \left(\frac{k}{y}\right)^* = \frac{s}{n+\delta}. \qquad \text{(Harrod–Domar formula)}$$

The Harrod–Domar formula is useful because it provides an explicit expression for the steady-state capital–output ratio in terms of the exogenous variables $s$, $n$ and $\delta$, which does not depend on the particular form of the production function. We can summarize the results of the Solow growth model so far:

1.  In steady state growth, output and capital grow at the same rate as the exogenously given growth rate of the labour force. There is no growth in output per capita in the steady state.

2.  The capital–output ratio in the steady state is higher, the higher is the savings rate and the lower are the labour force growth rate and depreciation.

We can show steady state growth in a diagram with the capital labour ratio on the horizontal axis and growth rates on the vertical axis. The horizontal line shows the growth rate of labour, $n$. There is a downward-sloping line showing the growth rate of capital, labelled $g_K = sAPK - \delta$. This is downward sloping because as we have already seen, the APK is a decreasing function of the capital–labour ratio. The line showing the growth rate of output labelled $g_Y$ lies between the growth rate of capital and of labour.[9] This is intuitively clear: output will grow at the rate of a weighted average of the growth rates of the two inputs, capital and labour. In steady state growth, all three curves intersect since $n = g_K$.

The diagram showing steady state growth rates (as in Fig. 8.8) is very useful for analysing the *growth of output*, whereas the standard Solow diagram, which we shall derive next and is shown in Fig. 8.9, is useful for analysing the *growth of output per capita*.

---

[9] To derive $g_Y$ we start with the Cobb-Douglas production function, $Y = K^\alpha N^{1-\alpha}$ (assuming $A$ is one for simplicity). We then take logs and differentiate it to get:

$$\frac{d\log Y}{dt} = \alpha\frac{d\log K}{dt} + (1-\alpha)\frac{d\log N}{dt}$$

$$\frac{d\log Y}{dY}\frac{dY}{dt} = \alpha\frac{d\log K}{dK}\frac{dK}{dt} + (1-\alpha)\frac{d\log N}{dN}\frac{dN}{dt}$$

$$\frac{\dot{Y}}{Y} = \alpha\frac{\dot{K}}{K} + (1-\alpha)\frac{\dot{N}}{N}$$

$$g_Y = \alpha g_K + (1-\alpha)n.$$

Hence, the growth rate of output is a weighted average of the growth rate of the capital stock and population growth.

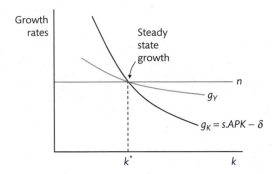

**Figure 8.8** Steady state growth rates in the Solow model: $g_Y$ is a weighted average of $g_K$ and $n$.

There is a second way of characterizing the steady state growth path, in which we use the intensive form of the production function. From above, we have

$$\dot{K} = sAK^\alpha N^{1-\alpha} - \delta K \text{ and, dividing through by } K \text{ and rearranging} \tag{8.4}$$

$$\frac{\dot{K}}{K} = sAk^{\alpha-1} - \delta. \tag{8.5}$$

Since

$$\frac{\dot{k}}{k} = \frac{\dot{K}}{K} - n,$$

we subtract $n$ from Equation 8.5 to get the equation for the growth rate of the capital–labour ratio

$$\frac{\dot{k}}{k} = sAk^{\alpha-1} - (n+\delta)$$

and multiplying both sides by $k$, we obtain the *Fundamental Solow Equation of Motion*, which describes how capital per worker varies over time:

$$\dot{k} = sAk^\alpha - (n+\delta)k. \tag{8.6}$$

It is worth exploring in some detail what Equation 8.6 tells us. The first term shows the extent to which investment is adding to the capital stock per worker. The second term shows the amount of investment needed to offset depreciation ($\delta k$) and to equip additions to the labour force at existing levels of capital per head ($nk$). Note that if there were no savings in the economy ($s = 0$) then $\dot{k} = -(n+\delta)k < 0$, that is, capital per head would be falling under the pressures of an increasing population, $n > 0$ and capital depreciation, $\delta > 0$.

We present this result in a standard Solow diagram (Fig. 8.9) by plotting the two parts of the right hand side of Equation 8.6. This is similar to Fig. 8.5a above. However, now there is the capital labour ratio, $k$, on the horizontal axis and output per worker, $y$, on the vertical one. Just as before, $sy$ is a curve shaped like the production function. The line from the origin is labelled $(n + \delta)k$. This line shows what is required to keep the capital labour ratio fixed and it reflects the need to replace capital stock as it depreciates at rate $\delta$, and the need to equip with capital new entrants to the labour force arriving at rate $n$. The difference between the two curves at any level of $k$ determines $\dot{k}$. For example, if $sAk^\alpha > (n+\delta)k$, capital per worker

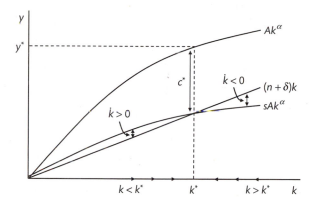

**Figure 8.9** The dynamics of capital and output in the Solow model.

increases because investment per head is greater than the reduction in capital per head due to an increasing population and depreciation.

The point where the two curves intersect is given by the level of capital per worker ($k^*$) where $sA(k^*)^\alpha = (n + \delta)k^*$. At this point $\dot{k} = 0$ and $\dot{y} = 0$, which means that the level of capital per worker and output per worker are constant. As we have noted above, this defines a *steady state* in the Solow model: at $k^*$ both $K$ and $N$ grow at the same constant rate $n$.

In Fig. 8.9, the steady state levels of output per head ($y^*$) and of consumption per head ($c^*$) are shown. We can easily see that the steady state level of output per head is given by

$$y^* = A(k^*)^\alpha$$

while the steady state level of consumption per head is also a constant and is a fraction of steady state income. It is given by

$$c^* = A(k^*)^\alpha - sA(k^*)^\alpha = (1 - s)A(k^*)^\alpha.$$

It is possible to solve for the steady state values of $k^*$ and $y^*$ explicitly. The equilibrium property $\dot{k} = 0$ implies $sA(k^*)^\alpha = k^*(n + \delta)$, where we can rearrange for $k^*$ and obtain the steady state value of capital and output per unit of labour:

$$k^* = \left(\frac{As}{\delta + n}\right)^{\frac{1}{1-\alpha}} \qquad\qquad \text{(steady state capital labour ratio)}$$

$$y^* = A(k^*)^\alpha = A^{\frac{1}{1-\alpha}}\left(\frac{s}{\delta + n}\right)^{\frac{\alpha}{1-\alpha}}. \qquad\qquad \text{(steady state output per capita)}$$

Although we have made substantial progress in understanding the role of capital accumulation in the economy, we still do not have an explanation of economic growth (that is, of output per capita) in the steady state.

### Does a higher savings/investment ratio always raise welfare?

In the Solow model, a higher savings rate will always raise output per capita. If welfare were measured in GDP per capita, then a higher savings/investment rate would always raise welfare. We can see from Fig. 8.10 that China's investment rate has increased markedly over the past 40 years, whereas investment rates elsewhere are lower and have on average

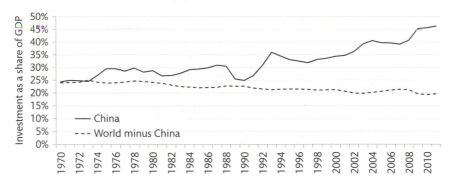

**Figure 8.10** Investment as a share of GDP: 1970–2011.

*Source:* United Nations Statistics Division, National Account Main Aggregates Database, December 2012.

declined. There is much discussion among observers of the Chinese economy about the need to reduce the investment share and the Solow model helps clarify the reasoning.

A preferable measure of welfare to GDP per capita is consumption per capita, denoted as $cy$ in the Solow model, where $c$ is the 'consumption rate' or the marginal propensity to consume. If this were taken as the yardstick for welfare, we can ask how a hypothetical social planner whose aim is to maximize welfare would set the savings rate to maximize welfare. The saving rate that would be chosen is called the Golden Rule saving rate.

It is very intuitive to illustrate the concept of the Golden Rule graphically, as is done in Fig. 8.11. The figure shows that consumption per worker (the gap between the production function and the savings function) is maximized at the steady state marked $k_{GR}^*$ at which the tangent to the production function has the same slope as the line $(n + \delta)k$. With competitive markets, the slope of the tangent to the production function, which is the marginal product of capital, is equal to $r + \delta$. The marginal product of capital has to cover the rental cost of capital, $r$, plus depreciation, $\delta$. As shown in the diagram, consumption per head is maximized when $r + \delta = n + \delta$, i.e. where $r = n$. The function $s_{GR}y$ will go through this point.

$$f'(k) = n + \delta = r + \delta$$
$$\rightarrow r = n. \qquad \text{(Condition for the Golden Rule savings rate)}$$

Using the Harrod–Domar formula, we can calculate the Golden Rule savings rate. For the Cobb-Douglas production function, the Golden Rule savings rate is equal to capital's share:

$$s_{GR} = \frac{(n + \delta)k_{GR}^*}{f(k_{GR}^*)} = \frac{(r + \delta)k_{GR}^*}{f(k_{GR}^*)} = \frac{f'(k_{GR}^*)k_{GR}^*}{f(k_{GR}^*)}$$
$$= \frac{\Pi}{Y_{GR}^*}.$$
$$\rightarrow s_{GR}Y_{GR}^* = S_{GR} = \Pi$$
$$\rightarrow s_{GR}y_{GR}^* = \frac{\Pi}{N}.$$

Two interesting results come from this. First, it says that at the Golden Rule, total savings, $S$, are equal to total profits, $\Pi$, and hence, total wages are equal to total consumption. Wages per worker and profits per worker are shown in Fig. 8.11 and the geometry of the result that

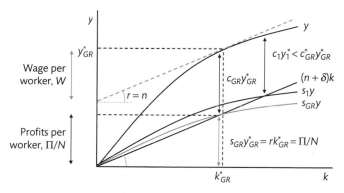

**Figure 8.11** The Golden Rule.

savings are equal to profits is shown. Second, for the Cobb Douglas production function, since $\alpha = \frac{f'(k)k}{f(k)}$, then it follows that the Golden Rule savings rate is equal to $\alpha$, capital's share of output.

It is clear from Fig. 8.11 that an increase in the savings rate above $s_{GR}$ actually reduces consumption per worker. It therefore also reduces welfare in this framework. The figure highlights an interesting point, if welfare is measured in terms of consumption per worker, then although it raises output per worker, raising the savings rate will not necessarily raise welfare.

### Policy experiment: a reduction in the savings rate

Let us now consider the following policy experiment: at time $t_1$, there is an exogenous fall in the savings rate. For example, a fall that takes China's investment share (savings rate) down toward levels elsewhere in the world. In Fig. 8.12, we trace the impact of this shock and show how $k$ and $y$ adjust as the economy moves to a new steady state. We assume that $A = 1$ for simplicity in the diagram. In the top left panel this is represented by a downward shift in the $sy$ curve corresponding to the decrease of the savings rate from $s_0$ to $s_1$. The economy slowly adjusts from the old steady state $k_0$ to the new steady state $k_1$, where capital per worker is lower than at $t_0$.

The transition dynamics are better illustrated in the bottom left panel, where we can inspect growth rates directly. The shock is illustrated by the downward shift of the $g_K$ curve. Immediately after the exogenous shock occurs at $t_1$, the growth rate of capital drops down to the rate shown on the new curve. Output growth drops as well. As the economy slowly converges to the new capital per worker long-run steady state $k_1^*$, the growth rate $g_K$ (and hence $g_Y$ too) rise back to their steady state values of $n$. The economy converges to point $B$. The paths of output and capital growth are shown explicitly in the top right panel.

The last panel (bottom right) shows how output per capita is permanently lower after the exogenous fall in the savings rate. As we have shown, however, if the economy began with a savings rate above the golden rule level, consumption per capita is higher in the new steady state if the new savings rate is closer to the golden rule level.

The explanation for what at first may seem to be a surprising result—namely, that a lower investment share does not reduce *growth* permanently—lies once again in the assumption of diminishing returns to capital accumulation in the Solow model. This means that the initial

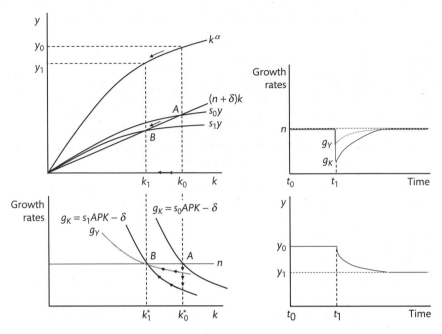

**Figure 8.12** How does a fall in the savings rate affect growth in the Solow model?

fall in the growth rate of the capital stock does *not* bring a proportionate decrease in output. Thus, along with the fall in capital per worker and productivity, there is an initial fall in the capital–output ratio. This means that the slower capital stock growth generated by the lower savings rate fades away as reduced depreciation eventually counterbalances the reduction in investment.

## 8.5 The Solow model and cross-country performance

### Cross-country differences in GDP per capita

At the start of the chapter (in Fig. 8.1), we saw that there have been periods of history where living standards have significantly diverged between countries (e.g. East and West during the industrial revolution), but that there have also been periods of noticeable convergence (e.g. East and West since 1980). In this section, we will more systematically compare the predictions of the Solow model to the real-world data, paying special attention to the concept of convergence.

We can use the equation derived earlier for output per worker in the steady state to set out the predictions of the Solow model.

$$y^* = A^{\frac{1}{1-\alpha}} \left( \frac{s}{\delta + n} \right)^{\frac{\alpha}{1-\alpha}}. \tag{8.7}$$

The model predicts that when the economy is in long-run steady state, output per head is: (1) increasing in the level of total factor productivity, $A$; (2) increasing in the savings rate

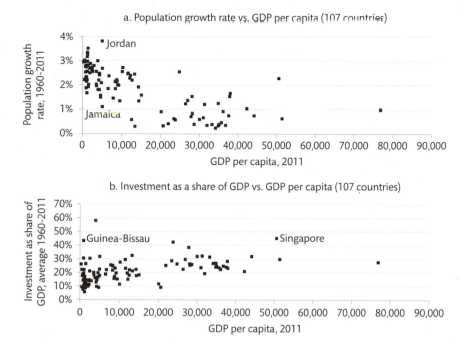

**Figure 8.13** Current levels of GDP per capita vs. population growth and investment as a share of GDP over the last 50 years.

*Source:* Penn World Table 8.0, July 2013.

(investment share) of the economy, *s*; (3) decreasing in the rate of population growth, *n*; and (4) decreasing in the depreciation rate, δ.

Figure 8.13 uses statistics from the Penn World Table to construct scatter plots of GDP per capita in 2011 and population growth and investment share over the last 50 years. The predictions of the Solow model suggest that there should be a negative association between population growth and GDP per capita, signalling that those countries that experienced slower population growth between 1960 and 2011 should be richer today. We can see from Fig. 8.13a that there is only weak evidence for this relationship in the data. It appears to be true that richer countries generally have slower population growth, but the relationship is far from perfect, especially for the poorer countries in the sample. For example, Jamaica and Jordan have almost identical GDP per capita today, but population growth has been substantially higher in Jordan since 1960.

When applied to cross-country performance, the Solow model also predicts that those countries that save more should have higher GDP per capita. We can use investment data to see if this prediction matches the cross-country data, as the Solow model assumes all savings are invested. Figure 8.13b shows a similarly weak relationship. Richer countries have had higher investment on average, but there is still a lot of unexplained variation in the data. For example, Guinea-Bissau and Singapore have invested a similar proportion of GDP over the past half century, but the former is one of the poorest countries in the world and the latter one of the richest.

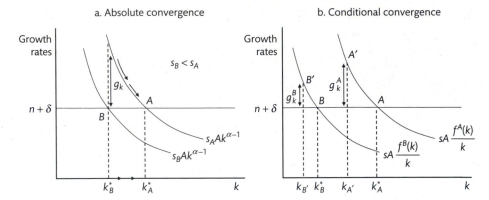

**Figure 8.14** Absolute and conditional convergence in the Solow model.

The cross-country scatter plots provide some weak evidence for the predictions of the Solow model, but the model cannot explain the large variation in living standards seen in the world today. It is also important to note that even if correlations in the data are consistent with the model's predictions, they do not provide evidence for the causal story provided by the model. For example, it is likely that richer countries are able to afford a higher saving rate than very poor ones; equally, families in richer countries may choose to have smaller families than in poor countries because they do not need to rely on their children to provide for them in old age.

### Convergence between rich and poor countries

To investigate convergence in the Solow model we start by introducing the concept of *absolute* convergence. If this holds, then poor countries will grow faster than rich countries and eventually catch up to their per capita GDP through the process of capital deepening, which is at the heart of the Solow model. To illustrate the idea of absolute convergence, we return to the Fundamental Solow Law of Motion,

$$\dot{k} = sAk^\alpha - (n + \delta)k,$$

and divide through by $k$ to find the growth rate of the capital–labour ratio:

$$g_k = \frac{\dot{k}}{k} = sAk^{\alpha-1} - (n + \delta). \tag{8.8}$$

Figure 8.14a shows the balanced growth paths for a rich country, A, and a poor country, B, which differ only in their savings rates. The poor country has a lower capital–labour ratio (i.e. $k_B^* < k_A^*$) and consequently has a lower output per capita than the rich country. In steady state, both economies are growing such that:

$$g_K = g_Y = n$$
$$g_k = g_y = 0,$$

hence output per capita growth is zero in both the poor and rich countries.

Is there anything the poor country can do to boost their capital–output ratio and increase their living standards to those of the rich economy? According to this simple version of

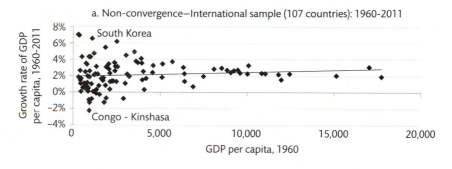

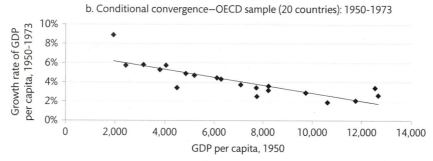

**Figure 8.15** Do we see economic convergence in the real-world?

*Source:* Penn World Table 8.0, July 2013.

the Solow model, an increase in the savings rate of the poor country will lead to a period of positive growth of capital per worker. The rich and poor countries now have identical parameters but the poor country is out of equilibrium. Given the rise in its saving rate, it is away from steady state. The model predicts that the poor economy will converge from its low output per capita level to that of the rich country: the doubled-headed arrow at point *B* shows the growth rate of the capital labour ratio (Equation 8.8) triggered by the rise in the savings ratio. The economy transits as shown in Fig. 8.14a to point *A* because the increase in the saving rate allows the poor country to take advantage of the high marginal product of labour at the low level initial level of capital intensity.

Is there any evidence of absolute convergence among the economies of the world? Figure 8.15a suggests not. It shows a sample of 107 economies, ranging from developing to frontier economies and plots their compound annual growth rate of GDP per capita between 1960 and 2011 against their GDP per capita in 1960. We would expect to see a negative association in the scatter plot if absolute convergence held (i.e. initially poorer countries growing faster). Instead, we find little relationship between the two variables. Whilst it is true that some poor countries like South Korea have grown rapidly in the last 50 years, others such as Congo-Kinshasa have significantly underperformed the richest economies.

This brings us to the idea of *conditional convergence*, which is where countries converge to their own steady states and more similar economies have steady states closer to one another. Let us consider the case in which the production functions differ between rich and poor countries. To this point we have assumed that poor and rich countries have the same Cobb-Douglas production function, $Y = AK^{\alpha}N^{1-\alpha}$. In other words, that poor and rich countries can produce the same amount of output from a given amount of labour and capital. This may well not be true; for example, richer economies could have more efficient production processes.

To illustrate the concept of conditional convergence, imagine there are a set of poor countries with intensive form production functions of $f^B(k)$ and a set of rich countries with $f^A(k)$. Figure 8.14b shows this example in a graphical form. The growth rate of capital per worker for each country depends on their distance from the steady state of their country group. For example, we can see that a poor country located at point $B'$ will experience capital per capita growth of $g_k^B$ and converge to the steady state capital per capita of the poor set of countries. The equivalent is true of a rich country at point $A'$. In this example, the rich country is actually predicted to grow faster, as it is further away from its own steady state. This highlights the key feature of conditional convergence: it is the distance away from your own steady state that dictates the speed of output per capita growth.

The weaker proposition of conditional convergence predicts that countries with similar steady states will converge, but that fundamentally different economies will not. The lack of convergence between rich and poor economies in this framework could be because poorer countries have inferior production functions, lower TFP or for other reasons, such as lower levels of savings or higher rates of population growth.

### Is there evidence of conditional convergence in the world economy?

There have been periods of history where conditional convergence has taken place within a group of countries. The best example of this is amongst the OECD economies in the so-called 'golden age' between 1950 and 1973. Figure 8.15b plots GDP per capita growth against initial GDP per capita for 20 OECD economies over the golden age. The figure shows a strong downward trend, meaning that the poorer OECD economies caught up to the richer ones over this period. This provides evidence for 'club convergence', where countries with similar structures and underlying production functions converge over time.

Mankiw, Romer and Weil (1992) test for the much weaker phenomenon of conditional convergence using the Solow model framework and find that the real world data shows evidence of conditional convergence, but that convergence is much slower in the real world than the model would predict. The next section takes this one step further and adds a new component to the model in a bid to bridge the divide between theory and reality.

### Human capital

Up to this point, we have been discussing the raw amounts of capital and labour across economies. To reconcile the theory and the cross-country data, we need an additional source of productivity that has thus far not been included in the model. If the productivity source is more abundant in rich economies then this would help to explain the lack of evidence for convergence seen in the empirics. One possibility is that more education increases the marginal product of labour for all given levels of raw physical capital and labour. In other words, more education enables workers to produce more with the same inputs.

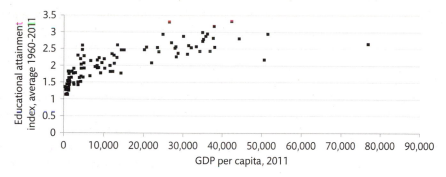

**Figure 8.16** Current levels of GDP per capita vs. educational attainment over the last 50 years.

*Source:* Penn World Table 8.0, July 2013.

Figure 8.16 plots GDP per capita in 2011 against average educational attainment over the past half century for 97 countries. The figure shows a clear upwards trend, with richer countries having higher educational attainment.

Setting the causality issue (i.e. is more education driving higher incomes or do rich countries simply spend more on education?) to one side, the Solow model can be extended to include human capital. In this context we can think of education as a proxy for human capital. Other components of human capital might include the health of the workforce and the quality of education. Once we have decided how to measure human capital the next question is how to incorporate it in the production function. In the standard Solow model, labour input is assumed to be the same for each worker across countries. We now relax this assumption and allow labour input per worker, $h$, to be different across countries. The augmented Cobb–Douglas production function is:[10]

$$Y = AK^{\alpha}(hN)^{1-\alpha},$$

where $h$ is a measure of the level of educational attainment in a country.

By taking $h^{(1-\alpha)}$ outside the bracket, the production function is now the same as that used in Section 8.4, except the $A$ in front of the production function has been replaced with $h^{(1-\alpha)}A$.

$$Y = h^{(1-\alpha)}AK^{\alpha}N^{1-\alpha}.$$

Following the same steps as the derivations in Section 8.4, we solve for the steady state level of output per head in the augmented Solow model.

$$y^* = (h^{(1-\alpha)}A)^{\frac{1}{1-\alpha}}\left(\frac{s}{n+\delta}\right)^{\frac{\alpha}{1-\alpha}}$$

$$= h\left[A^{\frac{1}{1-\alpha}}\left(\frac{s}{n+\delta}\right)^{\frac{\alpha}{1-\alpha}}\right].$$

The important thing to take away from this version of the Solow model is that it predicts that countries with higher levels of educational attainment will have higher levels of output per head in steady state (all other factors held constant). The model therefore provides a

---

[10] See Chapter 6 of Weil (2012).

potential explanation for the persistence of the gap in living standards between poor and rich economies.

Mankiw, Romer, and Weil (1992) estimate (a slightly different version of) the augmented Solow model from data for GDP per capita in 1985 for a sample of 98 countries. They find that the model accounts much better for the variation in GDP per capita across countries than does the model without human capital. They find strong evidence for conditional convergence, with the convergence rate close to that predicted by the augmented Solow model.

The result of augmenting the Solow model by including human capital provides a way of narrowing the gap between theory and empirical analysis. The model focuses on *broad* capital accumulation—of human as well as physical capital—as the engine of catch-up growth. However, to this point, the Solow model provides no account for the continuous growth of per capita GDP that has characterized the last 250 years in the advanced capitalist economies and which has transformed human lives. We turn now to show how the Solow model can be adjusted in a purely mechanical way to account for technological progress and for the steady growth of per capita GDP in the frontier countries. This provides the background for Section 8.7, which sets out a more satisfactory way of modelling innovation at the frontier.

## 8.6 Technological progress in the Solow model

### 8.6.1 Technological progress and steady state growth

Figure 8.6 shows a remarkably steady long-run growth rate of output per capita in the USA. Long-run growth since 1870 has been at the rate of 2.4% per annum. This fact provides the motivation for the modelling of technological progress in the Solow model. The Solow model does not attempt to explain the determinants of technological progress. But it pins down the form technological progress would have to take if it was to be consistent with the phenomenon of balanced or steady state growth.

Once we pose the problem like this, the answer is quite intuitive. Technological progress will have to be of the form that does not use up any resources in the economy (all investment is used to replace and increase the size of the capital stock) and that increases the productivity of labour. This is called exogenous Harrod-neutral (or labour-augmenting) technological progress.[11] It is usually described as a process that involves steady technological improvement, which raises output per worker by a constant rate, of $x$% per annum.

With exogenous technological progress at rate $x$, the Solow model requires only minor, mechanical adjustment. The Cobb-Douglas production function for output, $Y$, becomes,

$$Y = K^\alpha (A_t N)^{(1-\alpha)}$$

where $A_t = A_0 \exp(xt)$.

[11] Harrod-neutral technological progress is necessary for steady state growth with a general production function. If the production function is Cobb-Douglas, however, the three forms of technological progress (augmenting labour, capital or both factors) are identical and consistent with steady state growth. See the appendix to Chapter 13 of Carlin and Soskice (2006).

It is important to note the difference between $A$ in the standard Solow model from Section 8.4 and the $A_t$ introduced here. Up to this point, $A$ has represented the level of *TFP* in an economy. It could affect the level of steady state output per capita in the standard Solow model, but not the growth rate. The $A_t$ introduced in this section is an exponential growth process (see Section 8.3) that represents the growth of the technological frontier over time, hence it can affect steady state growth rates.

The model implies that the rates of growth of output and capital in actual and per capita terms on the balanced growth path are

$$g_Y = g_K = n + x, \text{ and}$$

$$g_y = g_k = x,$$

which means there is constant growth of output per worker in the steady state.

We can reconcile the Solow model with technological progress with the standard Solow model by introducing the concept of efficiency units, such that

$$\hat{y} = \frac{Y}{A_t N} = \frac{y}{A_t} \text{ and } \hat{k} = \frac{K}{A_t N} = \frac{k}{A_t},$$

where $\hat{y}$ is output per efficiency unit of labour and $\hat{k}$ is capital per efficiency unit of labour. When working in efficiency units, it is useful to remember that $y$ and $k$ can be retrieved by multiplying the corresponding values in efficiency units by $A_t$. Using these definitions we take the same steps as in the basic Solow model to arrive at the fundamental law of motion for the Solow model with technological progress. It is left to the reader to work through this derivation:

$$\dot{k} = s(\hat{k})^\alpha - (n + \delta + x)\hat{k}.$$

The economy is in the steady state when there is no change in capital per efficiency unit. As before, we can use the fundamental law of motion to derive the steady state levels of capital per efficiency unit and output per efficiency unit, where asterisk indicates steady-state level:

$$s(\hat{k}^*)^\alpha = (n + \delta + x)\hat{k}^*$$

$$\hat{k}^* = \left(\frac{s}{n + \delta + x}\right)^{\frac{1}{1-\alpha}}$$

$$\hat{y}^* = (\hat{k}^*)^\alpha = \left(\frac{s}{n + \delta + x}\right)^{\frac{\alpha}{1-\alpha}}.$$

We can also use this last expression to solve for the steady state value of output per worker:

$$y_t^* = A_t \left(\frac{s}{n + \delta + x}\right)^{\frac{\alpha}{1-\alpha}}.$$

This expression shows that at time $t$ after the economy has reached its long-run steady state growth path, output per head is: (1) increasing in the level of technological development $A_t$ at time $t$; (2) increasing in the savings rate of the economy, $s$; (3) decreasing in the rate of population growth, $n$; and (4) decreasing in the depreciation rate, $\delta$.

Consistent with our intuition, this shows that economies that save more, have lower fertility and are advanced technologically will have higher GDP per capita. But note that whilst higher

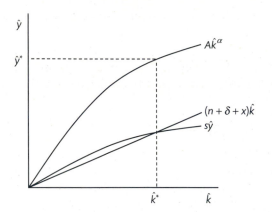

**Figure 8.17** The Solow model with technological progress.

savings and lower population growth mean a higher level of living standards, only faster technological progress (higher $x$) can raise the *growth rate* of living standards.

Figure 8.17 shows the Solow diagram with exogenous technological progress. It is very similar to the standard diagram except that it is in efficiency units and the line from the origin—$(n + \delta + x)\hat{k}$—includes the rate of technological progress $x$ and now shows what investment is required to keep capital per efficiency unit of labour fixed. In this model, a rise in the exogenous rate of technological progress raises output and creates new capital investment opportunities. It also puts the economy onto a higher growth path, permanently increasing the rate of growth of output per worker.

### 8.6.2 Growth accounting: measuring the impact of technology

At the start of Section 8.4, we introduced the idea of total factor productivity, or *TFP*. *TFP* is the contribution to economic growth that is unaccounted for by the growth of factor inputs (e.g. labour and capital). It captures the intangible aspects of human progress, such as efficiency gains and management quality, that improve the productivity of factor inputs (i.e. the amount of output that can be produced with a given amount of inputs).

Solow's method of calculating total factor productivity growth is known as *growth accounting*. To see how this works we can start from our standard Cobb–Douglas production function:

$$Y = AK^{\alpha}N^{1-\alpha}.$$

We then take logs and differentiate with respect to time to get:

$$\frac{\dot{Y}}{Y} = \frac{\dot{A}}{A} + \alpha\frac{\dot{K}}{K} + (1 - \alpha)\frac{\dot{N}}{N}$$

$$g_Y = g_{TFP} + \alpha g_K + (1 - \alpha)n.$$

*TFP* growth (also known as the Solow residual) is the difference between output growth and a weighted sum of the growth of factor inputs where the weights are given by the factor shares, i.e. it is the growth that is not attributed to the growth of either labour or capital inputs. Using national accounts data it is possible to calculate *TFP* growth.

$$TFP \text{ growth} = g_Y - \alpha g_K - (1 - \alpha)n.$$

In empirical analysis, it is often illuminating to work in per capita terms and we can rearrange this equation as follows:

$$TFP \text{ growth} = (g_Y - n) - \alpha g_K + \alpha n$$
$$= g_y - \alpha g_k,$$

where as usual, $y \equiv Y/N$ and $k \equiv K/N$. We can also turn the equation around and decompose the growth of labour productivity into the contribution from the growth of capital intensity, i.e. capital-deepening, and the contribution of TFP growth:

$$g_y = \alpha g_k + TFP \text{ growth}.$$

Over the years economists have come up with many objections to Solow's attempt to use a simple accounting decomposition based on the Cobb-Douglas production function to measure technological progress,[12] but as a way of organizing the data, the technique is widely viewed as valuable.

Table 8.2 is an example of how growth accounting can provide useful insights. It shows the contributions to growth of the different factors of production (labour and capital) and also of *TFP* (referred to as multifactor productivity in the table) to the growth of the market economy (i.e. excluding the government sector) in the US and the European Union for two periods since 1980. The table also decomposes the factor inputs further, which allows the contribution of the knowledge economy to growth through skilled labour and information and communications technology (ICT) capital to be quantified.

The table contains a large amount of information, and it is left to the reader to explore this in greater depth. We highlight two interesting findings:

1. Trends in *TFP* growth: the evolution of *TFP* is very different in the two regions. *TFP* growth was higher in the EU than in the USA between 1980 and 1995, but the trend reversed thereafter, with the USA seeing a significant productivity increase and the EU experiencing a marked slowdown between 1995 and 2004. The weakness of EU *TFP* growth after 1995 has been a cause for concern on the part of European policy makers.

2. The contribution of the knowledge economy (ICT capital deepening and labour composition): the US and the EU had the same contribution from the knowledge economy defined this way in the early period. In the latter period, however, the US moved ahead of the EU. The knowledge economy (ICT capital deepening and labour composition) contributed 0.4 percentage points more to US than EU growth between 1995 and 2004.

The interesting result is that although there was a modest US advantage in the contribution of the knowledge economy from 1995–2004, the advantage in *TFP* growth was almost three

---

[12] For a wide-ranging, recent and critical assessment, see Lipsey and Carlaw (2004).

**Table 8.2**  Contributions to growth of real output in the market economy, European Union and United States: 1980–2004 (annual average growth rates, in percentage points)

|  | European Union | | United States | |
|---|---|---|---|---|
|  | 1980–1995 | 1995–2004 | 1980–1995 | 1995–2004 |
| 1. Market economy output (2) + (3) | 1.8 | 2.2 | 3.0 | 3.7 |
| 2. Hours worked | –0.6 | 0.7 | 1.4 | 0.6 |
| 3. Labour productivity (4) + (5) + (8) | 2.4 | 1.5 | 1.5 | 3.0 |
| Contributions from |  |  |  |  |
| 4. Labour composition | 0.3 | 0.2 | 0.2 | 0.3 |
| 5. Capital services per hour (6) + (7) | 1.2 | 1.0 | 0.8 | 1.3 |
| 6. ICT capital per hour | 0.4 | 0.5 | 0.5 | 0.8 |
| 7. Non-ICT capital per hour | 0.8 | 0.5 | 0.2 | 0.4 |
| 8. Multifactor productivity | 0.9 | 0.3 | 0.5 | 1.4 |
| Contribution of the knowledge economy |  |  |  |  |
| to labour productivity (4) + (6) + (8) | 1.6 | 1.1 | 1.3 | 2.6 |

*Source:* Ark, O'Mahoney and Timmer, 2008.

times as great (a gap of 1.1 percentage points). The unexplained 'residual *TFP*' accounts for most of the difference in dynamism.

## 8.7  Endogenous growth: the Romer model

Using the Solow model, we obtained insight into the role of capital accumulation as a mechanism through which a society raises GDP per capita and how the presence of diminishing returns to factor accumulation imposes a limit on the extent to which changes in policy or institutions can affect growth in the long run. For the Solow model, changes in the rate of growth of output per capita in the long-run steady state come from changes in the rate of exogenous technological progress. Endogenous growth theory proposes a number of mechanisms that could overcome diminishing returns to capital and thereby open up the possibility that changes in policy can affect the growth rate in the long-run steady state.

In this section, we explain the mechanics of switching from exogenous to endogenous growth. There are many different channels—knowledge spillovers from the accumulation of physical capital, investment in human capital, and in research and development—that might drive endogenous growth. The way in which diminishing returns to capital accumulation is offset in each case is set out in detail in Chapter 14 of Carlin and Soskice (2006).

### 8.7.1  Research and development

This section introduces the role of ideas and technological innovation as the engine of economic growth. The approach to technological progress in the Solow model places the process outside the realm of economic forces. There are two aspects to this: on the one hand, improvements in productivity appear like manna from heaven at no resource cost, and on the other hand, access to the new technology is universal so it has the character of a public good that is non-excludable. Both aspects are challenged in growth models that put R&D at the centre of attention. These models centre on purposeful innovation activities undertaken with the aim of securing innovation rents because, at least for a time, the productivity enhancement is not available to imitators.

The ideas that form the output of the innovation process are different from many of the other goods we encounter in everyday life, and economists refer to them as possessing the properties of *non-rivalry* and *non-excludability*. By contrast, most goods are both rivalrous and excludable. Non-rivalry refers to the use of an existing idea at zero marginal cost. It is the rivalrous nature of most natural resources that lies behind much human conflict. More generally, your consumption of the additional food resources used in your meals today comes at a marginal cost and you can prevent others from eating the food.

Economists often visualize the ideas that result from innovation as blueprints. These blueprints are instructions on how to build the latest plane or what ingredients to put in the latest AIDS medicine. Once a blueprint becomes available, anyone who understands it can start to use it and market their own products based on it. This explains why we have generic drug companies that produce drugs that are chemically identical to their most famous branded cousins.

Hence ideas in the context of innovation are non-rivalrous. However, at least for some time period, they are excludable. The excludability property of ideas in the process of innovation naturally leads to an imperfect market structure in the market for blueprints.

The legal institution of patents is one method that allow firms to earn supernormal profits (or, equivalently innovation rents) for a limited period of time, which can be used to finance R&D. Pharmaceutical companies invest billions of dollars in developing new drugs. If new drugs were marketed immediately at marginal cost (think of how low the marginal cost of producing one pill is) firms would soon go out of business and innovation would slow. Setting prices above marginal cost in the market for ideas is entailed by the intrinsic properties of ideas as blueprints. On the other hand, the non-rivalrous nature of ideas promises social benefits as everyone can benefit from them without diminishing their availability to others. Before we return to the role in innovation of the extent of competition in the product market and of spillovers, we establish the relationship between endogenous growth and endogenous technological progress based on the production of ideas.

### 8.7.2 Endogenous growth and endogenous technological progress: the Romer model

At its most basic, a model of endogenous growth requires that the production function exhibits constant returns to a factor that can be accumulated—for example, capital, human capital or ideas. This contrasts with the production function in the Solow model, where there are diminishing returns to capital, or to human and physical capital. Taking the example of capital as the factor that can be accumulated, in Fig. 8.18, a production function with constant returns to capital is shown. It is linear rather than concave. In this case, where the $sY$ line coincides with the $\delta K$ line, saving (and investment) is just equal to depreciation and whatever level the capital stock is at, it will remain constant at that level. If the savings rate rises to $s_1$ then unlike the case with diminishing returns (illustrated in Fig. 8.5a), the capital

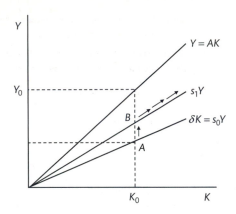

**Figure 8.18** A rise in the savings rate in the endogenous growth model.

stock will continue growing without limit; as will output. This is a model of 'endogenous growth'.

To incorporate the production of ideas into a simple growth model, we begin with a production function using capital and labour, but with a twist: we distinguish between workers who are employed in production and those employed in research. The population is assumed to be constant. We denote by $N_t^Y$ the total number of workers employed in the final goods market. These are the workers who use the blueprints in conjunction with physical capital and raw labour to produce final goods. We also denote by $N_t^R$ the number of workers employed in R&D. These are the researchers who increase the stock of knowledge in the economy through innovation. They create blueprints that will be used later on in production by workers in the final goods sector.

We use a Cobb–Douglas production function for final goods:

$$Y_t = K_t^\alpha (A_t N_t^Y)^{1-\alpha},$$

where $A_t$ now stands for ideas, which does not represent exogenous technological progress as in the Solow model, but is an integral component of the model. Total labour in the economy at time $t$ is given by $N_t = N_t^Y + N_t^R$, that is, the sum of the labour employed in the manufacturing sector producing the final output and the labour employed in the research sector producing the blueprints.

What can we say about the accumulation equation for blueprints or ideas, $A$? The source of endogenous growth in this model is the *constant returns* to the *accumulation of blueprints*. We begin with a general specification for endogenous technological progress and then show the constant returns case:

$$\dot{A}_t = c A_t^\eta N_t^R,$$

which says that ideas accumulate proportionally to the number of workers $N_t^R$ employed in R&D and in a way that is related to the current stock of ideas $A_t$, where $c$ is a constant. The size of the parameter $\eta$ is important for the accumulation of ideas equation. As long as $\eta > 0$, the equation captures the notion that the economy benefits from positive spillovers or externalities from the existing stock of ideas or blueprints. If $\eta = 1$, there are constant returns to the accumulation of ideas and this will be a source of endogenous growth. This version of the model is often referred to as the Romer model.[13]

Since we are especially interested in the possibility of endogenous growth, we concentrate on the special case where $\eta = 1$. In this case the accumulation equation for ideas is given by

$$\dot{A}_t = cA_t N_t^R,$$

where we divide both sides by $A_t$ to obtain the growth rate of ideas

$$g_A = cN_t^R.$$

Note that only with $\eta = 1$ do we get steady state endogenous growth from the model of endogenous technological progress: steady state endogenous growth requires constant returns to the accumulation of ideas. In this case, the growth rate of the factor that can be accumulated can be expressed entirely in terms of the exogenous variables. This gives a constant rate of technological progress in the steady state, $g_A \equiv \dot{A}_t / A$.

In the Solow model with exogenous technological progress (where $g_A = x$), the steady state growth rate of per capita output is equal to the growth rate of ideas, where $x$ is given exogenously. The difference here is that under the assumption that $\eta = 1$, $g_A = cN_t^R$, which means that the steady state growth rate of the economy is higher the more people are employed in the research sector.

To summarize, this is called a model of *endogenous growth* because unlike the Solow case, where an increase in the rate of technological progress, $x$, was exogenous, here a permanently higher growth rate of productivity can be achieved by a policy of increasing the number of R&D workers.

## 8.8 Schumpeterian growth: the Aghion-Howitt model

Innovation works through entrepreneurs who implement new discoveries and bring them successfully to the market. Schumpeter identifies the entrepreneur as the key agent in the process of innovation, which extends well beyond the idea of inventing a new product.[14] Innovations include developing a new route by which existing factors of production are channelled into the production process; a new product or improving the quality of an existing product; a completely new production process for an existing product; or a completely new market, where there previously was none.

Schumpeter's concept of creative destruction captures the dual nature of technological progress: in terms of 'creation', entrepreneurs introduce new products or processes in the hope that they will enjoy temporary monopoly profits, known as innovation rents, as they capture markets. In doing so, they make old technologies or products obsolete—this is the 'destruction'.

The motivation for innovators to make risky investments in new products is to make a temporary profit by stealing a march on other producers. This requires that the innovation

---

[13] This is an outline of the model developed by Paul Romer (1990). See Carlin and Soskice (2006) Chapter 14 for an extended presentation.
[14] Schumpeter (1934; 1961 edition: 66).

cannot immediately be copied by an imitator. Formal patents are only one method of protecting the temporary monopoly profits of the entrepreneur, trade secrets are another and being the first mover into a market is a third. The first mover method for capturing innovation rents highlights the important role in market economies of the emergence of new firms. One reason for the weakness of innovation in planned economies was the control by the state over new business activities.

For the process of creative destruction, it is also necessary that institutions are in place to ensure that the rents from innovation go to the entrepreneur and are not confiscated by the government or other powerful groups like organized crime. An investigation of the institutional pre-requisites for innovation and the sustained growth that began in the eighteenth century in England (see Fig. 8.1) is beyond the scope of this chapter. There has been a wealth of highly productive research on this question in the past 15 years complementing the work of economic historians and historians stretching back much further. A very good place to begin is the overview written by Acemoglu, Johnson and Robinson (2005), where they say:[15]

> Of primary importance to economic outcomes are the economic institutions in society such as the structure of property rights and the presence and perfection of markets. Economic institutions are important because they influence the structure of economic incentives in society. Without property rights, individuals will not have the incentive to invest in physical or human capital, or adopt more efficient technologies.

Instead of opening up the broad question of the role of institutions as a fundamental cause of economic growth, we concentrate on innovation as a proximate cause of growth and the narrower question of the incentives for innovation.

### Linking the Solow model to the Schumpeterian model

We can highlight the connection between the Solow model of growth with exogenous technological progress and a Schumpeterian model by bringing together the two proximate sources of growth in per capita GDP: factor accumulation and technological progress.

In the Solow model, we can compare different steady state growth paths for different rates of exogenous technological progress, $x$. Given the savings rate, population growth rate, and depreciation in the economy, a higher rate of technological progress implies a lower level of capital per efficiency unit of labour on the steady state growth path (the line labelled $(n + \delta + x)\hat{k}$ in Fig. 8.17 rotates to the left). This allows us to derive a downward-sloping relationship between the level of capital per efficiency unit of labour, $\hat{k}$, and $x$, the rate of technological progress, which in turn defines the growth rate of output per capita in the steady state. This downward-sloping line is shown in Fig. 8.19 and labelled the 'Solow steady state relationship'.

In the Solow relationship, the causality goes from the rate of exogenous technological progress to the steady state level of capital per efficiency unit. Faster technological progress means that at the initial steady state, less capital is now needed to equip new entrants to the labour force (since the newly arrived technology raises their productivity using the existing capital). This shifts the economy to a faster rate of growth with lower capital intensity measured in efficiency units. In Fig. 8.19, we can compare the initial equilibrium at point $A$ with the new equilibrium at point $B$ associated with the higher rate of technological progress.

---

[15] Excerpt taken from p. 389 of Acemoglu et al. (2005).

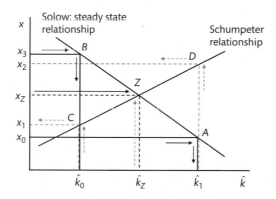

**Figure 8.19** Endogenous determination of $x$, the rate of technological progress.

Next, a Schumpeterian element is introduced by modelling the determinants of $x$, the rate of technological progress, as a function of innovative activities. In a model of endogenous growth based on endogenous technological progress, steady state growth will depend on the expected returns to innovative effort which are greater with higher capital (and output) per efficiency unit of labour, as depicted in the upward-sloping Schumpeter relationship. Schumpeter stressed the importance of the size of the market for the incentive to innovate, and a simple way of capturing this is to assume that a higher level of output or of capital per efficiency unit of labour implies a larger market for the innovator.

This gives a second relationship between the rate of technological progress, $x$, and capital intensity per efficiency unit, $\hat{k}$. This positively sloped relationship is labelled the 'Schumpeter relationship' in Fig. 8.19. Compare point C in Fig. 8.19 with point D. In the Schumpeter relationship, the causality goes from the size of the market, which is taken as given by the innovator and is proxied by the economy's capital per efficiency unit, to the rate of technological progress.

On the steady state growth path, the economy where both these forces are at work is characterized by the combination of capital per efficiency unit and rate of technological progress where the two relationships intersect. In the example shown in Fig. 8.19, the growth rate at point Z is $x_Z$.

### Policies to raise long-run productivity growth

We now consider how policy could be used to shift either of these relationships and promote higher steady state growth: first, an increase in the savings (and investment) ratio and second, an improvement in the expected returns to innovation. Each of these can be thought of as resulting from decisions by policy makers. Governments can use tax policy to stimulate saving and investment and shift the Solow relationship upwards. Typical policies to stimulate R&D and shift the Schumpeter relationship upwards are taxes and subsidies that reduce the marginal cost of R&D. Policies to increase investment in higher education, and as argued in the next section, well-designed competition policies could also have this effect.

If there is an increase in the savings rate in the economy, this shifts the Solow line outwards. At a given rate of technological progress, higher saving leads to an increase in capital per efficiency unit through the Solow (capital accumulation) mechanism.

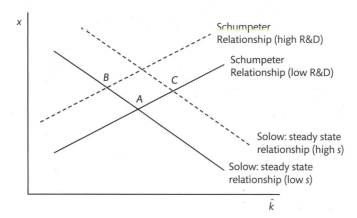

**Figure 8.20** Policy experiments and endogenous growth: rise in savings; rise in the intensity of R&D.

In the combined model, this increases the size of the market for innovators and prompts more R&D activity via the Schumpeter relationship. The economy moves to a new steady-state growth path fixed by a point to the north-east of point A at point C in Fig. 8.20.

In contrast to the standard Solow model, this means that higher saving produces a permanently higher growth rate. It is interesting to note as well that to the extent there is a causal link of this kind from capital per efficiency unit to R&D and via R&D to growth as suggested by the Schumpeter relationship, a regression framework based on the Solow model will overestimate the direct contribution of capital to growth by ignoring the fact that part of its contribution is via the R&D that it stimulates.

In the second experiment, we assume that the policy environment becomes more support-ive of R&D $\lambda$. As a result, R&D intensity rises, which shifts the Schumpeter line upwards. The more rapid technological progress takes the economy to a higher growth path at lower capital per efficiency unit along the Solow relationship. The new steady state growth equilibrium is to the north–west of point A at point B. Complementary policies could be adopted that would act on both relationships. Crafts (2007) applies this framework to addressing the question of why recent European economic growth was not like the Golden Age of the 1950s and 1960s.

### 8.8.1 Creative destruction, competition and Schumpeterian growth

The idea of modelling innovation as 'vertical', in the sense that it takes the form of a qual-ity improvement rather than 'horizontal' (the introduction of a new variety of good) allows Schumpeter's insight that new goods or techniques push out old ones to be formalized in an endogenous growth model. The most famous such model based on quality-improving innovations is due to Philippe Aghion and Peter Howitt.[16] In the production of ideas, the promise of innovation rents induces investment, which suggests that too much competition can dampen growth. But Schumpeter also stressed the positive role of rivalry in stimulat-ing innovation, suggesting—consistent with the observed absence of competition and of innovation in the planned economies—that competition is good for growth. The Aghion-

---

[16] For a comprehensive treatment, see Aghion and Howitt (1998). For a shorter and more accessible presen-tation, see Aghion and Howitt (2005).

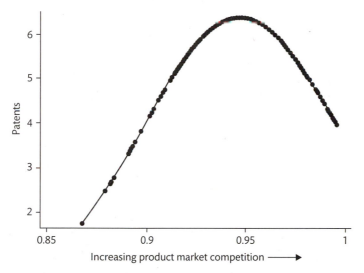

**Figure 8.21** The relationship between innovation and competition: UK firms.

Howitt model provides a way of explaining these two opposite effects of competition on innovation and has been used to test whether they are found in the data.[17]

Figure 8.21 shows the relationship between the innovation activities of British firms as measured by patents and a measure of the degree of competition in the product market. As product market competition increases to the right of the figure, innovation first increases but at high levels of competition, innovation falls. This inverse U-shaped relationship in the data suggests that both of the Schumpeterian effects can be in operation. For sectors where competition is low, more intense rivalry appears to stimulate patenting; whereas in sectors where competition is already intense, an increase in competition sees innovation fall off.

When modelling the inverse U-shaped relationship, the economy is divided into three sectors according to whether the sector begins the period with technology at the frontier, one step behind or two steps behind. Innovation is always 'step-by-step', which means that a firm can only upgrade its technology by one step as a result of innovation activity: there is no leapfrogging. Moreover, it is impossible for a sector to be more than two steps behind the frontier because it is assumed that there is an automatic spillover from innovation in the one step behind sector after one period. These assumptions mean that there are three sector types.

1. In frontier sectors, large or radical innovations are possible, which improve quality (cut costs) by so much that they confer temporary monopoly pricing power on the innovating firm. For such firms, more competition makes more attractive the carrot of monopoly rents that would follow a successful innovation. Hence, at the frontier, *more competition boosts innovation*. This is referred to as the 'escape competition' effect.

---

[17] This work is based on Aghion et al. (2001). It is presented in Aghion and Howitt (2009) and Aghion et al. (2014).

2. For the one-step behind sectors, it is assumed that the size of innovation these firms could make is sufficiently modest that an innovator is unable to charge the monopoly price. The reason is that the modest innovation does not force the other firms in the industry (referred to as the competitive fringe), which do not innovate, out of business. Since there is no chance to escape the competitive fringe, *more competition dampens innovation* by lowering the successful innovator's mark-up. With more competition, more firms can innovate and the mark-up for each of them will be lower.

3. For the two-step behind sectors, there is no incentive to innovate at all—they automatically gain from the spillover of innovation from the one-step behind sectors after one period.

As shown in Fig. 8.21, there is interesting empirical support for the existence of these effects. Aghion et al. (2005) use firm-level data from the UK on patents as a measure of innovation and on the price-cost margin as an inverse measure of the extent of competition in the product market.[18] The relationship is plotted using a quadratic estimator (which allows a non-linear relationship). The data suggest that at lower levels of competition, which are characteristic of frontier sectors, an increase in competition would stimulate innovation because firms have more incentive to escape the competition and seek the monopoly rents. In the more competitive environment inside the frontier, where only incremental innovations are possible and therefore the prize of monopoly rents is not available, the effect of an inverse relationship between competition and innovation dominates: more competition lowers innovation.

The idea that more intense competition boosts innovation in frontier firms but may discourage it among non-frontier firms is reflected in the results of another empirical test. Aghion et al. (2009) use UK firm-level data and measure the extent of competition by the entry of foreign firms into an industry. They find that as the entry rate of foreign firms rises (pushing up competition), a measure of innovation (TFP growth) rises for firms near the frontier but falls for firms far away from the frontier. This suggests that for frontier firms, policies to boost competition (for example, by encouraging entry of foreign firms) promote innovation through the incentives they create for firms to get a step ahead. But for firms far from the frontier, the additional competition is discouraging for innovation.

For frontier firms, policies that promote competition and policies favouring innovation are *complementary* for boosting growth. The reinforcing effect of greater competition and policies to raise the expected return from R&D, including stronger temporary protection of innovators' intellectual property, brings to the fore the subtle balance between the private incentives to take risky R&D decisions and the social benefits of the spread of new ideas.

### 8.8.2 Schumpeterian growth and business cycle fluctuations

At the beginning of this chapter, we took a look at how models of long-run growth can be related to short and medium-run models of business cycle fluctuations. The Schumpeterian

---

[18] Aghion et al. (2005). Data kindly provided by Nick Bloom.

model provides additional insights about the connection between growth and volatility. As we have seen, sustained growth in per capita GDP in the Schumpeterian model is due to purposeful investment in R&D and other productivity-enhancing activities. This prompts the question of how business cycle booms and recessions may affect investment in R&D, and whether this mechanism should influence the way macroeconomic stabilization policy is conducted.

### Creative destruction—the positive role of firm-level volatility

It is useful to emphasize Schumpeter's stress on the positive role of creative destruction in a market economy. Creative destruction means that higher quality products and methods of production displace inferior ones. This suggests that a particular kind of volatility related to the entry and exit of activities within and between firms themselves plays a crucial role in sustaining dynamism. Both incumbent firms and new entrants innovate: evidence from the USA suggests that about 25 percent of productivity growth comes from new entrants.[19] The pervasiveness of a 'soft budget constraint' for enterprises in planned economies, which meant that they could survive irrespective of their performance, was linked with the absence of dynamism in economies operating under central planning's 'rules of the game'.[20]

### Business cycle volatility and growth

We turn next to consider the impact on long-term growth of business cycle fluctuations caused, for example, by shocks to aggregate demand and supply. In the 3-equation model, the policy maker uses monetary and fiscal policy to keep the economy close to equilibrium output, and to reduce the damage caused by fluctuations in unemployment. The Schumpeterian model of growth provides additional reasons for active counter-cyclical policy intervention that would see governments increasing public deficits and central banks cutting real interest rates in recessions and doing the converse in booms.

The argument rests on the fact that the availability of credit to firms is tightened in recessions as firms appear less creditworthy to lenders. When firms are credit constrained, inadequate access to funding forces them to cut down on productivity enhancing investment in innovative activities. Moreover, the prospect that funding for innovation may dry up in a downturn is also likely to dampen long term growth-enhancing investments. This creates a role for government stabilization policy. Another channel through which stabilization policy is growth enhancing, suggested by the Schumpeterian approach, is its role in stabilizing the size of the market.

Recent studies using cross-industry cross-country data show that countries with more countercyclical fiscal and monetary policies ease the credit constraints on firms in industries that are especially credit or liquidity constrained. This provides evidence supportive of the mechanism through which countercyclical policy enhances growth by reducing the extent to which recessions depress access to finance for innovation.[21]

[19] See Bartelsmann and Doms (2000) and Foster, Haltiwanger and Krizan (2001).
[20] See Kornai (2013).
[21] For example, see Chapter 14 of Aghion and Howitt (2009), Aghion et al. (2012) and Aghion et al. (2014).

If we bring together the argument about creative destruction with the one about recessions exacerbating credit constraints and inhibiting innovation, we have the implication that in a dynamic economy, economic policy should promote micro volatility in the sense of firm entry and exit, but should control macro volatility by aiming to keep the economy close to equilibrium output.

## 8.9 Conclusions

This chapter has focused on the *proximate* causes of growth: factor accumulation and technological progress. The proximate causes of growth lie at the heart of why the capitalist system has achieved sustained growth in living standards across the Western economies since the industrial revolution. In short, this economic system succeeded both in mobilizing resources to raise the amount of physical and human capital employed in production and in providing the incentives for continuous technological innovation.

We have based our discussion of long-run economic growth around the most widely used models of growth; the Solow model and endogenous growth models. The Solow model shows how broad capital accumulation produces higher living standards in the long-run steady state. It suggests that there is a limit to the extent to which changes in policy or institutions can influence long-run growth, due to the assumption of diminishing returns to capital. Although the Solow model can be adapted to include technological progress, it can only account for long-run productivity growth in a mechanical way. It falls to the endogenous growth models to provide a framework for thinking about the central role of purposeful innovation in economic growth.

The key difference between the Solow model and endogenous growth models is that the latter assume there is a mechanism which offsets the diminishing returns to capital. Economists have explored a number of potential mechanisms that could achieve this, such as investment in human capital or research and development or knowledge spillovers from the accumulation of physical capital. The mechanisms open the door to the possibility that policy can affect long-run growth. The Schumpeterian model puts the concept of 'creative destruction' at the centre of the expansion of the technological frontier in successful economies. Innovation is driven by the promise of excess profits, and new products and production methods making old products and firms obsolete is a central part of that process.

## 8.10 Questions

### 8.10.1 Checklist questions

1. Assess the following statements S1 and S2. Are they both true, both false or is only one true? Justify your answer.

   S1. A rise in the saving rate will plunge the economy into recession.

   S2. A rise in the saving rate is good for growth.

2. How will an inflation-targeting central banker react to a fall in the savings rate? Answer very briefly using the 3-equation model and then extend your analysis using the standard Solow diagram to show what happens to the interest rate.

3. Using the data in Table 8.1, calculate the following:

   (a) The CAGR for US GDP per capita between 1950 and 2010.

   (b) The time it would take for US GDP per capita to double if it grew at the rate calculated in part (a).

4. Use Equation 8.6 to derive the steady state values of capital per worker and output per worker in the standard Solow model. Interpret these equations.

5. Discuss the following statement: 'increasing the savings rate in the economy always increases welfare as it leads to an increase in output per capita'.

6. Assume we are in a Solow world in which the population is growing at a constant rate (and there is no technological progress). Suppose from an initial steady state, there is a sudden fall in the growth rate of the population. Would you predict a rise or a fall in output growth? How about in the growth of output per head? Describe how and why the economy adjusts to a new steady state and how the new steady state differs from the old one. Show the time paths for the growth rates of output, output per head, the capital stock and the capital intensity of production. To help in answering the question, produce a set of diagrams similar to those in Fig. 8.12.

7. In the course of answering this question, explain the concepts of absolute and conditional convergence.

   (a) Explain the mechanism(s) through which, according to the Solow model, an initially poor country would be predicted to catch up to the living standards of a rich country. Set out carefully the assumptions that you are making to derive this result.

   (b) Now use the model to explain why catch up may not take place.

   (c) Comment on the likely validity of the assumptions in (a) and (b) when applying the model to the real world.

8. How do endogenous growth models explain the persistence of differences in living standards among economies? Explain the role played by the production function for goods and the accumulation function for ideas in coming to your conclusion.

9. What does the term 'creative destruction' mean? In a Schumpeterian growth model, what determines the growth rate of productivity? How does this compare to the mechanism driving growth in the Solow model with technological progress?

10. Assess the following statements S1 and S2. Are they both true, both false or is only one true? Justify your answer making reference to the objectives of the policy maker.

    S1. Economic policy should aim to limit firm-level volatility.

    S2. Economic policy should aim to limit macro-level volatility.

## 8.10.2 Problems and questions for discussion

1. In an economy characterized by a Cobb-Douglas production function (without technical progress), labour's share of income is 70% and the depreciation rate is 3% per annum. The economy is in a steady state with GDP growth at 4% per year and with a capital output ratio

of 2. Find the savings rate and the marginal product of capital. At time $t$ the savings rate in this economy increases to a new constant level, with the outcome that the economy converges to the Golden Rule steady state. What are the new savings rate, capital output ratio and marginal product of capital? Use diagrams with time on the horizontal axis to sketch the path of the capital–output ratio, the marginal product of capital and of consumption per unit of labour.

2. Download data on GDP per capita between 1950 and the latest available period for two countries of your choosing (other than the USA) from the latest version of the Penn World Table. Calculate the following and comment briefly on your findings:

   (a) The annual growth rate for the latest period (using both the normal and log difference methods)

   (b) The CAGR for the whole period (using both the normal and exponential methods)

   (c) The time it would take for GDP per capita to double if growth was equal to the trend rate calculated in part (b)

3. Study Table 8.2. Use the information in the table (and the paper it is taken from) to write a one page note on the role of innovation in the evolution of the EU and US economies since 1980.

4. 'More competition and stronger protection of IPR (intellectual property rights) will speed up technological progress.' Is this a recommendation you would take to a policy maker? You have 700 words to make your case.

# The 3-equation model in the open economy

## 9.1 Overview

In this chapter, we extend the macro-model to the flexible exchange rate open economy. How does the openness of the economy to trade and financial flows affect the way an inflation-targeting central bank approaches its stabilization role? In the closed economy, the central bank diagnoses shocks hitting the economy and chooses their interest rate response, taking into account the implications of the shock for future inflation. The main insight when we extend the discussion to the open economy is that the forward-looking foreign exchange market and the central bank will simultaneously analyse shocks, and their responses will take into account the response of the other party.

Just as a great deal of resources are deployed in central banks to analyse economic developments and forecast inflation based on the diagnosis of the nature of shocks, the same is the case in financial institutions operating in global financial markets. Foreign exchange traders look at what is happening in the domestic and world economy and at how the central bank is likely to respond to economic developments.

The motives of the central bank and the foreign exchange traders for employing resources to forecast the future are, however, different. The central bank is attempting the stabilize the economy, whereas the foreign exchange traders are attempting to profit from arbitrage opportunities.

### Expectations and the forward-looking foreign exchange market

In Chapter 4, we discussed the pervasiveness of uncertainty in the macroeconomy (predominantly in a closed economy context) and how this leads to agents forming expectations about the future so they can make better economic decisions today. In the baseline closed economy 3-equation model (introduced in Chapter 3), the central bank is forward looking with rational expectations. The central bank has to forecast both the *IS* and *PC* curves in the next period when setting interest rates in the current period. This is due to the assumption that interest rates can only affect economic activity with a one period lag.

When we move to the open economy, we introduce the foreign exchange market, where trades are also assumed to be forward looking and rational. We assume both interest rates and real exchange rates affect the economy with a one period lag. In the open economy 3-equation model, the central bank takes account of the reaction of the foreign exchange market when setting interest rates and the foreign exchange market moves when expectations about future central bank policy change.

*Arbitrage opportunities, the foreign exchange market and the government bond market*

When trade in financial assets across borders is possible, investors will want to take advantage of differences in rates of return on government bonds. In order to take advantage of arbitrage opportunities in the bond market, an agent must have the relevant national currency. For example, to buy US Treasury Bills, it is necessary to have US dollars; to buy German government Bunds, it is necessary to have euros. The exchange rate will depend on supply and demand in the foreign exchange market. An important source of demand and supply of foreign exchange arises from the desire of economic agents to buy and sell government bonds in order to take advantage of differences in interest rates.

Both the central bank and foreign exchange traders know that the extent of integration of international capital markets means that opportunities to make a profit from a difference in rates of return on bonds issued in different countries will be short-lived. Take the possibility of profiting from an interest rate differential opened up by a decision of one central bank to change its interest rate. This is a form of arbitrage opportunity. If, for example, the Bank of England increased the UK interest rate so that the return on UK bonds was higher than on US bonds, there would be a rush into UK pounds and out of US dollars until the chance of profiting from one rather than the other kind of bond has vanished.

*Defining the nominal and real exchange rates*

Let's take a step back for a moment and clarify the concept of the exchange rate. We need to define both the nominal and real exchange rates. Home's nominal exchange rate is 'the amount of home currency that can be bought with one unit of foreign currency'. For example, the nominal exchange rate for the UK pound (home economy) is defined in terms of the foreign currency (the US dollar) as the amount of UK pounds that can be bought with one US dollar (i.e. £/$). We use $e$ to denote the nominal exchange rate of the home economy:

$$e \equiv \frac{\text{no. units of home currency}}{\text{one unit of foreign currency}}. \qquad \text{(home's nominal exchange rate)}$$

An increase in $e$ means that one US dollar can buy more UK pounds, so that the pound has depreciated (or weakened). Note that since the nominal exchange rate is defined as the number of home currency units for one foreign currency unit, a depreciation of the pound is the same as $\uparrow e$.

The nominal exchange rate shows the rate at which the currencies of two economies can be exchanged for one another. To measure the rate at which domestic and foreign *goods and services* can be exchanged for each other, we also need to take into account the relative price level between the two economies. This is where we introduce the concept of the *real* exchange rate, which is defined as:

$$Q \equiv \frac{\text{price of foreign goods expressed in home currency}}{\text{price of home goods}} = \frac{P^* e}{P},$$

(home's real exchange rate, price competitiveness)

where $P^*$ is the foreign price level and $P$ is the home price level. The real exchange rate $Q$ is a measure of price competitiveness between two economies. If $Q$ increases, this reflects the fall in price of home goods relative to the price of foreign goods (when expressed in the same currency). This depreciation of the real exchange rate would make home's exports more attractive to foreigners and discourage the consumption of imports by domestic consumers. We assume throughout our modelling of the open economy that a depreciation of the real exchange rate (i.e. $\uparrow Q$)—an improvement in price competitiveness—will cause an increase in *net exports* (i.e. the real value of exports − the real value of imports).[1]

In the open economy model, aggregate demand not only consists of consumption, investment and government spending (as it does in the closed economy), but also net exports. This means that we assume an increase in competitiveness (a real depreciation) boosts aggregate demand through its effect on net exports.

### Two stabilization channels in the open economy: interest rate and exchange rate

Given the central bank's stabilization objective and the way the nominal exchange rate will respond to arbitrage opportunities, the response to a shock will be a combination of a change in the interest rate by the central bank and a change in the exchange rate resulting from the actions of foreign exchange traders. For example, if a shock pushed inflation above target, the response in the closed economy is for the central bank to raise the interest rate in order to depress next period's level of output and bring inflation down.

In the open economy, it is also the case that a negative output gap is required to begin to bring inflation down. However, foreign exchange market operators know that the central bank will raise home's interest rate and this creates an arbitrage opportunity. In this example, we assume that the UK is the home economy and the US is the foreign economy. There will therefore be a rush out of US dollars and into UK pounds, due to the higher return on UK bonds. What happens to the exchange rate between UK pounds and US dollars as a result of this?

In this example, the interest differential in favour of UK bonds results in stronger demand for UK pounds, which forces the currency to appreciate. An appreciated currency will increase the price of the home economy's exports in terms of foreign currency, depressing demand for home-produced goods in foreign markets. It will also reduce the price of foreign-produced goods that are imported to the home economy (in terms of home currency), boosting demand for foreign goods.

In other words, it will make the British economy less competitive and depress aggregate demand for home-produced goods and services. We can therefore see that in addition to the *interest rate channel*, there is a second channel operating to produce the central bank's desired negative output gap: this is the *exchange rate channel*. With the higher interest rate in the UK and the appreciation of the UK pound both bearing down on output, the central bank will know that it needs to raise the interest rate by less than would be the case in the closed economy to achieve the same negative output gap.

Both parties solve the central bank's stabilization problem—this implies an assumption that both the central bank and the foreign exchange market form expectations rationally. Together their actions will place the economy on the stabilization path desired by the central bank.

---

[1] This result will be derived formally when we discuss the Marshall-Lerner condition in Chapter 10.

In short, we shall see that the presence of the foreign exchange market means that the work of stabilization is shared between exchange rate and interest rate adjustments. As with any rational expectations assumption, we have to be careful about its relevance for understanding real-world phenomena. In the case of the 3-equation closed economy model, we used the idea of the central bank solving the model in order to make its best judgement about how to respond to a shock; here we are assuming that the profit-seeking motivation of foreign exchange traders will produce an outcome that can be captured by the rational expectations assumption.

This is a more dubious assumption than is the case for the central bank, as we know that financial markets are affected by fads and manias (see Chapters 1, 4 and 6). However, we continue to work with the rational expectations model for the foreign exchange market as it provides a useful basic model of a very complex situation. In addition to helping us to understand the way interest rate and exchange rate changes interact following a shock to the economy, the open economy model also helps to explain exchange rate overshooting and highlights the trade-off between the contribution of exchange rate changes to stabilization and the potential for the foreign exchange market to be a source of volatility in the real economy.

### How are the key aspects of the open economy reflected in the 3-equation model?

We now explore why central banks in flexible exchange rate economies are active in stabilization. Figure 9.1 shows that central banks frequently change the policy interest rate as they attempt to achieve their inflation target. We can think this through systematically by taking each of the three equations in the 3-equation model in turn.

### IS relation

Beginning with the demand side of the economy, the *IS*, we need to amend the model to recognize that home's households, firms and government spend on imported as well as home-produced goods, and that foreigners buy goods produced at home. Since imports will depend on the level of activity in the home economy, some of the additional demand generated by higher incomes will leak abroad because of purchases of imports. This means

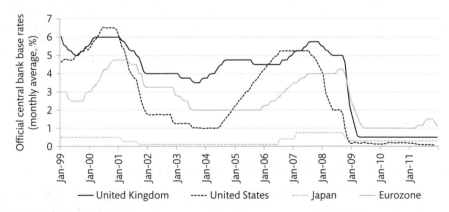

**Figure 9.1** Official central bank interest rates, monthly averages, per cent: 1999–2011.

*Source:* Bank of England; Board of Governors of the Federal Reserve System (US); Bank of Japan; European Central Bank (data accessed January 2012).

the multiplier will be lower, the higher is the marginal propensity to import. The other major change to the *IS* relationship will come from the impact on imports and exports of changes in the competitiveness of home's production, as noted above. An improvement in home's competitiveness, i.e. a depreciation of the real exchange rate, boosts the demand for exports and dampens the demand for imports as home goods become relatively more attractive both abroad and at home.

In graphical terms, the presence of imports in reducing the multiplier makes the *IS* curve steeper because a given fall in the interest rate is associated with a smaller increase in output; and a depreciation of the real exchange rate shifts the *IS* curve to the right. An appreciation of the real exchange rate—a deterioration in home's competitiveness—shifts the *IS* to the left. These results are derived step by step in Chapter 10.

### Phillips curve, PC

As in the closed economy, in this chapter, we shall assume that households use domestic inflation in their wage-setting calculations.[2] This means we can continue to work with a situation in which the equilibrium rate of unemployment is unique, i.e. it only shifts as a consequence of supply-side shifts in the *WS* curve (changes in the cost of job loss, wage-bargaining arrangements, employment regulation, etc.) or in the *PS* curve (changes in the degree of monopoly, the tax wedge, etc.).

### Central bank behaviour, MR

Finally, we turn to the policy maker, which is the central bank. There is no reason why opening up the economy to international trade and capital flows should affect the policy maker's preferences, and hence, the *MR* curve. We continue to assume that the central bank suffers a loss of utility according to how far away it is from its inflation target and from equilibrium output. But what is the inflation rate the central bank targets? It could target consumer price inflation, which includes the price changes of imported goods or it could target domestic inflation. In this chapter, we keep to the simple case where the central bank targets *domestic* inflation.

To summarize, in the open economy we need to modify the *IS* curve, making it steeper to reflect the lower multiplier, and noting that it will shift with a change in the real exchange rate. If the central bank targets domestic inflation and we assume wage setters use domestic inflation in their wage-bargaining calculations, we do not need to modify the *PC* or the determinants of equilibrium unemployment, $y_e$. Equilibrium employment remains determined in the same way as in the closed economy. In the $PC - MR$ diagram, the vertical axis is domestic inflation and the *MR* curve is derived in the same way as in the closed economy: from the tangencies of the Phillips curves with the loss circles, which capture the preferences of the central bank.

## How does capital market openness affect stabilization policy?

Two elements of global flows of capital play a crucial role: the foreign exchange market and the ability of home and foreign economic agents to buy home and foreign assets. This ties

---

[2] We shall explore the effects of imports on wage setting in the next chapter.

together the foreign exchange market and the money market where government bonds are bought and sold.

In a world without global financial markets, the supply and demand for foreign exchange and therefore exchange rates are driven by exports and imports (i.e. by the need to finance trade in goods and services). By the late 1980s, values traded in international markets for financial assets far exceeded the value of international trade in goods and services. As a consequence, it is trade in international financial markets that dominates the foreign exchange market. Market participants buy and sell currencies to take advantage of differences in rates of return on financial assets. Just as in the closed economy, we continue to assume there is just one asset, namely government bonds. Foreigners seeking to buy home bonds, need home currency in order to do this and vice versa. As market participants seek to take advantage of differences in interest rates on government bonds issued by different countries, this trading is a key determinant of exchange rate fluctuations. To understand the essential aspects of international financial markets, it is useful to make some simplifying assumptions.

1. There is *perfect international capital mobility*. This means that home residents can buy or sell foreign bonds with the fixed nominal world interest rate, $i^*$, in unlimited quantities at low transactions costs.

2. The home country is assumed to be *small* in the sense that its behaviour cannot affect the world interest rate.

3. Just as in the closed economy, we assume there are just *two assets* that households can hold—bonds and money. But now they can hold foreign or home bonds. We assume that they hold only home money.

4. There is *perfect substitutability* between foreign and home bonds. This assumption means that the riskiness of foreign and home bonds is identical, so the only relevant difference between them is the expected return.

The last assumption means we rule out differences in the risk of default of bonds issued by different governments and we assume that investors do not care about the balance between home and foreign bonds in their portfolio. Cross-country differences in default risk have always been highly relevant for the analysis of emerging and developing economies but much less so in developed economies, where bond yields converged at low levels during the Great Moderation. Default risk has, however, reemerged as a pertinent issue for developed economies with the Eurozone crisis in 2010–11, which centred on the diverging default risk on Eurozone government bonds. In this chapter, we assume away issues related to differences in default risk. We return to them when we discuss the Eurozone in Chapter 12.

### How do foreign exchange traders respond to interest rate differences? The uncovered interest parity (*UIP*) condition

If home households can hold home and foreign bonds in their portfolio, what will influence their choice? Assumption 4 (above) means there is no difference in risk between the bonds issued by the two governments. In this case, the only difference is the expected return on the two bonds and that will depend on two factors:

1. any expected difference in interest rates over a specific time horizon; and

2. a view about the likely development of the exchange rate over the same time horizon.

The second of these factors emphasizes the importance of forming expectations about the exchange rate in future periods. In this model, agents are therefore fully forward looking and take all available information into account when making decisions. How does this tally with our view that households form expectations of inflation in a backward-looking manner (i.e. the assumption that underlies the Phillips curve)?

Just as in Chapter 5, we assume that households save in the money market through pension funds or other sophisticated agents who are acting on their behalf. It is these agents that act in a forward-looking manner and are collectively referred to in our model as participants in the *foreign exchange market*. In contrast, workers are assumed to handle their wage negotiations personally or through a union, both of which form expectations in a backward-looking manner. To make this distinction clearer, when discussing households buying and selling home and foreign bonds we will refer to this as the actions of foreign exchange market participants. Following the definitions introduced in Chapter 4, the foreign exchange market participants are therefore assumed to have rational expectations.

*Example*

Suppose the UK is the 'home' economy and the US is the 'foreign' economy. As discussed earlier, if the interest rate on home bonds is higher than on foreign ones, that will make home bonds more attractive. This would be followed by appreciation of home's currency (i.e. UK pounds) as people sold US dollars in order to buy UK pounds, which they need to buy the UK bonds. But, we need a model to explain by how much the UK pound appreciates.

Suppose that initially the interest rate on both bonds is 4%. Now let us see what happens if the Bank of England suddenly raised the UK interest rate to 6.5%. This case is shown in Fig. 9.2, where $e$ is used to denote the UK pound nominal exchange rate (i.e. £/$), $t$ is used to denote the time period, $i$ is used to denote the home interest rate and $i^*$ is used to denote the world (or foreign) interest rate. The interest rate change makes UK bonds more attractive and investors will sell US dollars and buy UK pounds in order to take advantage of the higher expected return. But the move out of dollars and into UK pounds leads the US dollar to depreciate (weaken) and the UK pound to appreciate (strengthen).

As investors try to maximize their returns, the UK pound will appreciate by exactly 2.5% so that the expected return on UK and US bonds is identical. An American investor holding UK bonds for the duration of the interest differential (i.e. one year) gets 2.5% more in interest receipts than he would holding US bonds. On the flipside, however, the American investor loses 2.5% as the UK pound depreciates back to its 'normal' level over the course of the year. We assume that the underlying expected level of the exchange rate is exogenous and remains constant. The American investor will have to buy UK pounds at the start of the year in order to purchase the UK bonds, but wants US dollars at the end of the year to spend in the US (Assumption 3). Figure 9.2 shows how this process of arbitrage in the international bond markets works to equalize the expected return on bonds.

A survey of foreign exchange dealers in the UK asked: 'How fast do you think the market can assimilate the new information when the following economic announcements from

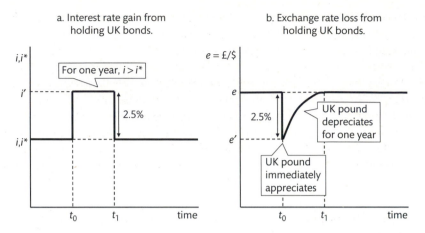

**Figure 9.2** Arbitrage in the international bond market.

the major developed economies differ from their market expectations?'[3] For an unexpected interest rate announcement, over 60% of the traders said 'less than ten seconds' with most of the rest saying less than one minute. According to this survey, speedy reaction is most common for news about interest rates, which also has a bigger impact on foreign exchange markets than announcements about inflation, unemployment, the trade deficit, the money supply or GDP. The survey findings suggest that any arbitrage opportunities that arise as a result of interest rate differentials (or expected interest differentials) are exhausted extremely quickly. This results in jumps in the exchange rate. In the example shown above, as soon as the interest differential is announced, the UK pound would immediately appreciate by 2.5%.

The result that the exchange rate will jump so as to eliminate differences in expected returns on bonds is called the uncovered interest parity condition (*UIP*). It is derived in detail in the modelling section (9.2) that follows. We can write it like this:

Interest gain from holding home currency (UK pounds) rather than US dollar bonds $=$ Loss from the expected depreciation of home currency (UK pounds) against the US dollar

(UIP condition)

With home's interest rate above the world (US bond) interest rate for one period between $t_0$ and $t_1$, the *UIP* condition states that the exchange rate will jump immediately to eliminate the arbitrage opportunity. Applying this to our example in Fig. 9.2, the *UIP* condition states that: the UK pound exchange rate will appreciate by exactly 2.5% so that the loss from the expected depreciation of the UK pound over this period is equal to the interest gain from holding the higher yielding UK bonds over the same period. All market participants are assumed to believe that the exchange rate will return to its initial level at the end of the period.

[3] See Cheung et al. (2004).

The *UIP* condition tells us that the 'unwinding' of the initial change in the exchange rate must be equal to the interest rate differential; hence we know that the interest differential pins down the size of the jump. The arbitrage condition also tells us that the exchange rate at any time during the period between $t_0$ and $t_1$ will be as shown on the path in the right-hand panel of Fig. 9.2. As the time comes closer to when the interest differential will disappear, the size of the interest gain from a UK bond shrinks and hence the matching expected depreciation of the pound must be smaller. The exchange rate must therefore be closer to its expected level of *e*. If this was not the case, there would be unexploited opportunities for profit-making by buying or selling pounds to buy or sell UK bonds. An important distinguishing characteristic of financial markets (as compared with goods and labour markets) is that *jumps* in prices are commonly observed.

### The reaction of the central bank and the foreign exchange market to an inflation shock

We have now discussed the key components and mechanisms driving the 3-equation model in the open economy. This allows us to use the model to think about the adjustment of a small open economy to an inflation shock. We will set out detailed, period-by-period adjustment paths to an inflation shock and a range of other shocks later in the chapter. This initial simple example aims to provide an overview of how the model works and to highlight the key differences from the closed economy model presented in Chapter 3.

We assume a flexible exchange rate economy, which is initially at equilibrium output and target inflation, is hit by an inflation shock. In this case, just as in the closed economy, the central bank will raise the interest rate in order to reduce output and dampen inflation. However, the foreign exchange market will also react to the knowledge that home's interest rate will be kept above that of the rest of the world for some time. The *UIP* condition tells us that home's exchange rate will therefore appreciate, as there will be increased demand for home's currency. This occurs as investors buy home currency to buy home bonds so as to take advantage of their higher yields.

We know from the *IS* curve that the appreciation of the exchange rate will depress demand by reducing net exports. This means the central bank will not have to raise the interest rate as much as they would in the closed economy, as they correctly anticipate some of the adjustment will take place through the foreign exchange market. In other words, in the open economy, the dampening of demand needed to get the economy back onto the *MR* curve occurs through a combination of a higher interest rate and exchange rate appreciation.

### Forward-looking behaviour of central banks and foreign exchange markets—real-world examples

The interaction between a forward-looking central bank and a forward-looking foreign exchange market is at the heart of the model of stabilization policy in the open economy. This is reflected in the publications of central banks and the financial press.

The link between the exchange rate and the monetary policy of the central bank in a flexible exchange rate regime is highlighted in Obstfeld and Rogoff (2009):[4]

---

[4] See p. 32 of Obstfeld and Rogoff (2009).

Under the pressure of very loose US monetary policy after the dot-com crash and 9/11, however, the dollar depreciated by more than 16% from early 2002 through the start of 2007, with a significant (but temporary) reversal over 2005 as the Fed tightened.

In the wake of the 9/11 attacks on the US, the Federal Reserve cut interest rates more aggressively than other developed economy central banks (e.g. the European Central Bank; see Fig. 9.1). This saw the emergence of an interest rate differential that contributed to the depreciation of the dollar over that period.

One of the main lessons of this chapter is the way a forward-looking foreign exchange market anticipates the actions of the central bank and facilitates the adjustment of the economy to a shock. On a minute-by-minute basis, the foreign exchange market is assimilating the latest macroeconomic data and making forecasts about how this could affect the interest rates set by the central bank. In light of this, changes in interest rate expectations are often built into the foreign exchange market a long time before the interest rate changes actually take place, as illustrated by this Bloomberg News article from mid-2004:[5]

> The dollar rose the most against the euro in a month on speculation government reports tomorrow will show faster inflation in the US, underscoring the potential for the Federal Reserve to raise interest rates more than some traders had expected.

In uncertain economic times, such as the UK's stop-start recovery from the 2008–09 financial crisis, it is harder to predict the path of the economy, and consequently of interest rate decisions. Mansoor Mohi-uddin, UBS's managing director of foreign exchange strategy alluded to this point in early 2011:[6]

> But do not pity the Sterling [i.e. UK pound] bulls. Foreign exchange investors have bolstered the pound this year on expectations interest rates would soon be raised. Yet it remains far from clear whether the Bank's Monetary Policy Committee will take such a step.

Foreign exchange traders make their best estimate with the information they have available in each time period but can be wrong, which might subject the market to corrections and jumps in the exchange rate. This could happen if the market anticipated a smaller (or larger) interest rate change than was actually observed. The extra unanticipated change would likely cause a jump in the exchange rate, as the market quickly takes advantage of the unexpected interest rate differential. In short, because the future is uncertain, basing current actions on forecasts and predictions can lead to volatility in the exchange rate.

Foreign exchange markets are complex and are influenced by a whole host of macroeconomic variables. The *UIP* condition is often hard to observe in exchange rate data, because these other factors influence the future expected exchange rate. In the recent economic downturn, the Bank of England kept a close eye on interest rate differentials and the ster-

---

[5] Excerpt taken from: Heather Bandur and Vivanne Rodrigues, June 9th 2004, 'Dollar Surges Against Euro as Traders Anticipate Fed Rate Moves,' *Bloomberg News*.

[6] Excerpt taken from: Mansoor Mohi-uddin, February 7th 2011, 'Pound Remains Vulnerable to Abrupt Reversal of Fortune,' *Financial Times*.

ling (i.e. UK pound) exchange rate and found a number of other factors contributing to the depreciation of the UK pound over this period:[7]

> Sterling had lost over a quarter of its value since mid-2007. To some degree, that depreciation had probably reflected the need to rebalance the UK economy away from domestic towards external demand. In addition over the past year, the global outlook had deteriorated with resultant downward revisions to interest rate expectations worldwide. But the downward revision to forecasts of the UK economy appeared to have been greater than for some other countries. And those perceptions may have contributed to sterling's decline. Another factor in sterling's decline over the past eighteen months could have been increased risk premia.

As discussed in Chapter 7, the recent recession of 2008–9 saw the limits of conventional monetary policy reached and central banks had to resort to unconventional monetary policy, such as quantitative easing, to avoid a deflation trap. These policies also affect the foreign exchange market. Quantitative easing aims to influence long term interest rates and therefore to affect interest rate differentials. An article in the *Financial Times* from autumn 2011 attributed moves in the pound exchange rate to changes in expectations about quantitative easing:[8]

> The pound dropped to an eight-month low against the dollar on Wednesday as expectations heightened that the Bank of England would engage in further quantitative easing in an effort to boost the UK economy.

### Summary

In this chapter, we extend the core 3-equation model introduced in Chapter 3 to set out a framework for analysing stabilization policy in the flexible exchange rate open economy. This involves opening up the economy to both international trade (i.e. imports and exports) and international capital flows (i.e. home and foreign bonds). The two main effects on the model of introducing the forex market are that:

1. following an economic shock, the central bank and foreign exchange market react to the shock, which means adjustment occurs through both exchange rate and interest rate channels; and

2. the forex market bases its actions partly on its expectations of the future, which can lead to jumps in the exchange rate and increased macroeconomic volatility.

## 9.2 Modelling

In the previous section, we provided an overview of how the 3-equation model works in the open economy. In this section, we get into the mechanics of the model. The first part of

---

[7] Excerpt taken from: Bank of England, *Minutes of the Monetary Policy Committee Meeting, 4 and 5 March 2009*, published 18th March 2009.
[8] Excerpt taken from: Peter Garnham, September 21st 2011, 'Dovish Bank Minutes Weigh on Pound,' *Financial Times*.

the section formalizes the *UIP* condition. In the second part, we explain what is meant by medium-run equilibrium in the open economy. We combine these components to build the open economy 3-equation model and use them to analyse the period-by-period adjustment of the economy to shocks. The new *RX* curve combines the interest rate and exchange rate channels through which the central bank's interest rate decision affects aggregate demand. Section 9.3 discusses the role of exchange rate overshooting in the open economy.

### 9.2.1 The foreign exchange market and the *UIP* condition

In Section 9.1, we introduced the concept of the *UIP* condition, which is central to the behaviour of the foreign exchange market in the open economy 3-equation model. In this subsection, we will set out the equation for the *UIP* condition and use a graphical analysis to explore the concept in more detail.

**The *UIP* condition**

The *UIP* can be represented as:

$$\underbrace{i_t - i^*}_{\text{interest gain (loss)}} = \underbrace{\frac{e_{t+1}^E - e_t}{e_t}}_{\text{expected depreciation (appreciation)}},$$

where $i$ is the home interest rate, $i^*$ is the foreign interest rate, $e$ is the nominal exchange rate of the home country and $e^E$ is the expected exchange rate of the home country. The equation says that given the values for $i_t$, $i^*$ and $e_{t+1}^E$, we can work out the value to which the exchange rate will jump, $e_t$.

In the example we introduced in Section 9.1, the initial shock is the rise in $i_t$. The world (i.e. US) interest rate, $i^*$, and the view of the exchange market traders about the expected exchange rate in a year's time, $e_{t+1}^E$, remain unchanged. From the point of view of the UK as the home country, there is an interest gain on the left hand side, which in the presence of arbitrage must equal the expected depreciation of the pound (on the right hand side). For the equation to hold therefore, the UK pound exchange rate $e_t$ must immediately appreciate (as people sell US dollars to buy UK pounds): it will appreciate by exactly 2.5% so that its subsequent expected depreciation just offsets the interest gain incurred by holding UK rather than US bonds (see Fig. 9.2 in Section 9.1).

So far we do not have a model of what determines the expected exchange rate: we simply assume it is expected to return to its previous value after one period. In Section 9.2.2, we introduce a model that pins down the equilibrium exchange rate and hence provides an anchor for exchange rate expectations. For the moment, we assume the expected exchange is constant.

We make use of the fact that we can approximate the percentage growth of the exchange rate by the change in the (natural) log of the exchange rate, i.e.

$$\frac{e_1^E - e_0}{e_0} \approx \log e_1^E - \log e_0 \text{ and in our example, } \log e_1^E - \log e_0 \approx 2.5\%.$$

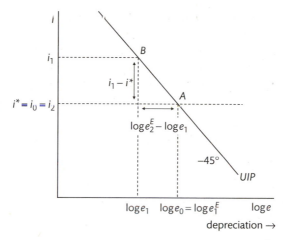

**Figure 9.3** The uncovered interest parity condition: $i_t - i^* = \log e_{t+1}^E - \log e_t$.

The great advantage of using the log formulation is that we now write the *UIP* condition as

$$\underbrace{i_t - i^*}_{\text{interest gain (loss)}} = \underbrace{\log e_{t+1}^E - \log e_t,}_{\text{expected depreciation (appreciation)}}$$

and we can draw this as a line with a $-45°$ slope as shown in Fig. 9.3 with the interest rate on the vertical axis and the log of the nominal exchange rate on the horizontal axis.[9] The *UIP* curve is pinned down by the world interest rate and the expected exchange rate.

Our understanding of the model is helped by looking at two points on the *UIP* curve. The first is point A in Fig. 9.3: this is where the home interest rate equals the world interest rate ($i = i^*$) and exchange rate expectations are fulfilled ($\log e_0 = \log e_1^E$) and the exchange rate does not change.

We now look at a second point on this *UIP* curve at B. This represents the situation where home's interest rate of $i_1$ above the world interest rate is expected to prevail for one year. Assuming the expected exchange rate remains fixed at $\log e_1^E$, then since home's interest rate is now above the world interest rate, there must be a change in the *actual* exchange rate away from $\log e_0$. According to the *UIP* condition, as soon as the interest rate differential opens up, home's exchange rate will appreciate immediately (jump) to $\log e_1$ so that its expected depreciation over the year is equal to the interest rate differential. In the diagram, the two double-headed arrows are equal.

---

[9] Natural logs often allow equations to be displayed and manipulated in a simpler manner. Taking the natural log of a variable is an example of a monotonic transformation, that whilst changing the values in the series preserves the order of the underlying variables. This ensures that taking natural logs does not change the meaning of the original data. Another useful property of natural logs is that (when percentages are small) the percentage change between two variables is approximately equal to the difference in the natural logs of those two variables. In the case of the *UIP* condition, using this property of natural logs allows us to represent the *UIP* condition as a $-45°$ degree line, which makes the graphical analysis less complex. In general, this property makes calculating percentages changes or growth rates easier and is often used when analysing time series data. We look at natural logs in more detail in the discussion on long-run growth in Chapter 8.

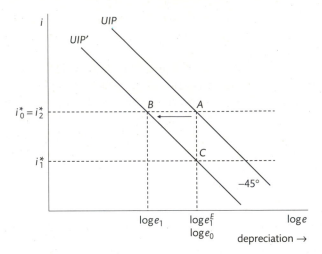

**Figure 9.4** The uncovered interest parity condition: a fall in the world interest rate leads to an immediate appreciation of the home exchange rate.

The key features of the *UIP* diagram with $i$ and $\log e$ on the axes are:

1.  each *UIP* curve has a slope of $-45°$ and must go through the point $(\log e^E, i^*)$;

2.  a change in home's interest rate causes a *movement along* the *UIP* curve (for a given $\log e^E$ and $i^*$);

3.  for a given expected exchange rate, any change in the world interest rate *shifts* the *UIP* curve;

4.  for a given world interest rate, any change in the expected exchange rate *shifts* the *UIP* curve.

To illustrate how the *UIP* curve works, suppose there is a fall in the world interest rate that will last for one period. What is the implication for the home country's exchange rate assuming that there is no change in the home interest rate? To answer this question, we assume there is no change in the expected exchange rate. The shift in the *UIP* curve from *UIP* to *UIP'* due to the fall in the world interest rate is shown in Fig. 9.4.

The economy is initially at point *A* on the *UIP* curve. With the expected exchange rate equal to $\log e^E$ and with home's interest rate unchanged and now above the world interest rate of $i_1^*$, arbitrage in the financial market will lead to an immediate appreciation of the home exchange rate as shown by point *B* on the new *UIP* curve, *UIP'*. At the end of the period, $i^*$ reverts to its initial level (and the *UIP* curve reverts to the original one). There is no interest differential and the exchange rate is back at its initial level.

If the home country is the UK, the pound depreciates continuously over the period during which the interest rates differ. As the *UIP* condition makes clear, for example, just before the US interest rate is raised at the end of the period, there is little to be gained by switching to UK bonds: the tiny expected interest gain would be matched by a tiny expected depreciation of the pound: hence $e_t$ would be very close to its expected level.

The diagram also illustrates that there will be no change in the exchange rate at all if the central bank in the home country immediately follows the interest rate move by the foreign central bank. The economy would shift from A to C . At the end of the period, if home again follows the interest rate move of the foreign central bank, then the move is from C back to A and the exchange rate does not change.

A final exercise is the analysis of a change in sentiment in the foreign exchange market. If traders suddenly change their view about the likely exchange rate in a year's time, the UIP curve will shift. If a depreciated home exchange rate is expected, the UIP curve will shift to the right. With the home and world interest rates equal, such a change in sentiment will have the effect of leading to an immediate depreciation of the actual exchange rate to its new expected value (so that the UIP condition holds). This illustrates that expectations about future developments are incorporated into today's exchange rate. Drawing the diagram for this case is left as an exercise for the reader.

### 9.2.2 Medium-run equilibrium in the open economy and the AD-ERU model

Before we can bring the foreign exchange market together with the 3-equation model, we need to analyse the characteristics of the constant inflation equilibrium of the open economy. This entails discussion of the supply side and the demand side.

We saw in Chapter 2 that the closed economy is in medium-run equilibrium when inflation is constant. For inflation to be constant, there must be equilibrium on the supply side, which occurs when wage and price setters have no incentive to change their behaviour—i.e. at the intersection of the WS and PS curves (see Chapter 2). The intersection between the WS and PS curves pins down the *equilibrium rate of unemployment*, which is why we shall call the supply-side schedule in the medium-run model the ERU curve. The use of the term ERU is a reminder that the supply side, and in particular the labour market, lies behind the determination of the constant inflation equilibrium.

In the open economy, the real exchange rate plays a central role and it is useful to present the medium-run model in a diagram with output on the horizontal axis and the real exchange rate on the vertical axis. The full medium-run model, which includes the trade balance, is introduced in the next chapter. Here we focus on the demand- and supply-side relationships, and we use the simplest model that allows us to understand stabilization policy problems in the open economy.

As we shall see in this section, the ERU curve captures the supply side of the economy. On the ERU curve, inflation is constant. The demand side in the open economy is represented by the *aggregate demand* curve (the AD curve). On the AD curve, the goods market is in equilibrium and the real interest rate is equal to the world real interest rate (i.e. $r = r^*$).

The medium-run equilibrium (MRE) in the open economy is defined by values of output, unemployment and the real exchange rate. In a MRE, which we shall see is at the intersection of the supply-side (ERU) curve and the demand side (AD) curves, output and the real exchange rate are at their equilibrium levels and inflation is constant. The medium-run model applies irrespective of the exchange rate regime. The type of exchange rate regime (i.e. fixed or flexible) affects the dynamics of adjustment to shocks, the available policy instruments and how the medium-rate inflation rate is determined. In this chapter, we concentrate on flexible exchange rate regimes and leave a discussion of fixed exchange rate regimes until Chapters 10 and 12. We look at the ERU and the AD curves in turn.

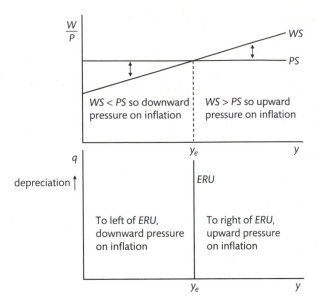

**Figure 9.5** Supply-side equilibrium and the *ERU* curve.

### Supply-side equilibrium: the *ERU* curve

The *ERU* curve is defined by the intersection of the wage- and price-setting curves. It shows the combinations of the real exchange rate and output at which there is supply-side equilibrium (i.e. constant inflation).

In this chapter, we continue to work with a single price level, $P$, which means the *WS* and *PS* curves are exactly the same as in the closed economy. Figure 9.5 shows the equilibrium output level, $y_e$, associated with supply-side equilibrium. At an output level to the right of $y_e$, the real wage defined by the *PS* curve is too low for wage setters given that unemployment is below equilibrium. This puts upward pressure on inflation. Similarly, an output level below $y_e$ where unemployment is higher than equilibrium means that the real wage (on the *PS*) is too high given the weakness of workers in the labour market: there is downward pressure on inflation. Although not shown in the diagram, the short-run Phillips curves are derived graphically from the *WS* and *PS* curves in exactly the same way as in the closed economy.

The $WS - PS$ intersection defines the *ERU* curve, which is vertical in the real exchange rate–output diagram at $y_e$.[10] For reasons that will become clear, we use the log of the real exchange rate rather than its level on the vertical axis in Fig. 9.5. We use $q$ to denote the natural logarithm of $Q$–i.e. $q \equiv \log Q$. We can write the *ERU* curve as:

$$y = y_e(z^W, z^P), \qquad\qquad (\textit{ERU curve})$$

where $z^W$ is the set of supply-side factors that shift the *WS* curve such as unionization, labour market regulations and unemployment benefits. $z^P$ is the set of factors that shifts the *PS* curve, such as the tax rate, the level of technology (i.e. labour productivity) and the degree

---

[10] In the next chapter, we shall see why the *ERU* may be downward sloping.

of product market competition. As we saw in Chapter 2, for example, a rise in unionization shifts the WS curve upwards and reduces equilibrium output. In the open economy diagram, this is represented by a leftward shift in the vertical *ERU* curve to the new lower level of equilibrium output.

The ERU curve is defined as the combinations of the real exchange rate and output at which the wage-setting real wage is equal to the price-setting real wage. At any point on the ERU curve, inflation is constant.

### 9.2.3 *AD curve*

The *AD* curve incorporates the demand side and the *UIP* condition in the medium-run equilibrium. To derive the *AD* curve, we use the version of the *IS* curve introduced in Chapter 3. This formulation captures the fact that aggregate demand responds negatively to the real interest rate ($r$) and positively to a depreciation in the real exchange rate ($q$), both with a one period lag. Hence

$$y_t = A_t - ar_{t-1} + bq_{t-1}, \qquad \text{(open economy IS curve)}$$

where $A$ includes the multiplier and demand shift variables in the open economy, such as world trade, as well as government spending ($G$) and the variables that shift the consumption and investment functions such as wealth and Tobin's $Q$. The open economy *IS* curve is discussed in detail in the next chapter.

The second step in deriving the *AD* curve is to incorporate financial integration. In medium-run equilibrium, the real exchange rate is constant and equal to its expected value. We shall see that this implies that $r = r^*$. We are considering a small open economy, which cannot affect the world real interest rate. To see why $r = r^*$ in a medium-run equilibrium, we begin by recalling the *UIP* condition:

$$i_t - i^* = \log e_{t+1}^E - \log e_t. \qquad \text{(UIP condition)}$$

From this, we know that for the nominal exchange rate to be unchanged (i.e. $\log e_{t+1}^E = \log e$), then $i_t = i^*$. We can derive the *UIP* condition in terms of the real rather than the nominal exchange rate (see Section 9.5.1 of the Appendix for the derivation):

$$r_t - r^* = q_{t+1}^E - q_t. \qquad \text{(real UIP condition)}$$

The real *UIP* condition says that if home's real interest rate is higher than the world's, then its real exchange rate is expected to depreciate. Since for a medium-run equilibrium, we require the real exchange rate to be constant, i.e. that the actual real exchange rate is at its expected level, then it is also the case that $r = r^*$. This produces the aggregate demand equation:

$$y = A - ar^* + bq. \qquad \text{(AD curve, } r = r^*\text{)}$$

Note, there are no time subscripts on the equation for the *AD* curve, because to be on the *AD* curve, $r$ has to be equal to $r^*$ and the real exchange rate must be constant. The *AD* curve is upward sloping in the exchange rate–output space (as shown in Fig. 9.6). This means a more depreciated exchange rate is associated with a higher level of output.

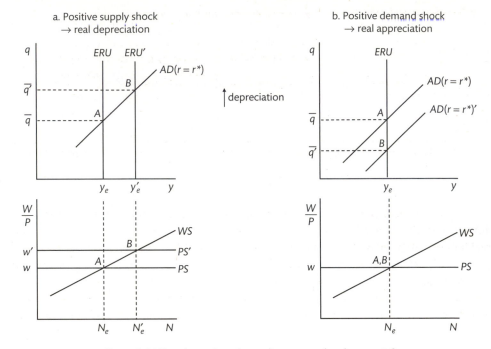

**Figure 9.6** What determines the medium-run real exchange rate?

*The AD curve shows the medium-run combinations of the real exchange rate, q, and level of output, y, at which the goods market is in equilibrium with the real interest rate equal to the world real interest rate (i.e. r = r\*).*

### The medium-run model (*AD-ERU* model)

The basic medium-run model for analysis in the small open economy consists of:

- The demand side represented by the *AD* curve. On the *AD* curve, the goods market is in equilibrium and $r = r^*$.

- The supply side represented by the *ERU* curve. On the *ERU* curve inflation is constant.

- In medium-run equilibrium, the economy is at the intersection of an *AD* curve with the *ERU* curve: $r = r^*$; $y = y_e$; $q = \bar{q}$; and inflation is constant. Being on the *AD* curve implies that the real exchange rate is equal to its expected value and hence, constant; being on the *ERU* curve means $y = y_e$ and hence, inflation is constant.

### What determines the medium-run real exchange rate?

In modelling the *UIP* condition, exchange rate expectations played a key role. The *AD* − *ERU* model helps to explain those expectations by showing how the real exchange rate is determined in the medium-run equilibrium.

**Table 9.1** Supply and demand shocks: implications for medium-run equilibrium.

| | Shock | | |
|---|---|---|---|
| | Rise in productivity | Fall in union bargaining power | Increase in autonomous consumption |
| Equilibrium unemployment | ↓ | ↓ | no change |
| Real exchange rate | depreciation | depreciation | appreciation |
| Real wage | ↑ | no change | no change |

*Note:* ↑ means the variable is higher in the new medium-run equilibrium, ↓ means it is lower and 'no change' means it is unchanged. We assume a flat PS curve throughout.

In the closed economy, there is a new stabilizing real interest rate at medium-run equilibrium following a permanent demand or supply shock. In the small open economy, the real interest rate is pinned down by the world real interest rate in medium-run equilibrium (i.e. $r = r^*$) and it is therefore the real exchange rate that varies in response to demand and supply shocks.

We assume the economy is initially at medium-run equilibrium on the *AD* and *ERU* curves, and look at the implications for the real exchange rate of a supply shock and a demand shock.

**A supply shock** A positive supply shock such as a wave of new technology raises productivity and the *PS* shifts up (assuming it takes time for the change in trend productivity to make its way into wage-setters' behaviour). This shifts the *ERU* curve to the right. At the new equilibrium, the real exchange rate has depreciated to $\bar{q}'$. Equilibrium output is higher (see point *B* in Fig. 9.6a). The intuition for this result is that for the level of output demanded to increase to the higher equilibrium level, the real exchange rate must be depreciated. All the other components of aggregate demand are unchanged.

**A demand shock** A positive demand shock such as an investment boom shifts the *AD* curve to the right and at the new equilibrium, there is an appreciated real exchange rate, $\bar{q}'$ (point *B* in Fig. 9.6b). Output is unchanged in the new equilibrium. In this case, an investment boom raises *A* in the *AD* equation; $r^*$ is fixed and therefore an appreciated real exchange rate is required to reduce aggregate demand such at $y = y_e$.

Table 9.1 compares the implications of a variety of permanent supply and demand shocks for unemployment, the real exchange rate and real wages in the new constant inflation equilibrium.

## 9.2.4 Stabilization under flexible exchange rates: 3-equation model and *RX* curve

To model stabilization policy in the open economy, we use the $AD - ERU$ model to characterize the medium-run equilibrium and extend the 3-equation model to explain how the central bank responds to a shock. To do this, we introduce a new curve, the *RX* curve, explained below, which gives the central bank's best interest rate response taking into account the reaction of the foreign exchange market.

To simplify the modelling, we assume the central bank targets domestic inflation. In reality, central banks target consumer price inflation, which includes the effect of changes in import prices.

In the closed economy, the central bank minimizes its loss function, which expresses its objective of keeping inflation close to target, $\pi^T$, subject to the constraint from the supply side, which is the Phillips curve ($PC$). This produces the monetary rule function ($MR$), which pins down the best response output gap ($y_t - y_e$). This is in turn implemented through the choice of the real interest rate ($r$) using the $IS$ equation.

Why should openness of the economy affect the central bank's inflation targeting behaviour? The answer is that the central bank will need to take account of the forward-looking behaviour in the foreign exchange market and the effect of changes in the exchange rate on aggregate demand. The examples in Section 9.1 highlighted why the central bank will need to build into its decision making the anticipation of the foreign exchange market response.

In the open economy, the central bank minimizes its loss function, which just as in the closed economy expresses its objective of keeping inflation close to its target, $\pi^T$

$$L = (y_t - y_e)^2 + \beta(\pi_t - \pi^T)^2, \qquad \text{(central bank loss function)}$$

1. Subject to the constraint from the supply side, which (again, just as in the closed economy) is the adaptive expectations Phillips curve ($PC$),

$$\pi_t = \pi_{t-1} + \alpha(y_t - y_e). \qquad \text{(Phillips curve, } PC\text{)}$$

2. Again this produces the monetary rule function ($MR$), which pins down the best response output gap ($y_t - y_e$),

$$(y_t - y_e) = -\alpha\beta(\pi_t - \pi^T). \qquad \text{(monetary rule, } MR\text{)}$$

3. But now this is implemented through the central bank's choice of $r$ using the *open economy IS curve* and *taking account of the reaction of the forward-looking forex market*,

$$y_t = A_t - ar_{t-1} + bq_{t-1}. \qquad \text{(open economy } IS \text{ curve)}$$

Earlier in the chapter, we introduced the $UIP$ condition, which showed how the exchange rate jumps in response to any news about home or foreign interest rates. When a shock hits the economy, this is news and both the central bank *and* the foreign exchange market will respond to it (see Fig. 9.7, starting at the top, for a summary of the dynamic adjustment of the economy to an inflation shock).

Instead of adjusting back to equilibrium along the $IS$ curve as in the closed economy, the central bank will adjust along a flatter 'interest rate − exchange rate' curve called $RX$. Smaller interest rate changes will be needed because the exchange rate channel operates as well.

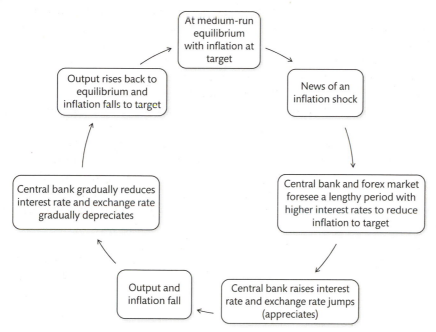

**Figure 9.7** Dynamic adjustment to an inflation shock under flexible exchange rates and inflation targeting.

## 9.2.5 Inflation shock: comparing closed and open economies

The first step is to recall that a temporary inflation shock shifts the Phillips curve for one period. The problem for the inflation-targeting central bank is to get inflation back to its target and in order to do that, it must push output below and unemployment above equilibrium by raising the interest rate. This is because of the persistence in the inflation process (indicated by $\pi_{t-1}$ in the *PC* equation): once inflation has been pushed up by the shock, it is built in to the behaviour of wage and price setters. For example, if food prices were pushed up by the effects of a drought, wage setters will expect in the next round of wage setting to get a wage increase that compensates them for the higher prices they face. In turn, firms will increase their prices to maintain their profit margins in the face of higher labour costs. This feature of inertia in wage and price setting means the central bank faces the constraint of the Phillips curve indexed by the inflation shock even though the shock was a temporary one.

Once inflation is back at target, the economy will be back at the initial equilibrium. This means that in the $AD - ERU$ model the new equilibrium coincides with the initial equilibrium—i.e. there is no change in the medium-run equilibrium real exchange rate.

A good way of introducing the open economy aspects of the problem faced by the central bank is to make a direct comparison with the closed economy. Figure 9.8 shows the *IS* and Phillips curve diagrams for the cases of the open and closed economies following an inflation shock.

### Closed economy

Figure 9.8a (the left-hand panel of Fig. 9.8), shows the adjustment of a closed economy to a temporary inflation shock, repeating the analysis from Chapter 3.

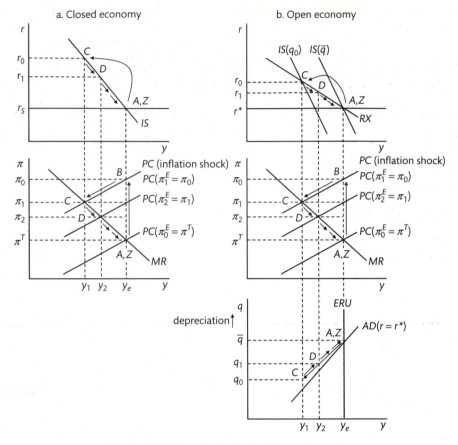

**Figure 9.8** Inflation shock: closed and open economies.

**Period 0** The economy starts at A—the central bank's bliss point. The economy is hit by an inflation shock which shifts the PC to PC(inflation shock) and the economy moves from A to B. Point B is not on the central bank's MR curve. The central bank forecasts the PC in the next period. This is $PC(\pi_1^E = \pi_0)$. Faced with this PC, the central bank would like to locate at point C, back on their MR curve. They therefore set the interest rate at $r_0$. The interest rate can only affect economic output with a one period lag, however, so the economy ends period 0 with inflation at $\pi_0$, output at $y_e$ and interest rates at $r_0$.

**Period 1** The new interest rate has had time to affect aggregate demand. The higher rate of interest dampens investment. This reduces output and the economy moves to point C, with output below equilibrium at $y_1$ and inflation at $\pi_1$. The central bank forecasts the PC in the next period. Based on last period's inflation, the PC it faces is $PC(\pi_2^E = \pi_1)$ and the central bank would like to locate at point D, back on their MR curve. They therefore reduce the interest rate to $r_1$. The interest rate can only affect economic output with a one period lag however, so the economy ends period 1 with inflation at $\pi_1$, output at $y_1$ and interest rates at $r_1$.

**Period 2 onwards**  In period 2, the economy moves to point $D$, as the lower interest rate stimulates demand. This increases output to $y_2$ and inflation falls to $\pi_2$. The same process now repeats itself until the economy is back at equilibrium at $Z$. The economy will move gradually down the $MR$ curve, as the central bank slowly adjusts the interest rate down from $r_1$ to $r_s$. The adjustment to the inflation shock ends when the economy is back at point $Z$, with output at $y_e$, inflation at $\pi^T$ and the interest rate at $r_s$.

## Open economy: introducing the **RX** curve

Figure 9.8b shows the adjustment of a small open economy to a temporary inflation shock.

**Period 0**  The economy starts at $A$ and the central bank's reasoning is the same as in the closed economy to locate its best response output gap at point $C$, on their $MR$ curve. The foreign exchange market foresees that the central bank will keep interest rates above world interest rates for a number of periods in order to squeeze inflation out of the system. The *UIP* condition implies this will cause an immediate appreciation of home's currency, so that it can depreciate for the *whole period* during which there is a positive interest differential between home and foreign bonds. To get the economy back on the $MR$ curve in the next period, the central bank therefore sets the interest rate at $r_0$ on the $RX$ curve—taking into account the appreciation in the exchange rate that will occur since the IS curve will shift to the left to IS($q_0$). The interest rate and the exchange rate can only affect economic output with a one period lag however, so the economy ends period 0 with inflation at $\pi_0$, output at $y_e$, the interest rate at $r_0$ and the exchange rate at $q_0$.

**Period 1**  The new interest rate and exchange rate have had time to affect aggregate demand. The higher rate of interest dampens investment and the appreciated exchange rate reduces net exports. These forces combine to reduce output and the economy moves to point $C$, with output below equilibrium at $y_1$ and inflation at $\pi_1$. The *IS* curve has shifted to the left on account of the more appreciated exchange rate. The central bank forecasts the $PC$ in the next period, $PC(\pi_2^E = \pi_1)$. Faced with this $PC$, the central bank would like to locate at point $D$, back on their $MR$ curve. In setting the interest rate, they again take into account the response of the foreign exchange market. The central bank foresees that a depreciation of the exchange rate will follow any reduction in the interest rate, as the *UIP* condition needs to hold in every period. They therefore reduce the interest rate to $r_1$ and the exchange rate depreciates to $q_1$ (point D on the $RX$ curve). The interest rate and the exchange rate can only affect economic output with a one period lag however, so the economy ends period 1 with inflation at $\pi_1$, output at $y_1$, the interest rate at $r_1$ and the exchange rate at $q_1$.

**Period 2 onwards**  In period 2, the economy moves to point $D$, as the lower interest rate and depreciated exchange rate stimulate demand. This increases output to $y_2$ and inflation falls to $\pi_2$. The *IS* curve has shifted to the right (back towards the initial equilibrium), due to the depreciation in the exchange rate. The economy is travelling down the curve labelled $RX$ curve, which is flatter than the *IS* curve. It shows the adjustment path of a small open economy (with flexible exchange rates) after an economic shock. Along the $RX$ curve the *UIP* condition always holds—i.e. it shows the central bank the interest rate to set to achieve a given output gap, taking into account the reaction of the forex market. The same process now repeats itself until the economy is back at equilibrium at Z.

The adjustment from D to Z will take a number of periods. The IS curve will gradually shift to the right and the economy will move gradually down the RX and MR curves, as the central bank slowly adjusts the interest rate down from $r_1$ to $r^*$ and the exchange rate depreciates from $q_1$ to $\bar{q}$. The interest rate needs to be back at the world interest rate for there to be no pressure on the exchange rate to change and for the economy to be in medium-run equilibrium. The movements in $r$ and $q$ reinforce each other, causing output to rise slowly from $y_2$ to $y_e$ and inflation to fall slowly from $\pi_2$ to $\pi^T$. The adjustment ends when the economy is back at point Z, with output at $y_e$, inflation at $\pi^T$, the interest rate at $r^*$ and the exchange rate at $\bar{q}$.

To complete the discussion of the open economy adjustment, the bottom panel of Fig. 9.8b shows the $AD - ERU$ diagram. In the case of an inflation shock, the positions of the AD and ERU curves are unaffected by the shock. For the whole of the adjustment process the economy is to the left of the ERU curve and as we saw in Fig. 9.5, this leads to downwards pressure on inflation. This causes inflation to fall until the economy is back at target inflation and once again on the ERU curve in medium-run equilibrium. From the top panel, we know that the real interest rate is above the world interest rate during the adjustment process. This means the adjustment along the MR curve from C to Z will lie to the left of the AD curve as shown in the bottom panel: at each level of $q$, $r > r^*$ so output is below the level shown by the AD curve on which $r = r^*$. The economy will only be back on the AD curve when it is once more in medium-run equilibrium with $r = r^*$.

### Comparing the closed and open economy cases

There are clear differences between the closed and open economy adjustment paths in Fig. 9.8:

1. The initial interest rate hike (to $r_0$) in response to the inflation shock is greater in the closed economy. This is because the appreciation of the exchange rate shoulders some of the burden of adjustment in the open economy.

2. The IS curve shifts in each period in the open economy but remains fixed in the closed economy. The open economy IS curve includes net exports, which are dampened by any appreciation of the real exchange rate and boosted by any depreciation. Net exports are part of the intercept term of the open economy IS curve, so the IS curve shifts if the real exchange rate changes. In contrast, a change in the real interest rate causes a movement along the IS curve (in both the closed and open economies).

3. The closed economy moves along the IS curve on its path back to equilibrium. This curve shows the interest rate the central bank must set to achieve their desired output gap on the MR curve. The open economy moves along the flatter RX curve on its path back to equilibrium. This curve shows the interest rate the central bank must set to achieve its desired output gap, whilst also taking into account the response of the forex market to any differential between home and world interest rates. The UIP condition holds at all points on the RX curve.

Figure 9.8 also highlights the important role played by expectations in the adjustment of the economy to an inflation shock in an open economy. The adjustment process relies heavily on the central bank and forex market foreseeing that a lengthy period with higher interest rates will be required to reduce inflation to target (see the third step in the flow diagram in Fig. 9.7). The central bank and foreign exchange market solve the dynamic adjustment problem simultaneously using the same model, which is an example of rational expectations modelling.

In Section 9.5.2 of the Appendix, we show in more detail how to calculate the initial jump in the exchange rate and therefore how to derive the *RX* curve mathematically and geometrically.

To use the *RX* curve, its key features are:

1. It goes through the intersection of $r^*$ and $y_e$ and therefore shifts only when either of these changes.

2. Its slope reflects the interest and exchange rate sensitivity of aggregate demand, the central bank's preferences and the slope of the Phillips curves:

   (a) it is flatter than the *IS* curve;

   (b) it is flatter, the flatter is the *IS* curve (i.e. when $a$ is higher indicating higher interest sensitivity of aggregate demand) and the higher is $b$ (i.e. the more sensitive is aggregate demand to the real exchange rate). When there is a larger aggregate demand response to a given change in the interest rate or exchange rate (i.e. a higher $a$ or $b$), the central bank has to change the interest rate by less, ceteris paribus;

   (c) it is flatter, the steeper is the *MR* curve (i.e. the lower is $\alpha$, flatter Phillips curves; or the lower is $\beta$, steeper loss circles). For example, when the central bank is less 'hard-nosed' the return to equilibrium following a shock will be slower and the central bank will raise the interest rate by less.

The response of the economy and the central bank to an inflation shock in both a small open economy with flexible exchange rates and a closed economy can be shown using the Macroeconomic Simulator available from the Carlin and Soskice webpage.[11] Figure 9.9 shows the impulse response functions after the economy experiences a 2% inflation shock in period five. We can see that the behaviour of inflation and GDP is the same in both cases, which is analogous to the bottom panels being identical in Fig. 9.8. The key difference in the

[11] The impulse reponse functions shown in Fig. 9.9 show the effect of a 2% positive inflation shock. To re-create these graphs, open the Macroeconomic Simulator available from the Carlin and Soskice website http://www.oup.com/uk/orc/carlin_soskice and choose the closed economy version. Then take the following steps:
(1) Click on the *reset all shocks* button on the left hand side of the main page. (2) Set a 2% positive inflation shock and change the sensitivity of expenditure with respect to interest rate to 0.5. (3) Click on the *inflation, income and interest rates figures* button on the left hand side to view the impulse response functions. (4) Return to the main page and click on the *save* button on the left hand side. This will store these graphs in memory. (5) Click the *change to a different simulator version* on the main page to switch to the open economy (with flexible exchange rates) version of the simulator and then apply the same shock, remembering to adjust the sensitivity of the exchange rate with respect to the real exchange rate to 1. (6) Save this data, then click on the *go to saved data* button on the main page to compare the two scenarios.

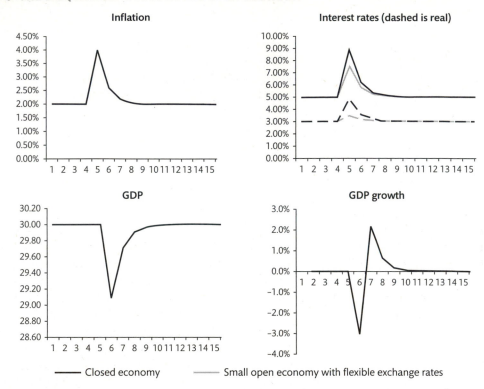

**Figure 9.9** Macroeconomic simulator example—Impulse response functions after an inflation shock (in period 5) in a closed economy and a small open economy with flexible exchange rates.

impulse reponse functions is the behaviour of interest rates. In the closed economy case, the central bank has had to raise the interest rate by more to stabilize the economy after the inflation shock. This is because in the open economy, some of the adjustment takes place through an appreciation of the real exchange rate.

## 9.3 Applications

### 9.3.1 Demand and supply shocks: the 3-equation and *AD-ERU* models

As we have seen in the closed economy (Chapter 3), it is only necessary for the central bank to manage the adjustment of the economy to an aggregate demand shock when it is unable to respond quickly enough to prevent any consequences of the shock for inflation from occuring. If it could act quickly enough by changing the interest rate to offset the effect of the demand shock on inflation, it could avoid the need to get the economy on to the *MR* curve. This is also the case in the open economy, where we have defined the *IS* curve such that output in period $t$ depends on the real interest rate and the real exchange rate in period $t - 1$:

$$y_t = A_t - ar_{t-1} + bq_{t-1}. \qquad \text{(open economy IS)}$$

This *IS* curve assumes it takes one period for the decisions of the central bank and the foreign exchange market to affect the real economy: a shock to $y_t$ cannot be offset by a change in

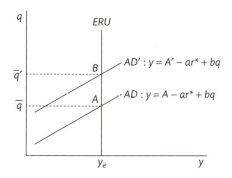

**Figure 9.10** Medium-run equilibrium: negative demand shock.

$r$ or in the real exchange rate $q$ within the period. The fact that interest rates typically affect the economy with a lag is taken into account when monetary policy is formulated in the UK. The Bank of England's mandate when making interest rate decisions is to target inflation two years ahead. If the real economy responded immediately to changes in the real interest rate and the real exchange rate, then the economy would return to equilibrium within the period, there would be no chance for the output gap to affect inflation and no need for the central bank to intervene to bring inflation back to target along the *MR* curve.

From Section 9.2.2 we know that demand and supply shocks change the medium-run exchange rate. The first step is therefore to look at the implications of the demand (or supply) shock for the medium-run equilibrium using the $AD - ERU$ model (Fig. 9.10). As our example, we take a permanent negative aggregate demand shock due, for example, to a fall in investment demand, which reduces the term $A$ in the $AD$ equation (shown in Section 9.2.3). This shock shifts the $AD$ curve to $AD'$. Since we know that in the small open economy the real interest rate in the new equilibrium is at the world real interest rate, it is clear that there will be a depreciated *real exchange rate* in the new equilibrium: for output to be equal to $y_e$, higher net exports must offset the lower investment. This contrasts with the closed economy, where a permanent negative demand shock implies a lower stabilizing *real interest rate* in the new medium-run equilibrium.

### Dynamic adjustment to the shock

Next, we analyse the dynamic adjustment of the economy to the shock using the 3-equation model, as shown in Fig. 9.11:

**Period 0** The economy starts at $A$—the central bank's bliss point. The economy is hit by a negative permanent demand shock which shifts the $IS$ curve to $IS(A', \bar{q})$. Output in the economy falls to $y_0$ and inflation falls to $\pi_0$. The economy moves from $A$ to $B$. Point $B$ is not on the central bank's $MR$ curve. The central bank forecasts the $PC$ in the next period. The $PC$ will move to $PC(\pi_1^E = \pi_0)$ next period. Faced with this $PC$, the central bank would like to locate at point $C$, back on their $MR$ curve. At point $C$, output is above equilibrium, so in order to reach this point, the central bank will need to reduce interest rates to stimulate investment and boost output. The foreign exchange market foresees that the central bank will keep interest rates *below* world interest rates for a number of periods in order to boost demand and return inflation to target. The *UIP* condition implies this will cause an immediate

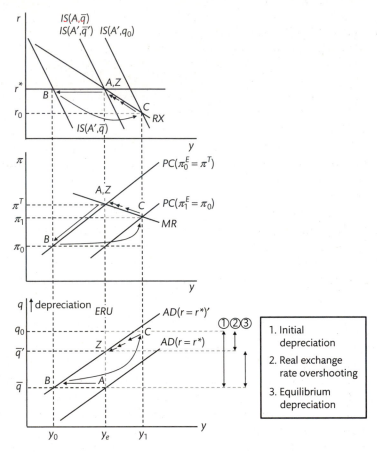

**Figure 9.11** Dynamic adjustment to a negative permanent demand shock.

depreciation of home's currency, so that it can appreciate for the whole period where home's interest rates are below world rates. The central bank therefore sets the interest rate at $r_0$—taking into account the immediate depreciation in the exchange rate that will occur—to get the economy back on the *MR* curve *in the next period*. The interest rate and the exchange rate can only affect economic output with a one period lag however, so the economy ends period 0 with inflation at $\pi_0$, output at $y_0$, interest rate at $r_0$ and exchange rate at $q_0$.

**Period 1 onwards** The new interest rate and exchange rate have had time to affect aggregate demand. The lower rate of interest boosts investment and the depreciated exchange rate increases net exports. The economy moves to point $C$, with output above equilibrium at $y_1$ and inflation at $\pi_1$. The *IS* curve has shifted to the right to $IS(A', q_0)$ due to the depreciation of the exchange rate. This is further to the right than the original *IS* curve. The adjustment process from point $C$ back to point $Z$ (not shown in the diagram) follows the process described for an inflation shock in Section 9.2.5 and will take a number of periods. The *IS* curve will gradually shift to the left and the economy will move gradually up the *RX* and *MR* curves, as the central bank slowly adjusts the interest rate up from $r_0$ to $r^*$ and the exchange rate appreciates from $q_0$ to $\bar{q}\prime$. The exchange rate appreciates from period 1 onwards to take account of the fact that home interest rates are below world interest rates. This ensures the *UIP* condition holds in every period. The interest rate needs to be back at the world interest rate for there to be no pressure on the exchange rate to change and for the economy to be in medium-run equilibrium. Adjustment to the demand shock ends when the economy is back at point Z, with output at $y_e$, inflation at $\pi^T$, the interest rate at $r^*$ and the exchange rate at $\bar{q}\prime$.

In the new medium-run equilibrium, the *IS* curve is indexed by lower autonomous demand (as a result of the permanent negative demand shock) and a depreciated real exchange rate (i.e. $IS(A\prime, \bar{q}\prime)$). This is because the permanent fall in autonomous demand needs to be offset by higher net exports for the economy to return to equilibrium output after the shock.

The bottom panel of Fig. 9.11 shows the $AD - ERU$ diagram. A permanent negative demand shock causes a leftward shift of the *AD* curve. The arrows plot the adjustment path of the economy. They show that the initial depreciation of the real exchange rate (from $\bar{q}$ to $q_0$) was greater than the equilibrium depreciation (from $\bar{q}$ to $\bar{q}\prime$). The label ② on the $AD - ERU$ diagram shows the difference between the initial and equilibrium movements in the real exchange rate, which is referred to as *real exchange rate overshooting*. We discuss real and nominal exchange rate overshooting in Section 9.3.2.

At point C on the $AD - ERU$ diagram, the exchange rate is $q_0$ and is expected to appreciate back to $\bar{q}\prime$: this is just what we would expect, given that during the period of expected appreciation, home's interest rate is below the world interest rate. Holders of home bonds are losing out in terms of the interest return on home bonds, but are gaining from the expected appreciation of home's exchange rate.

It is important to note that point C is not on the new *AD* curve, because at this point home's interest rate is below the world interest rate ($r$ must be below $r^*$ to produce the desired boost to demand to offset the shock, whereas $r$ must equal $r^*$ to be on the *AD* curve). Since $r < r^*$, $y$ must be greater than it is on the $AD(r = r^*)\prime$ line because the lower $r$ will stimulate higher interest-sensitive spending. Hence, point C is to the right of $AD\prime$.

## Summing up

The examples of an inflation shock (as shown in Section 9.2.5) and an aggregate demand shock (as shown in this section) highlight the similarities and differences between the way the 3-equation model works in the closed and open economies. The analysis of a supply shock is left as an exercise. Remember that in the case of a supply shock, the *ERU* curve will shift. In the $AD - ERU$ diagram, there will be a new equilibrium real exchange rate and a new equilibrium output level. Just as in the closed economy, a supply shock means the *MR* curve and the Phillips curves shift. In the open economy, the *RX* curve will shift to intersect the new equilibrium output level and $r^*$.

The new element in the open economy is the way the behaviour of the foreign exchange market interacts with that of the central bank. Table 9.2 contrasts the decision-making process in the central bank and the foreign exchange market in the closed and open economies using the example of a permanent demand shock.

### 9.3.2 **Exchange rate overshooting**

Exchange rate overshooting refers to the phenomenon of the nominal and real exchange rate jumping by more than the equilibrium adjustment in response to shocks. In the case of

**Table 9.2** Decision-making process of central bank and foreign exchange market after a permanent demand shock.

| Period | Closed economy | Small open economy |
|---|---|---|
| 0 | CB works out stabilizing interest rate in the new equilibrium, $r^S$. | CB and forex market work out real exchange rate in the new equilibrium, $\bar{q}$; $r = r^*$. Use *AD-ERU* model. |
| | CB works out implications of the shock for the Phillips curve and for its choice of output in period one on the *MR* curve. | |
| | | CB and forex market work out the path over time of the CB's desired output level along the *MR* to the new equilibrium. |
| | CB sets $r_0$ using the *IS* curve to achieve its desired output gap in the next period. | CB sets $r_0$ using the *RX* curve to achieve its desired output gap in the next $q$ jumps to $q_0$, as the forex market take advantage of the arbitrage opportunities brought about by the interest rate differential. Both parties take into account the response of the other when formulating their best response. |
| 1 | $r_0$ affects the real economy, shifting output to $y_1$, which is on the *MR* curve and minimizes the CB's loss function. | $r_0$ and $q_0$ affect the real economy. This shifts output to $y_1$ on the *MR* curve, which minimizes the CB's loss function. The *IS* curve shifts as the real exchange rate affects demand for net exports. |
| 2+ | CB adjusts $r$ to move economy along *MR* (and *IS*) to equilibrium. | CB adjusts $r$ (and forex market adjusts $q$) to move economy along *MR* (and *RX*) to equilibrium. |

an inflation shock, there is no change in the equilibrium real exchange rate, which means that all of the initial jump from $\bar{q}$ to $q_0$, which shifts the *IS* curve to the left in Fig. 9.8, is real exchange rate overshooting. In the case of a permanent demand shock, the new equilibrium real exchange rate is depreciated, but initially the depreciation overshoots this equilibrium as shown in Fig. 9.11.

Overshooting is integral to the 3-equation model of inflation targeting. It exists because of the combination of:

1. an internationally integrated financial market;

2. rational expectations in the foreign exchange market, which leads to jumps in the exchange rate; and

3. sluggish adjustment of wages and prices in the economy, which requires the central bank to keep the interest rate above (or below) the world interest rate until inflation returns to target.

When financial markets are integrated, the real *UIP* condition,

$$r_t - r^* = q_{t+1}^E - q_t, \hspace{4cm} \text{(real \textit{UIP} condition)}$$

holds each period. When $r > r^*$, the real exchange rate, $q$ must jump relative to its expected value. The greater the cumulative deviation of home's interest rate is expected to be above (e.g. in the case of a positive inflation shock) or below (e.g. in the case of a negative demand shock or a positive supply shock) the world interest rate, the more the real exchange rate must overshoot initially in order that it can adjust back to the equilibrium exchange rate during the period of the interest rate differential. Overshooting will be greater when shocks are larger.

We can define the *equilibrium change* as the difference in the real exchange rate between the inital equilibrium and the new medium-run equilibrium. Hence the initial jump in the exchange rate equals the equilibrium change plus the exchange rate overshooting. If the interest rate differential was expected to prevail for just one year, the initial jump will be $[(r_0 - r^*) +$ equilibrium change]; if it is expected to prevail for three years, the initial jump will be $[(r_0 - r^*) + (r_1 - r^*) + (r_2 - r^*) +$ equilibrium change].[12] In Section 9.3.1, we showed exactly how the initial jump in $q$ is determined in the case of inflation targeting, where the interest rate is gradually adjusted back to the world interest rate. This is shown by point C on the *RX* curve in Fig. 9.11.

Although exchange rate overshooting is an integral part of the modern modelling of a flexible exchange rate economy, this was not always the case. The German-American economist Rudiger Dornbusch developed the theory of exchange rate overshooting as a way of explaining the volatility of exchange rates following the end of the Bretton Woods system of fixed exchange rates at the end of the 1960s.[13] The idea of overshooting centres on the fact that the exchange rate is a variable that can jump easily—as we discussed when introducing the *UIP* condition in Section 9.1, within seconds of news arriving that changes the views of traders about the future, transactions take place and the exchange rate jumps. This is also true of the prices of other financial assets like shares and bonds. By contrast, the prices of most goods and services, and of labour, do not jump. Only the prices of goods that are homogeneous and traded on commodity exchanges, such as oil and wheat, behave like those of financial assets. It is the interaction of prices that jump with those that do not that produces exchange rate overshooting. It is because prices and wages *do not change immediately* to wipe out an inflation shock and return the economy to target inflation, or change to bring about the new equilibrium exchange rate to wipe out an aggregate demand shock, that overshooting occurs.

---

### Box 9.1  Dornbusch overshooting and the Thatcher recession

In 1979, Margaret Thatcher became Prime Minister of the UK and her government introduced an anti-inflationary monetary policy referred to as the Medium-Term Financial Strategy. Prime Minister Thatcher announced a reduction in the growth of the money supply with the objective of reducing inflation. Theory suggests that if no overshooting takes place, then a 10% reduction in the money supply produces a 10% fall in prices and output would remain unchanged. The nominal exchange rate would appreciate by 10%, leaving the real exchange rate unchanged.

---

[12] For example: $(r_0 - r^*) + (r_1 - r^*) + (r_2 - r^*) = (\bar{q}' - q_0)$. Add $(\bar{q} - \bar{q}')$ to both sides: $(r_0 - r^*) + (r_1 - r^*) + (r_2 - r^*) + \underbrace{(\bar{q} - \bar{q}')}_{\substack{\text{equilibrium} \\ \text{change}}} = \underbrace{(\bar{q} - q_0)}_{\text{initial jump}}$.

[13] The initial model of overshooting was developed by Rudiger Dornbusch (1976). For a very readable introduction to the Dornbusch model, see Rogoff (2002), who also describes the atmosphere in Dornbusch's PhD class at MIT when he first explained the model.

Dornbusch pointed out that if the foreign exchange market expects that a period with output below its equilibrium level is required to bring prices down, then they will also expect a prolonged period where real interest rates will remain high. This is because the central bank is expected to keep nominal interest rates high until they can see evidence that prices are adjusting downwards. The expectation of higher interest rates leads to an immediate appreciation of home's real exchange rate (i.e. overshooting of the real as well as the nominal exchange rate since the nominal exchange rate appreciates by more than 10%).

Applying this to the Thatcher case, an announcement of a lower money supply growth rate did not produce an immediate fall in inflation. In anticipation that a period of high interest rates was needed to push up unemployment and squeeze inflation out of the system, the UK pound appreciated sharply following the announcement of the tight money policy in 1979. Unemployment rose as a consequence of the appreciated real exchange rate and the higher real interest rates. The fall in inflation *followed* the rise in unemployment. Figure 9.12 shows the path of the real and nominal exchange rates, unemployment and inflation over the Thatcher period. Although some of the exchange rate appreciation was attributable to the discovery of North Sea oil, exchange rate overshooting in response to the tight monetary policy was an important part of the story. Exchange rate overshooting was viewed as having led to lasting damage to the UK's manufacturing industry.

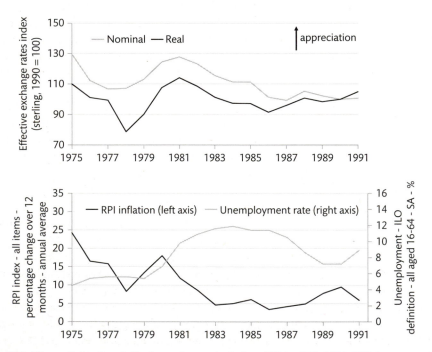

**Figure 9.12** UK nominal and real effective exchange rate indices (1990 = 100): 1975–1991 (upper panel) and UK unemployment and inflation: 1975–1991 (lower panel).

*Note:* An increase in the effective exchange rate indices represents an appreciation.

*Source:* Bank of England; IMF International Financial Statistics; UK Office of National Statistics (data accessed October 2011).

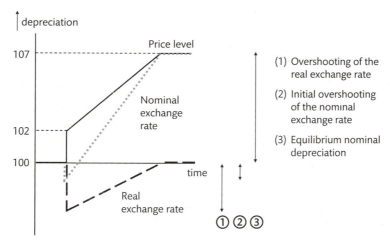

**Figure 9.13** Real and nominal exchange rate paths following an inflation shock.

## What determines the behaviour of the nominal exchange rate?

Our discussion of the 3-equation model to this point has been in terms of the real exchange rate—after all, it is the real exchange rate that affects aggregate demand and output, so that is the focus of attention of the central bank and the foreign exchange market in making their calculations. This is exactly the same logic as the focus on the choice of the real interest rate in the closed economy. However, it is interesting to know how the behaviour of the nominal exchange rate fits into the picture.

In Section 9.2.1, we used the *UIP* condition to see how the nominal exchange rate moved in response to a change in the home or world nominal interest rate, and in response to a change in the expected exchange rate. In the 3-equation model, the same logic is at work. However, we now have a full model of what determines the expected real exchange rate and what determines any gap between home and world real interest rates. This means that rational expectations in the foreign exchange market are oriented to producing the jump in the nominal exchange rate that is implied by solving the model.

It is useful to look at a particular example to understand the evolution of the nominal exchange rate. We take the case of an inflation shock. Looking back at Fig. 9.8b, we can see that the behaviour of domestic inflation is determined entirely by the Phillips curve and monetary rule mechanisms (in the middle panel). Since the model pins down how the real exchange rate (in conjunction with the central bank's monetary policy rule) must respond to the inflation shock, the behaviour of the *nominal* exchange rate is a residual. This follows from the definition of the real exchange rate: $Q \equiv \frac{P^*e}{P}$. Since we know that $P^*$ is exogenous to the small open economy because it is set in the rest of the world, and $P$ and $Q$ are pinned down by the inflation shock and the best response policy rule, it follows that the nominal exchange rate $e$ is just the residual.

Let us look at an example. Figure 9.13 shows the stylized paths of the domestic price level and the nominal and real exchange rates following an inflation shock using index numbers for each variable set initially at 100. For simplicity, we assume the inflation target and world inflation are both zero. With a target of zero inflation, the price *level* is therefore constant in medium-run equilibrium.

Following the inflation shock (say of 2%), the price level jumps from 100 to 102, and since home's inflation is higher than world inflation on the path back to target inflation, home's price level continues to rise until the medium-run equilibrium is reached (e.g. at a level of 107). The real exchange rate appreciates immediately and depreciates back to its initial level along the path to the medium-run equilibrium.

The nominal exchange rate depreciates more rapidly than the real exchange rate along the path to the medium-run equilibrium. At medium-run equilibrium, the price level has risen by 7% and the nominal exchange rate has depreciated by 7% relative to their starting levels: the real exchange rate is therefore back at its initial level. This reflects the fact that an inflation shock does not change the medium-run real exchange rate.

Two features of the response of the nominal exchange rate are worth pointing out. The first is that the initial nominal appreciation in period 0 is less than the real appreciation because part of the required real appreciation takes place through the initial inflation shock (and foreign exchange operators can work this out).[14] The second relates to the path back to equilibrium (from point B to Z in Fig. 9.8). In this phase, it is clear that home's inflation (although falling) is above world inflation, which would by itself imply an appreciating real exchange rate. However, the real exchange rate must be depreciating for two reasons:

1. in order to push the *IS* curve back to equilibrium (i.e. to the right); and

2. because home's real interest rate is above the world's, i.e. $r > r^*$. The gains from holding home bonds must be offset by the expected real exchange rate loss.

This accounts for the extent of the nominal depreciation, which outstrips the real depreciation, along the path back to equilibrium.

### 9.3.3 Exchange rate volatility

In this chapter, we have used the open economy $AD - ERU$ model to show that adjustment to demand and supply shocks requires changes in the real exchange rate. Under flexible exchange rates, the 3-equation model tells us that real and nominal exchange rate overshooting are an integral part of the adjustment process. Stabilization of shocks is successful under inflation targeting, but it is necessarily accompanied by exchange rate overshooting.

To this point, we have ignored an important characteristic of the foreign exchange market: its ability to generate shocks. Like other financial markets (see Chapters 1, 4 and 6), the foreign exchange market is subject to panics, waves of optimism and pessimism, and to herd and bandwagon effects. This means that the exchange rate can move—not in response to the mechanisms discussed in this chapter arising from shocks that shift the equilibrium real exchange rate and the overshooting that accompanies the adjustment to shocks—but because of changes in sentiment in the market.

---

[14] It can be useful here to rearrange the definition of the real exchange rate to $\overset{\downarrow}{e} = \frac{\overset{\downarrow}{Q}\overset{\uparrow}{P}}{P^*}$ to think about how changes in Q and P affect the nominal exchange rate.

An example occurred in 2011 as the Eurozone crisis took hold and growth prospects in the USA weakened. The Swiss franc became a 'safe haven' currency. The Swiss National Bank (SNB) was alarmed at the extent of the inflow of foreign currency and the appreciation of the franc, which was making its manufacturing sector uncompetitive. On September 6th 2011, the SNB took the extremely unusual step of announcing it would buy unlimited quantities of euros to weaken the franc. This amounted to the attempt to fix or peg the exchange rate to the euro. The threat was credible in the market and the pressure shifted to other currencies, creating potential distortions elsewhere in the world.

In Sections 9.3.2 and 9.3.3, we highlighted two features of flexible exchange rate regimes in highly integrated financial markets that complicate efficient resource allocation decisions by households and firms:

1. the presence of exchange rate overshooting due to sluggish adjustment of wages and prices; and

2. the noise arising from unpredictable and uncontrollable features of forex market.

In Chapter 12, we return to the discussion of the merits of different exchange rate regimes when we analyse the Eurozone.

## 9.4 Conclusions

This chapter has set out the basic framework for analysing economic shocks in the open economy. The framework has two key components; the $AD - ERU$ model, which determines medium-run equilibrium and the dynamic open economy 3-equation model, which shows how the central bank stabilizes the economy after an economic shock. The latter model extends the core closed economy 3-equation model of Chapter 3 by opening up the economy to international trade and capital flows. This requires the introduction of the foreign exchange market. In particular, we focus on the the behaviour of investors engaged in arbitrage between the bonds issued by different governments.

The open economy framework can be utilized to answer pertinent questions about economic policy and macroeconomic fluctuations in small open economies with flexible exchange rates:

1. What are the key features of the foreign exchange market? How do exchange rates respond to changes in interest rates? In an economy open to international capital flows, households have the option of holding both home and foreign bonds. Assuming there is no difference in default risk between the bonds issued by different governments, the only difference between these bonds is their expected return, which depends on the interest rate and any expected movements in the exchange rate. Households use sophisticated agents (e.g. pension funds) to allocate their investments between home and foreign bonds. These agents buy and sell foreign exchange and are assumed to be both forward looking and rational. Investors see that they can profit from arbitrage opportunities when there is an interest rate differential between home and foreign bonds. Arbitrage means that a movement into home bonds (e.g. as a result of a positive interest differential) causes home's currency to immediately appreciate, so that it can depreciate over the period of the differential. This

exchange rate response wipes out any potential gain from holding home bonds over foreign bonds. The relationship between the interest rate differential and the expected change in exchange rates is captured by the *UIP* condition.

2. How does the central bank's response to economic shocks compare in the closed and open economies? In the closed economy, the central bank responds to economic shocks by adjusting the interest rate. In the open economy, the central bank must also take into account the reaction of the forex market to any change in interest rates. The central bank and bond investors using the foreign exchange market are rational forward-looking agents who act simultaneously to solve the model after an economic shock. For example, if the central bank raises the home interest rate to squeeze an inflation shock out of the system, then the foreign exchange market will buy home bonds causing the currency to appreciate. This will dampen demand by reducing net exports. We can see from this example that the central bank does not have to change interest rates as much in response to shocks in the open economy, as some adjustment will occur through the real exchange rate channel.

3. How can the open economy model developed in this chapter shed light on the phenomenon of exchange rate overshooting? The overshooting of the exchange rate occurs when the initial jump in the exchange rate as the result of an economic shock is larger than the equilibrium change. This takes place in the model due to our assumption that there are rational expectations in the foreign exchange market, but that wages and prices are sluggish to adjust. The persistence of inflation in our model requires interest rates to diverge from world interest rates for a number of periods after a shock. The rational forex market responds to the interest differential and the exchange rate jumps. The exchange rate then slowly adjusts to equilibrium whilst the differential remains. Overshooting can have long term effects. For example, the over-appreciation of the exchange rate that accompanied the Thatcher disinflation in the UK in the 1980s is said to have done permanent damage to the UK manufacturing sector.

The next chapter looks more closely at the demand and supply sides in the open economy, providing the counterpart to the closed economy discussed in Chapters 1 and 2. Chapter 11 analyses the impact of oil price shocks and show how imbalances can occur between open economies even when inflation is low and stable. We end our analysis of the open economy by looking at the economics of the Eurozone in Chapter 12.

## 9.5 Appendix

### 9.5.1 Deriving the real *UIP* condition

The first step is to add $-\pi_{t+1}^E + \pi_{t+1}^{*E}$ onto both sides of the nominal *UIP* condition, which gives:

$$i_t - i^* - \pi_{t+1}^E + \pi_{t+1}^{*E} = \log e_{t+1}^E - \log e_t - \pi_{t+1}^E + \pi_{t+1}^{*E}. \tag{9.1}$$

If we now use the Fisher equation (i.e. $i = r + \pi^E$), then the left hand side of the equation becomes $r_t - r^*$.

In addition, if we recall that $Q = \frac{P^*e}{P}$ and that $\log Q = q$, then using the properties of logs we can express the log of the real exchange rate ($q$) as:

$$q = \log P^* + \log e - \log P. \tag{9.2}$$

We also know that the difference between a log variable at time $t+1$ and time $t$ is approximately equal to the growth rate of the underlying variable between those two periods, which means that:

$$\pi_{t+1}^E = \log P_{t+1}^E - \log P_t. \tag{9.3}$$

This is because inflation is defined as the growth rate of the price level. If we substitute back into Equation 9.1 then this gives us the real *UIP* condition,

$$i_t - i^* - \pi_{t+1}^E + \pi_{t+1}^{*E} = \log e_{t+1}^E - \log e_t - (\log P_{t+1}^E - \log P_t) + (\log P_{t+1}^{*E} - \log P_t^*) \tag{9.4}$$
$$r_t - r^* = (\log P_{t+1}^{*E} + \log e_{t+1}^E - \log P_{t+1}^E) - (\log P_t^* + \log e_t - \log P_t)$$
$$r_t - r^* = q_{t+1}^E - q_t. \tag{real \textit{UIP} condition}$$

## 9.5.2 The 3-equation model in more detail

In Section 9.2.4, we showed graphically how the openness of the economy affects the policy of an inflation-targeting central bank. In this Appendix, we set out more carefully how the model works. In particular, we show how rational expectations and arbitrage (captured by the *UIP* condition) in the foreign exchange market allow us to pin down precisely the interest and exchange rate responses to different shocks.[15]

It is convenient to repeat the equations for the structure of the economy, because it helps to clarify the origins of the parameters that will be used to derive the *RX* curve.

We begin with the Phillips curve and the monetary rule equations, which under the assumption of domestic inflation targeting, are the same as in the closed economy. This means the same methodology as Chapter 3 is used here to derive the *MR* curve.

Persistence in the inflation process is reflected in the Phillips curve, which is:

$$\pi_t = \pi_{t-1} + \alpha(y_t - y_e). \tag{Phillips curve, PC}$$

As in Chapter 3, the central bank is modelled as operating under discretion. Each period it minimizes a loss function:

$$L = (y_t - y_e)^2 + \beta(\pi_t - \pi^T)^2, \tag{central bank loss function}$$

where $\beta > 1$ characterizes a central bank that places less weight on output fluctuations than on deviations in inflation, and vice versa. The central bank optimizes by minimizing its loss function subject to the Phillips curve. This produces the monetary rule equation (the *MR* curve), which is the same as in the closed economy:

$$(y_t - y_e) = -\alpha\beta(\pi_t - \pi^T). \tag{monetary rule, MR}$$

---

[15] This section uses the formula for the sum of an infinite series, which is set out in full in Chapter 1.

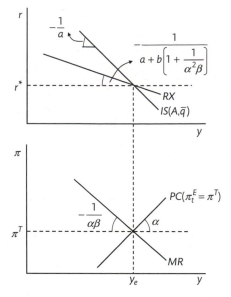

**Figure 9.14** The 3-equation open economy model.

The demand side of the economy is represented by the open economy *IS* curve, which captures the fact that demand responds negatively to the real interest rate and positively to a depreciation in the real exchange rate, $q$:

$$y_t = A - ar_{t-1} + bq_{t-1}. \qquad \text{(open economy \textit{IS} curve)}$$

The dynamics of the adjustment of the economy to a shock depend on the same aspects of the economy as in the closed economy. The additional open economy factors are the responsiveness of aggregate demand to the real exchange rate, $b$ and the real *UIP* condition:

$$r_t - r^* = q_{t+1}^E - q_t. \qquad \text{(real \textit{UIP} condition)}$$

The real *UIP* condition says that any positive (negative) real interest differential will be matched by an expected depreciation (appreciation) in the real exchange rate.

Figure 9.14 shows where the different structural parameters fit into the open economy model. In Chapter 3, we showed how the different parameters affect the curves underlying the core closed economy 3-equation model. In Fig. 9.14, we can see where the open economy elements fit in: the lower panel is exactly the same as in the closed economy. In the *IS* panel, the *IS* will shift by more in response to a given change in the real exchange rate if $b$ is larger: this flattens the *RX* curve and implies that a smaller rise in the interest rate is necessary to achieve a given output level on the *MR* curve.

### Deriving the *RX* curve

In order to pin down the interest rate that the central bank needs to set once a shock has been observed, we make the following assumptions about the agents in the model:

- forward looking with rational expectations. central bank, which targets domestic inflation, and foreign exchange market;
- backward looking: private sector as represented by *IS* and *PC* curves.

We break the problem into the following steps:

1. From these assumptions, we know we can use the same *PC* − *MR* diagram as for the closed economy. But to translate the chosen output gap from the *MR* line into the central bank's interest rate decision in the *IS* diagram, we must derive the *RX* line, which will incorporate the real *UIP* condition.

2. The key to understanding how the central bank and foreign exchange market solve the model is encapsulated in the *RX* line. For a period during which the economy moves down the *MR* back to equilibrium $r > r^*$, and we know from the real *UIP* condition that it must be the case that the real exchange rate is expected to depreciate. Hence, the forex market and the central bank work out that there must be an initial jump appreciation of the real exchange rate so that it can depreciate *in every period* as the economy moves down the *MR* during which $r > r^*$. This jump appreciation in $q$ causes an initial shift in the *IS* curve to the left. Hence the central bank's desired output gap in the first period after the shock is achieved by a combination of a shift of the *IS* ($\downarrow q$; i.e. appreciation) and the usual closed economy mechanism of a shift to the left along the *IS* ($\uparrow r$).

3. If we assume that $\sum_{t=0}^{\infty} (r_t - r^*) > 0$ then $q$ needs to immediately appreciate to $q_0$ such that $\sum_{t=0}^{\infty} (r_t - r^*) = \bar{q} - q_0$ so that the expected depreciation from holding £ bonds over the whole adjustment period to the new equilibrium exactly balances the interest rate gain. $\bar{q} - q_0$ is referred to as 'overshooting'. If the initial equilibrium exchange rate (and the initial actual exchange rate before the jump to $q_0$) is $\bar{q}'$ then it is still true that $\sum_{t=0}^{\infty} (r_t - r^*) = \bar{q} - q_0$. But we can see the size of the initial jump by expanding the RHS:

$$\sum_{t=0}^{\infty} (r_t - r^*) = \bar{q} - q_0 = (\bar{q} - \bar{q}') + (\bar{q}' - q_0) = eqm \; \Delta \; in \; q + initial \; jump. \tag{9.5}$$

If the equilibrium $q$ appreciates (as in a positive permanent demand shock), then $\bar{q}' - q_0 = (\bar{q} - q_0) - (\bar{q} - \bar{q}') > (\bar{q} - q_0)$ so the initial appreciation is greater than the subsequent depreciation.

4. The deviations in the rate of interest from its equilibrium value will decline at a constant rate and at the same rate at which the output gap declines on the path down the *MR*. Call this rate $(1 - \lambda)$. It reflects the CB preferences ($\beta$) and the constraint it faces, i.e. the slope of the Phillips curve, $\alpha$.[16] The rate of decline is $(1 - \lambda) = 1 - \frac{1}{1+\alpha^2\beta}$ and is lower, the lower are $\alpha$ or $\beta$ and hence, the steeper is the *MR*. Therefore, $(r_{t+1} - r^*) = \lambda(r_t - r^*)$ and we can write the left hand side of Equation 9.5 as:

---

[16] To see how $(1 - \lambda)$ is derived and why it must be the case that the rate of interest will decline at the same rate as the output gap declines then refer to Section 9.5.3 of the Appendix.

$$\sum_{t=0}^{\infty}(r_t - r^*) = (r_0 - r^*)\left[1 + \lambda + \lambda^2 + \lambda^3 + ...\right] = \frac{(r_0 - r^*)}{(1 - \lambda)}. \tag{9.6}$$

If we now substitute Equation 9.6 into Equation 9.5,

$$\frac{(r_0 - r^*)}{(1 - \lambda)} = \bar{q} - q_0, \tag{9.7}$$

we know the relationship between the initial rise in $r$ and in $q$.[17]

5. We can now work out the initial $r_0$ set by the central bank, once we know its chosen output gap: $(y_1 - y_e)$, which is found by using the Phillips curve and the $MR$, exactly as it was in the closed economy. The way to think about how the desired output gap in the open economy is achieved by the policy response is that it consists of two parts: one due to the appreciation of $q$ and the other due to the rise in $r$. We can write this as:

$$y_1 - y_e = -a(r_0 - r^*) + b(q_0 - \bar{q}). \tag{9.8}$$

Now, we just substitute 9.7 into 9.8 to get an expression for $r_0$ once the desired output gap for period 1 is known: this is the interest rate the central bank sets in period 0:

$$y_1 - y_e = -a(r_0 - r^*) + b(q_0 - \bar{q}) \tag{9.9}$$

$$= -a(r_0 - r^*) - b\left(\frac{(r_0 - r^*)}{(1 - \lambda)}\right)$$

$$= -\left(a + \frac{b}{1 - \lambda}\right)(r_0 - r^*). \tag{RX equation}$$

Since $a$, $b$ and $\lambda$ are all parameters and $r^*$ is a constant, once $y_1$ is known, the central bank can calculate $r_0$. This is the $RX$ equation. It is clear immediately from this equation that the $RX$ is flatter than the $IS$ line: if we think of an increase in $r$ above $r^*$, the $RX$ equation tells us that the fall in $y$ below $y_e$ will be greater (since we multiply by $\left(a + \frac{b}{1-\lambda}\right)$) than is the case on the $IS$, when we multiply by $a$.

To find the interest rate $r_0$ graphically, as shown in Fig. 9.15, we mark the desired output gap, $(y_1 - y_e)$ and then note that this can be broken into the two parts as shown in Equation 9.8. Once we find the length of $b(q_0 - \bar{q})$, we know the horizontal shift of the $IS$, since this shift is caused by the appreciation. To find the length of $b(q_0 - \bar{q})$, we note from the $RX$ equation that this is equal to $-\left(\frac{b}{1-\lambda}\right)(r_0 - r^*)$,

$$b(q_0 - \bar{q}) = -\left(\frac{b}{1 - \lambda}\right)(r_0 - r^*).$$

Rearranging gives $(r_0 - r^*) = -\left(\frac{1 - \lambda}{b}\right) \cdot b(q_0 - \bar{q}).$

Hence, if we draw a line from the point B with a slope of $\left(\frac{1-\lambda}{b}\right)$ to intersect the $IS$ curve, this will define a triangle with its base equal to $b(q_0 - \bar{q})$ and its height equal to $(r_0 - r^*)$. This pins

[17] This relationship can be plotted in the $r$–$q$ space. It is flatter than the $-45°$ of the real $UIP$ condition because a larger initial jump in $q$ is necessary when $r$ varies from $r^*$ for more than one period.

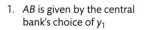

1. *AB* is given by the central bank's choice of $y_1$

2. Draw line *BC* with slope $(1 - \lambda)/b$

3. Point *C* shows the $r_0$ chosen by the central bank

4. This fixes the shift in the *IS* curve, *DC*, and in the interest rate chosen by the central bank, *BD*

5. The *RX* curve goes through *D* and *A*

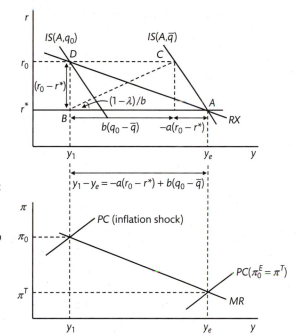

**Figure 9.15** The geometry of the *RX* curve-example of a positive inflation shock.

down the shift in the *IS* and the interest rate the central bank sets. By drawing a line through the period 0 interest rate at the central bank's desired output gap and the initial equilibrium (i.e. between point *D* and *A*), we have the path along which the interest rate will be adjusted on the return to equilibrium. This is the *RX* curve. Section 9.5.4 provides more discussion of the geometry of parameter changes in the *RX* diagram.

### 9.5.3 Derivation of $(1 - \lambda)$ and its properties

$(1 - \lambda)$ represents the rate of decline of deviations of inflation from target and output from equilibrium. It is derived from the equations for the Phillips curve and the monetary rule as follows:

$$\left(\pi_t - \pi^T\right) = \left(\pi_{t-1} - \pi^T\right) - \alpha^2 \beta(\pi_t - \pi^T)$$

$$\rightarrow \frac{\left(\pi_t - \pi^T\right)}{\left(\pi_{t-1} - \pi^T\right)} = \frac{1}{1 + \alpha^2 \beta} \equiv \lambda = \frac{y_t - y_e}{y_{t-1} - y_e}.$$

In the previous section of the Appendix, we stated that it must be the case that the rate of interest will decline at a constant rate and at the same rate at which the output gap declines on the path down the *MR*. If you want to see why this is true, you can go through the argument here. Let $y$, $r$ and $q$ be in deviation form (i.e. the deviation from $y_e$, $r^*$ and $\bar{q}$ respectively. Let $r_t = \rho r_{t-1}$ and $y_t = \lambda y_{t-1}$ along the best response adjustment path. We show that $\rho = \lambda$.

From the *IS* equation, $y_{t+1} = -ar_t + bq_t$.

From the *UIP* condition, $-q_t = \sum_{i=0}^{\infty} r_{t+i} = r_t \left[ 1 + \rho + \rho^2 + ... \right] = \dfrac{r_t}{1 - \rho}$

$$\to y_{t+1} = -\left( a + \frac{b}{1 - \rho} \right) r_t$$

$$\to y_t = -\left( a + \frac{b}{1 - \rho} \right) r_{t-1}$$

$$\to \frac{y_{t+1}}{y_t} = \frac{r_t}{r_{t-1}}$$

$$\therefore \rho = \lambda.$$

### 9.5.4 Geometry of the *RX* curve: varying the parameters

The *RX* equation is

$$y_1 - y_e = -\left( a + \frac{b}{1 - \lambda} \right) (r_0 - r^*), \qquad \text{(RX equation)}$$

where

$$\lambda = \frac{1}{1 + \alpha^2 \beta}.$$

One way of developing an intuitive understanding of the effect of parameter changes on the central bank's best response to shocks in the open economy is to conduct experiments of varying the parameters. Variations in $a$ and $b$, the coefficients in the *IS* curve, have simple graphical representations: an increase in $a$ means that interest-sensitive expenditure responds more to changes in the interest rate, and the *IS* curve is flatter. This has the effect of reducing the interest rate and exchange rate responses, and a larger share of the output gap is accounted for by the interest rate component (which increases from $(r_0 - r^*)$ to $-a(r_0 - r^*)$). The *RX* curve is flatter.

If $b$ increases, aggregate demand is more sensitive to changes in the real exchange rate. Geometrically, the line with slope $\left( \frac{1-\lambda}{b} \right)$ becomes flatter. This lowers the initial interest rate chosen by the central bank and the associated exchange rate appreciation, and increases the share of the output gap accounted for by the exchange rate component. The *RX* curve is flatter.

If $\alpha$ or $\beta$ decrease, then the *MR* curve is steeper. This means a lower $(1 - \lambda)$ and a slower rate of decline of the output gaps on the path back to equilibrium. For example, the central bank's preferences are weighted less strongly toward reducing inflation—it is a 'wetter' central bank. In the *RX* equation, a slower rate of decline of the output gap has the same effect on the slope of the *RX* as a rise in $b$: i.e. it makes the *RX* flatter. If we compare two economies identical in every way except that the first has a less hard-nosed central bank (lower $\beta$), then in the face of the same inflation shock, the first will be observed to have a smaller output gap and a lower interest rate.

# 9.6 Questions

## 9.6.1 Checklist questions

1. Use a *UIP* diagram to illustrate the following cases. Discuss the adjustment process in each case and show how it relates to the *UIP* equation.

   (a) Home's interest rate falls below the world interest rate for one period.

   (b) The world interest rate increases for one period and the home economy raises their interest rate in line.

   (c) The foreign exchange market changes their expectation of the exchange rate in a year's time to a more depreciated exchange rate.

2. Answer the following questions about the supply and demand sides in the medium-run model:

   (a) What does the *ERU* curve represent? What would happen to the *ERU* curve if unemployment benefits were raised? What would you expect to happen to inflation?

   (b) What does the *AD* curve represent? Derive the *AD* curve graphically from the *IS* curve. [Hint: draw the *IS* diagram below the *AD* diagram and think about how changes in the real exchange rate affect the *IS* curve. To derive the *AD*, map the combinations of $q$ and $y$ on each *IS* curve at $r = r^*$.]

   (c) How does a rise in the world real interest rate affect the *AD* curve? What is the effect on the medium-run real exchange rate?

3. What conditions need to hold for a small open economy to be in medium-run equilibrium?

4. In a small open economy, is a negative supply shock or a negative demand shock more damaging for medium-run output? Explain in words and use $AD - ERU$ diagrams to back up your argument. Describe the effects on the real wage, unemployment and the real exchange rate in medium-run equilibrium of an increase in unemployment benefits.

5. Use the 3-equation open economy model to answer the following questions:

   (a) Explain what the following statement means: 'after a demand shock in a small open economy, the exchange rate often overshoots'. Use an $AD - ERU$ diagram to help explain your answer.

   (b) What causes exchange rate overshooting?

   (c) What problems, if any, would you expect exchange rate overshooting to cause?

   (d) How could you modify the 3-equation open economy model so that exchange rate overshooting does not occur? Explain in words.

6. Is the following statement true or false? Explain your answer. 'Central banks have to be more aggressive when making interest rate changes in the open economy because the *IS* curve is steeper than in the closed economy.'

7. Consider a large negative demand shock that hits two small economies. The economies are identical except that one is closed and the other is open. Answer the following:

   (a) Briefly explain how a large negative demand shock can lead to a deflation trap.

   (b) Which of the economies is more likely to fall into a deflation trap following the shock? Justify your answer.

(c) What initial conditions would make it likely that both economies would fall into a deflation trap?

8. Compare the decision making process taken by the central bank (and forex market in the open economy) in a closed and open economy after a permanent positive supply shock. Create a table similar to Table 9.2. How does the real interest rate in the new medium-run equilibrium compare in the two cases?

9. Explain what is meant by this statement: 'The behaviour of the nominal exchange rate in the model is a residual'.

10. This question uses material from Sections 9.5.2 and 9.5.4 of the Appendix. For a benchmark case, draw the $PC - MR$ and the $IS - RX$ diagrams after an inflation shock. Now increase the interest sensitivity of aggregate demand (i.e. $a$) and redraw the graphs. What has happened to $r_0$ and $q_0$? Explain your results.

## 9.6.2 Problems and questions for discussion

1. 'Following an announcement from the Riksbank (the Swedish central bank) of an interest rate increase, an immediate depreciation of the Krona was observed'. How can you explain this outcome? In your answer explain the economics of the $UIP$ condition. Summarize your findings highlighting the role played by expectations and communication by the central bank. You are advised to take the following steps and in each case to draw a $UIP$ diagram:

(a) Show the 'normal case' in which the central bank announcement is followed by an immediate appreciation of the Krona.

(b) Suppose the rise in the interest rate had been widely expected in financial markets. Show in the $UIP$ diagram that there would be no immediate change in the exchange rate when the Riksbank made its announcement.

(c) Finally, show how an immediate depreciation in the Krona can be explained.

2. The Bank of England keeps a directory of the minutes from the monthly meetings of their Monetary Policy Committee online:
(http://www.bankofengland.co.uk/monetarypolicy/pages/decisions/decisions.apx)

(a) Pick a period following a shock such as after September 11th 2001 or following the 2008–09 financial crisis, and see how the Bank of England comments on the interaction between the interest rates they set and the UK pound exchange rate. Are interest rate differentials thought to be causing movements in the exchange rate? If not, then does the movement of exchange rates invalidate the $UIP$ condition?

(b) Find some news articles from the same period that talk about the reactions of the foreign exchange market (useful sources for market news include the Financial Times, Reuters and Bloomberg). Did the forex market anticipate changes in interest rates before they happened? If so, were their predictions proved correct?

3. Assume you are in a small open economy with flexible exchange rates. The economy experiences a permanent positive demand shock.

(a) Draw the $PC - MR$, the $IS - RX$ and the $AD - ERU$ diagrams to help you explain the path back to medium-run equilibrium.

(b) Draw a graph of the real exchange rate over time and give a brief explanation of its path.

(c) How does the medium-run equilibrium vary from that which would occur in a closed economy subjected to the same shock?

4. This question uses the Macroeconomic Simulator available from the Carlin and Soskice website http://www.oup.com/uk/orc/carlin_soskice to model supply-side reform in the open economy. Start by opening the simulator and choosing the open economy (flexible exchange rate) version. Then reset all shocks by clicking the appropriate button on the left hand side of the main page. Use the simulator and the content of this chapter to work through the following questions:

(a) Decide on a supply-side reform and describe briefly how it is modelled—i.e. does it affect the *WS* or *PS*? What effect does this have on the *ERU* curve?

(b) Apply a permanent 2% positive supply shock. (Note that a positive supply shock is one that reduces equilibrium unemployment; raises equilibrium employment.)

(c) Use the impulse response functions from the simulator or from your sketches to help explain the path of the economy following the above shock.

(d) Draw the *IS − RX* and *PC − MR* diagrams for this scenario. Draw the *AD − ERU* diagram for this scenario. [Hint: the path of the key variables (output, inflation, real interest rate, real exchange rate) will have to match the impulse response functions from the simulator. Remember that whenever the central bank sets the interest rate different from $r^*$ to get the economy on to the *MR* curve, the economy will be *off* the *AD* curve. Once the economy is back at a MRE, then $r = r^*$ and the economy is, once again, *on* the *AD* curve.]

(e) Briefly discuss one aspect of this way of modelling the adjustment of the economy to a supply-side reform that seems to you to be unrealistic. Express your concern in terms of the assumptions of the model.

5. This question uses material from Sections 9.5.2 and 9.5.4 of the Appendix. The parameters that underlie the economy are $a = b = \alpha = \beta = 1$, which implies that $\lambda = 0.5$. The economy is initially in equilibrium and experiences a positive inflation shock. Use the steps set out in Section 9.5.2 to graphically derive the *RX* curve. [Hint: you will need pick the initial equilibrium $r^*$ and use a grid to ensure accurate measurements.] What is the new $r_0$?

# 10 The open economy: the demand and supply sides

## 10.1 Overview

In Chapter 9, we extended the 3-equation model to the open economy to show how an inflation-targeting central bank interacts with the foreign exchange market in response to shocks to the economy. In this chapter, we look more carefully at how trade and capital market openness affect the demand and supply sides of the economy.

The world economy has become increasingly integrated since the Second World War. This process of globalization has seen a surge in trade and international capital flows, which has fundamentally changed the way goods and services are produced and consumed. Think for a minute about an item of clothing. In the past, clothing worn in the United States was often manufactured and sold inside the country by American firms. Now, however, even in a large country, the supply chain is likely to be much more international. For example, an item of clothing could use textiles from Bangladesh, be assembled in China to a French design using machinery manufactured in Germany and be transported via Hong Kong. And when the clothing finally arrives on the US high street it could be sold by a French clothing company. This is a stylized example of a modern day supply chain, which uses the comparative advantages of different countries to ensure goods (of a given quality) are produced as cheaply and efficiently as possible. We could tell an equally globalized story about how the finance was raised for each stage of the production process.

We begin with some data illustrating how the openness of economies to trade and how international capital flows have changed over recent decades. Figure 10.1 shows how external trade and financial flows have evolved in the post-World War II period. Trade openness is usually measured by the sum of exports and imports as a percentage of GDP, $((X + M)/GDP)$. Trade in the six major economies shown in Fig. 10.1 has steadily increased, albeit experiencing a temporary contraction during the recent financial crisis.

The cross-country patterns are interesting: for example, the UK's trade openness remained remarkably stable from the early 1970s at about 40% of GDP. By contrast, in two of the world's most export-oriented large economies, China from the early 1980s and Germany from the early 1990s, openness rose strongly to peak just before the global financial crisis at respectively 60% and 70% of GDP. India remains a much more closed economy than China, although the growth in international integration in the 2000s left it more open than the USA, the least open of the major economies.

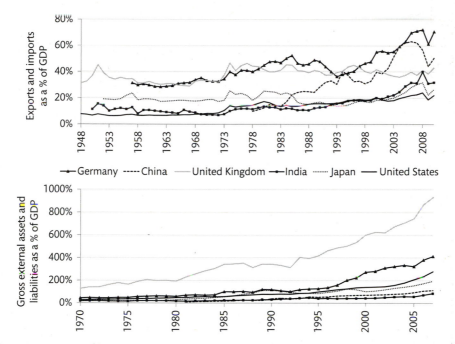

**Figure 10.1** Exports and imports as a percentage of GDP: 1948–2010 (upper panel) and gross external assets and liabilities as a percentage of GDP: 1970–2007 (lower panel).

*Source:* IMF International Financial Statistics (accessed September 2011); updated and extended version of dataset constructed by Lane and Milesi-Ferretti (2007).

The lower panel in Fig. 10.1 displays a commonly used indicator of financial globalization: gross external assets plus liabilities as a percentage of GDP. Historically, financial openness in the UK has been higher than elsewhere; however, all the economies in the sample have become more financially open over time, spurred by financial deregulation, which started in earnest in the late 1980s. Digging a little deeper into the underlying data shows that there was a dramatic build-up of cross-border debt financing in many of the developed economies over the last 20 years.[1] In contrast, China accumulated $1.5 trillion of foreign exchange reserves by 2007, largely as a by-product of its interrelated export-led growth strategy and exchange rate policy. Against the background of the increasingly integrated global economy, we clarify how openness affects the macro model.

### 10.1.1  The open economy accounting framework

The balance of payments accounts provide a useful way of clarifying important open economy concepts. The open economy accounting framework helps us to understand the sense in which changes in a country's external balance are of interest to a policy maker. The

---

[1] See the updated and extended version of the dataset, which was released in August 2009 and is available from Philip Lane's personal website: http://www.philiplane.org/EWN.html.

transactions between the home country and the rest of the world are recorded in the balance of payments account, which is divided into the current account and the capital and financial account.

The **trade balance** records the receipts from export sales less payments for imported goods and services, this is $BT \equiv X - M$.

The **current account** consists of the trade balance plus net interest and profit receipts. The current account reflects the fact that home and foreign residents can receive income, such as interest and profit payments, from assets that they own in each other's countries. Specifically, net interest and profit receipts in the home country's balance of payments accounts arise from earnings from foreign assets (e.g. bonds, equities) that are owned by residents of the home country less payments of interest and profit to foreigners who own home country assets.

The **capital and financial account** records changes in the stock of various types of foreign assets owned by home residents, home assets owned by overseas residents and changes in official foreign exchange reserves of the central bank.

To understand the balance of payments accounts, it is useful to separate the private and official parts of the capital account.

$$BP \equiv \left( \underbrace{(X - M)}_{\text{trade balance}} + \text{ net interest receipts} \right)$$

$$\underbrace{\phantom{(X - M) + \text{ net interest receipts}}}_{\text{current account, } CA}$$

$$+ \underbrace{(\text{private net capital inflows} - \text{change in official foreign exchange reserves})}_{\text{capital account}}$$

$$\equiv (BT + INT) + (F - \Delta R) \equiv 0,$$

where $BT$ is the balance of trade and $INT$ is net receipts of factor income from abroad. $F$ records private net capital inflows and $\Delta R$ is the change in official foreign exchange reserves. We have so far concentrated our open economy analysis on flexible exchange rate economies. To understand the role played by $\Delta R$ in the balance of payment accounts, however, we need to think about the two polar exchange rate regimes; *fully flexible* and *fixed*.

At one end of the spectrum of exchange rate regimes is the freely floating, *fully flexible* one (as seen in the previous chapter). In this case, neither the government nor central bank intervenes in the foreign exchange market to influence the price at which one currency trades with another. The exchange rate is then determined by supply and demand for that currency relative to other currencies. As discussed in the previous chapter, supply and demand of different currencies are in turn the outcome of foreign exchange traders' responses to news about interest rates and other economic developments that are viewed as influencing future interest rates and the longer run trajectory of the exchange rate. Under flexible exchange rates, the exchange rate is determined by market forces and there is no official intervention, which means that $\Delta R = 0$.

In a *fixed* exchange rate regime, the nominal exchange rate is kept fixed at a certain level (i.e. $e \equiv \frac{\text{home curr.}}{\text{foreign curr.}} = \text{constant}$) as a result of government policy. The home country's exchange rate is 'pegged' at a fixed rate to another country's currency (e.g. the Hong Kong dollar is pegged to the US dollar) or to a so-called 'basket' of other currencies. In the face of shifts in the demand for and supply of home's currency in the foreign exchange market, the government must actively intervene in the market (i.e. buy and sell foreign exchange) to keep the rate pegged. The purchase of foreign exchange by the home central bank is $\Delta R > 0$ and the sale of foreign exchange is $\Delta R < 0$. A central bank would buy foreign exchange to increase the supply of home currency in the market if excess demand for the home currency in the market is causing pressure for it to appreciate (and vice versa). An example of this would be the People's Bank of China buying US dollars in order to stop the yuan appreciating against the US dollar. If the government wishes to change the exchange rate peg, it announces the new rate at which it is prepared to buy and sell the home currency. It is a revaluation if it intervenes to support a rate where fewer units of home currency can be bought for one unit of foreign currency; the converse is a devaluation.

The balance of payments records the *sources* and *uses* of foreign exchange and sums to zero.[2] If there is a trade surplus, then exports exceed imports. This means that the home economy is increasing its wealth. The balance of payments identity helps explain this. The current account surplus is a source of foreign exchange. Something must be done with it, and the balance of payments identity highlights that it must either be used to purchase foreign assets or to increase home's foreign exchange reserves.[3] Both of these represent more wealth for the home economy because the assets can be used at a later date to increase consumption. The converse is true for a country running a deficit: its wealth is falling (or equivalently, its debt to the rest of the world is increasing).

A moment's reflection will suggest that running a trade deficit is not necessarily a problem. For example, a country with a trade deficit may be fast-growing with lots of highly profitable investment opportunities: being able to borrow from abroad allows it to take advantage of these opportunities. Equally, a country with a trade surplus may be slow-growing, and the opportunity to lend abroad enables its residents to take advantage of investment opportunities in other countries, which are better than those at home.

When analysing performance in a particular economy, it is important to bear in mind that trade or current account imbalances may reflect the optimizing behaviour of forward-looking agents, including governments, but they may not. For example, a trade deficit may reflect weak competitiveness, and high levels of private or government consumption (i.e. low savings rather than high investment). These are all reasons for monitoring the trade balance in our analysis of the open economy.

### 10.1.2  The demand side, trade balance and the supply side

*The demand side and trade balance*

What affects our demand for foreign goods and services and the demand of foreign residents for our tradable products? As noted in Chapter 9, one obvious influence is 'relative prices'. If our goods are relatively expensive, then demand for them by foreigners will be reduced and home residents will tend to buy more imported goods. In order to compare prices across

---

[2] In practice, the records are incomplete, with the result that an entry for errors and omissions has to be added to make the balance of payments sum to zero.

[3] At first sight it may seem paradoxical that a negative $F$ in the balance of payments represents home's *purchase* of foreign assets—but the purchase of foreign assets is a use of foreign exchange and therefore has a negative value in the balance of payments accounts.

countries, we need to convert them to a common currency, producing a measure of price competitiveness, which we call $Q$. As discussed in Chapter 9, $Q$ is the price of foreign goods expressed in home currency divided by the price of home goods, which are also expressed in home currency, $Q \equiv \frac{P^*e}{P}$. Higher $Q$ is a real depreciation for home—an improvement in its competitiveness, because its goods are cheaper relative to those of the rest or the world. Just as in the case of the nominal exchange rate, it is safest to avoid using the terms 'rise' or 'fall' or 'high' or 'low' in relation to the real exchange rate. It is better to stick to the terms 'appreciation' or 'depreciation'.

Of particular importance is the relationship between changes in the real exchange rate and the trade balance. In Chapter 9, we assumed that if the home economy's competitiveness improved, i.e. its real exchange rate depreciated, net exports would rise, shifting the *IS* curve to the right. In this chapter, we will show why it is reasonable to make that assumption. In doing so, we will highlight the two-sided character of exchange rate depreciation. The first is the link from the real exchange rate to competitiveness via the demand for exports and imports. As we saw in the previous chapter, an improvement in home's competitiveness increases exports because foreigners find our goods and services more attractive and it depresses imports, because home residents also switch toward home-produced output. The combination of more exports and less imports improves the trade balance.

However, there is another effect of an exchange rate depreciation. Why does a real depreciation lead home residents to switch away from imports? The answer is because they have become more expensive. Since a given volume of imports will be more expensive, there will be a second influence of the depreciation on the trade balance, one that worsens it. The two effects of a real depreciation on the trade balance go in opposite directions—the first improves it and the second causes a deterioration. The first effect is called the *volume* effect because it relates to how the quantities of imports and exports respond to the change in competitiveness. The second effect is called the *relative price* or *terms of trade effect* because it relates to the effect on a given volume of imports of the change in the relative price between home-produced and foreign goods. Which effect is stronger?

We can think this through intuitively as follows. When the exchange rate depreciates, say, by 10%, this will raise the cost to the home economy of a given volume of imports by 10%. They are 10% more expensive. For the volume effect to outweigh the depressing effect of the higher cost of imports on the trade balance overall, the boost to export volumes and the fall in import volumes must add up to more than 10%. This result is called the Marshall–Lerner condition. Fortunately the empirical evidence of its validity is reasonably clear-cut: the volume effect is strong enough to outweigh the terms of trade effect, so we can be confident that a real depreciation improves the balance of trade. As long as the Marshall–Lerner condition holds—and we will assume it always does—a rise in $Q$, i.e. a real depreciation or an improvement in home's competitiveness, increases net exports and shifts the *IS* curve to the right.

### The supply side in the open economy

In Chapter 9, we assumed that wage setting was based on real wages defined in terms of the domestic price level. In this chapter, we relax that assumption to explore how changes in import prices may affect the supply side and equilibrium unemployment. In the closed economy model and in the open economy model of Chapter 9 with a vertical *ERU* curve, the economy can only move to a new medium-run equilibrium with lower unemployment if there are supply shocks or policy reforms that have the effect of shifting the *WS* curve downwards or the *PS* curve upwards. We shall see that when wage-setting behaviour is defined by real wages, including the import component of the bundle of goods and services that households consume, the *ERU* curve is downward sloping. In this case, shifts in aggregate demand can also lead to new medium-run equilibria with constant inflation.

If the *ERU* curve is downward sloping, shifts in aggregate demand can move the economy to another constant inflation equilibrium. The intuition is that a positive aggregate demand shock can be associated with a new constant inflation equilibrium at lower unemployment and an appreciated real exchange rate. This is because the lower real cost of imports, due to the appreciation, allows real wages to rise: hence there can be a new $WS - PS$ intersection at lower unemployment, higher real wages, lower import costs and unchanged firm profit margins. The *PS* curve will shift up showing that workers get higher real consumption wages following a real appreciation. Wage and price setters will be content and there will be no pressure for inflation to change.

### The medium-run model: AD — BT — ERU

In Chapter 9, we introduced the $AD - ERU$ model to show how shifts in aggregate demand or supply-side shocks affected the real exchange rate in the constant inflation equilibrium. A positive aggregate demand shock was associated with an appreciated real exchange rate and vice versa. We can now include the more general downward-sloping *ERU* curve.

We also include the *BT* curve, to show the trade balance explicitly. The *BT* curve is upward sloping in the diagram with output on the horizontal axis and the real exchange rate on the vertical. Above the *BT* line, there is a trade surplus (lower competitiveness and/or higher output to boost imports is needed to get to balanced trade) and below the *BT* line there is a trade deficit (higher competitiveness and/or lower output to dampen imports is needed to balance trade). We can explain intuitively why the *BT* curve will be flatter than the *AD* curve—we set out the argument systematically in the modelling section. A real depreciation boosts net exports and raises aggregate demand. If the economy is initially in trade balance, then the question we must answer is whether at the new goods market equilibrium, there is a trade surplus. If so, then the economy must be above the *BT* curve and the *BT* must therefore be flatter than the *AD* curve. The answer is that there is a trade surplus at the new equilibrium, because the boost to net exports caused by the depreciation will raise output through the multiplier process. However, the multiplier process will not drive output up by enough to lead to increased imports equal to the boost to net exports due to the depreciation. This is because only a proportion of any increase in output is spent on imported goods.

Figure 10.2 uses the medium-run model to look at the predicted effects of demand shocks, supply shocks and policy reforms. We can see that, in contrast to the model with a vertical *ERU*, demand shocks as well as supply shocks are associated with changes in the equilibrium level of output if the *ERU* curve is downward sloping.

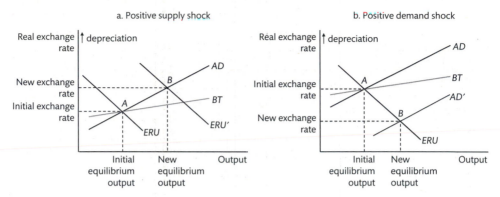

**Figure 10.2** The response of an economy with a downward-sloping *ERU* curve to economic shocks
a. Positive supply shock
b. Positive demand shock.

From the 1980s onwards, weaker trade unions in some countries and greater coordination among wage setters in others, and increased competition in the product market can be modelled by a rightward shift of the *ERU* curve. If we keep the demand side unchanged, then policies and structural reforms that shift the *ERU* to the right will be associated with lower equilibrium unemployment, a depreciated real exchange rate and an improvement in the trade balance (as shown in Fig. 10.2a).

Figure 10.2b shows that a positive demand shock boosts output and appreciates the real exchange rate. Examples where domestic demand shocks and appreciated real exchange rates appear to have been important in the 2000s include countries with private sector demand shocks (such as those with strong leverage cycles, like Spain or Ireland) or with expansionary government fiscal policies (such as the UK government's increased spending on health and education under Prime Minister Tony Blair, or the US government's tax cuts and increased military spending under President George W. Bush). If the demand shock is domestic— whether private or public—it will be associated with a deterioration of the country's external balance. A positive demand shock is modelled by a rightward shift in the *AD* curve.

Figure 10.3 shows key macroeconomic indicators for Spain and the UK in 1999 and 2007. One interpretation of the evolution of the Spanish economy over this period is that a large property bubble in the pre-recession years was responsible for the combination of lower unemployment, a more appreciated real exchange rate and a serious deterioration in the current account balance. The indicators for Spain are consistent with it experiencing a positive demand shock as shown in Fig. 10.2b. For the UK case, the data also suggest a positive demand shock played a role in the evolution of the economy in the pre-crisis years. In addition, the UK is expected to have benefitted from the lagged effects of supply-side reforms initiated under Prime Minister Thatcher in the 1980s. It is important to note that, even in the face of positive demand shocks, inflation remained low and stable in both economies. This is consistent with the presence of multiple constant inflation equilibria in the medium-run model with a downward-sloping *ERU* curve. The experience of the British economy during the Great Moderation is the subject of a case study in Section 10.3.

| | Spain | | UK | |
|---|---|---|---|---|
| | 1999 | 2007 | 1999 | 2007 |
| Unemployment rate (%) | 12.5 | 8.3 | 5.9 | 5.3 |
| Inflation rate (%) | 2.2 | 2.8 | 1.3 | 2.3 |
| Real exchange rate (1999 = 100); rise in the index is a real appreciation | 100 | 125 | 100 | 109 |
| Current account balance (% of GDP) | −2.7 | −8.8 | −1.8 | −2.8 |

**Figure 10.3** Macroeconomic indicators for the UK and Spain: 1999 and 2007.

*Source:* IMF World Economic Outlook, April 2011; OECD Economic Outlook Annex Tables, 2012.

## 10.2 Modelling

This section provides the detail behind the discussion in Section 10.1. We divide the modelling section into three subsections. The first covers the demand side. In the previous chapter, we used a simple *IS* equation to underpin the 3-equation model. In this chapter, we derive the open economy *IS* curve, paying particular attention to the relationship between the real exchange rate and the trade balance.

The second subsection covers the supply side and fills in the details behind the derivation of a downward-sloping *ERU* curve. We extend the model presented in the last chapter by assuming that wage setting is based on the real consumption wage. The real consumption wage is calculated by using the prices of both domestically-produced and imported goods. We shall see that this means the *PS* curve shifts with changes in the real cost of imports (i.e. the real exchange rate) and the *ERU* curve becomes downward sloping, which results in multiple levels of output being consistent with constant inflation.

The last subsection combines both the supply and demand sides into a new medium-run model. We use the *AD − BT − ERU* model to show the medium-run implications of supply and demand shocks and why current account imbalances of the kind observed in the years before the global financial crisis can persist in medium-run equilibrium.

### 10.2.1 The demand side and trade balance

**Summary**

In this subsection, four results about the demand side and the trade balance are explained. These results are used in both the open economy 3-equation model and in the *AD − BT − ERU* model. Readers familiar with these results can skim this section and go on to Section 10.2.2.

1. The open economy *IS* curve is steeper (a given fall in the real interest rate is associated with a smaller increase in output in the open economy). The reason is that the size of the multiplier is reduced in the open economy because of the marginal propensity to import. As income rises, not only do taxation and savings rise, but so does the level of imports. We show the results using a simple Keynesian consumption function. As explained in Chapter 1, due to the presence of credit constraints and uncertainty about whether income shocks are

temporary or permanent, a model that includes permanent income behaviour is also likely to have a sizeable multiplier, which will be dampened by the marginal propensity to import.

2. The open economy *IS* curve shifts in response to changes in the real exchange rate ($Q$) and world output ($y^*$). A depreciation of home's real exchange rate (i.e. an improvement in home's price competitiveness) or a rise in $y^*$ shifts the *IS* to the right. If the Marshall–Lerner condition holds, this boosts the trade balance and aggregate demand. The Marshall–Lerner condition says that the effects of an exchange rate depreciation in raising the volume of exports and reducing the volume of imports outweigh the terms of trade effect, which will increase the value of the import bill. A rise in world demand increases net exports. For any interest rate, goods market equilibrium will therefore occur at a higher level of output and the trade balance improves.

3. Although both a real depreciation and a rise in world demand raise output and improve the trade balance (at a given interest rate), there is an important difference between the cases. Depreciation entails a deterioration in home's terms of trade, which means higher import costs and lower living standards in the home economy.

4. Following a depreciation of the real exchange rate, there will be a trade surplus at the new goods market equilibrium. The increase in output at the new goods market equilibrium is equal to the multiplier times the boost to net exports caused by the depreciation. The increase in balanced trade output is equal to the reciprocal of the marginal propensity to import times the boost to net exports. Since the multiplier is smaller than the reciprocal of the marginal propensity to import, the goods market equilibrium is at a lower income level than the new balanced trade level of output: hence there is a trade surplus (see the equations for the goods market equilibrium and the trade balance).

**Goods market equilibrium in the open economy**

Recall the goods market equilibrium condition from Chapter 1:

$$y = y^D,$$

where $y$ is output and $y^D$ is aggregate demand. In the closed economy aggregate demand is:

$$y^D = c_0 + c_1(1 - t)y + I(r) + G.$$

Introducing trade in goods and services has two effects. First, demand for home's output is boosted by demand from abroad, in the form of exports, $X$. Second, it is dampened by goods imported from abroad, $M$, which substitute for domestic output. Remember that $(C + I + G)$ measures total spending by home agents on consumption, investment and government purchases *irrespective* of the origin of the goods or services. To calculate *total* demand for *home* produced goods and services, $y^D$, we subtract spending on imports, $M$, and add foreign demand for exports, $X$:

$$y^D = (C + I(r) + G) - M + X \equiv (C + I(r) + G) + BT,$$

(aggregate demand , open economy)

where the trade balance, $BT \equiv X - M$, is also called net exports.

To begin with, we assume that exports are exogenous and that imports depend only on the level of domestic output or income. We define exports and imports as

$$X = \overline{X} \text{ and } M = my,$$

where $m$ is a constant between 0 and 1 and is called the marginal propensity to import. At this stage, we keep the models as simple as possible so that we can highlight a key difference between the open and closed economy $IS$ curves: the size of the multiplier.

The economy is in goods market equilibrium when output and aggregate demand are equal, $y = y^D$:

$$y = y^D = c_0 + c_1(1-t)y + I(r) + G + \overline{X} - my. \tag{10.1}$$

Collecting the terms in $y$ on the left hand side and rearranging gives the goods market equilibrium condition in the form: output is equal to the multiplier times the exogenous components of demand plus investment at a given real interest rate. Thus:

$$y = \underbrace{\frac{1}{1 - c_1(1-t) + m}}_{\text{multiplier}} \left( c_0 + I(r) + G + \overline{X} \right), \qquad \text{(goods market equilibrium)}$$

If we compare the open economy multiplier to its closed economy counterpart (introduced in Chapter 1), we can see that the open economy multiplier is lower because of the marginal propensity to import, $m$:

$$\underbrace{\frac{1}{1 - c_1(1-t) + m}}_{\text{open economy multiplier}} < \underbrace{\frac{1}{1 - c_1(1-t)}}_{\text{closed economy multiplier}}. \tag{10.2}$$

When exogenous spending goes up, output rises by less than in the closed economy because some of the demand is satisfied by imports rather than by domestic production. This also means that output reacts less to any given change in the real interest rate in the open economy (all other things held constant)—hence, the open economy $IS$ curve is steeper.

### Exchange rates and competitiveness

*Price and cost competitiveness*

Since relative prices, $Q \equiv \frac{P^*e}{P}$, affect net exports, we need to know how they are set in the open economy and how they are related to costs. Given that firms normally operate under imperfect competition and thus face downward-sloping demand curves, we assume that firms set home prices on the basis of home costs using the price-setting rule for the closed economy explained in Chapter 2.

But when it comes to foreign markets, two alternative pricing rules for exports are suggested:

1. the first—*home-cost pricing*—is that firms set export prices in the same way as for goods sold at home, i.e. based on domestic costs;

2. the second—*world pricing*—is that firms set export prices based on the prices of similar products produced abroad.

To see how these differ, imagine there is an increase in costs in the home country but not abroad (and assume that the nominal exchange rate remains unchanged).

1.  Under the first pricing hypothesis, home's exports rise in price relative to the price of the output of firms abroad. Higher home costs make it less competitive, which represents a real appreciation for the home country ($\downarrow Q$).

2.  Under world pricing, export prices do not change, because by assumption prices in the foreign market are unchanged. In this case, there is no change in the *price* competitiveness of exports. However, we would expect higher home costs to affect the ability of home firms to compete internationally. If the costs of home firms rise relative to their competitors but prices are unchanged, then the profit margins of home firms are squeezed. This means home firms will be at a relative disadvantage in their access to internal finance to fund future investment, marketing, research and development or after-sales service. Although price competitiveness is maintained, 'non-price competitiveness' is reduced.

This suggests that an alternative way of defining the real exchange rate is based on relative *costs* rather than relative *prices*. One commonly used measure of competitiveness is called relative unit labour costs or *RULC* and is defined as follows:

$$RULC \equiv \frac{\text{foreign unit labour costs expressed in home currency}}{\text{home unit labour costs}}$$

$$\equiv \frac{ULC^* e}{ULC}. \qquad \text{(cost competitiveness; real exchange rate)}$$

Higher home costs reduce home's competitiveness: ($\downarrow RULC$): this is a real appreciation for home.[4]

### The Law of One Price and Absolute Purchasing Power Parity

The two pricing rules can be compared to the so-called Law of One Price (LOP) and to the hypothesis of Purchasing Power Parity (PPP). According to the Law of One Price, the common currency price of a traded good is identical in different countries. For any good, $j$, that is traded,

$$P_j = P_j^* e.$$

The logic of the LOP is straightforward: international trade should have the effect of equalizing prices for the same good in different countries, since as long as transport costs are not too high, profits can be made by transporting a good from a location where the price is low and selling it where the price is high. This process of arbitrage would tend to equalize the prices in the two locations. If the LOP holds for all goods *and* the same basket of goods is consumed in different countries, then this basket of goods will have the same common currency price

---

[4] Just as is the case with the price-based measure of the real exchange rate, conventions vary. Sometimes RULC is defined with home costs in the numerator, in which case a rise in RULC is a deterioration of home's competitiveness and hence a real appreciation.

anywhere in the world. This is referred to as Absolute Purchasing Power Parity. if for all goods $j$ in a basket of goods that is common to consumers in both countries,

$P_j = P_j^* e$ for all goods $j$, then $P = P^* e$

$\implies Q = 1.$                                 (Absolute Purchasing Power Parity)

The hypothesis of Absolute Purchasing Power Parity implies that the real exchange rate is always equal to one. If we add the assumption of perfect competition, then since under perfect competition, price is equal to marginal cost, marginal costs will be equalized in all countries and there will be no supernormal (i.e. economic) profits. Hence, unlike the world pricing hypothesis discussed above, where costs can differ across countries and profit margins can expand and contract, in a world of Absolute PPP and perfect competition, neither price nor cost competitiveness can vary.

The empirical evidence is not supportive of the LOP or Absolute PPP. Transport costs and barriers to international trade interfere with the LOP, and the presence of non-traded goods and services in the consumption bundle and differences in consumer tastes across countries prevent the Absolute Purchasing Power Parity hypothesis from holding. In evaluating the accumulated evidence, Obstfeld argues that '[a]pparently consumer markets for tradables are just about as segmented internationally as consumer markets for nontradables'.[5]

The main reason is that international markets are imperfectly competitive. Most tradables—both goods and services—are differentiated products, and producers pursue pricing strategies to maximize their long-run profits. For example, firms set different prices in different markets to take advantage of variations in the elasticity of demand. An extensive survey of pricing strategies is provided by Goldberg and Knetter.[6] They report evidence of the widespread use of so-called pricing to market and of the incomplete pass-through of exchange rate changes into prices: 'world pricing' incorporates both these effects.

In reality, firms' pricing strategies lie between the two alternatives of home-cost based and world pricing presented above. Fortunately, the main results of the macro model do not depend on which of these simple pricing hypotheses is used: the way that shocks and policy responses are transmitted varies, but the qualitative results are similar.

One of the big facts that has emerged since the era of floating exchange rates began in 1973 is that the fluctuations in nominal exchange rates have been accompanied by fluctuations in real exchange rates. To quote Obstfeld's evaluation of the evidence: 'Real exchange rate variability tends to be almost a perfect reflection of nominal rate variability, with changes in the two rates highly correlated and independent movements in price levels playing a minor, if any, role'.[7] A simple explanation is that nominal exchange rates are volatile and prices are sticky because they are based on the price-setting strategies of imperfectly competitive firms. Figure 10.4 illustrates this for the UK, where we see that the sharp nominal depreciation of sterling during the financial crisis was tracked closely by the real depreciation.

An appropriate model should accommodate this fact. Either the home-cost or world pricing rule would do (LOP plus perfect competition, i.e. Absolute PPP, will not). We stick to the home-cost pricing rule because it conveniently allows us to use the real exchange rate

[5] See p. 16 of Obstfeld (2001).     [6] See Goldberg and Knetter (1997).     [7] See p. 14 of Obstfeld (2001).

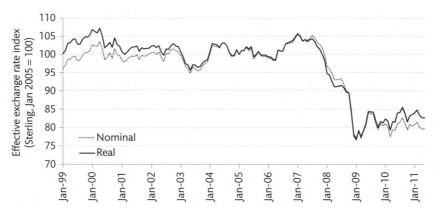

**Figure 10.4** UK nominal and real effective exchange rates indices (2005 = 100: 1999-2011).

*Note:* An increase in the index is an appreciation.

*Source:* Bank of England; IMF International Financial Statistics (data accessed Sept 2011).

defined in terms of price competitiveness. The assumption that prices are set by home costs implies that the price level of home-produced goods sold at home and in the export market is the same, and that the price in home currency of imports is set by the price in the rest of the world (i.e. by costs in those economies). After summarizing the evidence, Obstfeld states: 'These relationships are consistent with a model in which domestic marginal cost (consisting mainly of wages) is sticky in domestic-currency terms, and export prices are set as a (perhaps somewhat variable) mark-up over marginal cost.'[8]

Hence we have:

$$P_X = P = (1 + \mu) \cdot \text{unit cost} \qquad \text{(export price)}$$
$$P_M = P^*e, \qquad \text{(import price)}$$

where $\mu$ is the mark-up. This means that exports prices are set as a mark-up on domestic unit labour costs.

### The two sides of exchange rate depreciation

In this section, we set out the details of the two-sided character of changes in the real exchange rate, which was introduced in Section 10.1. On the one hand, a real depreciation makes our goods more attractive in export markets and makes imports less attractive to home consumers. Being more competitive sounds like good news. But on the other hand, a real depreciation means that any volume of imports that we buy is more expensive—this is the bad news. The first effect boosts the export industries and aggregate demand, but the second reduces real wages and living standards. The two effects push the trade balance in different directions: the first effect improves the trade balance but the second worsens it.

---

[8] See p. 24 of Obstfeld (2001).

By making some assumptions, we can give a definite answer to the question of whether a real depreciation improves the trade balance. This is called the Marshall–Lerner condition. The intuition is straightforward: if the effect of the depreciation in boosting the *volume* of net exports outweighs the fact that the import bill will go up one-for-one with the depreciation, then the trade balance improves. We shall see that another way of putting this is to say that if the sum of the price elasticities of demand for exports and imports is greater than one, the trade balance improves.

To show how the Marshall–Lerner condition works, we need to include the real exchange rate explicitly in the import and export functions. In the home market, home goods with price $P$ compete with imports (in home currency terms) with price $P^*e$. The relative price is therefore our measure of competitiveness, $Q \equiv \frac{P^*e}{P}$. In export markets, home produced goods (exports) with price $P$ compete with world goods priced (in home currency terms) at $P^*e$. Once again, the relative price is our measure of competitiveness, $Q$.

The nominal value of exports in home currency terms, $X_{nom}$, is equal to the price index of exports times the volume. The volume of exports can be expressed as a share of world output, where our share $\sigma$ (sigma) depends positively on competitiveness, and $y^*$ is world output:

$$X_{nom} = P_X \underbrace{\sigma\left(\frac{P^*e}{P}\right)}_{\text{home's share}} \underbrace{y^*}_{\text{world output}}.$$

To get the export function in real terms, we divide each side by the domestic price level, $P = P_X$:

$$X = \sigma\left(\frac{P^*e}{P}\right) y^* = \sigma(Q)y^*. \qquad \text{(export function)}$$

The value of imports $M_{nom}$ in home currency terms is the price index, $P_M = P^*e$ times the volume of imports. The volume depends on the marginal propensity to import, which will be a negative function of competitiveness, and on the level of domestic output.

$$M_{nom} = \underbrace{P_M \cdot m(Q)}_{\text{marginal propensity to import}} \cdot \underbrace{y}_{\text{home output}}.$$

To derive the import function in real terms, we divide each side by $P$.

$$\begin{aligned} M &= \frac{P_M}{P} m(Q)y \\ &= \frac{P^*e}{P} m(Q)y \\ &= Qm(Q)y. \qquad \text{(import function)} \end{aligned}$$

This means that the balance of trade is:

$$\begin{aligned} BT &= X - M \\ &= \underbrace{\sigma(Q)y^*}_{\text{volume}} - \underbrace{Q}_{\text{ToT}}\, \underbrace{m(Q)y}_{\text{volume}} \\ &= X(Q, y^*) - QM(Q, y). \qquad \text{(balance of trade)} \end{aligned}$$

The good news about a real depreciation for the home economy is the so-called volume effect and the bad news is the relative price, or terms of trade (ToT), effect. The volume effect is the effect on the volume of exports and of imports due to a change in $Q$. The volume effect is unambiguous: a rise in $Q$ boosts the volume of exports ($\sigma(Q)$ rises as home takes a larger share of world output) and reduces the volume of imports ($m(Q)$ falls as home's marginal propensity to import falls). But, a rise in $Q$ will raise the relative price of a given volume of imports.

Another way of expressing the 'relative price effect' of a change in $Q$ is to use the concept of the *terms of trade*. The terms of trade is defined as the price of exports divided by the price of imports:

$$\frac{P_X}{P_M} = \frac{P}{P^*e} = \frac{1}{Q},$$    (terms of trade)

where an increase in $\frac{P_X}{P_M}$ is an improvement in the terms of trade because a greater volume of imports can be bought for a given volume of exports. Conversely, an increase in $Q$ means a rise in the price of imports relative to exports: it is a deterioration in the terms of trade.[9] For a given volume of imports, this will produce a decline in the trade balance.

In summary, given the way that import and export prices are defined, a rise in $Q$ for the home economy is a

1.  rise in price competitiveness, which is the same thing as a depreciation of the real exchange rate

2.  deterioration in the terms of trade because it produces a rise in the real cost of imports.

As long as the volume effects are strong enough to outweigh the countervailing terms of trade effect, then a real depreciation (a rise in $Q$)—i.e. an improvement in home's price competitiveness—improves the trade balance. The converse is true for a real appreciation. This result is the famous Marshall–Lerner condition, which states that as long as the sum of the price elasticity of demand for exports and the price elasticity of demand for imports exceeds one, a depreciation will improve the balance of trade. The simplicity of the Marshall–Lerner condition depends on the assumption that goods are in perfectly elastic supply (i.e. the price does not change as output increases) and that we begin in trade balance, but the central insight of comparing the volume with the terms of trade effects is a general one.[10] There are many ways to prove the Marshall–Learner condition—one is shown in the Appendix to this chapter.

In the dynamic *IS* model introduced in Chapter 9, there is a one period lag from a change in the real exchange rate to the effect on output: this reflects the time for new orders to be placed and resources to be reallocated in response to the change in competitiveness.

---

[9] Our baseline pricing hypothesis is consistent with the evidence that a nominal depreciation is associated with a deterioration of home's terms of trade. See Obstfeld and Rogoff (2000b).

[10] It should be noted that the pricing assumptions that have been made imply that neither export nor import prices are affected by changes in the volume sold (within the range of variation considered). This is the traditional assumption made in the proof of the simple Marshall–Lerner condition that supply elasticities are infinite.

> ## Box 10.1  Numerical example of the Marshall–Lerner condition
>
> For example, suppose the home economy begins in trade balance with exports equal to imports, which are equal to 100. The elasticity of demand for exports is 0.75 and for imports is 0.50. Consider the implications of a 1% rise in competitiveness arising for example from a rise of 1% in foreign relative to domestic prices: export volume rises by 0.75 to 100.75; import volume falls by 0.50 to 99.50; the real price of imports rises by 1%, pushing the import bill up to 100.495 (since $1.01 \times 99.5 = 100.495$). In this case, the balance of trade improves because $BT = 100.75 - 100.495 = 0.255$.
>
> If, on the other hand, export demand elasticity was considerably lower at just 0.25, export volume would only rise by 0.25 to 100.25. Everything else stays the same so the balance of trade actually deteriorates ($BT = 100.25 - 100.495 = -0.245$).
>
> The elasticities used in the example are more 'pessimistic' than the consensus estimates from empirical studies. Dornbusch reports estimates for the absolute value of the price elasticity of demand for exports of 1.06 in Germany, 1.31 in the USA, and 1.68 in Japan and for imports of 0.50 in Germany, 0.97 in Japan, and 1.35 in the USA.[a] The requirement that the sum of the price elasticities of demand is greater than one is easily met for each of these countries.
>
> [a] See Dornbusch (1996).

In our model of the open economy, we assume the trade balance improves with a depreciation of the real exchange rate, given the level of output—i.e. we assume the Marshall–Lerner condition holds.

Empirical studies generally provide support for the Marshall–Lerner condition. The caveat to this result is that in the very short run when contracts are already in place, the volume effect is minimal but the terms of trade effect operates fully: this means that in the short run a real depreciation typically depresses the trade balance. This is referred to as the J-curve effect. The trade balance can worsen in the short run, for two reasons:

1. The short-run price elasticity of demand for exports and imports is much lower (approximately one half) its long-run value. This means that the volume response to the depreciation is initially weak.

2. To the extent that exports are invoiced in domestic currency, the dollar value of exports falls immediately, while imports invoiced in foreign currency remain unchanged in dollar terms. In home currency terms, export receipts are unchanged while the import bill rises immediately. Hence the trade balance worsens.

### Real exchange rate and trade balance

A real depreciation raises net exports via the Marshall–Lerner condition; higher net exports in turn raise output and pull up imports. What is the overall—or general equilibrium—effect on the trade balance once we allow output to adjust?

The trade balance is:

$$BT = X - M \qquad \text{(trade balance)}$$

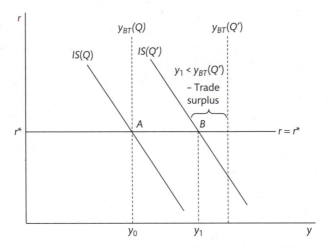

**Figure 10.5** Real depreciation ($\uparrow Q$): impact on output and the trade balance.

and we can therefore write the level of output at which trade is balanced (i.e. $BT = 0$), as $y_{BT}(Q, \sigma, y^*, m)$. A rise in price competitiveness increases the level of output at which trade is balanced and a higher level of world demand has the same effect: in each case the $y_{BT}$ line shifts to the right in the *IS* diagram. To the right of $y_{BT}$ there is a trade deficit and to the left there is a trade surplus.

What happens to output and the trade balance when the exchange rate depreciates, boosting net exports? The economy begins in goods market equilibrium and with balanced trade at $A$ in Fig. 10.5. The real depreciation from $Q$ to $Q'$ shifts both the *IS* curve and the $y_{BT}$ line to the right. We assume the interest rate remains unchanged at $r^*$. The rise in net exports due to the rise in $Q$ raises aggregate demand ($y^D$), which pushes up output and income until a new goods market equilibrium is established. This is where the higher savings, taxation *and* imports induced by the rise in exports are equal to the increase in demand: output rises from $y_0$ to $y_1$ in Fig. 10.5. At the new goods market equilibrium at $B$, output is to the left of the new $y_{BT}$ line (the level of income at which imports would be equal to exports at the depreciated exchange rate) and there is a trade surplus.

Another way to see this is to note that the increase in output at the new goods market equilibrium is equal to the multiplier times the boost to net exports caused by the depreciation. The increase in balanced trade output is equal to the reciprocal of the marginal propensity to import times the boost to net exports. Since the multiplier is smaller than the reciprocal of the marginal propensity to import, the goods market equilibrium is at a lower income level than the new balanced trade level of output: hence there is a trade surplus (see the equations for the goods market equilibrium and the trade balance).

## 10.2.2 The supply side in the open economy

### Multiple equilibria: a downward-sloping *ERU* curve

In Section 10.1, we introduced the logic of the existence of a range of constant inflation equilibrium unemployment rates in the open economy. In this section, we set out the derivation of the downward sloping *ERU* curve, beginning with the question of how workers calculate their real wage in the open economy. In the open economy we can no longer talk about a single price level. Assuming workers buy both home-produced and imported goods, the price level that is relevant in assessing the real value of nominal wages is the nominal wage in terms of consumer prices (i.e. $W/P_c$, where $P_c$ is the consumer price index). To define the consumer price index, $P_c$, it is assumed that consumers purchase a bundle of goods and services where the imported ones have a price of $P^*e$ and the home-produced ones have a price of $P$. The share of the consumption bundle that is imported we will call $\phi$, $\phi$ (pronounced 'phi') for 'foreign'. We assume that $\phi$ is constant for simplicity. The consumer price index is:

$$P_c = (1 - \phi)P + \phi P^*e.$$

Note that the standard of living of home households will fall if the prices of imported goods rise, even if the prices of home-produced goods remain fixed. This is because the real consumption wage, $W/P_c$, falls when $P_c$ increases. In Chapter 9, in order to focus on stabilization, we ignored this effect by assuming that workers defined the real wage relevant to wage setting only in terms of home-produced goods (i.e. $W/P$). This meant that the *WS* and *PS* curves were unchanged from the closed economy and there was a unique equilibrium unemployment rate and a vertical *ERU* curve.

We now look at the consequences for the medium-run model of taking on board the fact that the *WS* curve is defined in terms of the real consumption wage (i.e. $W/P_c$). The y-axis in the *WS* − *PS* diagram is now being defined in terms of $W/P_c$ and not $W/P$ as it was in Chapter 9 (see Fig. 10.6b). The wage-setting curve in the open economy is upward sloping just as in the closed economy: as employment rises and the labour market tightens, the real consumption wage workers can expect goes up. In this case, the real consumption wage depends on the price of both home produced goods and imports; this means that employers have to pay a particular real consumption wage ($W/P_c$) at a given level of employment on the *WS* curve to get workers to exert effort in the efficiency wage model or to strike a deal with their employees or with the union representing them. The main driver of wage-setting decisions is still the tightness of the labour market: the *WS* curve is upward sloping. Exactly the same factors as in the closed economy can cause the *WS* curve to shift in this model, such as changes in union bargaining power or unemployment benefits.

To find equilibrium output, we also need to define the *PS* curve in terms of the real consumption wage—it is then possible to draw *WS* and *PS* curves on the same diagram. When defined in terms of the real consumption wage, we shall see that the *PS* curve is a function of the real cost of imports i.e. of the real exchange rate. It will shift up and down as the real exchange rate changes. Why? Depreciation reduces the real wages workers get (i.e. on *PS*) because the price level of the imported goods they consume goes up.

The simplest way to think about how the *PS* curve is affected by changes in the real exchange rate is to go through an example step by step. We do this by considering what happens when there is a depreciation of the real exchange rate $Q$ (as a result of a depreciation of the nominal exchange rate, $e$).

The *PS* curve shows the real wage workers get after firms have set their prices, $P$. To show the *PS* curve in the labour market diagram with $W/P_c$ on the axis, we have to figure out the real wage workers get after firms set their prices, taking into account the additional effect on $W/P_c$ due to the inclusion of import prices.

A depreciation of the nominal exchange rate $e$, causes a depreciation of the real exchange rate, as $Q = \frac{P^*e}{P}$. Depreciation, an increase in $Q$, is an increase in the *real cost of imports*.

The consumer price index, $P_c$, is a weighted average of home and imported goods. As we saw above, $P_c = (1 - \phi)P + \phi P^*e$. The second term in the consumer price index equation has increased as a result of the increase in $e$.

We also need to check what happens to the price home firms set, $P$. Home firms set their price as a mark-up on their unit labour costs, i.e. $W/\lambda$. The real exchange rate does not come into this calculation. This means that home prices, $P$, remain the same (i.e. the first term in the consumer price index equation is not altered by the depreciation).

Hence, a depreciation will always increase $P_c$ in the model.

The increase in $P_c$ reduces the real consumption wage, $W/P_c$. Bananas and other imported elements in the consumption bundle become more expensive, making workers worse off. This results in a downward shift of the *PS* curve.

*Summary*

A depreciation of the real exchange rate shifts the *PS* curve down because it reduces the real consumption wage workers get after firms have set their prices. The real consumption wage is reduced because imports become more expensive following the depreciation. The opposite of this logic holds for an appreciation of the real exchange rate.

The example highlights the importance of correctly interpreting the *PS* curve. The curve shows the real wages that are available to workers after the firm has secured its profit margin, which it does by setting prices for home-produced goods. After a depreciation, workers cannot buy as many goods and services with the nominal wages firms pay them and the *PS* curve shifts downwards. After an appreciation, workers can buy more goods and services with the nominal wages firms pay them (bananas and other imported goods are cheaper) and the *PS* curve shifts upwards.[11]

When measuring real wages in terms of $W/P_c$, a real depreciation shifts the *PS* curve downwards. The intersection of the *WS* curve and the new *PS* curve is therefore at lower output as shown in Fig. 10.6b.[12] Translating this result into the real exchange rate–output diagram produces a downward-sloping supply-side equilibrium. This is the downward-sloping *ERU* curve.

- With a downward-sloping *ERU* curve, we can now show how a low level of unemployment and the associated high level of output can be sustained without inflationary pressure (point A in the top panel of Fig. 10.6b).

---

[11] Another possibility for modelling would be to think about the impact of imported inputs on firms' costs. We analyse this case when we model an oil price shock in the next chapter. To make the analysis as simple as possible here, we assume that no intermediate goods (i.e. firm inputs) are imported—i.e. the only imports in the economy are final goods consumed by workers. This assumption means that a depreciation cannot affect firms' costs. This means the only impact of imports on the *PS* curve in our model is to change $P_c$ and hence the real consumption wage of workers given the price set by firms for home-produced output.

[12] In Fig. 10.6 and all the other figures in this chapter we use $q = \log Q$ as our measure of the real exchange rate. This makes the analysis simpler and allows for all the diagrams in the chapter to be compatible with one another.

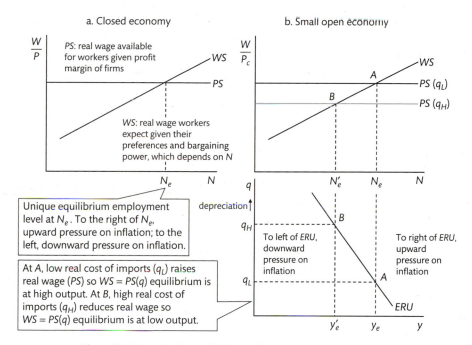

Figure 10.6 Supply-side equilibrium in the closed and open economy.

Just as in Chapter 2, where we introduced the closed economy WS curve, a low rate of unemployment means a low cost of job loss, which raises the wage-setting real wage (WS is upward sloping). For this to be a supply-side equilibrium (i.e. a WS − PS intersection), the value of the price-setting real wage must be at the same high level. This requires that the real cost of imported consumption goods be sufficiently low (i.e. by a sufficiently appreciated real exchange rate, which shifts the PS curve up). This gives point A at the combination of an appreciated value of $q$ and a high level of output. Exactly the same logic lies behind the location of point B.

### Deriving the equation for the downward-sloping ERU curve

To derive the downward-sloping ERU curve, we need to set out the details of wage and price setting in the open economy. We use the cost-plus pricing rule for home produced goods sold at home and exported:

$$P = P_X = (1 + \mu) \cdot \text{unit cost},$$

where $\mu$ is the mark-up. As we saw in the previous subsection, the consumer price index is defined as:

$$P_c = (1 - \phi)P + \phi P^* e,$$

where we use the fact that $P_M = P^* e$. The real consumption wage is defined in terms of consumer prices:

$$w = \frac{W}{P_c}.$$

## Wage setting

Wage-setting behaviour is the same as in the closed economy. The only modification is to make explicit the role of the consumer price index:

$$W = P_c \cdot b(N).$$

The wage-setting curve is defined by

$$w^{WS} = \frac{W}{P_c} = b(N),$$   (WS, wage-setting real wage equation)

where a rise in employment is associated with a rise in the wage-setting real wage (i.e. the WS is upward sloping).

## Price setting

In the absence of any imported inputs into production (e.g. oil), price setting in the open economy is the same as in the closed economy, i.e. prices are set as a mark-up on unit labour costs:

$$P = P_X = (1 + \mu) \cdot \frac{W}{\lambda},$$

where $P$ is the price of home goods sold at home and in export markets and $\lambda$ is the level of labour productivity. To work with the wage- and price-setting curves, both must use the same definition of the real wage. This means that we need to express the price-setting real wage in terms of the consumer price index, i.e. $W/P_c$.

The first step is to substitute the price equation into the equation for the consumer price index, $P_c$.

$$P_c = (1 - \phi)P + \phi P^* e$$
$$= (1 - \phi)\left[(1 + \mu)\frac{W}{\lambda}\right] + \phi P^* e.$$

In order to find the expression for the price-setting real wage, we need to do some algebra. The next steps are shown in the footnote.[13]

---

[13] The first line below shows the equation after dividing by $P = (1 + \mu) \cdot \frac{W}{\lambda}$. Then, we use the definitions of the real wage, $w = \frac{W}{P_c}$ and of the real exchange rate, $Q = \frac{P^* e}{P}$ to simplify the equation. In the third line, we rearrange the equation so that the real wage is in the numerator. Lastly, in the fourth line, we use the approximation that $\frac{1}{1+\mu} \approx 1 - \mu$.

$$\frac{P_c \lambda}{W(1+\mu)} = (1 - \phi) + \frac{\phi P^* e}{P}$$   (10.3)

$$\frac{\lambda}{w(1+\mu)} = (1 - \phi) + \phi Q$$   (10.4)

$$\frac{w(1+\mu)}{\lambda} = \frac{1}{(1-\phi)+\phi Q}$$   (10.5)

$$\frac{w}{\lambda(1-\mu)} = \frac{1}{(1-\phi)+\phi Q}.$$   (10.6)

In the final step, we rearrange the equation so that the price-setting real wage is on the left hand side:

$$w^{PS} = \frac{\lambda(1 - \mu)}{1 + \phi(Q - 1)}. \qquad \text{(PS, price-setting real wage equation)}$$

This can be approximated by $w^{PS} \approx \lambda(1 - \mu)(1 - \phi(Q - 1))$ so that the inverse relation between $w^{PS}$ and $Q$ is approximated by $\partial w^{PS}/\partial Q \approx -\lambda(1 - \mu)\phi < 0$.

We can see from this that the price-setting real wage in the open economy is equal to the closed economy price-setting real wage (i.e. $\lambda(1 - \mu)$) modified by the real exchange rate, $Q$. If there are no imported goods the weight of imports in the consumer price index is zero (i.e. $\phi = 0$) and it is easy to see that the price-setting real wage is indeed equal to its closed economy value,

$$w^{PS} = \lambda(1 - \mu). \qquad \text{(PS, closed economy)}$$

The *PS* curve also reverts to the close economy equation if $Q = 1$, which is the case when the prices of home and foreign produced goods are always identical in a common currency, as would be the case if the Law of One Price held.

The price-setting behaviour of firms means that regardless of the level of $Q$, nominal wages can purchase the same volume of *home* produced goods and services as they could in the closed economy. But in the open economy, workers choose to spend some of their wages on imported goods. If imports are more expensive (i.e. $\uparrow P^*$ or $\uparrow e$), then they can afford fewer consumption bundles. This means that a higher cost of imports reduces the real wage of workers: the *PS* curve shifts down with a rise in $Q$.

This shows another way of thinking about the case of the vertical *ERU* case: if wage setters do *not* take into account the effect of changes in the imported component of their consumption bundle in wage setting, then the *ERU* is vertical.

## 10.2.3 The medium-run model: *AD-BT-ERU*

### The *AD* curve

In Chapter 9, we used the dynamic open economy *IS* equation to underpin the 3-equation model:

$$y_t = A_t - ar_{t-1} + bq_{t-1}, \qquad \text{(open economy IS equation)}$$

where $q$ is defined as the log of $Q$. This version of the open economy *IS* curve is derived directly from the open economy *IS* relation, and highlights the inverse relationship of output with the real interest and the direct relationship with competitiveness.[14] The open economy

---

[14] As discussed in detail in Chapter 9, we use the natural log of the real exchange rate in the *IS* equation in the 3-equation model. This is because it makes the mathematics easier. It is a monotonic transformation and does not change the meaning of the equation—i.e. an increase in $Q$ always increases $q$ and vice versa.

multiplier is included in each of the terms $A$, $a$ and $b$.[15] In the dynamic version, we explicitly show the lagged effect of the real interest rate and the real exchange rate on output.

In turn, the *IS* curve is the basis for the *AD* curve in the medium-run model, which was derived in the previous chapter using the real *UIP* condition:

$$y = A(\sigma, y^*) - ar^* + bq, \qquad \text{(AD curve, } r = r^*\text{)}$$

where $r^*$ is the world real interest rate. The constant in the AD curve, $A$, includes both $\sigma$ and $y^*$ as demand shift variables. For the economy to be on the *AD* curve, it must be the case that home's interest rate is equal to the world interest rate (i.e. $r = r^*$). This is because the home economy's real exchange rate must be equal to its expected value for the economy to be in a medium-run equilibrium.

## The *BT* curve

As we saw in Section 10.2.1, the trade balance is an important factor in modelling the open economy. The last component of the medium-run model is the *BT* curve. *The BT curve shows the combinations of the real exchange rate, q, and the level of output, y, at which trade is balanced*: $X = M$. We summarize the *BT* curve using a simple linear equation as follows:

$$y^{BT} = B(\sigma, y^*) + cq, \qquad \text{(BT curve)}$$

where $y^{BT}$ is the level of output at which trade is balanced, $B$ is a constant, which includes the exogenous determinants of exports and imports: $\sigma$ is home's share of world trade, $y^*$ is world output and $m$ is the marginal propensity to import.[16]

As discussed previously, changes in $\sigma$ and $y^*$ will shift both the *AD* and *BT* curves.

### *Why is the BT curve flatter than the AD curve?*

The *BT* curve is flatter than the *AD* curve, i.e. $c > b$. This means that a rise in home's competitiveness (a real depreciation) improves the trade balance. As explained in Fig. 10.5 and the associated discussion, this reflects two factors:

- the Marshall–Lerner condition; and
- the fact that the multiplier is less than the reciprocal of the marginal propensity to import.

The exercise of deriving the *AD* and *BT* curves in the *q-y* diagram from the *IS* diagram (as in Fig. 10.5 but using *q* rather than *Q* for the real exchange rate) is left to the reader.

---

[15] To simplify the model, we use linear functions for investment and consumption, and for exports and imports. $X = x_0 + x_2q$ and $M = m_1y - m_2q$. The term $x_0$ includes home's share of world trade, $\sigma$, and world output, $y^*$. As usual, the multiplier is $k$. We can therefore write $A = k(c_0 + a_0 + G + x_0)$, $a = ka_1$ and $b = k(x_2 + m_2)$ in the *IS* and *AD* equations.

[16] Using the linear export and import equations, we write $y_{BT} = \frac{1}{m_1}x_0 + \frac{1}{m_1}(x_2 + m_2)q$. Hence, $B = \frac{1}{m_1}x_0$ and $c = \frac{1}{m_1}(x_2 + m_2)$ in the *BT* equation.

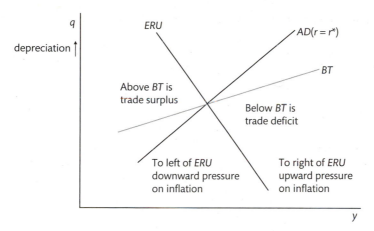

**Figure 10.7** The $AD - BT - ERU$ model.

## Using the *AD-BT-ERU* model

The medium-run model is formed by combining the *AD*, *BT* and *ERU* curves in the $q$–$y$ space, as shown in Fig. 10.7. The figure also shows how the position of the economy on the diagram can be used to diagnose the trade balance (a position off the *BT* curve) and whether there is any pressure on inflation to change (a position off the *ERU* curve).

*Supply, demand and external trade shocks in the open economy*

As we saw in Section 10.1, the key difference between the model presented here and the one in Chapter 9 is the introduction of a price-setting curve that depends on the real exchange rate and hence the downward-sloping *ERU* curve. We have also introduced the *BT* curve, which can of course also be used in the case of a vertical *ERU* curve.

   We first think about how a downward-sloping *ERU* curve affects the medium-run implications of demand and supply-side shocks. Figure 10.8 illustrates the $AD - BT - ERU$ and $WS - PS$ diagrams following (a) a positive supply shock and (b) a positive demand shock. We assume the economy is initially at medium-run equilibrium on the *AD*, *BT* and *ERU* curves, and look at the medium-run implications of the shocks for the real exchange rate, equilibrium unemployment, the trade balance and real wages.

**A supply shock**  A positive supply shock, such as a reduction in union bargaining power, shifts the *WS* curve downwards. This shifts the *ERU* curve to the right. There is a depreciated real exchange rate in the new medium-run equilibrium, as well as an increase in equilibrium output (see point *B* in Fig. 10.8a). The economy can operate at a new medium-run equilibrium with higher output. On the demand side, this is because of the higher competitiveness associated with the weaker unions. The depreciated real exchange rate means that real wages measured in terms of the consumer price index are lower. At point *B*, the economy is above the *BT* curve, which means the economy has moved into trade surplus.

**A demand shock**  A positive demand shock, such as a fall in the savings rate because households are able to get access to mortgages more easily, shifts the *AD* curve to the right, which results in an appreciated exchange rate at the new equilibrium. In light of the

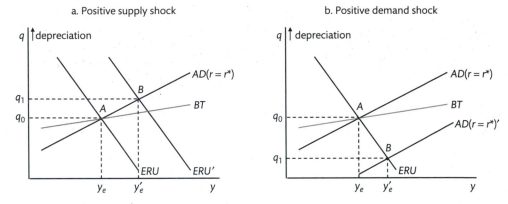

**Figure 10.8** What determines the medium-run equilibrium?

downward-sloping *ERU* however, it also leads to a reduction in the equilibrium rate of un-employment (see point *B* in Fig. 10.8b). This is markedly different from the outcome seen in the closed economy and in the open economy in Chapter 9 with a vertical *ERU* curve, where demand shocks could not affect the equilibrium rate of unemployment. By reducing the real cost of imported consumption goods, the appreciation of the real exchange rate that accompanies this shock shifts the *PS* curve upwards and results in a higher real wage for workers. At point *B*, the economy is below the *BT* curve, which means the economy has moved into trade deficit.

The extension of the model to the open economy means that it is not only domestic shocks to supply and demand that can affect the home economy. Economic shocks such as changes in world demand ($y^*$) or change in home's share of world exports ($\sigma$) can arise from outside the home economy, which will affect the medium-run equilibrium in the home economy. Such shocks are referred to as *external trade* shocks.

A positive trade shock due to higher world demand ($y^*$) because of a boom in a region of the world which constitutes a significant proportion of world GDP or a rise in home's share of world demand ($\sigma$) shifts the *AD* and *BT* curves to the right. An example of an external trade shock would be if France's share of world trade, $\sigma$, rises because preferences in the rest of the world shift from beer to wine, benefiting French exports of wine. Another example is where there is a change in the non-price attributes of the products of one country. For example, suppose that at a given price, the quality of cars made in India suddenly increases. This represents a positive external trade shock for India and a negative shock for its foreign competitors in the auto industry.

We show the $AD - BT - ERU$ diagram following a positive external trade shock in Fig. 10.9:

**An external trade shock** The *AD* curve shifts to the right because $A(\sigma, y^*)$ has increased and the *BT* curve shifts to the right because the term $B(\sigma, y^*)$ has increased. The new *AD* and *BT* curves are denoted by *AD′* and *BT′*. We know that medium-run equilibrium is at point *B*, where the new *AD* curve and the *ERU* curve intersect. At point *B*, there is an appreciated real exchange rate, higher output and a trade surplus. The economy is in trade surplus as it is above *BT′*. We can see that *AD′* and *BT′* intersect at point *C*, which is vertically below

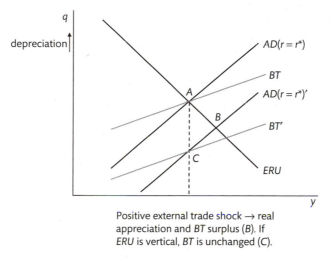

Positive external trade shock → real
appreciation and *BT* surplus (*B*). If
*ERU* is vertical, *BT* is unchanged (*C*).

**Figure 10.9** How does an external trade shock affect medium-run equilibrium?

**Table 10.1** Supply and demand shocks: implications for medium-run equilibrium in the $AD - BT - ERU$ model with a downward-sloping *ERU* curve.

|  | Shock | | | |
|---|---|---|---|---|
|  | **Rise in productivity** | **Fall in union bargaining power** | **Increase in autonomous consumption** | **Increase in world output** |
| Equilibrium unemployment | ↓ | ↓ | ↓ | ↓ |
| Real exchange rate | depreciation | depreciation | appreciation | appreciation |
| Trade balance | ↑ | ↑ | ↓ | ↑ |
| Real wage $(W/P_C)$ | ↑ | ↓ | ↑ | ↑ |

*Note:* ↑ means the variable is higher in the new medium-run equilibrium, ↓ means it is lower. We assume a flat *PS* curve throughout. For the trade balance, ↑ represents an improvement in the trade balance.

the initial intersection. This is because at point *C*, the appreciation of the real exchange rate is such that it causes net exports to fall by the exact amount that the external trade shock increases them. Trade is therefore balanced at point *C* and output is unchanged.[17]

In Chapter 9, we analysed how the medium-run equilibrium in the model with a vertical *ERU* curve is affected by supply and demand shocks. We repeat that exercise here with the downward sloping *ERU* curve and include an external trade shock. Table 10.1 summarizes the implications for the economy of a variety of permanent shocks. It shows the change in unemployment, the real exchange rate, the trade balance and real wages between the initial and the new constant inflation equilibria. The results hold for both flexible and fixed exchange rate regimes.

[17] Interestingly, a positive trade shock leaves the trade balance unchanged in the medium-run equilibrium in the case of a vertical *ERU* (at *C*). The reason is that, in this case, output in medium-run equilibrium is solely pinned down by the supply side.

Table 10.1 shows that:

1. The key differences from the model with a vertical *ERU* curve are that the reduction in union bargaining power now leads to a lower real wage since we are defining the real wage in terms of $W/P_c$ and that an increase in autonomous consumption now leads to both a higher real wage and a lower level of equilibrium unemployment.

2. The introduction of the *BT* curve also allows us to show how the economy reacts to an external trade shock and how different shocks are expected to affect the trade balance. The table shows that positive supply shocks are associated with a real exchange rate depreciation and hence an improvement in the trade balance, whereas positive demand shocks are associated with an appreciation in the real exchange rate and a deterioration in the trade balance. The table also shows that an external trade shock leads to a real appreciation, but because the *BT* curve also shifts, the shock improves the trade balance.

### Inflation in medium-run equilibrium: flexible and fixed exchange rates

What determines the medium-run inflation rate? At any medium-run equilibrium—i.e. at the intersection of an *AD* curve with the *ERU* curve—the real exchange rate is constant. If $Q = \frac{P^* e}{P}$ is constant, i.e. $\frac{\Delta Q}{Q} = 0$, we can use the definition of $Q \equiv \frac{P^* e}{P}$ to write the expression:

$$\frac{\Delta Q}{Q} = \frac{\Delta P^*}{P^*} + \frac{\Delta e}{e} - \frac{\Delta P}{P}$$

$$\text{For } \frac{\Delta Q}{Q} = 0, \quad \frac{\Delta P}{P} = \frac{\Delta P^*}{P^*} + \frac{\Delta e}{e}$$

$$\rightarrow \pi^{MRE} = \pi^* + \frac{\Delta e}{e},$$

which implies that home inflation is equal to world inflation plus the depreciation of home's nominal exchange rate.[18]

The intuition is that competitiveness remains constant as long as home and abroad's prices are rising at the same rate in a common currency (since the right hand side of the equation converts the growth of world prices in foreign currency into their growth in domestic currency terms). If home inflation is 5% and world inflation 2%, home's competitiveness will remain constant if its nominal exchange rate depreciates at a rate of 3% per annum.

---

[18] In continuous time, we find an expression for the growth rate of $Q$ by first taking logs, then differentiating with respect to time and using the fact that $d \log x / x = 1/x$:

$$\log Q = \log P^* + \log e - \log P$$

$$\frac{d \log Q}{dt} = \frac{d \log P^*}{dt} + \frac{d \log e}{dt} - \frac{d \log P}{dt}.$$

Use $d \log x / dx = 1/x$ to get

$$\frac{d \log Q dQ}{dQ dt} = \frac{d \log P^* dP^*}{dP^* dt} + \frac{d \log e de}{de dt} - \frac{d \log P dP}{dP dt}$$

$$\frac{dQ/dt}{Q} = \frac{dP^*/dt}{P^*} + \frac{de/dt}{e} - \frac{dP/dt}{P}$$

$$= \pi^* + \frac{de/dt}{e} - \pi.$$

What determines the rate of home inflation? In the closed economy, it is the monetary policy regime that fixes the medium-run inflation rate. With inflation targeting, the central bank's inflation target sets medium-run inflation.

In a small open economy with flexible exchange rates, the inflation rate in the medium-run is set by the central bank's inflation target (assuming that the inflation-targeting regime is credible), i.e.

$$\pi^{MRE} = [\pi^T], \qquad \text{(Medium-run inflation rate, flexible exchange rate regime)}$$

where MRE stands for medium-run equilibrium and the square brackets are used to indicate an exogenous variable, in this case chosen by the policy maker.

But what does this imply for the nominal exchange rate? Since both home and world inflation are now determined exogenously, the real exchange rate will only be constant if any discrepancy between home and world inflation is offset by a constant rate of change of the nominal exchange rate:

$$\frac{\Delta e}{e} = [\pi^T] - [\pi^*]. \tag{10.7}$$

If home's inflation target is below world inflation, then the exchange rate must steadily appreciate to keep the real exchange rate constant. Conversely, if home inflation is above world inflation, there will be a constant depreciation of home's exchange rate to keep the real exchange rate constant. Note that if home's central bank *chooses* $\pi^T = \pi^*$ then in the medium-run equilibrium, the nominal exchange rate will be constant. This may be one reason that central banks in different countries have chosen very similar inflation targets.

How can we reconcile Equation 10.7 with a fixed exchange rate regime, where the nominal exchange rate is not allowed to change? In this case, where $\frac{\Delta e}{e} = 0$, for the real exchange rate to be constant, home inflation must be equal to world inflation:

$$\pi^{MRE} = [\pi^*]. \qquad \text{(Medium-run inflation rate, fixed exchange rate regime)}$$

In turn, 'world' inflation will be set by the inflation target of the central bank to which the home economy's exchange rate is pegged. By choosing a fixed exchange rate regime, home loses control over monetary policy. A consequence of this is that its medium-run inflation rate is determined by world inflation.

### Establishing a credible low inflation monetary regime: flexible and fixed exchange rates

The Eurozone provides a real-world example of a fixed exchange rate regime. In 1999, the euro was introduced, irrevocably fixing the exchange rates between 11 European countries. The medium-run equilibrium rate of inflation in these economies was then pinned down by the inflation target of the European Central Bank, the Eurozone-wide institution to which each national government ceded control of monetary policy. Figure 10.10 shows how the inflation rates of three Eurozone economies (Italy, Spain and Germany) fell to low and stable levels after the introduction of the single currency. The countries that benefitted most from adopting the euro (in terms of reduced inflation) were the countries that had experienced difficulties establishing credible low inflation monetary regimes of their own, such as Italy and Spain.

The establishment of the single currency was signalled as early as 1992, via the provisions of the Maastricht Treaty. One explanation for the pattern observed in Fig. 10.10 is that the

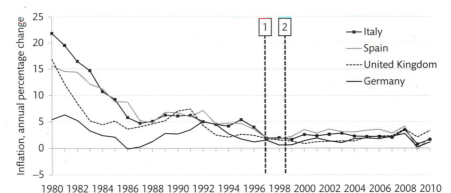

1. UK government establishes the Monetary Policy Committee to set interest rates independently
2. Introduction of the euro, which fixed the exchange rates of 11 countries

**Figure 10.10**  Inflation rates for selected European economies: 1980–2010.

*Source:* IMF World Economic Outlook, April 2011.

*expectation* of the establishment of a credible low inflation monetary policy regime helped to anchor inflation expectations in the years before the euro was introduced (in 1999).

The Eurozone example shows that giving up control of monetary policy to a credible pan-regional institution can help to create a low inflation environment. In this way, it can be viewed as a policy alternative to granting the national central bank independence (in a flexible exchange rate regime). Figure 10.10 shows the comparison between the countries acquiring low inflation credibility via membership of the Eurozone with the UK.

In 1992, the UK government chose to hand over responsibility for monetary policy to the Bank of England; in May 1997, it was made independent. The Bank's Monetary Policy Committee (MPC) is independent of political interference and meets on a monthly basis to set interest rates. The inflation target (i.e. $\pi^T$) of the MPC is 2% and we can see from Fig. 10.10 that inflation has been much lower and less volatile in the UK since the transfer of responsibility.[19]

### Medium- and long-run equilibrium

As we have seen, the key characteristic of the medium-run equilibrium is that inflation is constant. However, we have also seen that the economy may be in trade imbalance at the medium-run equilibrium. This was the case in Spain and the UK in the run-up to the financial crisis (see Fig. 10.3). We can define the long-run equilibrium as the situation in which the economy is not only at constant inflation, but also at trade balance. The difference between medium- and long-run equilibria in the basic model is illustrated by the example in Fig. 10.11. Let us compare the characteristics of points Z, B, and C.

---

[19]  The MPC has targeted the year-on-year change in the Consumer Price Index (CPI) since 2003. Prior to that, the MPC targeted the year-on-year change in the Retail Price Index excluding mortgage interest payments (RPI-X) and due to small differences in the baskets of goods used to calculate the two indices, the target for RPI-X was slightly higher, at 2.5%.

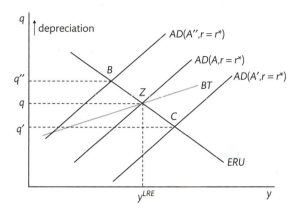

**Figure 10.11** Medium- and long-run equilibria in the open economy.

1. Medium-run equilibria with constant inflation are at points such as $Z$, $B$ and $C$, where the economy is on the $ERU$ curve, but not necessarily in trade balance. There is a trade surplus at point $B$, because it is above the $BT$ curve, and a trade deficit at point $C$. The economy can remain at points like $B$ and $C$ with stable inflation. However, in the longer run, pressures may emerge as a consequence of the external position that tend to push the economy toward point $Z$. (Don't confuse $A$ as autonomous demand in the $AD$ curves with $A$ as point in diagram.)

2. Long-run equilibrium is at point $Z$—on the $AD$, $ERU$, and $BT$ curves, where supply-side equilibrium coincides with the balanced trade level of output. This is likely to be a sustainable long-run position for the economy.

In the long-run, there may be pressures that tend to ensure that there is current account balance in the economy. We explore the sustainability of current account imbalances in Chapter 11.

## 10.3 Application

### 10.3.1 The UK economy before the crisis

This section provides a case study of the British economy between the mid-1990s and the onset of the global financial crisis in 2008. This study highlights how the model can provide insights into the factors driving macroeconomic performance when it is used alongside real-world macroeconomic data.

The second half of the 1990s through to the early years of the new century saw the most successful period of macroeconomic performance for the UK in the post-war era. Figure 10.12 illustrates the evolution of the UK economy between 1990 Q1 and 2007 Q4. The figures show that:

1. Unemployment declined dramatically over the period. Inflation fell in the early part of the period and stayed low and stable from then on.

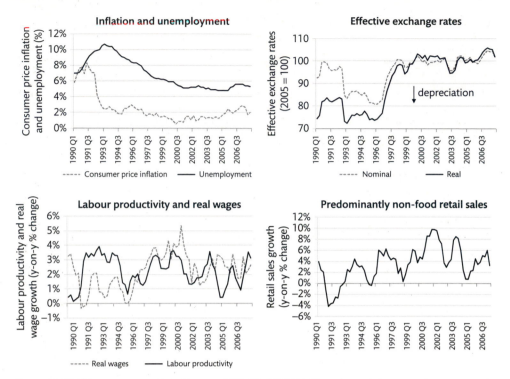

**Figure 10.12** UK macroeconomic indicators: 1990 Q1–2007 Q4. Note depreciation goes down not up in diagram.

*Source:* UK Office for National Statistics; Bank of England; IMF IFS (data accessed January 2012).

2. There was a large nominal and real appreciation in the mid to late-1990s.

3. Real wage growth and productivity moved in a similar manner, although real wage growth exceeded productivity growth for most of the period.

4. Retail sales experienced a strong upwards trend between the early 1990s and the mid-2000s.

The most striking feature of the UK's economic expansion over this period was that it was able to achieve such a marked decline in unemployment combined with low and stable inflation.

## Supply-side hypothesis

The argument that supply-side reform in the context of a sensible framework for macroeconomic policy accounts for the sustained fall in unemployment without rising inflation from 1997 can be illustrated in Fig. 10.13a. In 1996–97, the British economy was at a point like A, with trade balance and inflation at about the level of its trading partners. Let us consider a first scenario in which we assume that the *ERU* curve shifted to the right due to the lagged effects of supply-side reforms. The economy would be predicted to experience falling unemployment and inflation below its competitors as shown in Fig. 10.13a.

**Table 10.2** UK labour market institutions and government policy: 1983–2003.

| | 1983 | 1988 | 1993 | 1998 | 2003 |
|---|---|---|---|---|---|
| Average replacement rate | 21.7 | 18.1 | 18.5 | 17.5 | 16.5 |
| Tax wedge | 26.6 | 25.1 | 23.8 | 24.9 | 17.4 |
| Product market regulation | 4.5 | 3.8 | 2.2 | 1.4 | 1.0 |
| Union density | 48.0 | 42.6 | 36.1 | 31.5 | 30.5 |

*Source:* OECD Employment Outlook 2006, June 2006.

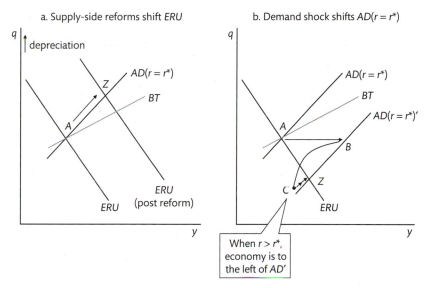

**Figure 10.13** Two hypotheses for the UK's shift to lower unemployment without inflationary problems.

Table 10.2 shows that during the 1980s and 1990s the UK saw a dramatic reduction in labour and product market rigidities such as the reduction in the power of unions and the progressive deregulation of product markets (to encourage competition). Each of these supply-side improvements is expected to have affected the *ERU* curve through their effect on the underlying *WS* − *PS* curves (see Chapters 2 and 15 for details of how changes in each variable would be expected to affect equilibrium unemployment). This hypothesis suggests that there are long lags associated with supply-side reforms—reforms that started in earnest the 1980s are thought to have contributed to the good economic performance of the UK economy in the late 1990s and early 2000s.

In these circumstances, the central bank would accommodate the supply-side improvement and adjust their estimate of the equilibrium rate of unemployment. In the new medium-run equilibrium, the real exchange rate would be depreciated and there would be a trade surplus.

However, it is obvious from the data in the top right hand panel of Fig. 10.12 that there is a problem with this as the sole explanation of British performance, because of the behaviour of the real exchange rate. From 1997, there was a large real appreciation, driven by an appreciation of the nominal exchange rate. Yet according to the pure supply-side reform story, the real exchange rate should depreciate.

## Demand shocks hypothesis

Let us now consider a different hypothesis to account for falling unemployment and modest inflation. For the sake of this example, suppose that the supply side remains unchanged but there is a boom in aggregate demand (e.g. a consumption boom). In the new medium-run equilibrium at point Z in Fig. 10.13b, the real exchange rate is appreciated and there is an external deficit.

As noted above, there was a sharp nominal (and real) appreciation of the pound in 1997. This is consistent with the prediction of the dynamic macro model set out in Chapter 9. In a flexible exchange rate regime, a consumption boom would boost output and inflation ($A \longrightarrow B$ in Fig. 10.13b). Using the logic of the dynamic model, the central bank would respond by raising the interest rate and the exchange rate would appreciate ($B \longrightarrow C$ in Fig. 10.13b). The economy shifts to lower output, because of the combined effect of the increase in interest rates and the appreciation.[20] Once inflation falls, the central bank begins to lower the interest rate and the economy adjusts to the new medium-run equilibrium at Z. The economy ends up with lower unemployment, a real exchange rate appreciation and a weaker external balance.[21]

As the diagrams in Fig. 10.13 show, both scenarios are consistent with the combination of lower unemployment and stable inflation in the new medium-run equilibrium at Z. Yet they imply very different outcomes for the real exchange rate, real wages and the trade balance. In the first scenario, the real exchange rate depreciates, real wages decline and the trade balance improves. In the second one, real wages rise, the real exchange rate appreciates and the trade balance deteriorates.

Do either of these stylized pictures fit the UK's experience? As we have seen, the first corresponds poorly with the behaviour of the nominal and real exchange rate. The second entails a real appreciation but ignores the supply-side reforms documented in Table 10.2.

There is some evidence that consumer behaviour was an important part of the post-1997 growth phase. The bottom right-hand panel of Fig. 10.12 shows how robust predominantly non-food retail sales growth was over this period, being particularly strong in the first half of the 2000s. A major trigger for the consumption boom was financial liberalization, which had the effect of lifting the liquidity constraints on some households—whereas previously they had been unable to borrow and smooth their consumption, they were now able to do so. This is highlighted by the household savings ratio in the UK, which fell from 11.7 in 1992 to

[20] Since the AD curve is defined for $r = r^*$, if $r > r^*$, then interest sensitive spending is dampened and the economy is to the left of the AD′ curve (at C).

[21] To use the dynamic model in the case of a downward-sloping ERU, it is necessary to locate the new $y_e$ at the output level of point Z. The new MR and RX curves would go through this level of output. Adjustment would then take place in the usual fashion. We do not discuss adjustment in the $RX - PC - MR$ diagrams with a downward-sloping ERU in order to make the analysis as simple and easily digestible as possible. This is left as an exercise for the reader.

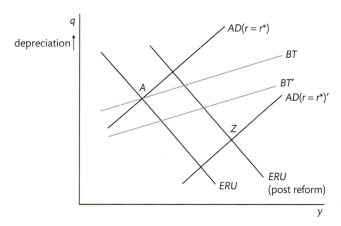

**Figure 10.14** UK from 1997—synthetic hypothesis.

just 2.7 in 2007.[22] Another contributing factor to the reduced savings rate was the perceived higher levels of household wealth that resulted from the stock market and real estate booms that took place over the period, and the ability of credit constrained households to increase consumption by withdrawing equity from their houses (as discussed in Chapters 6 and 7).

Other factors that are likely to have contributed to the consumption boom were the windfall gains to consumers due to changes in the financial sector (e.g. demutualization of building societies) and the high levels of real wage growth seen during the late 1990s and early 2000s. In this period, real wage growth outstripped productivity gains in the economy, as shown by the bottom left hand panel of Fig. 10.12. This matches the period where the pound appreciated strongly, thus making imports cheaper to domestic consumers and raising their real wages.

As the consumption boom slackened, public expenditure took over in maintaining the growth of demand. The Labour government elected in 1997 was able to consolidate the public finances during a period of robust private sector growth in its first term, which gave it the scope to introduce major public expenditure programmes in its second term from 2001.

In 1997, the Bank of England was made independent and began using a Taylor-type rule to adjust the interest rate. It raised the interest rate in 1997, but it is unlikely that this can account fully for the appreciation of the nominal exchange rate. One further change to the UK economy that is relevant to nominal exchange rate behaviour in the period from the mid-1990s is the emergence of export strength in knowledge-based services such as banking, finance, consulting and other business services.[23] This helps to explain the limited deterioration of the current account balance in the face of the large real appreciation. Such a shift in export capability (a rise in net exports at a given real exchange rate) is represented

[22] Source: OECD Economic Outlook, June 2012. Variable used is household and non-profit institutions serving households gross saving ratio.

[23] For an interesting analysis of the changing structure of the UK balance of payments (in an international perspective), see Rowthorn and Coutts (2004).

in the model by a rightward shift of the *BT* curve, and may help to explain the nominal appreciation.

By combining the aggregate demand, supply side and *BT* shifts as in Fig. 10.14, we have the elements for a systematic consideration of the driving forces behind the evolution of the British economy from the mid-1990s to the eve of the financial crisis.

## 10.4 Conclusions

This chapter has extended our understanding of the open economy by providing more detail on how the demand and supply sides operate when economies are open to international trade. On the demand side, we have shown that the open economy *IS* curve is steeper than the closed economy *IS* curve, due to the diversion of some aggregate expenditure away from home production towards imports from abroad in the open economy. We have also shown that exchange rate depreciation improves the trade balance, as long as the Marshall–Lerner condition holds. This assumption forms the backbone of the open economy *IS* and *AD* curves. In addition, we have introduced the concept of the trade balance, which can be modelled by the *BT* curve in the real exchange rate–output diagram.

On the supply side, we have altered a key assumption from the previous chapter, choosing to model wage setting based on workers' real consumption wages (which includes the price of imports). If workers' utility is defined in terms of their real consumption wage, the constant inflation equilibrium will be found by the intersection of the *WS* and the *PS* curves, where it is the real consumption wage on the vertical axis. In this modified model of the labour market, changes in the real exchange rate (i.e. the cost of imports), which affect the real wages that workers receive after firms have set their prices, shift the *PS* curve. For example, if the real cost of imports goes up (i.e. a real depreciation), the real consumption wage consistent with firms' pricing behaviour for a given nominal wage, goes down: this shifts the *PS* curve down.

This has an important effect on the medium-run model (i.e. the *AD* − *BT* − *ERU* model): the *ERU* curve becomes downward sloping, which means that there is a range of levels of output (and unemployment) consistent with constant inflation. This is in contrast to the medium-run model in the previous chapter, where there was a unique equilibrium rate of unemployment (exactly as in the closed economy) modelled by a vertical *ERU* curve.

The more detailed analysis of the demand and supply sides introduced in this chapter helps to illuminate interesting puzzles in the global economy, such as:

1. Why can real exchange rate depreciation be considered a 'double-edged sword'? There are two sides to a real exchange rate depreciation; the *volume effect* and the *relative price effect*. The volume effect occurs because a depreciation results in an improvement in home's competitiveness, which in turn affects the demand for exports and imports. Home's exports appear cheaper to foreigners after a depreciation, so export demand will increase. In addition, home consumers substitute away from imports and towards home-produced goods as imports rise in price. The volume effect therefore unambiguously improves the trade balance. In contrast, the relative price effect worsens the trade balance, as any volume of imports that home consumers purchase are more expensive following the

depreciation. Which effect is bigger? As long as the Marshall–Lerner condition holds, and we assume it always does, then a depreciation of real exchange rate will result in an improvement in the trade balance. Depreciation is a double-edged sword because although it improves the trade balance and helps the tradables sector, it reduces living standards by raising the real cost of imports.

2. How can we determine whether supply or demand shocks accounted for the good economic performance during the Great Moderation? Both supply and demand shocks can change constant inflation output in the $AD - BT - ERU$ model with a downward-sloping $ERU$ curve. Positive supply and demand shocks are both associated with reduced unemployment and stable inflation—but other characteristics of the medium-run equilibria are different. A positive demand shock is associated with an appreciation of the real exchange rate and a deterioration of the external balance, whereas a positive supply shock is associated with the opposite. In the case study of the UK economy in Section 10.3, we ruled out the robust economic performance being a result solely of supply-side policies, because the real exchange rate appreciated and the external balance deteriorated. The macroeconomic data instead seemed to suggest a combination of both supply and demand shocks.

3. How can current account imbalances persist in the medium-run? We introduced the $BT$ curve in this chapter. It represents the combinations of the real exchange rate and output at which the economy is in trade balance. It is flatter than the $AD$ curve: this reflects both the Marshall–Lerner condition and the fact that the multiplier is less than the reciprocal of the marginal propensity to import. The condition for a medium-run equilibrium is that the economy is on both the $AD$ and $ERU$ curves (i.e. at their intersection). At a medium-run equilibrium the economy does not have to be on the $BT$ curve: it can be in trade surplus, trade balance or trade deficit. In the long-run however, there are both economic and political forces that may drive the economy back towards external balance. These forces will be explored in the next chapter.

The next chapter applies the tools learnt so far to exploring the global economy further, using the open economy macro model to provide a framework for analysing global imbalances and oil shocks.

## 10.5 Appendix

### The Marshall–Lerner condition: a proof

Assume that trade is initially balanced and that the prices of exports and imports do not change in response to the volume sold. Since $BT = \sigma(Q)y^* - Qm(Q)y$, the change in the trade balance in response to a change in competitiveness is

$$\frac{dBT}{dQ} = \sigma'(Q)y^* - Qm'(Q)y - my$$

$$= \sigma y^* \frac{\sigma'(Q)}{\sigma} - Qm'(Q)y - my.$$

But by assumption, $BT = 0$, i.e. $\sigma(Q)y^* = Qm(Q)y$, and therefore

$$\frac{dBT}{dQ} = Qmy\frac{\sigma'(Q)}{\sigma} - Qm'(Q)y - my.$$

Dividing through by $my$,

$$\frac{1}{my} \cdot \frac{dBT}{dQ} = \frac{Q\sigma'(Q)}{\sigma} - \frac{Qm'(Q)}{m} - 1.$$

Since $my > 0$, $\frac{dBT}{dQ} > 0$ if and only if

$$\frac{Q\sigma'(Q)}{\sigma} - \frac{Qm'(Q)}{m} > 1.$$

Now, $\frac{Q\sigma'(Q)}{\sigma}$ is *minus* the elasticity of demand for exports, since $Q$ is the inverse of the real price of exports. Similarly, $\frac{Qm'(Q)}{m}$ is the elasticity of demand for imports. The Marshall–Lerner condition for an improvement in the balance of trade to follow from a rise in competitiveness is that the sum of the absolute values of the demand elasticities is greater than one; i.e.

$$\left|\frac{Q\sigma'(Q)}{\sigma}\right| + \left|\frac{Qm'(Q)}{m}\right| > 1.$$

## 10.6 Questions

### 10.6.1 Checklist questions

1. Explain the difference between the closed and open economy *IS* curves. Which curve is steeper? Explain both in words and with reference to equations why this must be the case.

2. Explain the sense in which an improvement in price competitiveness might be considered a 'good thing' for the economy. Might it also be considered a 'bad thing'? Is an improvement in the terms of trade the same as an improvement in price competitiveness?

3. Construct a numerical example to show how the Marshall–Lerner condition works. Why might its predictions not hold in the very short run?

4. How does the price-setting real wage equation differ in the case where you assume (a) a vertical *ERU* and (b) the downward-sloping *ERU* curve? Show how the price-setting real wage is derived in case (b).

5. Are real wages higher, lower or unchanged in the new medium–run equilibrium following a cut in unemployment benefits? Explain your answer.

6. Compare an economy with a vertical *ERU* curve with an otherwise identical economy with a downward-sloping *ERU* curve. Briefly explain how these economies differ. Consider a government facing an upcoming election. Does a downward-sloping *ERU* curve affect the policy maker's incentive to be fiscally disciplined ahead of an election?

7. Assume the home economy is a small open economy. It initially starts in trade balance with output at equilibrium. There is a sudden shift in preferences away from the home country's exports and towards the exports of their competitors (i.e. a reduction of $\sigma$ in the home economy). Are the following statements about the new medium-run equilibrium true or false? Justify your answers and use $AD - BT - ERU$ diagrams where appropriate.

(a) This shock will increase the level of output in the home economy if you assume a downward-sloping *ERU* curve.

(b) This shock will have no effect on world output.

(c) This will lead to an improvement in the trade balance in the home economy.

8. Explain in words with the help of a diagram (with a $q - y$ panel) why the *BT* curve is flatter than the *AD* curve. Show the result using equations.

9. What is the inflation rate in medium-run equilibrium in a fixed exchange rate economy? How will deviations in inflation from this rate affect the country's competitiveness?

10. A small open economy with flexible exchange rates is having trouble controlling inflation. What options does it have for establishing a credible low inflation monetary regime? Are there any downsides to these options?

## 10.6.2 Problems and questions for discussion

1. Use the website of *The Economist* magazine and search for the latest version of the 'Big Mac Index'. Answer the following questions:

(a) What does the index show and how does it relate to the concept of purchasing power parity?

(b) Describe some interesting cross-country comparisons in the data.

(c) What does the index tell us about the relative size of the Chinese and US economies?

2. Use the content of this chapter and Chapter 9 to answer the following questions:

(a) How would you expect an inflation-targeting central bank to respond to a fall in world trade? Explain the central bank's reasoning.

(b) Does the exchange rate overshoot as a consequence of the central bank's actions? Justify your answer.

3. This question uses content from both this chapter and Chapter 9. Read the following excerpt from *Economic luck that cannot last*:[24] 'The governor [of the Bank of England, Mervyn King] emphasizes four underlying causes of the improvement in UK performance: a monetary framework that evolved from inflation-targeting, in 1992, to the Bank's operational independence, in 1997; fiscal consolidation; 20 years of supply-side reforms; and a series of shocks that averaged out over time, rather than cumulated in either an upward or downward spiral. Yet, as Mr King notes, one beneficent shock did cumulate: to the terms of trade (the ratio of export to import prices), which improved by about 10% after 1996. This generated a substantial increase in real take-home pay without adding to employers' costs.'

How can we use the open economy models to explain the evolution of the UK economy over this period? In answering the question, you are advised to take the following steps:

(a) Link supply-side reforms to economic performance using the $AD - BT - ERU$ model.

(b) Use the 3-equation model to explain how an inflation-targeting central bank can respond to a shock and return the economy to target inflation.

---

[24] This excerpt is taken from Martin Wolf's article in the *Financial Times* on October 30th 2003 entitled 'Economic luck that cannot last'. Note that the article was written in 2003 (i.e. before the global financial crisis).

(c) Use the *AD − BT − ERU* model to explain how a demand shock could have 'beneficent' or good effects on economic performance and relate this to the UK.

(d) Identify the reasons why this 'good luck' cannot last (as in the headline of the article).

4. Pick a large Eurozone economy (e.g. France, Spain, Germany or Italy). Perform a short case study on the performance of your chosen economy between the mid-90s and the mid-2000s by following these steps:

(a) Use Eurostat to collect data on key macroeconomic indicators over the period (similar to that shown for the UK in Fig. 10.12)

(b) Use OECD.Stat to collect supply-side data over the period (similar to that shown for the UK in Table 10.2)

(c) What were the major macroeconomic developments in your chosen country over the period?

(d) Can the evolution of your chosen economy over this period be explained using the *AD − BT − ERU* framework (similar to that shown for the UK in Fig. 10.14)? Concisely summarize any problems you had in doing this.

# 11

# Extending the open economy model: oil shocks and imbalances

## 11.1 Overview

In this chapter, we extend the open economy model in a way that helps us to discuss some interesting puzzles. The puzzles relate to how economies were operating in the fifteen years that preceded the global financial crisis. This was the era of the Great Moderation. High and volatile inflation appeared to have been eliminated from the advanced economies and there were dramatic reductions in unemployment in many European economies, where it had remained stubbornly high in the 1980s. Whereas the oil price shocks of the 1970s had caused major economic disruption, oil shocks in the 2000s were absorbed relatively easily. Policy makers and some academic observers were confident that a decade of labour market reforms and a better policy-making environment, exemplified by the kind of inflation-targeting regime discussed in Chapters 3 and 9, had played a part in producing the improvements in performance.

Yet, the unfolding of the global financial crisis and the Eurozone sovereign debt crisis from 2008 revealed that beneath the surface of the Great Moderation, imbalances were building and with them, the pre-conditions for crisis. In Chapters 6 and 7 we focused on the build-up of a leverage cycle in a number of advanced economies. In this chapter, we introduce the tools that are useful in understanding the international dimensions of these crises. We extend the basic macroeconomic framework to allow us to analyse these issues.

First, we show how shocks to commodity prices, such as oil prices, can be analysed in the $AD - BT - ERU$ model. The analysis is motivated by the severe disturbance to the global economy caused by the oil shocks of the 1970s. The two oil shocks in 1973 and 1979 were followed by years of low growth, high inflation and rising unemployment—so-called 'stagflation'. It is striking that when the oil price increased sharply again in the 2000s, the macroeconomic effects were very different. In spite of near-record oil prices (in real terms), inflation remained subdued and unemployment in many countries was at its lowest level for several decades. This raises the question as to why the outcome was different. We shall see that the extended model can help provide insight into this.

The second extension to the open economy model in this chapter centres on imbalances and the interdependence of countries. Some countries run current account surpluses; others current account deficits. We need to have a way of thinking about whether these international payments patterns are problematic or whether they simply reflect benign differences among countries, for example, in investment opportunities or natural resource endowments.

Some observers argue that the very large build-up of global current account imbalances in the years before the financial crisis played a causal role in the crisis. But before tackling that issue, we need to extend the $AD - BT - ERU$ and 3-equation models to the two-bloc case. The simplest way of thinking about the interaction between economies is to assume the world is made up of just two large blocs of economies. We assume that in each bloc there is an inflation-targeting central bank. Using the extended model, we can explain how it was possible for inflation targeting central banks in the two blocs to successfully keep inflation close to target and yet for there to be persistently rising external imbalances.

### 11.1.1  How does a commodity price rise affect the macro-economy?

As far as an oil-importing country is concerned, we shall see that an oil shock is a combination of two different shocks: it is a negative external trade shock (which is also a negative aggregate demand shock) and a negative supply shock. However, in the contemporaneous analysis of the first oil shock in 1973, policy makers concentrated on the first feature of the shock. They were preoccupied with the depressing effects on aggregate demand, employment and the trade balance, and failed to take into account the impact on the supply side of the economy. We provide a more detailed description of the oil crises in Section 11.2.1. At this stage, we use our medium-run model of the open economy to answer some preliminary questions about oil shocks.

*Why does an oil shock depress aggregate demand?*

Oil is a key imported input to production and also an important element in the household consumption bundle. When the oil price rises, this depresses aggregate demand in oil import-ing countries. Thinking of the definition of aggregate demand, the higher oil price reduces net exports by raising the real import bill. From the perspective of households, when the oil price goes up, the price of petrol at the pump rises. Firms will also pass on the higher price of energy in the prices of their goods. These price rises reduce the real incomes of households and unless they can borrow to smooth this shock, consumption will fall. This reduction in aggregate demand (because of the fall in $(X - M)$ as the real cost of imported oil rises) shifts the $AD$ curve to the left in the $AD - BT - ERU$ model.

The fall in net exports (because of the higher import bill) also depresses the trade balance and we can show this in the model as a leftward shift in the $BT$ curve. The shifts in the $AD$ and in the $BT$ curves are shown in Fig. 11.1. As we saw in Chapter 10 (Fig. 10.9), it is not a coincidence that the new $BT$ curve intersects the new $AD$ curve vertically above the initial equilibrium. If we do the mental experiment of thinking about a real depreciation that would fully offset the effect on aggregate demand of the oil price shock and leave output unchanged at its initial level, this gives a point $B$ on the new $AD$ curve ($AD'$). This experiment works because, by improving competitiveness and restoring net exports to their initial level (in $AD$ and $BT$), it must be the case that there is also trade balance at point $B$.

From Fig. 11.1, we can see that the external trade shock would mean a new medium-run equilibrium at point $C$, with higher unemployment and a trade deficit. It is these aggregate

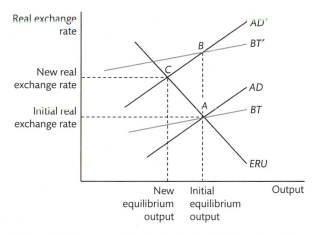

**Figure 11.1** The external trade effects of a rise in the price of oil.

demand and trade balance aspects of the shock that were at the top of policy makers' minds in 1973. They focused on trying to offset the implications of the shock for aggregate demand and the external balance.

### Why is an oil shock a negative supply shock?

It turns out that an oil shock is also a negative *supply shock*: this means not only that it raises unemployment as a consequence of the fall in aggregate demand, but that it also shifts the *ERU* curve to the left. Why is this? Think back to a household faced with a higher cost of living as a consequence of the energy price. In Chapter 10, we discussed the fact that households are likely to view their welfare in terms of their real consumption wage, i.e. they will evaluate the value of their nominal wage according to the consumption bundle they can buy with it. If the real value of their nominal wage is reduced by higher energy prices, this shifts the price-setting curve downwards (for a given real exchange rate), opening up a gap between the real consumption wage they expect at a given rate of unemployment and the real value of the wage they get. In Fig. 11.2, we can see that this downward shift in the *PS* curve has the effect of shifting the *ERU* curve to the left.

Thinking about an oil price increase as a negative supply shock helps to explain why the oil shock in 1973 led not just to a one-off increase in inflation, but to rising inflation—at a time when unemployment had also risen. There will be upward pressure on inflation as long as there is a gap between the *WS* curve and the new lower *PS* curve: unemployment must increase if the economy is to achieve stable inflation. In other words, if the policy maker tries to offset the effect of the fall in aggregate demand by monetary or fiscal stimulus, the economy will experience rising inflation.

For example, suppose the policy maker used a fiscal stimulus to shift the aggregate demand curve back to its initial pre-shock position (from *AD'* to *AD* in Fig. 11.3). Would this offset to the demand effects of the shock restore equilibrium in the economy? The answer is 'no' if the relevant post-shock supply-side equilibrium is on *ERU'*: the new equilibrium unemployment is higher as shown by point *B* in Fig. 11.3. Since at *A* the real wage has been pushed down by higher energy prices, wage setters will get higher money wages to compensate them and

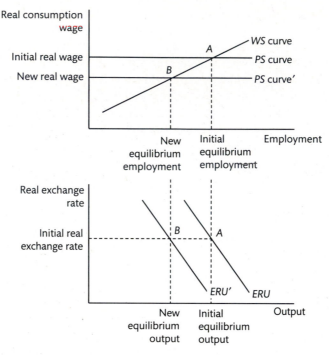

**Figure 11.2** A negative supply shock: an increase in the oil price shifts the *ERU* to the curve left.

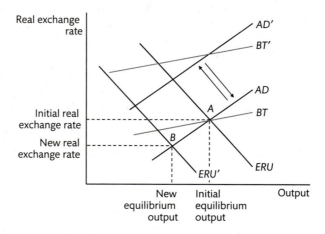

**Figure 11.3** An expansion of government spending in response to a rise in the price of oil.

inflation will no longer be constant (i.e. there is rising inflation at *A*). This is reflected in the diagram by the fact that point *A* is to the right of the relevant *ERU* curve labelled *ERU'*.

### What is the role of monetary policy?

In the analysis so far, the economy ends up at point *B* with constant inflation. Unemployment is higher than it was initially and there is a substantial deterioration in the economy's external balance (note the position of *BT'*). Although it is not shown explicitly in the diagram, it is also the case that the government's fiscal balance will have deteriorated due to the use of expansionary fiscal policy in boosting aggregate demand in addition to the operation of the automatic stabilizers. If the government wants to restore output and unemployment to their pre-oil shock levels, then it may try to use expansionary monetary policy.

Monetary policy can be used to stimulate aggregate demand by producing an exchange rate depreciation through a reduction in the interest rate. In a fixed exchange rate regime, the same result could be achieved by a devaluation. This would take the economy from *B* toward point *A*—the economy's starting point.

However, we can see immediately that this will provoke a rise in inflation. Why? Because at point *A*, the economy is to the right of the new *ERU'* curve: the depreciation will cut real wages and lead to compensation through higher nominal wage settlements. Higher wage and price inflation will result. As the impact of higher inflation on home's competitiveness kicks in, the economy will move to the south–west toward point *B*. To offset this recession, the government would have to implement another loosening of monetary policy. Another burst of inflation would ensue. (Although the cause is different, this is the same kind of inflationary process as described later in the chapter in Fig. 11.11.)

### How could a supply-side policy help?

Although many countries experienced the combination of high inflation and unemployment in the 1970s and 1980s, this was not true of all—see Fig. 2.1 in Chapter 2 for a comparison of advanced economy unemployment rates during this period. We can use the model to help provide a possible explanation. If the negative supply-side effect of the shock could be offset by an appropriate supply-side policy, then the stagflationary consequences of the oil shock would be mitigated.

One such policy is a wage accord. A wage accord, or incomes policy as it was sometimes called at the time, is typically a tripartite agreement between the government, employee unions and employer associations. The accord means that employees accept wage restraint in order to maintain higher employment than would be the case otherwise. These accords have the effect of shifting the wage-setting curve downward and hence offsetting (at least partially) the downward shift of the price-setting curve. If the wage accord fully offsets the effect of the oil shock, then the *ERU* curve will not shift to the left. Such a policy would reduce both the rise in unemployment and the rise in inflation associated with the oil shock. The downside of these policies is that they are hard to sell politically, as coupling rising oil prices with wage restraint means workers have to accept a reduction in their real incomes. The discussion in Chapter 15 about differences in institutional structures across countries helps to explain why the oil shocks of the 1970s resulted in stagflation in some countries but not others. Countries with coordinated wage-setting, such as those in Scandinavia and Austria, kept unemployment low in spite of these shocks.

### Why did the oil price hike in the 2000s not lead to stagflation?

Over the course of the period between 2002 and 2008, real oil prices almost doubled, taking them to a level above that of 1980. Yet, inflation remained low and unemployment was falling in many countries. An important reason that the depressive demand effects were muted in the 2000s was the very different behaviour of financial institutions. Banks were very keen to increase their lending and in the US for example, they allowed households to withdraw equity from their houses to enable them to maintain their consumption in the face of the oil price increases. The behaviour of banks is discussed at greater length in Chapter 7.

On the supply side, it seems that workers were less able or less inclined to get compensation through their wages for the higher oil prices in the 2000s than had been the case in the 1970s. This may be related to the decline in the role of unions in wage setting over this period (see Chapter 15). If this was the case, then in terms of the model, both the aggregate demand curve and the *ERU* curves would have shifted less to the left than was the case in the 1970s due respectively to bank and union behaviour. Finally, with their inflation-targeting mandates, central banks were not inclined to try to offset the effect on demand by loosening monetary policy in the 2000s.

### 11.1.2 Interpreting an economy's sector financial balances: does a current account imbalance matter?

To answer this question, it is useful to explain circumstances under which a current account imbalance is benign. The logic is familiar from the discussion of household decisions in Chapter 1. At different stages in their lifecycle, households would ideally like to borrow or lend in order to maintain a fairly smooth consumption path. A phase of borrowing would be expected when income is below its expected longer-term level; a phase of lending would be expected during years of higher than 'permanent' income. The ability to borrow and lend, i.e. access to the capital market, allows the household to improve its welfare relative to a situation in which its consumption is tied to its current income.

The same logic can be applied to a country. A good example is a situation in which a country gets a windfall increase in its wealth and hence in its 'permanent income' because of the discovery of a natural resource. Applying the same logic as in the household case, the country's permanent income has gone up, which means consumption can be higher now and into the indefinite future. If the country has access to borrowing on the international capital market, then current consumption of home residents can go up immediately on the discovery of the natural resource before any of it has been extracted. In practical terms, this means a rise in imports as home residents purchase more goods from abroad to sustain their higher consumption.

If we assume that the initial position was of current account and trade balance, we would observe a deterioration in the current account on discovery of the natural resource. In this example, the current account deficit is not a signal of any weakness in the performance of the economy: indeed, the current account deficit reflects the increase in long-run wealth of the country, which allows residents to improve their living standards immediately because they can borrow on international capital markets to fund the higher level of imports. Once the revenue from the natural resource comes on-stream, the accumulated debt associated with the years of current account deficits can be repaid.

However, just because we can think through an example in which a current account deficit is benign does not mean this is always the case. Let us take a very different example. Suppose the economy is characterized by a property price bubble. This can lead to a consumption boom as households feel wealthier as a consequence of rising house prices. For the economy

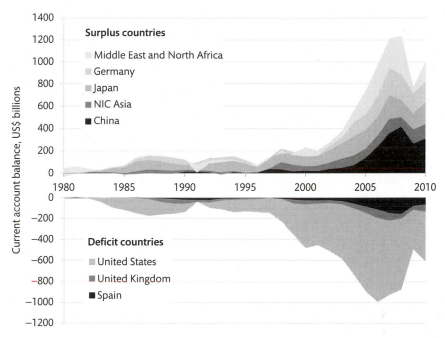

**Figure 11.4** Current account balances—countries with large surpluses or deficits: 1980–2010.

*Source:* IMF World Economic Outlook, September 2011.

as a whole, higher consumption leads to higher imports and to a deterioration in the current account. The country is accumulating debt to the rest of the world for as long as the current account deficit persists. Unlike the resource windfall case in which the means for repaying the debt are 'in the ground', the house-price boom does not create more wealth that can be used to repay the debt as it comes due. When the bubble bursts and house prices fall, the illusion of higher permanent income for the country is shattered and the country will have to find a way of servicing the higher debt it has accumulated. This will normally entail a fall in living standards.

### 11.1.3  Inflation targeting in a two-bloc world

One of the striking features of the global economy from the year 2000 in the late phase of the Great Moderation was the mounting external imbalances of a number of large economies. Figure 11.4 shows that the US, Spain and the UK had rising external deficits of a globally significant size. The counterpart to these deficits were the growing surpluses of China, the oil-producing countries and Germany. Japan's substantial surplus remained fairly stable over the 2000s.

In the same period, central banks in both developed and emerging and developing economies practiced inflation targeting and were seemingly successful at achieving low and stable inflation. Fig. 11.5 shows how inflation in these two country blocs remained low in the 2000s. This is in contrast to previous periods, which were blighted by high and volatile inflation, particularly in emerging and developing economies.

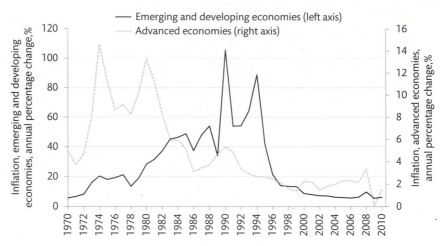

**Figure 11.5** Consumer price inflation, annual average percentage change: 1970–2010.

*Source:* IMF World Economic Outlook, September 2011.

In hindsight, the imbalances that emerged in the 2000s seem unhealthy, a sure sign of the troubles that were to come. In the wake of the financial crisis, politicians and economists have been quick to extol the virtues of 'rebalancing'—i.e. countries moving towards more balanced current account positions. We can use a two-bloc version of the 3-equation model to explore interdependence among countries and to show how the response of an inflation-targeting central bank in one bloc to a bloc-specific shock affects the economy and the policy maker in the other bloc. We show that both blocs can achieve their inflation target, but current account and real exchange rate divergences emerge if there are different shocks and/or patterns of demand in the two blocs. The two-bloc model will be set out and used to analyse the dynamic adjustment of two blocs to economic shocks in Section 11.2.5.

### 11.1.4 Different medium-run 'growth' strategies can cause global imbalances

One way of understanding the global imbalances that arose in the pre-crisis period is to see them as the outcome of the choice of different medium-run 'growth' strategies by significant global economies. For example, the US economy experienced consumption and housing booms and rising government spending under George W. Bush. From the analysis in Chapter 10, we know that a constant inflation equilibrium can be consistent with external imbalance in an open economy. For example, we showed there that a government in an economy (with a downward-sloping *ERU* curve) can encourage higher domestic demand (public or private), which will be associated with lower unemployment and higher real wages (via an appreciated real exchange rate), which in turn, is consistent with stable inflation.

If this were to improve a government's prospects for re-election, then why don't all countries act this way? If they all tried to do so at the same time, then since the world as a whole is a closed economy, this would be modelled by a rightward shift of the world *IS* curve in a closed economy model and it would not be possible to maintain constant inflation.

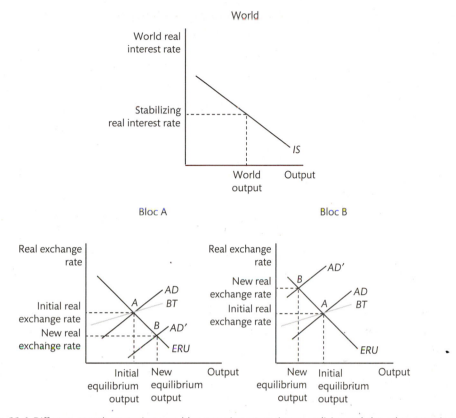

**Figure 11.6** Different growth strategies: one bloc pursuing expansionary policies and the other pursuing restrictive policies.

In Fig. 11.6, we provide a simple depiction of the medium-run equilibrium in the global economy in the pre-crisis years. Bloc A represents those economies who adopted a policy of supporting growth through domestic demand, such as the US, UK and Spain. At the level of the global economy, these expansionary policies were, however, offset by the bloc B economies, who depressed domestic demand in order to keep their real exchange rate depreciated and support their export-led 'growth' strategy. Two important countries where the attention of policy makers was on restraining domestic demand and promoting net exports in the 2000s were Germany and China.

In the stylized example in Fig. 11.6, bloc A is in a constant inflation equilibrium with lower unemployment and an external deficit and bloc B is in a constant inflation equilibrium with higher unemployment and a trade surplus. Assuming that the demand shifts are opposite and symmetric, the world economy remains at the unique constant inflation equilibrium as shown in the upper panel of the Fig. 11.6.

We can distinguish between an export-oriented growth strategy of China and Germany and a finance-oriented growth strategy of the US, UK and Spain. These strategies resulted in the emergence of large external imbalances developing from the beginning of the 2000s, with export surpluses rising sharply in China and Germany, and deficits rising rapidly in the US, and to a lesser extent in the UK and Spain (see Fig. 11.4).

As we discussed in Chapter 7, financial deregulation in the USA began in the early 1980s and culminated in 1999 with the repeal of the Glass Steagall act. In the UK, it was the 'big bang' of 1986 that signalled the start of rapid financial deregulation. In the US, this led to the extension of credit to low income households for mortgages. Financial deregulation fuelled housing booms in many other countries, including Spain, where the creation of the Eurozone also affected access to and the cost of loans. In many of the economies with finance-orientated growth strategies, household savings ratios fell to historically low levels in the 2000s.

However, not all countries were characterized by the same pattern. In particular, in terms of countries with global impact, China and Germany looked very different. Both countries had rapidly increasing current account surpluses. Looking first at China, in spite of a very high and rising investment rate (as a per cent of GDP) and rapid growth at rates close to 10% per annum, savings were even higher (reflecting increasing savings by firms offsetting a falling savings rate of households). The Chinese government favoured an export-led growth strategy to create a large globally competitive manufacturing sector. It was prepared to prioritize this over a more balanced growth pattern, which would have allowed the exchange rate to appreciate and real wages and domestic consumption to rise.

As Germany emerged from its period of financing reconstruction in East Germany following reunification in 1990, governments concentrated on setting policy so as to encourage the restoration of competitiveness in the export sector, which had been eroded during the post-unification boom in the early 1990s. The government kept fiscal policy tight and supply-side reforms focused on increasing the cost of job loss: both had the effect of encouraging wage restraint. Against the background of weak demand at home, German firms sought to take advantage of the opportunities available to reorganize production networks in Central and Eastern Europe and to sell to the rapidly growing markets in China and elsewhere in the emerging economies. Real wage growth was low, consumption depressed and the household savings rate was increasing. Although China was growing very fast and Germany slowly, the common factor of an export-orientated growth strategy meant that in both countries national savings were higher than investment and there was an export surplus.

In fact, the German preoccupation with export-led growth is not a recent development. As financial journalist John Plender points out, Germany has been characterized by a trade-orientated growth strategy and a mistrust of high finance for centuries:[1]

> Mercantilism and the fear of sophisticated finance have historically gone hand in hand in Germany and other parts of northern Europe. In the 15th century the cities of the Hanseatic League were profoundly suspicious of credit. They largely excluded foreign bankers. Merchants tried to balance trade bilaterally, relying partly on barter while making some use of coin. The economic historian Raymond de Roover reckoned the League's credit institutions were about two centuries behind the Italians in 1500.

The third important source of rising current account surpluses was the impact of the rapid economic expansion of emerging economies on the demand for oil and on oil prices and, hence, on the export surpluses of the oil-producing countries.

---

[1] Excerpt taken from: John Plender, December 29th 2011, 'How Goethe's Masterpiece is Shaping Europe' *Financial Times*.

By the mid-2000s, the magnitude of the surpluses relative to the global economy was unprecedented. Those surpluses were recycled to other regions. This echoed on a global scale the recycling of the surpluses of the oil exporters following the OPEC shocks of the 1970s to Latin America, which had created the basis for the subsequent regional debt crisis.

In a very stylized way, we can relate this discussion to Fig. 11.6. Bloc A represents the finance-orientated countries and bloc B represent the export-focused countries. Each bloc is assumed to have an inflation-targeting central bank. The boom in demand in bloc A causes an appreciation in the exchange rate and a current account deficit, whereas the opposite macroeconomic policy stance in bloc B ensures a depreciated exchange rate and a trade surplus. The strategies of the two blocs offset each other, which means that world interest rates could be kept low (as shown by the upper panel of Fig. 11.6) without causing either bloc to miss their inflation target.

## 11.2 Modelling

### 11.2.1 **Oil shocks**

In this section, we show how to include the role of imported raw materials in the macro model. As we have seen the most important real-world application of this for the advanced economies is to the oil shocks in the 1970s and 2000s. However, the insights from modelling shifts in the terms of trade faced by economies are much more broadly applicable.

**External supply shocks (e.g. oil shocks) in the *AD-BT-ERU* model**

An external supply shock is defined as an unanticipated change in the world terms of trade between manufactured goods and raw materials: a change in the world price of oil is a good example. This type of shock combines the effects of an external trade shock (as seen in the previous chapter) with a supply-side impact on the price-setting real wage curve. As explained in Section 11.1 the consequence is that there is a shift in the *AD* curve, in the *BT* curve, and in the *ERU* curve, with all three curves shifting in the same direction.

To see in more detail why the *ERU* curve shifts, we need to look closely at what is meant by a change in the world price of oil $P^*_{rm}$. If we say that the world price of oil rises, this means that it rises relative to the world price of manufactured goods $P^*_{mf}$, where $\tau = P^*_{rm}/P^*_{mf}$. In other words, we are talking about a change in *relative* prices, or to put it another way, a change in the *real* price of oil. The price-setting curve is defined for a given real exchange rate, $Q \equiv \frac{P^*_{mf} e}{P_{mf}}$, where now that we have introduced imports of raw materials, we need to specify that this is the relative price of manufactured goods: oil is excluded.

Now suppose that the world relative price of oil rises ($\uparrow \tau$). For a given real exchange rate ($q_0$ in Fig. 11.7), a rise in the price of an essential input like oil raises costs for firms in the home economy. These costs are passed on in higher consumer prices, which reduces the real consumption wage of workers. If firms are to protect their profit margins in the face of the oil price rise, then real wages must be lower. Hence the price-setting real wage curve shifts downward when the world price of oil rises (see Fig. 11.7). This implies a leftward shift in the *ERU* curve.

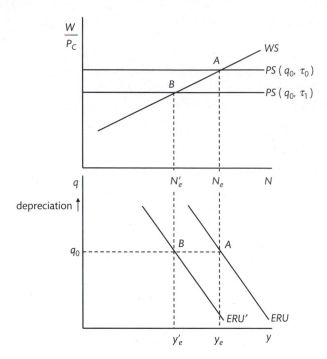

**Figure 11.7** A negative supply shock: an increase in the oil price ($\uparrow \tau$) shifts the *ERU* curve to the left.

A very simple way to model the impact of oil is to assume all imports are oil and that the consumer price index is the price index of home value-added (i.e. marked-up unit labour costs) plus the unit cost of imported oil. In this simple setting, petrol at the pump is a 'manufactured good'. Then

$$P_c = P_{mf} + v\tau P^*_{mf} e$$

where $P_{mf} = \frac{W}{(1-\mu)\lambda}$ is the price index of home value added and $v$ is unit materials requirement. This implies a price-setting real wage:[2]

$$w^{PS} = \frac{(1-\mu)\lambda}{1 + v\tau Q}.$$

Any rise in $\tau$ reduces the price-setting real wage. Note that any fall in unit materials requirement through increased energy efficiency, for example, would tend to offset this.

We can now analyse the full impact of an exogenous and permanent change in the world price of an essential commodity such as oil. We take the case of a rise in the price of oil. For simplicity, we assume that the home country only imports oil—it does not import final goods. This changes nothing essential and allows for a more direct examination of the issue at hand. We can investigate the three effects:

1. the impact on aggregate demand;

---

2 See footnote 13, Chapter 10 for a similar derivation.

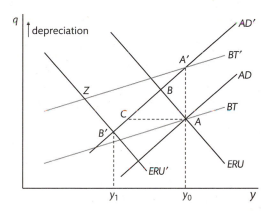

**Figure 11.8** A negative external supply shock: the combined effect an increase in the oil price ($\uparrow \tau$) in the $AD - BT - ERU$ model. The new long-run equilibrium is at point $Z$.

2.  the impact on the trade balance;

3.  the impact on price and wage setting and hence on the $ERU$ curve.

The aggregate demand and trade balance effects of an oil shock are modelled in the same way. In this case, there is a downward shock to net exports because the increase in the cost of the essential imported raw material absorbs a higher proportion of home income at a given real exchange rate. This shifts the $AD$ curve and the $BT$ curve to the left. We write out the trade balance equation from Chapter 10 to include the external terms of trade, $\tau$.

Since $P_M = P^*_{mf} e$ when imports are manufactured goods, $P_M = \frac{P^*_{rm}}{P^*_{mf}} P^*_{mf} e$ when imports are raw materials. Hence, imports in real terms, $M$, are:

$$M = \left( \frac{P^*_{rm}}{P^*_{mf}} \frac{P^*_{mf} e}{P_M} \right) M(\tau Q, y) = \tau Q M(\tau Q, y).$$

Holding all other variables constant, a rise in $\tau$ increases the import bill, depressing net export demand;

$$X - M = X(Q, y^*) - \tau Q \cdot M(\tau Q, y).$$

This reduces $X - M$, which shifts the $BT$ and the $AD$ curves to the left. The logic was explained in Fig. 10.9 in Chapter 10 and in Fig. 11.1 in Section 11.1. The new $AD$ and $BT$ curves intersect vertically above $A$ at $A'$.

Figure 11.8 summarizes the effect on all three curves of an oil shock. Given the shift in the $ERU$ curve, if the government tries to restore aggregate demand and output to its pre-shock level at point $A$, then the inflationary consequences of the commodity price rise are clear. Following the external supply shock, the initial equilibrium point $A$ is *above* the new $ERU$ curve labelled $ERU'$. This means that at $y_0$, the real wage is below the wage-setting real wage because the $PS$ curve has shifted down due to the increase in $\tau$. Point $A$ is no longer a medium-run equilibrium.

If the authorities did not attempt to offset the demand shock, the relevant $AD$ curve is $AD'$ and there would still be inflationary pressure until output had fallen to $y_1$.

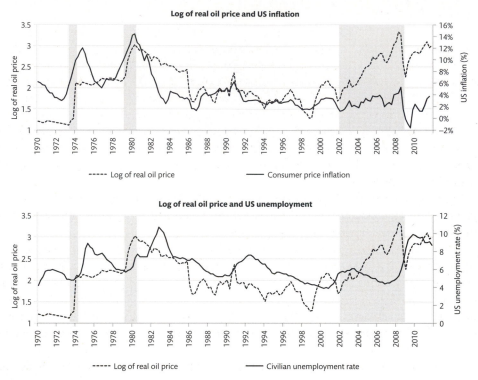

**Figure 11.9** Log of real oil prices and US macroeconomic indicators: 1970 Q1–2011 Q4.

*Source:* Federal Reserve Bank of St Louis - FRED (data accessed January 2012).

## Comparing three oil shocks

This section focuses on the three major global oil shocks since the early 1970s, comparing their causes, their macroeconomic implications and the associated policy responses. Figure 11.9 shows the path of oil prices over the last 40 years—to compare across periods, we show log real oil prices.[3] This approach allows for variations in the series to be interpreted as percentage changes. The shaded grey areas show the oil price shocks that we analyse in this section. The graphs also show the movement of US consumer price inflation and unemployment over the period, providing an insight into the macroeconomic consequences of each shock.

The three oil shocks we are investigating took place in 1973–1974, 1979–1980 and 2002–2008. We will go through each shock in turn, setting out its causes and its macroeconomic effects. We will also investigate the dominant monetary policy response of central banks in developed economies in relation to each episode.

---

[3] This way of presenting data means that an increase in the index from 1 to 2 is (approximately) a doubling of real oil prices. The first step is to produce the series for oil prices in real terms, by deflating nominal oil prices by the US GDP deflator (i.e. 2005 = 100). Next, the natural logarithim of this series is taken. Lastly, the series is multiplied by 100. This method is in line with that used in Blanchard and Gali (2007).

## OPEC I: 1973–1974

The Yom Kippur War began in the Middle East on October 6 1973. This did not directly affect oil shipments, but did lead to the Organization of Petroleum Exporting Countries (OPEC) cutting production of crude oil significantly towards the end of 1973. This is thought to have been the main driver of the more than doubling of crude oil prices seen over this period—the nominal oil price rose from $4.3 to $10.1 per barrel between 1973 Q4 and 1974 Q1. The overall impact of this event is estimated to have been between a 7% and 9% reduction in world oil supply.[4] In addition to this supply shock, demand pressures are thought to have played a complementary role in the oil price rise. Barsky and Killian (2002) suggest that general inflation and booming prices for other commodities contributed to the upward pressure on oil prices.

Figure 11.9 shows that this shock coincided with a rise in inflation to double digits. In contrast, the unemployment impact was largely felt in the year after the oil price hike, when the unemployment rate in the US nearly doubled.

In response to the first oil shock in 1973, many countries focused on the aggregate demand consequences and sought to offset them via expansionary fiscal and monetary policies. The example of expansionary fiscal policy was used in Section 11.1. We look now at the consequences of an accommodating monetary policy, which would allow the exchange rate to depreciate so as to offset the fall in aggregate demand. Referring back to Fig. 11.8, the aim would be to restore output to $y_0$ and move the economy from $B$ to $A'$ via a depreciation of the real exchange rate.

At point $A'$, however, the economy is to the right of the ERU curve. This causes inflation to rise, as workers' real wage expectations are not being met (as shown in Fig. 10.6 in Chapter 10). The increase in inflation ($\uparrow P$ relative to $P^*$) results in an appreciation of the real exchange rate, via the equation $Q = \frac{P^*e}{P}$. This leads to a movement leftwards down the AD curve, as net exports fall, until the economy is at $B'$, where the new AD and ERU curves intersect. This is the new medium-run equilibrium (MRE), where there is no pressure on inflation to change.

The consequence of the adoption of policies like this after 1973 was the onset of so-called stagflation: rising unemployment and rising inflation (as the economy eventually adjusted from $A'$ to the new medium-run equilibrium at $B'$ with unemployment rising and a burst of inflation). Any renewed attempt by the government to keep output at its pre-shock level would prompt a further increase in inflation (as the same process outlined above repeats itself).

In the UK, government policy exacerbated the stagflation. The government negotiated incomes policies during the 1970s to compensate workers for the rising cost of living. As firms sought to protect their profit margins the wage–price spiral continued. By encouraging real wage resistance (i.e. raising money wages to maintain real wages) this added to the sharp rises in actual and equilibrium unemployment and inflation seen in the UK after each of the oil shocks.[5]

---

[4] See Hamilton (2009).

[5] See David Walton's speech on February 23 2006 entitled, *Has Oil Lost the Capacity to Shock?* The speech is available from the Bank of England website.

*OPEC II: 1979–1980*

The second oil shock was once again the result of largely exogenous geopolitical events disrupting the production of crude oil in the Middle East.[6] This time, production was affected by both the Iranian Revolution in late 1978 and the Iran-Iraq War of 1980. As in 1973, these developments led to sharp rises in oil prices, which affected both US inflation and unemployment in a similar manner as the 1973–74 shock, as shown by Fig. 11.9. Again, the unemployment response lagged the inflation response, with unemployment not peaking until 1982, at a rate of over 10%.

When the 1979–80 oil shock struck, the nature of the shock was better understood and many countries attempted to use tight monetary policy to prevent exchange rate depreciation and hence prevent a big upsurge in inflation. For example, average UK official bank interest rates were 10% in 1978 Q3 and continued to rise during the shock, reaching 17% in the first half 1980. From here interest rates gradually fell, but stayed above 10% until the middle of 1983.[7] This shift of monetary policy regime to non-accommodation of inflation coincided with a change of government in the UK, as Thatcher took power in mid-1979. Her economic views were highly influenced by Milton Friedman's 'Monetarist' school of thought and this was reflected in her decision to squeeze inflation out of the system through tight monetary policy (even if it meant unemployment would be above equilibrium for some time). Thatcher's Monetarist experiment is discussed in more detail in Chapter 13.

In terms of Fig. 11.8, adoption of tight monetary policy would mean that output would fall from $A$ to $C$ to $B'$, but without the hike in inflation that accompanied loose monetary policy. The high rates of inflation and the sluggish adaptation of wage and price setters to tighter monetary policy meant that most countries experienced years of high unemployment before inflation was reduced to low levels in the 1990s. This shows that governments were generally unsuccessful in introducing the types of supply-side policies (e.g. wage accords) discussed in Section 11.1.1, which would have mitigated the inflation and output responses to the oil shocks.

*Oil price rises 2002–2008*

There was a persistent and marked rise in oil prices between 2002 and 2008, which culminated in a peak real oil price in 2008 Q2 that exceeded that reached in the 1979–80 oil shock.[8] The forces driving this movement in prices were distinctly different from the episodes in the 1970s, with demand factors in the global oil market playing a much larger role. The 2000s was a period of rapid economic expansion for emerging markets and especially China, whose demand for oil increased exceptionally fast over this period. In addition to this, world oil production stagnated between 2005 and 2007, partially driven by a decline in Saudi Arabian output. These demand and supply factors produced upward pressure on prices, as more nations were actively competing for a finite amount of resources.

A further component of the third oil shock that did not feature in the oil shocks of the 1970s was speculation in financial markets. Hamilton (2009) argues that the excessively high

---

[6] See Hamilton (2009).

[7] Source: Bank of England (data accessed January 2014).

[8] There were some brief periods between 2002 Q1 and 2008 Q2 where oil prices fell, but they were small and quickly reversed (see Fig. 11.9). In light of this, we treat the whole period as one oil shock.

oil prices reached in 2008 were in part influenced by the flow of dollars into commodity futures contracts. The path of the macroeconomy during this pronounced and consistent rise in oil prices was unexpected given past experiences. Instead of stagflation, the third oil shock coincided with a period of falling unemployment and low inflation (for the US, see Fig. 11.9).

What factors can account for the very different macroeconomic consequences? Can the model help explain why things were different this time around? On the demand side, two factors appear to have been important. Firstly, greater access to credit meant that households were able to cushion themselves against the increase in energy costs by withdrawing equity from their houses.[9] Secondly, there is some evidence that substitution away from energy-intensive activities was easier.

On the supply side, both labour market reforms and inflation-targeting macroeconomic frameworks appear to have made wage setters less inclined or able to secure compensation in their wages for higher imported energy costs. This would be reflected in a smaller left-ward shift of the *ERU* curve. The importance of labour market reform was emphasized by David Walton, a member of the Bank of England's Monetary Policy Committee in a 2006 speech, when he cited the increased flexibility of the UK labour market as a key reason for the oil price rises of the first half of the 2000s not disturbing the UK's low unemployment equilibrium.[10]

Central banks in the developed world have learnt through experience of the dangers of oil shocks for the macroeconomy and in particular for inflation. The change in policy stance since the early 1970s and the increased emphasis on keeping inflation expectations firmly anchored in the face of oil shocks was displayed in a 2004 speech by Edward M. Gramlich, then a member of the Board of Governors of the Federal Reserve:[11]

> I must stress that the worst possible outcome [of an oil shock] is not these temporary increases in inflation and unemployment. The worst possible outcome is for monetary policy makers to let inflation come loose from its moorings.

### 11.2.2 Current account imbalances

#### Do current account imbalances matter? An intertemporal approach to the balance of payments

Does it matter from an economic perspective if there is a current account or trade deficit or surplus in the economy? To answer this question, it is necessary to recall that any non-zero current account reflects a change in the country's wealth. If the home country has a current account surplus then this means that it is lending abroad—if it has a current account deficit, then it is borrowing from abroad. Since this borrowing will have to be repaid (with interest) in the future, the trade deficit represents a decline in the home country's wealth. A trade

---

[9] See Feldstein (2006).

[10] See David Walton's speech on February 23 2006 entitled, *Has Oil Lost the Capacity to Shock?* The speech is available from the Bank of England website.

[11] Excerpt taken from: Edward M. Gramlich's speech on September 16 2004 entitled, *Oil Shocks and Monetary Policy*. The speech is available from the Federal Reserve website.

deficit will imply a current account deficit unless the home country receives a sufficient net inflow of interest and profit receipts on the foreign assets that it owns.

A decline in wealth sounds like a bad thing—but this is not necessarily the case. When a student goes into debt to finance their university studies, their financial wealth falls. The wisdom of this move depends on the extent to which the university education increases the student's human capital and improves their earning capacity.

In the same vein, we can show how countries can rationally use borrowing from abroad to smooth consumption when there is an expectation that future income will exceed current income. Starting from the accounting identities, we can show the link between the current account and consumption.

$$X - M \equiv y - C - I - G$$
$$CA \equiv X - M + INT$$
$$\equiv y + INT - C - I - G = \tilde{y} - C,$$

where $\tilde{y} \equiv y + INT - I - G$.

By defining $\tilde{y} \equiv y + INT - I - G$ i.e. GDP plus net interest from abroad minus investment and government spending, we can see that the current account can be viewed as $\tilde{y} - C$, or savings plus taxes. We shall call $\tilde{y}$ aggregate household disposable income and note that it includes net interest from abroad. The intertemporal model of consumption of Chapter 1 focuses on the objective of consumption smoothing. Using the identity, we can see that in the open economy, fluctuations in the current account can allow aggregate consumption to remain constant in the face of fluctuations in income.

The intertemporal model of the current account (ICA) represents the CA as a forward-looking function of income and asset returns. And the cumulated value of past CA balances is defined as the net foreign asset (NFA) position. This model of the current account requires two key assumptions:

1. *Perfect international capital mobility*: home residents can buy or sell foreign bonds with the fixed world interest rate, $r^*$, in unlimited quantities at low transactions costs.

2. Domestic consumption is set by the infinite horizon *rational expectations permanent income hypothesis*. As discussed in Chapter 1, this amounts to perfect consumption smoothing in expectation when the real interest rate ($r$) is equal to the subjective discount factor ($\rho$).

Using the notation introduced in Chapter 1, we can write the ICA model as follows:

$$CA_t = -\sum_{i=1}^{\infty} (\frac{1}{1 + r^*})^i \Delta \tilde{y}_{t+i}^E,$$

where, $CA_t$ is the current account balance at time $t$, $\sum_{i=1}^{\infty}$ is the sum from period $t + 1$ to infinity, $r^*$ is the world interest rate, $\tilde{y}_{t+i}^E$ is aggregate household net income at time $t + i$, expected at the current period, $t$. In this framework, just like a household, a country has an intertemporal budget constraint. Consumption smoothing by borrowing and lending makes sense for individuals and the same can be said for countries. If a country experiences a temporary decrease in income this period (i.e. fall in $\tilde{y}_t$ due, for example, to an exogenous fall in exports), then there is an expectation that future income will be higher than current income (i.e. $\Delta \tilde{y}^E_{t+i} > 0$, in future periods, i.e. when $i > 0$).

In this scenario, a current account deficit in period $t$ would simply reflect optimal borrowing at the world interest rate, $r^*$, to smooth consumption against the adverse income shock. Borrowing from abroad needs to be repaid in the future, so from period $t+1$ onwards, the country would run a series of small current account surpluses as the debt is repaid (and the NFA gradually returns to zero). This illustrates that a country's current account deficit can be a reflection of its 'permanent income' and therefore that the possibility of borrowing from abroad is a rational method of increasing the utility of its citizens. The example shown here is analogous to a household borrowing to smooth their income when they have a bad income shock or when their expected lifetime income increases as was discussed in detail in Chapter 1.

Consider the example of a country that discovers a natural resource, such as oil or diamonds (see Fig. 11.10). This raises the country's wealth and therefore its permanent income (i.e. $\Delta \tilde{y}^E_{t+i} > 0$, when $i > 0$). The extraction of the resource commonly takes place some time after the discovery is made. However, the ability to borrow in international capital markets means the country can smooth its consumption, raising living standards even ahead of the first drop of oil being extracted. There are three separate factors that contribute to the emergence of a CA deficit upon the discovery of oil in this scenario:

1. Current consumption rises due to the expectation of higher future wealth.

2. Domestic investment increases to enable the extraction of the natural resources. The new investment is partly funded through international borrowing.

3. The nominal and real exchange rates appreciate, because the forex market anticipates that the real exchange rate that will balance the current account will be an appreciated one. The discovery is a positive external trade shock (as discussed in Chapter 10).

Figure 11.10 shows the time profile of the discovery of the resource, the period for which revenues are extracted and the period after the natural resource is exhausted. Following the discovery, such a country will have a current account deficit. Its consumption is permanently higher than would have been the case in the absence of the natural resource discovery. Once the revenue from the resource extraction begins to flow the current account balance improves. The current account eventually moves to a small surplus, which continues until the country has repaid the debt built up during the initial phase. This adjustment was observed in the UK in the 1970s with the discovery of oil in the North Sea.

If we think about current account imbalances more generally, for a country that does not have very profitable investment opportunities at home, it makes sense that domestic savings are used for net investment abroad. The purchase of foreign assets that the current account surplus represents may provide a higher return than would investment at home. High saving economies in Asia, such as Singapore, provide examples here.

### Causes and consequences of current account imbalances

If all economic agents act rationally by weighing up the relative returns from different investment opportunities, then a current account imbalance simply reflects the differences in preferences, in investment opportunities and in resource windfalls across countries. This is a useful benchmark case, but a persistent current account deficit is not always benign.

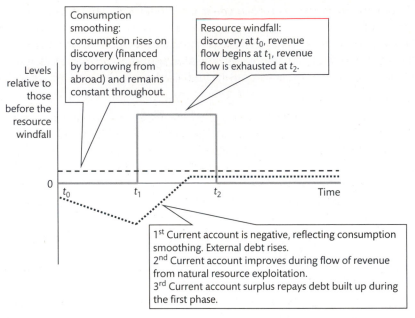

**Figure 11.10** Resource windfall and the current account.

For reasons of myopia and political pressures, a current account deficit may not reflect higher investment at home in response to especially attractive investment opportunities or because of a resource windfall—rather, it may reflect low savings because of high private consumption based, for example, on a property price bubble or unsustainably high government consumption, or it may reflect investment in wasteful projects.

We saw in Chapter 10 that a country does not have to be in trade balance to be in medium-run equilibrium. We also alluded to the fact that there are economic and political forces that can push countries back towards trade balance in the long run. These forces are likely to be stronger when the imbalance is viewed as being unsustainable (rather than benign).

There are a number of different channels through which persistent imbalances could come under pressure. To make the discussion as simple as possible, we assume that net interest and profit receipts from abroad are zero so that the current account balance and the trade balance are equivalent (see Chapter 10 for more information on the open economy accounting framework).

**Consumption effects of changes in wealth:** A trade surplus indicates rising wealth for the home country and a trade deficit the opposite. We saw from the PIH in Chapter 1 that changes in lifetime wealth can result in changes in consumption in the current period. For example, consumers in an economy with a persistent trade deficit may think that belt tightening will eventually be required for the home economy to service and repay their foreign debts. This could lead to estimates of permanent income being adjusted down and an associated fall in consumer spending, which would shift the AD curve leftwards and move the economy back towards long-run equilibrium.

**Willingness of financial markets to fund deficits:** If sentiment in financial markets is that a trade deficit reflects high home consumption or wasteful investment, then funds will cease to be available to the home country at the world interest rate. Our assumption that there is perfect international capital mobility would break down. This will tend to dampen private investment and may force the government to tighten demand policy to reduce the deficit.

**Exchange rate expectations:** In a fixed exchange rate regime, if private counterparties are not willing to purchase the home currency to finance the external deficit, this reduces demand for home currency and puts pressure on it to depreciate. To avoid this scenario, the home country will have to sell foreign exchange reserves to defend its exchange rate peg. Selling foreign exchange reserves will increase the demand for home currency and stop it from depreciating. However, the foreign exchange reserves of the central bank are limited, and borrowing to supplement them may be difficult, meaning the peg cannot be defended *indefinitely* in an economy with a persistent trade deficit. Eventually a currency crisis or the threat of one will lead to some combination of devaluation and fiscal tightening moving the economy back towards trade balance.

When analysing flexible exchange rates, up to this point we have assumed that exchange rate expectations are pinned down by the medium-run equilibrium value of $q$ (e.g. at $\bar{q}$ in Fig. 11.11). However, if we assume that the expected exchange rate is influenced by the trade balance, the ability of the central bank to achieve its inflation target is undermined. Let us now assume that the expected exchange rate adjusts immediately to deliver a real exchange rate consistent with trade balance: a trade deficit then becomes destabilizing for the economy. In Fig. 11.11 the economy is at medium-run equilibrium at point C with a trade deficit and constant inflation. Under the new assumption, the exchange rate will immediately depreciate, causing a movement along the AD curve as $q$ depreciates. This movement causes the economy to move to the right of the ERU curve. To the right of the ERU curve, there is a gap between the WS and PS curves and inflationary pressures will emerge. As home's inflation rises relative to that of its competitors, home will become less competitive. This implies a real appreciation for home: and the economy will move back in the direction of point C as net exports fall. We can imagine that such a process could repeat itself indefinitely. Once exchange rate expectations become unanchored in this way, there can be a spiral of rising inflation and nominal exchange rate depreciation until tighter *fiscal* policy is implemented and the AD curve is shifted to the left.

**Political pressures:** There could be political pressure to reduce imbalances, particularly in surplus countries. This pressure can come from within the country, as the population urges government to boost activity and operate at a lower unemployment rate, or from international trading partners. An example of external pressure to reduce imbalances is the tension between the US and China over China's manipulation of the yuan exchange rate.

As a result of these forces, long-run equilibrium is at a position on the ERU curve *and* at current account balance. As we have seen, when the current account is balanced, the country's wealth is constant—in the sense that it is not borrowing from or lending to the rest of the world. To make the exposition as simple as possible, we have ignored the difference between the trade balance and the current account. This allows us to define the long-run equilibrium in the $AD - BT - ERU$ model as the intersection of the ERU curve and the BT curve (as shown

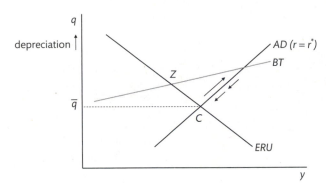

**Figure 11.11** Medium-run equilibrium at C (trade deficit) is disturbed by exchange rate depreciation.

by $y^{LRE}$ in Fig. 10.11 in Chapter 10 and labelled point Z in Fig. 11.11). Although economic pressures are more likely to make deficits unsustainable, external or internal political pressure may also lead a surplus country to adjust to the long-run equilibrium—or at least in the direction of a more balanced external position.

### 11.2.3 Sector financial balances

A major theme in the discussion of the background causes of the global financial crisis is global imbalances. What are these imbalances and how do they fit into the model? To understand what lies behind the emergence of global imbalances—current account (or trade) surpluses or deficits—it is helpful to see how the goods market equilibrium condition for one economy can be rearranged to show its sector financial balances. We can write the goods market equilibrium condition in terms of sectoral savings and investment balances.

Three sector balances are of interest: the private sector financial balance (private savings net of its investment), the government sector financial balance (taxation net of government expenditure), and the trade balance (net investment abroad). We assume that the economy is in a short-run equilibrium at which $r = r^*$. Ceteris paribus, a trade surplus means that stocks of foreign assets are increasing in the home economy. This measures the increase in the holdings of foreign wealth in the home economy and is therefore referred to as net investment abroad. We rearrange the outflows and inflows version of the goods market equilibrium condition to separate out taxation and show the sector financial balances:[12]

$$(S - I(r^*)) + (T - G) = X - M$$

$$\underbrace{(s_1 y^{disp} - c_0 - I(r^*))}_{\substack{\text{private sector} \\ \text{financial balance}}} + \underbrace{(ty - G)}_{\substack{\text{government} \\ \text{financial balance}}} = \underbrace{X(Q, y^*) - QM(Q, y)}_{BT \, = \, \text{net inv abroad}},$$

where $y^{disp}$ is disposable income, $y^{disp} = (1 - t)y$.

---

[12] To see this note that $S = y^{disp} - C = y^{disp} - \left(c_0 + (1 - s_1)y^{disp}\right) = s_1 y^{disp} - c_0$.

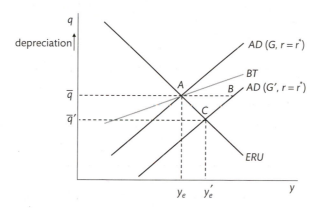

**Figure 11.12** Twin deficits arising due to an expansion of government spending.

This expression is useful because it highlights the flow equilibrium in the economy. One sector, for example, the private sector, can only run a financial deficit if it borrows from another sector: this would mean some combination of borrowing from the government (i.e. a government budget surplus) and borrowing from abroad (a foreign trade deficit). Whenever the goods market is in equilibrium, private savings net of investment (the private sector's financial balance) plus the government budget surplus (the government's financial balance) are equal to the trade surplus.

### How can 'twin deficits' arise?

The sector financial balances provide a useful lens with which to look at a country's macroeconomic developments, but the equation must be used with care. It is a goods market equilibrium condition, so in order to understand the implications of a shock or policy change it is first necessary to identify the shock and to work out the new goods market equilibrium.

In order to do this, we need to use a model. In our first example, we use the $AD - BT - ERU$ model to illustrate the twin deficits that arise following an expansionary fiscal policy. We begin in equilibrium at trade and government budget balance, and in private sector financial balance. As shown in Fig. 11.12, a rise in $G$ leads to a new constant inflation equilibrium at higher output (on the $ERU$ curve). Both in the temporary shorter-run equilibrium at point $B$ and in the medium-run equilibrium at $C$, there is a trade deficit. In both cases, output is higher than initially, which pushes up imports; in the new medium-run equilibrium, the exchange rate is appreciated, which depresses net exports (both $B$ and $C$ are below the $BT$ line).

What about the fiscal balance? To pin things down, let us concentrate on the new medium-run equilibrium. Higher output generates higher tax revenues but not by enough to prevent the government's budget balance from deteriorating.[13] Thus, in the new equilibrium, the

---

[13] The rise in G raises income, which raises savings and imports as well as tax revenue. The level of output in the new equilibrium will therefore be lower than the level that would raise taxes by the increase in G. Hence, there is a budget deficit in the new equilibrium. As an exercise, show this algebraically.

government's financial balance has deteriorated: there is a budget deficit. Higher $y$ also raises savings and improves the private sector balance (since nothing has happened to $s_1$, $c_0$, or $I$—remember that in the new equilibrium at $C$, $r = r^*$). To summarize, the increase in government spending results in a budget deficit. The financial sector balances equation highlights the fact that in the new equilibrium, this is partly financed by borrowing from the private sector (which goes into surplus) and partly by borrowing from abroad (the trade balance goes into deficit). So-called twin deficits (fiscal and trade) have emerged.

### Examples

Since the early 2000s, twin (or, as we shall see, triple) deficits have consistently been observed in the United States, as shown by Fig. 11.13. In the last decade, the budget deficit reflected a combination of tax cuts and expensive foreign wars. Government spending during this period was financed by borrowing from abroad: the fact that the current account deficit exceeded the government deficit indicates that the private sector was also borrowing from abroad. Hence, the triple deficit. US borrowing was the mirror image of Chinese lending (i.e. the purchase of US Treasury bills by the Chinese authorities as part of their intervention in currency markets).

Can the US current account be rationalized by using the intertemporal model of the current account? The future macroeconomic adjustment brought on by such a substantial current account deficit could be thought of as benign if the build-up of debt simply reflected optimal borrowing to smooth consumption. Some economists have pointed to expectations of rapid income growth and the presence of exceptionally low interest rates (which reduces the cost of financing the government debt and encourages consumption in the present) as possible reasons why this might be the case. However, these arguments have lost some weight since the onset of the global financial crisis, which means that the macroeconomic adjustment (i.e. repaying of debt) in the United States could indeed have painful economic ramifications. This will be explored in more detail in Section 11.2.4, as will the role of global imbalances in the recent economic downturn.

In our second example, we use the intertemporal model and for simplicity assume that the exchange rate is fixed. In this case, oil is discovered. We introduce a government sector into the model discussed above and assume that the rise in the economy's permanent income leads the government to increase its expenditure on education and other infrastructure by borrowing from abroad. In this example, the private sector also goes into deficit as consumption smoothing by households raises consumption when the discovery of oil is announced. Here there are 'triple deficits' in anticipation of the flow of oil.

A more complicated model would include the likely effect of the oil discovery on the exchange rate. Countries where there has been a natural resources windfall have typically experienced exchange rate appreciation and suffered from 'Dutch disease', named after the Netherlands' experience following the discovery of natural gas in the North Sea. Dutch disease captures the idea that the non-resource tradables sector endures a loss of competitiveness as a consequence of the exchange rate appreciation. The exchange rate appreciated when gas was discovered, because the foreign exchange market anticipated that the real exchange rate at which there would be current account balance was an appreciated one (as the $AD - BT - ERU$ model predicts when there is a positive external trade shock).

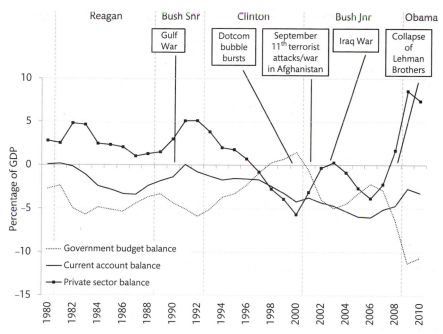

**Figure 11.13** United States Sector Financial Balances: 1980–2010.

*Note:* The private sector balance was computed using the sector financial balances equation (i.e. private sector balance = current account balance less government budget deficit).

*Source:* OECD (accessed September 2011).

### 11.2.4 Global interdependence and imbalances

As Fig. 11.4 showed, a notable characteristic of the period of the 2000s—the late phase of the Great Moderation (as discussed in the introduction to this chapter)—was the growth in external imbalances of large countries in the global economy. The US, Spain and the UK had rising external deficits of a globally significant size. The counterpart to these deficits were the increasing surpluses of China, the oil-producing countries and Germany. Japan's substantial surplus remained fairly stable in the 2000s. In the same period, central banks in both developed and emerging and developing economies were using inflation targeting and were apparently successful at achieving low and stable inflation. Figure 11.5 in Section 11.1 shows how inflation in these two country blocs remained low in the 2000s. This is in contrast to previous periods, where inflation, particularly in emerging and developing economies has proved difficult to control.

In hindsight, the imbalances that emerged in the 2000s seem unhealthy, a sure sign of the troubles that were to come. In the wake of the financial crisis, politicians and economists have been quick to extol the virtues of 'rebalancing'—i.e. countries moving towards more balanced current account positions. In the years preceding the crisis economists were divided over whether the current account imbalances were benign, reflecting rational optimizing by economic agents or whether they were unsustainable and posed a threat to medium-run economic stability.

Caballero et al. (2008) presented a unified model which sought to explain how large and rising US current account deficits could be coupled with low long-term interest rates and a rising share of US financial assets in world portfolios in a medium-run equilibrium. They divided the world into three regions: high-growth high-finance 'U' countries (e.g. US, UK, Australia), low-growth high-finance 'E' countries (e.g. Eurozone, Japan) and high-growth-low finance 'R' (i.e. the rest of the world). High finance referred to a high level of financial development. The core of the model is that there is fast economic growth in the R countries (i.e. emerging markets), but that their underdeveloped financial systems cannot provide enough high-quality savings instruments to satisfy demand. This pushes up demand for savings instruments from the U and E regions. The model assumes that U has higher growth potential than E, so a disproportionate amount of global savings flows into these countries. This model explained how three macroeconomic trends that defined the early and mid-2000s—a worsening of the US current account deficit, low global interest rates and a rising share of US assets in world portfolios—could co-exist. However, it has been criticized, particularly concerning the fact that the model assumptions better suit the 1990s (with the Asian financial crisis) than the mid-2000s. In the latter period, it could be argued that emerging markets did have the capacity to generate assets that others wanted.[14]

The Caballero et al. (2008) model emphasizes the importance of the US government's ability to create desirable financial assets. This is also highlighted in a paper by Richard Cooper on the eve of the financial crisis, which concluded that current account imbalances were benign, as they simply reflected rational savings decisions of individuals in economies with ageing populations (e.g. Germany, Japan, China).[15] Given the more favourable demographics in the US, the argument follows that these imbalances could persist until the baby boom generation in the ageing economies reached retirement, at which point the imbalances would naturally unwind as individuals sold these assets to finance consumption during retirement.

Not all economists held the view that these imbalances were sustainable. A number thought that the global imbalances, the vast majority of which were between the US and the major surplus countries (i.e. Japan, Germany and China), would inevitably lead to a large and potentially destabilizing depreciation in the dollar (Obstfeld and Rogoff, 2005; Feldstein, 2008). This would make US exports more attractive to foreigners and at the same time, make imports more expensive for US consumers. We know from Chapter 10, that if the Marshall–Lerner condition holds, a depreciation of the dollar would lead to an improvement in the trade balance.

### 11.2.5  A 2-bloc model with inflation-targeting central banks

The aim of this section is to set out a model which can provide a simple explanation of how two country blocs, each with an inflation-targeting central bank, but with different patterns in demand, could produce persistent imbalances in the global economy. We set out a 2-bloc model of the world economy and show how external imbalances can be consistent with successful inflation targeting.

---

[14]  See Frankel (2006).      [15]  See Cooper (2008).

In Section 11.1.4, we introduced the idea of medium-run global imbalances by using the downward-sloping *ERU* curve. It is easier to model the dynamic adjustment of two blocs to a shock, however, if we simplify on the supply-side and revert to a vertical *ERU*. The downward-sloping *ERU* is helpful in bringing out the incentive for a country to allow a domestic demand boom to take hold as discussed in Section 11.1.4. Here, we abstract from the motivation for different patterns of demand and concentrate on how the dynamic interaction takes place between two blocs where the supply-side is identical in each and is captured by a vertical *ERU* (i.e. there is a unique constant inflation equilibrium in each bloc).

### The role of q and r* in the 2-bloc model

In the model, there are two blocs, A and B. To fix ideas, think of bloc A as being the deficit countries (US, UK, Spain) and bloc B as the surplus countries (China, Germany, Japan, oil exporters). But note that in the model, the two blocs constitute the whole of the world economy and there is an inflation targeting central bank in each. In each bloc, the medium-run equilibrium is where aggregate demand is equal to equilibrium output (which is the same in each bloc at $y_e$), with $r = \bar{r}^*$ and $q = \bar{q}$.

To simplify the notation, we assume that the coefficients on the interest rate and real exchange rate are identical in each economy and equal to one. This means we can write the medium-run equilibrium for each bloc as follows:

$$y_e = A^A - \bar{r}^* + \bar{q} \qquad \text{(bloc A)}$$
$$y_e = A^B - \bar{r}^* - \bar{q}. \qquad \text{(bloc B)}$$

We can see why $q$ is positive for A and equal and opposite for B by writing out the definition of $q$ in the 2-bloc case,

$$q = \log\left(\frac{P^B e}{P^A}\right) \text{ and } e = \frac{\$_A}{\$_B}.$$

We assume that $A^A > A^B$ (i.e. that autonomous demand is higher in bloc A).

The first aspect of the model is that if we equate the right hand side of each equation, we can simplify and get an expression for the real exchange rate, $\bar{q}$:

$$A^A - \bar{r}^* + \bar{q} = A^B - \bar{r}^* - \bar{q}$$
$$2\bar{q} = A^B - A^A$$
$$\bar{q} = \frac{A^B - A^A}{2} < 0.$$

Since $A^A > A^B$, bloc A's real exchange rate is appreciated. This is reflected in $\bar{q} < 0$. It is also clear that bloc A's trade deficit (its net imports from bloc B), which is output minus domestic absorption, is negative ($BT^A = y_e - (A^A - \bar{r}^*) = \bar{q} < 0$) and this is equal to bloc B's trade surplus (its net exports to bloc A), which is positive: $BT^B = y_e - (A^B - \bar{r}^*) = -\bar{q} > 0$.

Changes in the real exchange rate between blocs ensures that in each bloc, aggregate demand is at equilibrium and hence inflation is constant. If the blocs were symmetric in their levels of autonomous aggregate demand, $\bar{q} = 0$, which means the real exchange rate $Q = 1$ and common currency prices are identical in each bloc. Trade would be balanced.

The second aspect of the model is to note the role of the world real interest rate: this adjusts to ensure that for the global economy (the combination of bloc A and bloc B), aggregate demand is consistent with output at its equilibrium level in the world as a whole. To see this, we write aggregate demand in block A as $y^{D,A}$ and similarly for bloc B. We need to ensure that

$$y^{D,A} + y^{D,B} = 2y_e.$$

Hence, $A^A - \bar{r}^* + \bar{q} + A^B - \bar{r}^* - \bar{q} = 2y_e$

$$A^A + A^B - 2\bar{r}^* = 2y_e$$

$$2\bar{r}^* = A^A + A^B - 2y_e$$

$$\bar{r}^* = \frac{A^A + A^B}{2} - y_e.$$

This shows that the world real interest rate adjusts to ensure a constant inflation equilibrium for the world as a whole. This happens as a result of the central banks of bloc A and bloc B adjusting the interest rate to guide inflation back to target in their blocs. Both of these central banks are forward looking and rational and solve the model taking into account the actions of the other central bank.

In the top panel of Fig. 11.14, the symmetric equilibrium is shown. In the lower panel, we show the new medium-run equilibrium in the world and in each bloc following a permanent positive demand shock in bloc A, which pushes $A^A > A^B$. The result is a higher world real interest rate, an appreciated real exchange rate and trade deficit in bloc A and a depreciated real exchange rate and trade surplus in bloc B. Inflation is constant in the new MRE. Next we examine how the economies move from the old to the new equilibrium.

### A permanent demand shock in bloc A

In Chapter 9, we showed how the central bank and foreign exchange market simultaneously solved the model to work out how the central bank would choose its interest rate response to a shock, and how the exchange rate would change. In the 2-bloc model, there are three parties involved in solving the model: the central banks in each bloc and the foreign exchange market. We need to use our imagination to think of these three rational actors playing a game with each other in which they have complete information about the model and about the shock.

To analyse how they react to a demand shock in one of them, we begin in a symmetric equilibrium with the blocs identical in every respect (the top panel of Fig. 11.14).

We assume a positive permanent shock to demand in bloc A in period zero. This pushes up output and inflation in bloc A in period zero and, just as in the closed economy, A's central bank will have to respond to this in order to get the economy on the path back to target inflation. As we shall see, the analysis we have used for a small open economy gives good guidance as to what happens in the 2-bloc case. In response to the demand shock in period zero, the central bank in bloc A increases its interest rate to dampen activity. As usual, this is accompanied by an appreciation of the real exchange rate in bloc A and in period one, bloc A is on the MR curve and on the path back to target inflation.

Meanwhile all three actors have to consider the spillovers from the shock to bloc B's economy. In this simple model, spillovers from A to B take place only through changes in the real exchange rate. In reality, there would also be feedback via the effect of changes in income in bloc A on imports from bloc B. In our simple model, the marginal propensity to import is zero. In a more realistic model, an increase in $A^A$ would not only push up output in bloc A, but also increase their demand for imports. As bloc A's imports are bloc B's exports,

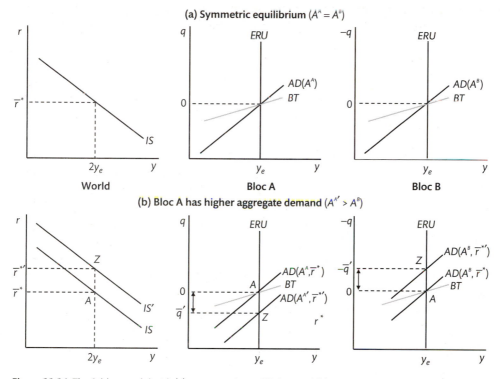

**Figure 11.14** The 2-bloc model with (a) a symmetric equilibrium and (b) a permanent positive demand shock in bloc A.

the initial increase in $A^A$ would also increase $A^B$. We exclude this feedback mechanism from the model as it complicates the analysis.

In the model, it takes one period for interest and exchange rate changes to have an effect: hence, in period zero, nothing happens to inflation or output in bloc B. However, bloc B's central bank observes the shock to bloc A in period zero and works out that in order to keep to its inflation target, it will need to act. Why? Because the appreciated real exchange rate in bloc A implies a depreciated real exchange rate for bloc B: whatever happens to the real exchange rate in bloc A happens (in reverse) to the real exchange rate in bloc B. Unless the central bank in bloc B raises its interest rate to offset the effect of the depreciation in its real exchange rate on aggregate demand in bloc B, there will be an increase in bloc B's inflation in period 1. By working through the model, the three parties will figure out that the central bank in bloc B will be able to fully offset the effects of the shock on inflation in its economy.

Figure 11.15 shows the new medium-run equilibrium (as in the lower panel of Fig. 11.14) and sketches the path of adjustment in each bloc. Figure 11.16 shows the adjustment process in the $PC - MR$ and $IS - RX$ diagrams for each bloc, which can be explained period-by-period as follows:

**Period 0** Both economies start at their respective bliss points–point $A$ in Fig. 11.16. There is a positive demand shock in bloc A, which is observed by both central banks and the forex market. This moves bloc A to point $B$ with output at $y_0$ and inflation at $\pi_0$. Bloc B has not

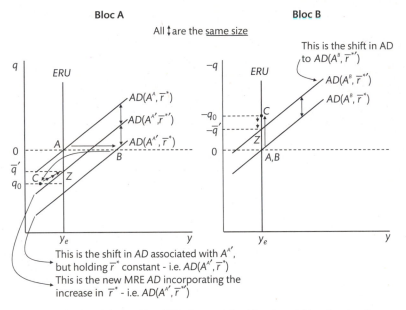

**Figure 11.15** The 2-bloc model: the $AD - ERU$ diagrams for bloc A and bloc B using the example of a permanent positive demand shock in bloc A.

moved from its original position. The central banks forecast their Phillips curves in the next period. In bloc A, the *PC* will move to $PC(\pi_1^E = \pi_0)$ next period. Bloc A is not on its *MR* curve at point B. Their desired position on next period's *PC* is point C. In order to achieve this, the central bank in bloc A raises the interest rate to $r_0^A$, taking account of the appreciation of the exchange rate that will occur (so the *UIP* condition holds).

Meanwhile, in bloc B, the central bank forecasts that the *PC* will not move next period, as inflation has not changed. They have, however, noted that the actions of bloc A's central bank will lead to a depreciated exchange rate in Bloc B (as an appreciation in bloc A is a depreciation in bloc B in this model). To counter this effect and keep the economy at its bliss point, the central bank of bloc B must raise interest rates to $r_0^B$. This rate hike is exactly what is required to offset the boost in output that would occur as the result of the depreciated exchange rate.

The new interest rates and exchange rates can only affect the economy with a one period lag. This means that bloc A ends period 0 with output at $y_0$, inflation at $\pi_0$, the interest rate at $r_0^A$ and the exchange rate at $q_0$. In contrast, bloc B remains at its bliss point, with a real interest rate of $r_0^B$ and an exchange rate of $-q_0$.

**Period 1 onwards** The new interest rates and exchange rates have had time to take effect and both blocs have moved to point C. In bloc A, the higher interest rate and the appreciated real exchange rate reinforce each other and dampen aggregate demand, causing output to fall to $y_1$ and inflation to fall to $\pi_1$. In bloc B, the interest rate and exchange rate effects exactly offset each other and the economy remains at its bliss point.

In bloc A, the adjustment from C to Z is very similar to the demand and supply shock cases in the open economy 3-equation model discussed in Chapter 9. The economy adjusts along the *RX* curve to the new medium-run equilibrium at point Z. The *RX* curve has shifted

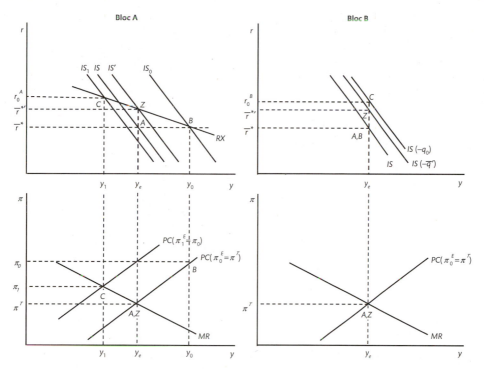

**Figure 11.16** The 2-bloc model: the $IS - RX$ and $PC - MR$ diagrams for bloc A and bloc B using the example of a permanent positive demand shock in bloc A.

upwards after the demand shock in bloc A. This is because the $RX$ curve is pinned down by the world rate of interest, which changes as a result of the demand shock. During the adjustment from C to Z in bloc A, the central bank slowly reduces the interest rate from $r_0^A$ to $\bar{r}^{*'}$ to stay on the $MR$ and $RX$ curves. The path of interest rates takes account of the depreciation that occurs each time the interest rate is reduced. This depreciation means the $UIP$ condition holds in all periods.

In bloc B, the adjustment from C to Z is simpler. The central bank can see that the exchange rate in bloc A is going to slowly depreciate over this period, meaning that bloc B's exchange rate is going to slowly appreciate. To offset the depressing effect from this appreciation the central bank will slowly reduce interest rates from $r_0^B$ to $\bar{r}^{*'}$. Throughout the entire adjustment period, bloc B does not move from its bliss point—i.e. where output is at equilibrium and inflation is at target.

The adjustment to the demand shock in bloc A ends when the blocs are at point Z, where inflation is back at target and output is back at equilibrium in both blocs. The new medium-run equilibrium is however characterized by a higher world interest rate (i.e. $\bar{r}^{*'} > \bar{r}^*$), a more appreciated exchange rate in bloc A and a more depreciated exchange rate in bloc B.

There are a number of important points to highlight from this process:

1. The initial interest rate hike in bloc A is greater than that in bloc B (i.e. $r_0^A > r_0^B$). This is because the permanent positive demand shock takes place in bloc A.

2. Throughout the adjustment process bloc B remains at equilibrium output and target inflation (i.e. its bliss point): all that the bloc B central bank has to do each period is to adjust its interest rate to offset the effects of the real exchange rate changes arising from bloc A's adjustment path.

3. When the adjustment process is complete, both economies are at equilibrium output with inflation at target and with the same real interest rate. As shown in the bottom left hand panel of Fig. 11.14, the common (i.e. world) real interest rate is higher than in the initial medium-run equilibrium to squeeze out the higher aggregate demand. Bloc A has an appreciated real exchange rate in the new medium-run equilibrium. It also has a trade deficit. Conversely, bloc B's exchange rate is depreciated and it has a trade surplus.

Lastly, Fig. 11.17 shows the impulse response functions for the key variables in each bloc. The details of the dynamic adjustment are set out in more detail in Section 11.4.1 of the Appendix.

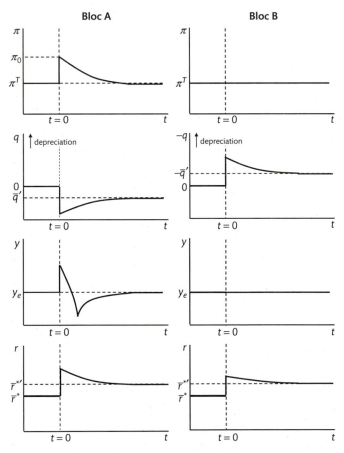

**Figure 11.17** The 2-bloc model: the impulse response functions (IRFs) for bloc A and bloc B using the example of a permanent positive demand shock in bloc A.

**Summary**  The model is very stylized and is based on very strong assumptions about ra-tionality and full information on the part of the three actors. Nevertheless, it brings out an important feature of an interdependent global economy: if economies differ in the kind of shocks they are exposed to—for example, as we saw in Chapters 6 and 7, the scale of financial and leverage cycles was very different in different countries—it is still possible for macroeconomic equilibrium to prevail in the sense of a constant inflation equilibrium in both blocs.

The 2-bloc model illustrates how current account imbalances can arise—when blocs are affected by different shocks and/or have different patterns of demand—and how they can be consistent with stable inflation. As highlighted by the intertemporal approach to the current account presented earlier in the chapter, such imbalances are not necessarily a problem: they may reflect an optimal response to differences in resource endowment (such as a natural resource windfall) or differences in preferences as countries take advantage of international capital mobility to smooth consumption.

## 11.3 Conclusions

This chapter has used open economy macro models to improve our understanding of oil shocks and global imbalances—two features of global macroeconomics that were particularly prominent in the years preceding the financial crisis. Setting out a framework within which to analyse these shocks and imbalances allows us to better understand their macroeconomic consequences and provides useful lessons for policy making.

We have shown how oil price (i.e. commodity) shocks can be modelled by introducing the world terms of trade between manufactures and raw materials. In this framework, an increase in the oil price is both a demand and a supply shock for an oil-importing economy, resulting in shifts in both the *AD* and *ERU* curves.

We have also introduced two new open economy models—the intertemporal model of the current account (ICA) and the 2-bloc model—which provide valuable insights into the sizeable current account deficits that characterized the global economy during the Great Moderation.

The ICA highlights that current account deficits can be either benign or potentially danger-ous, depending on whether they reflect optimizing forward-looking behaviour (e.g. borrow-ing to develop a newly discovered natural resource) or irrational myopia (e.g. a consumption boom based on an asset price bubble). The 2-bloc model can be used to show how two blocs in the world economy with different patterns of demand can result in both current account and real exchange rate divergences and successful inflation targeting.

This chapter allows us to shed light on some of the interesting puzzles that characterized the years of unprecedented macroeconomic stability that preceded the global financial crisis:

1.  Why did the oil price shock of the 2000s not lead to widespread 'stagflation', such as that experienced as a result of the 1970s oil shocks? The oil shocks of the 1970s were primarily driven by the supply side and reflected exogenous geo-political events disrupting oil supply, whereas an increase in oil demand (particularly in fast-growing emerging markets) played a

much more significant role in the 2000s shock. The latter shock coincided with a period of low inflation and falling unemployment, which was in stark contrast to the 'stagflation' of the 1970s. This is due to a combination of factors, including (a) the increased flexibility of labour markets in the 2000s and (b) the easier access to credit and ability to substitute away from energy-intensive activities in the latter period. In addition, inflation-targeting central banks used non-accomodating monetary policy to keep inflation expectations firmly anchored in the latter period, whereas policy makers mistakenly tried to keep output at its pre-shock level in the 1970s. This failure to account for the supply-side implications of the oil shock led to significantly worse economic outcomes in the 1970s than in the 2000s.

2. What were the macroeconomic consequences for economies following different growth strategies during the Great Moderation? There were two distinct blocs of economies during the Great Moderation; the deficit countries (the US, the UK and Spain) and the surplus countries (Germany, China and the oil exporters). The former favoured expansion of the financial sector. An emphasis on the export sector was very important in both China and Germany. Although China was growing rapidly, its growth was unbalanced: very high investment levels were associated with even higher saving rates. Germany grew very slowly: restrained domestic demand complemented restructuring of the export sector as a basis for export-led growth. The macroeconomic consequence of these different strategies was that although inflation targets were met, there was a build-up of large imbalances and interdependencies among countries.

3. Were the large current account imbalances accumulated during the pre-crisis years the result of intertemporal optimization? In the wake of the global financial crisis of 2008–09, it seems clear that the current account imbalances were not the result of rational forward-looking behaviour. Households in the United States borrowed excessively, which resulted in the build up of a dangerous leverage cycle (see Chapters 6 and 7), and made the global economy vulnerable to a financial crisis.

Chapters 9, 10 and 11 have primarily focused on open economy macroeconomics in relation to economies with flexible exchange rate regimes. In 2012, however, 17% of world output was accounted for by the Eurozone, a common currency area with irrevocably fixed exchange rates.[16] An economic model of the global economy would therefore not be complete without a proper treatment of the economics of a common currency area. The next chapter fills this gap, investigating how membership of the Eurozone affects macroeconomic adjustment and stabilization policy.

## 11.4 Appendix

### 11.4.1 Dynamic adjustment to a shock in the 2-bloc model

In this section, we will provide the mathematics behind the dynamic adjustment to shocks in the 2-bloc model. We will use the example of the case where there has been a positive

---

[16] Calculated using the IMF World Economic Outlook Database, October 2013.

permanent demand shock in bloc A (but not bloc B) in period 0. The intuition and explanation for this example is contained in Section 11.2.5 of the main body of this chapter.

We assume that bloc A and bloc B were in equilibrium in $t = -1$. So

$$y^A_{-1} = A^A - \bar{r}^* + \bar{q} = y_e$$
$$r^A_{-1} = r^B_{-1} = \bar{r}^*$$
$$\pi^A_{-1} = \pi^B_{-1} = \pi^T, \text{ and}$$

$$y^B_{-1} = A^B - \bar{r}^* - \bar{q} = y_e, \text{ such that}$$
$$A^A = A^B.$$

Then in $t = 0$, autonomous demand in bloc A increases permanently to $A^{A'}$. All three actors first work out the changes to equilibrium values. Bloc A and bloc B were identical before the shock, so that $\bar{q} = 0$ and $\bar{r}^* = A^A - y_e = A^B - y_e$. After the permanent demand shock in bloc A, the new medium-run equilibrium becomes:

$$y_e = A^{A'} - \bar{r}^{*'} + \bar{q}'$$
$$y_e = A^B - \bar{r}^{*'} - \bar{q}'$$
$$\bar{r}^{*'} = \frac{A^{A'} + A^B}{2} - y_e$$
$$\text{and } \bar{q}' = -\frac{A^{A'} - A^B}{2}.$$

What happens in period 0?

$$y^A_0 = y_e + A^{A'} - A^B$$
$$\pi^A_0 = \pi^T + (y^A_0 - y_e)$$
$$= \pi^T + (A^{A'} - A^B).$$

The central bank in bloc A, the central bank in bloc B and the foreign exchange market can now forecast that next period's Phillips curve in A will be

$$\pi^A_1 = \pi^A_0 + (y^A_1 - y_e).$$

It's also common knowledge that the central bank in bloc A has a monetary rule (MR) that defines the trade-off between output and inflation reductions each period—hence also next period, period 1. To simplify the notation, we assume $\alpha = \beta = 1$:

$$y^A_1 - y_e = -(\pi^A_1 - \pi^T). \hspace{2cm} \text{(monetary rule; bloc A)}$$

Putting period 1's Phillips curve and monetary rule equations together, all three rational actors can work out the combination of inflation and output in period 1 in bloc A that the central bank of bloc A will want to see. Thus:

$$\pi_1^A = \pi_0^A - (\pi_1^A - \pi^T)$$

$$\pi_1^A = \frac{(\pi_0^A + \pi^T)}{2}$$

$$y_1^A = y_e - \frac{(\pi_0^A - \pi^T)}{2} = y_e - \frac{A^{A'} - A^B}{2}.$$

Now all three actors know the output level, $y_1^A$, which the central bank in bloc A wants to achieve next period. To do so the only instrument bloc A's central bank has at its disposal is $r_0^A$. This has to be set to solve:

$$y_1^A = A^{A'} - r_0^A + q_0.$$

The problem is that $q_0$ depends on $r_0^A$ via the *UIP* condition:

$$r_0^A - r_0^B = q_1^E - q_0$$
$$r_1^A - r_1^B = q_2^E - q_1^E$$

....

The CBs in both A and B must respect this set of equations. Summing both sides we get $\sum_0^\infty (r_t^A - r_t^B) = \bar{q}' - q_0$ since $\lim_{t \to \infty} q_t^E = \bar{q}'$. Moreover $r_t^A, r_t^B \to \bar{r}^{*'}$. Hence

$$\sum_0^\infty (r_t^A - r_t^B) = \sum_0^\infty ((r_t^A - \bar{r}^{*'}) - (r_t^B - \bar{r}^{*'})) = \bar{q}' - q_0.$$

Now assume that $r^A$ and $q$ both converge to their new equilibrium levels $\bar{r}^{*'}, \bar{q}'$ at a proportional rate of $\lambda$. The derivation of $\lambda$ follows the same method as in the small open economy (see the Appendix of Chapter 9), so we no longer assume $\beta = 1$.

$$L = (\pi^A - \pi^T)^2 + \beta(y^A - y_e)^2$$
$$\implies (\pi^A - \pi^T) + \beta(y^A - y_e) = 0$$
$$\implies (y_1^A - y_e) = -\frac{1}{\beta}(\pi_1^A - \pi^T)$$
$$\implies (y_1^A - y_e) = -\frac{1}{1 + \beta}(\pi_0^A - \pi^T).$$

From this we derive $\lambda$:

$$(y_1^A - y_e) = -\frac{1}{\beta}(\pi_1^A - \pi^T) \text{ and } (y_1^A - y_e) = -\frac{1}{1 + \beta}(\pi_0^A - \pi^T)$$

$$\lambda = \frac{(\pi_1^A - \pi^T)}{(\pi_0^A - \pi^T)} = \frac{\beta}{1 + \beta}.$$

Hence $\sum_0^\infty ((r_t^A - \bar{r}^{*'}) - (r_t^B - \bar{r}^{*'})) = \frac{r_0^A - \bar{r}^{*'}}{1 - \lambda} - \frac{r_0^B - \bar{r}^{*'}}{1 - \lambda} = \bar{q}' - q_0$. Since $y_1^B = y_e$ that implies

$$y_1^B - y_e = 0 = -(r_0^B - \bar{r}^{*\prime}) - (q_0 - \bar{q}')$$

$$\rightarrow (r_0^B - \bar{r}^{*\prime}) = (\bar{q}' - q_0) \rightarrow \frac{(r_0^A - \bar{r}^{*\prime})}{1 - \lambda} - \frac{(\bar{q}' - q_0)}{1 - \lambda} = (\bar{q}' - q_0)$$

$$\rightarrow (r_0^A - \bar{r}^{*\prime}) = (\bar{q}' - q_0)(2 - \lambda).$$

This is now substituted into bloc A's *IS* curve in deviation form to get:

$$(y_1^A - y_e) = -(r_0^A - \bar{r}^{*\prime}) - \left(\frac{r_0^A - \bar{r}^{*\prime}}{2 - \lambda}\right)$$

$$= -(r_0^A - \bar{r}^{*\prime})\left(1 + \frac{1}{2 - \lambda}\right)$$

$$= -(r_0^A - \bar{r}^{*\prime})\left(\frac{3 - \lambda}{2 - \lambda}\right).$$

This is the *RX* curve showing the relation along the equilibrium adjustment path—through the relevant points of *IS* curves with different values of *q*. Notably the *RX* curve is shallower than the representative *IS* curve, implying that a given change in *r* has a greater impact on *y* in the open economy than in the closed. This is because the change in *r* both operates directly on *y* with coefficient −1 (or more generally *a*), and operates indirectly on *y* via its effect on changing *q* with coefficient $-\frac{1}{2-\lambda}$. Thus a much smaller change in *r* is needed in the open economy to have the same effect on *y* as in the closed economy. For example, if $\lambda = 0.5$, then *r* needs to change by only 3/5 of the amount as in the closed economy.

This is larger than in the small open economy case because of the 'bloc' effect. When *q* appreciates initially, $r^B$ has to rise to keep $y^B$ in equilibrium. This requires a bigger change in $r^A$ than would be the case in the small open economy: in effect the rise in $r^A$ has triggered a rise in the world rate of interest, which would have been fixed in the small open economy. The slope of the *RX* line here is $-\frac{2-\lambda}{3-\lambda}$ and in the small open economy case $-\frac{1-\lambda}{2-\lambda}$. The empirical implication here is that we might expect to see common patterns to interest rate changes across the world if there is a shock in any one big bloc.

## 11.5 Questions

### 11.5.1 Checklist questions

1. Explain using words and diagrams how an oil shock can be considered both a demand shock and a supply shock.

2. Use Section 11.2.1 to answer the following questions about the oil price shocks of the 1970s:

    (a) How did the misdiagnosis of the oil shock of 1973/74 affect policy choices and economic performance?

    (b) Was the same mistake made following the 1979 oil shock? If possible provide some evidence to support your answer.

    (c) Use the $AD - BT - ERU$ diagram to illustrate the basis of the policy error.

3. Oil prices fell dramatically in 1986. Use the $WS - PS$ and $ERU$ diagrams to explain the effect of this supply-side shock on a small open economy. At the initial real exchange rate, what has happened to real wages and the level of employment?

4. Assess the following statement: 'the 2002–08 oil shock had less negative macroeconomic consequences than those in the 1970s due to the success of inflation-targeting central banks at stabilizing their economies'.

5. A small open economy is initially in trade balance. There is a temporary increase in household income for one period (i.e. rise in $\widetilde{y}_t$). What effect does this have on the current account in period $t$ and the following periods? Does this story change if the increase in income is permanent?

6. What is meant by the term 'Dutch disease'? How does this relate to the intertemporal model of the current account?

7. Discuss the political and economic forces that could move a small open economy towards trade balance in the long run.

8. Use an $AD - BT - ERU$ diagram and the sector financial balances framework from Section 11.2.3 to show how a country whose government is restricting domestic demand could run 'twin surpluses' (i.e. government and current account surpluses).

9. Use Section 11.2.5 to answer the following questions about macroeconomic imbalances in the 2-bloc model:

    (a) Use a 2-bloc model to explain in words how there can be constant inflation in each bloc but current account imbalances.

    (b) Begin with 2 symmetric blocs. Now assume there is a permanent positive demand shock to bloc A and an equal and opposite permanent demand shock to bloc B. Describe the new medium-run equilibrium (MRE). [Hint: draw the $AD - BT - ERU$ diagrams for the world, bloc A and bloc B before and after the shock as in Fig. 11.14]. Your answer should focus on the differences between the initial and new MRE. Don't discuss the adjustment path to the new MRE. How could you adjust the nature of the shocks so that there was a lower real interest rate in the new MRE?

10. Why is it not possible for all countries to follow a demand-focused (i.e. expansionary) growth strategy? How did differing growth strategies across economies with global impact help current account imbalances emerge in the pre-crisis period?

## 11.5.2 **Problems and questions for discussion**

1. Use the online series for real oil prices from the Carlin and Soskice webpage http://www.oup.com/uk/orc/carlin_soskice. Pick an emerging and a developed economy and collect data from their national statistics or an international organization (e.g. IMF, OECD, Eurostat, World Bank) on the unemployment rate and the inflation rate from the start of the 1970s until the present. Do the patterns observed match those of the US in Fig. 11.9? If not, propose some potential reasons why?

2. Assess the following statement: 'economic policy makers should not directly intervene to reduce current account imbalances, because they simply reflect rational savings decisions and comparative advantages in an increasingly globalized world'.

3. Set out the $IS - RX$ and $PC - MR$ diagrams for bloc A and bloc B (as per Fig. 11.16) and the associated impulse response functions (as per Fig. 11.17) for the case where there is a positive demand shock in bloc A and a negative demand shock in bloc B (assume the shocks are equal and opposite and take place simultaneously).

4. Use the mathematics from Section 11.4.1 of the Appendix to derive the $RX$ curve after a negative demand shock in bloc B.

# 12 The Eurozone

## 12.1 Introduction

Among the 34 OECD member countries, 17 have floating exchange rates. Switzerland moved from floating to a managed exchange rate in September 2011, 15 have chosen to give up their own exchange rate and adopt the euro and one member's currency is pegged to the euro via ERM II (Denmark).[1] In Chapters 9 and 11, we concentrated on countries with independent central banks and floating exchange rates. We now turn our attention to the Eurozone, the members of which collectively accounted for 17% of global GDP in 2012.[2] In this chapter, we extend the macro model to analyse the macroeconomics of the Eurozone. We provide a set of tools for understanding the origins, successes and failures of the Eurozone—a large-scale experiment in the adoption of irrevocably fixed exchange rates, which began with 11 countries in 1999 and grew to 18 members by 2014.

*The Eurozone—successes and imbalances*

Before showing how the 3-equation model can be used to analyse macroeconomic policy in the Eurozone, we introduce the Eurozone and look at how it has operated. The Euro-zone's experience illustrates the role played by the central bank in a common currency area, and brings out the way the central bank responds to common shocks and how members are affected by country-specific shocks. The Eurozone celebrated its first ten years in 2009 and encountered its first crisis in 2010. The Eurozone's first decade was during the Great Moderation—a period of tranquility in the international macroeconomic environment. In this period, the European Central Bank functioned successfully, delivering an average infla-tion rate for the Eurozone just above its target of 2%.

In Chapter 11, we saw how low and stable inflation could be achieved in a global economy in spite of imbalances in the blocs that make it up. In this chapter we shall see another example of this general idea: if we think of the Eurozone as the 'global' economy, it achieved low and stable inflation during the 2000s, in spite of member countries experiencing different shocks, and imbalances building up. Different growth patterns were behind the build-up of imbalances in the Eurozone just as they were in the global economy. Figure 11.4 in Chapter 11 showed the evolution of current account balances in a number of large economies: two

---

[1] This information is taken from the IMF's de facto classification of exchange rate arrangements (at the end of April 2010), which can be found in Appendix II of the IMF Annual Report 2012.
[2] Calculated using the IMF World Economic Outlook Database, October 2013.

Eurozone economies feature in the chart. On the surplus side is Germany, with a rapidly growing surplus in the 2000s and on the deficit side is Spain, with a rapidly growing deficit. We shall see how these different growth patterns arose in the Eurozone and the role they played in the sovereign debt crisis.

## Common and country-specific shocks

The 3-equation model can be used to model the European Central Bank as an inflation-targeting central bank. The ECB responds to shocks to the common currency area as a whole, which are referred to as area-wide or common or symmetric shocks. But there will also be shocks that affect member countries differently. For example, there could be a housing boom in one country but not another: in the Eurozone, there was a housing boom in Spain but house prices fell in Germany during the same period of the 2000s. These are called country-specific or asymmetric shocks. An important task in this chapter is to extend the modelling framework to explain the different channels through which members of the Eurozone could adjust to country-specific shocks and how these channels played out in the first decade.

Countries in the Eurozone do not have independent monetary policy and it is obvious to think of fiscal policy being used as an alternative stabilization policy instrument. But in a common currency area, the use of fiscal policy by one member can have spillover effects for the currency area as a whole. This possibility led the Eurozone to adopt a fiscal policy framework for its members called the Stability and Growth Pact.

In the run-up to the global financial crisis, the private sector overheated in Ireland and Spain, and inflation was above the Eurozone average. We will apply the 3-equation model to show how national fiscal policy could have been used to 'lean against the wind' and dampen the boom. This was not done. We shall also see that self-stabilizing forces arising from the deteriorating competitiveness of the countries with higher inflation in the Eurozone were not strong enough to counteract the overheating. And, just as in the countries with flexible exchange rates like the US and the UK, measures were not taken before the financial crisis to halt the growth of leverage in the financial sector across the Eurozone (as discussed in Chapter 7).

## Vulnerability to a sovereign debt crisis

The Eurozone crisis brought to the fore the need to model the vulnerability of a member of a common currency area to a sovereign debt crisis, where financial markets attach very different risk premia to the government bonds issued by different member country governments. This requires an explanation of the relationship between banks, government and the central bank, which applies the analysis of Chapters 5 to 7.

The role of Eurozone membership is highlighted by the contrasting experiences of Spain and the UK. Although the underlying determinants of the solvency (the 'fundamentals') faced by the British and Spanish governments in 2011 were quite similar, interest rates on 10-year government bonds diverged sharply, reflecting differences in the market perception of the risk of sovereign default. This divergence demonstrated the vulnerability to a sovereign debt crisis of a country that borrows in a currency it does not issue. As a member of the Eurozone, the Spanish government borrows in euros, but it is the Eurozone central bank, the ECB, which issues euros.

### 12.1.1 **Origins of the Eurozone and the theory of an optimal currency area**

The political impetus for creating a common currency area in Europe was increased as a consequence of German reunification in 1990. The potential for a larger unified Germany to unbalance the achievements of post–war integration was defused by the idea that Germany would be tied more tightly to the European project through economic and monetary union. In economic terms, German industry favoured monetary union as a way of preventing its competitors in France, Italy and Spain from using exchange rate depreciation as a tool to regain competitiveness, as had happened under previous exchange rate arrangements. The private sector and policy makers in France, Italy and Spain saw Economic and Monetary Union as a means of acquiring a credible low inflation policy regime through a German–style inflation targeting central bank at the level of the common currency area. The themes of competitiveness and the behaviour of wage and price setters under the new rules of the game of a currency union play a big role in this chapter.

The theory of an optimal currency area points to the costs and benefits of a country giving up independent monetary policy (and an independent exchange rate). We divide the discussion into microeconomic and macroeconomic considerations.

#### Microeconomic benefits

The microeconomic benefits that arise from using a common currency increase with the degree of economic integration among the countries.

1. It is argued that monetary integration stimulates higher trade and investment, due to the fact that adoption of a single currency eliminates foreign exchange rate risk. As we saw in Chapter 10, an unexpected change in the exchange rate affects the profitability of production in different locations. Decisions about location often involve long-lived investment in physical plant and equipment. Where companies would previously have operated in two different countries to hedge the risk of a change in the exchange rate, in a common currency area, they can take advantage of economies of scale and achieve a more efficient allocation of resources by concentrating production in the best location.

2. Real resource savings arise from eliminating transactions costs that are incurred by currency conversion.

3. Competition in goods and labour markets would be expected to increase due to greater ease of price and wage comparisons. More competition, in turn, would be expected to produce both static and dynamic efficiency gains (as discussed in Chapters 8 and 15).

4. Monetary union is expected to increase the liquidity of financial markets. This is of particular benefit for small member countries. More liquid financial markets can also bring dangers of resource misallocation as explained in Chapters 6 and 7.

*Evidence*

A meta-analysis of 34 studies concluded that currency unions boost bilateral trade by between 30% and 90%.[3] Following the formation of the Eurozone, trade within it increased

---

[3] See Rose and Stanley (2005).

more than with non-EMU members.[4] It is also notable that before EMU, the EU countries that stayed out of the Eurozone (UK, Sweden, Denmark) had lower than average bilateral trade shares with Eurozone members.[5]

In relation to the competition effects, Holland (2009) concluded that

> trade liberalization, both on a global and European scale have reduced mark-ups, and that liberalization has had a clear effect on the sustainable level of employment in European countries. However, it does not appear that the transparency associated with the euro has had a significant impact on the mark-up.

## Macroeconomic costs and benefits

To pin down the macroeconomic costs and benefits of choosing to join a common currency area (CCA), the comparison is with a flexible exchange rate regime where the nominal exchange rate can aid the adjustment of the economy to shocks.

The theory of an optimal currency area highlights the main macroeconomic *cost* incurred by joining a common currency area: the policy maker is no longer able to use monetary policy (and the associated change in the nominal exchange rate) to adjust to country-specific shocks. This cost falls with the degree of integration between a country and the rest of the CCA. The more closely the business cycle of a member is correlated with that of other members, the better will be the stabilization performed by the CCA central bank.

There are a number of factors that influence the degree of integration among the members and how quickly they can stabilize against country-specific shocks in the absence of domestic monetary policy.

1. The degree of wage and price flexibility: domestic wage flexibility can substitute for a flexible nominal exchange rate since changes in prices influence the real exchange rate. For example, a period of wage and price growth below that of the other CCA members will make a country more competitive and boost net exports. There are different levels of wage flexibility across Eurozone members. We shall discuss the implications of this in Section 12.4.5.

2. The mobility of labour: in principle, closer economic integration makes labour more mobile and this provides a shock absorber that can help substitute for the loss of the exchange rate instrument. This channel works particularly well in the US, where the movement of workers across state borders is fluid. National differences in language, training and accreditation, and in the flexibility of housing markets are among the reasons for the limited mobility of labour across national borders in the Eurozone.

3. The size of fiscal transfers: the bigger the central (i.e. Eurozone level) tax and transfer system, the more automatic stabilization there is for country-specific shocks (see Chapter 14 for an explanation of the way automatic stabilizers work). This channel does not operate well in the Eurozone, as the EU budget is tiny. In comparison, in the United States, the federal tax and transfer system is much more substantial.

---

[4] See Micco et al. (2003) and Barr et al. (2003).     [5] See Barr et al. (2003).

There are a number of *benefits* of giving up flexible exchange rates and joining a CCA:

1. The reduction in exchange rate volatility and the removal of exchange rate overshooting from economic adjustment. We discussed the negative macroeconomic consequences of these two features of flexible exchange rate economies in Chapter 9.

2. By giving up control of monetary policy to the ECB, countries which could not successfully manage inflation through their own central bank could 'tie their hands' and establish a low inflation monetary policy regime. This was a key reason for the southern European economies to join the euro. The adoption of the euro can be seen as an alternative to delegating authority for monetary policy to an independent committee of an independent national central bank (as happened in the UK).

3. The other countries in the CCA can no longer competitively devalue. Ruling this out was a major selling point of EMU membership to the German public, who already had a credible low inflation monetary policy regime before joining the euro (i.e. the Bundesbank).

Macroeconomic adjustment in the Eurozone is discussed in detail in Section 12.4, where we set out the channels through which stabilization can occur in the absence of monetary policy and a flexible nominal exchange rate. We also look at the differences in labour market institutions across member states that meant some were more successful at stabilizing against country-specific shocks than others under conditions of monetary union.

### 12.1.2  The Eurozone's performance in its first ten years

One way of assessing the Eurozone's macroeconomic performance in its first decade is to use the same criteria we use for countries like the US or the UK: how close was the Eurozone on average to the inflation target set by the European Central Bank and to an output gap close to zero? Figure 12.1 shows the answer: where the two axes cross shows an average inflation rate of 2% and an output gap of zero. In its first decade and before the global financial crisis, the performance of the Euro area as a whole was close to target for inflation, with most

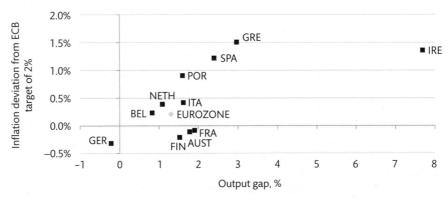

**Figure 12.1** Eurozone performance: inflation and output gap, 1999–2008 (average per cent per annum).

*Source:* OECD Economic Outlook Database (May, 2014). Inflation is consumer price index, harmonized, output gap is for total economy. Greece is from year of entry, 2001.

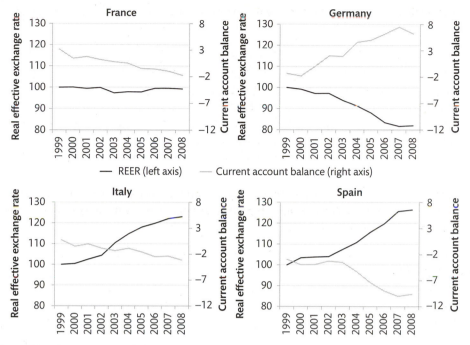

**Figure 12.2** Current account balances and intra-eurozone real effective exchange rates (REER)—France, Germany, Italy and Spain: 1999 to 2008. Increase in REER is a real appreciation.

*Source:* European Commission, January 2012; OECD Economic Outlook, December 2011.

countries displaying a small positive output gap. This suggests that the ECB was successful in managing shocks common to the Eurozone.

However, Fig. 12.1 shows very clearly how much variation there was in the performance of Eurozone member countries: at the top are the four Eurozone countries involved in the Eurozone crisis from 2010, Greece, Spain, Ireland and Portugal. These countries all had average inflation rates well above the ECB's inflation target of 2% and positive output gaps during the first decade of the euro. In the opposite corner with inflation below the target and with a negative output gap is Germany. Individual country performance was very diverse.

A second way of capturing the variation in country performance is to look at how real exchange rates and current account balances evolved. We introduced the difference between real and nominal exchange rates in Chapter 9. Figure 12.2 shows indexes for the intra-Eurozone real effective exchange rates (REER) and the current account balances for the four largest member countries (by GDP) between 1999 and 2008. The REER index is set at 100 in 1999 when the Eurozone was formed. The nominal exchange rate for each of the four countries is 100 for the whole period, reflecting the fact that nominal exchange rates are fixed between Eurozone members.

In Fig. 12.2, the current account balances are shown as a percentage of each country's GDP, where a negative value indicates a current account deficit and vice versa. The real exchange rates are defined in terms of relative unit labour costs and the index rises when the real exchange rate of the economy appreciates and competitiveness falls. This shows vividly how even when the nominal exchange rate is fixed, real exchange rates can move very differently: Spain's competitiveness relative to the Eurozone average fell by 26% over the first decade of the Eurozone, whereas Germany's improved by 17.5%. These divergences in external competitiveness were reflected in the build-up of current account imbalances, as shown in Fig. 12.2. We can see that Spain and Italy built up large current account deficits in the first ten years of the single currency, whilst Germany ran a large surplus.

This development was not anticipated when the formation of a common currency area was being discussed. It was assumed that once the nominal exchange rate had been given up—and with it, the opportunity to regain competitiveness through a nominal depreciation—wage and price-setting behaviour would adjust. What would adjustment mean? It would mean nominal wages taking the burden of adjustment to ensure that competitiveness evolved in a manner consistent with stability. To keep the real exchange rate unchanged, for example, would require that unit labour costs evolve in line with the Eurozone average, which itself would closely follow the inflation target.

Why might divergences in inflation rates and real exchange rates within a currency union matter? To the extent that expected inflation in a member country differs from the currency union average, the member country's real interest rate is affected. We shall see that this can be destabilizing: a country with higher than union average inflation (like Spain, Ireland, Portugal and Greece as shown in Fig. 12.1), has a lower real interest rate. If the higher inflation was the result of a country-specific positive demand shock, a lower real interest rate will reinforce rather than offset this shock.

Movements in the real exchange rate will also affect net exports and the trade balance. A member's external indebtedness will rise if it runs persistent current account deficits. Eventually this is likely to affect the terms on which the country can borrow i.e. their bond yields. In a common currency area, the only way a country can reverse an appreciation in its real exchange rate is by achieving a combination of slower nominal wage growth and faster productivity growth than the union average. In Section 12.4.5, we discuss the particular problems in the Eurozone that have arisen because of the differences among the countries in their wage-setting systems.

Public sector and household debt also evolved differently in member countries. The left hand side of Fig. 12.3 shows the long-run behaviour of the household debt to GDP ratio and the right hand side the government debt to GDP ratio for the large Eurozone countries. The UK, which remained outside the Eurozone, in also included for comparative purposes. The big differences across member countries in levels of debt when the Eurozone was formed are clear: Italy's public debt was very high but its household debt, relatively low. Public debt levels of Germany, France and Spain were similar in 1999 but evolved completely differently in the years before the global crisis: Spain's public debt ratio fell dramatically and household debt increased. In Germany, public debt increased but household debt fell. Spain's public debt problem arose only after the crisis, showing that fiscal recklessness during the 'good years' was not the root cause of Spain's later sovereign debt problems. In Chapter 14 Section 14.3.3, we use a model of debt dynamics to explain the behaviour of public sector debt in the Eurozone.

We shall see that the diversity of performance of member countries reflected policy choices at national level and differences in private sector behaviour, including the role of labour market institutions.

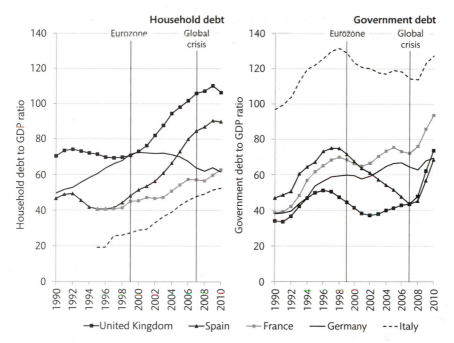

**Figure 12.3** Trends in household and public debt to GDP ratios for selected European countries between 1990 and 2010.

*Source:* Oxford Economics.

## 12.2 The Eurozone policy regime

### 12.2.1 The Maastricht policy assignment

The Maastricht Treaty of 1992 set out the basis for European Monetary Union. The first Chief Economist of the European Central Bank, Otmar Issing, used the term 'Maastricht policy assignment' to describe how the responsibility for economic policy was to be divided between the supranational ECB and the national governments.[6]

1. The ECB is responsible for using monetary policy to respond to Eurozone-wide shocks and for delivering low and stable inflation in the euro area.

2. National governments are responsible for fiscal sustainability and subject to that, for providing stabilization for country-specific shocks and for the asymmetric effects of common shocks (i.e. for dealing with the fact that common shocks may have different effects in different member countries).

3. The aim of the European Union's Stability and Growth Pact was to prevent governments from pursuing policies that might threaten the ECB's inflation objective.

---

[6] Otmar Issing (2004) 'A Framework for Stability in Europe' http://www.bis.org/review/r041130h.pdf?frames=0.

4. National labour and product markets, and national supply-side policies would determine equilibrium unemployment. However, supply-side reforms would be supported by
the European Union's 'Lisbon strategy'. The Lisbon strategy was a European Union programme for the 10 years from 2000 aimed at making the EU 'the most competitive and
dynamic knowledge-based economy in the world capable of sustainable economic growth
with more and better jobs and greater social cohesion' (Lisbon European Council, March
2000). In 2010, the Lisbon strategy was replaced by the EU's 'Europe 2020' programme.[7]

### 12.2.2 Monetary policy in the Eurozone

The European Central Bank began work as the single monetary policy maker in the Eurozone
in 1999. The Eurozone is a unique structure. It has one central bank for the whole currency
bloc, but independent national fiscal authorities and distinct labour market arrangements for
each member. The ECB is politically independent of governments—its constitution reflects
the legacy of the German central bank, the Bundesbank, and as a result it is more independent
than either the Federal Reserve in the US or the Bank of England. It sets its own monetary
policy in terms of its target (price stability, defined as an inflation rate of close to but below
2%). It uses its policy instrument, the interest rate, to achieve this target, considering both
economic and monetary 'pillars' discussed below.

The economic pillar uses forecasts of the output gap and the deviation of inflation from
target to inform the interest rate decision. The arguments set out in Chapters 3 and 4 about
the credibility of an independent inflation targeting central bank suggest the ECB is likely
to have delivered a lower inflation bias than some members could have achieved with a
national monetary policy.

In contrast to most other independent central banks (e.g. the Bank of England), the ECB has
an asymmetric inflation target. The target implies that the ECB would be happier with inflation
1% below target than 1% above target. The target has been criticized on the grounds that it
leaves the Eurozone more vulnerable to deflation than would be the case with a symmetric
target.

The interest rate decision also reflects the second pillar of the ECB's monetary policy
strategy. The second, or monetary pillar reflects the influence of the legacy of the German
central bank, the Bundesbank. Unlike many central banks, the Bundesbank had considerable
success in targeting the growth of the money supply as part of its price stability mandate.
This contrasts with the failure of monetary targeting elsewhere.[8]

In addition to using information from the economic pillar to set the interest rate, the ECB
also uses the monetary pillar. For this purpose, it uses a reference growth rate of a broad
monetary aggregate. The ECB's inflation target is a rate below but close to 2%. Its reference
for the growth rate of the money supply (the broad monetary aggregate, M3) is 4.5%. This
number is consistent with a growth rate of nominal GDP of approximately 4% (e.g. inflation

---

[7] For an independent evaluation in 2006, see Pisani-Ferry and Sapir (2006). http://aei.pitt.edu/8387/
01/BPC200603.ExitLisbon.pdf.

[8] For a comparison with the UK, see Carlin and Soskice (2006) Chapter 8 pp. 273 and 277.

of less than 2% and output growth of 2–2.5%) and with prevailing estimates of a trend decline in the velocity of circulation at a rate of decline of 0.5–1% p.a.).[9]

Although much of the Anglo-American commentary about the behaviour of independent central banks has been critical of the ECB's 'second pillar', monetary economist (and former member of the Bank of England's Monetary Policy Committee) Charles Goodhart (2006) argued that if inflation expectations come to be more closely anchored to target inflation, current inflation may no longer be a good signal of future inflationary pressure. Under these circumstances, relying only on the economic pillar could be misleading and the growth rate of a money aggregate may be a more relevant indicator of future inflation.

Goodhart picks out two episodes when monetary growth was much faster than 4.5% in the Eurozone. The first was in 2001–3 and the second from 2005. In the first case, the ECB did not respond to the monetary growth outside its target zone. It correctly diagnosed the cause as unusual and temporary monetary growth due to a blip in the demand for money arising from the bursting of the high-tech boom in 2001. Higher monetary growth reflected higher demand for money and did not signal inflationary problems.

The second episode of faster than target monetary growth from 2005 was accompanied by higher bank lending (unlike the first time). The ECB viewed this as signalling a potential inflationary problem in the future (a possibility not reflected in the well-anchored inflation expectations) and pointing toward the need to tighten monetary policy. In view of the subsequent credit-related crisis, this is an interesting example of how the ECB's second pillar could potentially play a useful role. But the need for careful interpretation highlights the problems with the naive use of a money growth indicator.

The ECB's performance has been viewed as broadly successful—inflation was stable and only just above the 2% target on average in its first decade. Its constitution is viewed as strong on independence but weaker on transparency and accountability and its asymmetric target (inflation close to but below 2%) has been criticized because it leaves the Eurozone more vulnerable to deflation (see Chapter 3 for the analysis of a deflation trap) than would be the case with a symmetric target.

### 12.2.3 Fiscal policy in the Eurozone

Together with the Maastricht Treaty, the Stability and Growth Pact set the macroeconomic framework for the Eurozone as a whole. The Stability and Growth Pact (SGP) specified that national budget deficits be kept below 3% and that the ratio of government debt to GDP be kept below 60%. The choice of these particular numbers can be rationalized by noting that a debt ratio of 60% was the average of the EU members in the years preceding the formation of the Eurozone; and with a debt ratio of 60%, the debt to GDP ratio will remain constant if the nominal growth rate is 5% and the budget deficit is 3% of GDP.[10]

Why should the state of a member country's deficit and debt levels be of any concern to the EU or the ECB? Is this not simply a matter of national policy? The reason for supra-national

[9] The calculation uses the so-called Quantity Equation: $MV = Py$, where $V$ is the velocity of circulation. Hence $\Delta M/M = \pi + \Delta y/y - \Delta V/V$ so we have $2 + 2 - (-0.5) = 4.5$. See also Chapter 13.
[10] In Chapter 14, we set out the mathematics behind government debt dynamics, which provides a simple way of checking this calculation.

concern about the deficits and debt levels in member countries arises because of fears of spillovers from national policy decisions to the Eurozone. There are several arguments about possible spillovers:

1. For any one small country, there may be an incentive to run a budget deficit in order to boost aggregate demand (shift the *AD* curve to the right) and move along a downward-sloping *ERU* curve to a lower unemployment rate. Of course if all members of the Eurozone were to do this, then this rightward shift in the *IS* curve for the Eurozone as a whole would lead to higher inflation and the ECB would have to raise the interest rate to dampen demand. The SGP seeks to prevent individual members from behaving like this.

2. A second source of spillover relates directly to government debt. In principle, the market should price any differential risk of default on government debt across Eurozone members into the price of that country's bonds. Until the Greek crisis of May 2010, the differences in the cost to different Eurozone governments of borrowing were very small. This is shown in Fig. 12.10 later in the chapter. The problem is that once the risk of default rises in one member, contagion can occur to other members. This is clearly a source of spillover from the fiscal policy of one member to others.

According to its own criteria for success, the Eurozone's record on fiscal policy in the Eurozone's first decade is not as satisfactory as that of monetary policy. The deficit target

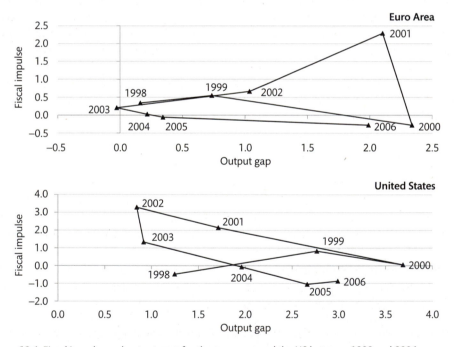

**Figure 12.4** Fiscal impulse and output gaps for the euro area and the US between 1998 and 2006.

*Note:* Fiscal impulse is defined as the change in cyclically adjusted primary budget deficit from the previous year. Output gap is for the whole economy.

*Source:* OECD Economic Outlook 89, June 2011.

of 3% was breached by a number of countries, including France. Figure 12.4 contrasts the pro-cyclical behaviour of fiscal policy in the Eurozone with the stabilizing counter-cyclical behaviour of the US. For example between 1999 and 2001, the Eurozone experienced a boom, with an increasing output gap. However, the fiscal impulse over this period was positive indicating an expansion and increase in government deficits. In contrast in the US, between 2000 and 2002, a falling output gap was associated with an increasing, counter-cyclical, fiscal impulse.

The SGP was revised in 2005. The aim was to discourage pro-cyclical fiscal policy by defining the fiscal rule in terms of the cyclically adjusted budget balance. There was greater emphasis on the sustainability of public debt and on structural issues such as the impact of future pension obligations. In addition, country-specific medium-term objectives were introduced, which ranged from a 1% of GDP deficit for countries with low debt and high potential growth to budget balance or surplus for countries with high levels of debt or with low potential for growth. Unlike the original formulation of the SGP, these amendments are consistent with the principles of a prudent fiscal policy rule set out in Chapter 14.

## 12.3 Stabilization in the Eurozone: common shocks

In the Eurozone, monetary policy is set by the ECB and the member states have no control over their own nominal interest or nominal exchange rates. The ECB responds to common shocks, that is, those that affect all members, by choosing the real interest rate to achieve its inflation target. Taking the example of an inflation shock that increases prices in the Eurozone as a whole, the ECB reacts in a similar fashion to a national central bank in a flexible exchange rate regime.

Figure 12.5 shows the adjustment of the economy to an inflation shock. Note that the interest rate in the rest of the world is indicated by $r^{row}$. We do not go through the period by period adjustment as it is exactly the same as the inflation shock example in Chapter 9, but the figure highlights some important points:

1. Although exchange rates are fixed between members, the Eurozone has a freely floating exchange rate with the rest of the world.

2. Adjustment to common shocks is therefore the same as for a country with a flexible exchange rate. In the case of an inflation shock in Fig. 12.5, the ECB raises its interest rate above the world interest rate, $r^{row}$, to get the economy on to the *MR* curve and return the Eurozone economy to target inflation.

3. The tool that helps return the economy to equilibrium after a common shock is the ECB's ability to influence aggregate demand by altering the interest rate, which in turn influences the exchange rate via the UIP condition.

The response of a national central bank in a flexible exchange rate regime to a range of macroeconomic shocks (e.g. inflation, supply and demand shocks) is analysed in detail in Chapter 9. This analysis also holds for the response of the ECB to common shocks in the Eurozone. We now go on to consider shocks that only affect one country within the Eurozone.

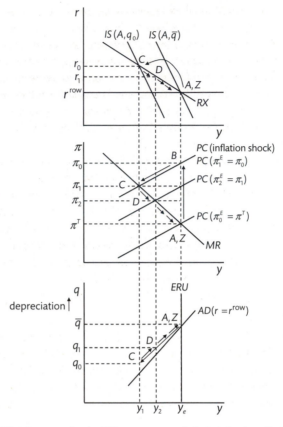

**Figure 12.5** Adjustment by the ECB to a common inflation shock to the Eurozone.

## 12.4 Stabilization in the Eurozone: country–specific shocks

### 12.4.1 Is stabilization policy necessary for country-specific shocks?

Before considering the case of a Eurozone member, it is useful to recall the way that stabilization policy works using monetary policy. One of the main results about stabilization in the closed economy and in the flexible exchange rate economy (set out in Chapters 3, 9 and 13) is the so-called Taylor principle. This says that the central bank should respond to forecast inflation by raising the *real* interest rate. This result was built into the operation of inflation targeting central banks around the world and has been credited with helping to keep inflation low and stable. In the case of an inflation shock, unless the central bank raises the nominal interest rate more than one-for-one with the expected increase in inflation, the real interest rate falls and the economy will move further away from equilibrium. The Taylor principle is discussed in detail in Chapter 13.

  Is a stabilizing policy intervention of this kind also needed in a CCA? Not necessarily. The reason is that when the nominal exchange rate is fixed as is the case for a member of the Eurozone, if inflation goes up, it makes the economy less competitive and this will dampen net exports and pull the economy back toward equilibrium without the need for policy intervention. This is called the 'real exchange rate' channel of adjustment. If this mechanism can be relied on, we would need to worry much less about how fiscal policy could be used to stabilize the economy. But can it be relied on? The example below from the recent history of the Eurozone suggests it cannot.

## De-stabilization in the Eurozone

An example of a country-specific inflation shock comes from the case of Ireland in the initial phase of the Eurozone. Following the adoption of the euro, the euro depreciated against both the US dollar and the pound sterling. Because Ireland has much stonger trade relations with the US and the UK than is typical in the Eurozone, the euro depreciation had a bigger effect in raising inflation in Ireland (as imported goods increased in price, which in turn triggered domestic wage increases) than was the case in other members. This represented a country-specific inflation shock for Ireland.

The Irish example highlights that there is another channel that can operate in a CCA to *destabilize* the economy and may prevent the 'no intervention' strategy via the appreciation of the real exchange rate from working to keep inflation in a member country close to the Eurozone target. This is the 'real interest rate' channel. When a member country's inflation is above the Eurozone average, this may affect *expected* inflation in that economy. If expected inflation rises, then the real interest rate falls and this boosts output, putting additional upward pressure on inflation as output rises above equilibrium. Instead of moving back to equilibrium as happens through the real exchange rate channel, the economy will move further away from equilibrium with rising output and rising inflation.

This helps to explain what happened in Ireland and Spain in their post-euro property booms: the combination of the low nominal interest rate set by the ECB with high domestic inflation (relative to the Eurozone average) pushed down the real interest rate. In conjunction with the operation of the financial accelerator and bubble mechanisms studied in Chapter 6, this stimulated investment in construction projects and consumption in those economies. It is said that 60% of Europe's concrete was being used in Spain in 2006. The real interest rate in Ireland and Spain was actually negative for much of the period from euro entry until 2007.

Under these circumstances, the government must intervene with a sufficiently contractionary fiscal policy to ensure that the economy returns to equilibrium. As noted above, the failure to do so fuelled the house price bubbles and construction booms in Spain and Ireland before the crash of 2007–8.

### The Taylor principle and the Walters critique

In a flexible exchange rate regime, the Taylor principle is built into the 3-equation model. For a member of a CCA, unless a similar principle is applied so that the required negative output gap is created to dampen inflation (through the combination of tighter fiscal policy and the operation of the real exchange rate channel), instability can arise. This is referred to as the Walters' critique. British economist Alan Walters argued against UK membership of the euro on the grounds of this kind of instability.

In the analysis of stabilization under *flexible* exchange rates, we did not mention the government's financial balance, i.e. whether it was in budget deficit or surplus. This is because under normal conditions, stabilization against a private sector shock is carried out by the

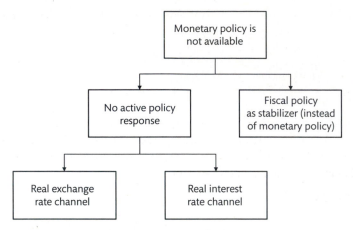

**Figure 12.6** Stabilization policy options as a member of a CCA.

central bank using the interest rate and once the economy has returned to medium-run equilibrium, the government's financial balance excluding interest payments, which is called its primary balance, will be back at its initial level.

We shall see that the result is different when fiscal policy is used as the stabilization policy by a member of a CCA. This draws attention to whether fiscal policy is a good substitute for monetary policy in stabilizing against shocks. In general, we find that fiscal policy is not a perfect substitute for monetary policy: concern about the consequences of stabilization for the budget balance make its use considerably more difficult than the use of monetary policy under flexible exchange rates.

Figure 12.6 summarizes the stabilization issues that arise for a member of a CCA because they do not have their own monetary policy. The government can choose to do nothing in response to a shock (the left-hand side of Fig. 12.6) or to use fiscal policy (the right-hand side). We look at the real exchange rate and real interest rate channels in turn, and then show why fiscal policy is not a perfect substitute for monetary policy in stabilization.

### 12.4.2 The real exchange rate (competitiveness) channel

As noted above, if the government decides not to use policy to respond to a shock, two adjustment processes arise automatically. These are the real exchange rate and real interest rate channels. Inflation in medium-run equilibrium in a member of a CCA is pinned down by the inflation target of the CCA's central bank, i.e. $\pi^{MRE} = [\pi^T]$. In the Eurozone, this is the ECB's inflation target.

The simplest way of explaining the two channels is by making an assumption about how inflation expectations are formed. In Chapter 9, we saw that in a fixed exchange rate economy, home's nominal interest rate is equal to the world nominal interest rate ($i = i^*$). In the case of a CCA, the 'world' nominal interest rate refers to the interest rate set by the CCA's central bank. Throughout this section, we shall refer to variables at the CCA level with a star and variables at a member level without a star (apart from the CCA's inflation target, $\pi^T$) and we ignore the rest of the world. If inflation expectations in a CCA member are firmly anchored to the CCA's inflation target, i.e. $\pi^E = [\pi^T]$, then from the Fisher equation, the real interest rate remains constant at the CCA real interest rate (i.e. $r^*$):

$$r = i - \pi^E \qquad \text{(Fisher equation)}$$

If $\pi^E = \pi^T$ and since $i = i^*$

then $r = i^* - \pi^T = r^*$.

Using the definition of the real exchange rate, $Q \equiv P^*e/P$ and taking logs, we have $q = p^* + \log e - p$, where $q$, $p$, and $p^*$ indicate the log of the variable. In a CCA, we can see that a CCA member's competitiveness improves (its real exchange rate depreciates) when its inflation is below CCA inflation and vice versa:

$$\Delta q = \Delta p^* - \Delta p = \pi^T - \pi.$$

The real exchange rate channel works like this: if we take the case of a positive inflation shock as our example, a rise in a CCA member's inflation reduces its competitiveness and depresses output via the $IS$ relation:

$$y_t = A_t - ar_{t-1} + bq_{t-1}.$$

The causal chain for the real exchange rate channel is:

$$\uparrow \pi \rightarrow \downarrow q \rightarrow \downarrow y \rightarrow \downarrow \pi... \text{ until } \pi < \pi^T \text{ when } \uparrow q \rightarrow \uparrow y.$$

Eventually, $y = y_e$ and $\pi = \pi^T$.

In Fig. 12.7a the upward shift in the Phillips curve due to the inflation shock is shown. As a consequence of the impact of the shock in reducing the CCA member's competitiveness, the $IS$ curve shifts to the left and the economy is at lower output (at point C on the $r = r^*$ line because of our assumption that $\pi^E = \pi^T$). What happens to inflation? As usual, this depends on inflation expectations. Because of our assumption that inflation expectations are firmly tied down to the CCA's inflation target, in the period after the inflation shock, the Phillips curve reverts to the one indexed by $\pi^E = \pi^T$. The fall in output caused by the CCA member's loss of competitiveness pushes inflation below $\pi^T$ and as we can see from the definition of the real exchange rate, this boosts their competitiveness. The following period, the $IS$ curve therefore shifts to the right ($IS(q_1)$) and the economy begins to recover. Eventually, it is back at equilibrium with the initial real exchange rate.[11] Nothing has happened to government spending or taxation, so the economy remains in fiscal balance.

### 12.4.3 The real interest rate channel

Let us now see what happens when inflation expectations are not firmly anchored to the CCA's inflation target. When there is a backward-looking element in inflation expectations, the Fisher equation indicates that a CCA member's real interest rate can deviate from the CCA real interest rate. This will be the case if agents believe that inflation will continue to behave as it has in the past. To make the explanation of this channel as clear as possible,

---

[11] For simplicity, we assume the economy moves smoothly to the new equilibrium and does not oscillate around it.

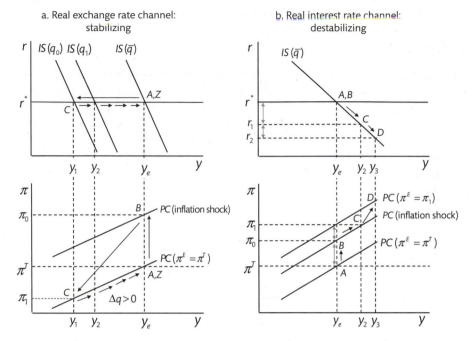

**Figure 12.7** Inflation shock: the real exchange rate and real interest rate channels.

we assume the *IS* curve does not shift with a change in the real exchange rate. Figure 12.7b illustrates how the real interest rate channel works. Inflation expectations are formed in a backward-looking way with $\pi^E = \pi_{-1}$. The inflation shock shifts the Phillips curve up as usual. This now raises *expected* inflation, which reduces the CCA member's real interest rate (to $r_1$). This leads to a rise in output and inflation (point *C*). Inflation expectations are updated and the Phillips curve shifts up again. Output rises further.[12]

The causal chain for the real interest rate channel works like this:

$$\uparrow \pi \rightarrow \uparrow \pi^E \rightarrow \downarrow r \rightarrow \uparrow y \rightarrow \uparrow \pi \dots \text{ destabilizing.}$$

In a more realistic model, the real exchange rate effect will operate alongside the real interest rate effect. But as long as the real interest rate effect is stronger, the problem of instability identified by Walters exists.[13]

### 12.4.4 Using fiscal policy to stabilize

Why might the government in a common currency area use fiscal policy for stabilization? Since it has no access to monetary policy to offset country-specific shocks, the government could turn to fiscal policy as a substitute for two reasons:

---

[12] The Macroeconomic Simulator available from the Carlin and Soskice website can be used to show the destabilizing real interest rate channel in action (see Question 4 in Section 12.7.2).

[13] See T. Kirsanova, D. Vines and S. Wren-Lewis (2006), 'Fiscal Policy and Macroeconomic Stability within a Monetary Union' CEPR DP 5584.

1. It may be necessary in order to prevent the instability of the Walters' critique effect.
2. Sluggish wage and price adjustment may make the real exchange rate channel slow and costly in terms of a period of elevated unemployment.

Even in an economy where the exchange rate channel dominates the interest rate channel, inflation expectations may adjust only slowly to the CCA's inflation target. Looking at Fig. 12.7a, if instead of jumping back to its original position in the period after the inflation shock, the Phillips curve shifts downward only a little, then inflation will remain above the CCA's inflation target and the CCA member's competitiveness will continue to deteriorate. The process will be stabilizing in the end, because eventually, the combination of the downward drift of the Phillips curve and the rise in the output gap will push the CCA member's inflation below the CCA's inflation target, and its competitiveness will begin to improve. In such a case, relying on the competitiveness channel may impose heavy costs on the economy in the form of inflation and output deviations from $\pi^T$ and $y_e$ respectively.[14]

### Inflation shock

It is important to carefully examine the use of fiscal policy for stabilization. A good place to start is to assume the policy maker in a CCA member has the same utility (i.e. loss) function as the monetary policy maker in a flexible exchange rate regime (or a closed economy) and faces the same constraints. In other words, the policy maker minimizes its losses subject to the constraint of the Phillips curve. To make the comparison with the flexible exchange rate economy as direct as possible, we use the same loss function and the same Phillips curve.

The policy maker is modelled as minimizing this loss function:

$$L_t = (y_t - y_e)^2 + \beta(\pi_t - \pi^T)^2, \qquad \text{(government loss function)}$$

where $\pi^T$ is the CCA's inflation target and $\beta > 1$ characterizes a government that places less weight on output fluctuations than on deviations in inflation, and vice versa. The only difference from the flexible exchange rate economy is that the government wants to minimize deviations from the CCA's inflation target and not a national inflation target.

The Phillips curve is the same as in the flexible exchange rate economy:

$$\pi_t = \pi_{t-1} + \alpha(y_t - y_e). \qquad \text{(Phillips Curve, PC)}$$

The government optimizes by minimizing its loss function subject to the Phillips curve. This produces the policy rule equation (the *PR* curve), which differs from the *MR* curve only in the replacement of a national-level inflation target with a CCA-level inflation target, $\pi^T$:

$$(y_t - y_e) = -\alpha\beta(\pi_t - \pi^T). \qquad \text{(Policy Rule, PR)}$$

Figure 12.8 provides a direct comparison between the use of fiscal policy in a CCA member and monetary policy in a flexible rate economy in response to an inflation shock. We see immediately that because of our assumptions about the policy maker's loss function and the

---

[14] The Macroeconomic Simulator available from the Carlin and Soskice website can be used to model the speed of adjustment to a negative demand shock in CCA member and flexible exchange rate economies (see Question 5 in Section 12.7.2). This highlights the costs imposed when fiscal policy is not used to stabilize country-specific shocks in a CCA.

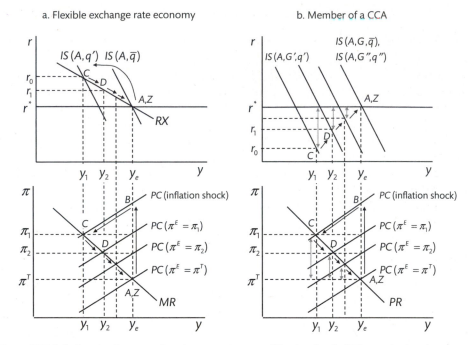

**Figure 12.8** Inflation shock: comparison between the use of fiscal policy (a CCA member) and monetary policy (a flexible exchange rate economy).

Phillips curve, the lower panel is virtually identical in each economy—the only differences are in the labelling of the policy rule curve, and the fact that at equilibrium, inflation is equal to the CCA's inflation target in the CCA member and equal to the national inflation target in the flexible exchange rate economy (both of which are labelled $\pi^T$).

The lower panels show that the optimizing policy maker in each type of economy chooses the same sequence of output gaps on the path back to equilibrium. However, how policy is used to implement those output gaps differs. The central bank in the flexible rate economy gets the economy on the path back to equilibrium by raising the interest rate and taking advantage of the exchange rate appreciation that will accompany it (left upper panel). The IS curve is shifted to the left by the appreciation and goes through point C.

In a CCA member, the government will decide on its initial fiscal policy stance, $G'$, (to achieve the output gap at point C) taking into account the fact that higher expected inflation reduces the real interest rate to $r_0$ and higher actual inflation reduces competitiveness to $q'$.

The crucial point to note is that once the CCA member is back at equilibrium with inflation at target, its real exchange rate will have appreciated. The reason is clear from the right hand lower panel of Fig. 12.8: its inflation is above the CCA's inflation target throughout the inflation shock episode. Hence, its price level will have risen relative to the other members of the CCA and with a fixed nominal exchange rate, $e$, its real exchange rate will have appreciated. In the flexible rate economy, the real exchange rate is back to its initial level $\bar{q}$: the burst of higher inflation at home is offset by the appropriate nominal depreciation to leave the real exchange rate unchanged. The appreciated real exchange rate ($q''$) at equilibrium in the CCA member

**Table 12.1**  Characteristics of the initial and new equilibria in the case of an inflation shock in a CCA member and a flexible exchange rate economy.

| | Member of a CCA | Flexible exchange rates |
|---|---|---|
| Initial equilibrium | $\pi = \pi^T; y = y_e; q = \bar{q}; G = G$ | $\pi = \pi^T; y = y_e; q = \bar{q}; G = G$ |
| New equilibrium | $\pi = \pi^T; y = y_e; q = q''\downarrow; G = G''\uparrow$ | $\pi = \pi^T; y = y_e; q = \bar{q}; G = G$ |

means that net exports are lower and therefore for the level of demand to be sufficient for output of $y_e$, government spending must be higher ($G'' > G$).

Table 12.1 shows the characteristics of the initial and new equilibria for the case of an inflation shock. Under flexible exchange rates, $\pi^T$ is the national inflation target and monetary policy is used to stabilize. In a CCA member, $\pi^T$ is the CCA's inflation target and fiscal policy is used to stabilize.

## Summary

In a *flexible* rate economy following an inflation shock, the central bank uses changes in the nominal interest rate to stabilize and it leaves no trace once the economy is back at equilibrium. However, in a CCA member, if fiscal policy has to be used to stabilize (because the real exchange rate channel is insufficiently effective), there is a fiscal deficit when the economy is back at equilibrium. Indeed, because net exports are lower and government spending is higher, the economy is characterized by twin deficits, a budget deficit and an external trade deficit.

In an $AD - ERU$ diagram (not shown, see Question 9 in Section 12.7.1), the flexible exchange rate economy returns to its starting point with budget balance. But the CCA member for which fiscal policy has been used to stabilize will be at a medium-run equilibrium with an appreciated real exchange rate and on a new AD curve indexed by the higher level of government spending. There is a budget deficit at the new medium-run equilibrium.

## Aggregate demand shock

If the economy is hit by a country-specific negative aggregate demand shock, the central bank in a flexible exchange rate economy will cut the interest rate. The exchange rate will depreciate and the economy will move on to the *MR* line at point *B* in the right hand panel of Fig. 12.9. At the new equilibrium at point *Z*, the flexible exchange rate economy is characterized by $r = r^*$ with a depreciated real exchange rate ($\bar{q}''$) and unchanged government expenditure. The primary fiscal deficit is unchanged.

In a common currency area, the *PR* line in the left hand panel of Fig. 12.9 shows the output gap the government has to choose in order for the economy to move back to equilibrium following the same path as the flexible rate economy. It raises G to G' at point B taking into account the fact that their real interest rate has been pushed up by lower inflation. To shift the economy to the new equilibrium at Z, the government adjusts government expenditure each period. Once the economy is at Z, the real exchange rate is depreciated (to $\bar{q}'$). The depreciation is not as large as in the flexible rate economy because it only reflects

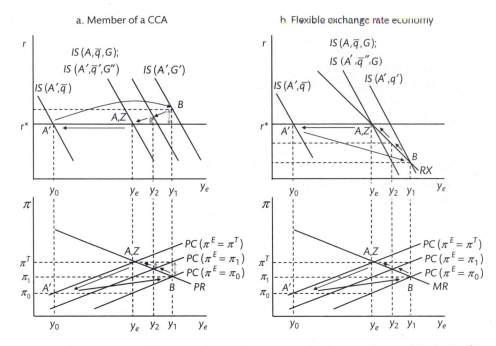

**Figure 12.9** Permanent negative aggregate demand shock: comparison between the use of fiscal policy (CCA member) and monetary policy (flexible exchange rates).

the cumulative inflation differential vis-à-vis the rest of the world: in the flexible exchange rate case, the depreciation consists of the same cumulative inflation differential plus some nominal depreciation. Hence, once the member of the common currency area is at the new equilibrium at $Z$, $r = r^*$, $\bar{q}' < \bar{q}''$ and $G'' > G$.

The bottom line is that in the face of a permanent negative demand shock, a CCA member that uses exactly the same policy rule as in the flexible exchange rate economy to return inflation to the CCA inflation target—but implements the desired output gaps by using fiscal rather than monetary policy—ends up with a primary budget deficit when it is back in equilibrium, whereas the flexible exchange rate economy does not.

## 12.4.5 The real exchange rate channel—internal devaluation

### The role of differences in wage-setting systems in the Eurozone

The role that fiscal policy plays in macroeconomic stabilization in a currency union could be shared with or substituted by wages policy or by the kind of coordinated wage-setting behaviour discussed in detail in Chapter 15. This possibility depends on institutional arrangements for collective bargaining and is relevant in the Eurozone because of the use made of it by Germany. In particular, we shall see that Germany's wage-setting system means that the real exchange rate channel explained in Section 12.4.2 operates there. This poses particular difficulties for some other member countries in which the real exchange rate channel does not operate as effectively.

As we have seen in Section 12.1.1, from a macroeconomic perspective, one attraction for a country on joining a common currency area with Germany is to acquire a credible commitment to low inflation. However, as noted in Section 12.1.2, one outcome has been divergent real exchange rates because inflation rates did not converge rapidly to the ECB's target *and* Germany's inflation was below the target.

Figure 12.2 shows that from 2000, Germany experienced a substantial real depreciation within the Eurozone. This took place through a combination of restraint in nominal wage growth and more rapid productivity growth than was the case in member countries in the southern Eurozone. Although this partly reflected the recovery of Germany's competitiveness, which had been depressed by the consequences of German reunification in the early 1990s, more importantly, it demonstrated the country's ability to engineer a real depreciation inside the Eurozone when required.

### German wage coordination

Whilst it does not have a classical flexible labour market, Germany, like some other northern Eurozone members (and some EU countries outside the Eurozone like Sweden and Denmark), has wage-setting institutions that enable nominal wage growth to be coordinated so as to achieve a real exchange rate target. The way in which different wage-setting institutions (coordinated, industry-level and firm level) operate is introduced in Chapter 2 and extended in Chapter 15. In the 2000s, unions in Germany agreed to modest nominal wage increases in multi-year deals, and works councils that represent workers in large companies negotiated over wage and hours flexibility in exchange for investment by firms in fixed capital and training.[15]

Germany's model of export-led growth relies on skilled workers in its core manufacturing industries. This places such workers in a strong bargaining position. As a result, unions and employers' associations in the export sector are important in wage setting. They play two roles in keeping the export sector competitive. First, agreements between unions and employers' associations are important in restraining the bargaining power of skilled workers in those industries. Second, unions and employers in the export sector lead the wage setting round in the economy as a whole so as to ensure that the pace of wage increases is pinned down by the competitiveness requirements of the export sector and not by the wage bargains in the non-tradeables parts of the economy, such as the public sector, where external pressure to contain cost increases is absent. Coordinated wage setting in Germany is the outcome of private sector behaviour—it is not the result of government policy.

The German model allows coordinated wage restraint to substitute for the use of stabilizing fiscal policy. To see how coordinated wage setting works, we can use the example shown in Fig. 12.7. The left-hand panel can be thought of as representing Germany and the right hand panel, a member county such as one in the periphery, where inflation expectations are not anchored to the ECB's inflation target. If there is an inflation shock to each country, the response in Germany is a reduction in wage increases, so that they are below the ECB's inflation target in order to restore the real exchange rate to its initial level. This restores

---

[15] See, for example, Carlin and Soskice (2009) and Dustmann et al. (2014).

competitiveness and the economy returns to equilibrium. Coordinated wage setting can make the real exchange rate channel work effectively.

A country without this kind of wage behaviour may experience destabilization as shown in the right-hand panel of Fig. 12.7. Weak and sluggish wage adjustment and inflation expectations that are backward looking and not anchored to the ECB's inflation target bring the destabilizing real interest rate channel into play. To return to equilibrium at the initial real exchange rate, such a country would have to use tight fiscal policy to implement the large negative output gap associated with the relevant Phillips curve (labelled $\pi^E = \pi_{-1}$) sufficient to bring inflation *below* the target. Only a period with inflation below $\pi^T$ will see the economy return to equilibrium without an appreciated real exchange rate.

To take another example, in the face of a negative aggregate demand shock, Germany is able to achieve a response similar to that implemented under flexible exchange rates whereby demand is stabilized by a real depreciation achieved via *wage restraint*. Under *flexible* exchange rates, the real depreciation takes place via a nominal depreciation triggered by a cut in the interest rate. By contrast, as we saw in Fig. 12.9, a Eurozone member without wage coordination can use fiscal policy to stabilize along the *PR* curve but will need to manage the consequences that arise for the government deficit.

For countries like Germany where the export sector is the dynamic part of the economy, it can be argued that it is important to limit the use of discretionary fiscal policy for stabilization since it weakens the incentive of wage setters to exercise wage restraint and to coordinate around the required real exchange rate.

### Living in the Eurozone with Germany

For Eurozone members that do not have wage–setting institutions that make the real exchange rate an effective stabilization mechanism, there are serious problems with achieving satisfactory macroeconomic performance. For example, a country entering the Eurozone with a higher growth rate of unit labour costs than the average will suffer from falling competitiveness. An attempt to offset the effects of this on aggregate demand by using expansionary fiscal policy will produce problems of fiscal imbalance; allowing a credit–fuelled housing boom to sustain growth (reflected in the trends in household debt shown in Fig. 12.3) brings the problems of potential instability explained in Chapters 6 and 7. The divergence of real exchange rates that characterized the Eurozone in its first decade (as shown in Fig. 12.2) reflects both the failure of domestic unit cost growth to adjust to the Eurozone inflation average of just above 2% and the success of Germany in achieving unit cost growth below 2% p.a.

Given the variation in institutional characteristics among members and Germany's export-oriented growth strategy, this problem is likely to remain a source of tension for the Eurozone.

### 12.4.6   Conclusions about stabilization policy in the Eurozone

In response to country-specific shocks, policy makers in a common currency area can choose not to intervene and rather, to rely on the stabilizing mechanism of the real exchange rate channel. But this may not produce rapid stabilization because of the countervailing operation of the destabilizing real interest rate channel and/or because the operation of the real exchange rate channel is sluggish. Hence, the government may use fiscal policy to stabilize. But fiscal policy is not a panacea.

Our results show that:

1. A fiscal policy rule can be used to stabilize output and inflation in a CCA member. However, although using the same loss function as in the flexible rate economy will return the economy to a medium-run equilibrium with inflation at the CCA's inflation target, the economy will not in general return to an equilibrium in which the government budget is balanced.

2. If the government wishes to ensure budget balance at medium-run equilibrium, then its stabilization task is more complex.

3. Labour market institutions matter for the ability of member states to adjust without the use of fiscal policy. The presence of coordinated wage bargaining that increases the flexibility of wages improves the operation of the real exchange rate channel. These institutions are typical in Germany and the other Northern European economies, which is beneficial for *their* adjustment, but can cause imbalances in real exchange rates and current accounts at the Eurozone level.

## 12.5 Eurozone governance, sovereign risk and the banking system

In this chapter, we have seen that a CCA member loses access to the nominal exchange rate as a mechanism for adjustment to shocks and that neither adjustment via domestic wages and prices (the real exchange rate channel) nor via the use of fiscal policy is problem-free. On the other hand, the economy is free of the disturbances that can come from the foreign exchange market itself. Until 2010, this was a reasonable summary of the issues facing a country deciding whether to join the euro.

The new issue that emerged was familiar to observers of emerging economies, but not to those whose expertise was limited to developed countries like Eurozone members. The new issue was the possibility of sovereign default—the inability of the government to honour the repayment of bonds it has issued. The first market signal that there was a problem of sovereign debt in the Eurozone came from the emergence of large interest rate differentials between bonds issued by Germany (and France) and those issued by the periphery countries (Greece, Portugal, Spain and Ireland). This was a new development and followed the collapse of Lehman Brothers in 2008 (see Chapter 7).

During the Eurozone's first decade, interest rate spreads on government bonds among Eurozone members shrank dramatically. Prior to the formation of the Eurozone, the interest rate differentials reflected both the exchange rate risk and the government default risk. Once inside the Eurozone, the exchange rate risk (e.g. the risk that the Italian lira would depreciate against the German D-Mark) vanished because all members used the euro, leaving only differences in government default risk to account for the variation in interest rates on long-term (e.g. ten-year) government bonds.

Extending the uncovered interest parity condition (*UIP*) to include the risk of a government defaulting on its debt highlights the exchange rate and default risk:

$$i = i^* + \left(\log e_{t+1}^E - \log e_t\right) \qquad\qquad\qquad \text{(\textit{UIP} condition)}$$

$$i = i^* + \underbrace{\left(\log e_{t+1}^E - \log e_t\right)}_{\text{exchange rate risk}} + \underbrace{\rho_t}_{\text{default risk}} , \qquad \text{(\textit{UIP} condition with default risk)}$$

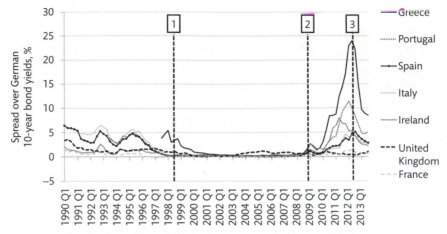

1. Introduction of the euro, which fixed the exchange rates of 11 countries
   (Greece joined in 2001, the UK did not join the Eurozone)
2. Lehman Brothers files for Chapter 11 bankruptcy protection (i.e. onset of financial crisis)
3. ECB President Mario Draghi announces "the ECB is ready to do whatever it takes to preserve
   the euro". Shortly after, the ECB announces Outright Monetary Transactions, a programme
   of government bond buying in secondary markets with the "aim of safeguarding an
   appropriate monetary policy transmission and the singleness of monetary policy".

**Figure 12.10** Long term interest rate differentials on 10-year government bonds vis-a-vis Germany between 1990 Q1 and 2013 Q3.

*Source:* OECD (accessed December 2013).

where $\rho_t$ is the default risk on government debt. The risk-adjusted *UIP* condition says that a CCA member's interest rate will be above the CCA interest rate to the extent that its nominal exchange rate is expected to depreciate and its risk of default on government debt exceeds that of the benchmark CCA government. In the Eurozone, the benchmark government debt is that issued by Germany (so-called German Bunds) and exchange rate risk is zero (as exchange rates are fixed between members). Hence, the difference between German and, for example, Greek interest rates on ten-year bonds reflects only the difference in default risk.

Figure 12.10 shows the differential between the interest rate on long-term government bonds issued by a number of European countries and the German Bund rate.[16] The data include the period before the Eurozone was formed (in 1999). The countries shown include those caught up in the Eurozone crisis of 2010 in addition to France and the UK. The UK is not a member of the Eurozone: its interest differential therefore reflects both the exchange rate risk and the default premium throughout the period. For the countries (i.e. excluding Greece) who joined the Eurozone when it began, the sharp fall in the interest differential with Germany when the exchange rate parities with the euro were announced in 1998 is clear. The same happened with Greece prior to its entry in 2001.

During the Eurozone's first decade, interest differentials with Germany on long-term government bonds were very small. How can this be explained?

[16] See Section 12.5.2 for a list of sources for the ECB quotes in Fig. 12.10.

1. The markets viewed the likelihood of a default by a Eurozone government as being very low. For example, they considered the risk of a systemic banking crisis in a Eurozone member that would require a government rescue of banks as a very low probability event.

2. The markets did not connect the divergent performance among Eurozone members with the possible implications for government solvency.

3. The markets did not believe the Eurozone's 'no bail-out clause' and took the view that any problem in one member government's ability to service its debts would be solved by the ECB and/or by the other Eurozone governments.

When the global financial crisis took hold in 2008 and large banks in small countries (like Ireland) began to fail, this market perception changed dramatically. Knowing that governments would rescue solvent but illiquid banks and would bear the burden of restructuring insolvent ones, the markets suddenly began to differentiate between the bonds issued by different Eurozone member governments. The emergence of very large interest rate spreads indicated that the markets were not confident that national governments that got into difficulty as a result of increases in national public debt due to bank failures and recession would be bailed out by the Eurozone.

### 12.5.1 Governance arrangements: banks, governments and central bank

At the root of the Eurozone's vulnerability to a sovereign debt crisis were the relationships among banks, national governments and the ECB that were put in place when the Eurozone was created. A coherent set of relationships among these three groups that was robust to a financial crisis was not established. In the Maastricht policy assignment discussed in Section 12.2.1, banks were not mentioned. This was a key omission. In terms of the relationships among member governments and between them and the ECB, the central elements were:

1. Government to government: the 'no bail-out' clause stated that other member governments could not be called upon to bail out a government in trouble.

2. ECB to government: the 'no monetary financing' clause stated that the ECB would not provide credit to governments (i.e. it would not be the lender of last resort to governments).

3. The fiscal rules: the entry rules for deficits and debt and the Stability and Growth Pact, which were designed to support (1) and (2).

Prior to 2010, this governance structure was believed to be sufficient. In particular, it was believed to make a supra-national *government* redundant. To highlight the problems that have arisen, it is useful to review the relationships among banks, government and central bank in a nation state with an independent central bank.

### Comparison between the Eurozone and USA

Both for understanding the problems in the Eurozone and for thinking about reforms, it is helpful to compare the governance arrangements in the USA and the Eurozone before the crisis. The US is a federal system, and parallels can be drawn between the US states and the member countries of the Eurozone. In the USA,

- the Federal Reserve stabilizes common shocks, is responsible for financial stability and is the lender of last resort to the federal government and to the banking system.
- The federal budget provides stabilization to the states in the face of asymmetric shocks (e.g. federal contributions to unemployment benefit and federal taxes). In the US, stabilization of state-specific aggregate demand shocks through federal taxes and transfers lies between 10 and 20%.[17]
- The states have balanced budget rules.
- The failure of a bank headquartered in a state is not the responsibility of the state but of the federal regulators and the federal government.
- The federal government does not bail out delinquent states—they are allowed to default.

In the Eurozone prior to the sovereign debt crisis,

- The ECB stabilized common shocks and, as was demonstrated by its actions in the financial crisis, was the lender of last resort to the banking system (although this was not explicitly part of the Maastricht Treaty). However, it was not responsible for financial stability and was not the lender of last resort to member governments.
- There was no federal government and no stabilization through the EU budget (it is too small).
- Member countries had national fiscal autonomy subject to rules (i.e. the SGP).
- The failure of a bank headquartered in a member country was the responsibility of the country and not of Eurozone federal regulators or a Eurozone government (there is no Eurozone government).
- The Maastricht Treaty included a 'no bail-out clause' that stated that member governments would not be bailed out.

In conjunction with Figs. 12.11 and 12.12, this comparison between the US and the Eurozone highlights the incoherence of the Eurozone governance structure prior to the sovereign debt crisis. In addition, the analysis presented in this section so far suggests that the problems brought to the fore by the financial crisis involve three key parties: banks, governments and the central bank. We will discuss the changes the Eurozone has made to the governance structure in the wake of the sovereign debt crisis in Section 12.5.2. At this stage, we focus on the original governance structure of the Eurozone and show why it left the currency union vulnerable to a sovereign debt crisis.

Figure 12.11 illustrates the relationships among commercial banks, the government and the central bank in a nation state. We begin with the *commercial banks*. In Fig. 12.11, which was introduced in Chapter 5, the *central bank's role of lender of last resort (LOLR) to the banking system* is represented by the dashed arrows labelled 'liquidity'. As we have seen in Chapter 5,

---

[17] See Melitz and Zumer (2002).

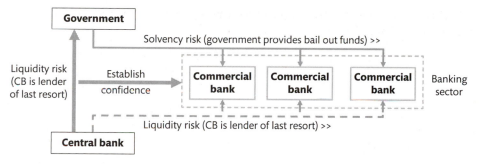

**Figure 12.11** Governance arrangements in a nation state.

*Source:* adapted from Winckler (2011).

a key role of the central bank is to provide liquidity in a situation where a bad shock to the economy has raised the possibility that banks may become insolvent (i.e. that their assets are worth less than their liabilities). Under such circumstances, there can be a run on banks as depositors do not want to be the last in line to turn their potentially risky deposits into safe cash.

The institutional response to this source of fragility in the banking system was to create a lender of last resort to the banking system in the form of a central bank. The central bank's LOLR role to the banking system rests on its judgement that the panic in the market is misplaced: i.e. that the problem is in fact not one of solvency, but of liquidity (i.e. a bank has insufficient liquid assets to cover its due liabilities). In the case where a bank is insolvent, the central bank and government work together. The central bank controls the panic by providing liquidity and the government, with its access to tax revenue (current and future), is responsible for the restructuring, recapitalization or orderly closure of the bank. This role is captured in Fig. 12.11 by the arrows labelled solvency.

We turn now to the role of the *government as borrower*. Households and firms make use of banks and the bond market to finance long-term investment projects using shorter-term loans. Governments also borrow shorter-term in the bond market to finance long-term projects. The service provided by banks and the bond markets that allows this is called maturity transformation, and whether the borrower can service the debt is called rollover risk. When the government is the borrower, it is relying on its ability to raise tax revenue to provide confidence to the bond market that it will service its debts. It is clear that if the government is being called upon to use tax revenue to support failing banks (or there is a possibility it will have to do so), its ability to service its debt via tax revenue is reduced. This highlights the interconnection between the banks, the government and the bond market. We can see the parallel with the 'last in line' liquidity problem for banks (Chapter 5): if fear emerges that the government will not be able to service its debts, holders of bonds will sell them, prices will fall and, reflecting the rise in the risk premium, interest rates will rise.

How can this be prevented? If the *central bank is the lender of last resort to the government*, it can be relied upon to step in and buy government bonds. How is this possible and why would the central bank do this? The parallel with the case of banks is again useful. If we

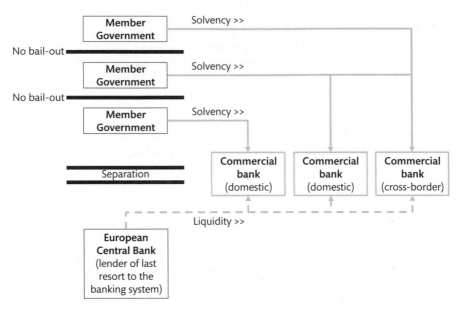

**Figure 12.12** Governance arrangements in the Eurozone prior to the crisis.

*Source:* adapted from Winckler (2011).

assume that the flight from government bonds is inconsistent with the underlying ability of the government to service its debts (i.e. the government is solvent) then the government is suffering from a liquidity problem. The central bank can step in by printing money (just as it does in the case of dealing with the liquidity problem of the banking system) and buying government bonds. The central bank would end up with more government bonds on its balance sheet and the counterpart on the liability side is an increase in high-powered money. The mutual support of the government and central bank for each other—the taxpayer base is the ultimate guarantee of the solvency of the government and of the central bank's ability to buy government bonds in unlimited quantities (LOLR)—is shown by the double-ended arrow in Fig. 12.11. This means that even when the market has doubts about the solvency of the government, the existence of the LOLR prevents runs on government bonds. If this structure of mutual confidence completely breaks down, reflected for example in the unwillingness of citizens to hold home's money, the economy can plunge into hyperinflation.

### Comparison between a country with an independent central bank and a Eurozone member

We can now compare the situation of a country with an independent central bank with that of a member of the Eurozone prior to the crisis. Figure 12.12 illustrates the governance structure of the Eurozone prior to the crisis. We begin with the banks. Once the financial crisis began, the ECB played the role of lender of last resort to the banks of member countries. Just like the Bank of England and the Federal Reserve, the ECB made liquidity available to banks in unlimited amounts, as highlighted by (then President of the ECB) Jean-Claude Trichet in a speech in April 2009 (at the nadir of the global financial crisis):[18]

> Our primary concern was to maintain the availability of credit for households and companies at accessible rates. We significantly adapted our regular operations in the crisis. Since then, we have followed a new 'fixed rate full allotment' tender procedure and we have significantly expanded the maturity of our operations. This means that banks have been granted access to essentially unlimited liquidity at our policy interest rate at maturities of up to six months.

In the Eurozone, responsibility for dealing with insolvent banks rested with member country governments (see Fig. 12.12). This meant that governments had to use national borrowing to pay for the recapitalization of banks headquartered in their country during the global financial crisis. The burden on governments increased (just as it did in the US and the UK, for example). However, the big difference is that for a Eurozone member, it could not rely on a lender of last resort to support its bond sales if required. There was no central bank that would—in extremis—purchase its bonds. There are two aspects to this: first, the member countries were issuing bonds in a currency (the euro) that they did not control and second, the central bank that issues the euros (the ECB) was prevented by its mandate from acting as lender of last resort to the governments of member states.

This created the fear of illiquidity of the government, i.e. that it would not be able to rollover its debts as they became due. As a result, interest rates on government bonds increased. We can see the same element of self-fulfilling prophecy here as arises in the case of a bank run: even if the bank is solvent, once doubts emerge about the liquidity of an institution, panic begins and depositor behaviour can produce insolvency. The circuit can be interrupted by the existence of a LOLR which quashes liquidity fears. Similarly, in the bond market, a LOLR to the government can prevent the negative feedback loop from taking hold.

---

### Box 12.1 Spain and the UK: sovereign risk inside and outside the Eurozone

To highlight the difference between the risk of sovereign default between a country inside and outside the common currency area it is useful to compare Spain and the UK. In this box, we show that on the basis of the determinants of government solvency, there was little to separate these two countries. However, interest rates on ten year government bonds in Spain at the end of November 2011 were 6.5% whilst they were 2.3% in the UK.

Table 12.2 compares the two countries and shows that the UK government was more indebted than that of Spain in 2010. GDP growth forecasts in the two countries were broadly similar at that point in time, with Spain expected to grow slightly more slowly in 2012 and 2013.

---

[18] Excerpt taken from. Jean-Claude Trichet, 27th April 2009, *The financial crisis and our response so far*, keynote address at the Chatham House Global Financial Forum

**Table 12.2** Macroeconomic and government finance indicators for the UK and Spain.

| Variable | Year | Spain | UK |
|---|---|---|---|
| General government underlying primary balances (as a % of potential GDP) | 2010 | −5.6 | −5.5 |
| Maastricht definition of general government gross public debt (as a % of nominal GDP) | 2010 | 61.0 | 79.9 |
| Real GDP growth (%, Dec 2011 forecast) | 2012f | 0.3 | 0.5 |
| Real GDP growth (%, Dec 2011 forecast) | 2013f | 1.3 | 1.8 |
| Ten year government bond yields (%, average) | 2010 | 4.3 | 3.6 |
| Ten year government bond yields (%, average, Dec 2011 forecast) | 2011f | 5.4 | 3.1 |

*Source:* OECD Economic Outlook, December 2011.

Given these figures, we would expect both countries to have had similar ten year government bond yields (i.e. default risks), but this was not the case. We can see from Table 12.2 that Spanish bond yields were higher than the UK's for 2010. We can also see that the UK's cost of borrowing fell in 2011, whilst Spain's continued to rise, culminating in interest rates on Spanish bonds being 2.3 percentage points higher than those on UK bonds (on average) over 2011. This apparent inconsistency between government solvency and perceived sovereign default risk is summed up by Pisani-Ferry (2012):

> This comparison is prima facie evidence that the fiscal situation per se fails to explain tension in the euro-area government bond markets. Or, to put it slightly differently, although their levels of deficit and public debt are the same, euro-area countries seem to be more vulnerable to fiscal crises than non-euro area countries.

As we saw in Chapter 10, in the 1990s, Spain and the UK both solved their high inflation problem by adopting a new monetary policy regime: the UK chose to establish a credible monetary policy through inflation-targeting and an independent central bank and Spain chose to borrow a credible monetary policy by giving up its exchange rate and joining the Eurozone. Both countries enjoyed buoyant domestic economies in the 2000s, and both suffered bank failures and a subsequent deterioration of the public finances in the global financial crisis. Yet, Spain faced much higher interest rates on government borrowing than the UK and was identified in 2011 as one of the so-called PIIGS. PIIGS refers to Portugal, Ireland, Italy, Greece and Spain and became a synonym for the Eurozone economies threatened by a sovereign debt crisis.

De Grauwe (2011) suggested that this was a consequence of Spain entering the European Monetary Union and the UK not doing so. The argument is that when Spain adopted the euro, it lost control over the currency it issued debt in, which meant that the financial markets could force the Spanish sovereign into default (or at least cause a sovereign liquidity crisis). De Grauwe highlights two important factors that make the UK less vulnerable to being forced into default by financial markets than a eurozone country (in a similar fiscal situation). Firstly, the UK has a freely floating exchange rate, which will depreciate if government bonds are sold off. This should help to raise growth and increase inflation, both of which are positive for debt dynamics. Secondly, if the UK cannot roll over its debts at a reasonable interest rate, then it could force the Bank of England (in its role as LOLR) to buy government securities. In summary, the governance structure of the Eurozone prior to the crisis (and particularly the lack of a credible LOLR to member governments) helps to explain the reason for seemingly solvent Eurozone governments (e.g. Spain and Italy) ending up in liquidity crises.

## Bank problems

Given its original mandate, the ECB concentrated on supporting the European banking system during the global financial crisis (and more recently during the sovereign debt crisis). This approach is helpful to the extent that the problems of European banks are ones of liquidity and not solvency. But if it postpones the required cleaning up of insolvent banks, it is only a holding mechanism. This delicate balancing act reflects the close relationship between the health of the banks and of governments in the Eurozone.

In the Eurozone, banks are major holders of government bonds. For example, the percentage of national government bonds that were held by domestic banks in Spain, Italy and Germany was 28.3%, 27.3% and 22.9% respectively in mid-2011. The equivalent figure for the UK was 10.7% and for the US was just 2%. The close ties between the governments and the banks in the Eurozone adds to the vulnerability of the system. When government bond prices fall, bank solvency is called into question; in turn, when banks are more likely to be insolvent, the contingent liabilities of the government (to recapitalize and restructure them) rise and government solvency comes into question.

The absence of a pan-European or Eurozone bank resolution scheme during the crisis meant countries were faced with dealing with bank solvency on their own. The fact that banks were often large relative to the size of the country helped turn the bank solvency issue into a sovereign debt problem. For example, the Irish commercial bank, Bank of Ireland, had total assets that were equal to 99% of Irish GDP in 2007. This can be compared to Bank of America that had total assets that were equal to only 12% of US GDP in the same year. This meant that the US government could bail out Bank of America (BoA) and other financial institutions without the government finances becoming unsustainable, this was not the case in Ireland and would not have been the case had North Carolina (the US state where BoA is headquartered) been responsible for bailing out BoA—BoA had total assets equal to 431% of North Carolina's GDP in 2007.[19]

A second difficulty faced in the Eurozone arose because of the presence of cross-border banks, where two (or more) national governments are responsible for dealing with solvency issues. This is illustrated by the inclusion of a cross-border bank in Fig. 12.12. We can see from the figure, that two member governments are jointly responsible for the restructuring, recapitalization or orderly closure of the cross-border bank (as indicated by the 'solvency' arrows).

In the US, the federal government's responsibility for the solvency of banks meant that although the liquidity support to the banks from the Fed quelled the panic, the government moved swiftly to recapitalize the banks through the Troubled Asset Relief Program (TARP) schemes (see Chapter 7 for discussion of the US government's response to the bank solvency crisis).

## Government problems

Governments of Eurozone countries have high levels of debt compared with states in the US. This reflects the fact that the US is a federal system. The *nation* is the major fiscal policy

[19] These figures were calculated by the authors in March 2012 using data from the 2007 annual reports of Bank of Ireland (BoI) and Bank of America (BoA), the IMF World Economic Outlook Database and the US BEA. The figures for total assets for BoI are as of March 31st 2007 and for BoA are as of December 31st 2007. GDP data for all regions are in current prices and for 2007.

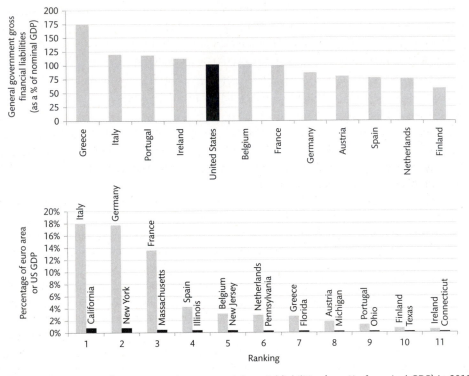

**Figure 12.13** Upper panel: gross general government financial liabilities (as a % of nominal GDP) in 2010. Lower panel: Eurozone government debt (as a % of Eurozone GDP) and US state debts (as a % of US GDP) in 2007.

*Source:* OECD Economic Outlook, December 2011; Eurostat (data accessed March 2012), US Census Bureau, 2007 Census of Governments.

player in both cases: the federal government in the US and the member countries in the Eurozone. The upper panel of Fig. 12.13 compares the debt to GDP ratios of the US and the Eurozone member countries in 2010. In contrast, the lower panel shows how the debts of the individual Eurozone countries compare to Eurozone GDP and how the debts of the individual US states compare to US GDP just before the onset of the financial crisis.

From the upper panel of Fig. 12.13, we see that the aggregate public debt burden of the US is comparable to that of the Eurozone. The key difference is that this is *federal* debt in the USA and *member country* debt in the Eurozone. This has major consequences for the resilience of the governance mechanism. If a state—even a large one like California—in the US defaults, this represents a small shock to US GDP. As the lower panel of Fig. 12.13 shows, this is not the case in the Eurozone.

### 12.5.2 Governance solutions

Creating a coherent governance structure for the Eurozone requires addressing the inter-connection among banks, governments and the central bank. European policy makers have been trying to tackle these problems since the onset of the sovereign debt crisis in 2010, with varying levels of success. This subsection sets out some of the governance solutions that have been implemented or are still being negotiated, and relates them to our analytical framework. We also discuss some of the problems with the proposed solutions and the challenges still facing the Eurozone if it wishes to be sustainable in the long run.

### Government to government: the bail-outs and the Fiscal Compact

The Eurozone governments broke the 'no bail-out' clause that separates member governments in the governance structure of the Eurozone (see Fig. 12.12). At the height of the crisis in 2010–11, Greece, Ireland and Portugal were all bailed out and forced into pursuing austerity policies by the creditor nations.[20] We discuss the macroeconomic impact of the adoption of austerity policies in Chapter 7.

In order to avoid getting into a situation where governments require bail-outs at the expense of Eurozone taxpayers, European policy makers introduced the Fiscal Compact at the start of 2013. The Compact provides a timetable for reducing government debt and brings in a balanced budget rule, similar to those often used at the state level in the United States.[21]

The balanced budget rule could have negative consequences for stabilization policy in Eurozone countries where the real exchange rate channel does not operate well, as it tightly circumscribes the use of discretionary fiscal policy in economic downturns. In addition, the credibility of the Compact could be threatened from a number of sources, such as the moral hazard problem created when countries were bailed out, the failure of the Stability and Growth Pact and the lack of a legitimate enforcement mechanism, and the high levels of government debt and deficit levels upon entering the Compact.

### The ECB to government: establishing a LOLR to member governments

The turning point in the sovereign debt crisis came in the second half of 2012, as shown by the reduction in peripheral bond yields after point 3 in Fig. 12.10. Two actions by the ECB prompted the turnaround. First, Mario Draghi, the President of the ECB, publically stated that the ECB was 'ready to do whatever it takes to preserve the euro'.[22] Second, the ECB announced the Outright Monetary Transactions (OMT) programme, which promised to buy peripheral country bonds on secondary markets until pressure in the bond markets eased off (subject to some conditionality clauses i.e. promises for structural reform).[23]

In 2012 and 2013, the ECB did not actually use OMT, but bond yields fell substantially regardless. This is because the ECB's actions removed the 'separation' between the central bank and the member governments in the governance structure of the euro (see Fig. 12.12). By

---

[20] See Lane (2012) for a good summary of the Eurozone sovereign debt crisis.

[21] The Fiscal Compact is the fiscal part of the Treaty on Stability, Coordination and Governance (TSCG). Further information on the Compact can be obtained from the European Commission website: http://ec.europa.eu/economy_finance/articles/governance/2012-03-14_six_pack_en.htm.

[22] Excerpt taken from a speech by Mario Draghi, President of the European Central Bank, at the Global Investment Conference in London on 26 July 2012.

[23] The details of the OMT programme are available from the ECB website: http://www.ecb.europa.eu/press/pr/date/2012/html/pr120906_1.en.html.

effectively changing the role of the ECB to be a lender of last resort to member governments, the ECB lowered the default risk for the PIIGS and their borrowing costs fell accordingly.

The conditionality attached to OMT is one possible cause for concern in the future, as it could impede the ECB's role as the lender of last resort to governments. National central banks, by contrast, are unconditional lenders of last resort.

### Banks to governments: the banking union

The dangerous interconnectedness of banks and sovereigns in the Eurozone played a significant part in the sovereign debt crisis. The solution to this governance problem is to create a banking union, where Eurozone member countries are jointly responsible for the solvency of banks located in the Eurozone.

At the end of 2013, the EU Council agreed on a general approach for the Single Resolution Mechanism (SRM). The SRM is the EU's banking union, which will raise resolution funds from national bank levies and use them to resolve failing banks across the EU.[24]

The mutualization of resolution funds will be phased in over a ten-year period, however, which poses a short-term problem for the banking systems in vulnerable peripheral economies. In the short term, responsibility for national banking systems ultimately resides with national governments. If they cannot afford to provide solvency to their banking systems, then they will again have to seek bail-outs from other Eurozone members and endure the harsh conditionality (i.e. austerity and structural reform) that accompanies the loans. The phasing in of the SRM may therefore delay the clean up of bad banks in the peripheral economies and, as a consequence, their economic recovery.

The SRM also stopped short of creating Eurobonds. Eurobonds are politically contentious, as they would raise borrowing costs in the Northern European creditor nations. However, making countries jointly responsible for each others' government debt in this way would have broken the nexus between member states and their banks once and for all.

### Impediments to further integration

The Eurozone could go a long way to solving its governance problems if it replicated the governance structure of a nation state (see Fig. 12.11). The governance structure of the Eurozone has changed considerably since the onset of the crisis, but it could have gone further. For example, a fully-fledged political and fiscal union like that in the US could have been created.

In the Eurozone, however, there is no natural solidarity across member countries comparable to that in a nation state. There is wide variation in political traditions and in the role of the state among member countries. There is no basis for pan-Eurozone solidarity that would permit a large federal budget (with transfers stabilizing member country shocks) or the joint issuance of debt through Eurobonds.

The Eurozone requires a different governance solution from that of a federal country, as there is little appetite or scope for further political or fiscal integration. The Eurozone has taken important steps towards a closer union in the wake of the sovereign debt crisis, but it

---

[24] For a summary of the Council's agreed general approach on the Single Resolution Mechanism, see: http://www.consilium.europa.eu/uedocs/cms_data/docs/pressdata/en/ecofin/140190.pdf.

remains to be seen whether these steps will be enough to secure the long-term sustainability of the currency union.

## 12.6 Conclusions

This chapter has focused on the Eurozone economy; the largest common currency area of nation states in the world. The introduction of the euro had both microeconomic benefits, such as increased trade and investment, and macroeconomic benefits, such as the provision of a credible low inflation monetary regime. However, relinquishing exchange rate flexibility and monetary policy also created problems for stabilization against country-specific economic shocks and produced increased vulnerability to a sovereign debt crisis.

The thrust of this chapter has been to think about common currency areas, and particularly the Eurozone, in the framework of the 3-equation model. We can use the 3-equation model to answer interesting questions about macroeconomic adjustment in a common currency area (CCA):

1. How does a CCA stabilize against common shocks? The central bank of the CCA (the ECB in the case of the Eurozone) will stabilize against common shocks through the use of monetary policy and the associated changes in the nominal exchange rate (against the rest of the world). In other words, adjustment is the same as in a flexible exchange rate economy (discussed in Chapter 9).

2. How does a CCA member stabilize against country-specific shocks? The model can be used to compare policy responses when a member country is hit with a country-specific shock: to do nothing, or to use fiscal policy to stabilize. If it decides to do nothing, there are two channels that operate automatically. The first is the real exchange rate channel, which arises because inflation differentials between members affect their external competitiveness. The second is the real interest rate channel, which arises because inflation differentials between members can affect their real interest rates. The first channel is stabilizing and the second is destabilizing. If the economy is put on a destabilizing path after a shock, the government can use fiscal policy to guide it back to equilibrium. The use of fiscal policy can help to limit deviations from equilibrium output and target inflation, but unlike monetary policy, it can also leave the government in deficit when back at equilibrium.

3. Why do wage-setting institutions matter in the adjustment to shocks? Wage-setting institutions, such as the coordinated wage bargaining that takes place in Germany, affect how well the real exchange rate channel works. The more flexible wage and price setting, the better the channel works at stabilizing the economy. Members with these institutions will have to do less active stabilization using fiscal policy, and hence are less likely to build up government and external deficits.

The euro was adopted at the start of 1999. By a number of measures its first ten years were successful; average inflation was kept close to the ECB's 2% target and member states became more economically and financially integrated. Beneath the surface, however, the picture was not quite so rosy. Large imbalances arose in real exchange rates and current accounts between the northern and southern parts of the currency bloc. The peripheral economies became very externally indebted; Greece's government borrowed excessively and Spain and Ireland had wild, credit-fuelled construction and consumption booms.

In a nation state, the external imbalances and indebtedness might not have led to a sovereign debt crisis. However, the unique governance structure that was put in place at the inception of the euro made it vulnerable to a government debt crisis after a large negative demand shock. The global financial crisis provided that shock, and the responsibility of members to stand behind the banks headquartered in their countries combined with the lack of a credible lender of last resort to governments proved to be fatal.

The Eurozone sovereign debt crisis did huge damage to the economies of its members, but the currency union survived. It persevered primarily as a result of the changes made to the governance structure, particularly the ECB's decision to act as a lender of last resort to member governments. Whilst reform has taken place in the Eurozone, its pace and scope has been held back by political considerations. There is not enough cross-country solidarity for the level of integration that would ensure the currency union is sustainable in the long-term. Therefore, only time will tell whether the Eurozone has a long-term future.

## 12.7 Questions

### 12.7.1 Checklist questions

1. What are the microeconomic benefits of a currency union?

2. Germany had a credible central bank before the introduction of the euro. What was their macroeconomic incentive to join the currency union? Was this incentive shared by the countries in Southern Europe?

3. Explain the factors that contributed to the difference in inflation rates between Germany and Spain between 1999 and 2008. What effect did this differential have on the external competitiveness of these two economies?

4. What are the two pillars of the ECB's monetary policy? Discuss the pros and cons of the ECB's strategy.

5. Use your knowledge of common currency areas (CCAs) to assess whether the following statements (S1 and S2) are both true or whether only one of them is true. Justify your answer:

   S1. If country A in a CCA undertakes an expansionary fiscal policy then they can reduce the unemployment rate.

   S2. The rate of unemployment in country A will be reduced even more should the other countries in the union also undertake expansionary fiscal policy.

6. Explain the difference between the real exchange rate channel and the real interest rate channel. Which of these channels has to dominate for the economy to revert to equilibrium after a shock without any active policy response?

7. What is the Walters' critique and why was it used as an argument for the UK not joining the single currency?

8. Use the 3-equation model to show how fiscal policy can be used to stabilize the economy after a positive demand shock in a country that is a member of a CCA. What effect does this have on the budget balance?

9. Use an $AD - ERU$ diagram to show the new medium-run equilibrium of a flexible exchange rate economy and a member of a CCA following a negative demand shock. Assume that the CCA member uses fiscal policy as a stabilization tool. What are the differences in $y$, $q$ and $G$ between the two economies in the new medium-run equilibrium?

10. How could the 2-bloc model from Chapter 11 be used to shed light on the economic divergence between the Northern and Southern European countries during the first ten years of the single currency? Explain in words.

11. Describe why the following factors made the Eurozone vulnerable to a sovereign debt crisis:

   (a) Member countries issued debt in a currency they did not control

   (b) National governments were responsible for the solvency of their banks.

## 12.7.2 Problems and questions for discussion

1. 'The ECB's success in achieving low and stable inflation during the Eurozone's first decade disguised the build-up of dangerous imbalances among the members.'
   Provide an explanation and assessment of the claims in this statement.
   Use the models presented in Chapters 9–12 to

   (a) Discuss reasons why countries that wish to achieve low inflation may join a common currency area. Discuss how the ECB achieved its inflation objective.

   (b) Explain what could be meant by 'dangerous imbalances' among the members.

   (c) Use the $AD - BT - ERU$ model to explain how imbalances could occur consistent with the ECB achieving its inflation target. Relate this to the performance of specific countries.

2. When joining a common currency area each country relinquishes the use of monetary policy.

   (a) Explain how fiscal policy can be used as a substitute when undertaking stabilization policy. Use the 3-equation model to provide an example.

   (b) Are there any drawbacks to stabilizing using fiscal policy?

   (c) What advantages have euro area economies gained by having an independent monetary authority? Give an example of a country where this has been particularly important.

3. What steps do you think need to be taken for the Eurozone to be sustainable in the long-run? Are your proposals politically feasible?

4. This question uses the Macroeconomic Simulator available from the Carlin and Soskice website http://www.oup.com/uk/orc/carlin_soskice to show the destabilizing real interest rate channel. Begin by opening the simulator and selecting the open economy (fixed exchange rates without endogenous fiscal policy) version. Then reset all shocks by pressing the appropriate button on the left hand side of the main page. Use the simulator and the content of this chapter to work through the following:

   (a) Apply a 2% inflation shock.

   (b) Use the impulse response functions to describe the path of the economy after the shock.

   (c) Is the economy self-stabilizing in this scenario?

   (d) Use the 3-equation model to explain how the real interest rate channel can lead to this outcome.

5. This question uses the Macroeconomic Simulator available from the Carlin and Soskice website http://www.oup.com/uk/orc/carlin_soskice to compare the effects of a negative demand shock in two economies; one with a fixed exchange rate regime and one with a flexible exchange rate regime. Begin by opening the simulator and selecting the open economy (flexible exchange rate) version. Then reset all shocks by pressing the appropriate button on the left hand side of the main page. Use the simulator and the content of Chapters 9–12 to work through the following:

(a) Apply a permanent 2% negative demand shock (i.e. −2%). Save your data.

(b) Switch to the open economy (fixed exchange rates without endogenous fiscal policy) version of the simulator by pressing the relevant button on the left of the main page. Set the degree of inflation inertia to 0.2. Apply a permanent 2% negative demand shock (i.e. −2%). Save your data.

(c) How long does it take for the economy to return to medium-run equilibrium in each case? Why is the speed of adjustment different?

(d) Can fiscal policy be used in the fixed exchange rate (i.e. CCA) case to speed up the adjustment? Are there any disadvantages of doing this? Suggest a real world setting in which you could you apply this analysis? (Hint: what happens to the adjustment of the economy in the simulator if public expenditure is permanently increased by 1.5%?)

# 13 Monetary policy

## 13.1 Introduction

In previous chapters, we have built up a macroeconomic model with the following structure:

1. Supply-side institutions and policies pin down the equilibrium level of output and unemployment in the economy.
2. Wages and prices do not adjust flexibly so as to keep the economy at equilibrium output in the presence of shocks. This implies there is a role for stabilization policy and that disinflation is costly in terms of higher unemployment.
3. When available, monetary rather than fiscal policy is the preferred stabilization policy.
4. The economy's nominal anchor (the inflation rate in medium-run equilibrium) is established by the adoption of an inflation target by a credible central bank.

In this chapter, we look in more depth at the reasoning and evidence behind the central role that monetary policy plays in contemporary macroeconomic management.

The chapter begins in Section 13.2 with a brief discussion of the Quantity Theory of Money. This theory can be used to argue that money supply targets provide a nominal anchor for the economy. Grappling with high inflation, policy makers in the late 1970s and 1980s introduced money supply targets. The 'Monetarist' policy of the UK's Thatcher government provides a striking example of the failure of monetary targeting.

This experience contributed to the shift toward the modern monetary policy framework, which combines explicit targets for inflation with the use of the interest rate as the policy instrument. The 3-equation model is based on this framework.

In Section 13.3, we extend the modelling of the modern monetary policy framework from Chapter 3. We firstly look at the underlying determinants of the sacrifice ratio, which is the unemployment cost of reducing inflation. This is followed by a subsection in which we combine the central bank's *MR* equation with the *IS* equation to derive the interest rate setting rule of the central bank. This is the best-response interest rate rule and is sometimes referred to as the optimal Taylor rule.

The practice of central banks that operate within the modern monetary policy framework is the subject of Section 13.4, which begins with the Bank of England's explanation of the transmission mechanism of monetary policy. This is followed by a comparison of central bank mandates and interest rate rules across countries.

Section 13.5 focuses on monetary policy and the global financial crisis. It begins with the debate, which began before the crisis, about whether central banks should intervene to burst asset price bubbles such as the dot-com bubble of the late 1990s. The general approach taken by central bankers before the crisis was to refrain from targeting asset price bubbles, to wait until they burst and then to 'mop up' after them by providing liquidity. We use this section to set out both sides of the debate and then discuss whether the central banks' strategy of mopping up after bubbles can still be justified in light of the financial crisis.

The second half of this section analyses the use of unorthodox monetary policy during the Great Recession. With interest rates at or close to the zero lower bound, the modern monetary policy framework was clearly inadequate and central banks across the world reached for other instruments to keep inflation close to target and to prevent a deflation trap. Central banks engaged in large-scale asset purchases (known as quantitative easing, or QE) in an attempt to boost asset prices. The aim of QE is to reduce the cost of long-term borrowing and to boost wealth, both of which are expected to stimulate spending and close the output gap. Following on from the modelling of QE in Chapter 7, we assess how QE is supposed to work, whether there is evidence of its effectiveness, if there are longer term dangers arising from the expansion of central bank balance sheets (as they acquire assets) and how central banks will exit from QE.

The chapter ends with Section 13.6, which links the failures of the conventional macroeconomic policy framework that were exposed by the global financial crisis to the debates about policy reforms aimed at safeguarding the world economy against future financial crises. This section covers both banking regulation and macro-prudential policy and is closely linked to the discussion of banking, financial cycles and crises in Chapters 5 and 6 and the analysis of the global financial crisis in Chapter 7.

## 13.2 Monetary policy and the economy's nominal anchor

### 13.2.1 The classical dichotomy and the nominal anchor

The classical dichotomy refers to the possibility of identifying different factors that pin down the real (output, employment) and the nominal sides (price level, inflation rate) of the economy. In a textbook, classical, perfectly competitive economy without imperfections or rigidities, this separation characterizes the economy at all points in time. Prices and wages always adjust immediately to keep the economy at equilibrium output. Technology and preferences (the most basic supply-side building blocks of household and firm behaviour) pin down output and the money supply pins down the price level. The Quantity Theory of Money encapsulates the classical dichotomy:

$$Py = MV, \qquad \text{(Quantity Theory of Money)}$$

where $P$ is the price level, $y$, the level of output, $M$, the money supply and $V$ is called the velocity of circulation of money. In the Quantity Theory, $y$ is the outcome of goods and labour market clearing. To gain policy insights from the Quantity Theory of Money it is necessary to convert the equation into growth rates. Using discrete time notation, we have:

$$\frac{\Delta P}{P} + \frac{\Delta y}{y} = \frac{\Delta M}{M} + \frac{\Delta V}{V}. \tag{13.1}$$

Equation 13.1 shows that the growth rate of prices plus the growth rate of output must be equal to the growth rate of the money supply plus the growth rate of the velocity of circulation. To make the maths as simple as possible, we make the assumptions that output growth is zero and that the velocity of circulation is constant. This gives us a simple expression for inflation:

$$\frac{\Delta P}{P} = \frac{\Delta M}{M} \tag{13.2}$$

$$\rightarrow \pi = \left[\frac{\Delta M}{M}\right]. \tag{13.3}$$

Under these assumptions, the growth rate of the money supply chosen by the policy maker fixes the growth rate of prices and hence, the rate of inflation.

To summarize, since the assumption that wages and prices are perfectly flexible means the economy is always in the medium-run equilibrium (or steady state, that is, $y = y_e$), the choice by the policy maker of $M$, pins down the price level, $P$; the choice of the growth rate of $M$ pins down inflation, $\pi$.

### 13.2.2 From theory to practice: monetary policy and inflation in the 1970s and 1980s

If the classical dichotomy and the Quantity Theory of Money are taken at face value, they imply that controlling the growth rate of the money supply will allow policy makers to control the rate of inflation. This idea was influential in the adoption of monetary targeting in 1974 as the method to secure low inflation in Germany and Switzerland. Monetary policy was back on the agenda of policy makers in the early 1970s in many countries following the collapse of the fixed exchange rate era of the Bretton Woods system.[1]

The Bundesbank was successful in using the language of monetary targeting to communicate to the public the orientation of monetary policy toward the long-run stability of inflation at a low rate.[2] One way of expressing this is to say that by describing its behaviour in terms of monetary targeting, the Bundesbank succeeded in establishing a value close to one for the coefficient on the inflation target, $\chi$, in the Phillips curve with anchored inflation expectations introduced in Chapter 4:

$$\pi_t = [\chi\pi^T + (1 - \chi)\pi_{t-1}] + \alpha(y_t - y_e). \tag{13.4}$$

As we saw in Chapter 4, a higher level of credibility reduces the costs of disinflation in this model.

In Chapter 4, we also explained that in a model economy where agents have rational expectations and there are fully flexible wages and prices, the announcement of a lower inflation target would lead to an immediate fall in inflation to the new target without cost.

---

[1] See Section 10.2.3 in Chapter 10 on the determinants of the medium-run inflation rate under fixed and flexible exchange rates.

[2] See Mishkin (1999).

Applying those assumptions to the use of the growth rate of the money supply as the nominal anchor, the announcement of a lower target for money growth would reduce inflation at no unemployment cost.

Once we abandon fully flexible wages and prices, a policy of tighter money has its effects through raising the real interest rate, creating a negative output gap and bearing down on inflation in the usual way via the Phillips curve. Under these conditions, for a policy of monetary targeting to be successful in its objective of controlling inflation, two conditions must hold: (1) the central bank must be able to control the chosen monetary aggregate and (2) the relationship between inflation and the targeted monetary aggregate must be reliable.

Problems can arise at both points. These problems undermined monetary targeting in the US, Canada and the UK. The UK provides a nice case study because both problems were present. Although the central bank can control a narrow money aggregate (such as notes and coins), the relationship between narrow money and inflation is weak, undermining the role of the target in shaping inflation expectations, which we can model as limiting the maximum value of the $\chi$ term to below 1 in Equation 13.4.

In the UK, it was argued that whenever the monetary authority attempted to control a particular monetary aggregate as its target, there would be a response by the financial system in the form of the emergence of close substitutes or near-moneys that would lie outside the target and therefore serve to undermine it.[3] This phenomenon is referred to as Goodhart's law.

In relation to the second condition, shifts in the demand for money (often referred to as velocity instability) will alter the relationship between the targeted money supply aggregate and inflation, making monetary targeting an inaccurate way of controlling aggregate demand.

### The failed Thatcher experiment with money supply targeting

Economic policy making in the United Kingdom from the end of the Second World War to the late 1970s focused on achieving multiple objectives. Governments used all the policy levers at their disposal to pursue low inflation, high employment, economic growth and a sustainable external balance.

The Conservative government that came to power under Margaret Thatcher in June 1979 broke from this framework, choosing instead to concentrate its macroeconomic policy on reducing inflation. At the same time, the government introduced a range of supply-side policies to reduce equilibrium unemployment, which are discussed in Chapter 15.

The path of inflation and unemployment over the Thatcher years is shown in Fig. 3.3 in Chapter 3. The year that Thatcher took office, retail price inflation stood at 13.4%, which was very high for the post WWII period.

The Conservatives attempted to achieve their desired disinflation by setting 'intermediate financial targets'. In practice, this translated into fixed targets for the growth rate of the money supply and public sector borrowing in each of the next four years, as set out in Thatcher's Medium-Term Financial Strategy (MTFS).[4] As discussed in Chapter 3, the Thatcher disinflation entailed large costs in terms of higher unemployment. Table 13.1 shows that inflation in the

---

[3] For details, see Goodhart (1989).

[4] The key papers used in this subsection are: Buiter and Miller (1981 and 1983) and Goodhart (1986 and 1989).

**Table 13.1** Money supply targets vs. outturn and UK macroeconomic performance: 1980–1983.

|  | 1980 | 1981 | 1982 | 1983 |
|---|---|---|---|---|
| M3 growth target range (%) | 7–11 | 6–10 | 8–12 | 7–11 |
| M3 growth outturn (%) | 19.4 | 13 | 11.1 | 9.5 |
| RPI inflation (%) | 18 | 11.9 | 8.6 | 4.6 |
| Unemployment (%) | 6.9 | 9.8 | 10.9 | 11.6 |
| Manufacturing output growth (%) | –8.7 | –6.2 | 0 | 2.1 |

*Source:* Goodhart (1986); UK Office for National Statistics.

*Note:* Money supply targets and outturn run from February to April—e.g. 1980 refers to the period from February 1980 to April 1981.

UK fell dramatically from 18% to 4.6% between 1980 and 1983, but unemployment rose from 6.9% to 11.6% over the same period.

The government targeted the growth of broad money, M3, which consists of currency, central bank reserves, demand deposits, savings deposits and time deposits. It can be argued that the central bank cannot directly control broad money, but rather only narrow money, M0, which consists of just currency and central bank reserves. This can translate into control of M3, but only when the relationship between M0 and M3 is stable over time.

What the government had not anticipated was that the early 1980s would see substantial shifts in the demand for money. This primarily came through two channels. One was the outcome of regulatory changes which removed restrictions on bank lending behavior and liberalized the scope for building societies to attract deposits. The second was related to the government's own anti-inflation policy. The severity of the recession in the early 1980s and the sharp appreciation of sterling (see Chapter 9 for a discussion of the associated exchange rate overshooting) had squeezed the non-bank financial sector (particularly in manufacturing, see Table 13.1). This led to an increase in the demand for loans from these companies as they fought to stay in business.

The Thatcher government missed its targets for M3 during the early years of the MTFS, with M3 expanding faster than intended (see Table 13.1). Changes in economic policy, financial innovation and the severe economic downturn had changed the relationship between M0 and M3, leading to the government losing control of M3. Goodhart's law (proposed by Charles Goodhart) takes this concept one stage further, stating that any observed regularity between a monetary aggregate and inflation will break down once a central bank tries to exploit it.

The outcome was the perverse combination of money supply growth above target (which would suggest policy was looser than intended) with an overall effect on the economy of a tighter squeeze than the one targeted by the MTFS.

In Chapter 9, we discussed the over-optimism of the Thatcher experiment in terms of the anticipated effects of the announced money growth target on inflation expectations: the unemployment cost of disinflation was much higher than anticipated. Here we have seen that the use of a money supply target as the anchor for inflation was flawed. Both problems tarnished the image of Monetarism as a practical policy doctrine. In debates about British economy policy, the Thatcher experiment was referred to by its proponents and opponents as 'Monetarist'. Box 13.1 explores what is meant by Monetarism and how it affected macroeconomic thinking.

## Box 3.2   Monetarism, inflation and monetary policy

The term 'Monetarism' is defined by The New Palgrave Dictionary of Economics as:[a]

> Monetarism is the view that the quantity of money has a major influence on economic activity
> and the price level and that the objectives of monetary policy are best achieved by targeting the
> rate of growth of the money supply.

This definition echoes Milton Friedman's famous quote that 'inflation is always and everywhere a monetary phenomenon'.[b] A core tenet of Monetarism (following the Quantity Theory of Money) is that inflation arises when there is a more rapid increase in the quantity of money than in output.

Friedman's Monetarism proposed that monetary policy be conducted through targeting the growth of the *money supply*. This approach is very different to what has become the mainstream view today—i.e. central banks adjusting interest rates to achieve a fixed inflation target. In its heyday in policy circles in the early 1980s, Monetarism was also associated with policies of reducing the size of the state and limiting the scope for government intervention in the economy.

Monetarism came to be very closely associated with the policies of the Thatcher government in the UK, including the willingness of the government to accept a high sacrifice ratio in terms of unemployment to get inflation down (see Fig. 3.3 in Chapter 3 and Section 13.3.2), supply-side policies of privatization and labour market reforms (see Table 10.2 in Chapter 10) and the broad objective of reducing the size of government. Monetarism also placed stress on the potential of credibility and expectations to reduce the costs associated with disinflation, as reflected in Thatcher's famous 'the lady's not for turning' speech.[c]

Monetarist ideas have not all stood the test of time. The experience of the US, the UK and Canada in the 1980s clearly discredited monetary targeting. In fact, it was discredited to such an extent that Milton Friedman himself admitted in 2003 that it had 'not been a success' and that he would no longer advocate the policy as strongly as he once did.[d] Monetarism has, however, had an enduring influence on the evolution of macroeconomics and economic policy. For example, in contrast to other major central banks the ECB still retains a target for the growth rate of money (see Chapter 12). More generally, Monetarism played a part in the shift in mainstream economic analysis toward the following ideas:

1. At least in the closed economy and leaving aside the possibility of hysteresis (see Chapter 15), the constant inflation rate of unemployment is pinned down by the supply-side of the economy, and systematic attempts by policy makers to run the economy at lower unemployment would lead to rising inflation. This was one of the central ideas put forward by Milton Friedman in his influential 1968 presidential address on Monetarism.[e]

2. When available, monetary rather than fiscal policy is the instrument of choice to stabilize the economy. This was partly a reflection of the shift at the time from fixed exchange rates under the Bretton Woods system to flexible exchange rates, where monetary policy gains effectiveness.

3. It follows that if the central bank is the policy maker and there is a unique equilibrium rate of unemployment, then achieving low and stable inflation at least cost is the appropriate policy goal.

[a] See Phillip Cagan's entry on *Monetarism* in The New Palgrave Dictionary of Economics, Second Edition (2008).
[b] See Friedman (1970).
[c] This refers to Margaret Thatcher's speech at the Conservative Party Conference on 10 October 1980.
[d] Excerpt taken from an interview with Milton Friedman published in the Financial Times in June 2003.
[e] See Friedman (1968).

### 13.2.3 **The inflation target as the nominal anchor**

The failure of the British experiment with money supply targeting helps to explain the emergence of the modern monetary policy framework, where the nominal anchor is the inflation target and the central bank uses a monetary rule as modelled by the *MR* curve in the 3-equation model to keep the economy close to target. Instead of using the intermediate target of the money supply, the modern framework uses an announced inflation target to anchor inflation expectations and chooses the desired degree of tightening by setting the interest rate directly. This eliminates the problems of velocity instability that can undermine a money supply target.

## 13.3 Modelling

### 13.3.1 **Active rule-based policy**

At the end of Chapter 2, we saw that a passive monetary policy that keeps the nominal interest rate fixed in the face of shocks will not stabilize the economy around the constant inflation equilibrium. This motivated the analysis in Chapter 3 of the 3-equation model and the *MR* curve, where the central bank actively intervenes to guide the economy back to the constant inflation equilibrium. We have now filled in a piece of economic history and doctrine by looking at the attempt to respond to the problem of rising inflation in the 1970s by adopting money supply targets. The failure of this experiment helped to pave the way for the widespread adoption of the inflation–targeting framework.

Frequent adjustments are made to the interest rate as the central bank seeks to achieve its inflation objective at least cost. It is therefore quite consistent to think of the central bank as following a 'rule-based' approach to monetary policy yet having to be very active. Figure 13.1 shows central bank interest rates in key developed economies between 1999 and 2011 and provides evidence that central banks regularly make adjustments to interest rates to keep inflation close to target. This active central bank behaviour was witnessed between 1999–2007, which corresponded to a period of unprecedented macroeconomic stability.

### 13.3.2 **Central bank preferences: sacrifice ratios and costly disinflation**

This section looks at the role of central bank preferences, investigating how different preferences affect the slope of the *MR* curve and what this implies for the trade-off between inflation and unemployment deviations on the path to the new equilibrium. We will also set out the two approaches to disinflation, the so-called 'cold-turkey' and the 'gradualist' approaches, which can be seen as descriptions of how inflation averse the central bank is.

*Central bank preferences and the slope of the MR*

To begin with, we recall the results from Chapter 3, where we derived the *MR* curve by minimizing the central bank's loss function subject to the Phillips curve constraint. The key equations are:

$$L = (y_t - y_e)^2 + \beta(\pi_t - \pi^T)^2. \qquad \text{(Central bank loss function)}$$

**Figure 13.1** Official central bank interest rates, monthly averages, %: 1999–2011.

*Source:* Bank of England; Board of Governors of the Federal Reserve System (US); Bank of Japan; European Central Bank (data accessed January 2012).

$$\pi_1 = \pi_0 + \alpha(y_1 - y_e). \qquad\qquad \text{(Phillips curve (PC))}$$

$$(y_1 - y_e) = -\alpha\beta(\pi_1 - \pi^T). \qquad\qquad \text{(monetary rule (MR) curve)}$$

We saw in the Modelling section in Chapter 3 that the central bank's preferences influences its chosen adjustment path for the economy after a shock. The degree of inflation aversion of the central bank is captured by $\beta$ in the central bank loss function.[5] If $\beta > 1$, the central bank attaches more importance to being away from the inflation target than from equilibrium output. This results in a flatter monetary rule, as shown in Fig. 13.2a. Given these preferences, any inflation shock that shifts the Phillips curve upward implies that the optimal position for the central bank will involve a more significant output reduction and hence a sharper cut in inflation along that Phillips curve than in the neutral case.

The second factor that determines the slope of the monetary rule is the responsiveness of inflation to output (i.e. the slope of the Phillips curve). Intuitively, the higher the value of $\alpha$, the steeper the Phillips curves, such that any given cut in output has a greater effect in reducing inflation. As we can see from Fig. 13.2b, a higher value of $\alpha$ also makes the *MR* curve flatter.

Our intuition tells us that steeper Phillips curves make things easier for the central bank, since a smaller rise in unemployment (fall in output) is required to achieve any desired fall in inflation. We can show this in a diagram. In Fig. 13.3a we compare two economies, one with flatter Phillips curves (dashed) and one with steeper ones. As we have already shown, the *MR* line is flatter for the economy with steeper Phillips curves: this is $MR_1$. Suppose there is a rise in inflation in each economy that shifts the Phillips curves up: each economy is at

[5] The central bank's preferences can be presented in this simple way if we assume that the central bank's discount rate is infinite. This means that it only considers one period at a time when making its decision. In a more realistic model, the central bank would minimize its losses over the whole adjustment path. A simple way to capture this is to use a larger weight for $\beta$ since lower inflation this period, reduces it in the next period via the Phillips curve.

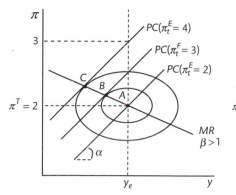

a. Inflation averse policy maker

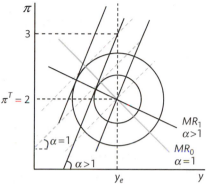

b. High responsiveness of inflation to the output gap

**Figure 13.2** How varying the parameters in the 3-equation model affects the MR curve:
a. Inflation-averse policy maker: flat $MR$ line ($\beta > 1$)
b. High responsiveness of inflation to output: flat $MR$ line ($\alpha > 1$).

*Note:* The angle marked $\alpha$ in the diagrams is in fact the angle whose tangent is $\alpha$. We adopt this convention throughout.

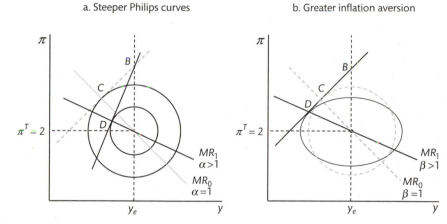

**Figure 13.3** Comparing the response of the central bank in two cases: steeper Phillips curves and a more inflation-averse central bank.

point $B$. We can see that a *smaller* cut in aggregate demand is best response in the economy with the steeper Phillips curves (point $D$). This reflects our intuitive argument above.[6]

In Fig. 13.3b, we compare two economies with identical supply sides but in which one has an inflation-averse central bank (the oval-shaped indifference ellipse), and show the central

[6] For those who are curious, with $\beta \geq 1$, the output cut in response to a given inflation shock is always less when $\alpha > 1$ as compared with $\alpha = 1$. For $\beta < 1$, the output cut is less as long as $\alpha > (1/\beta)^{\frac{1}{2}}$.

bank's reaction to inflation at point R The more inflation averse central bank always respond to this shock by cutting aggregate demand (and output) more (point D).

### Disinflation strategies

Disinflation is costly whenever a negative output gap has to be created to bring inflation down. This is captured by the concept of a sacrifice ratio. This ratio represents the percentage point rise in unemployment experienced for a one percentage point reduction in inflation during a disinflationary episode.

To get an empirical feel for the costs of disinflation, Lawrence Ball examines 28 episodes of disinflation in nine OECD countries and finds that with only one exception, disinflation was contractionary, with sacrifice ratios ranging from 2.9 in Germany (i.e. for a one percentage point reduction in inflation, the increase in unemployment was 2.9 percentage points for a year) to 0.8 in the United Kingdom and France.[7]

A recent study by Carvalho and Gonçalves extends the empirical research on disinflation, showing that amongst the OECD countries, countries with inflation targeting central banks have suffered smaller output losses during disinflations when compared to non-targeters[8].

We have also seen that the immediate response of a more inflation-averse central bank to an inflation shock is to dampen output by more than would a less inflation-averse one. It is willing to see a sharper rise in unemployment to get a faster fall in inflation. And this means that unemployment can consequently return more rapidly to equilibrium. The terms 'cold turkey'[9] or 'shock therapy' are sometimes applied to this strategy and are contrasted with a more 'gradualist' approach in which unemployment rises by less, but the process of disinflation takes longer.

An interesting question is whether cumulative unemployment is higher under the cold turkey or gradualist approach: in other words, if we add up the unemployment rates in every period after the inflation shock until inflation returns to target and unemployment to equilibrium, with which strategy will there have been a higher total amount of unemployment?

If the Phillips curves are linear and parallel, the cumulative amount of unemployment to achieve the reduction of inflation to target is the same under both strategies. In other words, in this case, the sacrifice ratio (cumulative unemployment to achieve a given reduction in inflation) is independent of the degree of inflation aversion of the central bank. But if the Phillips curves are flatter at higher unemployment (i.e. convex), then cumulative unemployment will be higher under the cold turkey strategy.[10]

### 13.3.3 The MR equation and Taylor rules

In the 3-equation model, the MR equation shows the central bank's response to a shock. The IS curve is used by the central bank in a closed economy to find out what interest rate to set given its best response output–inflation combination in the Phillips diagram, i.e. once

---

[7] See Ball (1994).      [8] See Carvalho and Gonçalves (2009).

[9] The analogy is to the treatment of alcohol or drug addiction: a cold turkey strategy reduces drug intake dramatically at the outset whereas a gradualist treatment, reduces it slowly. The choice thus ranges between severe discomfort for a short time or less pain for a longer period of time.

[10] Section 4.2 of Chapter 3 of Carlin and Soskice (2006) provides a simple geometric proof of these results.

it has located the best available position on the *MR* line. We now show how to derive a best-response *interest rate rule*, which directly expresses the interest rate the central bank should choose to achieve its objectives in terms of the current state of the economy.

The behaviour of central banks is often described by an interest rate rule of this kind. These rules have come to be known as Taylor rules, because of John Taylor's original claim in his landmark 1993 paper that the historical behaviour of the US Federal Reserve was well described by the following rule:[11]

$$r_0 - r_S = 0.5(\pi_0 - \pi^T) + 0.5(y_0 - y_e), \tag{13.5}$$

where $\pi^T$ is the central bank's inflation target, $y_e$ is the equilibrium level of output, and $r_S$ is the stabilizing interest rate. The Taylor rule states that if output is 1% above equilibrium and inflation is at the target, the central bank should raise the interest rate by 0.5 percentage points relative to stabilizing interest rate. As above we interpret the difference between $y$ and $y_e$ as the percentage gap; this is the equivalent of defining $y$ as the log of output. And if inflation is one percentage point above the target and output is at equilibrium, then the Taylor rule says that the real interest rate needs to be 0.5 percentage points higher.

We return to the question of how well a Taylor rule describes real-world central bank behaviour in the next section. First, we show how the best-response or optimal Taylor rule for the interest rate is derived in the 3-equation model.

### The best response Taylor rule in the 3-equation model

We can reorganize the 3-equation model to derive a rule for the interest rate the central bank *should* set if it is minimizing its loss function. This is called a best-response Taylor rule because it is derived from a model of optimizing behaviour of the central bank. In contrast, the original Taylor rule (Equation 13.5) was an empirical relationship inferred from historical data.

To derive a simple version of the best response Taylor rule, we bring together the three equations of the model:[12]

$$\pi_1 = \pi_0 + \alpha(y_1 - y_e) \qquad \text{(Phillips curve)}$$
$$y_1 - y_e = -a(r_0 - r_S) \qquad \text{(IS)}$$
$$(y_1 - y_e) = -\alpha\beta(\pi_1 - \pi^T). \qquad \text{(MR)}$$

From these equations, we can derive a formula for the interest rate, $r_0$ in terms of the period zero observation of inflation in the economy. If we substitute for $\pi_1$ using the Phillips curve in the *MR*, we get

$$\pi_0 + \alpha(y_1 - y_e) - \pi^T = -\frac{1}{\alpha\beta}(y_1 - y_e)$$

$$\pi_0 - \pi^T = -\left(\alpha + \frac{1}{\alpha\beta}\right)(y_1 - y_e)$$

---

[11] See Taylor (1993). Taylor assumed that $r_S = 2\%$ but we write the Taylor rule in the more general form, which allows $r_S$ to vary.

[12] We use the three equations as derived in the Appendix to Chapter 3. We use the deviations form of the *IS* curve.

and if we now substitute for $(y_1 - y_0)$ using the *IS*, and rearrange, we get the interest-rate rule:

$$r_0 - r_S = \frac{1}{a\left(\alpha + \frac{1}{\alpha\beta}\right)} \left(\pi_0 - \pi^T\right).$$    (best response Taylor rule)

We can see that

$$r_0 - r_S = 0.5 \left(\pi_0 - \pi^T\right),$$    (13.6)

if $a = \alpha = \beta = 1$.

All the parameters of the 3-equation model matter for the central bank's response to a rise in inflation. If each parameter is equal to one, the coefficient on the inflation deviation is one half. This says that if inflation is one percentage point above the target, then the real interest rate needs to be 0.5 percentage points higher. Since inflation is higher by one percentage point, the *nominal* interest rate must be raised by $1 + 0.5$, i.e. by 1.5 percentage points in order to secure a rise in the *real* interest rate of 0.5 percentage points. The requirement—if the central bank's response is to be stabilizing—that the nominal interest rate has to be raised sufficiently to push up the real interest rate is called the *Taylor principle*.

The central bank should respond to any deviation of inflation from target as follows:

1. As $\beta$ increases to reflect a more inflation averse central bank, its best-response output gap goes up, and from the best response Taylor rule equation, this means the central bank will respond to an inflation shock with a larger rise in the interest rate.

2. As $\alpha$ increases, i.e. as the Phillips curve gets steeper, the *MR* gets flatter, and as shown in Fig. 13.3, the central bank's desired output gap in response to an inflation shock falls (as long as $\beta \geq 1$). Hence the central bank's interest rate response to an inflation shock will be smaller.

3. As $a$ increases, i.e. as the *IS* curve gets flatter, reflecting greater interest-sensitivity of aggregate demand, the central bank's best response change in the interest rate to an inflation shock is reduced.

## 13.4 The modern monetary policy framework—practice

In the modern monetary policy framework, the central bank adjusts the interest rate to keep inflation at target. Figure 13.4 shows how the Bank of England sees the transmission mechanism of monetary policy to inflation.[13]

Domestic inflationary pressure occurs when aggregate expenditure exceeds equilibrium (or potential) output. In a growing economy, it is when aggregate expenditure grows more rapidly than potential output. The central bank aims to affect the level of expenditure in the economy (i.e. aggregate demand) by setting interest rates. There are four main channels through which interest rates can affect expenditure:

---

[13] This subsection is based on the 'How Monetary Policy Works' section of the Bank of England website (as of June 2012).

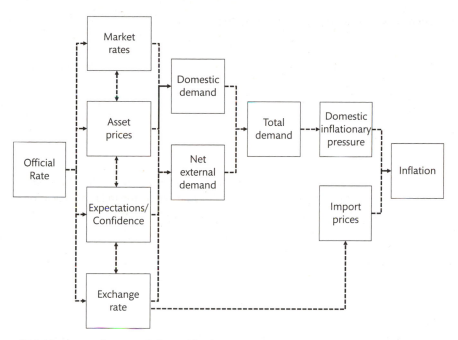

**Figure 13.4** Monetary policy transmission mechanisms.

*Source:* Bank of England (accessed June 2012).

**Market rates:**  Official rates directly influence market interest rates as discussed in Chapter 5. Lower interest rates will stimulate aggregate demand (i.e. consumption and investment) by making borrowing more desirable and savings less desirable. The opposite is true of a rate rise.

**Asset prices:**  Market interest rates can affect asset prices, such as equities and house prices. For example, lower interest rates encourage borrowing that can be spent on assets, pushing up their prices. Higher household wealth viewed as permanent pushes up consumption via the permanent income hypothesis (see Chapter 1). In some countries, higher house prices will also allow households to undertake additional borrowing by refinancing their mortgage (home equity loans). This practice was widespread in the US in the mid-2000s as discussed in Chapter 7.

**Expectations/confidence:**  Interest rate changes provide information about the central bank's future policy stance, which can affect current behaviour. For example, a rate reduction could signal a commitment to an accommodative policy stance and help to bring expenditure plans forward.

**Exchange rate:**  As we saw in Chapter 9, in a globally integrated financial market, interest rates directly affect exchange rates. Exchange rates affect both net external demand and import prices. The former affect aggregate demand, whilst the latter directly feed into the calculation of consumer price inflation as discussed in Chapter 10.

The labour market plays a key role in this process. Changes in aggregate demand affect employment, wage costs and workers' expectations of inflation. This feeds through to producer prices and eventually to consumer price inflation.

The magnitude and timing of the four channels can vary considerably. The Bank of England estimates lags in the transmission of monetary policy, such that:[14]

- the impact of interest rates on output is estimated to take up to (a maximum of) one year; and

- the impact of interest rates on inflation is estimated to take up to (a maximum of) two years.

### 13.4.1 Taylor rules in practice

*Central bank mandates: cross country differences*

In the developed world, not all inflation-targeting central banks have the same mandate. What the mandates have in common is that they tend to concentrate on the objectives of price stability (low and stable inflation) and supporting full employment and economic growth. Where the central banks differ is on the weight they place on each of these objectives.

The primary focus of the Bank of Japan until its change of course in early 2013 was on keeping inflation at target:[15]

> The Bank of Japan Act states that the Bank's monetary policy should be 'aimed at achieving price stability, thereby contributing to the sound development of the national economy'.

The fact that price stability will help create a favourable environment for economic growth and employment was taken as a given by the Bank of Japan.

At the other end of the scale are a number of central banks that have objectives to achieve both price stability and full employment, such as the Sveriges Riksbank (the Swedish central bank), the Reserve Bank of Australia and the Federal Reserve (the US central bank). The Federal Reserve is said to have a *dual mandate* for monetary policy, as set out by the Board of Governors of the Federal Reserve System:[16]

> The Congress established the statutory objectives for monetary policy—maximum employment, stable prices and moderate long-term interest rates—in the Federal Reserve Act.

The dual mandate refers to the Federal Reserve's goals of achieving stable prices and maximum employment. The Federal Reserve under Alan Greenspan (1987–2006) did not have an official inflation target. This set it apart from other modern central banks, which saw having an explicit target as the cornerstone of a credible inflation-targeting monetary regime. A target of 2% (in line with other developed economies) was, however, introduced by Ben Bernanke in January 2012 in order to help keep long-term inflation expectations firmly anchored.[17]

---

[14] This excerpt is taken from the 'How Monetary Policy Works' section of the Bank of England website (as of June 2012).

[15] Excerpt taken from the 'Monetary Policy Outline' on the Bank of Japan's website (accessed May 2012).

[16] Excerpt taken from the Federal Reserve website's Current FAQs section: What are the Federal Reserve's objectives in conducting monetary policy? (accessed May 2012).

[17] See Federal Open Market Committee (FOMC) statement of *Longer-run goals and policy strategy*, January 25 2012.

It is important to clarify that central banks that have a dual mandate are not targeting both output and inflation. Modern inflation-targeting central banks operate under the assumption that there is a unique equilibrium rate of unemployment, such that in the medium-run, targeting a level of unemployment lower than the equilibrium will only lead to higher inflation (and no output gain). It can be said however, that central banks that put more focus on output (a smaller $\beta$ in the loss function) experience bigger welfare losses when output deviates from target than those that focus more on inflation. This means they are less willing to accept large reductions in output to bring inflation back to target quickly after an economic shock—i.e. they would prefer a 'gradualist' to a 'cold turkey' approach to disinflation (see Section 13.3.2).

Lastly, there are also some central banks that fall somewhere in the middle, such as the ECB and the Bank of England. These two central banks have a primary objective of price stability, and a secondary objective of full employment. This is highlighted in the monetary policy framework of the Bank of England:[18]

> The Bank's monetary policy objective is to deliver price stability–low inflation–and, subject to that, to support the Government's economic objectives including those for growth and employment. Price stability is defined by the Government's inflation target of 2%.

### Taylor rules: cross-country differences

We have seen that central banks have different stated objectives, but how is this reflected in their actual behaviour? For example, does the ECB care less about deviations in the output gap than the Federal Reserve, as would be implied by their mandates? In this subsection, we present evidence on empirical Taylor rules for the Federal Reserve, the ECB and the Bank of England during the inflation-targeting period to try and answer these questions.

A recent paper by Castro (2011) uses econometric techniques to estimate Taylor rules for the periods through to the onset of the global financial crisis:

**Bank of England: 1992–2007**  The starting point is when the Bank of England began inflation targeting.

**ECB: 1999–2007**  This covers the period since the formation of the ECB (i.e. when they assumed responsibility for Eurozone monetary policy).

**Federal Reserve: 1982–2007**  This starts when the so-called Volcker disinflation began.

The basic form of the Taylor rule uses contemporaneous output and inflation gaps to determine the nominal interest rate the central bank should set in this period:

$$r_t = r_S + 0.5(\pi_t - \pi^T) + 0.5(y_t - y_e). \qquad \text{(TR for the real interest rate)}$$

This is the rule from Taylor's landmark 1993 paper in real terms.[19] The coefficients were chosen as they fitted US historic data well. In more general models, the coefficients on the

---

[18] Excerpt taken from the 'Monetary Policy Framework' on the Bank of England's website.

[19] Unlike the optimal Taylor rule derived above, the empirical Taylor rule has a term for the output gap as well as for inflation. As shown in Carlin and Soskice (2006) pp. 153-7, if in the Phillips curve, inflation responds to the output gap with a lag, the optimal Taylor rule will also have a term for the output gap.

**Table 13.2**  Estimated coefficients for linear Taylor rules.

| Central bank (time period) | Inflation gap coefficient | Output gap coefficient |
| --- | --- | --- |
| Bank of England (1992–2007) | 1.87 (4.89) | 0.91 (2.8) |
| ECB (1999–2007) | 2.77 (2.85) | 1.99 (5.84) |
| Federal Reserve (1982–2007) | 1.53 (5.18) | 1.40 (2.77) |

*Source:* Castro (2011).
*Note:* T-statistics using robust standard errors are shown in brackets, all coefficients are significant at the 1% level.

output and inflation gaps will vary depending on the preferences of the central bank, and the rule is often expressed in terms of the nominal interest rate (as this is the interest rate central banks actually control). A general Taylor rule in nominal terms would be:

$$i_t = \bar{i} + \gamma_1(\pi_t - \pi^T) + \gamma_2(y_t - y_e),$$ (TR for the nominal interest rate)

where $\bar{i}$ represents the nominal interest rate that prevails when output is at equilibrium and inflation is at target (it is the nominal counterpart to the stabilizing real rate of interest, $r_S$). The coefficients $\gamma_1$ and $\gamma_2$ will vary depending on the relative weight the central bank assigns to stabilizing deviations of inflation and output from target.

In order for monetary policy to be stabilizing, the *Taylor principle* states that the coefficient on the inflation gap, $\gamma_1$, has to exceed one, such that an increase in inflation (above target) leads to an increase in the *real* interest rate. Monetary policy is said to be destabilizing if a rise in inflation above target leads to a reduction in the real interest rate.[20]

Table 13.2 shows the coefficients on the output and inflation gap for forward-looking Taylor rules for the Bank of England, the ECB and the Federal Reserve:[21]

The coefficients show that all three central banks react to deviations in both inflation and output. In line with the central bank mandates, the ECB and the Bank of England react more strongly to inflation gaps than output gaps, whereas the US has a more balanced response (as per the dual mandate). However, perhaps unexpectedly, the results suggest that it is the ECB (in the short period of observation) and not the Federal Reserve that reacts most strongly to movements in the output gap.[22]

[20] Equivalently, in a general Taylor rule in real terms, the Taylor principle dictates that the coefficient on inflation has to be greater than zero, such that an increase in inflation (above target) leads to an increase in the real interest rate.

[21] Castro (2011) bases his modelling on forward-looking Taylor rules that take into account expected output and inflation gaps for 6 to 12 months into the future. This matches how modern central banks operate.

[22] Not all macroeconomic models produce a best response Taylor rule in which the coefficients $\gamma_1$ and $\gamma_2$ vary depending on the central bank's preferences (as captured by $\beta$, their level of inflation aversion). However, in line with much of the applied and policy literature, we assume this interpretation in our discussion of the estimates from Table 13.2. For further discussion, see Carlin and Soskice (2006): pp. 153-7.

## 13.5 Monetary policy and the global financial crisis

### 13.5.1 Asset price bubbles and central bank intervention

An asset price bubble occurs when financial market valuations become unrealistic—i.e. when the market price of an asset far exceeds its fundamental value. It is a source of much contention in macroeconomic and policy circles as to whether central banks should intervene to burst asset prices bubbles, such as the dot-com boom in the late 1990s or the sub-prime mortgage boom in the mid-2000s.[23] In both those cases, central bankers made little attempt to prick the bubbles and instead chose to 'mop up' after they burst. This involved providing liquidity to the market through both rapidly lowering interest rates and exploring more unconventional channels (e.g. quantitative easing).

The first question to ask when considering this debate is whether asset bubbles are inherently a bad thing. The answer is uncontentious. Asset price bubbles are seen as undesirable because they distort resource allocation, affect the central bank's target variables (e.g. inflation and output) both now and in the future and can cause financial instability.

The key question is therefore whether the central bank should intervene to burst asset price bubbles. The argument for doing this relies on the central bank:

1. being able to identify bubbles before the financial markets;

2. refraining from identifying bubbles that do not exist; and

3. bursting bubbles without causing excessive damage to the wider economy.

The former Federal Reserve Chairman Alan Greenspan believed that central banks were unable to fulfil these criteria, so he strongly advocated ex post rather than ex ante intervention. This position is known as the 'Greenspan doctrine'. We now discuss the reasons why central banks may be unable to fulfil the criteria.

The central bank and the financial markets have the same information available to them. There is little to suggest that central bankers are better placed to judge a bubble emerging than the financial markets. In fact, it is likely to be the opposite, as financial asset prices are an aggregation of the views of a very large number of market participants, whereas the central bank's view is likely to be informed by far fewer people. It is also often the case that a bubble only appears as a bubble in hindsight. This makes bubbles very hard to identify. Moreover, there is a significant risk that a central bank could intervene to pop a bubble that turned out not to be a bubble. For example, Alan Greenspan thought a bubble was forming in the US stock market as early as 1995–1996. In reality, the bubble didn't emerge until 1998–99. If rates had been raised in 1995–96 this could have wiped out the significant economic gains that accrued to the US economy between 1995–96 and the onset of the dot-com boom.

Let's assume for a moment that the central bank could correctly identify bubbles. How would they then go about bursting them? The main tool that central bankers have at their disposal is the interest rate. This is a very blunt intrument, and would be unable to pop a bubble without also harming the rest of the economy (by dampening consumption and investment in sectors not affected by the inflated asset prices). It is also not clear that a

---

[23] This section is based on the discussion and analysis in Blinder and Reis (2005).

moderate rise in interest rates would be sufficient to burst a bubble. For example, investors were expecting returns of up to 100% per annum during the height of the dot-com boom. It seems fanciful that a small rise in interest rates would have had a major effect on the decisions made by these investors.

The debate on central bank intervention to stop bubbles forming is back on the economic agenda following the global financial crisis. This is primarily because the 'mop up after' strategy did not work anywhere near as well in the late 2000s as it did in the early 2000s. When the tech bubble burst there was a very mild recession and no major bank failures. In contrast, the global financial crisis caused a severe downturn and the near collapse of the global financial system. It has also been followed by an anaemic recovery in most of the developed world. Chapter 7 provides a detailed discussion of the causes and consequences of the global financial crisis.

The bubble in US sub-prime mortgage markets that led to the global financial crisis was not foreseen by the majority of central bankers, investment bankers or economists. It is therefore not feasible to argue that the central bank should have intervened to burst the bubble. It is striking that the most consistent voice among central bankers to argue for leaning against the asset price bubble forming in the 2000s was the Bank for International Settlements in Basel.[24] The near meltdown of the global financial system that caused the global financial crisis was however precipitated by the high level of interlinkages between major banks, meaning that a problem in one bank could potentially compromise the integrity of the entire system. This has led central banks to rethink their role as the guardians of financial stability. Central banks admit that their pre-recession regulatory frameworks overlooked *systemic risk* in the banking system. They have tried to rectify this by focusing more on *macro-prudential regulation*, which is aimed at tackling the key sources of systemic risk (see Section 13.6). As we have seen, central banks might not be in the position to intervene and burst asset price bubbles that may emerge in the future, but with macro-prudential regulation they are seeking to mitigate the spillovers that occur when a bubble bursts in one market; and avoid the bad choices of one bank threatening the system as a whole.

### 13.5.2 Unorthodox monetary policy in the Great Recession

**Taylor rules and the Great Recession**

As background to looking at the use of unorthodox monetary policy in the Great Recession, we show the nominal interest rate that is implied if a simple Taylor rule is applied to the output gaps and inflation deviations for the US, Japan, UK and the Eurozone.[25] As we shall see, the Taylor rule calls for negative nominal interest rates in most cases. The zero lower bound means that the central bank cannot always choose the interest rate that would produce the desired output gap (as determined by the *MR* curve) to stabilize the economy. In extreme cases, this can lead to a deflation trap, in which the economy becomes stuck in a downward spiral of deflation and falling output. This highlights the motivation of central banks to adopt other instruments to stimulate aggregate demand.

---

[24] See for example, Borio and White, 2004.
[25] Using the same method as Sheets and Sockin (2012).

The Taylor rule for the nominal interest rate introduced in equation TR for the nominal interest rate is:

$$i_t = \bar{i} + \gamma_1(\pi_t - \pi^T) + \gamma_2(y_t - y_e),$$

where the following assumptions are made for setting the parameter values:

1. $\bar{i}$, to the average policy rate between 1999 and 2011,

2. $\pi_t$, to core consumer price inflation (i.e. excluding energy and food prices) in period $t$,[26]

3. $\pi^T$, to the core consumer price inflation target for each central bank—assumed to be 2% for the Fed, the BoE and the ECB and 1% for the BoJ,

4. $(y_t - y_e)$, to the output gap (i.e. the difference between actual and potential GDP) in period $t$ as a percentage of potential GDP,

5. $\gamma_1$, to 1.5 and

6. $\gamma_2$, equal to either 0.5 or 1, to show the effect on implied policy rates of two different levels of unemployment aversion.[27]

The results of the analysis are shown in Fig. 13.5. The solid black lines show the actual central bank interest rates in the four countries between 1999 and 2011, the grey lines show the interest rates implied by the Taylor rule when the coefficient on the output gap is set to 0.5 (bold line) and 1 (dotted line). The important points to take away from the charts are explained in the following paragraphs.

In Japan, the Eurozone and the US, the zero lower bound on interest rates was hit during the global financial crisis, as shown by the fact that the Taylor rule predicts negative nominal interest rates for this period. This is important for discussions of the optimal level of the inflation target in Chapter 3 and the deflation trap in Chapters 3 and 7.

In fact, the BoJ has kept policy rates at near zero for the entire period, suggesting that Japan has been at (or very near) the zero lower bound of monetary policy for over 20 years, rendering conventional monetary policy an ineffective tool for stabilizing the Japanese economy in response to economic shocks. Core inflation has also been negative for almost the entire period, providing further evidence that Japan has been victim to a deflation trap.

The UK has experienced CPI inflation above target during the recovery phase of the global financial crisis, which leads the Taylor rule to predict interest rates higher than those that have prevailed. However, the above target CPI inflation was mainly the result of two factors: 1) increases in Value Added Tax (VAT), and 2) the depreciation of the pound. In both these cases, the view of the Bank of England was that these were one-off sources of inflation and given the weakness of the economy over this period, would not translate into persistent

---

[26] Core inflation was used instead of headline inflation, because using headline inflation produced large variations in the implied policy rate due to the big swings in commodity prices over this period. We did not see these large movements in the policy rate in reality, suggesting that central banks were more focused on core inflation when making their monetary policy decisions. The Eurozone measure is for the Harmonized Index of Consumer Prices (HICP). All the others are for the Consumer Price Index (CPI). The Eurozone and UK indices of core inflation also exclude alcohol and tobacco on top of energy and food.

[27] These rules follow Taylor (1993) and Taylor (1999).

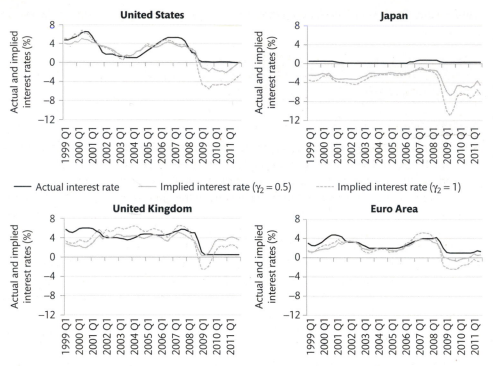

**Figure 13.5** Nominal interest rates implied by Taylor rules vs. observed central bank policy rates: 1999 Q1–2011 Q4.

*Source:* National statistical offices, national central banks, OECD, Eurostat (data accessed May 2012); Oxford Economics (June 2012).

inflation via wage increases. Indeed, wage growth has been modest during the recovery phase.

In summary, Fig. 13.5 shows that in many developed economies, monetary policy hit the zero lower bound during the Great Recession, rendering conventional monetary policy an ineffective tool for macroeconomic stablization.

## Quantitative easing

As shown above, conventional monetary policy reached its limits during the crisis so central banks had to turn to other policies. The main unconventional policy used was quantitative easing (QE), which was a largely untested policy (outside of Japan) and had never before been used on such a widespread scale.

Quantitative easing can take many forms, but in essence, the central bank uses its ability to create central bank money to buy financial assets. In the UK, these assets were mainly government bonds (bought from non-financial companies in secondary markets), whereas in the US, the Fed bought predominantly mortgage-backed securities from financial institutions, but also some government bonds and agency debt.

The use of unconventional policies can help central banks to stabilize demand and avoid undershooting their inflation targets when conventional policies are constrained by the zero lower bound. This point is captured by the Federal Reserve's announcement on the eve of their second bout of QE at the end of 2010:[28]

> To promote a stronger pace of economic recovery and to help ensure that inflation, over time, is at levels consistent with its mandate, the Committee decided today to expand its holdings of securities.

*Quantitative easing: transmission mechanisms*

Conventional monetary policy has a clear transmission mechanism (see Fig. 13.4). In a simplified form, the central bank sets the interest rate, which then influences the level of aggregate demand (and hence the output gap and inflation) through its effects on interest-sensitive behaviour in the economy and on the exchange rate in the open economy. Unconventional monetary policy does not have such a clear transmission mechanism. In theory, it could potentially affect the economy through a number of channels.

Figure 13.6 is taken from the *Bank of England Quarterly Bulletin (2011 Q3)* and shows the ways in which the Bank believes that their asset purchases can affect the real economy.[29] The majority of the channels work through raising asset prices. This will lead to increases in total wealth and a reduction in the cost of borrowing (as bond prices are inversely related to the interest rate), which could potentially raise consumption and investment.

We have seen that QE was introduced as a result of interest rates being limited by the zero lower bound. How then can QE reduce interest rates when we are already at the ZLB? Firstly, QE is not aimed at affecting short-term policy rates, which are set by the central bank, but long-term interest rates, which are set in financial markets as discussed in Chapters 5 and 7. As explained in Chapter 7 (see Section 7.5.2 and Fig. 7.12), QE is aimed at altering the term structure of interest rates and flattening the yield curve. Secondly, in times of financial distress, interest rates on assets previously viewed as very safe (e.g. interbank loans) can diverge from the policy rate, increasing the cost of borrowing. QE can help reduce the interest rate wedge by boosting market confidence and increasing market liquidity (see below). A more detailed discussion of yield curves and interest rate premia can be found in Chapter 7.

In Fig. 13.6, there are five transmission channels, which can be simply explained as follows:

**Confidence** Quantitative easing might help improve the public's perception of the economic outlook. In addition to this, a higher level of confidence could directly affect asset prices.

**Policy signalling** The introduction of QE signals the central bank's commitment to meeting the inflation target and might help to anchor inflation expectations at target. If inflation expectations were allowed to fall below the target, this would raise the real interest rate (via the Fisher equation: $r = i - \pi^e$) and depress activity. Central banks are also very scared of falling into the deflation trap and unconventional policies send a strong signal that the central bank is willing to do whatever is necessary to avoid this situation. The deflation trap is modelled using the 3-equation model in Chapters 3 and 7.

---

[28] Excerpt from the FOMC statement on 3 November 2010.     [29] See Joyce et al. (2011).

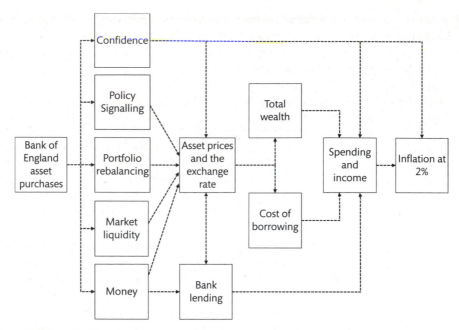

**Figure 13.6** Quantitative easing transmission channels.

*Source:* Joyce et al. (2011).

**Portfolio rebalancing**  The purchases of government bonds by the central bank will directly push up the price of government bonds, but it will also indirectly increase the price of other assets. Firms that sell their bonds to the central bank will be left with money. To the extent that money and assets are not perfect substitutes, sellers will rebalance their portfolios, buying other financial assets and pushing up their prices. This will reduce the interest rates on financial assets, lowering borrowing costs for households and firms and stimulating demand. In a situation in which banks are re-building their balance sheets, this channel seeks to facilitate borrowing by firms through the issue of bonds.

**Market liquidity**  QE can actively encourage trading in times of financial market distress, which increases liquidity in temporarily dysfunctional markets. This can influence asset prices by reducing the premia associated with illiquidity. This channel is likely to be most prominent when the actual asset purchases are taking place.

**Money**  The sellers of government bonds to the central bank will be left with cash, which they could choose to deposit in financial institutions. A higher level of liquid assets could induce the financial institutions to lend more, stimulating activity. This route is less likely to take place during financial crises when financial institutions are under pressure to reduce the size of their balance sheets.

*Quantitative easing: does it work?*

The key difficulty in measuring the impact of quantitative easing on the economy is the lack of a counterfactual—i.e. we do not know what would have happened in the absence of the policy. There are, however, some impacts that are easier to measure than others such as the effect of QE on government bond yields. The empirical evidence for the UK and the US suggests that QE brought down long-term government bond yields by up to 100 basis points (i.e. 1 percentage point). In addition, the policy had wide-ranging effects on the markets for housing agency debt and mortgage-backed securities in the US.[30]

It is more difficult to predict the effect of QE on output and inflation, as there were so many other factors affecting these variables during the Great Recession. Kapetanios et al. (2012) attempt to isolate the impact of QE by using advanced modelling techniques to construct counterfactuals for output and inflation in the UK. They find that QE may have had a peak effect on the level of real GDP of around 1.5% and a peak effect on annual consumer price inflation of about 1.25 percentage points.

We can see from Fig. 13.5 that the best response nominal interest rate was negative in a number of developed economies during the global financial crisis (i.e. conventional monetary policy was constrained by the ZLB). We can also see that QE expanded central bank balance sheets rapidly over this period (Fig. 13.7). QE was used as a substitute for conventional monetary policy during the crisis. The impact of QE can also be quantified by looking at what the equivalent effect would be on the central bank policy rate. In the UK, Joyce et al. (2011) summarize several previous studies and find that QE was equivalent to a 150–300 basis points cut in the policy rate. Similarly in the US, Chung et al. (2012) find that the Fed's QE during the crisis was equivalent to a 200 basis points reduction in the federal funds rate. These studies suggest that QE made some contribution to bridging the gap between the ZLB and the central banks' best response interest rate during the crisis.

### Quantitative easing: is it dangerous?

Figure 13.7 shows the rapid expansion of central bank balance sheets that accompanied the onset of the global financial crisis. At the start of the period in mid-2006, the total assets of the Fed were equal to $847bn, which was equal to 6.3% of US GDP in that year. It was quite another story after the financial crisis: by mid-2011 the Fed's total assets had swelled to 2.87 trillion dollars, which amounted to 19% of GDP.[31] The two channels that led to the striking increase in central bank total assets over this period were liquidity support for the financial system (e.g. short-term loans to financial institutions) and the direct purchasing of financial assets (e.g. quantitative easing).

Figure 13.7b shows that the Bank of England and the Federal Reserve saw larger increases in total assets than the ECB over the period. In the case of the Bank of England, their total assets quadrupled between 2006 and 2012. This highlights the extent to which the role and scope of central bank policy has been redefined by the global financial crisis.

The unprecedented size of central bank balance sheets does not come without risks—to both economic stability and to the operation of monetary policy. There are a number of key dangers of undertaking quantitative easing:

---

[30] See Joyce et al. (2011) and Gagnon et al. (2011).

[31] Mid-year values for total assets refer to the value of the series in the last week of June. GDP data used to calculate total assets as a percentage of current price GDP are taken from the IMF World Economic Outlook Database, April 2012.

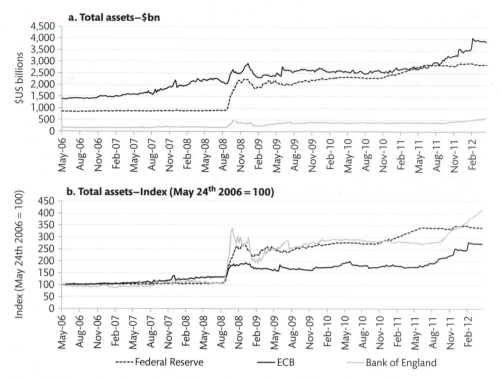

**Figure 13.7** Expansion of central bank balance sheets during global financial crisis and the recovery phase:
a. Total assets ($bn)
b. Total assets index (24th May 2006 = 100).

*Source:* Board of Governors of the Federal Reserve System; Bank of England; ECB (data accessed May 2012).

*Note:* In top panel, total assets converted into US dollars at spot exchange rates.

**Central bank independence and credibility:** The movement towards central bank independence has been one of the key trends of the inflation-targeting era, but this has been compromised by the extended role taken on by central banks during the Great Recession. If the extension of the central bank remit into areas previously deemed off-limits (e.g. large purchases of financial assets by the Fed) and higher levels of political interference (e.g. the political pressure the ECB came under during the Eurozone sovereign debt crisis) lead to a perceived reduction in credibility, then inflation expectations could become less firmly anchored to the inflation target and stabilization policy could become more costly (in terms of unemployment fluctuations).

**Inflation expectations:** Quantitative easing represents a huge expansion of central bank balance sheets. Although some observers view this as representing a potential future danger of higher inflation (along the lines of the Quantity Theory of Money), under conditions of a deep recession, it was intended to boost inflation expectations. This was viewed as a necessary step to guard against deflation in the midst of the financial crisis.

**Financial cycle:**  Central banks resorted to QE because the collapse of the upswing of the financial cycle was so serious that it rendered conventional interest rate–based monetary policy inoperative. There is a danger that, under conditions of prolonged low interest rates and official asset purchases, the search for yield will reemerge to inflate housing and other asset price bubbles in the global economy. This points to the importance of financial and macro-prudential regulation and is discussed in Section 13.6.

**Excess reserves:**  Banks are required to hold reserves at their national (or supranational) central bank. Over the course of the crisis, some banks built up large excesses of reserves in their central bank (i.e. reserves over and above the required amount). A high level of excess reserves means that banks can quickly create large amounts of new loans and deposits without putting pressure on deposit rates and without any change in central bank policy. This carries inflationary risks if the central bank does not respond by raising the interest rate on reserves or is slow to react.[32]

**Exit:**  The policy of quantitative easing is not unwound when the central bank stops purchasing assets, but rather when the assets accumulated on the central bank's balance sheet mature or are sold back into the market. This could pose dangers for both inflation (by putting downward pressure on it) and macroeconomic stability. Exit strategies are discussed further in the next subsection.

In the years that immediately followed the crisis, none of these dangers materialized; inflation remained low and stable across the developed world.

### Quantitative easing: exit strategies

The sheer scale of asset purchases by central banks has led to concerns over the *exit strategy*—how central banks plan to unwind their positions and reduce the size of their balance sheets. In theory, the selling of assets by the central bank will have the exact opposite effects to those mentioned earlier, such that it will depress asset prices and raise long-term yields. This would be expected to have a contractionary effect on the economy and exert downward pressure on inflation.

In an effort to reduce the costs associated with exit, the Federal Reserve has already begun communicating its 'strategies for normalizing the stance and conduct of monetary policy'. The strategy focuses on a gradual selling of its large portfolio of financial assets (known as the System Open Market Account, or SOMA) back into the market:[33]

> Sales of agency securities from the SOMA will likely commence sometime after the first increase in the target for the federal funds rate. The timing and pace of sales will be communicated to the public in advance; that pace is anticipated to be relatively gradual and steady, but it could be adjusted up or down in response to material changes in the economic outlook or financial conditions. Once sales begin, the pace of sales is expected to be aimed at eliminating the SOMA's holdings of agency securities over a period of three to five years, thereby minimizing the extent to which the SOMA portfolio might affect the allocation of credit across sectors of the economy.

---

[32]  See Ennis and Wolman (2010).

[33]  Excerpt taken from the *Minutes of the Federal Open Market Committee*, June 21st-22nd, 2011.

The statement above highlights the importance of timing in exiting QE. The Fed is keen not to reverse its position too rapidly for fear that it might hinder a fragile recovery. The other side of that coin is that central banks could wait too long to tighten unconventional policy and cause a build up of inflationary pressure if aggregate demand is higher than consistent with equilibrium unemployment.

Central banks have purchased some assets through their QE programmes that the market considered to be very risky, such as mortgage-backed securities in the US and periphery country sovereign debt in the Eurozone. There is a chance that central banks could take losses on the sale of these assets, which are ultimately borne by the taxpayer. This raises again the interconnectedness of monetary and fiscal policy that has emerged under the conditions of the Great Recession.

### The role of forward guidance in the crisis and post-crisis period

As we have seen, central bank communication stretches far beyond the publishing of current interest rate decisions. A key reason that central banks invest so heavily in communication is to help households and firms to form more accurate expectations about the future paths of inflation and interest rates. *Forward guidance* is one method of achieving this objective and is based on the expectations hypothesis linking the short term policy interest rate and long term rates along the yield curve. The idea is that greater confidence about the path of the policy rate produces greater confidence about the long term rate, which is relevant to investment decisions. The term forward guidance is used to describe any communication by a central bank aimed at signalling the likely future path of policy rates.[34]

The Reserve Bank of New Zealand pioneered the publication of the interest rate path it intended implementing in 1997; the central banks of Norway and Sweden followed in 2005 and 2007. Alan Greenspan (Fed Chairman from 1987–2006) was initially sceptical of the advantages of transparency, claiming it could add to market instability. Monetary policy for the majority of his tenure was characterized by little indication of the future path of policy rates.[35] The Fed has become gradually more transparent over time, however, and now provides calendar-date guidance—i.e. communicating the amount of time that the current policy stance is expected to be maintained for. The Federal Open Market Committee (FOMC) started taking this approach in 2003, with the Committee's assertion that 'policy accommodation can be maintained for a considerable period'.[36]

Forward guidance has been particularly important during and after the global financial crisis, as conventional monetary policy has been constrained by the zero lower bound. In an environment of near zero interest rates and a weak recovery, it becomes very important for the central bank to signal its commitment to accommodative policy. The Federal Reserve provides a good example of post-crisis forward guidance in practice. In January 2012, the FOMC committed to keep rates exceptionally low at least through late

---

[34] See Woodford (2008).      [35] See Blinder and Reis (2005).
[36] Excerpt taken from the *Federal Open Market Committee Statement*, August 12 2003.

2014.[37] They took this even further in December 2012, committing not to raise interest rates until unemployment fell below 6.5% (assuming inflation projections were close to target).[38]

The policy of forward guidance fits into the trend of central banks moving towards greater levels of transparency and communication. Forecasts of future policy rates will of course often be wrong, as interest rate decisions are highly dependent on the latest economic developments. Nevertheless, the forecasts are valuable because they set out explicitly the policy stance of the central bank, giving a clear indication of the speed with which rates are expected to be returned to 'normal' levels. The forecasts should therefore benefit household and firm decision making, aid the anchoring of inflation expectations and help ensure that policy is as tight or loose as the central bank intends. In principle, this helps to educate the public about the central bank's best response function. As a practical matter however, given the extent of uncertainty facing policy makers and market participants (see Chapter 4), it may be difficult for policy makers to achieve a consensus on the interest rate path. This may limit the feasibility of forward guidance.

## 13.6 Post-crisis reform of financial regulation and the macro policy framework

Central banks extended their reach during the global financial crisis by pursuing unconventional monetary policies and rapidly expanding their balance sheets. In the wake of the crisis, debate turned to how to reform the monetary policy framework and financial regulation in order to safeguard the world economy against future financial crises. The remit of many globally important central banks, such as the Bank of England and the ECB, was widened significantly in the post-crisis period, with central banks taking on more responsibility for banking regulation and the monitoring of systemic risk and financial stability.

This section discusses post-crisis macroeconomic and regulatory reforms and draws on the models and analysis of the financial system presented in Chapters 5–7.

### 13.6.1 The failures of the conventional macroeconomic policy framework

The financial crisis concentrated the attention of economists and policy makers on the following features of conventional macroeconomic policy:

1. Inflation-targeting monetary policy alone cannot be relied on to safely stabilize the economy when it is in the upswing phase of a financial cycle.

2. In the upswing of a financial cycle, there is more than the socially optimal level of borrowing and risk-taking in the financial and non-financial sectors, which make the economy vulnerable to a financial crisis.

---

[37] See the *Federal Open Market Committee Statement*, January 25 2012.

[38] See the page entitled *How does forward guidance about the Federal Reserve's target for the federal funds rate support the economic recovery?* in the Current FAQs section of the Federal Reserve website.

3. In a normal recession, monetary policy relies for its effectiveness on reducing interest rates to induce more borrowing and risk-taking by households and firms (a move along the *IS* curve to the right). It is therefore especially ill-suited to work well in a recession following a financial crisis because of the zero lower bound, and the excessive levels of indebtedness and risk-taking that characterized the upswing.

4. The state of government finances is flattened by the upswing of a financial cycle because the housing and financial sectors provide strong inflows of tax revenue.

5. A financial crisis dramatically worsens the government's fiscal position for three reasons: a) operation of the automatic stabilizers; b) discretionary fiscal stimulus in the crisis phase; c) bailing out banks.

6. The specific features of a crisis that follows a financial cycle upswing lead governments to use fiscal policy to support aggregate demand and to save banks. This worsens the government's fiscal position and leads to a rapid increase in government debt. Early implementation of fiscal austerity can delay recovery.

The experience of the crisis revealed major shortcomings in the use of monetary and fiscal policy in the upswings and downswings of financial cycles.[39] The spotlight is now on the need to reform the banking system in order to dampen financial cycles and minimize the chance of crises happening.[40]

As we saw in Chapter 6, banks pay insufficient attention to the downside risks of their activities because they take no account of how their behaviour contributes to the risk of a systemic crisis via contagion and moreover, they know that there is a chance of being bailed out by governments who cannot afford the catastrophic costs that would come with the collapse of the supply of core retail banking services.

Banks choose *higher leverage* and *lower liquidity* than is socially optimal. In addition, as we have seen in Chapter 6, there are positive feedback processes that produce increases in leverage and vulnerability to a crisis. We illustrated how in a situation in which perceived risk is falling, aggregate risk in the financial system can build up through the positive feedback process that operates in the market for financial assets when systemically important banks use a Value at Risk business model.

This immediately suggests a policy response: the regulator should force banks to have higher capital ratios (equivalently, lower leverage) so that they have a big enough private cushion against losses and do not require a public one provided by taxpayers.

The aim of this section is to connect the question of how to create a safe and re-silient banking system to the core macro model. Prior to the financial crisis, macro-economics and finance were separate subjects in the economics curriculum, and macro-economic policy and financial regulation were separate spheres of policy making. Since the financial crisis, bank regulation and its connection with macroeconomic policy have been widely debated in the economics press, research literature and by policy making bodies.

---

[39] See Borio (2012).      [40] See Vickers (2012).

### 13.6.2 **Post-crisis reforms for a safer financial system**

*Higher capital ratios (Policy 1)*

An important policy proposal is that banks should have substantially higher capital cushions. This would make them safer and reduce the chance of failure of a systemically important bank, the threat of a financial crisis and the need for a state bail-out.

The argument that a higher capital ratio makes a bank safer is straightforward and we have seen it already: when a bank (or any other entity like a household or a firm) has high leverage (a low capital cushion), it only takes a small fall in the value of assets for the equity to be wiped out and the bank to be insolvent. For example, if a bank has a capital cushion or so-called capital ratio of 3% (i.e. equity is 3% of assets), then a loss of 1% in the value of assets (due for example to a fall in asset prices by 1%) wipes out one-third of the equity of the bank. By contrast, if equity amounts to 25% of assets, then a 1% fall in the value of assets wipes out only 4% of equity. In the first case the solvency of the bank is clearly threatened by a 1% fall in the price of assets; in the latter it is not.

Figure 6.10 in Chapter 6 shows the median leverage of UK banks between 1960 and 2011. The upswing in the financial cycle is clearly shown by the sharp rise in the series in the years preceding the crisis. The series peaks in 2008 at leverage of nearly 50. To put this into the discussion of capital ratios above, a leverage of 50 is equivalent to a capital ratio of 2%. The high leverage and low capital ratios of the UK banks meant they were vulnerable to solvency crises once the downswing in the financial cycle took hold.

The models of bank behaviour developed in Chapters 5 and 6 assume the bank is maximizing its expected profits. Banks borrow from the money market in order to finance their lending. Even for banks that take in deposits, decision-making runs from their desired lending to how it is funded. When desired lending is higher than deposits, the bank borrows from the money market. In these models, we have assumed that the number of bank shares remains constant. However, like other publically quoted companies, banks can increase their equity by selling more shares. Equity can also be raised to a higher level by not paying dividends to their shareholders (or bonuses to their managers) for a period.

Figure 13.8 contrasts the initial situation (the left hand panel) with two approaches to comply with a higher capital ratio. Figure 13.8b shows the bank responding to the new regulation by increasing its equity, leaving the scale of its operation unchanged (total assets). It increases its equity by some combination of the methods mentioned above: selling new shares, selling assets, reducing dividend pay-outs and bonuses/salaries. In the right-hand of the figure, panel (c), the adjustment to the capital ratio regulation takes the form of leaving equity unchanged and shrinking the bank's assets.

There is strong opposition by banks to regulation that would require substantially higher capital ratios. One reason banks favour debt finance over equity is because tax systems favour debt. Leaving to one side the tax treatment, we now set out the arguments about whether higher capital ratios would be costly to the economy and/or to banks.[41]

---

[41] See Vickers (2012) for a clear discussion of these issues.

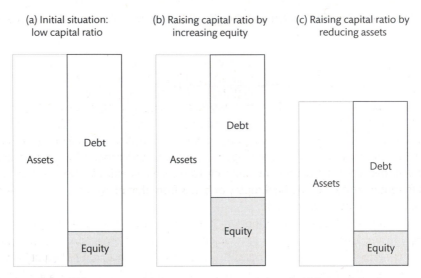

**Figure 13.8** Two potential responses to new regulation of a higher capital ratio.

*Does the funding structure between debt and equity matter for companies?*

Having a higher capital ratio means that banks would have to finance a higher proportion of their business with equity rather than with debt. We begin by asking whether
for a company, its cost of capital depends on the relationship between debt and equity
in its funding. In an important result in the theory of corporate finance, the Modigliani-
Miller (MM) (1958) theorem showed the conditions under which the overall cost of
finance to a firm does *not* depend on the balance of financing between debt and
equity.[42]

   The logic of the result is reasonably intuitive and goes as follows. The equity (or share)
holders in a company are the residual owners, which means they get any returns to the firm's
activities once the parties with contracts with the firm have been paid (i.e. suppliers, workers,
tax owed to the government, interest owed to banks, interest owed to bondholders). As well
as having the chance of upside returns, equity owners bear more risk than the suppliers of
debt finance. To compensate them for the additional risk, equity owners require a higher
return. At first sight, this makes it sound as if imposing a higher capital ratio would increase
the cost of capital to a company because of the need of the equity owners for a higher return
than the suppliers of debt. However, this ignores the effect of the change in financing mix
on the riskiness of the firm: a firm with higher equity is less risky because it has a larger
capital cushion to absorb any losses. Hence, a higher share of equity in the firm's finances
lowers risk, which in turn lowers the required return to the equity holders: the overall cost
of capital to the firm does not change. The cost of capital to the firm depends on the value
of the firm and underlying risks and not on the financing mix: if it did not, it would be

_____

[42] See Modigliani and Miller (1958).

possible to make a profit through arbitrage by either buying debt and selling equity or vice versa.

### Does the Modigliani–Miller theorem apply to banks?

The direct application of MM to banks would say that the argument that higher capital ratios would raise the cost of capital to banks ignores the effect of a higher capital ratio in reducing risk: with lower risk, equity holders would require a lower rate of return and overall funding costs would be unchanged. But we know that banks differ from ordinary companies because the government is unlikely to allow a systemically important bank to fail. The different treatment of the bankruptcy of banks from that of ordinary companies affects the interpretation of the MM result.

We have already discussed an important reason why from a social cost perspective, the funding mix of banks is not irrelevant. Acting in their own self-interest, banks will choose a lower than socially optimal capital ratio. The public suffers if the share of equity is too low (leverage is too high) because of the greater risk of financial crisis and of state bail-out. If the capital ratio is raised, this reduces the taxpayer liability (in the event of insolvency) and increases the private cost of capital. By reducing the potential liability of the government, the cost of finance to the government goes down but goes up for the private bond and shareholders of the bank.

John Vickers, who chaired the UK's Independent Commission on Banking, concludes: 'So MM might hold taking the public and private sectors together, while it fails for the private sector in isolation. Again we have a reason why private and social incentives for greater bank capital may diverge'.[43] The results of recent research are presented in the economist Anat Admati's November 2012 Congressional Testimony.[44] The conclusion is that there are few clearly identifiable social costs associated with the imposition of higher capital ratios on banks to offset the substantial social gains associated with reducing the risk of financial crisis.

### Is there empirical evidence about the effect of higher capital ratios?

The empirical evidence provided by Miles et al. (2013) suggests that better capitalized banks would reduce the likelihood of financial distress, would be in a better position to make good loans because they will avoid very risky ones, and would probably be smaller because of the reduction in the probability of state support. This points toward substantial net benefits for the economy. A recent empirical study of German bank lending finds that better capitalized banks do not lend less.[45]

---

[43] Excerpt taken from p. 11 of Vickers (2012).

[44] The testimony is available online from: http://financialservices.house.gov/uploadfiles/hhrg-112-ba15-ba04-wstate-aadmati-20121129.pdf. Also see Admati and Hellwig (2013) for a more thorough overview of their research on financial regulation.

[45] See Buch and Prieto (2012).

## Box 13.2   Leverage and capital ratios before and after the crisis

The Basel II regulatory regime was first introduced in 2004. At its centre was a minimum requirement that banks should hold at least 4% regulatory (Tier 1) capital against their risk-weighted assets (see Chapter 7 for a discussion of risk weights). Doubts about the reliability of risk weights are underscored by a report in 2013 by the global banking regulator, which shows that banks implement risk weighting in very different ways.[a] Basel II did not include any limit on simple leverage (i.e. total assets/equity). This is in contrast to the US regulation which did have such rules for non-investment banks.

The differences in regulation before the crisis were reflected in the simple leverage of European and US banks. For example, in 2007, a leading German bank (Deutsche Bank) had leverage of 49 (i.e. total assets were 49 times larger than equity). Similarly, the leverage of the median UK bank in 2008 was 48.[b] In contrast, the leverage of the big six US banks varied between 12 and 34 in 2007.[c] A simple leverage of 12 is equivalent to a ratio of capital to (non-risk-weighted) assets of 8%, whereas leverage of 49 is equivalent to a ratio of just 2%. Leverage has come down in the post-crisis period but it is still high by historic standards.

In the wake of the financial crisis, policy makers have recommended raising capital ratios. Basel III states that banks should hold at least 6% regulatory (Tier 1) capital against their risk-weighted assets and that global systemically important banks should hold 8.5%.[d] A report by the UK's Independent Commission on Banking went further, recommending banks hold Tier 1 capital of 10%.[e] Policy makers are also considering the introduction of caps on simple leverage to run alongside the new risk-weighted capital requirements.

The academic literature is largely supportive of raising capital ratios. Some of the main proponents believe that the current proposals from policy makers will be insufficient to safeguard the financial system. For example, Miles et al. (2013) propose Tier 1 capital ratios be raised to between 16% and 20% and Admati and Hellwig (2013), who oppose the use of risk weights altogether, propose a ratio of capital to (non-risk-weighted) assets of 20–30%.

[a] See http://www.bis.org/publ/bcbs256.pdf.

[b] Source: Kalemli-Ozcan et al. (2012); Bank of England, Financial Stability Report, June 2012.

[c] Source: Kalemli-Ozcan et al. (2012). Note that the US big 6 are Bank of America Merrill Lynch, Citigroup, Goldman Sachs, JP Morgan, Morgan Stanley and Wells Fargo.

[d] Source: Bank for International Settlements (data accessed June 2013).

[e] See ICB (2011).

### Problems with higher capital ratios

Higher capital ratios will not solve the problem entirely for several reasons. Bulow and Klemperer (2013) report that in 2008–11, the US federal deposit insurance corporation (FDIC) lost money on 413 bank failures. Had capital ratios been 20% (more than three times as high as the prevailing regulatory ratio), this would have been insufficient to cover losses in 90% of the cases.

It is difficult to get banks to raise their equity to safer levels because given the existing overhang of debt, the extra equity would go to reducing the expected losses of creditors of the bank (including the government). Because of these initial conditions, existing shareholders will not see a benefit and raising new equity will be expensive. Hence banks respond to higher capital ratios by shrinking their assets as illustrated in Fig. 13.8c. In a post-financial crisis recession, this effect is pro-cyclical and inhibits banks from financing good investment projects.

Higher capital ratios will also lead banks to shift their operations geographically or institutionally to avoid regulation. Geographical arbitrage means banks shift their operations to jurisdictions with lower regulatory capital ratios. In addition, we discussed the operation of the shadow banking system in Chapter 7. If higher capital ratios are imposed on banks, they will have more incentive to shift their activities to unregulated entities.

Given the difficulties with moving toward sufficiently high capital ratios, a number of other methods of improving the safety of the financial system are under debate.[46]

### Living wills, resolution schemes, bail-ins (Policy 2)

The common feature of a variety of schemes called 'living wills', 'resolution schemes' and 'bail-ins' is to replace the situation in which failing banks are rescued by taxpayer funded bail-outs with a system in which the interests of the taxpayer are placed above those of the bondholder. This second line of defence aims to create mechanisms that ensure that if there is a threat to the solvency of a systemically important bank, the core banking services can continue uninterrupted whilst some part of the bank is taken through a partial bankruptcy or resolution procedure.

With ordinary companies, bankruptcy is commonplace and there is a clear pecking order through which the remaining assets of the firm are distributed to meet its obligations. The firm's resources are distributed in the form of payments to suppliers, wages to workers and taxes owed to the government. Only when these have been paid can bondholders receive something for their bonds: the size of the 'haircut' applied to bonds will depend on the remaining assets of the firm. Equity holders typically receive nothing; they are completely wiped out when the firm goes bankrupt.

By contrast, when a bank is in trouble, the value of its equity falls and the bank's owners bear this cost directly as a consequence of the operation of the market. But if the bank is systemically important and on the verge of bankruptcy, what happens is that the state steps in and bails out the bank by providing capital in exchange for shares. In the case of banks, by preventing bankruptcy because of the threat to the continuity of core banking services, the action of the government places costs on the taxpayer and leaves the bank's bondholders unscathed. It would only be in a situation in which the bank actually went bankrupt that the bondholders who had lent to the bank would lose money.

Resolution and bail-in arrangements are not credible—i.e. they will not remove the presumption of rescue by the state, and hence of risky behaviour, unless the loss-absorbers in the bank are sufficiently high. To this end, reformers recommend that the capital cushion be augmented by other features such as contingent capital, which is debt (bonds) that is converted into equity (and therefore goes to the bottom of the queue for repayment) in a near-bankruptcy situation. More of the losses are absorbed by the private sector and state rescue is avoided (or reduced in size). Bail-in refers to compulsory haircuts

---

[46] See, for example, the UK's Independent Commission on Banking (ICB (2011)) and Vickers (2012).

applied to bondholders that write down the value of bonds when the bank is on the point of failing.

### Structural reform—retail versus investment bank activities (Policy 3)

For the private resolution of failing banks to be credible, it is also necessary that there is a mechanism to ensure that the provision of core banking services can be maintained whilst the problematic activities of the bank are wound up or restructured. In our simple modelling framework of two types of bank (retail banks and investment banks) and universal banks that combine both, the retail banks are responsible for the provision of core banking services relating to the payments system, deposits and lending (including overdrafts) to households and small and medium-sized firms. Hence, in addition to Policy 2, governments could introduce a policy of structural reform to restrict the presumption of government rescue to those parts of the bank that are essential to core banking services. The UK, EU and US have moved in broadly similar directions to alter the institutional structure of banking in pursuit of these aims.

### Macro-prudential regulation (Policy 4)

If we recall the difference between the financial cycle and the business cycle from Chapter 6, it is clear that relying on the central bank to stabilize the business cycle is not a guarantee of financial stability. In addition to policies 1-3, this has led to proposals for the introduction of policies to be implemented by a financial policy committee to stabilize the financial cycle. Such policies are referred to as macro-prudential policies.

One way of implementing macro-prudential regulation is that in a financial cycle upswing, loan-to-value ratios for housing would be reduced and bank capital ratios would be raised. This would help to dampen the boom by interrupting the financial accelerator processes and asset price bubbles in housing and the financial sector. In a downswing, the opposite would happen. By raising loan-to-value ratios, macro-prudential intervention would help the economy to recover from the consequences of the downswing of the financial cycle by helping to revive the housing sector.

Goodhart (2013) argued that it is likely to be difficult to operate macro-prudential capital ratios in the symmetric fashion sketched above. This is well-illustrated by the desire of regulators to *raise* capital ratios in the aftermath of a financial crisis whereas a macro-prudential remit would wish to loosen them.

## The interaction of policies for financial and macroeconomic stability

The distinction between the financial cycle and the business cycle is helpful in considering the interaction of policies for financial and macroeconomic stability. The task of a financial policy committee is to find ways of identifying the build-up of a financial cycle. It would implement macro-prudential policies as described above, which include sectoral measures especially in relation to housing. Macro-prudential policies are described as counter-cyclical but they need to be counter-cyclical in relation to the upswing of the *financial* cycle.

This distinction helps to highlight why there may be tension between the decisions of the bodies responsible for financial and macroeconomic stability. Note first, by looking at the financial cycle figures in Chapter 6 (Figs. 6.3 and 6.5), that business cycle recessions coincide with many different phases of the financial cycle. Suppose the economy is in a business cycle recession. Following its policy rule, the monetary policy committee seeks to boost aggregate demand to get the economy on to the *MR* curve, and it does this by reducing the interest rate. Yet at the same time, the financial policy committee may be worried about the longer-run build-up of a housing-collateral fuelled financial cycle and it would therefore like to see a reduction in loan-to-value ratios. Policies in relation to housing credit are therefore pulling in opposite directions.

In a post-financial crisis recession, there is a tension between the objectives of:

1. stabilizing the business cycle by reviving banks so they can increase their lending and contribute to a recovery of economic activity, and

2. permanently dampening the financial cycle by making the banking system safer.

The lesson from considering the interaction between the policy maker's business cycle and financial stability objectives is that effective management of financial cycles may be extremely difficult. Hence, the policy priority is to dampen their magnitude by serious reforms to the financial sector.

## 13.7 Conclusions

Building on the foundations of Chapters 3 to 6, this chapter deepened the analysis of monetary policy. We can summarize the main conclusions of the chapter as follows:

1. Monetary policy has evolved dramatically over the last 30 years. Monetary targeting was used with mixed success in the 1980s, but was ultimately replaced by the inflation-targeting framework with central banks that use Taylor rule-type behaviour to set interest rates. This sea-change in approach to monetary policy and the movement away from Monetarist ideas was partly the result of the failure of monetary targeting in the UK and North America in the 1980s. The Monetarist version of inflation targeting was undermined by the inability of monetary authorities to control their chosen monetary aggregate and the instability of the relationship between monetary growth and inflation.

2. The modern inflation-targeting central bank has preferences over output and inflation deviations, as represented in a loss function by the parameter for the degree of inflation aversion, $\beta$. The level of $\beta$ affects the slope of the *MR* and consequently the central bank's best policy response to shocks. A more inflation-averse central bank will be more aggressive in raising interest rates in response to an inflation shock. This type of central bank would prefer an adjustment path that reduced inflation quickly, even if this caused a large rise in unemployment ('cold turkey'), as opposed to an adjustment path that entailed a smaller initial reduction in unemployment, but brought inflation back to target more slowly ('gradualist'). The *MR* curve is also flatter if inflation is more responsive to changes in output (i.e if $\alpha$ in the Phillips curve is higher).

3. The best-response or optimal Taylor rule is derived from the 3-equation model and shows the interest rate the central bank should set to minimize its loss function. The size of the

best interest rate response to an economic shock in the closed economy will depend on the inflation aversion of the central bank ($\beta$), the supply-side structure as reflected in the slope of the Phillips curve ($\alpha$) and the interest-sensitivity of aggregate demand ($a$). Central banks around the world have different preferences, which are reflected in their mandates. The nominal interest rates implied by simple Taylor rules in some countries were negative during the financial crisis, suggesting that conventional monetary policy had reached its limits.

4. We have seen a number of times in the recent past that asset price bubbles arise in financial markets, such as the tech boom of the late 1990s and the sub-prime mortgage-backed securities boom in the mid 2000s. Should central banks intervene to burst these bubbles? There are some arguments against doing so. The interest rate is the main policy tool of modern inflation-targeting central banks and raising it is not guaranteed to cool the asset market in question, where returns are typically extremely high (whilst the bubble is inflating). There is also little evidence that central bankers are better placed to identify bubbles than financial markets and a significant risk they might make errors. In light of this, the central banks' preferred approach has been to wait until bubbles burst and then mop up after them. As argued in Chapters 6 and 7, the severe recession following the global financial crisis highlighted the dangers of leverage-fuelled bubbles in a highly interdependent banking system. Central banks have responded to this by focusing more on macro-prudential regulation, which aims to limit systemic risk. Regulators have been urged to concentrate on structural reforms to the banking system and caps on leverage to reduce the scale of leverage cycles.

5. The global financial crisis saw a number of countries introduce unconventional monetary policies in response to interest rates being stuck at the zero lower bound. Quantitative easing—the central bank using newly printed money to buy financial assets—was the most commonly used of these policies. The early research suggests this policy had some limited success in increasing asset prices, reducing long term interest rates, boosting GDP and putting upward pressure on inflation. The policy is not without its dangers, however, such as its impact on central bank credibility and independence, medium-term inflation and the as yet unknown macroeconomic effects of exiting the policy (i.e. selling the assets purchased back into the market).

6. In the post-crisis world, central banks have seen their remits widened to include more responsibility for banking regulation and financial system oversight. The crisis exposed the inadequacy of the conventional inflation-targeting macroeconomic framework to stabilize fluctuations in the financial cycle. Options available to policy makers include raising capital ratios, imposing leverage caps, improving insolvency processes, undertaking structural reforms and introducing macro-prudential regulation. When deciding which options to take, policy makers will also need to consider how pursuing stabilization of the financial cycle could conflict with their primary objective of stabilizing the business cycle and controlling inflation.

This chapter sets out one side of macroeconomic stabilization policy—monetary policy. The modern monetary policy framework of central bank independence saw politicians delegating this policy lever to central bankers in the majority of developed economies. Governments do, however, directly control tax and spending decisions through fiscal policy. This is the subject of the next chapter.

## 13.8 Questions

### 13.8.1 Checklist questions

1. Section 13.2.2 sets out two conditions that must hold if monetary targeting is going to succeed in controlling inflation. Briefly explain these two conditions and why they were violated during the Thatcher experiment with monetary targeting in the UK.

2. Margaret Thatcher started an aggressive disinflationary policy when she came to office as the UK's prime minister in 1979. In October 1980, she delivered her famous 'the lady's not for turning' speech. What was the aim of this speech and how was it influenced by Monetarist views on the importance of credibility and managing inflation expectations?

3. Use the central bank's loss ellipses and Phillips curves to derive the MR curve in the following cases:

   (a) When $\alpha = 1$ and $\beta = 1$

   (b) When $\alpha = 1$ and $\beta < 1$

   (c) When $\alpha < 1$ and $\beta = 1$.

   In cases (b) and (c) how can the changes in $\alpha$ and $\beta$ be interpreted? What do they suggest for the central bank's best response to an inflation shock?

4. Use a $PC - MR$ diagram to show that the cumulative unemployment caused by disinflation is independent of the degree of inflation aversion ($\beta$) of the central bank. How does this finding change if:

   (a) The Phillips curves are convex

   (b) The Phillips curves are steeper (i.e. $\uparrow \alpha$)?

5. Use the $IS - PC - MR$ diagram to show the logic behind the equation

$$r_0 - r_S = \frac{1}{a\left(\alpha + \frac{1}{\alpha\beta}\right)} \left(\pi_0 - \pi^T\right).$$

(best response Taylor rule)

   Approach the question as follows:

   (a) Use the diagrams to show how the initial interest rate response to an inflation shock varies with the slope of the MR.

   (b) What parameters affect the slope of the MR?

   (c) Are your findings consistent with the best response Taylor rule equation?

6. Assess the following statement: 'asset price bubbles played a major role in the global financial crisis, so central banks should have stepped in to burst them in their early stages'.

7. Explain how the Taylor rule could find the best response nominal interest rate to be negative.

8. Compare the transmission mechanisms of conventional monetary policy with quantitative easing. Can the two policies be viewed as substitutes?

9. Assess the following statement: 'during the financial crisis, central banks significantly expanded their balance sheets through quantitative easing and this did not cause inflation expectations to become less firmly anchored to the inflation target, thus we can say that QE does not pose a danger to macroeconomic stability'.

10. Evaluate the following claim: 'higher capital ratios for banks are costly for society as they increase banks' cost of capital'.

## 13.8.2 Problems and questions for discussion

1. Pick a developed economy (outside of the UK) that experimented with monetary targeting in the 1980s. Use the concepts in this chapter and the available academic literature to answer the following questions:

    (a) Was the policy successful?

    (b) What were the reasons that led to the policy being successful or unsuccessful?

    (c) How do these reasons relate to the Quantity Theory of Money?

2. A central bank has the following loss function:

$$L = -(y_t - y_e) + \beta(\pi_t - \pi^T)^2. \tag{13.7}$$

Use the information in this chapter to answer the following questions:

    (a) What can we interpret about the central bank's preferences from this loss function (Equation 13.7)?

    (b) Briefly explain how this loss function compares to the standard loss function and a loss function with $y^T > y_e$.

    (c) Find the inflation bias for a central bank with this loss function (Equation 13.7). [Hint: see Section 4.6 in Chapter 4].

3. Pick an economy (outside of the US, the Eurozone, the UK and Japan) with an inflation-targeting central bank. Use their central bank's website to gather information on interest rates and total assets for the period from 2006 to 2011. Present the data in a graph (as per Fig. 13.7). Use the graph to answer the following questions:

    (a) Did the central bank hit the zero nominal bound during the Great Recession? If so, did they employ quantitative easing?

    (b) Use your own knowledge and macroeconomic indicators e.g. from the IMF World Economic Outlook Database to provide a picture of your chosen economy before and during the crisis. Does this help to shed light on why it did or did not reach the ZLB during the global financial crisis? [Hint: think about your chosen economy's strength entering the recession, the severity of their recession, other policies used to stimulate demand (e.g. fiscal policy), their reliance on exports etc.]

4. Use this chapter and your own research to answer the following questions. Why might the factors listed below have compounded Japan's macroeconomic problems in its so-called 'lost decades'? Do Japan's lost decades provides strong evidence for the impotence of conventional and unconventional monetary policy at the zero lower bound?

    (a) The refusal to adopt an explicit inflation target.

    (b) Tightening monetary policy too soon in the 1990s.

    (c) Banks continuing to lend to firms in severe financial distress in order to avoid recognizing bad loans on their own books (see Chapter 7, Section 7.5.4).

# 14 Fiscal policy

## 14.1 Introduction

Fiscal policy refers to decisions by governments about raising revenue through taxation and distributing that revenue as public expenditure. In the modern monetary policy framework reviewed in the previous chapter, monetary policy is the preferred tool for stabilization policy. Why then, does fiscal policy continue to play such an important role in the macroeconomy? There are three reasons.

1. *Discretionary* fiscal policy is still used as a stabilization tool by governments around the world, as shown, for example, by the coordinated fiscal stimulus programs implemented during the global financial crisis. This policy lever is particularly important when conventional monetary policy is constrained by the zero lower bound and for countries with fixed exchange rates, including members of a common currency area.

2. Fiscal policy provides *automatic stabilizers*, which insulate the economy to some extent from shocks to aggregate demand, even in the absence of changes in the fiscal policy stance. For example, in a recession, automatic stabilizers will help boost the economy, by increasing social security spending (e.g. unemployment benefits) and reducing tax burdens.

3. Fiscal policy affects the burden of public debt in the economy. The global financial crisis has revealed the economic consequences of high levels of government debt. As we saw in Chapter 7, debt levels rose rapidly as a consequence of bank bail-outs and deep recessions. In the background, the advanced countries have ageing populations and rising health costs, which imply rising long-term debt ratios, assuming, for example, that policies such as pensionable age are not automatically linked to increases in longevity.

In this chapter, we set out some more formal models of fiscal policy and government finances. We aim to provide the reasoning and evidence behind the use of fiscal policy in modern macroeconomic management, as well as assessing the necessary conditions for government debt to be kept on a sustainable path. The rest of the chapter is organized as follows.

In Section 14.2, we analyse the use of fiscal policy for stabilization in the economy. There are two key components to fiscal policy—*automatic stabilizers* and *discretionary* fiscal policy. The former refers to the changes in the budget deficit that occur automatically as a response to the economic cycle (e.g. unemployment benefits), whereas the latter refers to changes in the fiscal policy stance of the government.

Section 14.3 focuses on a key downside of using discretionary fiscal policy—the build up of public deficits and debt. We use a simple model to show how government debt (as a percentage of GDP) evolves and the factors that can influence its path. The section ends by discussing debt reduction—what is the impact of high debt on GDP growth? What methods can governments employ to reduce their debt ratios? Can fiscal consolidation have expansionary effects on the economy?

Section 14.4 introduces the concept of *Ricardian equivalence*. This links back to the discussion of the permanent income hypothesis in Chapter 1. We show how the impact of fiscal policy on the economy differs when households are rational and fully forward-looking, and where they incorporate the government's budget constraints into their own saving decisions. We also use this framework to look at the difference between tax and bond-based financing and temporary and permanent changes to fiscal policy.

In Section 14.5, we report a number of explanations for the tendency of governments to run budget deficits and for debt ratios to rise—the so-called *deficit bias*. We also look into why the extent of deficit bias varies across countries. We end the section by discussing the two approaches commonly used to tackle deficit bias: *fiscal rules* and *fiscal policy councils*.

## 14.2 Fiscal policy's role in stabilization

### 14.2.1 The scope of fiscal policy

In addition to its role in stabilization, fiscal policy is used to meet a distinct set of government objectives related to income redistribution, resource allocation and the provision of public goods.

**Income redistribution**  Fiscal policy involves raising revenue through taxation and redistributing that money through government expenditure. This process can be used to redistribute income between different sections of society. Tax and transfer systems in developed economies are normally designed to redistribute income from those with higher incomes to those with lower incomes. This can be embedded in the structure of taxes, such as an income tax where tax rates increase as income increases (i.e. a progressive tax). Social security transfers, such as unemployment and housing benefits, also redistribute income towards those with lower income. There are substantial cross-country differences in the extent of redistribution. For example, redistribution is a much higher political priority in Continental Europe and Scandinavia than it is in the United States.

**Resource reallocation**  Fiscal policy can be used to intervene and alter the market allocation of resources. The government could do this by providing subsidies to a particular industry. This would encourage more of the economy's resources to be devoted to that industry than would otherwise be the case. Taxing undesirable activities is the other side of this coin. This approach has been widely used to discourage the consumption of goods that harm the environment or public health, such as petrol and cigarettes.

**Provision of public goods**  Governments have an obligation to provide public goods, as they would not be provided by the market. These goods are said to be non-excludable and non-rivalrous, such as lighthouses, clean air and defence.[1] The government typically also provides some quasi-public goods, such as health, education and libraries. These goods are termed 'quasi' because individuals could potentially be excluded from consuming them. Quasi-public goods are often underprovided by the market and the government might want to ensure no one is denied access to them (for example, on the grounds of price). It is the quasi-public goods that are politically contested. Left-leaning governments generally prefer a higher government provision of these goods than right-leaning governments. For example, the provision of quasi-public goods, particularly universal healthcare, was a driving force behind the creation of the modern welfare state in the United Kingdom by the Labour government following the Second World War.

### 14.2.2  The effects of discretionary fiscal policy

To understand debates about the likely effectiveness of fiscal policy, we need to know (1) the initial state of the economy (e.g. recession or equilibrium output), (2) the model that is being used and (3) the timescale (e.g. short or medium run).

We shall restrict the use of the term discretionary fiscal policy to stabilization–oriented fiscal policy measures. And in the discussion of discretionary fiscal policy, we are going to focus on government spending changes that solely affect the demand side of the economy. We discuss the implications of government policies that affect the supply side in Chapter 15. Supply-side government policies are those that shift the *WS* and *PS* curves, such as changes in the tax wedge or unemployment benefits.

*Multipliers: short and medium run*

A great deal of discussion about fiscal policy is couched in terms of 'the multiplier'. This has mushroomed in the last few years in the macroeconomics blogosphere.[2] In Chapter 1, we defined the multiplier in the simple Keynesian model and showed how it can be modified by introducing more sophisticated forward-looking behaviour of households and firms. We can use the simple Keynesian case to clarify an important distinction, namely between the short-run multiplier in the *IS* curve, which assumes everything else remains unchanged and the medium-run multiplier, which tells us by how much output increases once we take into account any monetary policy response and the possibility of crowding out responses.

The short-run multiplier tells us the partial equilibrium effect of a change in government spending: i.e. holding everything else constant, by how much does a change in government spending affect output? We derived the short-run multiplier in Chapter 1 and

---

[1] Non-excludable means that no one can be excluded from using the good once it has been provided. Non-rivalrous means that consumption of the good by one person does not diminish the availability of that good to others. For example, if the government cleans up the air in a city, none of the city's inhabitants can be excluded from breathing that air. In addition, if one person breathes the clean air it does not diminish the amount of air available for others to breathe.

[2] See, for example, Paul Krugman's blog post from 10 November 2009 entitled *Depression multipliers* or John Cochrane's blog post from 21 March 2012 entitled *Austerity, Stimulus, or Growth Now?*

we can use it to calculate how much a change in government spending ($\Delta G$) will change output ($\Delta y$):

$$\Delta y = \underbrace{\frac{1}{1 - c_1 (1 - t)}}_{\text{multiplier}} \Delta G = k \Delta G. \tag{14.1}$$

The short-run or Keynesian multiplier is equal to $k$ or $\frac{1}{1-c_1(1-t)}$ and since $c_1$ and $t$ are between zero and one, the multiplier is always greater than one. The change in output (keeping everything else constant) that is associated with a change in government spending is $k\Delta G$, which means that the change in output exceeds the initial change in government spending.

We are generally interested not only in the short-run multiplier—i.e. what happens in period 0 before wages, prices and policy respond to the stimulus—but in the 'full effect' of the increase in government spending. As we shall see, the full effect depends on the model (and what is being assumed e.g. about monetary policy) and on the initial conditions of the economy. This is because the general equilibrium outcome of a rise in government spending will be different depending on the way other elements of the economy are assumed to respond. In the two scenarios below, we shall see that although we assume the short-run multiplier is the same in each case, i.e. $k = \frac{1}{1-c_1(1-t)}$, the medium-run multiplier showing the full effect of the change in government spending on output differs.

### Fiscal scenarios

We compare two different scenarios where a fiscal stimulus is used by the government. In the first case, the economy is affected by a severe negative demand shock. In the normal course of events, the central bank would respond by cutting interest rates. However, in this case, monetary policy is disabled because of the zero lower bound and stabilization therefore falls to fiscal policy. In the second scenario, the economy is at equilibrium but the government wishes to run the economy at lower unemployment. To pursue its objective, it prevents the central bank from independently targeting inflation. The fiscal policy maker takes charge and we look at the consequences. In both cases to emphasize the fiscal channel, we model our assumptions by fixing the interest rate at the stabilizing rate.

### Scenario 1: deep recession

The economy is in a deep recession—a negative demand shock has pushed output below equilibrium (i.e. the *IS* has shifted leftwards and the economy has moved from point *A* to point *B* in Fig. 14.1a). One reason why fiscal policy comes to the fore as a policy instrument in a deep recession is that monetary policy is limited by the zero lower bound (ZLB)—i.e. nominal interest rates cannot fall below zero. A more detailed discussion of the ZLB is provided in Chapters 3 and 7, where the policy rule curve, *PR*, is introduced.

With output below equilibrium, inflation will have fallen below target and the government will have to increase government spending to $G_1$ to shift the *IS* curve to $IS(A', G_1)$ and get the economy back onto the policy rule curve labelled *PR* (as shown by the movement from point *B* to point *C* in Fig. 14.1a). From point *C* on the *PR*, the policy maker then gradually eases the fiscal stimulus to guide the economy back to *A*, with output at equilibrium and inflation at target. A value of the multiplier greater than one lies behind the strategy of using

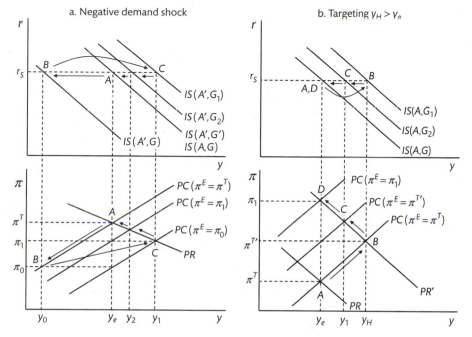

**Figure 14.1** Using fiscal policy to:
a. stabilize the economy following a negative demand shock.
b. target a level of output greater than equilibrium output (i.e. $y_H > y_e$).

fiscal policy to shift the *IS* curve. The increase in government spending will increase output, as $\Delta y = k\Delta G$.

In the new medium-run equilibrium (MRE), the real interest rate remains unchanged at $r_S$, so interest-sensitive private spending will be at its pre-recession level. The new MRE is however characterized by higher government spending and lower private spending—autonomous private spending remains depressed at $A'$, so government spending must be higher in the new MRE to make up the shortfall: $\Delta G = G' - G = (y_e - y_0)/k = \Delta y/k$.

Since we have assumed in this scenario that the policy maker incurs losses whenever inflation deviates from target or output from equilibrium, it will be very focused on forecasts of private sector demand. Once the negative demand shock begins to recede, the policy maker will reverse the fiscal stimulus to keep the economy at the MRE. One argument for the use of stabilization policy (whether monetary or fiscal) is that, by making clear its objective of keeping output close to equilibrium, private sector expectations are stabilized and less stabilization is required following economic shocks.

## Scenario 2: an over-ambitious output target

In this scenario, the economy is initially at equilibrium output (point *A* in Fig. 14.1b). The government decides to introduce an expansionary fiscal policy. This means that the *PR* curve goes through $y_H > y_e$. Under inflation targeting, the central bank would respond to the fiscal expansion by pushing up the interest rate and squeezing the inflation caused by the government's policy out of the system in the usual way. However, to bring out the consequences of a government using fiscal policy to target output above equilibrium, we have to assume it is able to prevent the central bank from responding to its expansionary policy by tightening monetary policy.

The economy is initially at equilibrium output and target inflation (at point A in Fig. 14.1b). The government decides to try and take advantage of the short-run trade-off between output and inflation by increasing output to $y_H$. This move to target a higher level of output ($y_H > y_e$) shifts the PR curve rightwards to PR' in Fig. 14.1b. The government undertakes a fiscal expansion ($G_1 > G$) to increase output and the economy moves to point B, where output is at $y_H$. We assume the government's new inflation target is at $\pi^{T'}$.

Point B is not a medium run equilibrium, however, as workers' inflation expectations are not being fulfilled. Inflation expectations are backward looking in the 3-equation model, which causes the Phillips curve to shift upwards in the next period. Faced with $PC(\pi^E = \pi^{T'})$, the government will reoptimize (and minimize its loss function) by part reversing the expansionary policy in order to get the economy on to the PR curve at point C in Fig. 14.1b. At point C, output is still above equilibrium, so there is positive pressure on inflation and the Phillips curve shifts up again. This process will continue until the economy arrives at point D—the new MRE. Under rational inflation expectations, the economy moves directly to point D as explained in Chapter 4.

What is the overall outcome of the fiscal expansion? At the new MRE, output is back at $y_e$, but inflation has risen to $\pi_1$. The government is worse off at point D than it would have been by staying at point A. This is the same result as the inflation bias outcome from Chapter 4 and highlights the pointlessness of using a fiscal stimulus in Scenario 2—unless the government is seeking a short-term gain, for example prior to an election. The medium-run multiplier in this case is zero because once the dynamic adjustment of the economy is complete, there is no increase in output in the medium run. In addition, if the government subsequently wishes to return to point A without inflation bias, it will have to incur the costs of disinflation as discussed in Chapter 4.

### What do we learn from these examples?

1. For a given size of $k = \frac{1}{1-c_1(1-t)}$, the short-run multiplier in the IS curve, the change in y ultimately associated with the change in G depends on the model, the context and the behaviour of the central bank.

2. In an economy with spare capacity, the government can boost aggregate demand and raise output. This is welfare-enhancing.

3. In an economy with output at equilibrium, if the central bank keeps the real interest rate unchanged in the face of the government's expansionary fiscal policy, the economy ends up at the new MRE at point D in Fig. 14.1b, with inflation bias and higher government debt.

### Tax finance and the balanced budget multiplier

In the two scenarios discussed above, we implicitly assumed that the government financed its expenditure plans by borrowing, i.e. by selling bonds. Later in the chapter, we look in more detail at the special case in which a bond- and a tax-financed expansion have the same effects on consumption behaviour (so-called Ricardian equivalence). However, before doing so, it is useful to calculate the short-run multiplier in the simple Keynesian model when government expenditure is tax-financed.

Suppose the government increases taxation by enough to finance its increased government spending so that there is no deficit at the new short-run equilibrium. We assume that the interest rate is fixed throughout. What is the effect on the economy of a *fully* tax-financed expenditure programme? Suppose the government increases government spending and taxation revenue by exactly the same amount. The argument is transparent when taxation is lump-sum—i.e. it does not depend on the level of income. Firstly, we need to restate the aggregate demand equation that underlies the *IS* equation introduced in Chapter 1, but using a lump-sum tax instead of a proportional tax rate:

$$y^D = c_0 + c_1(y - T) + (a_0 - a_1 r) + G. \tag{14.2}$$

Next, let us consider the impact on output of the change in $G$:

$$\Delta y = \Delta G + c_1 \Delta G + c_1(c_1 \Delta G) + \cdots \tag{14.3}$$

and then, the impact on output of the equal and opposite change in $T$:

$$\Delta y = -c_1 \Delta T - c_1(c_1 \Delta T) - \cdots \tag{14.4}$$

We add the two effects together to get the total effect on output and use $\Delta G = \Delta T$:

$$\Delta y = \Delta G + c_1 \Delta G + c_1(c_1 \Delta G) + \cdots - c_1 \Delta T - c_1(c_1 \Delta T) - \cdots$$
$$= \Delta G, \tag{14.5}$$

i.e. $\dfrac{\Delta y}{\Delta G} = 1.$ (balanced budget multiplier)

The balanced budget multiplier result is interesting: it does not depend on the assumption that taxes are lump sum. It hinges on the fact that the government spending on goods and services ($\Delta G$) generates extra output and income (Equation 14.3), whereas the increase in taxation *redistributes* spending power from taxpayers to those who provide the goods and services (Equation 14.4). If these two groups have the *same* marginal propensity to consume (as is assumed here, i.e. $c_1$ is the same in Equation 14.3 and Equation 14.4), then the balanced budget multiplier is equal to one. Why? Because *aggregate consumption* remains unchanged as a consequence of the redistribution of spending power. The only impact on output comes from the first round effect of the government's purchases of goods and services, $\Delta G$. All the other terms cancel out.

The balanced budget multiplier result is important for practical policy purposes: a government that is unable or unwilling to use debt financing can still raise the level of *aggregate demand* in the economy by engaging in a balanced budget expenditure programme. In the 3-equation model, if the economy is in a deep recession where monetary policy is ineffective and if the government does not want to increase its deficit, a balanced budget expansion is a valuable policy option.

## Empirical evidence on the size of the multiplier

The debate on the size of the multiplier has raged among economists for decades, but has recently been in the spotlight again due to the widespread use of stimulus packages during the global financial crisis and the subsequent adoption of austerity policies. It is important to try to pin down the size of the multiplier, because it has serious implications for the design of government economic policy. For example, a large multiplier would provide support for the use of fiscal stimulus during a recession and would caution against a premature switch from stimulus to austerity.

There is no firm consensus in the empirical literature on the size of the multiplier. Studies on this topic all face the same problem: it is very difficult to isolate the impact of changes in fiscal policy on output when other economic variables are changing at the same time (as is always the case in the real world). There is a specific problem when trying to estimate the size of the multiplier. The aim is to find the effect of a change in government spending or taxation on output, but the data will also include episodes where a change in output (such as a recession) led to a change in government spending or taxation. When looking for the size of the causal effect *from* a change in fiscal policy *to* output in the data, the estimated size of the effect will be contaminated by the presence of the reverse causal effect from a weaker economy to the use of looser fiscal policy. A variety of econometric techniques have been used to address these problems and to provide an estimate of the size of the multiplier. They have led to a range of estimates.

Ramey (2011) summarizes the empirical literature on the size of the multiplier in the US for a temporary, deficit-financed increase in government purchases (e.g. a fiscal stimulus).[3] Looking at around 30 aggregate level and cross-state studies for the US, she concludes that the multiplier is probably between 0.8 and 1.5.

The resurgence of interest in the multiplier since the global financial crisis has not just focused on estimating its size, but also on investigating whether its size is dependent on context. The first strand of this literature assesses whether the size of the multiplier is dependent on the economic characteristics of individual countries. Ilzetzki, Mendoza and Végh (2013) use data on government expenditures across 44 countries and find that the multiplier is:

1. larger in developed than developing countries (in developing countries there may be more waste or diversion of the fiscal stimulus from its intended purpose because of weaker governance);

2. larger in closed than open economies (due to leakages of aggregate demand to imports in a more open economy);

3. zero in economies operating under a flexible exchange rate regime, but relatively large for countries with fixed exchange rates (monetary policy can offset the effects of fiscal stimulus in flexible but not in fixed exchange rate regimes); and

4. negative in high-debt countries (due to its anticipated effects on macroeconomic stability such as provoking a sovereign debt or exchange rate crisis).

The second strand of this literature assesses whether the size of the multiplier differs over the economic cycle. In other words, is the multiplier different during recessions and expansions?

---

[3] There is also a literature on the multiplier effect of tax cuts. For studies that use narrative information on policy changes to uncover the causal effect of a tax cut on GDP, see Romer and Romer (2010) for the USA and Cloyne (2013) for the UK.

A number of empirical studies have found that the multiplier is larger during recessions. For example, the IMF (2012a) study analysed data on 28 economies during the Great Recession and found multipliers for that period in the range of 0.9 to 1.7, which is significantly higher than the value of 0.5 typically used in growth forecasts.[4] There is also some contrasting evidence that multipliers are not bigger in times of economic slack. For example, Owyang, Ramey and Zubairy (2013) use a dataset spanning the twentieth century to estimate the size of multipliers in Canada and the US. They find evidence that multipliers are higher during recessions in Canada, but find no such evidence for the US.[5]

The empirical evidence largely supports the idea that the size of the multiplier is dependent on context. This fits nicely with the modelling approach taken in this book. The two scenarios shown earlier in this section highlighted the importance of the state of the economy and the behaviour of the central bank for the impact of discretionary government spending on output. We showed that in the 3-equation model, fiscal stimulus can help boost aggregate demand and return the economy to medium-run equilibrium in a recession. We also discussed how fiscal policy is one of the only tools available to policy makers to stabilize the economy when monetary policy is constrained by the zero lower bound (as it was in the global financial crisis). In addition to this, the impact of openness to trade and exchange rate regimes on the fiscal multiplier is covered in detail in Chapters 9–12.

### 14.2.3  The automatic stabilizers

From the formula for the short-run multiplier, it is clear that taxes related to the level of income reduce the size of the multiplier and hence dampen the impact on aggregate demand of a demand shock. Similarly, because unemployment benefit payments vary with the numbers unemployed, transfers increase as the level of output falls and this, too, reduces the size of the short-run multiplier. Note that government spending on unemployment benefits is a transfer payment and shows up in the model in $T$, which is taxes less transfers, and not in $G$, which is government spending on goods and services.

Recall that a smaller multiplier is reflected in a steeper $IS$ curve that shifts less far horizontally in response to a change in exogenous expenditure (see Chapter 1). This inbuilt dampening of shocks is what is meant by the 'automatic stabilizer' role of the tax and social security system. A consequence of this feature of the fiscal structure is that the budget deficit rises (automatically) when activity falls and declines when activity rises.

To interpret the significance of the budget deficit recorded at any particular time, it is necessary to know whether output is below, at, or above equilibrium. To assist policy makers, the cyclically-adjusted budget deficit is calculated. This is the budget deficit that would prevail given existing tax and transfer commitments if the economy was operating at equilibrium output. Assuming we know equilibrium output, the concept of the cyclically-adjusted deficit indicates whether fiscal policy is expansionary or contractionary. One practical problem with

---

[4] See also Auerbach and Gorodnichenko (2013) and Fazzari, Morley and Panovska (2012).
[5] See also Crafts and Mills (2012).

using the cyclically-adjusted deficit as a measure of fiscal stance is in estimating the level of equilibrium or *potential* output, as it is often called.[6]

Let us define the relationship between the different concepts of the fiscal balance as follows.

cycl. adj. or structural budget deficit ≡ budget deficit−impact of aut. stabilizers

discret. fiscal impulse ≡ budget deficit−impact of aut. stabilizers

$$G(y_e) - T(y_e) \equiv [G(y_t) - T(y_t)] - a(y_e - y_t), \tag{14.6}$$

where $a$ is a constant and the term $a(y_e - y_t)$ captures the impact on the budget deficit of the automatic stabilizers. Note that here we are only concerned with the budget deficit *excluding* interest payments on the outstanding government debt. This is known as the *primary* budget deficit.

If current output, $y_t$, is below equilibrium output, $y_e$, the economy is in a recession. The automatic stabilizers will automatically help to stabilize the economy by raising government expenditure on transfers and depressing tax revenue ($a(y_e - y_t) > 0$), thereby pushing up the actual deficit [$G(y_t) - T(y_t) > 0$]. If these two effects on the right hand side of Equation 14.6 cancel out, then the change in the deficit simply reflects the automatic stabilizers: there is no discretionary fiscal impact on aggregate demand (and the cyclically-adjusted deficit is zero).

By definition, the impact on the budget deficit of the automatic stabilizers is zero when output is at its equilibrium level. A cyclically-adjusted budget deficit of zero implies a *discretionary* fiscal impulse on aggregate demand of zero, whereas a deficit ($G(y_e) - T(y_e) > 0$) implies an expansionary fiscal impulse, and a surplus, implies a contractionary impact on aggregate demand.

If the economy is in recession with output below the equilibrium and the cyclically-adjusted deficit or surplus is zero, then the actual deficit simply reflects the automatic stabilizers and will disappear once the economy returns to the equilibrium. In this case, fiscal policy is providing no additional discretionary stimulus to push the economy back toward the equilibrium (i.e. in 3-equation model terminology, there is no rightward shift of the IS curve).

Equally, if *discretionary* fiscal policy is used to stimulate the return of the economy to equilibrium (a rightward shift of IS), a cyclically-adjusted deficit would be observed. In this case, when the economy returns to equilibrium output, it will be characterized by a larger debt stock, i.e. T will return to $T(y_e)$ and the deficit will disappear, but debt will be higher because each year the government runs a deficit, the debt stock increases. The government has to recognize that it will eventually have to reduce the increase in debt that has built up as a result of this policy stance. Such an opportunity would arise if, when the economy is above equilibrium output, the government undertakes discretionary fiscal tightening. We shall return to this issue when we analyse the medium-run problem of fiscal policy and public sector debt in Section 14.3.

Figure 14.2 provides a picture of UK government finances since the 1970s. Recessions are highlighted by the light grey shaded areas.[7] The top panel shows the primary budget

[6] The difficulties with measuring potential output and its implications for government policy are discussed in the Web Appendix to this chapter.

[7] We define recessions as periods of two or more consecutive quarters of negative GDP growth. The data on real GDP used to calculate the series is from the UK Office for National Statistics (accessed June 2012).

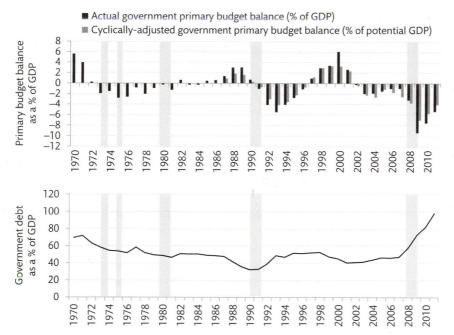

**Figure 14.2** UK government debt and primary budget balance as a percentage of GDP: 1970–2011.

*Source:* OECD Economic Outlook, June 2012.

*Note:* The actual primary balance has been calculated by adding net interest payments back onto the government budget balance. Data for the cyclically-adjusted primary balance is only available from 1987 onwards.

balance as a percentage of GDP (a negative value implies a primary budget deficit). The black bars show the actual government primary budget balance, which has been in deficit for the majority of the four decades shown. The primary budget deficit worsened sharply during (and after) recessions, such as in the early 1990s and the late 2000s. The grey bars show the cyclically-adjusted government primary budget balance, for which a deficit represents the use of discretionary fiscal expansion. There were large cyclically-adjusted deficits in the two most recent recessions, suggesting that the UK government undertook fiscal stimulus on top of the stabilization provided by automatic stabilizers. However, in the years of growth directly preceding the global financial crisis, the government also ran an expansionary fiscal policy, as shown by the cyclically-adjusted deficit being larger than the actual deficit in all bar one of the years between 2002 and 2008. This suggests that the Labour government ran a potentially destabilizing, pro-cyclical fiscal policy during their second and third terms in power.

The lower panel of Fig. 14.2 shows the evolution of UK government debt as a percentage of GDP between 1970 and 2011. We can see that periods of high budget deficits usually translate into increases in the government debt burden (e.g. during the Great Recession). This was not the case however in the 1970s, where the government ran persistent deficits, but the debt ratio followed a downwards trend. This can be explained by the role of inflation in reducing the real burden of debt, which will be discussed in more detail in the box on government debt and inflation in Section 14.3 (see Box 14.2 and Fig. 14.6) on p. 523.

*How effective are the automatic stabilizers?*

This question was investigated for the USA at the turn of the century. Auerbach and Feenberg (2000) focus on the stabilization role of federal taxes and unemployment compensation. They find that the US tax system offsets about 8% and unemployment benefits about 2% of any initial shock to GDP. This is rather modest, and the effects are greater in Central and Northern European countries, which typically have higher taxation and more generous unemployment benefits.[8]

Recent cross country research highlights the importance of the size of government in accounting for the role of the automatic stabilizers.[9] A mental experiment helps clarify this. Let us take a simple example where the tax system is proportional, i.e. a 1% fall in income leads to a 1% fall in tax revenue. If consumption depends on current disposable income, this means that the tax system provides no stabilization in the face of the shock. The assumption of a proportional tax system highlights the role in stabilization played by the size of government. Under the assumption that government spending is acyclical, i.e. it does not change with a fall in GDP, then following a fall in income, the budget deficit increases and helps to dampen the impact of the fall in income. The larger is $G$, the larger is this dampening or counter-cyclical effect.

From their study of 23 OECD countries over the period 1960–2010, Fatas and Mihov (2012) report two interesting empirical results:

1. As expected, countries with larger government sectors (i.e. $G/y$) have larger automatic stabilizers.

2. Countries with larger governments and hence larger automatic stabilizers undertake less discretionary fiscal policy.

One interpretation of the second result is that even if governments place similar weight on the benefits of stabilization, their ability to achieve it is affected by the size of government—hence, discretionary and automatic stabilizers substitute for each other. They contrast the USA and Germany. In the USA, the share of government in GDP is 37% and in Germany it is 48%.[10] For the USA, they find that counter-cyclical discretionary policy is almost as large as the automatic stabilizer effect; in Germany, with its much larger government and larger automatic stabilizers, all the counter-cyclical behaviour comes from the automatic stabilizers.

## 14.3 Debt dynamics

### 14.3.1 The government's budget identity

Each period, the government must finance its expenditure plans and also pay interest on the outstanding government debt. Government debt is the stock of government bonds that

---

[8] See Dolls et al. (2011). This paper also includes a useful summary of the academic literature on automatic stabilizers.

[9] See Fatas and Mihov (2012).

[10] The variable used is: total disbursements, general government, as a percentage of GDP. These values are an average for the period 1991–2010. The data is from the OECD Economic Outlook, June 2012.

have been sold to the private sector in the past. The government can use taxation, the sale of new bonds or the printing of money to finance its expenditure. The sources of funds are on the right hand side of the identity and the uses of funds are on the left hand side. In *nominal* terms, the government's budget identity in each period is:

$$\underbrace{G_t}_{\text{govt. exp.}} + \underbrace{i_t B_{t-1}}_{\text{interest}} \equiv \underbrace{T_t}_{\text{tax revenue}} + \underbrace{\Delta B_t}_{\text{new bonds}} + \underbrace{\Delta M_t}_{\text{new money}} ,$$

where $G_t$ is government expenditure on goods and services in nominal terms, $i_t$ is the nominal interest rate, $B_{t-1}$ is the outstanding stock of bonds and hence the value of the national debt at the beginning of the period, $T_t$ is tax revenues measured net of transfers, $\Delta B$ is the value of the new bonds issued in the current period and $\Delta M$ is the new central bank money issued by the government. Note that we use $G_t$ and $T_t$ to represent nominal values in this section. This is different from the use of $G_t$ and $T_t$ elsewhere in the book, where they represent real values. We do this to make the notation of the debt dynamics model simpler, which will become apparent as we derive the model. The $t$ subscript denotes that value of the variable in period $t$, $\Delta B = B_t - B_{t-1}$ and $\Delta M = M_t - M_{t-1}$.

A time subscript will only be shown when referring to the variable in a period other than $t$. For example, $G_t$ becomes $G$, but the value of $G$ in period $t - 1$ would be written as $G_{t-1}$. We use this approach so that the notation is less cluttered and easier to follow.

## Box 14.1 Monetary financing

When the central bank finances public expenditure through printing money, this is referred to as *monetary financing*. In the government's budget constraint this is represented by the term $\Delta M$. Monetary financing is a last resort and a state of extreme political dysfunction that only arises when the government cannot raise money through taxation or borrowing due to, for example, a small tax base, high levels of tax evasion or investors being unwilling to lend to the government.

The creation of new money by the central bank produces *seignorage revenues* for the government, but it also increases the growth rate of the money supply, which, if maintained, ultimately causes inflation to rise. The danger of continued monetary financing is that it will lead to hyperinflation, which is where the inflation rate is in excess of 50% per month. Modern examples of hyperinflations include some Latin American countries in the 1980s and 1990s (e.g. Nicaragua and Brazil) and some African countries in the 2000s (e.g. Zimbabwe).

We choose not to focus on the topic further in this chapter, as monetary financing of government deficits is not part of the modern inflation-targeting macroeconomic regime that is at the heart of the modelling approach taken in this book. This is not necessarily the case in developing or emerging economies, however, where political institutions are often weaker and central banks less independent (as shown by the recent hyperinflations listed above).[a]

[a] See Chapter 6 of Carlin and Soskice (2006) for a detailed discussion of monetary financing, seignorage and hyperinflation.

### 14.3.2 Debt dynamics

What determines the path of the government's debt over time? If the debt is rising, will it continue rising indefinitely? To answer these questions, we need to move beyond the government's single period budget identity.

Before we do that, we exclude the possibility that the government can borrow from the central bank (i.e. that it can use the creation of central bank money to finance its deficit). As discussed in Box 14.1, monetary financing is not a viable option in an economy with an independent central bank. The budget identity therefore becomes:

$$\underbrace{G}_{\text{govt. exp.}} + \underbrace{iB_{t-1}}_{\text{interest}} \equiv \underbrace{T}_{\text{tax revenue}} + \underbrace{\Delta B}_{\text{new bonds}}.$$

We begin by distinguishing between the budget deficit, which is the difference between total expenditure and revenue (i.e. actual deficit $\equiv G + iB_{t-1} - T$) and the primary deficit, which excludes the interest payments on the debt (i.e. primary deficit $\equiv G - T$). It is important to note that the stock of bonds in the economy (held by the public) is equal to the stock of government debt. By rearranging the budget identity, we can see that the actual deficit is equal to the change in the stock of government debt:

$$\Delta B \equiv (G - T) + iB_{t-1} \tag{14.7}$$

change in debt $\equiv$ primary deficit + interest on outstanding debt

change in debt $\equiv$ budget deficit.

It is the government debt relative to national income that is of central concern. We therefore define the debt ratio at the start of period $t$ as

$$\text{debt ratio} \equiv b_t \equiv \frac{B_{t-1}}{P_t y_t},$$

where $P$ is the price level and $y$ is real national income, which means that $Py$ is nominal national income. The next step is to rewrite the budget identity (Equation 14.7) by dividing through by $Py$. This gives us the budget deficit to GDP ratio ($\frac{\Delta B}{Py}$):

$$\frac{\text{budget deficit}}{\text{GDP}} = \frac{\Delta B}{Py} \equiv \frac{G - T}{Py} + \frac{iB_{t-1}}{Py}$$

$$\equiv d + ib, \tag{14.8}$$

where the ratio of the primary deficit to national income is:

$$\frac{\text{primary deficit}}{\text{GDP}} = d \equiv \frac{G - T}{Py}.$$

In order to pin down the determinants of the growth in the debt to GDP ratio, i.e. $\Delta b$, we begin with the definition of $b$:

$$B \equiv bPy,$$

use the approximation that

$$\Delta B \approx Py\Delta b + by\Delta P + bP\Delta y$$

and divide each side by $Py$ to give:

$$\frac{\Delta B}{Py} = \frac{b\Delta Py}{Py} + \frac{b\Delta yP}{Py} + \frac{\Delta bPy}{Py}$$
$$= b\pi + b\gamma_y + \Delta b,$$

where as usual, we write the growth rate of prices (i.e. the rate of inflation), $\frac{\Delta P}{P}$, as $\pi$ and the growth rate of output, $\frac{\Delta y}{y}$, as $\gamma_y$. Using the Fisher equation $r = i - \pi$, we get the following expression for the change in the debt to GDP ratio:

$$\Delta b = d + (i - \pi - \gamma_y)b$$
$$= d + (r - \gamma_y)b. \tag{14.9}$$

For an explanation of the role of inflation, see Fig. 14.6 and Box 14.2. Equation 14.9 explains four key determinants of the growth of the debt to GDP ratio:

(1) the primary deficit ratio, $d$

(2) the real interest rate, $r$

(3) the growth of real GDP, $\gamma_y$

(4) the existing ratio of government debt to GDP, $b$.

   It also provides a framework for looking at the fiscal rules that governments have introduced or may consider introducing. To interpret the equation, let us consider two cases:

**Case 1** The real interest rate is above the growth rate (i.e. $r > \gamma_y$): the arithmetic of Equation 14.9 says that in this case, the debt to GDP ratio will be rising unless $d$ is negative, i.e. unless there is a primary budget surplus. The explanation is straightforward: with the real interest rate above the growth rate, the interest payments on the existing debt are rising faster than is GDP. Hence servicing the debt interest is pushing up the debt burden. The only way that this can be offset so that the debt ratio does not rise (i.e. for $\Delta b = 0$) is for the government to run a primary budget surplus.

**Case 2** The real interest rate is below the growth rate (i.e. $r < \gamma_y$): this case represents a benign scenario from the perspective of the government's finances. Since the growth of the economy is sufficient to reduce the impact of interest payments on the debt burden, some level of primary deficit is consistent with a constant ratio of debt to GDP. Indeed if the government were to run a primary surplus in this scenario, it would eventually end up with negative public debt. The *public* sector would own financial assets issued by the *private* sector.

   A diagram helps to clarify the relationship between the primary deficit, the real interest rate, the growth rate and the debt ratio and to highlight the difference between Case 1 and Case 2. We use a diagram with the existing debt to GDP ratio ($b$) on the horizontal axis and the change in the debt to GDP ratio ($\Delta b$) on the vertical axis. The primary deficit, $d$, is the intercept term and the relationship between the real interest rate and the growth rate determines the slope of the line showing the growth of the debt ratio. For any economy, in order to draw the appropriate 'phase line' (the name for the line showing $\Delta b$ as a function of $b$), we need to know the current primary deficit, the real interest rate and the growth rate.

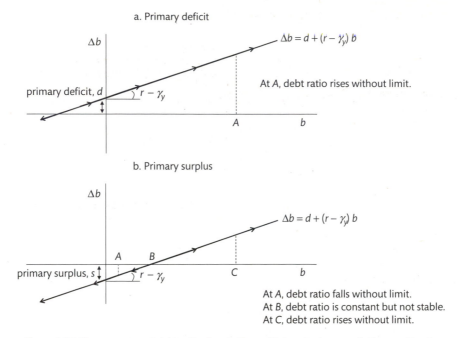

a. Primary deficit

$\Delta b = d + (r - \gamma_y)\, b$

At A, debt ratio rises without limit.

b. Primary surplus

$\Delta b = d + (r - \gamma_y)\, b$

At A, debt ratio falls without limit.
At B, debt ratio is constant but not stable.
At C, debt ratio rises without limit.

**Figure 14.3** The government debt ratio. Case 1: the real interest rate exceeds the growth rate.

The existing level of debt, $b$, then tells us where we are on the phase line. Of course, unless the initial position of the economy is on the horizontal axis with $\Delta b = 0$, the debt ratio will have changed if we look at the economy at a later time.

Figure 14.3 illustrates Case 1: the real interest rate exceeds the growth rate. Figure 14.3a shows an economy with a primary deficit. Once we know the existing level of debt, we can fix the economy's position on the phase line. But note that the economy will not remain stationary: it will be moving north-east along the phase line as shown by the arrows. When next observed, the debt ratio will be higher.

Figure 14.3b shows an economy with exactly the same interest rate and growth rate as in Fig. 14.3a but with a primary surplus (hence the intercept is below the horizontal axis). Here, we note the situation with three different initial debt ratios. If an economy happens to have an initial debt ratio shown by point A, its debt ratio will be falling (as shown by the arrows in the south-westerly direction). Why is this? This is because it is a situation in which the primary surplus is sufficiently large to offset the $(r > \gamma_y)$ effect so that the debt ratio declines. If the debt ratio is as at point B, then the debt ratio will remain constant: the primary surplus (reducing the debt ratio) and the $(r > \gamma_y)$ effect (raising it) exactly offset each other. But, note that point B is not *stable*: a slight increase in the debt ratio triggers an ever-increasing debt ratio and a slight fall triggers an ever-falling debt ratio. An appropriate primary surplus can hold the debt ratio constant, but it cannot mitigate the underlying dynamics of the debt, which is determined by the relationship between $r$ and $\gamma_y$. An economy with a debt ratio as at point C is characterized by an ever-increasing debt ratio.

Figure 14.4 illustrates Case 2: the growth rate exceeds the real interest rate. In this case, the phase line has a negative slope. At point C in Fig. 14.4a, the debt ratio is rising as

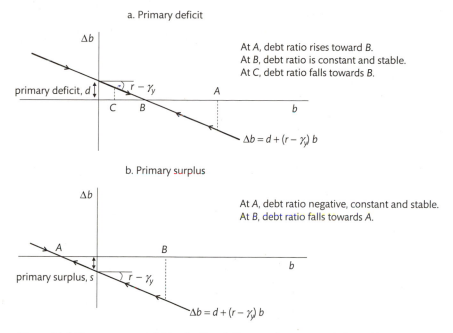

**Figure 14.4** The government debt ratio. Case 2: the growth rate exceeds the real interest rate.

shown by the arrows to the south-east. But what happens when we observe this economy some time later and the debt ratio has risen to the level shown by point *B*? As long as the primary deficit and interest and growth rates remain unchanged, the economy will remain at point *B*. Moreover, unlike point *B* in Fig. 14.3b, this debt ratio is *stable*: a slight increase in the debt ratio will put the economy on to the segment with the north-westerly arrows taking it back to the equilibrium (and vice versa). How can we explain this? Let us compare point *B* in Fig. 14.3b with point *B* in Fig. 14.4a. In Fig. 14.3b, the fact that $r > \gamma_y$ means that when there is a small increase in the debt ratio, the interest burden of the debt reinforces the increase in the debt ratio. By contrast in Fig. 14.4a, the fact that $r < \gamma_y$ means that the increase in the debt is dampened because output grows faster than the interest cost of the debt.

The lower panel of Fig. 14.4 shows the case where a primary surplus characterizes an economy in which the growth rate exceeds the real interest rate. As the diagram shows, such an economy will converge toward a negative debt ratio. The government will be a net holder of private sector financial assets.

We can use the debt diagram to explore some interesting examples. In the first example (Fig. 14.5a), the initial situation is one in which there is a primary deficit, the growth rate exceeds the real interest rate, and the debt ratio is declining (at time *t*, the economy is at point *A*); we assume that the economy suddenly experiences a rise in the interest rate and/or a fall in the growth rate so that $r > \gamma_y$. What happens? The new phase line is shown by the upward-sloping line and the economy jumps from point *A* to point *B*. The debt ratio begins to rise and will rise without limit unless the interest rate, growth rate or the primary deficit changes.

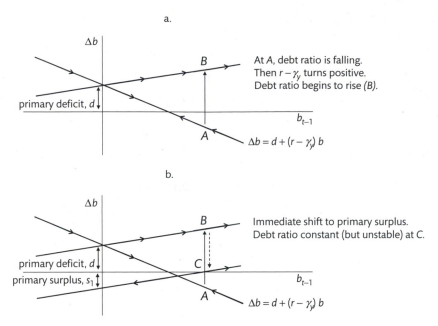

**Figure 14.5** Switch from the case where the growth rate exceeds the real interest rate to the case where the growth rate is less than the real interest rate.

In the second example (Fig. 14.5b), we follow the same economy but this time as soon as the switch in $r - \gamma_y$ occurs, the government immediately tightens fiscal policy so that the primary deficit is replaced by a primary surplus ($s_1$). This would require a dramatic cut in government spending and/or rise in taxation. If this could be done instantaneously, then the economy would move from point A to point C and the debt ratio would be constant (although unstable).

### Sovereign default risk

Until the global financial crisis it was customary in discussions of debt dynamics for the advanced economies to assume that there was essentially no risk that the government would not honour its bonds, i.e. pay the interest and repay the principal. This is no longer the case, as vividly demonstrated by the crisis in the Eurozone.[11] A positive default risk alters the debt dynamics since the risk premium, $\rho$, is added to $r^{\text{risk-free}}$, the risk-free real interest rate. A non-zero risk of sovereign default affects the path of the debt ratio:

$$r = r^{\text{risk-free}} + \rho$$

$$\Delta b = d + (r^{\text{risk-free}} + \rho - \gamma_y)b. \tag{14.10}$$

From Equation 14.10 it is clear that a positive risk premium worsens the debt dynamics.

---

[11] See Chapter 12 for an explanation of why the sovereign debt crisis affected member countries of the Eurozone.

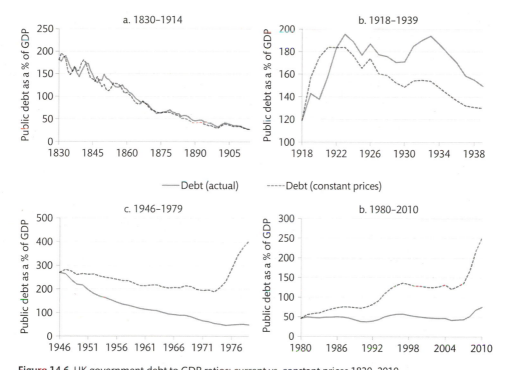

**Figure 14.6** UK government debt to GDP ratios: current vs. constant prices 1830–2010.

*Source:* Debt data from the IMF Historical Public Debt Database (see Abbas et al. 2010). Consumer prices data from the ONS (accessed June 2010).

*Note:* The constant price data was calculated by multiplying the nominal debt data (from the IMF) by the consumer price index in the current year relative to that in the base year (for each chart separately).

## Box 14.2  Government debt and inflation

The link between inflation and the government debt ratio is given by:

$$\Delta b = d + (i - \pi - \gamma_y)b. \qquad \text{(debt dynamics and inflation)}$$

We can see that inflation contributes to reducing the change in the debt ratio.[a] This is intuitive, as we can think of inflation as reducing the real value of debt. When the debt level is high, governments may be tempted to allow inflation to rise and erode the real debt burden. This highlights the fact that the equation showing the relation between inflation and the change in debt does not express causality. Causality can clearly go in either direction: for a given debt burden, higher inflation will reduce it; but higher inflation may be a consequence of a policy response to a higher debt burden.

The extent to which inflation can influence government debt ratios can be shown by analysing the evolution of public debt in the UK over four historical episodes.[b] Figure 14.6 compares the actual government debt to GDP ratio to that which would have prevailed had prices been held constant in four different time periods; 1830–1914, 1918–1939, 1946–1979 and 1980–2010.[c] We can study each period in turn to highlight the importance of inflation to the path of the debt ratio. In each case, it is interesting to keep in mind the possibility of reverse causality and to think about what lay behind the very different behaviour of inflation. A high debt ratio was not always followed by high inflation.

**1830–1914**  The actual debt ratio started the period at 182% due to the large amount of debt the government built up during the Napoleonic wars. The ratio had fallen to 27% by the end of the period. The evolution of the constant price debt ratio almost exactly matches the actual debt ratio, as the price level stayed roughly constant throughout this period (i.e. inflation was zero on average). In other words, inflation did not contribute to the fall in the debt burden.

**1918–1939**  In the interwar period, the actual debt ratio rose sharply, to 196% by 1923, and did not fall substantially until the years directly preceding World War II. The debt ratio would have fallen much faster and more consistently had the price level been held constant. The period was, however, marred by deflation, which made debt reduction more difficult.

**1946–1979**  The post-World War II period was one of inflation, prices were over eight times higher in 1979 than they were in 1946. This aided the government in reducing the substantial debt incurred during WWII. The actual debt ratio started the period at 270% and fell to around 50% by 1973. In the absence of the effects of inflation, debt would have only fallen to 189% by this time. The period from 1974–1979 was one of very high inflation (partly as a result of the OPEC oil shocks discussed in Chapter 11) and poor economic performance. The debt ratio would have risen sharply to over 400% of GDP in this period without this rapid increase in prices, as it was, the actual debt ratio finished the period just below the 50% mark.

**1980–2010**  The three decades from 1980 were also characterized by positive inflation, albeit typically at much lower levels than those seen in the 1970s. In this period, the actual debt ratio hovered around 50% of GDP before climbing to 75% in the second half of the 2000s as a result of the global financial crisis. The constant price series shows that the debt ratio would have risen to over 250% had there been no inflation over the post-1980 period.

This analysis highlights two important points. Firstly, high levels of government debt decline slowly. It can takes years to reduce debt to sustainable levels. Secondly, the path of the debt ratio is influenced by inflation. High inflation may also be a response to high debt.

[a] This box investigates the impact of inflation on the government debt ratio. For a discussion of the impact of inflation on other fiscal policy factors, such as revenue, expenditure and debt interest costs, see Box 4.3 in the Office for Budget Responsibility's *Economic and Fiscal Outlook*, March 2011.

[b] Hall and Sargent (2010) undertake a similar analysis for the United States in the post-WWII period. The authors ascertain the contributions to changes in the US debt ratio from both inflation and the other variables in the debt dynamics equation (e.g. the interest rate, economic growth and the primary deficit).

[c] This section uses the same methodology as the analysis presented in Chapter 4 of Eichengreen et al. (2011).

**Table 14.1** Growth rates, real interest rates, and real rates of return.

| | USA | | | Germany | | |
|---|---|---|---|---|---|---|
| | 1960s & 1970s | 1980s | 1990s | 1960s & 1970s | 1980s | 1990s |
| Growth rate (% p.a.) | 3.7 | 3.2 | 3.1 | 3.5 | 1.4 | 1.8 |
| Real interest rate (%) | 0.9 | 5.4 | 4.5 | 2.7 | 4.5 | 4.2 |
| Real profit rate (%) | 10.0 | 7.8 | 8.6 | 14.1 | 8.9 | 10.3 |

*Note:* Prior to 1995, Germany is West Germany.
*Source:* OECD, Historical Statistics (various years); the real profit rate is for the business sector and calculated for the USA from Bureau of Economic Analysis National Income and Product Accounts and for Germany from the Statistisches Bundesamt, Volkswirtschaftliche Gesamtrechnungen.

### 14.3.3 The costs of high and rising government debt

In the examples we have discussed, it is clear that the cost of high public debt differs according to whether the real interest rate (including the risk premium) is higher or lower than the growth rate. If the growth rate is higher than the interest rate, then the economy is converging to a stable debt ratio—there is no problem with solvency. The problematic situation is one in which the real interest rate exceeds the growth rate. Although the latter was typical of the advanced economies in recent decades, the former was characteristic of the 1960s and 1970s. Table 14.1 provides data for the USA and Germany for the 1960s to the 1990s. It is interesting to note that in the years when the growth rate exceeded the real interest rate, it was nevertheless the case that the real rate of return on capital remained above the growth rate. For the evolution of the debt ratio, it is the relationship between the real growth rate and real interest rate on government debt that matters. In the advanced countries, it is typically the case that the real interest rate on government bonds is risk free. This means that it is well below the real rate of return on fixed investment as illustrated in the data for Germany and the USA.

As we have seen, with $r > \gamma_y$, a substantial primary *surplus* may be required to stop the debt ratio rising further and an even larger primary surplus is required to reduce the debt burden. This is likely to create problems for the economy for a number of reasons. Increasing the primary surplus either requires painful cuts in expenditure or politically unpopular increases in taxation. Because of their supply-side effects, increases in taxation are also likely to raise equilibrium unemployment (*PS* shifts down) and make macroeconomic management more difficult (see Chapter 15).

A high level of debt that is rising without limit may trigger concerns that the government may default on its debt. If so, the government will face a higher interest rate on its borrowing to incorporate the premium for default risk, $\rho$. A higher interest rate will in turn feed back to worsen the debt burden as in Equation 14.10, as well as dampening investment. In addition, at some point, credit to the government may be cut off. To continue to finance its expenditure the government may resort to monetizing the debt, as explained in the box on monetary financing in Section 14.3 on p.517.

In explaining the mechanics of debt dynamics, we have assumed that the interest rate and the growth rate are exogenous. However, we have now highlighted the potential feedback from the debt ratio to the interest rate via the risk premium. To see why this matters, let us consider the case of a government operating in the benign regime in which the growth rate exceeds the real interest rate. As we have seen, in this regime, a primary budget deficit is consistent with a stable debt ratio, and a larger primary deficit is associated with a larger stable debt ratio. The higher is the debt ratio, the more vulnerable is the government in the event that the relationship between the growth rate and the real interest rate becomes adverse: it has to undertake greater fiscal tightening in order to stem the rise in the debt ratio. This possibility may in turn lead to a rise in the risk premium and trigger such an adverse shift. This provides an argument for the government to be concerned about the size of the debt ratio even when there is no immediate threat of an ever-increasing debt ratio because the growth rate is above the real interest rate.

The government's intertemporal budget identity can also be interpreted as its solvency constraint and as the requirement for the absence of a default risk on its debt. We begin with Equation 14.9, we assume that there is positive government debt (i.e. $b > 0$) and focus on the conditions necessary for the debt ratio not to increase, i.e. for $\Delta b \leq 0$:

Since $\Delta b = d + (r - \gamma_y)b$,

this implies that for $\Delta b \leq 0$,

$$b \leq \frac{-d}{r - \gamma_y}$$

i.e. existing debt/GDP $\leq \dfrac{\text{primary surplus/GDP}}{(r - \gamma_y)}$.

In order to interpret the budget constraint in this way, we have to think of each variable in terms of its 'long-run' or 'permanent' value. The equation says that for long-run sustainability, with a given long-run real interest rate in excess of the expected long-run growth rate, there must be a long-run primary surplus if the debt ratio is to be constant. When interpreted in this way, as we shall see in Section 14.5.3, this equation provides a method for evaluating the sustainability of a fiscal policy programme.

### The Eurozone sovereign debt crisis

The Eurozone provides a good example of how government (or sovereign) debt can become unsustainable. We can apply the debt dynamics model presented in this section to a real-world situation. Figure 14.7 shows the government debt ratios for selected Eurozone members from 1995 to 2011.

The government debt to GDP ratios (i.e. $b$) of all countries in Fig. 14.7 increased (i.e. $\Delta b > 0$) between 2008 and 2011. This trend was particularly marked in Greece, Ireland and Spain. We can use the debt dynamics equation, including the risk premium on sovereign debt, to trace the cause of this increase in debt burdens:

$$\Delta b = d + (r^{\text{risk-free}} + \rho - \gamma_y)b.$$

For debt to be increasing, the right hand side of the debt dynamics equation needs to be positive. There were a number of factors that meant this was indeed the case in the peripheral Eurozone economies between 2008 and 2011. The severity of the recession caused by the global financial crisis and the need to bail out banking systems meant these countries all ran

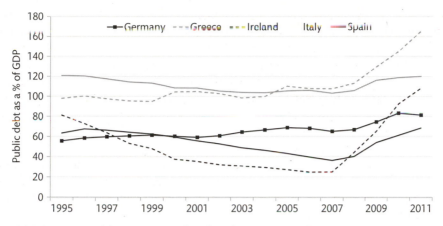

**Figure 14.7** Government debt to GDP ratios for selected Eurozone members: 1995–2011.

*Source:* OECD Economic Outlook, June 2012.

*Note:* Variable used is gross public debt, Maastricht criterion, as a percentage of GDP.

large primary budget deficits between 2008 and 2011, that is, $d > 0$. The collapse in aggregate demand that accompanied the global financial crisis (and the subsequent debt crisis) negatively affected economic growth in these countries, reducing $\gamma_y$. The risk premium on peripheral economy sovereign bonds increased substantially upon fears of default, that is, $\uparrow \rho$.

The experience of these countries shows that even low and stable government debt ratios are inherently vulnerable to negative economic shocks and a sudden increase in ($r^{\text{risk-free}} + \rho$) relative to $\gamma_y$. This can put debt on an explosive path—Ireland provides a poignant example of this: their debt ratio was only 25% in 2007, but shot up to 108% by 2011.

## Empirical evidence on the relationship between high debt and GDP growth

The rise in government debt levels associated with the global financial crisis and the Eurozone sovereign debt crisis has led to much research activity on the relationship between high government debt and GDP growth. The literature has primarily focused on the question of whether high government debt acts as a drag on economic growth. An influential paper by Reinhart and Rogoff (2010) ignited this debate. The authors analysed historical episodes of debt overhang and reported that periods in which government debt to GDP ratios exceeded 90% were associated with roughly 1% lower growth annually.

The Reinhart and Rogoff paper was widely cited by policy makers implementing austerity policies. It has been criticized on two grounds. Herndon, Ash and Pollin (2013) uncovered a number of coding errors in the spreadsheet underpinning the Reinhart and Rogoff analysis, which when corrected reduced the strength of the negative relationship between high debt and GDP growth in their findings. More substantively, economists have questioned the direction of causality in the association between high debt and slow growth found in the data. Reinhart and Rogoff claim that high debt causes low growth; other economists claim that it is more likely to be slow growth causing the build up of debt.[12] It is important to establish

---

[12] See for example, Irons and Bivens (2010) and Paul Krugman's blog post from 11 August 2010 entitled *Reinhart and Rogoff Are Confusing Me*.

the true direction of causation, as the two potential explanations imply very different policy recommendations (for example, on austerity).

The use of advanced statistical techniques can help to overcome the problem of disentangling the causal effect of higher debt on growth from the reverse effect of weaker growth leading to higher debt, which is at the centre of this debate. The academic literature has taken a number of different approaches to this, such as using instrumental variables and distributed lag models. The literature has yet to come to a consensus: some of the articles find statistical support for Reinhart and Rogoff's assertions, whereas others find evidence that the correlation between debt and growth is due to slow growth causing the accumulation of government debt.[13]

Policy makers in Europe used Reinhart and Rogoff's paper as evidence to justify the implementation of frontloaded fiscal consolidations (i.e. austerity measures) in the wake of the sovereign debt crisis. However, even a finding that high debt is bad for long-run growth does not necessarily lead to this policy recommendation. Cottarelli and Jaramillo (2013) support the view that high public debt to GDP ratios are bad for long-term growth. However, they also find that fiscal consolidation is bad for short-term growth and can delay improvements in fiscal indicators, particularly when frontloaded. In the case where there is no immediate market pressure, the authors therefore recommend a more gradual pace of consolidation to balance the short-term costs of consolidation against the long-term gains.

The next subsection looks more closely at the debate surrounding policies aimed at reducing government debt ratios, asking whether there are circumstances under which fiscal consolidation can be positive for GDP growth in the short run as well as the long run.

### 14.3.4  Can fiscal consolidation be expansionary?

In the discussion of the costs of fiscal consolidation, it has been assumed so far that an increase in the primary budget surplus (i.e. a cut in government expenditure on transfers, consumption or investment and/or a rise in taxation) will have the short-run consequence of reducing the level of aggregate demand and output (because the *IS* curve shifts to the left). Arguments have been developed—partly in response to the experience of fiscal consolidation in the 1980s of a number of European countries—that a contractionary short-run effect may not necessarily occur. Denmark (1983–86) and Ireland (1987–89) in the 1980s provide two examples of periods where fiscal consolidations ran alongside expansions in consumption, investment and GDP.[14]

Why might fiscal consolidation directly stimulate aggregate demand? If the economy is already in a state of so-called fiscal stress (an unsustainable fiscal position), then because of the risk premium ($\rho$) the interest rate will be higher than it otherwise would be and the country's sovereign bond yields (i.e. government borrowing costs) will diverge from the risk-free rate. In addition, in the expectation of some kind of crisis, households may have

---

[13] For examples of articles that find evidence that high debt causes slow growth, see Kumar and Woo (2010), Cecchetti, Mohanty and Zampolli (2011) and Baum, Checherita-Westphal and Rother (2013). For examples of articles that find evidence that slow growth causes high debt, see Bivens and Irons (2010), Basu (2013) and Dube (2013).

[14] See Giavazzi and Pagano (1990).

lowered their estimates of their wealth. In a situation of fiscal stress, it is also likely that there is considerable uncertainty about future economic developments, which will typically depress investment and spending more generally. A fiscal consolidation that was viewed by the public as credible may boost both investment and consumption by resolving uncertainty as well as by reducing the risk premium and restoring optimism about expected wealth.

Less dramatic arguments may also hold weight. If the government announces a fiscal consolidation plan that is based on cutting government consumption (e.g. the public sector wage bill) rather than cutting government investment or raising taxation, the public may believe that this signals a commitment to long term fiscal reform. This may lift households' expectations of lifetime wealth because they believe that taxes in the future will be lower (see Section 14.4.1). If wealth goes up, then for households that are not credit constrained and behave according to the permanent income hypothesis, consumption spending should rise.

The idea that the *composition* rather than simply the size of the fiscal consolidation programme determines its short-run impact is an interesting one. Some empirical support for this is provided in the studies of European fiscal consolidations in the 1980s and 1990s.[15] The arguments centre on the expectational effects of the programmes: cutting government consumption is believed to be more costly in political terms than is either cutting government investment or raising taxes. Hence a government embarking on a consolidation programme based on reductions in consumption may more effectively signal its seriousness about fiscal reform and hence have a stronger effect on expectations in the private sector.

The insights from the macro model highlight the need to take account when analysing the impact of a fiscal consolidation programme of (1) the supply-side impact of the consolidation policy (e.g. an increase in tax would shift the *PS* curve down and prompt monetary policy tightening whereas a consolidation based on cuts in public sector pay would shift the *WS* curve down permitting an easing of monetary policy), (2) the stance of monetary policy, and (3) other supply-side policies.

An analysis of the details of fiscal consolidation programmes that were implemented in the 1980s and 1990s suggests that the impact of the programmes on output in the short run was influenced by the balance between expenditure cuts and tax increases in the programmes, the associated stance of monetary policy and by wage accords. In particular, features of policy in countries observed to have expansionary fiscal consolidations were the following: expenditure-based consolidations, implementation of a devaluation of the exchange rate and a wage accord at the same time as the consolidation.[16]

Alesina and Ardagna (2010) analyse 107 fiscal consolidations in OECD economies between 1970 and 2007. The authors find that 26 of these episodes (roughly a quarter of the total) were expansionary and that all episodes were mostly associated with spending cuts rather than tax increases.

More recent literature is less supportive of the expansionary fiscal consolidation hypothesis. Two influential papers by the IMF (IMF, 2010 and Guajardo et al., 2011) criticize the methodology used in the earlier studies. They adopt a different approach by using policy

---

[15] See, for example, Alesina et al. (1998).

[16] See, for example, Alesina and Ardagna (1998 and 2010). For a summary of the evidence, see Briotti (2004). For a recent reevaluation of four cases originally thought to support the idea of expansionary fiscal consolidation see Perotti (2013).

documents to identify tax hikes or spending cuts that were explicitly undertaken to improve the public finances. In this way, the IMF can identify episodes which were based on fiscal policy actions motivated by deficit reduction, irrespective of their success. In contrast, the method used by Alesina and co-authors identifies periods of consolidation by looking at successful budget outcomes, which can can bias the results towards finding expansionary effects.[17]

The IMF papers find that:

1. Fiscal consolidation is typically contractionary—a consolidation of 1% of GDP typically reduces GDP by around 0.5% within two years. It also reduces domestic demand by 1% and increases unemployment by 0.3 percentage points.

2. The pain of consolidation is eased by accommodative monetary policy, exchange rate depreciation and an adjustment that relies more heavily on spending cuts than tax rises. Although the latter is largely a result of monetary policy providing more stimulus in spending-based consolidations.

3. Consolidations are less contractionary in countries with high perceived default risk but expansionary effects are still unusual.

4. Fiscal consolidation is likely to be beneficial for GDP in the long term.

Moreover, consolidation will be most painful when undertaken simultaneously in economies with fixed exchange rates and little scope for monetary stimulus. This provides a bleak picture for the Eurozone economies undergoing austerity in the wake of the global financial crisis and the Eurozone debt crisis.

## 14.4 The government's budget constraint and Ricardian equivalence

In the previous section, we used the government's budget identity to investigate the determinants of the path of the debt to GDP ratio. Here we show the connection between that discussion and the analysis of household consumption behaviour using the permanent income hypothesis (PIH) in Chapter 1. In the RE–PIH (Ricardian equivalence–permanent income hypothesis), the government's intertemporal optimization problem is set up in the same way as the household's, i.e. maximizing utility subject to an intertemporal budget constraint. Households and government are connected through their budget constraints.

Looked at in this light, and recalling the permanent income hypothesis from Chapter 1, we can see that the household will take into account the consequences for its budget constraint of how the government finances its expenditure. If the government sells bonds (to households) to fund its spending, the household will figure out that higher taxes will be required later on to service the debt and repay the principal. Under some circumstances therefore, deficit-financed spending will be viewed as identical to tax-financed spending. The term Ricardian equivalence is used to refer to this case.

---

[17] Alesina's response to the IMF approach can be found in an online article on Vox entitled *Fiscal adjustments and the recession*, November 2010.

We address the following questions:

1. Under what conditions is the household indifferent between taxes now and in the future, i.e. when does Ricardian equivalence hold?

2. Is there empirical evidence for this behaviour?

3. If the world is Ricardian in this way, what does it imply for the effectiveness of fiscal policy, in particular, what are the implications of a tax cut or a rise in government spending for aggregate demand and output?

### 14.4.1 Ricardian equivalence and the PIH

The core idea of the RE–PIH, is that households will fully internalize the consequences for them over an infinite time horizon of government spending and financing decisions. Any increase in the government deficit will be analysed by households for its consequences for their permanent income and they will behave accordingly. As we shall see, this may or may not mean that aggregate demand changes in response to a change in the government deficit. The answer depends on the implications for household permanent income. This argument has a pedigree stretching back to the nineteenth-century classical economist David Ricardo and was revived in the 1970s by Robert Barro and is known as 'Ricardian equivalence'.[18]

It is simplest to think about the Ricardian equivalence hypothesis by modelling the economy over an infinite time horizon as in Chapter 1. We assume that the permanent income hypothesis describes consumption behaviour. As we showed in Chapter 1, households prefer a smooth path of consumption independent of current income and since it is assumed that they can borrow at the interest rate $r$, they will be able to implement this.

We begin by writing the households' intertemporal budget constraint (in the absence of government) as follows:

$$\sum_{i=0}^{\infty} \frac{y_{t+i}}{(1+r)^i} = \sum_{i=0}^{\infty} \frac{c_{t+i}}{(1+r)^i} \qquad \text{(HH intertemporal budget constraint)}$$

where $\sum_{i=0}^{\infty} \frac{1}{(1+r)^i} y_{t+i}$ is total lifetime labour income and noting that in this model, consumption is the only type of expenditure. To simplify, we omit the expectation operator, assume a constant real rate of interest $r$, and ignore assets held at the beginning of the period. This says that the present value of the income of the household sector, which is assumed to live forever, is equal to the present value of its spending.

Households maximize their utility subject to the intertemporal budget constraint. As discussed in Chapter 1, the solution to the maximization problem takes the form of the Euler equation,

$$c_t = \frac{1+\rho}{1+r} c_{t+1}, \qquad \text{(Euler equation)}$$

[18] Barro (1974).

which highlights the consumption smoothing result of the PIH.[19] $\rho$ is the subjective discount rate of the households and when $\rho = r$, households consume the same in every period. We will assume $\rho = r$.

*Step 1: introduce the government with tax-financed spending*

We now introduce the government. It is assumed that the government undertakes spending in each period and that the spending is financed through lump-sum taxation, i.e. there is a balanced budget in each period ($T = G$). It is assumed that government spending does not provide utility to households. How does this affect our results for consumption? We modify the intertemporal budget constraint for the households by explicitly including the tax that has to be paid each period to finance the government spending:

$$\sum_{i=0}^{\infty} \frac{y_{t+i} - T_{t+i}}{(1+r)^i} = \sum_{i=0}^{\infty} \frac{C_{t+i}}{(1+r)^i}. \qquad \text{(HH intertemporal budget constraint with government)}$$

We compare the housholds' intertemporal budget constraint with and without the government, noting the following: the tax is lump-sum, so it cannot affect incentives; and government spending does not affect either future income (e.g. via infrastructure spending) or utility. The latter leaves the household utility function unaffected by government spending.

Given this set-up, when households maximize utility, they will smooth consumption, just as in the case without government. Their behaviour is captured by the Euler equation and the only difference is that the *level* of consumption in the Euler equation will be *lower* because taxation reduces permanent income. Consumption will therefore be constant over time, but at a lower level than in the case without government.

We have assumed that $r = \rho$, such that the household's optimal comsumption path is to consume the same amount in each period. How much do they consume when government spending is tax financed? When the economy is in equilibrium, they will consume their permanent disposable income, which is equal to $y_e - T$ (or equivalently $y_e - G$).

*Step 2: what happens if the government switches to financing government spending through borrowing rather than taxation?*

We now assume that the government reduces tax in period 0 to zero and finances government spending through borrowing. The government borrows $B = G$ in each period by selling a bond of value $B$ and must then pay interest of $rB$ in perpetuity on that period's borrowing. We assume that the government has to raise taxes to pay the interest and that they do this as the interest comes due (i.e. tax in period 1 is $rB$, tax in period 2 is $2rB$, and so on). The interest bill (and hence taxation) increases in each period because the government has to pay interest of $rB$ for every bond of value $B$ it sells and it sells one every period from period 0 onwards.

How much disposable income do households have in each period in this scenario? Again assuming the economy starts at equilibrium, they will have $y_e$ minus the tax in each period.

---

[19] As discussed in the Appendix of Chapter 1 the Euler equation takes this form if and only if we assume a log utility function of the form: $U(C_{t+i}) = \frac{\log C_{t+i}}{(1+\rho)^i}$.

Hence, disposible income in period 0 is equal to $y_e$, disposible income in period 1 is equal to $y_e - rB$, disposible income in period 2 is equal to $y_e - 2rB$ and so on.

In our model, we have assumed that $r = \rho$, so that households want to consume the same amount in each period. How much would the household need to save in each period in order to earn interest that would exactly cover the amount they will be required to pay in taxation in the future? The answer is obvious, they would need to save $B$ in each period, in effect buying the bond the government has sold. The stream of income from the bonds bought by the households will then exactly cover their tax bill and as $B$ is the same in each period, consumption smoothing is preserved.

What is the permanent disposible income of households in this scenario? It is simply $y_e - B = y_e - G = y_e - T$. Hence, the permanent consumption of households is the same whether government spending is financed by taxes or by borrowing. Under the RE–PIH, households do not take advantage of the higher disposable income they have in period 0 to increase consumption, because they want to smooth consumption in order to maximize their utility.

In short, the household takes action in period 0 to completely neutralize the effect of the shift from tax to bond finance. Once the interdependence between the government and the household sector is made transparent, the strong result of Ricardian equivalence can be clearly seen.

The Ricardian equivalence result depends on the following assumptions:

1. the absence of credit constraints on households, i.e. households are able to borrow against expected future income at the current interest rate (permanent income hypothesis);

2. the interest rate and time horizon faced by households and the government are the same; and

3. households have children or heirs and incorporate the utility of their heirs into their consumption behaviour, i.e. households behave 'as if' they last forever.

Let us take each of these in turn. If households are credit constrained, then as we saw in Chapter 1, they are unable to implement consumption smoothing. If this is the case, Ricardian equivalence will not hold, because being unable to borrow, the household will *not* be indifferent to the timing of changes in its income.

Unlike the Ricardian equivalence assumption that the government is just the aggregate of all the households in the economy, in the real world, governments can often borrow more cheaply than households. This makes government borrowing more attractive to the household than higher current taxation. This is also the case if households are more myopic or short-sighted than governments, or if they care more about their own welfare than that of their children or of other new households, including those who arrive as immigrants and enter the economy in the future. In all these cases, households will prefer to defer taxes and hence will raise consumption by more in the first period in the case of the deficit-financed spending programme.

After a clear statement of the nature of the assumptions required to deliver Ricardian equivalence, John Seater, in a survey in the *Journal of Economic Literature*, concludes:[20]

[20] Seater (1993: 155–6).

Finite horizons, non-altruistic or inoperative bequest motives, childless couples, credit constraints, and uncertainty can all lead to failure of Ricardian equivalence and it seems virtually certain that some of these sources of non-equivalence are operative. It appears likely that the world is not Ricardian.

The consensus view is that changes in fiscal policy are only partly offset by changes in private sector savings: the sources of 'non-equivalence' in the real world mean that Ricardian equivalence is not a good representation of macroeconomic behaviour.[21] Recent literature has shown that standard macroeconomic models can be made to better fit the empirical data by allowing for the presence of some rule-of-thumb consumers—i.e. a proportion of consumers act as if they follow a Keynesian consumption function instead of being fully forward looking.[22]

In addition, recent research has found that Ricardian effects are stronger the more developed are financial markets.[23] This finding not only suggests that credit constraints are a salient source of 'non-equivalence', but also that the global trend towards financial development could see the world economy becoming more Ricardian over time. This could have important implications for stabilization policy, as we shall see in the next subsection.

### 14.4.2 Ricardian equivalence and fiscal policy effectiveness

We turn our attention to the implications of the RE–PIH for the effectiveness of fiscal stimulus packages, i.e. the use of *temporary* changes in taxation or government spending to boost aggregate demand.

*Temporary tax cuts*

In the RE–PIH framework, a temporary tax cut entails a tax increase later in order that the intertemporal budget constraint is met. Because the tax cut is saved (as in Step 2 above), consumption and hence aggregate demand do not change at all. Attempting to stimulate the economy by increasing aggregate demand via a temporary tax cut like this is completely ineffective if the economy is characterized by Ricardian equivalence (remember that this is a lump-sum tax cut so it has no effect on incentives).

*Temporary rise in government spending financed by borrowing*

The case of a temporary rise in government spending financed by borrowing is different. If we return to Step 1 above, we can easily see that higher government spending in period 0 reduces permanent income for households. They will therefore re-optimize and reduce consumption in every period. To calculate the net impact of the increased government spending on aggregate demand in period 0, we therefore need to add together the extra

---

[21] For a study focusing on OECD countries, see de Mello, Kongsrud, and Price (2004). A summary is provided in OECD, *Economic Outlook*, 76 (2004), ch. V. For further evidence on the real world being only partially Ricardian see Holmes (2006) and Brittle (2010).

[22] Galí et al. (2007) shows how adding rule-of-thumb consumers to a New Keynesian DSGE model can account for existing evidence on 'non-equivalence'. See Chapter 1 for a discussion of the different types of consumption function. See Chapter 16 for a discussion of New Keynesian DSGE models.

[23] See Röhn (2010).

government spending and the reduced level of consumption. Since the impact of the higher government spending on the household's budget constraint is spread across all periods (saving goes up in all periods to pay the higher taxes in order to satisfy the intertemporal budget constraint), the fall in consumption must be less than the rise in government spending: hence there is a positive boost to aggregate demand in period 0. This assumes that the real interest rate remains unchanged.

To summarize, if Ricardian equivalence (and hence the PIH) holds:

1. Temporary tax cuts have no impact on aggregate demand (and cannot therefore affect output).

2. Temporary higher government spending financed by borrowing boosts aggregate demand, because the offsetting effect on consumption is spread over future periods whereas all of the government spending affects aggregate demand in period 0. Note that the increase in government spending is partially offset by lower consumption, so the multiplier must be less than 1.

3. Combining the first and second results, a temporary increase in government spending financed by higher taxes (i.e. a balanced budget spending boost) will have the same effect as the case where the spending is financed by borrowing.

These results contrast with a model with Keynesian consumption behaviour, where holding the interest rate constant, the multiplier is greater than 1 in the case of a temporary rise in government spending financed by borrowing and equal to 1 when it is a balanced budget fiscal expansion.

## 14.5 Deficit bias and the political economy of debt

Figure 14.2 for the UK highlights what is called 'deficit bias'. This is the tendency for budget deficits to rise in recessions, but not to fall in a sufficiently offsetting way in booms. The bias leads to a preference for financing government spending through borrowing rather than taxation.

The result is the upward trend in debt ratios reported in Section 14.3. Relating these data to the debt dynamics equation in the form that includes inflation, we can infer that a tendency toward deficit bias has been mainly interrupted by bursts of inflation (e.g. the UK in the 1970s; see Figure 14.6) or especially rapid GDP growth relative to the real interest rate (e.g. Spain and Ireland in the 2000s; see Figure 14.7).

In this section, we set out briefly some of the hypotheses that have been proposed to explain deficit bias behaviour.[24] Some of the explanations help to account for a general tendency for deficit bias and others are more helpful in explaining why the problem appears to be more severe in some countries than in others. We end the section by discussing fiscal rules and fiscal policy councils, two commonly used approaches to tackle deficit bias.

---

[24] Calmfors and Wren-Lewis (2011) provide a very useful summary and relate the different explanations for deficit bias to the role of a fiscal council.

## 14.5.1  Causes of deficit bias

*Over-ambitious output target*

At the beginning of this chapter, we looked at the case of a government with an over-ambitious output target (e.g. it seeks to achieve unemployment below the equilibrium rate). The medium-run impact of this policy stance is that the economy returns to equilibrium output at constant inflation, but the new medium-run equilibrium is characterized by both inflation bias and higher government debt.

*Uncertainty about growth forecasts*

This explanation is related to the previous one. In the previous example, we assumed that the government knows potential output and chooses to ignore this by opting for a higher output target—possibly for reasons of electoral gain. The government can implement its favourite spending plans or provide tax cuts to its target voters prior to an election. However, even if neither the government nor the voters have these preferences, it is still possible, given the extent of uncertainty about the future evolution of the economy, that they believe growth will be higher than it turns out to be. Since more optimistic forecasts for growth will produce higher estimates for tax revenue, this may encourage the government to adopt tax and spending plans that raise the debt level if the outturn for growth is lower than expected.

*Intergenerational conflict*

The current generation of voters may take insufficient account of the future burden that will arise, for example, if current fiscal policy places too low a weight on the higher future spending that will be associated with an ageing population. This effect will be exacerbated to the extent that politicians have shorter time horizons than voters.

## 14.5.2  Why deficit bias may vary across countries

A number of theories have been put forward to explain why some countries are more affected by deficit bias than others.

*Different preferences for public goods*

Song et al. (2012) propose a theory in which there are differences across countries in the extent to which public goods are valued relative to private consumption. They point to the stylized fact that in Scandinavian type countries, where public goods are highly valued and quality is high, governments run *tighter* fiscal policies than do those in countries like Greece and Italy where public goods are provided less efficiently. The idea is that when young and old members of the current generation vote and when there is no intergenerational altruism, the current generation are tempted to pass on the cost of public spending to the next generation (non-voters). This can only be avoided in countries where the current young voters are sufficiently confident about the quality of the public goods supply in the future (i.e. in their lifetime) that they vote to restrict spending and debt accumulation in the short-term in order to secure the supply of valued public goods later on.

Another application of this idea is the impact on the debt ratio of partisan politics, where political parties have different preferences for public goods. The following quote from the

New York Times about President Reagan's State of the Union address in January 1987 captures this:[25]

> This deficit is no despised orphan. It's President Reagan's child, and secretly, he loves it ... The deficit rigorously discourages any idea of spending another dime for social welfare.

Since parties of the right are typically associated with small government, at first it seems paradoxical that this preference might contribute to deficit bias. The explanation is as follows: if one party, the right, values public goods less than does the left, and if there is uncertainty about who will win the next election, it is in the interests of the right party to cut taxes, increase the deficit and thereby make it harder for a left government if it wins the next election to spend on public goods. Song et al. (2012) find empirical evidence for this prediction. In a panel of OECD countries from 1980 to 2005, the authors find that a political shift from left to right increases the debt to GDP ratio by 0.7 percentage points per year.

### Common pool problems and budgetary processes

These explanations centre on the political process and suggest, for example, that countries with systems of government based on proportional representation, where coalitions are common, may face different pressures in budget making from countries with majoritarian systems. The core idea is that public spending projects or tax cuts may favour particular groups in the economy and ministers of spending departments may fail to fully internalize the costs to the current and future budget. Proportional representation electoral systems are more likely to lead to the fragmented governments that will exacerbate this overspending problem.

### 14.5.3  Approaches to tackle deficit bias

This subsection discusses two commonly used approaches to mitigating deficit bias: fiscal rules and fiscal policy councils. The discussion is limited to introducing the two approaches, showing how they can alleviate deficit bias and providing examples of their use in the real world. A much more detailed discussion of fiscal rules and fiscal policy councils can be found in the Web Appendix for this chapter.[26]

The discussion of deficit bias and the approaches used to mitigate it can be seen as analogous to the discussion of inflation bias in Chapter 4. In that case, government control over monetary policy led to a sub-optimal equilibrium, providing the motivation for the adoption of monetary policy rules, independent central banks and the delegation of monetary policy to monetary policy committees.

### Fiscal rules

Fiscal rules set out a guideline for how fiscal policy should be conducted. The central aim of the rules is to keep the public finances sustainable in the medium and long term. In practice

---

[25]  *New York Times*, 25 January 1987, 'The State of the President' (accessed online June 2012).

[26]  Additionally, Chapter 6 of Carlin and Soskice (2006) has a detailed discussion of fiscal policy rules.

the rules are typically numerical limits for fiscal aggregates such as government debt to GDP ratios and budget deficit to GDP ratios. Fiscal rules are typically written into government legislation and viewed as long term (i.e. they are not changed when governments change hands). The adoption of rules can help limit deficit bias by constraining the government's ability to use discretionary fiscal policy and by providing a benchmark against which the government's management of the public finances can be judged.

There are two sides to our discussion of fiscal rules. The first looks at an optimal fiscal policy rule and the second looks at how fiscal policy rules have been used in practice. This comparison parallels the discussion of the optimal Taylor rule in monetary policy and the monetary policy rules that are used in practice.

### What is the optimal fiscal policy rule?

In thinking about the optimal fiscal policy rule, we begin with the government's intertemporal budget constraint and the associated solvency condition that we set out in the Section 14.3.[27] We can use the intertemporal budget constraint $\Delta b = d + (r - \gamma_y)b$, which shows how government debt evolves over time, to provide the basis of a fiscal policy rule that ensures that the government debt to GDP ratio does not increase over time. An optimal or prudent fiscal policy rule (PFPR) is to set the share of tax in GDP at a constant level equal to the 'permanent' or long-run level required to satisfy the constraint (the rule is derived in the Web Appendix to this chapter):

$$\overline{(T/y)} = (T/y)^P \geq (G/y)^P + (r^P - \gamma_y^P)b, \qquad \text{(prudent fiscal policy rule)}$$

where the superscript $P$ refers to the long-run or permanent value.

The PFPR has a number of key implications for fiscal policy:

1. Any permanent increase in government expenditure, such as a rise in long-run government pension obligations, should be financed through a rise in taxation.

2. Any temporary increase in government expenditure, such as rising government transfers in a recession, should be financed through borrowing.

3. Any major government infrastructure spending that could take government expenditure above its permanent level for years (or even decades), such as renewing the transportation system, should be financed through borrowing.

4. Borrowing should be permitted to rise if the interest rate is confidently known to be temporarily higher than its permanent value or if growth is depressed relative to its long-run value.

5. Government expenditure must be reduced below its permanent level in upswings. Averaged over the cycle there is no case for divergence between $G/y$ and $(G/y)^P$.

The PFPR advocates a constant tax share. This is because taxes are distortionary and the distortions are assumed to increase with the amount of taxation raised. Hence, the optimal way for the government to behave is to smooth tax revenue collection over time by

---

[27] This discussion of fiscal rules relies heavily on the work of Willem Buiter. See for example Buiter (2001) and Buiter and Grafe (2004).

borrowing and saving. This is analogous to the household smoothing consumption through borrowing and saving under the permanent income hypothesis that we saw in Chapter 1. The government's optimal tax share therefore only changes when there is a permanent change to the government's intertemporal budget constraint. Temporary and/or unforeseen fluctuations in expenditure (due to the business cycle, wars, natural disasters etc.) are dealt with solely by changes in borrowing.

### Fiscal policy rules in practice

We focus on the Stability and Growth Pact (SGP) of the European Union because it applies across so many countries and has important differences from the PFPR discussed in the previous subsection.[28]

As discussed in Chapter 12, the original SGP contained two central rules: the budget deficit to GDP ratio must be less than 3%, and the government debt to GDP ratio must be less than 60%. The main drawback of these rules is that they might not allow adequate room for stabilization in a deep recession. The PFPR indicates that there is no economic reason that the deficit ratio should be limited to a fixed number. In contrast to the SGP, the PFPR advocates as much borrowing as is necessary after a temporary shock, even if this exceeds 3% of GDP.

Another, less formalized, rule within the SGP is that cyclically-adjusted budget balances must be close to balance or in surplus. The rule aims to stop governments running persistent deficits that are unsustainable in the medium term. The rule has one large disadvantage, however, as it limits the extent to which fiscal policy can be used for long-term government infrastructure investment projects. In contrast, the PFPR would allow the project to be financed through borrowing as long as the discounted present value of the expected social benefits exceeded the expected social costs.

The SGP is widely viewed as a failure. The deficit ceiling was broken by the Eurozone's two largest economies, Germany and France, in the early 2000s. The breaches should have been met with repercussions (e.g. fines) but were not, which undermined the legitimacy of the Pact. We also saw in Chapter 12, that the Pact did nothing to discourage destabilizing pro-cyclical fiscal policy during the first ten years of the single currency. Lastly, the SGP was shown to be too restrictive for stabilization in a deep recession, with nine out of the 11 core economies exceeding the deficit ceiling during the global financial crisis.[29]

### Fiscal policy councils

A fiscal policy council (FPC) is an independent (or semi-independent) body whose main role is to be a *fiscal watchdog*—i.e. to make sure government fiscal policy is sustainable over the long term.[30] It is the FPC's mandate to guard against deficit bias by providing independent

---

[28] The SGP and other fiscal rules are discussed in more detail in the Web Appendix to this chapter.

[29] The core Eurozone countries are the 11 which joined in 1999, minus Luxembourg plus Greece (who joined in 2001). The breaches of the deficit ceiling were calculated using data on net lending (+)/net borrowing (-) under the Excessive Deficit Procedure (EDP) from Eurostat (data accessed June 2012).

[30] For more information on fiscal policy councils (e.g. definitions, international examples and relevant academic literature) see Simon Wren-Lewis' website: http://www.economics.ox.ac.uk/members/simon.wren-lewis/fc/fiscal.councils.htm.

forecasts of the evolution of the public finances and calling the government to account when their tax and spending plans are unsustainable.[31]

FPCs have been in operation in some countries for many years, such as the Central Planning Bureau (CPB) in The Netherlands (established in 1947) and the Congressional Budget Office (CBO) in the US (established in 1975), but they were not widespread before the global financial crisis. Sweden, the UK and Slovenia have all set up FPCs since 2007, highlighting the renewed interest in fiscal watchdogs in the wake of the Great Recession.

There are three main reasons for the re-emergence of FPCs as an approach to limiting deficit bias following the global financial crisis:

1. The success of independent inflation-targeting central banks during the 1990s and 2000s.

2. The fact that fiscal rules proved insufficient to ensure prudent management of the public finances in the years preceding the crisis.

3. The fact that politically unpopular austerity packages were introduced to repair the damage done to the public finances by Great Recession. FPCs can boost the credibility of fiscal consolidation packages and act as a commitment device for successive governments when consolidation is spread over a number of years.

### The mandates of existing fiscal policy councils

There is currently no consensus 'best-practice' framework for FPCs. The list below shows some of the features of existing FPCs, starting with those with the narrowest remits.

1. To produce forecasts for growth, the output gap and the public finances on which the government's fiscal decisions conforming to their targets must be made (e.g. the UK's Office for Budget Responsibility (OBR)).

2. To carry out *positive* policy analysis—i.e. to assess the fiscal cost of different policies, but to remain objective and non-partisan (e.g. the US CBO and The Netherland's CPB).

3. To make *normative* recommendations based on the government's stated economic objectives—i.e. the FPC is actively engaged in the public debate about fiscal policy decisions (e.g. the Swedish Fiscal Policy Council and the Economic Council in Denmark).

It is important to note that even the FPC with the widest remit does not have the power to set fiscal policy in the same way that an independent central bank sets monetary policy. Fiscal policy has largely remained in the hands of elected politicians and has tended to be more discretionary than rules based. This is because fiscal policy is inherently political. It has more policy levers than monetary policy and different winners and losers are created depending on which lever is pulled. For example, raising duties on cigarettes and alcohol disproportionately affects the poor, whereas raising capital gains tax disproportionately affects the rich. Although there are distributional effects of monetary policy—for example, lower interest rates redistribute income from savers to borrowers—monetary policy is perceived as more neutral, so in contrast to fiscal policy, the public and politicians are happier to see it put in the hands of an independent expert.

---

[31] This subsection relies heavily on the work of Lars Calmfors. See for example Calmfors (2010) and Calmfors and Wren-Lewis (2011).

The mandates of existing FPCs and the difficulties associated with forecasting the public finances are addressed in more detail in the Web Appendix to this chapter.

### The future of fiscal policy councils

An unprecedented fiscal expansion was required to avoid the collapse of banking systems and economies in the developed world during the financial crisis. The implosion of the world economy might have been avoided, but the rescue left a mountainous government debt overhang (see Figure 14.7). Fiscal consolidation and the sustainability of the public finances are likely to be central to macroeconomic debate and policy over the medium term. This is likely to enhance the visibility and influence of existing fiscal councils; and lead to the establishment of more fiscal councils (as advocated by international organizations, such as the IMF and the OECD and European policy makers, such as the ECB and the European Commission (EC)).

## 14.6 Conclusions

This chapter on fiscal policy is a counterpart to the previous chapter on monetary policy. In combination with the analysis of the special features of the Eurozone set out in Chapter 12, they provide an analytical framework for thinking about the role of stabilization policy in modern economies. We can summarize the main findings of this chapter as follows:

1. The predicted effects of *discretionary* fiscal policy on the economy and the size of the short- and medium-run multipliers are highly dependent on the initial conditions in the economy and the modelling framework being used. In the 3-equation model, fiscal stimulus can be effective in raising output and welfare if the economy is hit by a negative demand shock (and monetary policy is unavailable). The other side of fiscal policy is its role in *automatically stabilizing* the economy—the presence of the government as a major source of injections and withdrawals of spending power in the economy helps to mitigate aggregate demand shocks. The stabilization provided by the automatic stabilizers is largely a by-product of the structure of the tax and social security systems. Although these systems are typically designed to meet the government's income distribution and microeconomic goals rather than its macroeconomic objectives, they nevertheless play an important role in stabilization.

2. We set out a model to determine the path of government debt over time. The evolution of the government debt ratio is influenced by the primary budget deficit ($d$), the differential between the interest rate and the growth rate ($r - \gamma_y$) and the existing stock of government debt ($b$). We use the model to show that public debt ratios can be reduced by shrinking $d$, ($r - \gamma_y$) or ($b$). As we can see in the Eurozone, austerity is one method of reducing $d$, but it is likely to have detrimental effects on economic growth. In some cases, fiscal consolidation has taken place alongside economic expansion, but economists are divided whether this was due to the non-Keynesian (i.e. expectations) effects of consolidation or because of the complementary policies enacted in parallel (i.e. monetary stimulus, exchange rate depreciation and wage accords). It is largely agreed, however, that consolidations that rely on spending cuts instead of tax rises exert less contractionary effects on output.

3. Under certain conditions, it does not matter whether permanent changes in government spending are financed by taxation or by borrowing; the consumption response will be the same—this is the *Ricardian equivalence* result. The result relies on households being rational and forward looking so that they *internalize* the government's intertemporal budget constraint when making decisions. This theory also implies that temporary fiscal stimulus packages will have no effect on consumption and hence on aggregate demand and output if they are based on tax cuts. In contrast, we show that they will boost output in the current period although with a multiplier of less than one if they are based on government spending; this is the case regardless of whether they are financed by taxation or borrowing.

4. *Deficit bias* is the tendency for budget deficits to rise in recessions, but not to fall in a sufficiently offsetting way in booms. The bias leads to a preference for financing government spending through borrowing rather than taxation. Common causes of deficit bias are: governments targeting a level of output above equilibrium, uncertainty around economic growth forecasts and intergenerational conflict. The extent of deficit bias can also vary across countries depending on preferences for public goods, political systems and partisan politics. *Fiscal rules* and *fiscal policy councils* are two methods of guarding against deficit bias. The optimal fiscal rule is a *prudent fiscal policy rule*, which is analogous to the optimal Taylor rule for monetary policy introduced in the previous chapter. This rule is preferable to existing rules, such as the Stability and Growth Pact, as it ensures the long-term sustainability of the public finances, whilst allowing for stabilization in downturns and for long-term public investment projects. Fiscal policy councils (FPCs) have re-emerged as a method to tackle deficit bias in the wake of the global financial crisis. Although the mandates of existing FPCs vary across countries, their central role is to be a *fiscal watchdog*—i.e. to make sure the government's fiscal policy is sustainable over the long term.

## 14.7 Questions

### 14.7.1 Checklist questions

1. What are the automatic stabilizers? How could the method of local income-based or property-value based government taxation affect the automatic stabilizers?

2. Explain the logic of the balanced budget multiplier result. Investigate whether this result continues to hold if there is a proportional income tax (rather than a lump sum tax).

3. What is meant by the cyclically-adjusted primary budget deficit? How can it be calculated? Why is it conceptually equivalent to the discretionary fiscal impulse? Is such a deficit sustainable?

4. Is the view that automatic stabilizers are effective consistent with the view that discretionary fiscal policy is not?

5. Explain in words the intuition behind the debt dynamics equation: $\Delta b = d + (r - \gamma_y)b$.

6. Discuss how each of the following can help to reduce the debt burden on governments. What are the problems and potential negative consequences associated with each method?

   (a) reducing the primary deficit, $d$

   (b) increasing the growth rate, $\gamma_y$

(c) reducing the interest rate, $r$

(d) reducing the existing stock of debt, $b$.

7. Explain the concept of an expansionary fiscal consolidation. Why is consolidation less likely to be expansionary for a country in a common currency area where all the countries are simultaneously undertaking austerity measures?

8. Assume an economy with lump-sum taxes is hit by a large negative demand shock (e.g. financial crisis). In response, the government introduces a large fiscal stimulus package to try and boost economic activity and help to stabilize the economy. Assess whether the policy will be successful in each of the following cases:

    (a) In the 3-equation model, when stimulus is financed through borrowing.

    (b) In the 3-equation model, when the stimulus is financed by raising taxes (i.e. a balanced budget expansion).

    (c) In the $RE - PIH$ model, when the stimulus is financed through borrowing.

    In which case will output expand the most? Justify your answer.

9. Explain the concept of deficit bias. Use Section 14.5 (and IMF Fiscal monitor and OECD Economic Survey of UK and Greece) and your own knowledge to identify the different sources of deficit bias in the UK and Greek economies between 2001 and 2007.

10. Explain in words what is meant by the prudent fiscal policy rule. What is the main reason for 'tax smoothing'? Under this rule, how should a government react in the following scenarios:

    (a) Defence spending is cut for the foreseeable future due to the end of the Cold War.

    (b) The government compensates farmers following a disease outbreak.

    (c) The Treasury releases a report forecasting that the cost of the tax-funded health service will treble within twenty years.

    (d) The government decides to contribute troops to a war that it expects to be over in a matter of weeks.

11. Why has there been a resurgence of interest in fiscal policy councils (FPCs) since the onset of the global financial crisis? Can FPCs be seen as a substitute for fiscal rules?

## 14.7.2 Problems and questions for discussion

1. Use the 3-equation model to discuss whether contractionary fiscal policy should be used in the following situation—the economy is initially at equilibrium and there is a positive shock to aggregate demand from improved consumer confidence.

2. Begin with the scenario in Fig. 14.5a. Following the shift to an explosive debt path, and assume that the debt ratio has risen further before the government reacts. If its objective is to return the debt ratio to its initial level, explain using a diagram how it could achieve this by using fiscal policy.

3. This question uses the UK Office for Budget Responsibility's (OBR's) 2011 Fiscal Sustainability Report (July 2011). The report can be downloaded from the publications section of the OBR website:

    (http://budgetresponsibility.independent.gov.uk/category/publications/).

Table 5.1 (on page 112) shows the adjustment to the primary balance needed to ensure the long-term sustainability of the public finances. How do each of the following factors affect the extent of adjustment (i.e. tightening) required to reach the target debt to GDP ratio by 2060? In each case, you must give an explanation of how you think the factor influences the debt dynamics equation (14.9).

(a) interest rates

(b) productivity

(c) migration

(d) age structure

(e) increased health spending

(f) lower morbidity rates.

4. This question uses the Macroeconomic Simulator available from the Carlin and Soskice website http://www.oup.com/uk/orc/carlin_soskice to model the evolution of the public finances. Start by opening the simulator and choosing the closed economy version. Then reset all shocks by clicking the appropriate button on the left hand side of the main page. Use the simulator and the content of this chapter to work through the following questions: [Hint: for all these questions the real interest rate is 3%].

(a) Set long-run economic growth to 'yes' and the growth rate to 2%. Set the initial public expenditures/GDP to 21% (giving a primary budget deficit of 1%) and the initial public debt/GDP to 60%.

(b) Click on the 'public finance figures' button on the top left of the main page. Is public debt sustainable? Justify your answer by using the debt dynamics equation (14.9).

(c) Change the long-run growth rate to 4% and then 6%. Is the debt sustainable in these cases? If so, why?

(d) For each of the three cases, draw a diagram (with the primary deficit on the y-axis and the debt ratio on the x-axis) showing the evolution of the public debt ratio (see Section 14.3).

(e) Do the result for parts (b) and (c) still hold if the initial public expenditures/GDP is set to 25% (giving a primary budget deficit of 5%)? Why?

5. This question uses the Macroeconomic Simulator available from the Carlin and Soskice website http://www.oup.com/uk/orc/carlin_soskice to model fiscal consolidation. Start by opening the simulator and choosing the closed economy version. Then reset all shocks by clicking the appropriate button on the left hand side of the main page. Use the simulator and the content of this chapter to work through the following questions: [Hint: for all these questions the real interest rate is 3%].

(a) Set long-run economic growth to 'yes' and the growth rate to 2%. Set the initial public expenditures/GDP to 23% (giving a primary budget deficit of 3%) and set the initial public debt/GDP to 60%.

(b) Click on the 'public finance figures' button on the top left of the main page. Click on the 'change the time span in figures' button on the left hand side. Change the timespan to run from 1 to 25 years. Is public debt sustainable in the medium term?

(c) Add a permanent decrease in public expenditure in period 10 of 3%. This is equivalent to a fiscal consolidation. Is public debt sustainable in the medium run after the consolidation package is introduced?

(d) Given that the primary budget to GDP ratio is now positive, why does the debt to GDP ratio not fall over time?

(e) Click on the 'inflation, income and interest rate figures' button on the left hand side. What is the short-term impact of the consolidation package on GDP growth? Explain why using the 3-equation model. What does the path of interest rates tell us about the central bank's role in supporting fiscal consolidation?

# 15 Supply-side policy, institutions and unemployment

## 15.1 Introduction

Understanding the causes of the unemployment patterns shown at the start of Chapter 2 in Fig. 2.1 for the rich countries of the world is a challenge for economists and policy makers. The economist Richard Layard emphasizes the research results on the consequences of unemployment for human well-being:

> From the new science of happiness we now know enough of the causes of human happiness to make some quite firm statements. When a person becomes unemployed his welfare falls for two reasons—first the loss of income, and second the loss of self-respect and sense of significance (the psychic loss).

Layard, 2004

By looking back at Fig. 2.1, we can see that unemployment was low virtually everywhere in the 1960s. It went up in most countries in the 1970s—with an extraordinary dispersion in unemployment rates emerging among European countries. The Great Recession that followed the global financial crisis saw the rapid reversal of the downward trends in unemployment over the previous two decades – the Great Moderation – and pushed concern about unemployment once more toward the top of the policy agenda.

The varied experiences of unemployment led to a major research effort to uncover the underlying causes of the trends and cross-country patterns, and to identify policies that governments could implement to reduce unemployment on a lasting basis.

In Chapter 2, we introduced the basic supply-side model of the economy and showed that supply-side equilibrium is defined by the intersection of the wage- and price-setting (WS and PS) curves. In this framework, there is a unique rate of unemployment at which inflation is constant. At equilibrium, there is involuntary unemployment. Factors shifting the equilibrium rate of unemployment can be divided into wage-push factors that shift the WS curve and price-push factors that shift the PS curve.

Equilibrium unemployment rises with a downward shift of the price-setting or an upward shift of the wage-setting curve. From Chapter 2, we write the equation for the price-setting curve:

$$\frac{W}{P_c} = \lambda F(\mu, \mathbf{z_p}), \qquad\qquad\qquad (PS \text{ curve})$$

where $P_c$ is the consumer price index and $\mathbf{z_p}$ is a set of price push variables including the tax wedge. The PS curve shifts down when there is a rise in the tax wedge, a rise in the mark-up, $\mu$, due, for example, to a weakening in the enforcement of competition policy, a fall in productivity, $\lambda$, or a rise in the oil price.

We write the WS equation:

$$\frac{W}{P_c^E} = B(N, \mathbf{z_w}) \qquad\qquad\qquad (WS \text{ curve})$$

where $\mathbf{z_w}$ is a set of wage push variables. The $\mathbf{z_w}$'s include institutional, policy, structural and shock variables. The WS curve shifts up when there is a rise in the level of unemployment benefits or its duration because this reduces the cost of job loss at any given unemployment rate, increasing the wage-setting real wage required to elicit effort; when unions are stronger; and when they choose not to exercise bargaining restraint in the context, for example, of the collapse of a wage accord between unions and government. Such an accord may be part of a broader settlement in which the government agrees to undertake policy measures supported by the unions and/or to give the unions an enhanced role in government economic policy making.[1]

The aim of this chapter is to push that analysis further. We begin by extending the set of models introduced in Chapter 2. We then apply the models to analysing empirical data on labour markets from the OECD countries, focusing on two time periods:

**1960-mid 2000s** We report the results of studies that use cross-country data over this period to try and better understand the trends and cross-country differences in the unemployment experienced in developed economies over the past five decades.

**Great Recession: post 2008** We investigate the changes in rates, duration and composition of unemployment experienced in the aftermath of the global financial crisis.

The data in Fig. 2.1 provide a graphic illustration of the dispersion of unemployment rates across the OECD countries in the last fifty years by showing the five-yearly average unemployment rates for selected OECD countries. The OECD's standardized measure of unemployment is used. It is constructed using comparable labour market survey based definitions of unemployment, which allows cross-country comparisons to be made. Although not all countries are shown in the chart, the patterns are as follows:

1. There is a cloud of countries with unemployment rates below the USA up to the early 1980s, which moves above the USA thereafter until the global financial crisis in 2008.

---

[1] An example in Europe is the 1982 Wassenaar Accord in The Netherlands between employers and unions, which was later endorsed by the government and which continues to affect wage setting (see Nickell and van Ours (2006)). Unions offered wage restraint and more local flexibility in wage setting; employers agreed to a reduction in working hours. The unions agreed that reductions in working hours would not increase labour costs. Although the accord was bilateral between the unions and employers, the government agreed to deal with its fiscal problems (a burgeoning public sector deficit).

2. Several European countries had spectacular improvements in their unemployment performance in the 1990s: the UK, Ireland, The Netherlands and Denmark are said to have experienced 'employment miracles' over this decade.

3. Austria, Norway and Japan have very low rates throughout. Sweden and Finland had very low unemployment until the early 1990s.

4. Spanish unemployment has been the highest in the sample in every period since the start of the 1980s. It has also fluctuated substantially, for example, it fell from over 20% in the late 1990s to under 10% by 2005–08.

5. The heterogeneity in the unemployment experience of European countries, where some highly unionized countries with high taxation have *low* unemployment, and where there were many changes in labour market policy provides a good testing ground for theories linking unemployment to policy and institutions.

Figure 2.1 also provides data for 2009–2012 to show how unemployment reacted to the global financial crisis. It shows that:

1. The US unemployment rate rose dramatically during the global financial crisis and was higher than most OECD economies during 2009–12.

2. Countries with yet higher unemployment were the Eurozone countries that became embroiled in the Eurozone debt crisis (see Chapters 12 and 14). For example, Ireland and Spain saw their employment miracles rapidly unravel during the Great Recession, with unemployment rates of 14% and 21% respectively between 2009 and 2012. Germany stands out as a country where the labour market performed very well during the crisis, with the unemployment rate falling to levels not seen since before German unification in the early 1990s.

As we shall see, the fact that there are:

1. large differences in unemployment across countries; and that

2. performance changes dramatically,

is consistent with the main theme of this chapter, namely that policies and institutions matter for unemployment, and some of these can be changed over relatively short time periods. Moreover, shocks to demand such as occured as a consequence of the global financial crisis can have persistent effects on unemployment.

The rest of the chapter is organized as follows. Section 15.2 explains the essence of the *flow approach* to the labour market, which centres on search and matching models. This approach is complementary to the *WS-PS* framework. Job search theory analyses the *flows* of workers into and out of employment and unemployment. In the efficiency wage model introduced in Chapter 2, a key element is the probability that a worker who enters the pool of unemployment gets a new job. The flow approach focuses on this. It assumes that workers and jobs are heterogeneous and that an important aspect of how well the labour market works is how well it achieves the matching of unemployed workers with unfilled job vacancies. We show how the insights of the flow approach can be integrated with the *WS-PS* framework.

We then look in more detail at the way unions operate and at the macroeconomic implications of their behaviour for equilibrium unemployment in Section 15.3. We explain the famous Calmfors–Driffill model, which suggests a hump-shaped relationship between the degree of centralization of wage setting and the equilibrium rate of unemployment.

Section 15.4 extends the discussion of efficiency wages introduced in Chapter 2 by setting out a simple micro-based model. This is a way of highlighting the key determinants of the cost of job loss and how changes in technology, the growing role of services in the economy and policies related to working conditions can affect equilibrium unemployment.

Section 15.5 focuses on long-term unemployment and the permanent damage this can do to the supply-side of the economy. We introduce the concept of *hysteresis*, in which the equilibrium of the system depends on what has happened in the past. The main result is that if actual unemployment stays above equilibrium for an extended period, then it could raise the equilibrium itself. For example, being out of work tends to make people less effective competitors for jobs because their skills atrophy (i.e. deteriorate). This reduces the cost of job loss for those in work and weakens the dampening effect that higher unemployment has on inflation.

The last two sections use the models presented in this chapter to analyse unemployment in the OECD economies from the 1960s to the present. Section 15.6 concentrates on the longer term patterns in unemployment, whereas Section 15.7 focuses on the impact of the recent financial crisis on OECD labour markets. At the turn of the century, it might have seemed as if high and persistent unemployment was a thing of the past. This is evidently not the case. An analysis of changes in unemployment during the global economic downturn after 2008 raises interesting questions:

1. Did different government policies account for some of the cross-country differences in unemployment changes during this period?

2. How was Germany able to keep unemployment on a downward trend during its worst peacetime recession since the Great Depression?

## 15.2 Flows, matching and the Beveridge curve

The *flow* or *matching* approach to the labour market belongs to part of labour economics known as job search theory. This theory was recognized by the award of the Nobel Prize in 2010 to three of its pioneers; Peter Diamond, Dale Mortensen and Christopher Pissarides. Pissarides' 1990 book entitled *Equilibrium Unemployment Theory* sets out the main foundations of this approach.[2]

In this section, without getting into the technical details, we explain the essence of this approach and show how it can be used to enrich the *WS − PS* model. We start by providing some data on flows into and out of unemployment, which will aid our understanding of the model. Figure 15.1 shows labour market flows in the UK between October and December 2011. A snapshot of the labour market reveals three key groups: the employed, the unemployed and the economically inactive (i.e. those not in work or looking for work). As we can see from Fig. 15.1, in any given period, thousands of people move between these different

---

[2] See Pissarides (1990).

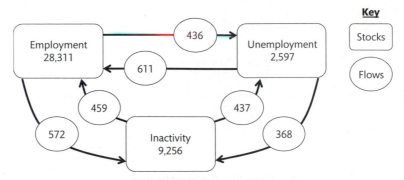

**Figure 15.1** Labour market flows between employment, unemployment and inactivity (in thousands): October to December 2011.

*Source:* Labour Force Survey, UK Office for National Statistics, Feb 2012.

labour market states. For example, 459,000 people moved from inactivity to employment in the last quarter of 2011.

In the job search tradition, unemployment is in equilibrium when flows into and out of unemployment are equal. With a constant labour force, labour market equilibrium in the flow approach means that hires, $H$, are equal to separations, $S$, from employment. The idea is that workers and jobs are heterogeneous (a factor that has been largely neglected until now) with the consequence that an important aspect of how the labour market works is how well it achieves the matching of unemployed workers with unfilled job vacancies.

A simple version of the matching function can be explained as follows. It is assumed that $U$ is the number of unemployed, $V$ is the number of vacancies and $\alpha$ is the parameter that describes the efficiency of the matching process in the economy. We can write the matching function as

$$H = \alpha \cdot m(U, V),$$

where a higher number of new hires is associated with higher matching efficiency ($\alpha > 0$). It is important to note that $H$ and $S$ are flows per period and that the period can be of any length as long as hires and separations are measured consistently. The matching function describes how the unemployed are matched with the vacancies. Holding the matching efficiency and the number of vacancies constant, higher unemployment is associated with more matches since there are more applicants for each job. Similarly, holding unemployment constant, more vacancies are associated with more matches. If we assume that the flow of workers from employment to unemployment is $S = sN$ where $s$ is the proportionate exit rate from employment, then the labour market will be in a flow equilibrium when the flow *into* unemployment, $sN$ is equal to the flow *out of* unemployment into jobs:

$$sN = \alpha \cdot m(U, V).$$

Using the assumption that matching takes place under constant returns to scale and assuming for simplicity that the separation rate is an exogenous constant (e.g. firms are randomly affected by shocks that result in separations), we can divide through by $N$, which gives us:

$$s = \alpha \cdot m\left(\frac{U}{N}, \frac{V}{N}\right).$$

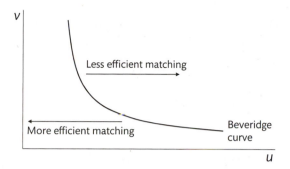

**Figure 15.2** The Beveridge curve.

If we draw a diagram with the 'unemployment rate' ($u \equiv U/N$) on the horizontal axis and the vacancy rate ($v \equiv V/N$) on the vertical axis, the labour market equilibrium can be plotted as shown in Fig. 15.2. The vacancy/unemployment curve depicting labour market equilibrium in the flow model is called the Beveridge curve. The curve is downward sloping because at high unemployment, with a given matching technology, it will be necessary for vacancies to be low to deliver the constant number of matches required to balance the fixed separation rate, $s$. Conversely at low unemployment with fewer people looking for work, more vacancies are required to ensure that the number of those taking jobs is equal to the separation rate. Any decline in the efficiency of matching, $\alpha$, will shift the curve to the right, with the implication that flow equilibrium at a given unemployment rate will require a higher rate of vacancies in the economy.

But how does this approach to labour market equilibrium relate to the *WS-PS* model, which concentrates on the *stock* of unemployment (see Fig. 15.1)? To this point in the *WS-PS* model, vacancies have been ignored. However, once heterogeneity between workers and jobs is introduced, vacancies represent a measure of pressure in the labour market. Holding all the other determinants of the wage- and price-setting curves constant, for a given employment (or unemployment) rate, higher vacancies in the economy increase the wage workers can bargain for, or that employers need to set to attract good workers. The *WS* equation written in terms of the unemployment rate is:

$$\frac{W}{P_c^E} = b(u, v, z_w),$$

where the function is called $b$ rather than $B$ because it is in terms of unemployment. Here, $v$ is the vacancy rate and $u$ is the unemployment rate. Holding everything else constant, the *WS* curve shifts up when the vacancy rate increases since it increases the probability of exit from the unemployment pool. As Fig. 15.3a shows, a higher rate of vacancies implies a lower equilibrium employment rate and hence higher equilibrium unemployment: there is a positive relationship between vacancies and equilibrium unemployment (at which *WS* and *PS* are equal). In the Beveridge curve diagram, we now include the positively sloped line showing the wage- and price-setting equilibrium (Fig. 15.3b). In the Beveridge curve diagram, full equilibrium in the labour market is shown by the intersection of the Beveridge curve and the *WS = PS* line.

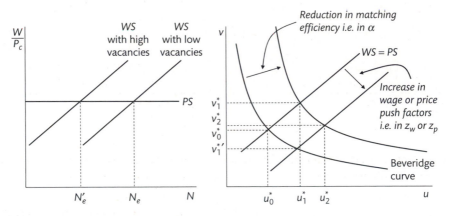

**Figure 15.3** Reconciling the flow approach and the $WS - PS$ model:
a. The $WS - PS$ equilibrium and vacancies
b. The Beveridge curve and the $WS - PS$ equilibrium.

It is clear from the diagram that there will be higher unemployment if the ability of the economy to match workers to jobs worsens (an outward shift of the Beveridge curve). In this case, both unemployment and vacancies will be higher in the new equilibrium (at $u_1^*$, $v_1^*$). The adjustment of the economy to the new equilibrium can be explained as follows: if a deterioration in matching occurs, vacancies rise, thereby pushing the $WS$ curve upwards and raising inflationary pressure (as in Fig. 15.3a). Equilibrium unemployment has gone up: an inflation targeting central bank would tighten policy and guide the economy to the higher unemployment rate consistent with constant inflation at its target at, i.e. at $u_1^*$ (in Fig. 15.3b).

Alternatively, if there is a rise in wage (or price) push in the economy but the Beveridge curve remains unchanged, then the $WS = PS$ curve shifts to the right and equilibrium occurs at higher unemployment (at $u_1^*$) but with a lower vacancy rate ($v_1^{*'}$). The intuition in the second case is that higher unemployment is associated with a lower vacancy rate (for matching reasons) and this somewhat offsets the effect of higher wage pressure, leaving equilibrium unemployment lower than would be the case if the vacancy rate did not fall. If equilibrium unemployment goes up with little change in the vacancy rate, this suggests that there has been a shift in both the $WS/PS$ curves and in the Beveridge curve (as in the move from $u_0^*$ to $u_2^*$ and $v_0^*$ to $v_2^*$).

By introducing the flow approach to the labour market, we have widened the set of factors that can account for changes in equilibrium unemployment. In addition to those that shift the $WS$ or the $PS$ curves, we now include features of the way the labour market brings workers and jobs together, for example:

1. Barriers to occupational and geographic mobility imply weaker matching and will shift the Beveridge curve outward; similarly policies to overcome these barriers by improving the efficiency of employment and training agencies or the operation of the housing market can have the opposite effect.

2. Forms of employment protection legislation may affect the ability of employers to hire workers, weakening the matching process.

**Table 15.1**  Shifts in the Beveridge curve.

| Beveridge curve shift | 1960–mid-1980s | Mid-1980s–1999 |
| --- | --- | --- |
| No change | Nor, Swe | |
| Right | all others | Bel, Fin, Fr, G, J, Nor, Sp, Swe, Swi |
| Left | | Can, Den, Neth, UK, US |
| Unclear | | Aus, Austria, NZ, Por |

*Source:* Nickell et al. (2003).

3.  Some factors will in principle shift both curves: for example, an increase in unemployment benefit duration weakens search intensity and shifts the Beveridge curve to the right and, as a wage-push factor, also shifts the *WS* upwards shifting the *WS* = *PS* curve in the Beveridge curve diagram to the right. These effects reinforce each other, worsening equilibrium unemployment.

Nickell et al. (2003) estimate a Beveridge curve equation and an unemployment equation. Their plots of Beveridge curves in each country show that for every country except Sweden and Norway there was an outward shift in the Beveridge curve between the 1960s and mid-1980s, indicating a deterioration in the ability of the labour market to match the unemployed to vacancies. After the mid-1980s countries can be divided into three groups (see Table 15.1): those with a further deterioration in matching, with the Beveridge curve shifting further to the right; those where it has shifted back to the left; and a group where the situation is unclear.

The Beveridge curve is estimated by regressing the annual unemployment rate on the vacancy rate, a proxy for the separation rate, and a set of shift factors. The downward-sloping Beveridge curve is obtained because there is a highly significant negative coefficient on the vacancy rate. The shift factors that appear to be empirically important in shifting the Beveridge curve to the right are longer benefit duration, a higher home owner occupation rate; and higher union density.

Higher employment protection is associated with a leftward shift of the Beveridge curve. This could indicate its role in increasing the incentive for firms to invest in policies to achieve better matching (because of the higher costs of severance). But a strong conclusion is hard to draw because other important variables, such as active labour market measures, that may be correlated with employment protection were omitted from the estimated equation because of a lack of data. We return to Beveridge curves in Section 15.7 when we discuss the labour market response to the global financial crisis and plot the Beveridge curves for the US and Germany (Fig. 15.12).

It is argued that a higher owner occupation rate reduces worker mobility and therefore inhibits the matching process. New empirical evidence from a study of the US labour market provides support for an important role of owner occupation in raising equilibrium unemployment (Blanchflower and Oswald, 2013). Blanchflower and Oswald use data on long run changes over half a century in home ownership and unemployment rates for US states. Their results suggest that rises in a state's home ownership rate results in later rises in the unemployment rate in the state. In quantitative terms, the estimated effects are large: a doubling of home ownership would in the long run see more than a doubling of the unemployment rate. The study does not suggest that home owners are more likely to be unemployed than renters—the opposite is likely to be the case. Instead, the argument rests on the effects of increased home ownership on the broader functioning of the labour market and new firm creation. Blanchflower and Oswald suggest that higher home ownership impairs matching efficiency in the labour market by reducing geographic mobility. Lower mobility in turn reduces the positive externalities on everyone's productivity from the flow of knowledge as better matching occurs. At a more basic level, higher home ownership increases commuting times and raises congestion. A third channel is that home owners may be more inclined to inhibit new business development in their area by blocking new zoning.

## 15.3 Unions and wage-setting arrangements

A standard argument is that greater union strength measured by the proportion of employees that belong to a union (union density) or by the proportion of employees whose wages are covered by union wage agreements (coverage) is a wage push factor that implies a higher *WS* curve and therefore higher equilibrium unemployment. However, an influential article written by Lars Calmfors and John Driffill in the late 1980s argued that there was a hump-shaped relationship between the degree of centralization of wage setting and the equilibrium rate of unemployment.[3]

The Calmfors–Driffill model showed low unemployment is consistent with either very decentralized wage setting or with very centralized wage setting; the worst institutional arrangement was a so-called intermediate level of wage setting. This is interesting because it provides a possible explanation for the persistence of very low unemployment rates in a number of highly unionized Nordic countries and Austria in the 1970s and 1980s, when unemployment rose elsewhere as illustrated in Fig. 2.1.

The insights of the Calmfors–Driffill model can be explained intuitively. The model assumes that all workers are unionized and compares three different contexts for wage setting: at firm level, at industry level and at the level of the economy as a whole.

1. 'Firm level' or 'decentralized' means a situation in which there is a union specific to each firm that sets the wage in the firm.

2. 'Industry level' or 'intermediate' means there is a union that sets the wage for all workers in an industry (e.g. the engineering industry union or the banking industry union).

3. 'Economy-wide' or 'centralized' means there is a single union that sets the wage for all workers in the economy. As we shall see, wage setting does not have to be literally centralized for the economy-wide outcome to prevail: what matters is the extent to which wage setters take into account the economy-wide implications of their wage-setting decision. For this reason, the term 'coordinated' is often preferred to 'centralized'.[4]

To be able to compare the predictions for unemployment across the different wage-setting structures, it is important to rule out other possible influences on the outcome. For

---

[3] Calmfors and Driffill (1988).

[4] For further discussion about how coordination in wage setting takes place see Soskice (1990).

this reason, we assume that the union's utility function is the same for each of the cases we look at. One way of modelling the union's utility function is that it simply mirrors the preferences of its members. This will give a utility function where well-being increases with employment and with the real wage. For simplicity, we also assume that the wage is chosen by a monopoly union rather than by bargaining between the union and the employer. The union unilaterally sets the wage and the employer chooses the level of employment.

There are two different forces for wage moderation:

1. How does the union expect employment of its members to respond to a change in the wage?

2. To what extent does the union take into account the impact of its decisions on the economy-wide price level and hence, on the macroeconomic equilibrium?

In relation to the first, as wage setting becomes more decentralized, the union becomes more concerned about the effect on the employment of its members if it increases the wage. If we think of the case where there is one union per firm, the union will worry that a wage increase in the firm will make the firm less competitive than others producing similar goods. As a consequence, the firm will lose market share and decrease employment, which will have a negative impact on the utility of union members. This acts to limit the exercise of union power when wages are set by the union at firm level.

By contrast, when wages are set by an industry union, the union will view the impact of its wage increase on the demand for industry output and hence on industry employment as limited. This is because the degree of substitutability between the products of different industries (e.g. between engineering equipment and textiles) is much less than between the products of different firms in the same industry (e.g. between the fork-lift trucks produced by firm A and firm B). Hence, the industry union will exercise less restraint and choose a higher wage than the firm-level union.

The second force for wage moderation is of a quite different kind. It arises from consideration of the general equilibrium or economy-wide effects of the wage increase. A union that is operating at the level of the firm takes as given the economy-wide price level and, when setting the money wage, assumes that this sets the real consumption wage for the workers in the firm (i.e. $\frac{W_i}{P_c}$, for firm $i$), which is what its members care about. Its decision on $W_i$ does not affect $P_c$. However, if the union is setting the wage for all workers in the economy, the impact of its decision on the economy-wide consumer price level cannot be ignored. The union will therefore recognize that any increase in the wage it sets (e.g. a 4% increase) will generate an increase in the price level in line (i.e. by 4%) as costs in the economy rise by 4%. Since its decision on $W$ affects $P_c$, the outcome will be that the real consumption wage does not rise.

### The Calmfors–Driffill model in a diagram

To see the above argument graphically, we begin with the union indifference curves (see Fig. 15.4a). These comprise two components: on the one hand, workers are interested in maximizing the wage bill and this produces a downward-sloping indifference curve in the real wage–employment diagram. The second component is that there is a disutility of work so eventually the indifference curve slopes upward. We assume that the indifference curves

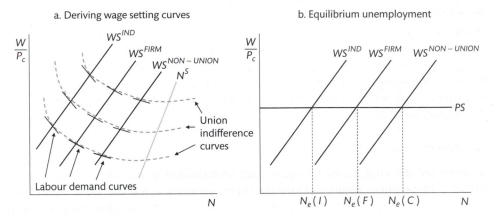

**Figure 15.4** The Calmfors–Driffill model
a. Deriving wage-setting curves under different institutional arrangements
b. Equilibrium employment with no unions (or centralized union), firm-level unions and industry-level unions.

of the individual workers form the basis of the union's indifference curves.[5] The labour supply curve, $N^S$ is derived by taking any real wage and finding the amount of labour supplied so this goes through the minimum points of the indifference curves. As argued in Chapter 2, the labour supply curve is very inelastic (i.e. steep). The WS curves lie to the left of the labour supply curve as discussed in Chapter 2. Equilibrium unemployment in the case where there are no unions in the economy is shown by the intersection of the $WS^{non-union}$ and PS curves.

### Centralized (or coordinated) wage setting: a single union

The centralized union takes into account the fact that the economy will end up on the price-setting curve after wages and prices have been set. The centralized union realizes that it cannot achieve a real wage higher than that on the PS curve. In the simple case of a horizontal PS curve, the real wage is constant so when the centralized union picks its best point along the PS curve, it will choose to maximize employment. This implies that the centralized union chooses not to exercise its monopoly power in wage negotiations: its utility is maximized at the employment level where the WS curve determined by efficiency wages in the absence of unions cuts the PS curve. This curve is labelled 'Non–union'.

### Industry level wage setting

If unions are organized at industry level, then as explained above, they believe that their wage decision will have little impact on employment since the degree of substitutability between the products of different industries is low. This is reflected in the rather steep downward sloping industry-level labour demand curves. The industry-level union optimizes by choosing the highest indifference curve subject to the constraint of the labour demand curve. Three labour demand curves for different levels of aggregate demand in the economy are shown. By joining up the points of tangency, the wage-setting curve for the case of wage setting by industry-level unions is derived, $WS^{IND}$ (see Fig. 15.4a).

[5] See Chapter 15 of Carlin and Soskice (2006) for the derivation of the formal model.

*Firm-level wage setting*

As we move to a more decentralized context for wage setting, the union becomes more concerned about the impact of its wage decision on employment of its members: if it raises its wage, the firm will raise its price and consumers will switch to other suppliers. The greater elasticity of demand produces flatter labour demand curves as shown in the diagram, with the consequence that the wage-setting curve for decentralized wage setting lies below that for industry-level wage setting, $WS^{FIRM}$.

## Macroeconomic equilibrium

To draw out the implications for equilibrium unemployment, we note that once wages are set, firms set prices. Returning to the level of the economy as a whole, we therefore have the *PS* curve as shown in Fig. 15.4b. Equilibrium employment for the case of industry-level wage setting is shown by the intersection of the $WS^{IND}$ and the *PS*. This is below that for the case of firm-level wage setting.

As argued above, the centralized case brings in the second element in the Calmfors–Driffill story: the wage decision affects prices and as the coverage of wage setting increases, it becomes impossible for the union to ignore the consequences of its wage decision for the economy-wide price level and hence for the real consumption wage, which enters its utility function. Given that the centralized union knows it cannot achieve a higher real wage than determined by the *PS* curve, it maximizes utility by going for the highest possible level of employment. This is at the intersection of the *PS* curve and the non–union *WS* curve (since this shows the minimum real wage the employer would set consistent with workers exerting effort). Hence equilibrium employment in this case is at $N_e(C)$.

These results predict a hump-shaped relationship between the centralization of wage setting and equilibrium unemployment. Soskice (1990) introduced the looser concept of wage coordination, and the OECD provides estimates of the structure of wage setting using both 'centralization' and 'coordination' (OECD, 2006). The Nordic countries and Austria have highly coordinated wage setting (see Table 15.2 below). Aidt and Tzannatos (2008) review the empirical literature on collective bargaining, coordination and macroeconomic performance. They find that the hump-shaped relationship receives little empirical support and that high levels of collective bargaining are generally associated with poor economic performance. They do, however, find that high levels of *coordination* in wage setting between unions and employers, which are found in some—but not all—countries with high union density, are often associated with lower unemployment. Coordination means that the economy-wide effects on employment of wage setting are taken into account. In Section 15.6, we look at the role of different arrangements for wage setting in accounting for cross-country differences in unemployment patterns.

## 15.4 Efficiency wage models

Although unions continue to play an important role in wage setting in many countries, they are not important everywhere. Yet involuntary unemployment is a characteristic of market economies. What prevents employers who are free to do so from paying the lowest possible wage? When they do not pay the lowest possible wage, there will be a pool of people who are prepared to work at the prevailing wage but who cannot get a job offer. This means the labour market does not clear and there is involuntary unemployment. Explanations of efficiency wages focus on the special characteristics of labour and the problems these pose for motivation, recruitment and retention of workers.

Shapiro and Stiglitz (1984) developed the shirking efficiency wage model. Their explanation was the basis of the discussion in Chapter 2, which we set out in more detail below. It is based on purely rational behaviour given the incentives faced by the employer and the worker when the worker's effort cannot be observed. Because of the information problem, the employer cannot write a contract for a specific amount and quality of output to be produced in exchange for the hourly wage or monthly salary. This leads to the—at first sight— apparently paradoxical feature of efficiency wages, because employers cannot monitor the worker's effort perfectly they will choose to pay them a premium in order to get them to work effectively.

In a separate contribution, Akerlof (1982) uses a psychological or behavioural rather than a purely rational explanation for efficiency wages, which he refers to as a gift exchange. This amounts to the employee saying to herself: this firm treats me well since my wage is above my fallback wage (alternatively called the reservation wage or the opportunity cost of working) so I will respond in kind by working hard. This highlights that a worker paid efficiency wages has something to lose by quitting. Since turnover is costly to the employer this is another reason for paying efficiency wages as discussed in Chapter 2.

A combination of shirking, fairness and turnover cost considerations provides the firm with an incentive to pay workers more than the minimum required to attract them to the job. The firm would like to ensure that the employee has something to gain by getting the job and something to lose by losing it. The firm thus sets the wage so that taking into account the likely consequences of being fired for low quality work, the worker will work hard and well so as to avoid this outcome. To determine how high this wage must be, the firm puts itself in the shoes of the worker and reasons as follows: how much better is it for me (as a worker) to keep the job, than to lose it, get by on unemployment benefits while searching for a new job and eventually land another (perhaps less attractive) one. The answer to this "how much better...?" question is called the employment rent, namely the difference between the value of having the job (and working hard on the job) on the one hand and losing the job (and so for a period not working and living on a reduced income). For a given wage, the employment rent will be greater the more unemployment there is, as this will increase the workers' expected duration of a spell of unemployment, should this occur. So for higher levels of unemployment the firm can pay a lower wage, while still sustaining an employment rent sufficient to motivate the worker not to shirk. Lower levels of unemployment have the opposite effect. This is why the wage curve slopes upwards.

### 15.4.1  A micro model of efficiency wage setting

This section sets out a simple microeconomic efficiency wage model, based on the Shapiro-Stiglitz shirking model, and integrates it into the macro $WS - PS$ framework. It also provides an overview of the empirical evidence to highlight the pervasiveness of efficiency wages in market economies.

The key features of the efficiency wage model are that:

1. Providing effort is costly for workers (i.e. there is a disutility to working as hard as the employer requires).

2. Unemployment is also costly to workers. They get the unemployment benefit if they are unemployed and they cannot immediately get another job at the prevailing wage.

3. The level of effort workers exert depends on the wage and other aspects of the work environment.

4. Firms cannot monitor the effort of their workers perfectly, so they must pay a wage higher than the wage at which a worker would take a job in order to make losing the job costly and thereby induce the worker to provide effort.

At the crux of the efficiency wage model is the idea of 'shirking', which is where workers provide a lower level of effort than the minimum required by the employer. This hinges on the reasonable assumption that there is a difference of interest in the employment relationship between the employer and the worker. We assume that firms will not fire workers as long as they provide effort at a level higher than $\underline{\varepsilon}$, but that workers will be fired with a probability of $\tau$, where $0 < \tau < 1$, if they provide effort lower than $\underline{\varepsilon}$.[6]

Why would firms not fire all workers who put in too little effort? They would like to, but the problem is that they cannot perfectly monitor the effort of their workers. The ability of firms to monitor effort will vary by industry and with technology. In some manufacturing activities, monitoring effort may be possible as there will often be clearly defined units of output. Even so, production is often team–based and this will make monitoring the effort of *individual* workers challenging. Moreover, in modern service-based industries monitoring effort and output may be more difficult. Another interpretation of $\tau$ would therefore be the probability of a firm detecting a shirking worker. It would then be the case that those workers who are caught shirking are dismissed. Information technology makes detection of shirking workers easier in some occupations and industries. For example, truck drivers can be tracked by in-cab monitoring devices and GPS navigation equipment in a way that was impossible before such technologies became low cost.

In this framework, and to simplify the analysis, there are just two discrete levels of effort; $\varepsilon = 0$ or $\varepsilon = \underline{\varepsilon}$. As exerting effort incurs a cost, workers will either provide no effort or they will provide the minimum amount of effort necessary to avoid the risk of being fired. Workers who provide $\underline{\varepsilon}$, will receive a utility of $V$ which is equal to their wage, $w$, minus the disutility of effort, $\underline{a}$. The employer will set the wage, $w$, as the lowest possible wage such that the worker does not prefer shirking.

If the worker provides inadequate effort (i.e. $\varepsilon = 0$) there are three possible outcomes: (a) with a probability of $(1 - \tau)$ they will not be fired and will receive a wage of $w$, with probability $\tau$ they will be fired, and then there are two possible outcomes. (b) With probability $h$ the worker finds another job immediately and receives a payoff of $w$ or (c) they could fail to find another job (with probability $(1 - h)$) and receive unemployment benefits of $b$ for the period.

Figure 15.5 shows this framework in the form of a one-shot game, which greatly simplifies the problem because we assume that the sequence of moves occurs simultaneously. In this

---

[6] We assume that $\underline{\varepsilon}$ is exogenously determined to make the mathematics as simple as possible. The results are qualitatively the same if $\underline{\varepsilon}$ is allowed to vary continuously and depends on $w$ (see Bowles, 2006).

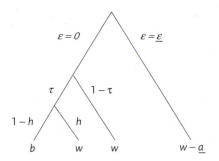

**Figure 15.5** A one-shot game showing the payoffs to shirking in an efficiency wage model.

game, workers pick an effort level (once and for all). If they are fired, they then either get another job with the pay-off $w$ (remember, they do not exert effort in this branch of the tree) or they go onto unemployment benefits. The payoffs to the worker from each outcome are shown in the bottom row.

What is the optimal wage for firms to pay their workers in this model? They will pay the lowest possible wage that will induce workers to provide effort $\underline{\varepsilon}$. Any wage offered below this and workers will shirk, any wage above this and firms' costs increase without any benefit to them. Firms set wages to minimize the costs of acquiring a given amount of effort. In other words, they minimize the cost of an 'efficiency unit of labour', which is where the term 'efficiency wages' comes from. We can infer from Fig. 15.5 that workers will be indifferent between providing no effort and effort of $\underline{\varepsilon}$ when the expected utilities of the two actions are equal. We can therefore use this equation to find the wage that will be set by firms:

$$V_{\text{not shirking}} = V_{\text{shirking}}$$
$$w - \underline{a} = (1 - \tau)w + \tau(hw + (1 - h)b). \tag{15.1}$$

Rearranging, we get the efficiency wage:

$$w^* = b + \frac{a}{\tau(1 - h)} \tag{15.2}$$
$$= b + \frac{a}{\tau u}, \tag{15.3}$$

(optimal wage, efficiency wage model)

where the unemployment rate, $u$, $u = (1 - h)$.

The optimal wage equation, which is commonly referred to as the No-Shirking Condition, shows that the optimal wage set by firms will depend (a) positively on the the level of unemployment benefits, $b$, and the disutility of work, $\underline{a}$; (b) negatively on the probability of being dismissed if shirking, $\tau$; and (c) negatively on the unemployment rate, $u = 1 - h$.

A higher unemployment rate increases the cost of shirking and reduces the efficiency wage that the employer has to pay to deter it. Note that in the general case where there is a positive chance of dismissal and a positive unemployment rate, $(0 < \tau u < 1)$, the employee who is working receives a rent because the wage is greater than opportunity cost of working, which is just $b + \underline{a}$. The jobless worker (with utility $b$) is involuntarily unemployed (she would prefer to be working at a job, since she would then get utility $w^* - \underline{a}$, which is greater than $b$).

We now want to scale up this firm-level model to find the macroeconomic equilibrium. We set out the *WS* and *PS* curves, and analyse how changing different parameters affects the equilibrium rate of unemployment in the economy.

*Efficiency wages in the WS-PS model*

We have already determined the wage that minimizes the cost of acquiring effort and hence maximizes firms' profits:

$$w^{WS} = b + \frac{a}{\tau u}.$$        (*WS* curve, efficiency wage model)

The efficiency wage falls with the unemployment rate; in our macro model, this means the *WS* curve is upward sloping in the real wage–employment diagram. Note that there cannot be full employment ($u = 0$) or labour market clearing in this model because the efficiency wage goes to infinity as unemployment goes toward zero.

The price-setting curve relies on the fact that all firms in the economy are symmetric, so all will set the same profit-maximizing price, such that the price-setting real wage is equal to:

$$w^{PS} = \frac{\eta - 1}{\eta} \varepsilon,$$        (*PS* curve, efficiency wage model)

where $\eta$ is equal to the elasticity of demand and $\varepsilon$ is equal to effort. In this model, effort is equal to labour productivity and firms set wages such that workers are induced to supply effort at the minimum level required by the employer of $\underline{\varepsilon}$.[7]

We can now use the efficiency wage *WS-PS* diagram in Fig.15.6 to illustrate the channels by which the equilibrium rate of unemployment is pushed up.

1. An increase in the rate of unemployment benefits (i.e. ↑ *b*) shifts the *WS* curve upwards, as shown in Fig. 15.6a. Since a higher unemployment benefit reduces the cost of shirking it increases unemployment because a higher efficiency wage is required to persuade workers to work diligently. The economy moves from *A* to *B*.

2. An increase in the disutility of work (i.e. ↑ *a*) or reduction in the probability of a shirking worker being dismissed (i.e. ↓ *τ*) increases the slope of the *WS* curve as shown in Fig.15.6b. A higher disutility of work shifts the trade-off between work and leisure and the worker requires higher compensation to work and exert effort—a higher efficiency wage will be set at any level of employment and hence, equilibrium unemployment will be higher. This highlights the benefits for the economy of changes in work organization that make work more pleasant for workers. For a given unemployment benefit and disutility of work, a lower probability of detection/dismissal means a higher wage has to be paid to induce effort, thereby raising equilibrium unemployment in the economy.

This analysis shows that there are alternative ways of organizing work in an economy in order to keep equilibrium unemployment low. The 'sticks' of lower unemployment benefits and or harsher monitoring of work effort are substitute instruments for the 'carrot' of

---

[7] Note that this is the same equation as in Chapter 2 for the price-setting wage curve, where instead of λ for labour productivity, we have $\underline{\varepsilon}$.

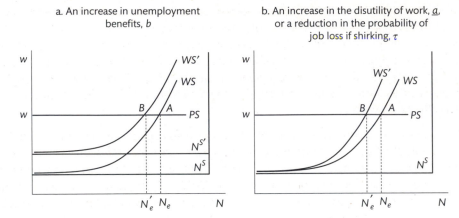

**Figure 15.6** Supply-side shocks in an efficiency wage model of the labour market:
a. An increase in unemployment benefits, *b*
b. An increase in the disutility of work, *a*, or a reduction in the probability of job loss if shirking, *τ*.

improving working conditions in order to reduce the disutility of work. To the extent it becomes more difficult to detect shirking in a services based economy, then as economies move away from producing goods, the benefits of making work less onerous go up.

### 15.4.2 What is the empirical evidence on efficiency wages?

In Chapter 2, we discussed a historical example of the use of efficiency wages: Henry Ford raised wages in his car factory from $2.34 for a nine-hour shift to $5 for an eight-hour shift. Raff and Summers (1987) found that this reduced absenteeism and worker turnover substantially between 1913 and 1915, resulting in higher productivity and profits for Ford. This is cited as a dramatic illustration of the payment of efficiency wages, but there is a further rich empirical literature that documents different mechanisms that drive the relationship between wages, effort, productivity and profits. This subsection provides a brief overview of the wider academic literature on efficiency wages:[8]

1. Agell and Lundborg (1995) undertook interviews with senior wage negotiators and personnel managers and found that they believed work effort would increase if local unemployment increased. This is consistent with the unemployment rate (closely related to the probability of the worker finding another job after being dismissed) acting as a disciplining device to induce workers to provide effort.

2. Fleisher and Wang (2001) provide evidence for the effects of higher wages on worker effort and the prevalence of shirking. The paper uses data from Chinese urban and rural nonagricultural firms to investigate efficiency-wage effects for technical, managerial and production workers. They collected survey data from a large sample of firms and used panel

[8] For a more thorough overview of the academic literature see Chapter 8 of Bowles (2006).

data regression models to investigate how excess wages (i.e. wages above the average wage for a given level of experience and schooling) affect gross output (and hence productivity). They report strong evidence of productivity-enhancing wage setting behaviour in both state, collectively and privately owned companies. The survey also collected data from workers on how frequently they observe shirking amongst their co-workers. These data were included in the regression models, and the results show that employees are less liable to shirk if they are paid higher wages.

3. Evidence to support the existence of efficiency wages comes from econometric studies that measure the loss of earnings of an employee when they lose their job as a result of a plant closure.[9] Interestingly, the loss of earnings is not restricted to those who fail to find another job after plant closure. For example, Farber (2005, p. 25) finds that 'counting foregone earnings increases enjoyed by non-losers, full-time job losers who find new full-time jobs earn up to 17% less on average in their new jobs than they would have had they not been displaced'.

4. Other evidence comes from studies that compare productivity under different compensation schemes. The evidence shows that workers exert more effort and produce more output when they are on piece-rates (i.e. a payment per unit of output). For example, Foster and Rosenzweig (1994) use longitudinal data from rural farming households in the Philippines to investigate the relationship between effort and contractual arrangements. They find that work effort was substantially higher under piece-rates than under time-wage (i.e. a fixed wage per hour) contracts. It is also clear that piece rates are a fairly rare method of payment—especially in modern service-based economies—highlighting the likely prevalence of efficiency wages.

5. At the macroeconomic level, a time series study of productivity in the US motivated by trying to explain the slowdown of productivity growth in the 1970s found that controlling for the standard determinants, productivity varied positively and strongly with the expected income loss from job loss (Bowles, Gordon and Weisskopf, 1983). More effort (higher productivity) was forthcoming when the threat of job loss was higher.

6. In related work, Lazear et al. (2013) use data from 20,000 workers in a large firm to investigate the cause of the rise in productivity observed in the United States during the global financial crisis. They find that the productivity increase was mainly driven by workers putting in more effort during the recession. This fits with the idea of firms 'making do with less'; workers are laid off, but instead of output falling equivalently, the existing workers are made to take on the extra workload. What makes the existing workers willing to put in extra effort for the same wage? An interpretation using the efficiency wage model is that the recession increased unemployment and lowered the probability of finding another job if dismissed.

The literature has also provided evidence for the effects of efficiency wages on recruitment and retention. These effects are outside of the scope of the simple model presented in the

---

[9] See, for example, Farber (2005).

last subsection, but are further important reasons why firms pay efficiency wages. Campbell and Kamlani (1997, p. 785), find support for explanations that focus on the effect of wages on retention:

> [F]irms fear the loss of firm-specific human capital when experienced workers quit almost as much as they fear the cost of hiring and training replacements.

There is also evidence that firms are reluctant to cut wages, even in recessions (Bewley, 1999). The managers surveyed by Bewley said that they feared cutting wages, even in difficult trading conditions, because of the effect it would have on their ability to recruit, retain and motivate workers.

## 15.5 Hysteresis and persistence in unemployment

We have seen that the equilibrium rate of unemployment is shifted by a range of supply-side factors. The policy implication is twofold:

1. Aggregate demand shocks have a short-run effect on unemployment but no effect in the medium run.
2. Whilst aggregate demand policies have a role to play in stabilizing the economy around equilibrium unemployment, they cannot influence its level.

However, it has been argued that if unemployment stays above equilibrium for an extended period, it could have a damaging effect on the supply side of the economy with the result that equilibrium unemployment is raised. This is an example of so-called hysteresis, in which the equilibrium of the system depends on the history of the system. Often the term 'path dependence' is used to describe this phenomenon.

Hysteresis is often referred to in conjunction with European unemployment in the 1970s and 1980s, where cyclical increases in unemployment appeared to permanently increase the rate of structural unemployment. Figure 15.9 shows the path of European unemployment between 1960 and 2012. We can see the ratchet pattern in European unemployment from the start of the 1970s though to the mid-80s, where the recessions associated with the oil shocks seem to have permanently increased unemployment. In the period since the mid-80s, European unemployment has remained between 7 and 10%, more than three times its rate at the start of the 1970s.

The issue of hysteresis was low on the macroeconomic agenda during the years of the Great Moderation from the 1990s to the eve of the global financial crisis, partly due to the impressive reductions in unemployment seen in the United States and some European economies (e.g. Ireland, Netherlands and the UK) over this period. It returned to the spotlight following the global financial crisis, however, as a large number of OECD economies experienced high and persistent unemployment.

In this section, we provide examples of unemployment persistence stemming from mechanisms that work through the *WS* curve:

1. The insider–outsider effect, where wages are set to benefit those in work, i.e. the insiders;[10] and

2. The long-term/short-term unemployment effect, where the long-term unemployed (the outsiders) lose touch with the labour market and cease to influence wage setting.

## The insider–outsider effect

We assume the economy is initially at equilibrium employment, $N_e$ in Fig. 15.7 and that there is a fall in aggregate demand that reduces employment to $N_1$. Our usual assumption is that the falling inflation at $N_1$ leads the central bank to cut the interest rate and boost aggregate demand so that the economy returns to $N = N_e$. If, however, the central bank is inactive, or the economy is at the zero lower bound (ZLB) after a balance sheet recession (see Chapter 6), and if the impact of falling inflation on aggregate demand is weak, then the economy may remain for some time at $N_1$.

Two groups of workers may then be identified: (1) the unemployed outsiders; and (2) the insiders who remain employed at $N_1$.

The insiders are in a strong bargaining position because, for example, their firm-specific skills mean that the firm cannot simply sack them and replace them with new workers. Insiders are presumed to be interested in maintaining their own employment and increasing their real wage; they attach no importance to the creation of employment for those currently unemployed.[11]

The consequence is that the WS curve becomes vertical at $N_1$ as shown in Fig. 15.7. Any increase in aggregate demand will simply be reflected in a rise in the real wage until the $w^{WS} = w^{PS}$, after which, higher aggregate demand will produce rising inflation: equilibrium employment has fallen to $N_1 = N'_e$. This is a model of pure hysteresis in the sense that once unemployment has risen and insiders have emerged with wage-setting power, equilibrium unemployment goes up and remains at the new level. Although the rise in equilibrium unemployment originated with a fall in aggregate demand (that was not offset), only a supply-side change, which alters wage-setting arrangements can reduce equilibrium unemployment.[12]

## Long-term unemployment and unemployment persistence

As an example of the interaction between aggregate demand and equilibrium unemployment, we look at the phenomenon of long-term unemployment in the labour market.[13] The long-term unemployed are viewed as having in effect withdrawn from participation in the labour market because of a progressive loss of skills and erosion of psychological attachment

---

[10] The original articles on the insider-outsider effect were: Lindbeck and Snower (1986) and Blanchard and Summers (1986).

[11] Note that implicitly in our usual discussions of wage setting, the utility function of workers (and unions) is based on a representative (or average) worker's preferences before they know whether they are employed or unemployed.

[12] The microeconomic working of the model is set out in more detail in Chapter 15 of Carlin and Soskice (2006).

[13] See Layard and Nickell (1986).

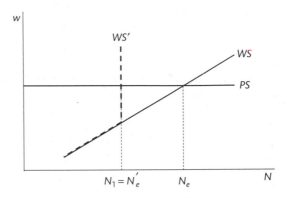

**Figure 15.7** Hysteresis: the insider–outsider model.

to working life. They are therefore only poor substitutes for those in work and exert little competitive pressure in the labour market. The higher is the proportion of the long-term unemployed in the overall pool of unemployment, the less impact will any given level of unemployment have on wage setting.

If this is the case, then since a long period of high unemployment is likely to eventually push up the proportion of the long-term unemployed, equilibrium unemployment will rise. In the *WS/PS* diagram, the *WS* curve shifts upwards. This in turn weakens the self-equilibrating process through which high unemployment dampens wage inflation. The objective of reducing the scarring effects of unemployment lies behind 'welfare-to-work' programmes. The aim of such programmes is to reconnect unemployed workers with the labour market by using combinations of sticks (e.g. loss of benefits if active search is not undertaken) and carrots (e.g. grants for travel to job interviews, training for interviews).

To explain how the emergence of long-term unemployment can lead to a prolonged period of high unemployment, we take as an example the case of an economy initially in equilibrium with constant inflation at point $A$ in Fig. 15.8. Let us assume that inflation is stable but high at point $A$ and a newly elected government wishes to reduce inflation to $\pi_L$ or adopts a policy of austerity aimed at reducing the level of government debt.

This leads it to reduce aggregate demand to $N_1$ and to keep activity low until inflation has been reduced to $\pi_L$. However, with high unemployment at $N_1$, the share of long-term unemployment begins to rise: it rises to $LTU_H$, at which point it stabilizes. With a large pool of long-term unemployed, the *WS* curve shifts upward as explained above: this is $WS(LTU_H)$. As is clear from the diagram, disinflation is slowed down by the upward shift of the *WS* curve. If we assume that inflation is brought down to $\pi_L$ then the government will want to move the economy back to $N_e$. However, because of the presence of higher share of long-term unemployed, equilbrium unemployment is now at $N_2$. But unlike the insider–outsider model, in this case, the economy will eventually return to equilibrium at $A$. The reason is that at point $D$, the share of long-term unemployed will begin to decline since unemployment is lower than at $N_1$ and the $WS(LTU)$ curve will shift down.

Gradually, as employment recovers, the share of long-term unemployed will shrink and the economy will return to $A$. If the 'scarring' effect of long-term unemployment is very serious, specific policies targeted at reintegrating the long-term unemployed back into jobs may be

- Begin at A. Government cuts N to $N_1$ in order to reduce inflation.
- At B, LTU rises to $LTU_H$ (equilibrium LTU associated with $N_1$); WS shifts up (B to C) and disinflation is weaker.
- New equilibrium employment at D.
- At D, LTU begins to fall to $LTU_M$ (equilibrium LTU associated with $N_2$) and WS shifts down.
- Initial equilibrium at A is attainable as LTU is reduced.

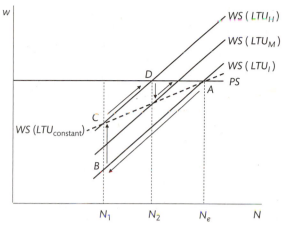

Figure 15.8 Unemployment persistence: the role of long-term unemployment.

necessary in order for the equilibrium at A to be attained. Once back at A, the government will have achieved its objective of reducing inflation but the process will be protracted if workers become disconnected from the labour force during the phase of high unemployment. The flatter WS curve (dashed) in the diagram shows the wage-setting curve when the long-term unemployment share is unchanging. It is the intersection of the dashed WS curve and the PS curve that fixes the 'long-run' equilibrium rate of unemployment: the shifting WS curve slows down the return to A and the economy will be observed at 'medium-run' constant inflation equilibria such as at point D.

## Hysteresis (Ball, 1999 and 2009)

Lawrence Ball set out to test whether there was evidence that macroeconomic policy choices by governments and central banks influenced equilibrium unemployment by virtue of their effect on actual unemployment. His first claim in his 1999 paper was that some countries pursued excessively tight macroeconomic policies in the early 1980s, which led to prolonged recessions and produced more long-term unemployment. As we have seen in the previous subsection, if the long-term unemployed are ineffective in dampening wage pressure, equilibrium unemployment is pushed up. 'Over-tight' policies became a self-fulfilling prophecy because the upward shift in the WS curve then requires tighter macro policy to stabilize inflation.

His second claim was that countries where unemployment fell substantially in the 1990s were those that undertook expansionary macro policies, i.e. hysteresis operated in reverse with strong aggregate demand reducing unemployment, which in turn brought down equilibrium unemployment.

Ball's 2009 paper used data from 20 OECD countries between 1980 and 2007 to investigate periods of significant change in the equilibrium rate of unemployment (NAIRU)—i.e. periods where the NAIRU changed by at least three percentage points within a period of ten years. He found that large increases in the NAIRU were associated with periods of disinflation and large decreases were associated with run-ups in inflation. He interpreted these facts as providing further evidence for hysteresis, arguing they could not be reconciled with the theory that the equilibrium rate of unemployment is independent of aggregate demand.[14]

Ball pointed out that the central banks in the USA and Canada cut interest rates much more vigorously than their European counterparts in the early 1980s recessions. The US and Canadian central bank reports from this period show the apparently greater concern to impart a counter-cyclical stimulus. Nevertheless, it is difficult to confirm or refute the hysteresis hypothesis: how can the hypothesis that central banks pursued tight policy for longer in Europe because the supply side had deteriorated (i.e. tighter policy was needed to ensure disinflation) be distinguished from Ball's one that the supply side deteriorated because the central banks in Europe failed to cut interest rates aggressively to promote recovery?

## 15.6 Unemployment in OECD countries

### 15.6.1 Definitions: employment, unemployment and inactivity

As emphasized in the discussion of the flow approach, there is not a one-for-one relationship between changes in employment and in unemployment. The working age population is divided into three labour market states: employed, unemployed (actively looking for work and able to begin) and inactive. Thus:

$$Pop \equiv U + N + I \equiv LF + I$$

where $Pop$ is the population of working age, $U$ is the number unemployed, $N$ the number employed, $I$ the inactive, and $LF$ the labour force. We can use Fig. 15.1 to find the composition of the UK working age population in 2011 Q4–28.3m individuals in employment ($N$), 2.6m unemployed individuals ($U$) and 9.3m inactive individuals ($I$).

The unemployment rate, $u$, is defined in terms of the labour force:

$$u \equiv \frac{U}{LF} \equiv \frac{U}{N + U}$$

whereas the employment rate, $n$, is defined in terms of the working age population:

$$n \equiv \frac{N}{Pop}.$$

The connection between the unemployment and employment rates is provided by the participation rate, which shows the proportion of the working age population active in the labour market:

$$PR \equiv \frac{LF}{Pop}.$$

Taking the labour flows data in Fig. 15.1, we can calculate the rates of employment ($n$), unemployment ($u$) and the participation rate ($PR$) for the UK economy in 2011Q4:

$$u \equiv \frac{U}{N + U} = \frac{2.6}{28.3 + 2.6} = 8.4\%$$

[14] For further empirical evidence for hysteresis effects see Stanley (2004) and Stockhammer and Stern (2012).

$$n \equiv \frac{N}{Pop} = \frac{28.3}{28.3 + 2.6 + 9.3} = 70.4\%$$

$$PR \equiv \frac{LF}{Pop} = \frac{28.3 + 2.6}{28.3 + 2.6 + 9.3} = 76.9\%.$$

The definitions shown above imply that:

$$n \equiv PR(1 - u) \text{ and that } u \equiv 1 - \frac{n}{PR}.$$

Thus, a rise in the employment rate will only be reflected in a fall in the unemployment rate to the extent that it is not offset by a rise in participation as the economically inactive are brought back into the labour force. The participation rate is not fixed: during a recession, when unemployment rises, participation rates tend to fall. The opposite happens in upswings. There are also important long-run trends, as women's participation has risen over the last half-century and men's has tended to fall.

In addition, policies affect participation. From the perspective of interpreting trends in Europe, the most important have been sickness and disability regulations and retirement practices, especially the use of early retirement schemes. Attempts to reduce the unemployment rate by lowering participation through early retirement schemes or easy access to disability benefits are likely to have serious consequences for macroeconomic management. Such measures can be counterproductive. They can reduce equilibrium employment through two channels: first, if these schemes have the effect of raising the tax burden, then equilibrium employment goes down because the price-setting curve shifts downwards. Second, measures to remove people from the labour force may reduce competition for jobs, which shifts the wage-setting curve upwards.

### 15.6.2 Overview

In Chapter 2 we showed the evolution of unemployment in 19 OECD countries between 1960 and 2012. This section examines OECD unemployment data to assess what factors caused the trends and cross-country differences observed over this period. Figure 15.9 helps shed more light on key global economies, showing the path of unemployment in Japan, the US and Europe between 1960 and 2012. Setting aside for the moment the variation of unemployment performance *within* Europe, we can see that:

1. Unemployment in Europe rose dramatically in the 1970s and despite periods of falling unemployment, it has remained high ever since.

2. From the early 1980s until the onset of the global financial crisis, the US unemployment rate was below that of Europe and on a downward trend.

3. Japan's unemployment was below that of Europe and the US for the majority of the period, but has been on a slow upward trend since 1990—the beginning of Japan's so-called lost decades of stagnation and deflation.

4. Unemployment rose in all three regions during the financial crisis, but the increase was largest in the US.

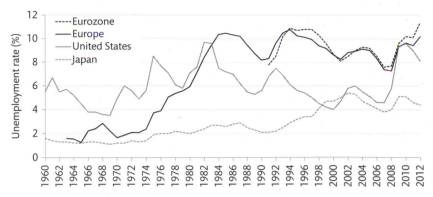

**Figure 15.9** Unemployment in Japan, the US, Europe and the Eurozone: 1960–2012.

*Note:* Data for Japan, the US and the Eurozone is OECD harmonized unemployment rates and data for Europe is OECD unemployment rates - all persons - total. Europe consists of all European countries in the OECD.

*Source:* OECD (data accessed December 2013).

5. In the years following the financial crisis, unemployment has continued to worsen in Europe and the Eurozone, but has fallen slightly in the US and Japan.

The ingredients that are useful in accounting for both the path of average European unemployment shown in Fig. 15.9, and for the cross-country variation in unemployment shown in Fig. 2.1 can be divided into the following.

1. **The determinants of shifts in unemployment around the equilibrium.** These can be policy-induced, arising, for example, from the use of tighter domestic aggregate demand policy to push unemployment up in order to reduce inflation. Alternatively, they can be caused by shocks. Aggregate demand fluctuates in response to domestic *IS* shocks or because of international shocks to trade or world commodity prices, as discussed in Chapter 11.

2. **The determinants of equilibrium unemployment**, as discussed earlier in this chapter and Chapter 2. These centre on factors shifting the wage-setting and/or price-setting curves or the unemployment/vacancy (Beveridge) curve:

(a) The *WS* curve shifts up with a rise in union bargaining power and with a fall in the cost of job loss (e.g. a rise in the unemployment benefit replacement rate). The degree of coordination of wage setting also affects the *WS* curve.

(b) The *PS* curve shifts down with a rise in the tax wedge; an unanticipated fall in trend productivity growth; a fall in the pressure of competition in the product market; or a rise in the oil price.

(c) The unemployment-vacancy (Beveridge) curve shifts to the right in unemployment-vacancy space when there is a rise in the mismatch between jobs available and potential employees (see Fig. 15.2).

3. **Interactions between shocks and institutions**: this is where the effect of a shock on unemployment depends on the supply-side institutions in the country. For example,

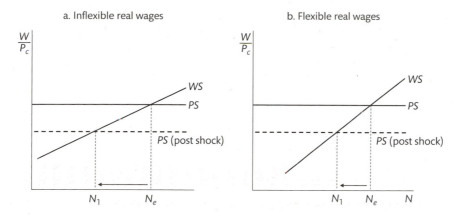

**Figure 15.10** Common shock: interaction with flexible and inflexible real wages
a. Inflexible real wages: large fall in $N$
b. Flexible real wages: small fall in $N$.

a supply-side shock such as an oil shock or a slowdown in productivity growth shifts the *PS* curve down: the impact of this on equilibrium unemployment depends on the slope of the *WS* curve, i.e. on how sensitive are real wages (of wage setters) to unemployment. One way of characterizing a flexible labour market is one in which the *WS* curve is very steep—i.e. real wages are very responsive to changes in unemployment. If the *WS* is very flat, then for a given negative external terms of trade shock, a much larger rise in unemployment is required to bring about the necessary downward adjustment of real wage claims (see Fig. 15.10 for an illustration). When wage-setting is highly coordinated as in the Nordic economies, for example, the wage setting curve is steep as in the flexible wage case illustrated.

4. **Hysteresis and persistence mechanisms**: as we have seen, a sustained period of high unemployment caused by weak aggregate demand can in turn cause a deterioration in the supply side of the economy so that the equilibrium unemployment rate is pulled up too.

### 15.6.3 **Empirical studies**

Starting from the *WS-PS* and matching models (Beveridge curve), many attempts have been made to sort out the role of institutional factors and of shocks (technology; terms of trade; etc.) in explaining unemployment. The OECD's *Jobs Study* of 1994 is a standard reference, which was followed in 1999 by its *Implementing the Jobs Study*.[15] The framework of analysis used in the OECD's studies is broadly similar to that used in the academic papers reported in this section.

Table 15.2 provides summary information about cross-country labour market performance and a set of determinants of the *WS* and *PS* curves (i.e. the $z_w$ and $z_p$ terms in the *WS* and *PS* equations). The data relates to a year in the early-mid 2000s before the financial crisis.

[15] See OECD (1994) and OECD (1996).

**Table 15.2** Employment and institutional patterns across country groups.

| | | Six liberal economies | Six high unemployment European countries | Six low unemployment European countries |
|---|---|---|---|---|
| 1. | Unemployment rate 2004 (%) | 5.2 | 9.1 | 5.0 |
| 2. | Employment rate 2004 (%) | 70.8 | 62.6 | 73.7 |
| 3. | Employment rate–less than high school education (%) (% of population with less than high school education) | 59.4 (27) | 56.0 (38) | 63.9 (23) |
| 4. | Wage differentials: ratio of median wages to lowest decile approx. year 2000 | 1.9 | 1.6 | 1.5 |
| 5. | Employment Protection Legislation 2003 (Index) | 1.2 | 2.6 | 2.2 |
| 6. | Unemployment benefits–Net Replacement Ratio 2002 (%) | 52 | 72 | 77 |
| 7. | Trade union membership 2000 (% employees) | 26 | 36 | 47 |
| 8. | Collective bargaining coverage 2000 (% of employees) | 36 | 83 | 76 |
| 9. | Co-ordination of bargaining 2000 (index) | 1.7 | 3.8 | 3.9 |
| 10. | Tax revenue as % GDP 2004 | 32 | 41 | 43 |
| 11. | Active Labour Market Policies 2004 (% of GDP) | 0.5 | 1.0 | 1.2 |

*Source:* Table 2 in Howell et al. (2007); underlying data from the OECD (see paper for full list of sources).

Eighteen advanced economies are divided into three groups: a group of 'liberal' economies, which comprises Australia, Canada, Ireland, New Zealand, UK and USA; a group of high unemployment European countries (Belgium, Finland, France, Germany, Italy, Spain); and a group of low unemployment European countries (Austria, Denmark, Netherlands, Norway, Switzerland, Sweden).

The data reported are the mean values for each country group. The unemployment rate is similar in 2004 in the liberal economies and in the low unemployment European countries at around 5%; and higher at 9.1 % in the other group of European economies. The interesting feature of the data in the table, which is reminiscent of predictions of the Calmfors–Driffill model presented in Section 15.3, is that there are two groups of countries with low unemployment in which institutions are quite different. As compared with the low unemployment European countries, the liberal economies have lower tax wedges, lower unemployment benefits, weaker employment protection, lower union membership and coverage and lower coordination of bargaining. They also spend much less on active labour market policies. These variables are among those most commonly included in cross-country unemployment regressions.

Most of the unemployed in Europe at that time lived in the four large countries of France, Germany, Italy and Spain (as we shall see below, unemployment in Germany began to fall from 2004 and continued to do so through the financial crisis and Great Recession). The employment rate is higher in the low unemployment European group than in the liberal group, which in turn is higher than in the high unemployment European group. The same pattern is repeated for the measure of the employment rate of the population with less than completed high school education. Overall, the labour market performance of the low unemployment European group is superior to that of the other two groups; those countries also have lower wage dispersion (row 4).

Although the results of studies that attempt to confirm the role of the factors in Table 15.2 are disputed, it is useful to explain briefly the three main strategies that have been undertaken in the empirical work. Policy makers frequently refer to studies of this kind to justify labour market reform measures.

1. The simplest kind of study attempts to explain the cross-country variation in unemployment rates across the OECD countries. Studies of this type focus on the relative *position* of the WS and PS curves in different countries. A widely cited cross-sectional study is that of Nickell (1997), which uses data for 20 OECD economies for two five year periods to investigate the impact of a range of labour market institutions on unemployment.

2. The second type of study, pioneered by Blanchard and Wolfers (2000), tests the hypothesis that it was the interaction between different (stable) institutions and common shocks to which countries were subjected that accounts for cross-country variation in employment over time. The idea is that some institutions translated bad shocks (e.g. to productivity) into more persistent unemployment problems than others. This can be illustrated using the $WS - PS$ model by considering a common shift in the PS curve that interacts with WS curves of differing slopes, as shown in Fig. 15.10. Testing this hypothesis requires using panel data—i.e. data that varies across both countries and time—and introducing interaction terms between time dummies and a set of institutional variables into the regression model.

3. The last type of widely used study design attempts to identify the role of institutional *change* in accounting for the time-series variation in unemployment across the OECD countries: i.e. *within country* shifts in the WS or PS curve due to institutional changes. This requires a panel dataset. A prominent example of this type of analysis was published in the OECD Employment Outlook 2006.[16] The analysis took advantage of recent OECD efforts to harmonize (i.e. make comparable) the data on labour market institutions across countries, using data from 1982–2003 for 20 OECD economies.

Table 15.3 summarizes the results of the three studies. The first thing that is immediately clear is that for some of the labour market institutions (e.g. employment protection and active labour market policies (ALMP)) there is no robust evidence for their effect on unemployment. In other cases, there seems to be more consensus. For example, the studies find that increases in the tax wedge and the level of unemployment benefits exert a statistically significant and positive effect on the unemployment rate (i.e. they increase it). In contrast, they find that

[16] See OECD (2006). In this vein, Soskice and Iversen (2000) show that non-accommodating central banks reinforce coordinated wage bargaining to reduce equilibrium unemployment.
D. Soskice and T. Iversen (2000), 'The Non-neutrality of Monetary Policy with Large Price or Wage Setters', Quarterly Journal of Economics, Vol 115 (1), 265-284.

**Table 15.3**   Estimated effects of institutions on unemployment: three studies.

|  | Nickell (1997) | Blanchard and Wolfers (2000) | OECD EO (2006) |
|---|---|---|---|
| Institutions: |  |  |  |
| Employment protection (+ 1 unit) | No effect | 0.24 | No effect |
| Unemp. benefit replacement ratio (+ 10 pp) | 0.88 | 0.70 | 1.20 |
| Unemp. benefit duration (+ 1 yr) | 0.70 | 1.27 | – |
| ALMP (+10 pp) | –1.92 | No effect | – |
| Union density (+ 10 pp) | 0.96 | 0.84 | No effect |
| Union bargaining coverage (+ 10 pp) | 3.60 | No effect | – |
| Bargaining coordination (+1 unit) (scale 1–3) | –3.68 | –1.13 | –1.42 |
| Taxes (+ 10 pp) | 2.08 | 0.91 | 2.80 |

*Note:* For detailed discussion see Howell et al. (2007). pp means percentage points. 'No effect' means not statistically significant. – means variable not included in study.
*Source:* Howell et al. (2007). Table 3.

bargaining coordination reduces unemployment. Table 15.3 was constructed using Howell et al. (2007), which provides a wider comparison of ten studies.[17] The most notable lesson from the comparison of cross-country studies is that even for variables where there is more consensus, the studies do not appear to give precise answers to the question of the likely *magnitude* of the effect of institutional and policy differences on unemployment outcomes.

## 15.7 Labour market behaviour in the crisis

The recent financial crisis came after a prolonged period of economic stability. From the mid-80s, as shown for the US in Fig. 1.3, the OECD economies entered a phase of reduced macroeconomic volatility, which was accompanied by falling unemployment rates in the majority of these economies. The so-called Great Moderation came to a sudden end when the collapse of American investment bank Lehman Brothers triggered a global financial crisis (see Chapter 7). The effect this had on global labour markets stretched far beyond the sectors immediately affected in housing and financial services.

The top line in the right panel of Fig. 15.11 shows that in the OECD, unemployment fell to below 6% in the years immediately preceding the financial crisis, but leapt to over 8% in 2009 and remained at this level in both 2010 and 2011. We can also see from Fig. 15.11 that the crisis caused a sharp rise in long-term unemployment (i.e. those unemployed for a year or longer) in the OECD. These facts highlight the severity and synchronicity of the Great Recession across developed economies, but also the persistence of unemployment, which remained stubbornly high during the recovery phase.[18]

[17] The study by Howell et al. (2007) provides a systematic comparison of the cross-country empirical evidence and provides results for ten studies. Heckman (2007) provides comment on this paper and other literature investigating the impact of labour market institutions on unemployment.

[18] The majority of developed economies returned to positive but weak GDP growth in the second half of 2009. Some European economies experienced economic contractions since that period as a result of the Eurozone sovereign debt crisis, which is discussed in Chapters 12 and 14.

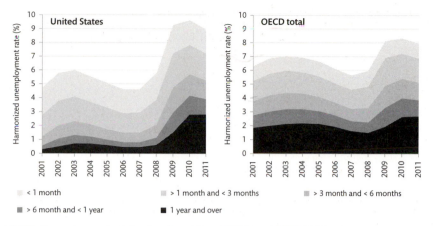

**Figure 15.11** Unemployment rate by duration—US and OECD total: 2001–2011.

*Source:* OECD (data accessed January 2013).

*Note:* Data was calculated by multiplying the harmonized rate of unemployment by the percentage shares of total unemployment by duration.

### 15.7.1 **US unemployment during the crisis**

The problem of long-term unemployment was new and particularly acute in the United States, where as a percentage of total unemployment it jumped from 10% in 2007 to over 31% in 2011. The shaded black area in the left hand panel of Fig. 15.11 shows the striking rise in long-term unemployment between 2007 and 2011.

Elsby et al. (2010) analyse the impact of the Great Recession on the US labour market and compare it to previous downturns. The authors find that the labour market response to the global financial crisis initially bore distinct similarities to other postwar recessions. The demographic groups that suffered most were young, male, less-educated and ethnic minority workers. The impact on youth unemployment was particularly acute, with youth unemployment averaging nearly 18% between 2009 and 2011.[19]

The flow approach to unemployment introduced in Section 15.2 is used to analyse the flows into and out of unemployment during the crisis. They find that the composition of separations from employment shifted from quits toward layoffs; workers laid off typically moved into unemployment and not straight into another job. This was a major driver of the rise in unemployment during the crisis.

As the recession progressed, the labour market response diverged from the recessions of the early 1990s and early 2000s. The exit rate of unemployed workers from joblessness dropped to historically low levels. The level of unemployment during the recession was higher than that implied by the historic Beveridge curve, which signifies a loss of efficiency in matching workers with vacancies (see Section 15.2). This contributes to long-term unemployment. The authors stop short of predicting hysteresis on the scale of Europe in the

[19] Source: OECD labour market statistics—unemployment rate for all persons aged 15–24 (data accessed January 2013).

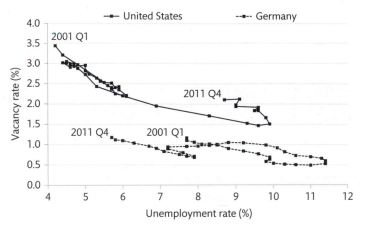

**Figure 15.12**  Beveridge curves in the US and Germany: 2001 Q1–2011 Q4.

*Source:* OECD Employment Outlook 2012.

*Note:* Rates are expressed as a percentage of the labour force.

1980s, as whilst exit rates were at record lows, they were still four times higher than those in continental Europe in the 1980s.

The view presented in Elsby et al. (2010) is in line with the latest Beveridge curve data for the US. Figure 15.12 plots the US Beveridge curve between the early 2000s and the end of 2011. It shows that the relatively stable Beveridge curve of the 2000s shifted out markedly during the crisis and remained there as growth resumed.

### 15.7.2  European unemployment during the crisis

From Fig. 15.9, we see that European unemployment rose by around two percentage points, on average, during the global financial crisis. This headline figure masks a divergence of performance across the individual countries however, as shown by Fig. 2.1 in Chapter 2 and Fig. 15.13. The worst affected Eurozone economies were Ireland and Spain. These countries had sizeable credit-fuelled consumption and property booms prior to the recession (see Chapter 12), which collapsed in the crisis. The increase in long-term unemployment in these economies was particularly marked; long-term unemployment as a percentage of total unemployment was 42% in Spain and 59% in Ireland in 2011.

In 2006, 34% of workers in Spain were on temporary contracts, compared to an OECD average of only 12%. The shedding of temporary workers (many of whom were in the construction industry), who had little employment protection, was a major contributor to the rise in Spanish unemployment seen between 2007 and 2011 (see Fig. 15.13).

Another quirk of the Spanish labour market is the concentration of temporary contracts among youth workers. This contrasts with older workers, whose extensive employment protection makes them very expensive to lay off. Spanish youth unemployment rose from 18% in 2007 to 46% in 2011.[20] These levels of youth unemployment led to social unrest reflected, for example, in the youth protests in Madrid in May 2011.

[20] Source: OECD labour market statistics—unemployment rate for all persons aged 15–24 (data accessed January 2013).

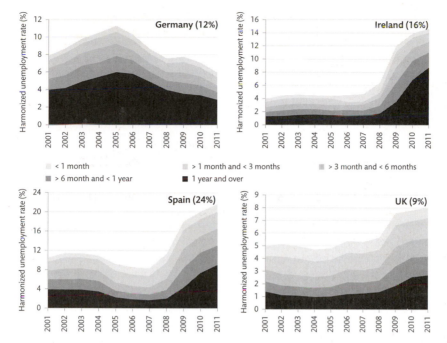

**Figure 15.13** Unemployment rate by duration—selected European economies: 2001–2011.

*Source:* OECD (data accessed January 2013).

*Note:* Data was calculated by multiplying the harmonized rate of unemployment by the percentage shares of total unemployment by duration. The percentages in brackets after the country labels show the scale of each graph.

Figure 15.13 shows that UK unemployment rose by three percentage points between 2007 and 2011, which is just slightly worse than the average of the OECD economies for this period (see Fig. 15.11). We can see that unemployment rose sharply between 2008 and 2009, but then stabilized, fluctuating around 8% until the end of the period. In contrast, GDP growth was anaemic in the years after the financial crisis and real GDP was still well below its pre-crisis level in autumn 2012.[21]

This presents a puzzle; why was UK unemployment so stable during the long recession that followed the financial crisis? The puzzle can be posed in another way: why was productivity growth so weak in the UK? Part of the answer is that real earnings for those in work fell substantially after the crisis.[22] One potential hypothesis for the stability of unemployment following the recession is that UK labour markets are more flexible than they were in previous recessions, due to the supply-side reforms initiated under Margaret Thatcher and carried on under Tony Blair.[23] The evidence points toward a downward shift in the *PS* (weakness in productivity) accompanied, due to labour market flexibility, by a downward shift in the *WS* curve resulting in falling real wages and hence having a limited impact on the unemployment rate.

---

[21] Source: UK Office for National Statistics—GDP (chained volumes measures, $bn, 2009 prices, seasonally adjusted) (data accessed December 2013).

[22] For a detailed analysis see Blundell et al. (2013).

[23] UK supply-side reform is discussed in more detail in Chapter 11.

**The German labour market miracle**

Germany's experience of the global financial crisis was very different from other OECD economies as its headline unemployment rate *fell* substantially between 2008 and 2011, as shown in Fig. 15.13. This cannot be attributed to a smaller impact of the crisis on Germany: its economy contracted by over 5% in 2009.[24] Until the mid 2000s, the German labour market was frequently described as very rigid or sclerotic, which makes its performance in the crisis yet more remarkable. To understand this, a number of features of the state of the German economy when the crisis occured along with characteristics of its labour market must be taken into account.[25]

The German economy was in a better position to weather the crisis than most of its European counterparts. In 2007, the public finances were in good shape, household debt was low and there was no house price bubble (see Chapter 7). This gave the German government greater scope to introduce a sizeable fiscal stimulus (Chapter 7). In addition to this, a substantial restructuring of the core manufacturing (i.e. export) sector took place during the 2000s. Wage restraint due to weakened unions and decentralized negotiations between works councils and employers (a downward shift of the *WS* curve) restored international competitiveness (Chapter 12).

In the years preceding the crisis, German GDP growth depended heavily on exports to fast-growing emerging markets (e.g. China). World trade collapsed as the recession hit, falling by 19% between September 2008 and January 2009.[26] To the extent that the contraction in world trade was due to macroeconomic uncertainty in the wake of Lehman brothers' collapse, it was efficient for firms to retain skilled workers and reduce their hours. World trade rebounded quickly during the recovery phase, driven by emerging market growth, and German workers increased their working hours accordingly. In contrast, in Ireland and Spain, the recession spelled the end of labour intensive contruction booms, which resulted in widespread layoffs in the construction sector. Demand for labour in those sectors was not expected to return.

The core manufacturing sector in Germany responded to the drop off in global trade by cutting hours and not workers. This was primarily through voluntary agreements between employees (or their works councils) and employers, reductions in overtime and the adjustment of working-time accounts, which reflected flexible arrangements that had developed in the 2000s.[27] The government also played a role through the longstanding reduced hours compensation scheme (Kurzarbeitergeld). The OECD suggests that 25% of the reduction in hours during the crisis was covered by this scheme. Firms could dramatically cut the hours of their employees, but the employee would still be compensated with up to 60% of their net salary for up to 24 months by the federal government.

Other OECD economies, such as the US and Spain, saw sharp rises in youth unemployment during the recession. This was not the case in Germany, where companies maintained apprenticeships in spite of the collapse in demand. This is partly a result of the skills shortages

---

[24] Source: IMF World Economic Outlook database, April 2012

[25] For a more detailed discussion of the German labour market and economy prior to and during the global financial crisis see Carlin and Soskice (2009) and Dustmann et al. (2014).

[26] Source: CPB World Trade Monitor, January 2012.

[27] See OECD Employment Outlook 2010, Box 1.6.

experienced prior to the recession and the shrinking size of the cohort of school leavers. The unions played a role by prioritizing training in their collective bargaining negotiations in 2009 and 2010 (alongside job stability). For example in the engineering industry, the union and employers' association agreed that trainees would continue to be employed for a year following the completion of their training.[28]

The flexibility of the German labour market during the Great Recession is highlighted in Fig. 15.12, which shows that the German Beveridge curve shifted inwards during this period. This represents an improvement in labour market matching in the German economy.

## 15.8 Conclusions

This chapter built on the foundations set out in Chapter 2 to provide a more detailed picture of the supply side of the economy. A key aim of the chapter was to answer the question of what determines the equilibrium rate of unemployment in the economy. To help answer this question we extended the modelling from Chapter 2, reviewed the empirical evidence and looked at the evolution of unemployment in the OECD countries since the 1960s.

There are a number of theoretical models of the labour market presented in the chapter.

*WS-PS* **model**  Any wage-push factors ($z_w$) that shift the *WS* curve can influence the equilibrium level of unemployment, such as the bargaining power of unions or the benefit replacement rate. Any price-push factors ($z_p$) that shift the *PS* curve can influence both the equilibrium level of unemployment and the real wage, such as productivity, the tax wedge and the level of product market competition. The famous Calmfors–Driffill model provides richer insights into the impact of different forms of union wage setting on unemployment.

**The matching or flow approach**  This approach centres on the heterogeneity of workers and is complementary to the *WS-PS* model. An important aspect of the labour market is how well it matches individuals who are out of work with unfilled vacancies. This theory introduces the concept of a Beveridge curve, which shows the negative relationship between the vacancy rate and the unemployment rate in the economy. The curve is shifted by factors that influence *matching efficiency*, such as barriers to occupational and geographic mobility including home ownership, and changes in unemployment benefit duration.

**Efficiency wage model**  By setting out the micro-foundations of the model that lies behind the *WS* curve, the role of a number of determinants of the cost of job loss in affecting equilibrium unemployment was highlighted. Changes in the balance of jobs toward those where monitoring of worker effort is more difficult tend to raise unemployment, whereas policies that raise the cost of job loss by, for example, improving working conditions, will reduce it.

**Hysteresis model**  The central insight of these models is that changes in aggregate demand that lead to persistently high unemployment can influence equilibrium unemployment. This is different from the benchmark $WS - PS$ model where only supply-side factors shift

[28] Bosch (2011) explains other agreements that were undertaken related to training in the crisis.

equilibrium unemployment. There are two main theories of hysteresis; the insider–outsider model and the long-term unemployment model. In the former, insiders (i.e. those in employment) set wages to benefit only themselves and force up equilibrium unemployment. In the latter case, the long-term unemployed become detached from the labour market, their skills atrophy and they cease to influence wage-setting, which also pushes up equilibrium unemployment.

The economic theories of the labour market presented in this chapter can help us to shed light on cross-country differences in employment outcomes in the last 50 years.

1. Empirical tests of how labour market institutions affect unemployment have typically used macroeconomic data for OECD countries and implemented cross-sectional or panel data methods. With the exception of the role of the tax wedge and unemployment benefit ratio in raising unemployment and of coordination among unions in wage setting in lowering it, the results have not been conclusive. Different regression specifications using similar data have often led to very different quantitative and in some cases qualititative results.

2. The global financial crisis has put unemployment back at the top of the policy agenda. The sharp increase and persistence of unemployment in OECD economies following the crisis has called into question the idea that the supply-side labour market reforms implemented following the OECD's 1994 Jobs Report had spelled the end of high and persistent unemployment.

3. Germany was one of the only major developed economies to avoid rising unemployment between 2008 and 2010. Germany's employment miracle was due to a combination of factors, including the state of the economy entering the recession, the temporary nature of the drop off in world trade and the high level of cooperation between employees (or works councils) and employers in the core manufacturing sector.

4. Following the growth of long–term unemployment in the Great Recession, concern about hysteresis due to the scarring effect of elevated unemployment has re-emerged not only in Europe but also in the USA.

During the Great Recession, countries with more generous welfare states and where labour markets are flexible but not deregulated, such as the Nordic countries and Germany, performed relatively well.[29] The behaviour of labour markets across OECD countries continues to throw up challenges for economic analysis and policy design.

## 15.9 Questions

### 15.9.1 Checklist questions

1. In the WS – PS model, use diagrams to show what happens following:

    (a) A rise in the tax wedge

    (b) A reduction in union bargaining power

    (c) A tightening in the enforcement of competition policy

---

[29] See the European Commission's report entitled *Employment and Social Developments in Europe 2012*.

In each case, briefly explain the implications for the real wage and the equilibrium level of employment.

2. Use the Calmfors–Driffill model to determine whether the following statements are true, false or uncertain. Briefly explain your answer.

   (a) Industry level unions face more inelastic product demand than firm-level unions

   (b) Industry level unions take into account their effect on the economy-wide price level when negotiating wages

   (c) Centralized wage setting secures the lowest level of unemployment because centralized unions have the most bargaining power

   (d) The hump-shaped (inverse U) relationship between centralization of wage setting and unemployment would be more pronounced in an open economy than in a closed one.

3. Why is unemployment referred to as a 'worker discipline device' in the efficiency wage model? What is meant by the term 'the opportunity cost of working'?

4. Draw the efficiency wages $WS - PS$ diagram for the following cases:

   (a) A reduction in unemployment benefits

   (b) An improvement in working conditions

   (c) A new camera system is installed that improves monitoring.

5. Use the Beveridge curve and $WS - PS$ model to assess the impact of the introduction of a wage accord on an economy's vacancy and unemployment rates.

6. How can the insider–outsider model explain persistently high levels of unemployment? Can this form of hysteresis be mitigated by increasing aggregate demand?

7. Use the long-term unemployment model to explain how the OECD economies could have seen a rise in *equilibrium* unemployment during the global financial crisis.

8. Use Table 3 from Howell et al. (2007) to answer the following questions:

   (a) Do the estimated effects of institutions on unemployment match the predictions of the theories presented in this chapter?

   (b) Do the studies present robust evidence for the effect of labour market institutions on unemployment?

9. Use the matching functions and the Beveridge curve shown in Section 15.2 to explain the assertion in Elsby et al. (2010) that the fall in the exit rate from unemployment contributed to the build up of long-term unemployment in the US during the global financial crisis.

10. Discuss three reasons why the Spanish and German unemployment trends were so different in the aftermath of the global financial crisis. Could the Spanish government have done anything different to mitigate the rise in unemployment?

## 15.9.2 Problems and questions for discussion

1. Use the matching functions, Beveridge curve and $WS - PS$ model from Section 15.2 to discuss how the following events and policies could affect unemployment:

   (a) An extension of unemployment benefit duration during a downturn

   (b) Increasing expenditure on active labour market policies

(c)  A cap on skilled immigration

(d)  Joining a single currency (e.g. the Eurozone)

(e)  A policy to encourage home ownership.

2.  Use Section 15.6, the OECD 1994 Jobs Report and other relevant empirical evidence to discuss the following question: does the use of more refined econometric techniques and the availability of better data since the original OECD Jobs Report in 1994 provide an evidence-based consensus for labour market reform in Europe? Explain your answer.[30]

3.  Take the position of either Agell or Heckman and defend your position and what it implies for labour market reform in Europe following the global financial and Eurozone crises.

   • 'Labour market reforms failing to distinguish between good and bad rigidities will do more harm than good.' Jonas Agell (2003) CESifo Forum

   • 'A substantial portion of European unemployment is a symptom of the deeper problem that incentives to innovate, to acquire skills, and to take risks have been thwarted by the welfare state and regulation.' James Heckman (2003) CESifo Forum

4.  Use Fig. 2.1 in Chapter 2 to pick two economies, one which saw a dramatic fall in unemployment between the mid-80s and the millenium and one that did not (for example, The Netherlands and Germany). Following that, download data from the OECD on the harmonized rate of unemployment for your two countries between 1985 and 2000. Use the OECD data on labour market institutions referred to in Table 15.2 to discuss whether the different paths of unemployment in these two countries are consistent with the changes in labour market institutions. What other factors might have influenced the employment outcomes in the two countries over this period?

---

[30]  The OECD 1994 Jobs Report is available online from: http://www.oecd.org/dataoecd/42/51/1941679.pdf.

# 16 Real Business Cycle and New Keynesian models

## 16.1 Introduction

In this chapter we introduce the New Keynesian (NK) and Real Business Cycle (RBC) approaches, which dominate contemporary business cycle research, as well as graduate macroeconomics. Blanchard's review (2009) of the 'state of macroeconomics' is sympathetic to but also critical of NK, and rather more critical of RBC models.

The 3-equation model used in this book is in some respects a radically simplified version of the NK model. Both models are based on the same three equations – *AD* (or *IS*), *PC*, and *MR*, with the actors being households, wage and price setters and the central bank respectively. In both, firms have enough monopolistic power to set prices and to respond to increases in aggregate demand by increasing output, and firms face timing constraints in setting prices. In these respects they both have 'Keynesian' elements. The NK approach diverges from the 3-equation model in two main ways: first, it assumes that *all* the actors are forward-looking and use rational expectations; by contrast, the 3 equation model assumes that it is only the central bank and foreign exchange markets that use rational expectations. Second, it is associated with *Dynamic Stochastic General Equilibrium (DSGE)* modelling.

While this represents a very active research frontier in modern macroeconomics, there has been considerable criticism of the approach as a reflection of how the economy works: '... the first two equations are patently false ... The *AD* equation relies on an intertemporal substitution effect in response to the interest rate which is hard to detect in the data on consumers. The inflation equation implies a purely forward-looking behaviour of inflation which again appears strongly at odds with the data' (Blanchard, 2009, p. 216). The notion that households, in response to shocks, behave as if they work out the expected future path of the output gap from a rational forecast of future central bank behaviour seems unrealistic. In pedagogic terms working with *DSGE* models does not provide the intuitive understanding of macroeconomics, which the 3-equation model can provide. Unlike RBC and NK models, business cycles in the 3-equation model are *disequilibrium* phenomena, where the economy is shifted by a shock away from equilibrium and the central bank gets the economy on to the stable path back to equilibrium. In RBC and NK models since all agents have model-consistent expectations, the economy is in a rational expectations equilibrium even when it is away from the steady state equilibrium.

In Chapter 4, we introduced the New Classical school of macroeconomics and its role in bringing the rational expectations hypothesis into macroeconomic modelling. If agents form expectations rationally, they are forward-looking and take into account all available information, including how the model works, and they do not make systematic errors. Real Business Cycle models stem directly from this tradition. The RBC model proposes that business cycles are the result of exogenous technology shocks, which are propagated through the economy because the shocks themselves are assumed to be persistent and because of the *intertemporal (or Frisch) elasticity of labour supply*. This means that workers shift both their hours of work and their consumption between periods to make best use of the changes in the returns to working and to saving arising from the shock. Fluctuations in employment arise from this behaviour and not from the hiring and retrenchment behaviour of firms responding to demand shocks as in the 3-equation model.

The early RBC models were criticized on many grounds, such as the lack of information about the source and nature of the 'technology shocks' driving the model and the importance of the unmodelled persistence of the shocks, and of intertemporal optimization, in generating the dynamics of the model. Nevertheless, the model did refocus macroeconomics on investigating the supply-side causes of business cycles (such as productivity shocks, oil shocks). It also provided a new methodology for conducting macroeconomic analysis, which has had a huge influence, not only in academic research, but also in a range of policy settings measures over the past two decades. The RBC model is the basis of the New Keynesian DSGE models, which are to be found in the research departments of most central banks around the world. However, the many quotes we have used from central bank policy makers suggest that they use a model closer to the 3-equation framework.

The New Keynesian model is best understood as descending directly from the RBC model, modified by the introduction of sticky prices, which gives a role for inflation-targeting monetary policy. The first stage of constructing the New Keynesian model, as distinct from the RBC, is to derive the New Keynesian Phillips curve. This relation states that current inflation depends on the entire future path of expected output gaps, which leads to substantially different implications for inflation than the standard adaptive expectations (i.e. backward-looking) Phillips curve used in the core 3-equation model.

Using the New Keynesian Phillips curve, it is possible to explain the impact of a central bank being able to credibly commit to a given adjustment path after economic shocks and to compare the commitment strategy to a strategy of discretion. We show that when policy makers operate under discretion (i.e. they can readjust interest rates in each period) rather than commitment (where they cannot deviate from a predetermined adjustment path), output and inflation losses from stabilization policy are larger. This is the 'stabilization bias' of a policy of discretion.

In the RBC model, business cycles can be viewed as *equilibrium phenomena*, because cyclical behaviour is the result of agents optimally adjusting their labour–leisure choice in response to exogenous and persistent technology shocks. Moreover, given that there are no imperfections in this model, welfare cannot be improved by the intervention of a policy maker. Hence there is no role for stabilization policy in the macro-economy in an RBC model. We shall see that although cycles in the NK model are also equilibrium cycles, the presence of imperfections in the economy (namely sticky prices) means that welfare can be improved by the presence of an inflation-targeting central bank.

## 16.2 The real business cycle model

### 16.2.1 Introduction

Against the background of dissatisfaction with the empirical performance of the dominant large-scale forecasting models of the economy in the 1970s and the vulnerability of models with backward-looking expectations to the Lucas critique, a completely new research programme in macroeconomics was established (see Chapter 4). The real business cycle model was developed from New Classical macroeconomics and the early developers were Robert Lucas, Thomas Sargent, Finn Kydland and Edward Prescott.[1] Their objective was to build a model of business cycles based on the neo-classical growth model, creating a unified model of growth and cycles with intra- and inter-temporally optimizing agents.

We introduced the standard Solow model in Chapter 8. The RBC model takes the Ramsey version of the Solow model, i.e. where a constant savings ratio is replaced by optimizing households who choose their savings rate. To this are added rational expectations and shocks to technology. The behaviour of all agents is captured by the so-called deep parameters, which characterize the production and utility functions. The macro model built on these foundations is invariant to policy. The name real business cycle (RBC) comes from the source of the fluctuations, which is on the supply side. It is shifts in the production function, referred to as 'technology shocks', which are believed to be the source of the fluctuations in economic activity that are observed in real world economies.

A fundamental feature of this approach is that business cycles arise because of exogenous technology shocks, and that these shocks result in economic fluctuations because of the way agents respond to the new opportunities they face as a consequence of the shocks. For example, following a negative technology shock, which reduces real wages, the economy is in a business cycle trough and the reduction in aggregate hours worked in the economy is the outcome of employees choosing to supply less labour. Since fluctuations in employment are due to choices made by workers about their labour supply, the unemployment in a business cycle trough is voluntary. When cycles are equilibrium phenomena, as they are in the RBC framework, there is no presumption that policy intervention to 'stabilize' the economy would improve welfare.

By comparison, in the 3-equation model, business cycles can result from shocks to equilibrium output (as in the case of an oil shock or a shift in union bargaining power or in the rate of productivity growth) or from shocks to aggregate demand, which shift the economy away from the equilibrium. In both cases, because of the sluggish adjustment of economic agents, output is shifted away from equilibrium and there is a role for economic policy to minimize the costs of the shock. Cycles are therefore modelled as *disequilibrium* phenomena in the 3-equation model, even if the source of the shock is on the supply side, and as *equilibrium* phenomena in the RBC model.

As an example, take a negative shift in aggregate demand, which in the context of imperfect competition in the 3-equation model, leads firms to cut back their production. The reduction in hours worked in the economy in a recession is interpreted as the consequence of there being fewer jobs available: weak aggregate demand in the economy leads firms to cut back

---

[1] See Lucas (1972); Sargent and Wallace (1975); Kydland and Prescott (1977).

employment and hours of work, by reducing overtime, for example. In contrast to the RBC model, in the 3-equation model, unemployment in a recession is involuntary and above the equilibrium level (where there is also involuntary unemployment). Welfare can be improved by policy intervention.

### Shocks and their propagation in the RBC model

The major propagation mechanism in the RBC model, which turns random shocks to technology into business cycle fluctuations, is the way that households react to changes in the real interest rate and the real wage. Household consumption and labour supply behaviour are at the core of the model because households care about their utility now and in the future. To maximize their utility over their planning horizon, households will make decisions about both savings and consumption, and work and leisure.

In Chapter 1, we modelled how households conforming to the permanent income hypothesis choose *consumption* by optimizing subject to their intertemporal budget constraint. They look ahead and make a calculation about their permanent income in order to choose between consumption today and consumption in the future. Higher consumption in the future will require households to undertake additional saving today. The three ingredients in their decision are their permanent income, the real interest rate and their subjective discount rate.

In the RBC models, we add to the consumption/saving decision the consumption/leisure choice, in which households decide how many hours to work today (and earn income, which they then decide to save or consume). Just as with the unconstrained households in Chapter 1, where they could borrow and lend freely to implement their optimal consumption plan, the extension to include the work–leisure choice assumes that households freely choose between leisure and consumption each period. If this assumption holds, then households can respond to economic shocks by raising or lowering their hours of work. The labour market is modelled as perfectly competitive so a worker can always increase or decrease their hours of work at the prevailing real wage and it is assumed that complete employment contracts exist. The microeconomic foundations of the labour market are like the hiring hall case explained in the Appendix to Chapter 1. The *intertemporal elasticity of labour supply* plays an important role in propagating shocks.[2] The intertemporal elasticity (also known as the Frisch elasticity) of labour supply is the percentage change in hours that arises as a result of a given percentage change in wages (holding constant the marginal utility of wealth).

### 16.2.2 The RBC model and business cycle facts

In addition to the core ideas about the source of fluctuations and the way they are propagated in the economy to produce cycles, the RBC approach has established a methodology for characterizing business cycles. The method is to take quarterly GDP data and to use a statistical procedure called filtering to separate trend growth from business cycle fluctuations. Figure 16.1 shows an example of this using the most commonly used filter, the H-P or Hodrick-Prescott filter, for the USA for the period from 1952 Q1 until 2012 Q1.[3] The H-P filter

---

[2] Landmark articles include the following: Kydland and Prescott (1982); Long and Plosser (1983).

[3] The business cycle facts shown in this subsection have been compiled based on the methodology used in King and Rebelo (1999).

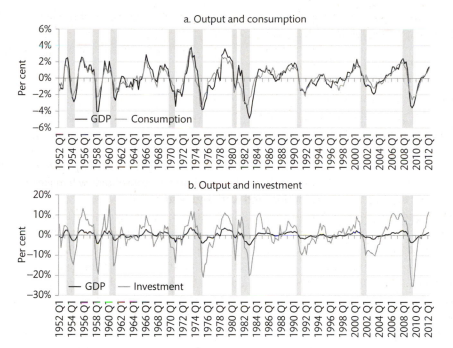

**Figure 16.1** Cyclical components of US macroeconomic indicators: 1952 Q1–2012 Q1
a. Output and consumption
b. Output and investment.

*Source:* US Bureau of Economic Analysis; US Census Bureau (data accessed June 2012).

*Note:* All variables have been detrended using a Hodrick-Prescott filter. Output, consumption and investment are in per capita terms. Grey shaded areas represent recessions as defined by NBER.

is a more sophisticated method of detrending a logged data series than using a linear trend as it solves a minimization problem that takes into account both the 'goodness of fit' and the 'smoothness' of the detrended series.[4] The RBC literature is concerned with explaining the cyclical component of macroeconomic time series isolated from long-run trends in this way.

As shown in Fig. 16.1, this method of estimating the cyclical component in the GDP data shows that output is up to 4% above trend in the peaks and up to 5% below trend in the troughs. We can also see that the magnitude of fluctuations in output and consumption are very similar, whereas investment is much more volatile (note the difference in the scale used to compare output and consumption in panel (a) with that used to compare output and investment in panel (b)). The shaded bands are the recessions as defined by the National Bureau of Economic Research (NBER).

Using the filter procedure to remove the trend from the various series, the RBC modellers begin their analysis by presenting a set of business cycle facts. They focus on the *volatility* of the key variables, the extent to which the variables move together over the cycle (this is called *co-movement*) and how *persistent* are the series. The initial aim of RBC modellers was

---

[4] A linear trend would be completely 'smooth', but it is not likely to provide a very good 'fit'.

**Table 16.1**   Business cycle statistics for the US economy.

| | Volatility | | Comovement | Persistence |
|---|---|---|---|---|
| | Standard deviation | Relative standard deviation | Contemporaneous correlation with output | First-order autocorrelation |
| Output | 1.61 | 1 | 1 | 0.85 |
| Consumption | 1.28 | 0.80 | 0.89 | 0.86 |
| Investment | 7.42 | 4.61 | 0.89 | 0.80 |
| Output per hour | 1.08 | 0.67 | 0.44 | 0.72 |
| Hours per worker | 0.53 | 0.33 | 0.73 | 0.82 |
| Real wages | 0.90 | 0.56 | 0.17 | 0.74 |
| Employment | 1.38 | 0.86 | 0.80 | 0.92 |
| Unemployment | 13.24 | 8.22 | −0.82 | 0.89 |

*Note:* All variables are in logarithms and have been detrended using a Hodrick-Prescott filter. Output, Consumption and Investment are in per capita terms.
*Source:* US Bureau of Economic Analysis; US Bureau of Labor Statistics; US Census Bureau (data accessed June 2012).

to build a model based on microfoundations that was capable of replicating the business cycle facts seen in the aggregate level data (see Section 16.2.4).

Table 16.1 shows the facts that motivate the modelling. In the first column is the standard deviation of GDP, consumption, investment, hourly productivity, hours per worker, real wages, employment and unemployment. The second column shows the standard deviation of each variable relative to that of GDP. This matches the facts we saw in Chapter 1, namely, that consumption is less volatile than output and investment is much more volatile. In addition, we see that the real wage is much less volatile than GDP whereas unemployment is much more volatile.

Lastly, we see that hours per worker are much less responsive to changes in output than employment (see also Fig. 16.2). This business cycle fact is not supportive of a key propagation mechanism of RBC models—that workers adjust their hours in response to exogenous technology shocks (which affect real wages).

The third column shows the co-movement (or correlation) of each series with GDP. Consumption, investment, employment and hours of work are pro-cyclical (positive co-movement with output), whereas unemployment is counter-cyclical. Productivity is also pro-cyclical, but real wages are only weakly (positively) correlated with GDP. The final column reports the persistence of each series. In all series, there is a strong correlation between the variable in period $t$ and in period $t - 1$. Growth above trend in one year is typically followed by growth above trend the following year: the economy does not jump from boom to bust year by year.

### 16.2.3 **The model and its properties**

It is important to keep in mind that the RBC modellers did not work backwards from the facts or from apparently important features of the real world to make their modelling decisions. Instead of such an inductive approach, they deliberately began with a very simple (and manifestly unrealistic) model and wanted to see how well such a model was able to match

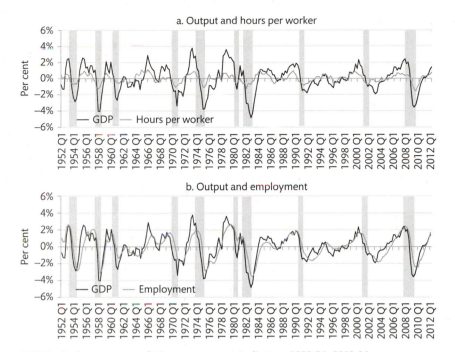

**Figure 16.2** Cyclical components of US macroeconomic indicators: 1952 Q1–2012 Q1
a. Output and hours per worker
b. Output and employment.

*Source:* US Bureau of Economic Analysis; US Bureau of Labor Statistics; US Census Bureau (data accessed June 2012).

*Note:* All variables have been detrended using a Hodrick-Prescott filter. Output is in per capita terms. Grey shaded areas represent recessions as defined by NBER.

the business cycle facts described above. Viewing the RBC approach as one of explicitly adopting a deductive method makes it easier to understand (a) the rationale for the very unrealistic assumptions and (b) the focus on whether an economy with these features can generate fluctuations that match those in a real economy. It contrasts with the inductive approach in the 3-equation model where the microfoundations are based on incomplete contracts and imperfect competition to reflect the presence of involuntary unemployment in equilibrium and the response of output and employment to shocks to aggregate demand.

At its simplest, a RBC model makes the following assumptions (see Web Appendix).

1. The economy is made up of a large number of identical agents who are assumed to live forever. Each agent is referred to as a 'representative agent'.

2. When saving goes up, it is invested and this therefore results in a larger capital stock the following period.

3. There is perfect competition and perfect information.

4. Expectations are formed rationally.

5. There is full flexibility of nominal wages and prices. We shall therefore work entirely in real terms.

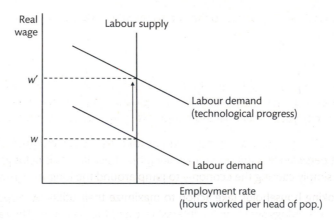

**Figure 16.3** Steady state growth in the Ramsey model.

6.  The economy is disturbed by so-called technology shocks that temporarily and randomly shift the production function. These technology shocks have inbuilt persistence, which means that they die out slowly.

*Long-run properties*

It is useful to begin by briefly describing how the economy evolves over the long run in the RBC world. At the heart of the model is the famous Solow growth model (from Chapter 8), modified to include optimizing households. In Solow's model, the economy is characterized by a production function, a constant saving rate and a constant growth rate of the population. In the simplest case, the economy grows along a steady state growth path with a constant real wage and real interest rate. Solow then introduced a special form of technological progress into the model. This exogenous technological progress appears like manna from heaven to raise output per worker hour every period. In the Solow model with technological progress, the output per head and real wage in the economy therefore grow in steady state at a constant rate fixed by the rate of exogenous technological progress. When optimizing households are introduced to the Solow model, it is called the Ramsey model: instead of a constant saving ratio, the saving rate is decided by households in the same way as in the permanent income model of Chapter 1 and depends on the real interest rate and the subjective discount rate.

Figure 16.3 summarizes steady state growth in the Ramsey model: in the steady state, with a constant rate of population growth, the employment rate (i.e. hours worked per head of the population) is also constant. This is shown by the vertical labour supply curve in Fig. 16.3. The labour demand curve shifts upward each period at the rate of exogenous technological progress. Labour productivity and real wages rise at this constant rate. The predictions of the long-run growth model accord with the fact that productivity has grown at approximately 2–2.5% per annum in the advanced countries over the long run and there has been no long-run tendency for the employment rate to rise. In the RBC model, the fact that a rising real wage over long periods has not been accompanied by a rising employment rate is interpreted as an inelastic labour supply curve. We follow that interpretation, which is consistent with the vertical labour supply curve used in Chapter 2. This allows all attention in the model to be on the household's response to the change in *intertemporal* opportunities caused by technology shocks.[5]

### Short-run properties

The RBC model can be thought of as providing an account of cycles based on introducing shocks to the process of exogenous technological change in the Ramsey model. A technology shock produces an equilibrium business cycle for two main reasons:

1. The shock itself is assumed to hit the economy and then to die out gradually over time. This in-built persistence is important in making the shock last. This helps generate cycles rather than simply causing the economy to jump around the long-run growth trend.

2. Forward-looking households take action to maximize their utility by responding to the effect of the technology shock on the interest rate and the wage rate. They are motivated to respond because they prefer a smooth path of consumption. This behaviour helps to sustain the effects of the technology shock on output, employment and the capital stock.

The economy begins in equilibrium and is disturbed by a random positive shock to the economy's production function. This shifts the production function in a way that increases both the marginal product of labour and the marginal product of capital. In the competitive model, this means a higher real wage and a higher real interest rate (which in this model is the same as the rate of return on capital).

The representative household makes its choices in response to the change in the rate of interest and the real wage, taking into account the way the shock affects its future choices. The agent makes decisions based on the fact that there is an infinite future. As we emphasized in Chapter 1, households value a smooth consumption path. This means the agent will want to optimize on two margins. The agent will ensure that the last unit of consumption today provides the same utility as the last unit of consumption *tomorrow* is expected to provide, by responding to the higher interest rate (adjusting savings) and to the higher real wage (adjusting hours).

First, the agent will want to ensure that the subjective marginal rate of substitution (MRS) between consumption today and consumption tomorrow is equal to the objective marginal rate of transformation (MRT) between consumption today and consumption tomorrow. The subjective MRS reflects how much consumption tomorrow would be required to compensate households for giving up one unit of consumption today if utility is to be held constant. And the objective MRT reflects how much consumption can be increased tomorrow by sacrificing one unit of consumption today (and saving it). The reason the MRS and the MRT have changed is that the *technology shock increased the rate of interest*, making the (objective) returns from saving now go up (i.e. the MRT increases)—the agent rationally expects the interest rate to go down later. This makes saving in this period more attractive, which will boost consumption tomorrow at the expense of consumption today (i.e. because of the household's response, the MRS increases in line with the increase in the MRT).

Second, the agent will want to ensure that the subjective MRS between consumption today and consumption tomorrow is equal to the objective MRT between the return from

---

[5] For further discussion, see for example, Chapter 4 of Romer (2011).

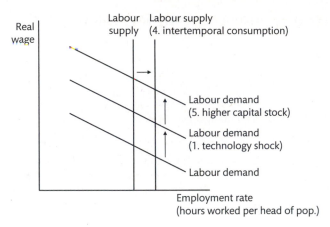

**Figure 16.4** The real business cycle model: an exogenous positive technology shock (see the summary below for the interpretation of the numbers).

working today and the return from working tomorrow. In this case, the MRS is the same as above, but the interpretation of the MRT changes. It now reflects how much consumption can be increased tomorrow by sacrificing one unit of leisure today, i.e. working one unit more and saving that income. The reason that the MRS and the MRT have changed is that the *technology shock increased the wage*, making working relatively more attractive in this period (i.e. the MRT increases). Again, this will boost consumption tomorrow, at the expense of consumption today (i.e. because of the household's response, the MRS increases in line with the increase in the MRT).

The changes in consumption have resulted in an increase in savings in the current period. In the RBC model, savings are entirely transformed into investment—this is easiest to imagine if households are also the firms in the model. Although this is not necessary in the model it helps highlight how different it is from the important feature of the 3-equation model that decisions about savings are made by different agents in fundamentally different ways from decisions about investment (see Chapter 1). In a Keynesian model, an important problem for the macro-economy is that there is no automatic mechanism that transforms savings into investment. In an RBC model, an increase in savings as a result of the shock to technology also increases investment, leading to an expansion of the capital stock. The higher capital stock further boosts labour demand.

*Summary*

The shock has the following effects. In each case the effect is measured relative to the steady state equilibrium of the economy.

1. Output goes up because of the technology shock (with the same inputs, there is higher output).

2. The wage and interest rate go up (because of the technology shock).

3. Consumption goes up but not by as much as output (households smooth the temporary shock over all future periods). Saving and therefore investment go up (the rise in saving is the other side of the coin of consumption smoothing).

4. Hours of work go up (which reflects the shift in labour supply due to intertemporal substitution).

5. The savings are automatically invested in new capital stock, which shifts the labour demand curve the following period helping to amplify the initial shock.

6. As the technology shock peters out, the economy gradually returns to the steady state growth path.

Steps 1–3 and 5 and their unwinding over time generate a cycle for output, consumption and investment as a result of the technology shock. Step 4 is necessary in order to get fluctuations in employment (hours). In Fig. 16.4, we show a stylized picture of how the positive shock to the underlying process of technical change shifts the economy away from the long-run equilibrium growth path and produces an equilibrium real business cycle.

### 16.2.4 **Results**

To test how well the RBC model 'fits the data', the output of the model is used to create a set of business cycle statistics. This table can then be compared to the actual US business cycle data from Table 16.1 to ascertain the extent to which fluctuations in the US economy are consistent with those predicted by the model. The process of calibrating and solving the model to build a table of business cycle statistics entails a number of steps:[6]

1. Choose functional forms for the equations that underpin the basic neoclassical model (such as the production function and the utility function of households). These choices fix the important parameters in the model that need to be estimated.

2. Calibrate the model by assigning values to these parameters (e.g. as we shall see below, capital's share, $\alpha$, in the Cobb Douglas production function) based on their long-run values from actual data or estimates from studies using, for example, microeconomic data in the economy being studied.

3. Use historical data to find the Solow residual, which is a proxy for the technology shocks (see below).

4. Use the Solow residual to shock the *calibrated* model and produce *simulations* of the path of the *model economy* over time.

5. Detrend the simulations from the model economy using the HP filter. This splits out each macroeconomic variable into a cyclical and a trend component.

6. Use the cyclical components of the simulations from the model economy to create a table of business cycle statistics. Compare the moments (e.g. standard deviations and correlations) produced by the simulated model economy with those calculated from the actual economy (see Table 16.1).

---

[6] This set of steps follows the methodology used in King and Rebelo (1999).

The basic business cycle model produces outcomes that are viewed as matching many aspects of the data, as stated in the conclusion to King, Plosser and Rebelo (1988):[7]

> When driven by highly persistent technology shocks, the basic neoclassical model is capable of replicating some stylized facts of economic fluctuations. First, the model generates procyclical employment, consumption and investment. Second, the model generates the observed rankings of relative volatility in investment, output and consumption.

The ability of this very simple model to fit the fluctuations observed in the macroeconomy has been part of its lasting appeal among an influential group of macroeconomists. It seemed to provide a new way of doing macroeconomics that was immune to the Lucas critique. It was also welcomed as offering the possibility of rigorous analysis of government intervention because the building blocks of the model reflect the optimizing decisions of the micro-agents not empirical correlations that could be policy dependent. After setting out the model we discuss its shortcomings in Section 16.2.5.

### Calculating the Solow residual

The key impulse mechanism for business cycles in RBC models is technology shocks. The Solow residual is the most commonly used proxy for technology shocks in the RBC tradition. We introduced the concept of the Solow residual when we discussed growth accounting in Chapter 8.

This subsection will elaborate on step 3 of the process described above and show how the Solow residual can be calculated from historical macroeconomic data.[8] This will also allow us to see how the US Solow residual has evolved over the past 60 years. The calculation of the Solow residual begins with the production function. For the RBC, a Cobb-Douglas production function is typically used:

$$y_t = B_t K_t^\alpha N_t^{1-\alpha}, \qquad \text{(production function)}$$

where $y_t$ equals output, $K_t$ is the capital input, $N_t$ is the labour input and $B_t$ is total factor productivity or the *Solow residual*. The $\alpha$ in the production function is a constant between zero and one. We can rearrange the production function to find an expression for the Solow residual:

$$B_t = \frac{y_t}{K_t^\alpha N_t^{1-\alpha}}. \qquad \text{(Solow residual)}$$

The Solow residual is a measure of output per weighted factor input; a measure of productivity. The change in the Solow residual is the portion of economic growth that cannot be accounted for by changes in measurable factor inputs (e.g. labour and capital), hence it is often referred to as total factor productivity growth.

The next stage is to find macroeconomic data corresponding to the variables and to the parameter $\alpha$ on the right hand side of the equation. In a competitive equilibrium (which the RBC model assumes), $\alpha$ is the share of national income that goes to the capital input and $1 - \alpha$ is the share that goes to the labour input. In the postwar US data, labour's share of

---

[7] See p. 231 of King, Plosser and Rebelo (1988).

[8] This calculation of the Solow residual follows the methodology used in Chapter 8 of Williamson (2011).

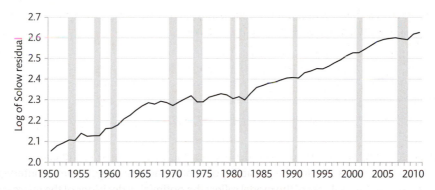

**Figure 16.5** Natural log of the US Solow residual (total factor productivity): 1950–2011.

*Source:* US Bureau of Economic Analysis; US Bureau of Labor Statistics (data accessed August 2012).

national income is on average around two-thirds. We therefore set $1 - \alpha$ at 64% (i.e. 0.64), which is the value used by Prescott (1986). This means $\alpha$ is set at 0.36 and that the equation becomes:

$$B_t = \frac{y_t}{K_t^{0.36} N_t^{0.64}} \quad \text{(Solow residual)}$$

We can use macroeconomic data to find the Solow residual in any given year in the past. We use real GDP as a measure of $y_t$, the real net stock of private fixed assets as a measure of $K_t$ and total employment as a measure of $N_t$. Figure 16.5 shows the path of the natural log of the Solow residual between 1950 and 2011. We can see from the figure that:

1. total factor productivity has trended upwards over time (a long-run trend rate of TFP growth of 0.94% p.a.)[9];

2. recessions are typically associated with falls in TFP (as shown by the shaded grey bars in Fig. 16.5)[10]; and

3. from the late 1960s through the early 1980s, there was a period of substantial productivity slowdown.

Many economists, including Solow himself, disagree with using the Solow residual to proxy for short-run technology shocks. We discuss their criticisms in Section 16.2.5.

## A fundamentally different approach to macroeconomic analysis

The RBC modellers championed a fundamentally new approach to macroeconomic analysis. One of the fathers of the RBC movement, Edward Prescott, states that 'business cycle theory uses *deductive* or *quantitative theoretic inference*'.[11] In this approach, the model is not the outcome of the research, but it is a tool that is used to deduce the implications of theory. The RBC modellers marked a distinct departure from the existing macroeconomic literature, which

---

[9] The long-run trend rate of TFP growth is calculated as the compound annual growth rate of TFP between 1950 and 2011.

[10] The shaded grey bars are recessions as defined by the National Bureau of Economic Research (NBER).

[11] See p. 1 of Prescott (1998).

was seen as being more *inductive*. In inductive research, the model or law is the outcome of the research. Prescott saw using empirical estimation or induction as the tool for deriving models, which were then used to make deductive inferences, as bad scientific practice.[12]

The cornerstone of RBC modelling is that it uses a model based on micro-foundations to answer quantitative questions about the macro-economy. For example, RBC models could be used to answer questions such as; what is the quantitative effect of a rise in income tax on hours worked and output? Or, what are the size and persistence of aggregate fluctuations following a positive technology shock?

The general process for these deductive studies is as follows. Firstly, pose a quantitative question. Then, use theories that have been subject to rigorous empirical testing, such as neoclassical growth theory, to construct a model economy. Thirdly, calibrate that model using long-run real-world data. And lastly, use the model economy to answer your quantitative question. Prescott and Kydland also referred to this research procedure as 'the computational experiment' and practitioners are often said to be 'building quantitative laboratories'.[13]

There are many examples in the literature of the quantitative laboratory tradition, which has become increasingly sophisticated over time:

1. Kydland and Prescott's landmark paper used a competitive equilibrium model to explain aggregate fluctuations in the US economy. The authors state that the 'preference technology environment was the simplest one that explained the quantitative co-movements and the serial correlation properties of output'.[14]

2. Krusell and Smith altered the original RBC framework to test the quantitative implications of removing the representative agent assumption and replacing it with a more realistic model of consumer behaviour, which allowed for heterogeneity in income and wealth.[15]

3. More recent literature has sought to use RBC-type modelling to gather practical insights for public policy. For example, Heathcote et al. (2010) use a dynamic macroeconomic model to study the quantitative and welfare implications of prominent US labour market trends, such as the increase in the returns to college education and a closing of the gender pay gap.

### 16.2.5 Criticisms of the RBC model

#### The impulse and propagation mechanisms

In the RBC model, it is exogenous shocks to technology that are the principle impulses driving business cycles, but what are these technology shocks? Little evidence is provided in the literature on the source or nature of these shocks. As we have seen, for lack of a better alternative, the 'Solow residual' is often used by RBC proponents to proxy for technology. The Solow residual is the portion of economic growth that cannot be accounted for by changes in measurable factor inputs (e.g. labour and capital).

---

[12] See Prescott (1998).

[13] See Pavoni (2008) for a more thorough discussion of the history of RBC modelling.

[14] See Kydland and Prescott (1988).        [15] See Krusell and Smith (1998).

The Solow residual had its origins in the growth accounting literature. These economists are sceptical of the RBC theorists' use of the Solow residual as a measure of short-run technology shocks, as perfectly summed up by King and Rebelo (1999):[16]

> The stated goal of that [growth accounting] literature was to measure the long-run evolution of disembodied technical progress, not the short-run behavior of productivity. Its hidden agenda was to make the Solow residual negligible, that is, to measure production inputs well enough that all growth in output could be accounted for by movements in factors of production. For this reason the residual was often referred to as a 'measure of our ignorance'. Growth accountants were horrified when they saw the measure of their ignorance recast as the main impulse to the business cycle.

Another important criticism of using this proxy is that movements in the Solow residual might not just reflect technological change, but also market imperfections, such as labour hoarding and monopoly power.[17] These imperfections produce problems of measurement error, where the Solow residual implies a change in total factor productivity when in fact none has taken place. Labour hoarding, for example, is the name given to the phenomenon when labour is underutilized during a recession. Labour hoarding occurs when firms expect a recession to be temporary and are reluctant to lay off expensively trained staff. If the Solow residual is calculated using employment (as we have in Fig. 16.5), then underutilization of labour during a recession will imply that TFP has fallen, when in fact the reduction in output is simply the result of employees working less hard (or less hours) than they did before the downturn.[18]

Another key criticism of the model is that it requires there to be periods of technological regress to produce business cycles. It is hard to imagine periods since WWII where technology went backwards. To address this, RBC modellers widened the scope of what they consider to be technology shocks. Hansen and Prescott (1993) argue that changes in regulatory and legal systems within a country can be considered as technology shocks and could be negative. The plausibility of this interpretation of technology shocks as a good fit is disputed by Calomiris and Hanes (1995), who believe it is incompatible with the long-run macroeconomic data. They cite the fact that regulatory and legal interventions in the US economy were much smaller before the First World War but business cycles were much larger.[19] If regulatory and legal shocks were in fact causing business cycles, you would expect business cycles to be larger *after* the First World War.

An alternative approach to make the model more realistic is to adjust the model itself. King and Rebelo (1999) formulate an RBC model with varying capital utilization, which can produce realistic business cycles (judged by the behaviour of the moments from the simulated model economy as discussed above) from small, nonnegative changes in technology.

Lastly, and very importantly, the propagation of the technology shock through the economy requires the initial impulse to be very persistent. The 'memory' coefficient on the productivity shock must be very high (typically around 0.9) to produce the business cycles we see in the data. There is no economic justification or micro-foundation for this assumption. Without a persistent shock the model produces very weak dynamics and does not fit the data well.

---

[16] See pp. 962–3 of King and Rebelo (1999).     [17] See Summers (1986).
[18] See Chapter 12 of Williamson (2011).     [19] See Hartley et al. (1997).

## The labour market

The original form of the RBC model relies on the intertemporal substitution between labour and leisure to help drive business cycles. To match the model in this regard, we would expect the actual data to show that aggregate hours and productivity vary closely with output, which would imply that hours per worker vary closely with output and that the real wage would be strongly procyclical, as this is one of the mechanisms that induces agents to substitute between labour and leisure.

In the data for the US economy presented in Kydland and Prescott (1982), aggregate hours worked are much more variable than productivity, which is not supportive of the model. What is driving the observed variability in aggregate hours if it is not movements in hours per worker? Figure 16.4 shows that employment varies more with output than does hours per worker, suggesting that changes in employment are the key factor driving changes in aggregate hours.

Again, the RBC model can be modified to better fit the data in this regard. As an example, Hansen (1985) uses a model of indivisible labour (where workers can either work a set amount of hours or not at all) and Christiano and Eichenbaum (1992) allow government consumption shocks to influence labour market dynamics. The output of these models is capable of replicating the actual US labour market data much more closely than the original RBC model.

The second labour market prediction of the model is for a strongly procyclical real wage. The real wage is shown to be acyclical or mildly procyclical in the data. An acyclical or mildly procyclical real wage is consistent with the imperfect labour market model introduced in Chapter 2. In such a model, shocks are mainly demand shocks and the economy moves around the equilibrium rate with the real wage lying in between the upward–sloping wage-setting and the fairly flat price-setting curve. The inconsistency between the RBC model and the data could be rectified by modifying the model, by using indivisible labour (see above) or by allowing labour supply shocks to coincide with productivity shocks.[20]

The key labour market propagation mechanism in the model is the intertemporal (or Frisch) elasticity of labour supply, which indicates how readily workers are willing to substitute labour and leisure over time. Microeconomic studies have shown little evidence that workers carry out enough intertemporal substitution to justify the fluctuations in aggregate hours shown in the data.[21] This point is emphasized in Chetty et al. (2011), who conduct a review of existing studies and find that:[22]

> micro estimates of intertemporal substitution (Frisch) elasticities are an order of magnitude smaller than the values needed to explain business cycle fluctuations in aggregate hours by preferences.

## Modelling approach

Real business cycle models have become more sophisticated in recent years. The early models were built on microfoundations, but these model economies were composed entirely

---

[20] See Holland and Scott (1998).      [21] See Ashenfelter (1984).      [22] See p. 471 of Chetty et al. (2011).

of identical representative agents solving dynamic optimization problems. They did not undertake a serious analysis of heterogeneity or aggregation, which limited the extent to which they could provide accurate quantitative conclusions.[23] Hartley at al. (1997) provide a detailed critique of this phase of RBC modelling. They found that alternative models (e.g. those based on Keynesian assumptions) do as good a job of mimicking the data, on the usual aesthetic standards, as does the RBC model. Over the past 15 years there has been a major research effort in constructing heterogeneous agent RBC models.

The Hodrick-Prescott detrending method is at the heart of the original RBC models. This filtering technique strips out the steady state trend from macroeconomic data series and leaves only the cyclical fluctuations. The use of the H-P filter as a method of detrending data has been criticized on many grounds. Common criticisms are that it induces spurious cycles and that it makes the implicit assumption that the extracted trend is a good approximation of the steady state, for which no evidence is offered.[24]

Canova (1998) analyses the effects on the 'business cycle facts' of using different filtering techniques. He finds that the detrending method used can substantially alter the business cycle facts produced from a real-world dataset. His findings warn against building theoretical models to mimic the fluctuations in data detrended using a particular filter because the data the models are trying to mimic changes drastically if, for example, an alternative filtering technique to the H-P one is used.

### 16.2.6 The impact of RBC modelling

RBC modelling has had a huge impact since its introduction in the early 1980s, which was reflected in Kydland and Prescott winning the Nobel Prize for Economics in 2004. The approach has both supporters and detractors and is the subject of much debate. Agreement may be possible on the following contributions RBC modelling has made to the development of academic macroeconomics:

1. The models focus on micro-foundations. In other words, they attempt to pin down how the reaction of individual agents to shocks generates aggregate fluctuations. This was influenced by the desire of macroeconomists to build models that were more robust to the Lucas critique. However, the choice of microfoundations remains open to dispute.

2. Since they are micro-founded structural models, RBC models are better able to analyse the causal effects of policy—assuming the behaviour incorporated in the structural equations is a good representation of the economy under study—than are ad hoc empirical models. Recent econometric developments where RBC models are estimated have allowed for proper shock decompositions to be carried out to determine what has driven changes in the data.

3. It refocused macroeconomics on real causes of business cycles.

4. The device of building a model economy is a potentially valuable methodology. More realistic microeconomic foundations can be introduced, which is what the widely used New Keynesian DSGE models have done (see Section 16.3). Dynamic macroeconomic models

---

[23] See Hartley et al. (1997).      [24] See Hartley et al. (1997).

(i.e. quantitative laboratories) can be useful tools for quantifying the welfare implications of economic policy or changes in society such as ageing (as shown by the Heathcote et al. (2010) paper discussed in Section 16.2.4).

## 16.3 The New Keynesian model and stabilization policy

### 16.3.1 The New Keynesian Phillips curve

The *New Keynesian Phillips curve (NKPC)* is the result of deriving a model of inflation by combining price stickiness with long-sighted decision-making. Price stickiness is modelled via the assumption introduced by Calvo (1983) that firms can change their price if they get the 'green light', which occurs randomly for each firm. Hence only a fraction of firms are able to adjust their price in each period. Interestingly, this way of modelling price rigidities has the consequence that when a firm gets the green light, it will take a forward-looking view and adjust its price taking into account the expected future sequence of output gaps. This will produce a jump in the prices set by the firms who are able to adjust: only being able to adjust price infrequently produces jumps in the price when adjustment is allowed. Hence inflation in the economy as a whole jumps in response to shocks. We shall see that the *NKPC* has some strange features, which have led Robert Solow to comment that although it might be new, it is neither Keynesian, nor a Phillips curve.[25]

The *NKPC* is derived from first principles in the Web Appendix to this chapter. This derivation produces the equation for the New Keynesian Phillips curve:

$$\pi_t = \psi E_t \pi_{t+1} + \frac{\delta(1 - (1 - \delta)\psi)}{1 - \delta}\alpha x_t. \qquad (NKPC)$$

When prices are set on the Calvo basis, inflation in period $t$ can be expressed as a function of two terms: (a) the rate of inflation that is expected to prevail *next period*, i.e. $E_t \pi_{t+1}$ multiplied by the discount rate, $\psi$, and (b) the output gap term, $\alpha x_t$, multiplied by a constant that depends on the share of firms that are able to change their price, $\delta$, and the discount rate. In this case, we express the output gap as $x_t \equiv \log y_t - \log y_e$.

*Comparing the NKPC and the adaptive expectations Phillips curve*

Before discussing the *NKPC* further, we write the adaptive expectations (i.e. backward-looking) Phillips curve using the same notation to make the comparison easier:

$$\pi_t = E_t \pi_t + \alpha x_t \qquad (16.1)$$

$$= \pi_{t-1} + \alpha x_t \qquad \text{(adaptive expectations Phillips curve)}$$

where, $E_t \pi_t = \pi_{t-1}$.

Unlike the standard Phillips curve discussed in Chapters 2 and 3, the expected inflation term in the *NKPC* relates not to the expected value of current inflation, but to next period's inflation. Second in the standard Phillips curve, the coefficient on the output gap is $\alpha$. In the *NKPC* it is $\frac{\delta(1-(1-\delta)\psi)}{1-\delta}\alpha$. As the proportion of firms that can adjust their price increases towards

---

[25] See Carlin et al. (2012)

one (i.e. $\delta \to 1$), the final term in the *NKPC* equation tends to infinity (i.e. $\frac{\delta(1-(1-\delta)\psi)}{1-\delta}\alpha \to \infty$). This implies that for $\delta = 1$, the output gap must be zero for inflation to be non-infinite. This says that with fully flexible prices, the Phillips curve is vertical.

An interesting feature of the *NKPC* is that unlike the adaptive expectations case, there is a *long-run* trade-off between output and inflation. With sticky prices, this is the case unless the discount factor, $\psi$, is equal to one. For $\psi < 1$, i.e. where the future has less weight than the present period, then in long-run equilibrium where $\pi_t = E_t\pi_{t+1}$, we have

$$\pi_t = \psi E_t\pi_{t+1} + \frac{\delta(1-(1-\delta)\psi)}{1-\delta}\alpha x_t$$

$$\pi_t = \psi\pi_t + \frac{\delta(1-(1-\delta)\psi)}{1-\delta}\alpha x_t$$

$$\pi_t(1-\psi) = \frac{\delta(1-(1-\delta)\psi)}{1-\delta}\alpha x_t$$

$$\pi_t = \frac{\delta(1-(1-\delta)\psi)}{(1-\psi)(1-\delta)}\alpha x_t = \text{constant} \times \alpha x_t. \qquad (\textit{NKPC}, \text{long-run equilibrium})$$

This means that a higher output gap is associated with a higher inflation rate in the long run—i.e. the 'long-run Phillips curve' is not vertical. The reason for this result is that because sluggishness is built into pricing via the Calvo process, with a discount factor less than one, a positive output gap forever is consistent with constant inflation. The lower is the discount factor, the bigger is the trade-off. Only with $\psi = 1$ does the trade-off disappear.

How does the term in inflation expected next period affect the *NKPC*? Because the *NKPC* includes expected future inflation and the adaptive expectations *PC* includes last period's inflation, very different predictions arise. There are three important ones. We compare the response of inflation to a temporary positive output gap using the standard adaptive expectations Phillips curve and the *NKPC* in Fig. 16.6.

Note that these differences are solely between the adaptive expectations Phillips curve and the *NKPC*. We are not comparing the differences between the 3-equation model and the New Keynesian (DSGE) model, to which we turn in the next subsection. This means that there is no policy maker in the example shown in Fig. 16.6—i.e. the figure shows the effects on inflation of an expected positive output gap, in the absence of any policy intervention.

1. First, a positive output gap is associated with rising inflation with the standard adaptive expectations Phillips curve and with falling inflation with the *NKPC*. Figure 16.6 sketches the time path of inflation and the output gap for the the two types of Phillips curve. The details of these results are set out in the Web Appendix to this chapter. The impulse response functions provide a number of interesting insights:

   (a) Adaptive expectations *PC*: as shown in Fig. 16.6a inflation begins to rise when the output gap occurs; it continues to rise until the positive output gap disappears. A positive output gap is associated with rising inflation.

   (b) *NKPC*: as shown in Fig. 16.6b, a positive output gap, which is anticipated by agents, is accompanied by a jump up in inflation as the firms that get the green light to adjust their price do so. Since this price adjustment happens instantly in the *NKPC* model,

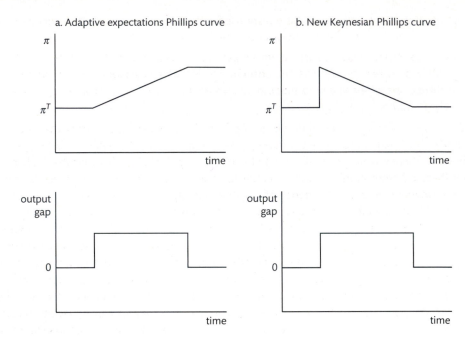

**Figure 16.6** The response of inflation to a temporary output gap
a. Adaptive expectations Phillips curve
b. New Keynesian Phillips curve.

over the period of the positive output gap, inflation is *falling*. At any point during the period when there is a positive output gap, firms are optimizing—e.g. just before the output gap disappears, inflation is just above the equilibrium level.

(c) Comparison between the *NKPC* model of price setting and arbitrage behaviour in the foreign exchange market: the behaviour of inflation and the output gap in the *NKPC* model is analogous to the uncovered interest parity (*UIP*) condition discussed in Chapter 9. In that case, when agents take the view that there will be an interest rate differential vis-à-vis the rest of the world for a period of time, home's nominal exchange rate jumps. If there is a positive interest differential, home's exchange rate appreciates and then depreciates over the period the interest differential prevails. This reflects arbitrage behaviour in a market (for foreign exchange) where prices jump to ensure that the expected return from holding home and foreign bonds (where the default risk is assumed to be identical) is the same. In the *NKPC* model, firms are forward-looking and predict that the output gap will only last for a set amount of time. The model only makes sense when they assume the output gap disappears at some future date, $T$. Given this, their optimal pricing strategy is to increase prices faster than normal (i.e. $\pi > \pi^T$) whilst there is a positive output gap and to return to their original pace of price increases (i.e. $\pi = \pi^T$) when the output gap disappears. Put another way, it is optimal for the firm's initial price rise to be more aggressive, the longer the output gap is expected to persist. This gives rise to the downward-sloping section of the inflation impulse response function in Fig. 16.6b, which coincides with the period when there is a positive output gap.

(d) In the *NKPC* model, a positive output gap is associated with falling inflation, which is the opposite pattern to the one observed under adaptive expectations. Inflation only falls in the adaptive expectations model when the output gap is *negative*.

2. Second, inflation is inertial in the standard Phillips curve: inflation this period is equal to its level last period modified by the output gap. By contrast, in the *NKPC*, inflation jumps whenever there is new information about the output gap. An interesting case that highlights why these different predictions may matter for policy makers is the global financial crisis (or the ongoing Japanese experience of negative output gaps and deflation). It was widely expected that the global financial crisis would be followed by a lengthy period of negative output gaps because of the impact of the banking crisis on the ability of firms and households to borrow and spend (see Chapters 6 and 7) and the limited ability of central banks to offset the shock because of the zero lower bound problem. For the purpose of this argument, we assume monetary policy is completely ineffective because the nominal interest rate is zero and we therefore compare the implications of the two different Phillips curves in the absence of a policy maker. The adaptive expectations Phillips curve predicts gradually falling inflation along with the negative output gaps. The *NKPC* predicts a jump drop in inflation in anticipation of the expected phase of output below equilibrium, followed by rising inflation during the period with output below equilibrium (i.e. the exact opposite of the path shown in Fig. 16.6b). The implications of the two models are different: from the Fisher equation, we know that $r = i - \pi_t^E$, and that aggregate demand depends on the real interest rate. If behaviour is captured by the *NKPC*, the rising expected inflation over the period with negative output gaps would reduce the real interest rate and help stimulate demand. In contrast to the *NKPC*, if behaviour is best characterized by adaptive expectations, then falling inflation over the period of negative output gaps pushes up the real interest rate and weakens aggregate demand further, highlighting the need for policy intervention to stimulate demand.

3. Third, with the adaptive expectations Phillips curve, disinflation is costly, because for inflation to be falling, there has to be a negative output gap. By contrast, if agents believe that expected future inflation will be lower, i.e. $E_t \pi_{t+1}$ goes down, then according to the *NKPC*, this will feed directly into current inflation via the term $E_t \pi_{t+1}$ and does not require a negative output gap. We return to this below where we introduce the policy maker explicitly.

The contrast between the way the two types of Phillips curve work can be highlighted by writing the *NKPC* in an alternative way, which brings out the fact that inflation depends on the entire future sequence of expected output gaps.[26] Since the *NKPC* relates current inflation to expected future inflation and the current output gap, it is possible to use

---

[26] See Rudd and Whelan (2007). This paper also provides a useful critical assessment of the NK model and tests its ability to fit the inflation data.

the method of repeated substitution explained in the footnote[27] to re-write the equation *NKPC* as

$$\pi_t = \Lambda\alpha \sum_{i=0}^{\infty} \psi^i E_t x_{t+i}, \text{ where we write} \qquad (NKPC, \text{alternative form})$$

$$\frac{\delta(1 - (1-\delta)\psi)}{1-\delta} \text{ as } \Lambda \text{ to simplify the notation.} \qquad (16.2)$$

This expression makes it very clear that inflation in period $t$ will jump in response to any news about future output gaps and that there is no role here for costly disinflation. It also highlights the role of credibility: the key to achieving low inflation now is for the central bank to commit to a sequence of future output gaps of zero, i.e. to forego targeting an output level above equilibrium.

### 16.3.2 Stabilization bias

The New Keynesian Phillips curve allows us to investigate the impact of the central bank being able to *commit* to a given adjustment path following economic shocks. In the cases we have looked at so far in this book, the policy maker has been characterized by *discretion*. Monetary policy makers in contemporary central banks practice discretion: they are able to re-optimize their policy stance (i.e. readjust interest rates) in each period.

We shall see that, even when the policy maker targets equilibrium output, a sub-optimal outcome occurs under discretion. Time inconsistency means that if it were possible to impose commitment, adjustment to shocks would be less costly. More costly adjustment to shocks under discretion is called 'stabilization bias'.

When considering the operation of stabilization policy under discretion and commitment in a macro model with a *NKPC*, two related results arise:

1.  Both the rise in inflation and the size of the negative output gap required to counteract an inflation shock are smaller under commitment than under discretion. This is called the *stabilization bias* of a policy of discretion. The response of the policy maker is 'too harsh' because it is unable to commit not to change the policy once the private sector sets prices.

---

[27] The first step is to take the original NKPC:

$$\pi_t = \psi E_t \pi_{t+1} + \Lambda\alpha x_t.$$

We can then use this relation to move the equation forward by one period and find an expression for $\pi_{t+1}$:

$$\pi_{t+1} = \psi E_{t+1}\pi_{t+2} + \Lambda\alpha x_{t+1}.$$

This is then substituted back into the original NKPC, such that:

$$\pi_t = \psi E_t(\psi E_{t+1}\pi_{t+2} + \Lambda\alpha x_{t+1}) + \Lambda\alpha x_t.$$

The process then carries on, hence the term 'repeated substitution'. The next stage is to get an expression for $\pi_{t+2}$ (using the original NKPC) and to substitute that into the equation above. This process is repeated an infinite number of times. We can then use a summation to get an expression for $\pi_t$ in terms of the entire future sequence of output gaps:

$$\pi_t = \Lambda\alpha \sum_{i=0}^{\infty} \psi^i E_t x_{t+i}.$$

Note that this derivation is based on the rule of iterated expectations, which implies that $E_t E_{t+1} = E_t$ etc.

2. The optimal policy rule under discretion is one that targets inflation (and produces stabilization bias), whereas the optimal rule with commitment targets the price level. This suggests that one reason we do not observe price-level targeting is that in the real world of policy making, achieving commitment is difficult. As a result, we see the time-consistent but sub-optimal policy of inflation-targeting.

The full dynamic stochastic general equilibrium (DSGE) model that lies behind these results is set out in Galí (2008) Chapter 5 and Walsh (2010) Chapter 11. We sketch the intuition, emphasizing the two results above.

The simplest way to see both the welfare benefits of commitment (price-level targeting) and the difficulty of achieving it is to consider a temporary (i.e. one period) inflation shock. We assume throughout this model that the central bank has an inflation target of zero. This implies a constant price level in equilibrium and is used for convenience.

We take first the situation of discretion, where the central bank re-optimizes each period. This looks similar to the familiar case of the 3-equation model: there is a downward-sloping *MR* curve in the inflation-output diagram (Fig. 16.7). The central bank responds to the infla-tion shock by 'leaning into the wind' and choosing its optimal response, which will entail a negative output gap. Since the shock lasts for only one period and price setters are forward looking (but cannot all adjust immediately to the shock), the one period with output below equilibrium induces firms who can adjust to re-set their prices downwards. This produces point A in Fig. 16.7a. In the following period, the economy is once more at Z, with output at equilibrium and inflation at target.

If the policy maker could announce its plan of minimizing its losses over a lengthy period of adjustment to the shock and could commit to sticking to it, it is able to respond to the shock with a smaller deviation of inflation from target and a smaller negative output gap. We can see this in Fig. 16.7, by comparing points A and A' and noting that $\pi_1 > \pi_1' > \pi^T$ and $y_1 < y_1' < y_e$.

What such a policy maker would do is to take advantage of its commitment to the least cost policy plan in order to influence private sector expectations. The plan would be to return more gradually to equilibrium: a smaller initial negative output gap would be followed by a further sequence of negative output gaps on the path to equilibrium. As shown in Fig. 16.7b the optimal plan under commitment sees inflation falling below target and gradually returning to target as the output gap is reduced.

Figure 16.8 highlights the differences in the outcomes under discretion and commitment. We can see that:

1. The 'footprint' (size of the deviations) of the adjustment path in the inflation-output di-agram is smaller under commitment (see Fig. 16.7). The more muted response under commitment highlights the stabilization bias that arises under discretion. Welfare is lower in the case of discretion because the higher costs in the first period outweigh the dis-counted value of the deviations in output and inflation over the adjustment period under commitment.

2. The price level is permanently higher in the case of discretion, whereas it returns to its initial level in the case of commitment (Fig. 16.8b). Only by having some time with inflation below target, which is possible with commitment but not discretion, can the price level return to its starting point (shown by $P = 100$ in Fig. 16.8b).

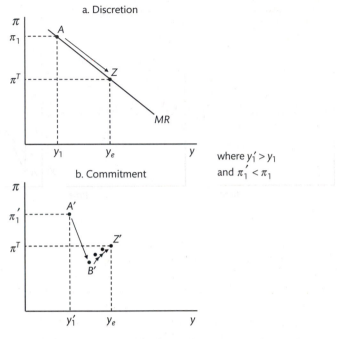

**Figure 16.7** Stabilization bias: commitment vs discretion—the adjustment path in the inflation-output diagram after an inflation shock.

3. The comparison between the two policies illustrates how time inconsistency works: since there is no persistence in the inflation shock itself, once inflation falls, the central bank will be tempted to abandon its plan and return to an output gap of zero. From that point forward, this would boost its welfare relative to sticking to the plan set out under commitment, since the squared deviations of inflation from target and output from equilibrium would be zero and hence less than the corresponding positions and welfare loss on the commitment plan. It is because the central bank would not stick to its announced plan when it has discretion that it is forced to tighten more than it would under the 'no choice to change' commitment policy: this produces the bias toward too much stabilization, i.e. stabilization bias.

### 16.3.3 NK DSGE modelling

The New Keynesian Dynamic Stochastic General Equilibrium (NK DSGE) model is the workhorse model for much of modern macroeconomics and it was adopted by research departments in central banks around the world in the years leading up to the global financial crisis.[28] It is derived from a RBC model and combines rational expectations of all agents with price stickiness. The model is expressed in terms of three equations: the New Keynesian Phillips curve equation (*NKPC*) introduced in the last subsection, the *IS* equation, which

---

[28] This section is not intended as standard teaching material at intermediate level but is a guide to the connection between the modelling in this book and widely used New Keynesian models.

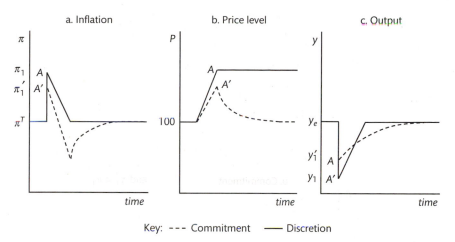

**Figure 16.8** Stabilization bias: commitment vs. Set out under commitment, discretion—impulse response functions for inflation, the price level and output after an inflation shock.

reflects the permanent income hypothesis, and a monetary rule equation that captures the behaviour of an inflation-targeting central bank (*MR*). Figure 16.9 shows the evolution of the NK DSGE model from its origins in the real business cycle model.

The structure of the NK model provides the basis for describing the policy regime often referred to as Taylor rule macroeconomics. The central bank in the NK model effectively picks both output and inflation using a Taylor rule consistent with the Taylor principle.[29] This contrasts with the example in Fig. 16.6 of the working of the *NKPC* in which the opening up of an output gap caused a response from forward-looking price setters. When a forward-looking central bank is added to the *IS* and the *NKPC* to create the NK model, output and inflation are jointly determined by equilibrium decisions at each point in time. We highlight the difference between this interpretation of Taylor rule macroeconomics and how it is interpreted in the 3-equation model below.

The NK model is different from the 3-equation model (but similar to the RBC model), because rational expectations and intertemporal optimization behaviour are assumed in both the *IS* and the *PC* relations (as well as in the *MR*). It is similar to the 3-equation model (but different from the RBC model), because it has real (imperfect competition) and nominal (sticky prices) rigidities. This means a policy rule incorporating the Taylor principle is required to ensure the economy stabilizes after a shock.

It is useful to clarify a number of important concepts that help when comparing the models as we have described them in this chapter. These are shown in Fig. 16.10.

1. A crucial concept in all three models is the flexible price equilibrium. When the economy is undisturbed by a shock, it is said to be in steady state equilibrium defined by the flexible price equilibrium. The flexible price equilibrium is the equilibrium level of output when prices and wages are flexible. It is often referred to as the natural rate in the NK model; in the 3-equation model, we use the term equilibrium rate or medium–run equilibrium.

---

[29] See Chapter 13 for a discussion of Taylor rules and the Taylor principle.

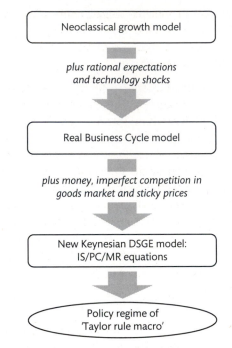

**Figure 16.9** The evolution of the New Keynesian DSGE model.

| | RBC model | NK DSGE model | 3-equation model |
|---|---|---|---|
| **Steady state equilibrium** | Flexible price equilibrium in the absence of shocks | | |
| **Flexible price equilibrium** | • first best | • natural rate of output given imperfect competition in product market<br>• *real* rigidity of imperfect competition in product market implies economy is not at first best equilibrium<br>• no involuntary unemployment | • equilibrium rate of output & unemployment given imperfect competition in labour and product markets<br>• *real* rigidities in labour and product markets mean economy is not at first best equilibrium<br>• involuntary unemployment |
| **Actual output and employment** | • shocks produce (efficient) equilibrium cycles around (efficient) flexible price equilibrium<br>• no role for stabilization policy | • shocks produce (inefficient) *equilibrium* cycles because of *nominal rigidity* (sticky prices) around (inefficient) flexible price equilibrium<br>• no involuntary unemployment<br>• underemployment as compared with flex price<br>• role for stabilization policy | • shocks produce (inefficient) *disequilibrium* cycles around (inefficient) flexible price equilibrium<br>• involuntary unemployment<br>• role for stabilization policy |

**Figure 16.10** Concepts of equilibrium in macroeconomic models as discussed in this chapter.

2. In the RBC model, the flexible price equilibrium is also the first best equilibrium. It is not possible to achieve higher welfare than at this equilibrium. However in the NK model, the flexible price equilibrium is not efficient (first best) because of the presence of imperfect

competition in the goods market. In principle, welfare could be improved if this imperfection could be removed. In the 3-equation model, there are imperfections in both labour and product markets. Because of the imperfections in the labour market, there is involuntary unemployment in the flexible price equilibrium.

3. When the economy is disturbed by shocks, the cycles that arise in the RBC model are equilibrium cycles. They are also efficient cycles because they represent first best outcomes: the labour market always clears. There is no role for a policy maker to improve welfare. In the NK model, a second kind of imperfection in addition to monopoly power in the goods market, namely price rigidity, keeps the economy away from the flexible price equilibrium in a way that could be improved on by the intervention of a policy maker. This explains the welfare-enhancing role of the central bank in this model and the rationale for a Taylor rule. Nevertheless, these cycles are still equilibrium cycles as they result from forward-looking best-response decision making by all parties. In the 3-equation model on the other hand, the deviations from the flexible price equilibrium are *disequilibrium* cycles. It is disequilibrium in the labour market that feeds back into price setting. Using a Taylor rule, the forward-looking central bank can improve welfare by steering the economy back to the flexible price equilibrium at least welfare cost.

Focusing just on the NK model and the 3-equation model, there are three important differences in the mechanisms at work. The first difference is that because all the private sector agents in the NK model are forward-looking with rational expectations, they 'solve the model' and inflation jumps immediately to the level required to ensure that the cycle is stabilized.[30] This requires the presence of a credible inflation-targeting central bank that is committed to zero output gaps in the future. By contrast, in the 3-equation model, given the absence of a NK Phillips curve, the economy is stabilized by the behaviour of the forward-looking central bank that uses the monetary rule to choose the output gap and in that way to get the economy on to the stable path to equilibrium.

The second difference is the behaviour of employment. There is no unemployment in the NK model and the response of employment to a shock is explained by the RBC mechanism of intertemporal substitution in response to changes in the real wage. There is *under*employment because fewer hours are worked than in the RBC flexible price equilibrium. As highlighted in the discussion of the RBC model earlier in the chapter, the welfare implications of employment fluctuations are quite different when business cycles entail involuntary unemployment as is the case in the 3-equation model.

The third difference is that in the NK model there is no chain of causation from what is happening in the labour market to inflation. Output and inflation are determined simultaneously in the NK model: inflation is caused by firms changing their prices in order to maximize profits given their expectations about future costs represented by the expected path of the output gap. In the 3-equation model, by contrast, in response to inflation above target, it is the

---

[30] Cochrane (2011a) provides a critique of the New Keynesian model from a neo-classical (RBC) perspective by highlighting the strength of the assumption that inflation must jump to one particular value in order that the economy stabilizes. Section VI of Cochrane's paper provides a useful comparison between what he refers to as Old and New Keynesian models.

loosening of the labour market caused by the central bank's decision to raise the interest rate that pushes wage inflation down; price inflation falls as a consequence of the fall in cost inflation.

### Sources of persistence in state-of-the-art NK models

In the NK DSGE models found in central banks, many adjustments are made to the model to allow it to capture the persistence in inflation and in the output response to shocks that characterize real economic data. The model which many central banks have used is a version of the Smets–Wouters (2003; 2007) model. This model incorporates features which are introduced to better match the sluggish adjustment of the economy such as:

1. partial indexation of prices and wages, which introduces lagged inflation into the *Phillips* curve;

2. habit formation in consumption and investment adjustment costs, which introduces a role for lagged output in the *IS* curve;

3. lags in the Taylor rule, which introduces the lagged interest rate in the Taylor rule.

The hybrid Phillips curve is an example of how models used in the policy arena seek to overcome unsatisfactory features of both the adaptive expectations Phillips curve (it is empirically successful, but is subject to the Lucas critique; lacks micro-foundations and rational expectations; and lacks a channel for credibility to affect inflation) and the *NKPC* (which is forward looking and therefore not subject to the Lucas critique; has micro-foundations and rational expectations with a role for credibility, but counterfactual empirical predictions). The hybrid includes forward-looking inflation expectations but acknowledges that inflation appears to be persistent or inertial, i.e. that it depends on lagged values of itself.

$$\pi_t = \lambda \pi_{t-1} + (1 - \lambda) E_t \pi_{t+1} + \Lambda \alpha x_t. \qquad \text{(hybrid PC)}$$

The hybrid Phillips curve can be rationalized by the assumption that some proportion, $\lambda$, of firms use a backward-looking rule of thumb to set their inflation expectations while the remainder use forward-looking expectations. This parallels the consumption function discussed at the end of Chapter 1, where a proportion of households are assumed to use rule of thumb behaviour and base their consumption decisions on current income, whilst the rest are modelled as using the forward-looking permanent income hypothesis. Another frequently used rationalization is the idea of habit formation in consumption, which produces slow adjustment to income shocks. These sources of persistence are necessary for NK DSGE models to fit the data. They considerably complicate the models and make it difficult to uncover the role played by the micro-foundations that stem from the origins of the model in the RBC modelling tradition.

## 16.4 Conclusions

The work of Lucas and his contemporaries fed directly into the real business cycle (RBC) models of the 1980s, which form the basis of the dynamic stochastic general equilibrium (DSGE) models that dominate modern academic macroeconomics today. RBC models use microfoundations, such as representative dynamically optimizing agents and perfect competition, to build a model of the economy that seeks to match the economic fluctuations observed in the data. The key features of these models are that business cycles are caused by exogenous technology shocks and are propagated through the economy by agents smoothing consumption and optimizing between leisure and consumption over time. Proponents emphasize how well such stripped down models fit the data; critics point to the way technology shocks are modelled, the filtering method used and the discrepancy between the predictions and the labour market data.

The New Keynesian (NK) model includes elements from both the 3-equation model (e.g. sticky prices) and the RBC model (e.g. rational expectations of all agents). At the heart of the NK model is the NK Phillips curve, which states that current inflation depends on the entire future path of expected output gaps. The introduction of the NK Phillips curve allows us to set out the stabilization bias problem that arises when monetary policy makers operate with discretion (i.e. they can readjust interest rates in each period). Only when a central bank can credibly commit to a given adjustment path following shocks to the economy can stabilization be achieved at least cost (in terms of deviations from target inflation and equilibrium output). In the absence of commitment, the central bank cannot follow the least cost adjustment path because it is time inconsistent.

The NK DSGE model was widely adopted as the workhorse model of the research departments of central banks before the financial crisis. It is a common misconception that the NK DSGE model is simply a more complicated version of the basic 3-equation model. There are significant differences between the two models. The NK DSGE model is grounded in the RBC model, so the intertemporal substitution of labour is the mechanism driving business cycles and there is no involuntary unemployment. In addition, all the agents are forward-looking and 'solve the model', which leads to jumps in inflation. In contrast, in the 3-equation model there are incomplete contracts and involuntary unemployment at equilibrium, and cycles are driven by the response of price–setting firms and to demand and supply shocks; wage and price inflation respond to the output gaps that arise. In this model, the central bank is forward looking and has to adjust interest rates to set the economy on a stable path to equilibrium. Introducing some forward-looking behaviour of private sector agents to the 3-equation model dampens cyclical fluctuations, but does not change the nature of the propagation mechanisms or of the role of the central bank. The sharp differences between the NK model and the 3-equation model highlighted in this chapter are somewhat blurred in the NK DSGE models used in central banks where a large number of sources of persistence are introduced.

## 16.5 Questions

### 16.5.1 Checklist questions

1. List the key assumptions behind the RBC model. Are these assumptions realistic? To justify your answer, provide some real-world examples where these conditions do not hold. Is this an objection to the modelling strategy adopted?

2. Explain in words how exogenous technology shocks produce business cycles in the RBC model. Why are business cycles considered to be *equilibrium phenomena* in this model?

3. Use a diagram (as per Fig. 16.4) to explain the movements of the labour supply and demand curves after a negative technology shock. What might constitute a negative technology shock?

4. Explain in words what the *Solow residual* is. Use the production function to derive an equation for the Solow residual. Are there any problems with using the Solow residual as a proxy for technology shocks in the RBC model?

5. What are some common criticisms of the RBC model? Suggest how the model could be modified to deal with these problems.

6. Is the following statement true or false? Justify your answer. 'The RBC and New Keynesian models both view agents as rational and optimizing, hence they both view business cycles as equilibrium rather than disequilibrium phenomena.'

7. Write out the equations for the adaptive expectations and New Keynesian Phillips curves. What are the main differences between the two? Use the equations to explain the costs associated with disinflations.

8. This question requires using the 3-equation and New Keynesian models to analyse the adjustment of the economy after a negative demand shock. Assume the economy is initially in equilibrium and the negative output gap lasts for a set amount of time.

   (a) Draw the impulse response functions for inflation and the output gap for each model (as per Fig. 16.6).

   (b) Explain why the paths of inflation are different in each model.

   (c) How would the adjustment path change for the 3-equation model if a proportion of households exhibit permanent income behaviour and have rational expectations?

9. Assess the following statements S1 and S2. Are they both true, both false or is only one true? Justify your answer.

   S1. A monetary policy maker will achieve stabilization at least cost by committing to a price-level target.

   S2. When a monetary policy maker has discretion to choose the interest rate in each period, they will follow the same adjustment path as under commitment because this minimizes the cost of adjustment to shocks.

10. Discuss the following statement: 'the 3-equation model is just a simple version of the NK model'. When comparing the two different models make sure you discuss:

   (a) How different agents interact to 'solve the model'.

   (b) The propagation mechanism driving business cycles.

   (c) The implications for inflation of economic shocks.

   (d) The link between the labour market and inflation.

   (e) The impact of business cycles on unemployment.

## 16.5.2 Problems and questions for discussion

1. Choose a large developed European economy (e.g. Germany, UK, France etc.). Use the OECD. Stat website to gather a quarterly economic time series of macroeconomic indicators (see the list of variables used in Table 16.1). Take the natural logarithm of each series and then

pass it through a H-P filter (an Excel add-in can be downloaded from: http://www.web reg.de/hp_addin.html). The difference between the actual and detrended log series is equiva-lent to the cyclical component of each series. Create graphs comparing the cyclical component of each variable to the cyclical component of GDP (as per Figs. 16.1 and 16.2). Use the STDEV.P and the CORREL functions in excel to compute the volatility and co-movements with GDP of each of your series (as per Table 16.1). Answer the following questions:

(a) How far does the business cycle data of your chosen country match the predictions of the original RBC model (as shown in Kydland and Prescott (1982))?

(b) What do your findings suggest about the success of the original RBC model at mimicking business cycles outside of the United States?

2. Use Section 16.2 and other relevant academic literature to assess the following statement: 'real business cycle models are preferable to traditional Keynesian macroeconomic models as they are not based on ad hoc assumptions, but rather solid microfoundations, such as dynamic optimizing individuals and perfectly competitive markets'.

3. This question focuses on the predictions of the 3-equation and NK models and how they compare to the real-world data. Use Section 16.3 and your own analysis to answer the following questions:

(a) What do the two models predict should have happened to inflation during the global financial crisis (i.e. a large negative output gap that is expected to persist for a number of periods)?

(b) Choose two OECD economies and use the OECD.Stat website to download inflation data from 2006 to the end of 2011. Plot this data on a graph. Describe the path of inflation for each of these economies over the period.

(c) Does the data more closely match the predictions of the 3-equation model or the NK model? Are there significant differences across the two countries?

(d) What other factors might have influenced the path of inflation in these countries over this period?

4. Macroeconomic policy is about controlling the economy in the sense of keeping it close to the constant inflation equilibrium. Read the following statement and answer the accompanying questions: 'when thinking of controlling a classroom full of children, one would probably think it wise to base classroom rules on the actual behaviour of children rather than on how they would behave if they solved a forward-looking problem'.

(a) Does the line of reasoning in the statement have any implications for the RBC and NK DSGE models? [Hint: think about the assumptions behind the models].

(b) Are there any insights from the microeconomic literature on behavioural economics that would suggest that the RBC and NK DSGE models place too much weight on agents solving complicated problems forward over distant time horizons? [Hint: a useful starting point is the work of Nobel Prize winners Daniel Kahnemann and Amos Tversky].

# Bibliography

Abbas, S.M.A., Belhocine, N., ElGanainy, A.A. and Horton, M. (2010) A historical public debt database. *IMF Working Papers*, No. 10/245:1–26.

Acemoglu, D., Johnson, S. and Robinson, J. (2005) 'Institutions as the Fundamental Cause of Long-Growth' in *Handbook of Economic Growth*, eds Philippe Aghion and Stephen Durlauf, Elsevier, Amsterdam.

Acemoglu, D. and Robinson, J. (2012) *Why Nations Fail: The Origins of Power, Prosperity and Poverty*. Profile Books, London:

Admati, A. (2012) 'Examining the impact of the proposed rules to implement Basel III capital standards: Testimony for hearing of subcommittee on financial institution and consumer credit and subcommittee on insurance, housing, and community opportunity'. Technical report.

Admati, A. and Hellwig, M. (2013) *The Bankers' New Clothes: What's Wrong with Banking and What to Do about It*. Princeton University Press, Princeton, NJ.

Adrian, T. and Shin, H. S. (2011) 'Financial Intermediaries and Monetary Economics' in *Handbook of Monetary Economics*, eds Benjamin M. Friedman and Michael Woodford, volume 3, chapter 12, pp. 601–650. Elsevier, Amsterdam.

Agell, J. (2002) On the determinants of labour market institutions: Rent seeking vs. social insurance. *German Economic Review*, **3**(2):107–135.

Agell, J. and Lundborg, P. (1995) Theories of pay and unemployment: Survey evidence from Swedish manufacturing firms. *The Scandinavian Journal of Economics*, **97**(2):295–307.

Aghion, P., Akcigit, U. and Howitt, P. (2014) 'What Do We Learn From Schumpeterian Growth Theory?' in *Handbook of Economic Growth: Volume 2*, eds P. Aghion and S. N. Durlauf. North Holland, New York.

Aghion, P., Angeletos, G.-M., Banerjee, A. and Manova, K. (2010) Volatility and growth: Credit constraints and the composition of investment. *Journal of Monetary Economics*, **57**(3):246–265.

Aghion, P., Bloom, N., Blundell, R., Griffith, R. and Howitt, P. (2005) Competition and innovation: An inverted-u relationship. *The Quarterly Journal of Economics*, **120**(2):701–728.

Aghion, P., Blundell, R., Griffifth, R., Howitt, P. and Susanne Prantl. (2009) The effects of entry on incumbent innovation and productivity.

*Review of Economics & Statistics*, **91**(1): pp. 20–32.

Aghion, P., Farhi, E. and Kharroubi, E. (2012) Monetary policy, liquidity, and growth. *NBER Working Paper*, No. 18072.

Aghion, P., Harris, C., Howitt, P. and Vickers, J. (2001) Competition, imitation and growth with step-by-step innovation. *The Review of Economic Studies*, **68**(3):467–492.

Aghion, P., Hemous, D. and Kharroubi, E. (forthcoming) Cyclical fiscal policy, credit constraints and industry growth. *Journal of Monetary Economics*.1

Aghion, P. and Howitt, P. (1998) *Endogenous Growth*. MIT Press, Cambridge, MA.

Aghion, P. and Howitt, P. (2005) 'Growth with quality-improving innovations: An integrated framework' in Volume 1, Part A of *Handbook of Economic Growth*, pp. 67–110. Elsevier, Amsterdam.

Aghion, P. and Howitt, P. (2009) *The Economics of Growth*. MIT Press, Cambridge, MA.

Aghion, P. and Marinescu, I. (2007) 'Cyclical Budgetary Policy and Economic Growth: What Do we Learn from OECD Panel Data?' in *NBER Macroeconomics Annual 2007, Volume 22*, pp. 251–278. University of Chicago Press, Chicago.

Aidt, T.S. and Tzannatos, Z. (2008) Trade unions, collective bargaining and macroeconomic performance: a review. *Industrial Relations Journal*, **39**(4):258–295.

Akerlof, G. A. (1982) Labor contracts as partial gift exchange. *The Quarterly Journal of Economics*, **97**(4):543–569.

Alesina, A. and Ardagna, S. (1998) Tales of fiscal adjustment. *Economic Policy*, **13**(27):487– 545.

Alesina, A. and Ardagna, S. (2010) 'Large Changes in Fiscal Policy: Taxes versus Spending' in *Tax Policy and the Economy, Vol. 24*. Cambridge, MA: National Bureau of Economic Research.

Alesina, A., Perotti, R. and Tavares, J. (1998) The political economy of fiscal adjustments. *Brookings Paperson Economic Activity*, **1998**(1):197–266.

Alesina, A. and Summers, L. H. (1993) Central bank independence and macroeconomic performance: Some comparative evidence. *Journal of Money, Credit and Banking*, **25**(2):151–162.

Alessandri, P. and Haldane, A. G. (2009) *Banking on the state*. Bank of England, London.

Alvarez, L. J., Dhyne, E., Hoeberichts, M., Kwapil, C., Le Bihan, H., Lnnemann, P., Martins, F., Sabbatini, R., Stahl, H., Vermeulen, P. and Vilmunen, J. (2006) Sticky prices in the euro area: A summary of new micro-evidence. *Journal of the European Economic Association*, **4**(2/3):575–584.

van Ark, B., O'Mahony, M. and Timmer, M. P. (2008) The productivity gap between Europe and the United States: Trends and causes. *The Journal of Economic Perspectives*, **22**(1):25–44.

Armantier, O., de Bruin, W. B., Topa, G., van der Klaauw, W. and Zafar, B. (2011) Inflation expectations and behavior: Do survey respondents act on their beliefs? *Federal Reserve Bank of New York Staff Reports*, No. 509.

Armstrong, P., Glyn, A. and Harrison, J. (1991) *Capitalism Since 1945*. Basil Blackwell.

Aron, J., Duca, J. V., Muellbauer, J., Bauer, J., Murata, K. and Murphy, A. (2012) Credit, housing collateral, and consumption: Evidence from Japan, the UK and the US. *Review of Income and Wealth*, **58**(3):397–423.

Ashenfelter, O. (1984) Macroeconomic analyses and microeconomic analyses of labor supply. *Carnegie-Rochester Conference Serieson Public Policy*, **21**(1):117–156.

Ashraf, N., Karlan, D. and Yin, W. (2006) Tying Odysseus to the mast: Evidence from a commitment savings product in the Philippines. *The Quarterly Journal of Economics*, **121**(2):635–672.

Auerbach, A. J. and Feenberg, D. (2000) The significance of federal taxes as automatic stabilizers. *The Journal of Economic Perspectives*, **14**(3):37–56.

Auerbach, A. J. and Gorodnichenko, Y. (2013) 'Fiscal Multipliersin Recession and Expansion' in *Fiscal Policy after the Financial Crisis*, pp. 63– 98. National Bureau of Economic Research: University of Chicago Press, Chicago.

Ball, L. (1994) 'What determines the sacrifice ratio?' in *Monetary policy*, ed. N. Mankiw, pp. 155–193. The University of Chicago Press, Chicago.

Ball, L. (1999) Efficient rules for monetary policy. *International Finance*, **2**(1):63–83.

Ball, L. (2009) Hysteresis in unemployment: Old and new evidence. *NBER Working Paper No. 14818*.

Ball, L., Leigh, D. and Loungani, P. (2012) Okun's law: Fit at 50? *Paper presented at the 13th Jacques Polak Annual Research Conference: Hosted by the International Monetary Fund*.

Ball, L., Mankiw, N. G. and Nordhaus, W. D. (1999) Aggregate demand and long-run unemployment. *Brookings Paperson Economic Activity*, **1999**(2):189–251.

Barattieri, A., Basu, S. and Gottschalk, P. (2010) Some evidence on the importance of sticky wages. *NBER Working Paper*, No. 16130.

Barksy, R. and Killian, L. (2002) 'Do We Really Know that Oil Caused the Great Stagflation? A Monetary Alternative' in *NBER Macroeconomics Annual 2001*. Cambridge, MA, MIT Press.

Barr, D., Breedon, F. and Miles, D. (2003) Life on the outside: economic conditions and prospects outside euroland. *Economic Policy*, **18**(37):573–613.

Barro, R. J. (1974) Are government bonds net wealth? *Journal of Political Economy*, **82**(6):1095–1117.

Barro, R. J. (1977) Unanticipated money growth and unemployment in the United States. *The American Economic Review*, **67**(2):101–115.

Bartelsman, E. J. and Doms, M. (2000) Understanding productivity: Lessons from longitudinal microdata. *Journal of Economic Literature*, **38**(3):569–594.

Bassanini, A. and Duval, R. (2009) Unemployment, institutions, and reform complementarities: re-assessing the aggregate evidence for OECD countries. *Oxford Review of Economic Policy*, **25**(1):40–59.

Basu, D. (2013) Guest post: 'The time series of high debt and growth in Italy, Japan, and the United States'. *Next New Deal: The Blog of the Roosevelt Institute*. http://www.nextnewdeal.net/

Baum, A. Checcherita-Westphal, C., and Philipp R. (2013) Debt and growth: New evidence for the euro area. *Journal of International Money and Finance*, **32**(0):809–821.

Bean, C. (1998) The new UK monetary arrangements: A view from the literature. *The Economic Journal*, **108**(451):1795–1809.

Belot, M. and van Ours, J. C. (2004) Does the recent success of some OECD countries in lowering their unemployment rates lie in the clever design of their labor market reforms? *Oxford Economic Papers*, **56**(4):621–642.

Bernanke, B. (2000) 'Japanese Monetary Policy: A Case of Self-Induced Paralysis?' in *Japan's Financial Crisisandits Parallels to US Experience*, eds By Adam S. Posen and Ryoichi Mikitani, Institute of International Economics, Washington DC.

Bernanke, B. and Gertler, M. (2001) Should central banks respond to movements in asset prices? *The American Economic Review*, **91**(2):253–257.

Bernanke, B., Gertler, M. and Gilchrist, S. (1999) 'The Financial Accelerator in a Quantitative Business Cycle Framework' in *Handbook of Macroeconomics, Volume*

1, eds John B. Taylor and Michael Woodford, pp. 1341–1393. Elsevier Science B.V., Amsterdam.

Bertola, G., Blau, F.D. and Kahn, L. M. (2001) Comparative analysis of labor market outcomes: Lessons for the us from international long-run evidence. *NBER Working Paper No. 8526.*

Bewley, T. (1999) *Why Wages Don't Fall Duringa Recession.* Harvard University Press, Cambridge, MA.

Bewley, T. (2007) 'Fairness, Reciprocity and Wage Rigidity' in *Behavioral Economics and its Applications,* eds Peter Diamond and Hannu Vartiainen, pp. 157–188. Princeton University Press, Princeton, NJ.

Blanchard, O. (2009) The State of Economics. *Annual Review of Economics,* Vol 1: 209-232.

Blanchard, O., Amighini, A. and Giavazzi, F. (2010) *Macroeconomics: A Euro-pean Perspective.* Pearson Education Limited, Harlow.

Blanchard, O., DellAriccia, G. and Mauro, P. (2010) Rethinking macroeconomic policy. *Journal of Money, Credit and Banking,* **42**:199-215.

Blanchard, O. and Gali, J. (2007) The macroeconomic effects of oil shocks: Why are the 2000s so difierent from the 1970s? *NBER Working Paper,* No. 13368.

Blanchard, O. and Giavazzi, F. (2003) Macroeconomic effects of regulation and deregulation in goods and labor markets. *The Quarterly Journal of Economics,* **118**(3):879-907.

Blanchard, O. and Philippon, T. (2004) The quality of labor relations and unemployment. *NBER Working Paper No. 10590.*

Blanchard, O. and Summers, L. (1986) Hysteresis and the european unemployment problem. *NBER Macroeconomics Annual 1986,* **1**:15-90.

Blanchard, O. and Watson, M. W. (1982) 'Bubbles, Rational Expectations and Financial Markets' in *Crises in the Economic and Financial Structure,* ed. Paul Wachtel, pp. 295–316. Lexington, MA, D.C. Heathand Company.

Blanchard, O. and Wolfers, J. (2000) The role of shocks and institutions in the rise of European unemployment: the aggregate evidence. *The Economic Journal,* **110**(462):1-33.

Blanchflower, D. G. and Oswald, A. J. (1995) An introduction to the wage curve. *The Journal of Economic Perspectives,* **9**(3):153-167.

Blanchflower, D. G. and Oswald, A. J. (2013) Does high home-ownership impair the labor market? *NBER Working Paper,* 19079.

Blinder, A. S. (1999) *Central Banking in Theory and Practice (Lionel Robbins Lectures).* MIT Press, Cambridge, MA.

Blinder, A. S., Canetti, E. R. D., Lebow, D. E. and Russ, J. B. (1998) *Asking about prices: A new approach to understanding price stickiness.* Russell Sage Foundation.

Blinder, A. S., Ehrmann, M., Fratzscher, M., de Haan, J. and Jansen, D. (2008) Central bank communication and monetary policy: A survey of theory and evidence. *Journal of Economic Literature,* **46**(4):910-945.

Blinder, A. S. and Reis, R. (2005) Understanding the Greenspan standard. *Paper presented at the Federal Reserve Bank of Kansas City symposium, The Greenspan Era: Lessons for the Future, Jackson Hole, Wyoming, August 25–27, 2005.*

Blinder, A. S. and Solow, R. M. (1973) Does fiscal policy matter? *Journal of Public Economics,* **2**(4):319-337.

Blinder, A. S. and Solow, R. M. (1976) Does fiscal policy matter?: A correction. *Journal of Public Economics,* **5**(12):183-184.

Bloom, N. (2009) The impact of uncertainty shocks. *Econometrica,* **77**(3):623-685.

Bloom, N. (2011) The uncertainty shock from the debt disaster will cause a double-dip recession. *Vox,* http://www.voxeu.org

Blundell, R., Bond, S., Devereux, M. and Schiantarelli, F. (1992) Investment and Tobin's q: Evidence from company panel data. *Journal of Econometrics,* **51**(12):233-257.

Blundell, R., Crawford, C. and Wenchao, J. (2013) What can wages and unemployment tell us about the UK productivity puzzle? Institute of Fiscal Studies Working Papers W13/11, IFS, London.

Bolt, J. and van Zanden, J. L. (2013) The first update of the Maddison project; re-estimating growth before 1820. *Maddison Project Working Paper,* No 4.

Boltho, A. (1989) Did policy activism work? *European Economic Review,* **33**(9):1709-1726.

Boltho, A. and Corbett, J. (2000) The assessment: Japan's stagnation—can policy revive the economy? *Oxford Review of Economic Policy,* **16**(2):1-17.

Bond, S. and Cummins, J. (2001) Noisy share prices and the q model of investment. *IFS Working Paper W01/22.*

Borio, C. (2012) The financial cycle and macroeconomics: What have we learnt? *BIS Working Papers,* 395.

Borio, C. and Lowe, P. (2002) Asset prices, financial and monetary stability: Exploring the nexus. *BIS Working Papers*, 114.

Borio, C. and White, W. (2004) Whither monetary and financial stability? the implications of evolving policy regimes. *BIS Working Papers*, 147.

Bos, F. and Teulings, C. (2010) Lessons from the Netherlands. *Paper to Conference on Independent Fiscal Institutions, 18-19 March, Fiscal Council Republic of Hungary, Budapest.*

Bosch, G. (2011) 'The German labour market after the financial crisis: Miracle or just a good policy mix. Work inequalities in the crisis' in *Inequalities in the World of Work: The Effects of the Crisis*, ed. D. Vaughan-Whitehead, Geneva: International Labor Organization, 255-286.

Bourne, R. (2011) From spot on to inaccurate: the recent history of MPC inflation forecasts. *Centrefor Policy Studies: Statistical Fact sheet 6.*

Bowles, S. (2006) *Microeconomics: Behaviour, Institutions and Evolution.* Russell Sage Foundation. Princeton University Press, New Jersey.

Bowles, S., Gordon, D.M. and Weisskopf, T. E. (1983) Hearts and minds: A social model of U.S. productivity growth. *Brookings Paperson Economic Activity*, **1983**(2):381-450.

Brayton, F., Levin, A., Lyon, R. and John C. Williams. (1997) The evolution of macro models at the federal reserve board. *Carnegie-Rochester Conference Series on Public Policy*, **47**(0):43-81.

Briotti, M. G. (2004) Fiscal adjustment between 1991 and 2002: Stylised facts and policy implications. *ECB Occasional Paper Series*, No. 9.

Brittle, S. (2010) Ricardian equivalence and the efficacy of fiscal policy in Australia. *Australian Economic Review*, **43**(3):254-269.

Broadberry, S. (2013) Accounting for the great divergence. Economic History Working Papers, 184/13. London School of Economics and Political Science, London.

Broda, C. and Weinstein, D. E. (2005) 'Happy News from the Dismal Science: Reassessing Japanese Fiscal Policy and Sustainability' in *Reviving Japan' sEconomy*, eds Takatoshi Ito, Hugh Patrick and David E. Weinstein, pages 40-78. MIT Press, Cambridge, MA.

Brunnermeier, M. K. (2009) Deciphering the liquidity and credit crunch 2007-2008. *Journal of Economic Perspectives*, **23**(1):77-100.

Buch, E. M. and Prieto, E. (2012) Do better capitalized banks lend less? Long-run panel evidence from Germany. *CESifo Working Paper Series*, No. 3836.

Buiter, W. (2001) Notes on 'a code for fiscal stability'. *Oxford Economic Papers*, **53**(1):1-19.

Buiter, W. (2003) Deflation: Prevention and cure. *CEPR Discussion Paper*, No. 3869.

Buiter, W. and Grafe, C. (2004) Patching up the pact. *Economics of Transition*, **12**(1):67-102.

Buiter, W., Miller, M., Baily, M. N. and Branson, W. H. (1981) The Thatcher experiment: The first two years. *Brookings Papers on Economic Activity*, **1981**(2):315-379.

Buiter, W., Miller, M., Sachs, J. D. and Branson, W. H. (1983) Changing the rules: Economic consequences of the Thatcher regime. *Brookings Papers on Economic Activity*, **1983**(2): pp. 305-379.

Bulow, J., Goldfield, J. and Klemperer, P. (2013) Market-based bank capital regulation. *Vox*, http://www.voxeu.org

Caballero, R. (1999) 'Investment' in *Handbook of Macroeconomics*, eds. John B. Taylor and Michael Woodford. Elsevier Science B.V., Amsterdam.

Caballero, R., Farhi, E. and Gourinchas, P.-O. (2008) An equilibrium model of 'global imbalances' and low interest rates. *The American Economic Review*, **98**(1):358-393.

Cagan, P. (1956) 'The Monetary Dynamics of Hyperinflation' in *Studies in the Quantity Theory of Money*, ed. M. Friedman, pp. 25-117. University of Chicago Press, Chicago.

Calmfors, L. (2010) The Swedish fiscal policy council experiences and lesson. *Paper for Conference on Independent Fiscal Policy Institutions, Budapest, 18-19 March 2010.*

Calmfors, L. and Driffill, J. (1988) Bargaining structure, corporatism and macroeconomic performance. *Economic Policy*, **3**(6):13-61.

Calmfors, L. and Wren-Lewis, S. (2011) What should fiscal councils do? *Economic Policy*, **26**(68):649-695.

Calomiris, C. W. and Hanes, C. (1995) 'Historical Macroeconomics and Macroeconomic History' in *Macroeconometrics: Developments, Tensions, and Prospects*, ed. Kevin D. Hoover, pages 351-416. Kluwer, Dordrecht.

Calvo, G. A. (1983) Staggered prices in a utility-maximizing framework. *Journal of Monetary Economics*, **12**(3):383-398.

Campbell, C. M. and Kamlani, K. S. (1997) The reasons for wage rigidity: Evidence from a survey of firms. *The Quarterly Journal of Economics*, **112**(3):759-789.

Campbell, J. Y. and Mankiw, N. G. (1989) Consumption, income, and interest rates: Reinterpreting the time series evidence. *NBER Macroeconomics Annual*, **4**:185-216.

Canova, F. (1998) Detrending and business cycle facts. *Journal of Monetary Economics*, **41**(3):475-512.

Carlin, W., Gordon, R. J. and Solow, R. M. (2012) 'Round Table Discussion: Where is Macro Going?' in *What's Right with Macroeconomics?* eds Robert M. Solow and Jean-Philippe Touffut. Edward Elgar, Cheltenham, UK and Northampton, MA, USA.

Carlin, W., Schaffer, M., and Seabright, P. (2013) Soviet power plus electrification: What is the long-run legacy of communism? *Explorations in Economic History*, **50**(1):116–147.

Carlin, W. and Soskice, D. (2005) The 3-equation New Keynesian model — a graphical exposition. *The B.E. Journal of Macroeconomics*, **0**(1):13.

Carlin, W. and Soskice, D. (2006) *Macroeconomics: Imperfections, Institutions, and Policies*. Oxford University Press, Oxford.

Carlin, W. and Soskice, D. (2009) German economic performance: disentangling the role of supply-side reforms, macroeconomic policy and coordinated economy institutions. *Socio-Economic Review*, **7**(1):67–99.

Carlin, W. and Soskice, D. (2010) A New Keynesian Open Economy Model for Policy Analysis, CEPR Discussion Papers 7979.

Carroll, C. D. (1997) Buffer-stock saving and the life cycle/permanent income hypothesis. *The Quarterly Journal of Economics*, **112**(1):1–55.

Castro, V. (2011) Can central banks' monetary policy be described by a linear (augmented) Taylor rule or by a nonlinear rule? *Journal of Financial Stability*, **7**(4):228–246.

Cecchetti, S. G., Mohanty, M. S. and Zampolli, F. (2011) The real effects of debt. Bank for International Settlements, Monetary and Economic Department.

Chadha, B., Masson, P. R. and Meredith, G. (1992) Models of inflation and the costs of disinflation. *Staff Papers—International Monetary Fund*, **39**(2): 395–431.

Chetty, R., Guren, A., Manoli, D. and Weber, A. (2011) Are micro and macro labor supply elasticities consistent? a review of evidence on the intensive and extensive margins. *American Economic Review*, **101**(3):47175.

Cheung, Y.-W., Chinn, M. D. and Marsh, I. W. (2004) How do UK-based foreign exchange dealers think their market operates? *International Journal of Finance & Economics*, **9**(4):289–306.

Chevalier, J. and Goolsbee, A. (2009) Are durable goods consumers forward-looking? evidence from college textbooks. *The Quarterly Journal of Economics*, **124**(4):1853–1884.

Chirinko, R. S. (1993) Business fixed investment spending: Modeling strategies, empirical results, and policy implications. *Journal of Economic Literature*, **31**(4):1875–1911

Christiano, L.J. and Eichenbaum, M. (1992) Current real-business-cycle theories and aggregate labor-market fluctuations. *The American Economic Review*, **82**(3):430–450.

Christiano, L. J., Eichenbaum, M. and Evans, C. L. (2005) Nominal rigidities and the dynamic effects of a shock to monetary policy. *Journal of Political Economy*, **113**(1):1–45.

Chung, H., Laforte, J.-P., Reifschneider, D. and Williams, J. C. (2012) Have we underestimated the likelihood and severity of zero lower bound events? *Journal of Money, Credit and Banking*, **44**:47–82.

Claessens, S., Pozsar, Z., Ratnovski, L. and Singh, M. (2012) Shadow banking: Economics and policy. *IMF Staff Discussion Note*, SDN/12/12.

Clarida, R. and Gertler, M. (1997) 'How the Bundesbank Conducts Monetary Policy' in *Reducing Inflation: Motivation and Strategy*, eds. Christina D. Romer and David H. Romer. University of Chicago Press, Chicago.

Clark, A. E. and Oswald, A. J. (1994) Unhappiness and unemployment. *The Economic Journal*, **104**(424):648–659.

Cloyne, J. (2013) Discretionary tax changes and the macroeconomy: New narrative evidence from the United Kingdom. *American Economic Review*, **103**(4):1507–28.

Cochrane, J. H. (2011a) Determinacy and identification with Taylor rules. *Journal of Political Economy*, **119**(3):565–615.

Cochrane, J. H. (2011b) Understanding policy in the great recession: Some unpleasant fiscal arithmetic. *European Economic Review*, **55**(1):2–30.

Cooper, R. N. (2008) Global imbalances: Globalization, demography, and sustainability. *The Journal of Economic Perspectives*, **22**(3):93–112.

Corbett, J. (2012) Has Japan's lost decade(s) changed economic thinking? *The Economic Record*, **88**(s1):100–105.

Cottarelli, C. and Jaramillo, L. (2013) Walking hand in hand: Fiscal policy and growth in advanced democracies. *Review of Economics and Institutions*, **4**(2).

Crafts, N. (2007) Recent European economic growth: why can't it be like the golden age? *National Institute Economic Review*, **199**:69–81.

Crafts, N. and Fearon, P. (2010) Lessons from the 1930s Great Depression. *Oxford Review of Economic Policy*, **26**(3):285–317.

Crafts, N. and Toniolo, G. (1996) (eds) *Economic Growth in Europe since 1945*. Cambridge University Press, Cambridge.

Crafts, N. and Mills, T. C. (2012) Rearmament to the rescue? New estimates of the impact of Keynesian policies in 1930s Britain. CAGE Online Working Paper Series 102, Competitive Advantage in the Global Economy (CAGE).

Crowe, C. and Meade, E. E. (2008) Central bank independence and transparency: Evolution and effectiveness. *European Journal of Political Economy*, **24**(4):763–777.

Deaton, A. (1992) *Understanding Consumption*. Clarendon Press: Oxford.

DeLong, B. (1998) Estimates of world GDP, one million B.C.–Present. http://www.delong.typepad.com/delong.long.form/

DeLong, J. B. and Summers, L. (2012) Fiscal policy in a depressed economy. *Brookings Papers on Economic Activity*, pp. 233–297.

Demertzis, M. and Hughes Hallett, A. (2007) Central bank transparency in theory and practice. *Journal of Macroeconomics*, **29**(4):760 –789.

D'Hulster, K. (2009) The leverage ratio. Technical report, The World Bank Group.

Dincer, N. and Eichengreen, B. (2009) Central bank transparency: Causes, consequences and updates. *NBER Working Paper*, No. 14791.

Dixit, A. (1992) Investment and hysteresis. *The Journal of Economic Perspectives*, **6**(1):107–132.

Doi, T, Hoshi, T. and Okimoto, T. (2011) Japanese government debt and sustainability of fiscal policy. *NBER Working Paper No. 17305*.

Dolls, M., Fuest, C. and Peichl, A. (2011) *Automatic stabilizers, economic crisis and income distribution in Europe. Vol. 32*. Emerald Group Publishing Limited, Bingley.

Dornbusch, R. (1996) The effectiveness of exchange-rate changes. *Oxford Review of Economic Policy*, **12**(3):26–38.

Dornbusch, R. (1976) Expectations and exchange rate dynamics. *Journal of Political Economy*, **84**(6):1161–1176.

Drehmann, M., Borio, C. and Tsatsaronis, K. (2012) Characterising the financial cycle: Don't lose sight of the medium term! *BIS Working Papers*, 380.

Du Caju, P., Gautier, E., Momferatou, D. and Ward-Warmedinger, M. (2008) Institutional features of wage bargaining in 23 European countries, the US and Japan. *National Bank of Belgium Working Paper Research*, No. 154.

Dube, A. (2013) Guest post: Reinhart/rogoff and growth in a time before debt. *Next New Deal: The Blog of the Roosevelt Institute*, http://www.nextnewdeal.net/

Durlauf, S. and Blume, L. (2008) (editors) *The New Palgrave Dictionary of Economics: 2nd edition*. Palgrave Macmillan, London.

Dustmann, C., Fitzenberger, B., Schoenberg, U. and Spitz-Oener, A. (2014) From Sick Man of Europe to Economic Superstar: Germany's Resurgent Economy. *The Journal of Economic Perspectives*, **28**(1):167–188.

Eggertsson, G. B. and Krugman, P. (2012) Debt, deleveraging, and the liquidity trap: A Fisher–Minsky–Koo approach*. *The Quarterly Journal of Economics*, **127**(3):1469–1513.

Eichengreen, B. (2007) *The European Economy Since 1945: Coordinated Capitalism and Beyond*. Princeton University Press, Princeton.

Eichengreen, B., Feldman, R., Liebman, J, von Hagen, J. and Wyplosz, C. (2011) *Public Debts: Nuts, Bolts and Worries (Geneva Reports on the World Economy, No. 13)*. Centre for Economic Policy Research.

Eliasson, A.-C. (2001) Is the short-run Phillips curve nonlinear? Empirical evidence for Australia, Sweden and the United States. *Sveriges Riksbank Working Paper Series No. 124*.

Elsby, M. W., Hobijn, B. and Sahin, A. (2010) The labor market in the great recession. *NBER Working Paper No. 15979*.

Ennis, H. M. and Wolman, A. L. (2010) Excess reserves and the new challenges for monetary policy. *Richmond Fed Economic Brief* (March).

Estrella, A. and Fuhrer, J. C. (2002) Dynamic inconsistencies: Counterfactual implications of a class of rational-expectations models. *The American Economic Review*, **92**(4): pp. 1013–1028.

European Commission. (2012) *Employment and social developments in Europe*. Technical report, European Commission.

Farber, H. S. (2005) What do we know about job loss in the United States? evidence from the displaced workers survey, 1984-2004. *Federal Reserve Bank of Chicago Economic Perspectives*, (QII):13–28.

Fatás, A. and Mihov, I. (2012) Fiscal Policy as a Stabilization Tool. CEPR Discussion Paper No. DP8749.

Fazzari, S. M., Morley, J. and Panovska, I. (2012) State-dependent effects of fiscal policy. *Australian School of Business Research Paper No. 27*.

Fehr, E. and Falk, A. (1999) Wage rigidity in a competitive incomplete contract market. *Journal of Political Economy*, **107**(1):106–134.

Fehr, E. and Tyran, J.-R. (2001) Does money illusion matter? *The American Economic Review*, **91**(5):1239–1262.

Feldstein, M. (2006) The 2006 economic report of the president: Comment on chapter one (the year in review) and chapter six (the capital account surplus). *Journal of Economic Literature Internet*, **44**(3):673–79, 2006.

Feldstein, M. (2008) Resolving the global imbalance: The dollar and the U.S. saving rate. *The Journal of Economic Perspectives*, **22**(3):113–126.

Fischer, S. (1977) Long-term contracts, rational expectations, and the optimal money supply rule. *Journal of Political Economy*, **85**(1):191–205.

Fischer, S., Sahay, R. and Vegh, C. A. (2002) Modern hyper- and high inflations. *Journal of Economic Literature*, **40**(3):837–880.

Flanagan, F., Soskice, D. and Ulman, L. (1983) *Unionism, Economic Stabilization, and Incomes Policies: European Experience.* Brookings Institution, Washington.

Flavin, M. A. (1981) The adjustment of consumption to changing expectations about future income. *Journal of Political Economy*, **89**(5):974–1009.

Fleisher, B. M. and Wang, X. (2001) Efficiency wages and work incentives in urban and rural China. *Journal of Comparative Economics*, **29**(4):645–662.

Fliessbach, K., Weber, B., Trautner, P., Dohmen, T., Sunde, U., Elger, C. E. and Falk, A. (2007) Social comparison affects reward-related brain activity in the human ventral striatum. *Science*, **318**(5854):1305–1308.

Fostel, A. and Geanakoplos, J. (2012) Why does bad news increase volatility and decrease leverage? *Journal of Economic Theory*, **147**(2):501–525.

Foster, G. and Frijters, P. (2012) The formation of expectations: Competing theories and new evidence, http://tinyurl.com/Foster-Frijters-2012

Foster, L., Haltiwanger, J. C. and Krizan, C. J. (2001) 'Aggregate Productivity Growth. Lessons from Microeconomic Evidence' in *New Developments in Productivity Analysis*, eds Charles R. Hulten, Edwin R. Dean, and Michael J. Harper. University of Chicago Press, Chicago.

Foster, A. D. and Rosenzweig, M. R. (1994) A test for moral hazard in the labor market: Contractual arrangements, effort, and health. *The Review of Economics and Statistics*, **76**(2):213–227.

Frankel, J. A. (2006) Global imbalances and low interest rates: An equilibrium model vs. a disequilibrium reality. *KSG Working Paper*, No. RWP06-035.

Friedman, M. (1957) *A Theory of the Consumption Function.* Princeton University Press, Princeton.

Friedman, M. (1969) *The Optimum Quantity of Money and Other Essays.* Aldine, Chicago.

Friedman, M. (1968) The role of monetary policy. *The American Economic Review*, **58**(1):1–17.

Friedman, M. (1970) *The Counter-Revolution in Monetary Theory (First Wincott Memorial Lecture).* Institute of Economic Affairs.

Friedman, M. (1977) Nobel lecture: Inflation and unemployment. *Journal of Political Economy*, **85**(3): pp. 451–472.

FSB. (2012) Consultative document: Strengthening oversight and regulation of shadow banking. Technical report, Financial Stability Board.

Fujiki, H. and Shiratsuka, S. (2002) Policy duration effect under the zero interest rate policy in 1999–2000: Evidence from Japan's money market data. *Monetary and Economic Studies*, **20**(1):1–31.

Gächter, S. and Thoni, C. (2010) Social comparison and performance: Experimental evidence on the fair wage-effort hypothesis. *Journal of Economic Behavior & Organization*, **76**(3):531–543.

Gagnon, J., Raskin, M., Remache, J. and Sack, B. (2011) The financial market effects of the federal reserve's large-scale asset purchases. *International Journal of Central Banking*, **7**(1):3–43.

Gai, P., Haldane, A. and Kapadia, S. (2011) Complexity, concentration and contagion. *Journal of Monetary Economics*, **58**(5):453–470.

Gali, J. (2008) *Monetary Policy, Inflation and the Business Cycle.* Princeton University Press, Princeton.

Gali, J., López-Salido, J. D. and Vallés, J. (2007) Understanding the effects of government spending on consumption. *Journal of the European Economic Association*, **5**(1):227–270.

Geanakoplos, J. (2010) 'The Leverage Cycle' in *NBER Macroeconomics Annual 2009 Volume 24*, eds Daron Acemoglu, Kenneth Rogoff and Michael Woodford. pp. 1–65.

Giavazzi, F. and Pagano, M. (1990) Can severe fiscal contractions be expansionary? Tales of two small European countries. *NBER Macroeconomics Annual*, **5**:75–111.

Goldberg, P. K. and Knetter, M. M. (1997) Goods prices and exchange rates: What have we learned? *Journal of Economic Literature*, **35**(3):1243–1272.

Gonçalves, C., Eduardo S. and Carvalho, A. (2009) Inflation targeting matters: evidence from OECD economies' sacrifice ratios. *Journal of Money, Credit and Banking*, **41**(1):233–243.

Goodhart, C. (1986) Financial innovation and monetary control. *Oxford Review of Economic Policy*, **2**(4).

Goodhart, C. (1989) The conduct of monetary policy. *The Economic Journal*, **99**(396):293–346.

Goodhart, C. (2006). The ECB and the conduct of monetary policy: Goodhart's law and lessons from the euro area. *Journal of Common Market Studies*, **44**(4):757–778.

Goodhart, C. (2013) How to organize macro-prudential policies in Europe. Available at http://tinyurl.com/goodhart-macroprudential

Gordon, R. J. (1977) Can the inflation of the 1970s be explained? *Brookings Papers on Economic Activity*, **1977**(1):253–279.

de Grauwe, P. (2011) 'European monetary union' in *The New Palgrave Dictionary of Economics*, eds Steven N. Durlauf, and Lawrence E. Blume. Palgrave Macmillan, Basingstoke.

Griffith, R., Harrison, R. and Macartney, G. (2007) Product market reforms, labour market institutions and unemployment. *The Economic Journal*, **117**(519):C142–C166.

Gross, D. B. and Souleles, N. S. (2002) Do liquidity constraints and interest rates matter for consumer behavior? Evidence from credit card data. *The Quarterly Journal of Economics*, **117**(1):149–185.

Guajardo, J., Leigh, D. and Pescatori, A. (2011) Expansionary austerity: New international evidence. *IMF Working Paper No. 11/158*.

Haldane, A., G.and May, R. M. (2011) Systemic risk in banking ecosystems. *Nature*, **469.7330**:351–355.

Hall, R. E. (1978) Stochastic implications of the life cycle-permanent income hypothesis: Theory and evidence. *Journal of Political Economy*, **86**(6):971–987.

Hall, G. T. and Sargent, T. J. (2010) Interest rate risk and other determinants of post-WWII U.S. government debt/GDP dynamics. *NBER Working Paper No. 15702*.

Hall, R. E. and Mishkin, F. S. (1982) The sensitivity of consumption to transitory income: Estimates from panel data on households. *Econometrica*, **50**(2):461–481.

Hamilton, J. D. (2009) Causes and consequences of the oil shock of 2007-08. *Brookings papers on economic activity*, **40**:215.

Hansen, G. D. (1985) Indivisible labor and the business cycle. *Journal of Monetary Economics*, **16**(3):309–327.

Hansen, G. D. and Prescott, E. C. (1993) Did technology shocks cause the 1990-1991 recession? *The American Economic Review*, **83**(2):280–286.

Hartley, J. E., Hoover, K. D. and Salyer, K. D. (1997) The limits of business cycle research: assessing the real business cycle model. *Oxford Review of Economic Policy*, **13**(3):34–54.

Hayashi, F. and Prescott, E. C. (2002) The 1990s in Japan: A lost decade. *Review of Economic Dynamics*, **5**(1):206–235.

Heathcote, J., Storesletten, K. and Violante, G. L. (2010) The macroeconomic implications of rising wage inequality in the United States. *Journal of Political Economy*, **118**(4):681–722.

Heckman, J. J. (2013) Comments on Are Protective Labor Market Institutions at the Root of Unemployment? A Critical Review of the Evidence by David Howell, Dean Baker, Andrew Glyn, and John Schmitt (January 24, 2013). *Capitalism and Society*, **2**(1), Article 5, 2007. Available at SSRN: http://ssrn.com/abstract=2206513

Heitger, B. (1993) Comparative economic growth: Catching up in east Asia. *ASEANE conomic Bulletin*, **10**(1):68–82.

Herndon, T., Ash, M. and Pollin, R. (2013) Does high public debt consistently stifle economic growth? A critique of Reinhart and Rogoff. *Cambridge Journal of Economics*, doi:10.1093/cje/bet075

Hicks, J. R. (1937) Mr. Keynes and the 'classics'; a suggested interpretation. *Econometrica*, **5**(2):147–159.

Holland, A. and Scott, A. (1998) The determinants of UK business cycles. *The Economic Journal*, **108**(449):1067–1092.

Holland, D. (2009) The impact of European and global integration on the mark-up of prices over costs. *National Institute Economic Review*, **208**(1):118–128.

Holmes, M. J. (2006) To what extent are public savings offset by private savings in the OECD? *Journal of Economics and Finance*, **30**(3):285–296.

Honohan, P. and Walsh, B. (2002) Catching up with the leaders: The Irish hare. *Brookings Papers on Economic Activity*, **2002**(1):1–57.

Hoover, K. D. (1988) *The New Classical Macroeconomics*. Wiley-Blackwell, Oxford.

Howell, D. R. and Azizoglu, B. M. (2011) Unemployment benefits and workincentives: the US labour market in the great recession. *Oxford Reviewof Economic Policy*, **27**(2):221–240.

Howell, D. R., Baker, D., Glyn, A. and Schmitt, J. (2007) Are protective labor market institutions at the root of unemployment? A critical review of the evidence. *Capitalism and Society*, **2(1)**.

Howitt, P. (2001) *Learning about Monetary Theory and Policy*. Mimeo, Brown University.

Iacoviello, M. (2005) House prices, borrowing constraints, and monetary policy in the business cycle. *The American Economic Review*, **95**(3):739–764.

ICB (2011) Final report recommendations. Technical report, Independent Commission on Banking (ICB).

Ilzetzki, E., Mendoza, E. G. and Végh, C. A. (2013) How big (small?) are fiscal multipliers? *Journal of Monetary Economics*, **60** (2):239–254.

IMF (2009) World economic outlook: From recession to recovery: How soon and how strong? Technical report.

IMF (2010) 'Will it Hurt? Macroeconomic Effects of Fiscal Consolidation' in *World Economic Outlook: Recovery, Risk and Rebalancing*, pp. 93–124.

IMF (2010) Global financial stability report: Durable financial stability — getting there from here. Technical report.

IMF (2011) IMF fiscal monitor, September 2011. Technical report.

IMF (2012) IMF fiscal monitor, April 2012. Technical report.

IMF (2012) World economic outlook: Coping with high debt and sluggish growth. Technical report.

Irons, J. and Bivens, J. (2010) Government debt and economic growth: Over-reaching claims of debt 'threshold' suffer from theoretical and empirical flaws. *EPI Briefing Paper*, 271.

Issing, O. (2004) 'A framework for stability in Europe'. Speech at the University of London, European Economics and Financial Centre, London, 19 November.

Iwata, Y. (2009) Fiscal policy in an estimated DSGE model of the Japanese economy: Do non-Ricardian households explain all? *ESRI Discussion Paper Series*, No. 216.

Jappelli, T. (1990) Who is credit constrained in the U.S. economy? *The Quarterly Journal of Economics*, **105**(1):219–234.

Jappelli, T. and Pistaferri, L. (2010) The consumption response to income changes. *Annual Review of Economics*, **2**(1):479–506.

Johnson, S. and Kwak, J. (2010) *13 Bankers: The Wall Street Takeover and the Next Financial Meltdown*, Pantheon books, New York.

Johnson, D. S., Parker, J. A. and Souleles, N. S. (2006) Household expenditure and the income tax rebates of 2001. *The American Economic Review*, **96**(5):1589–1610.

Jones, C. I. and Vollrath, D. (2013) *Introduction to Economic Growth: Third Edition*. W.W. Norton & Company, New York.

Joyce, M., Tong, M. and Woods, R. (2011) The United Kingdom's quantitative easing policy: Design, operation and impact. *Bank of England Quarterly Bulletin, 2011.*

Kalemli-Ozcan, S., Sorensen, B. and Yesiltas, S. (2012) Leverage across firms, banks, and countries. *Journal of International Economics*, **88**(2):284–298.

Kapetanios, G., Mumtaz, H., Stevens, I. and Theodoridis, K. (2012) Assessing the economy-wide effects of quantitative easing. *Bank of England Working Paper No. 443.*

Keynes, J. M. (1921) *A Treatise on Probability*, Macmillan, London.

Keynes, J. M. (1936) *The General Theory of Employment, Interest and Money*, Palgrave Macmillan, London.

Keynes, J. M. (1937) The general theory of employment. *The Quarterly Journal of Economics*, **51**(2):209–223.

Kindleberger, C. P. and Aliber, R. Z. (2011) *Manias, Panics and Crashes: A History of Financial Crises*, Sixth Edition. Palgrave Macmillan, London.

King, M. (1997) Changes in UK monetary policy: Rules and discretion in practice. *Journal of Monetary Economics*, **39**(1):81–97.

King, R. G., Plosser, C. I. and Rebelo, S. T. (1988) Production, growth and business cycles: I. The basic neoclassical model. *Journal of Monetary Economics*, **21**(23):195–232.

King, R. G. and Rebelo, S. T. (1999) 'Resuscitating real business cycles' in volume 1, Part B of *Handbook of Macroeconomics*, eds John B. Taylor and Michael Woodford, pp. 927–1007. Elsevier Science B.V., Amsterdam.

Kirsanova, T., Vines, D. and Wren-Lewis, S. (2006) Fiscal policy and macroeconomic stability within a currency union. No. 5584. CEPR Discussion Papers.

Klomp, J. and De Haan, J. (2010) Inflation and central bank independence: A meta-regression analysis. *Journal of Economic Surveys*, **24**(4):593–621.

Knight, F. (1921) *Risk, Uncertainty, and Profit*. Houghton Mifflin, New York.

Koo, R. C. (2003) *Balance Sheet Recession: Japan's Struggle with Uncharted Economics and Its Global Implications*. JohnWiley & Sons, Singapore.

Koo, R. C. (2011) The world in balance sheet recession: Causes, cure, and politics. *Real-world economics review*, **58**:19–37.

Kornai, J. (2012) Centralization and the capitalist market economy. *Economics of Transition* **20**(4).

Kornai, J. (2013) *Dynamism, Rivalry, and the Surplus Economy: Two Essays on the Nature of Capitalism.* Oxford University Press, Oxford.

Krueger, A. B. (1991) Ownership, agency, and wages: An examination of franchising in the fast food industry. *The Quarterly Journal of Economics*, **106**(1): 75-101.

Krugman, P. R., Dominquez, K. M. and Rogoff, K. (1998) It's baaack: Japan's slump and the return of the liquidity trap. *Brookings Papers on Economic Activity*, **1998**(2):137-205.

Krusell, P. and Smith Jr., A. A. (1998) Income and wealth heterogeneity in the macroeconomy. *Journal of Political Economy*, **106**(5):867-896.

Kumar, M S. and Woo, J. (2010) Public debt and growth. *IMF Working Paper No. 10/174*.

Kuttner, K. N. and Posen, A. S. (2001) The great recession: Lessons for macroeconomic policy from Japan. *Brookings Papers on Economic Activity*, **2001**(2):93-160.

Kuttner, K. N. and Posen, A. S. (2002) Fiscal policy effectiveness in Japan. *Journal of the Japanese and International Economies*, **16**(4):536-558.

Kydland, F. E. and Prescott, E. C. (1977) Rules rather than discretion: The inconsistency of optimal plans. *Journal of Political Economy*, **85**(3):473-492.

Kydland, F. E. and Prescott, E. C. (1982) Time to build and aggregate fluctuations. *Econometrica*, **50**(6):1345-1370.

Lane, P. R. (2012) The European sovereign debt crisis. *Journal of Economic Perspectives*, **26**(3):49-68.

Lane, P. R. and Milesi-Ferretti, G. M. (2007) The external wealth of nations mark II: Revised and extended estimates of foreign assets and liabilities, 1970-2004. *Journal of International Economics*, **73**(2):223-250.

Laxton, D., Meredith, G. and Rose, D. (1995) Asymmetric effects of economic activity on inflation: Evidence and policy implications. *Staff Papers - International Monetary Fund*, **42**(2):344-374.

Layard, R. (2004) Good jobs and bad jobs. *CEP Occasional Paper No. 19*.

Layard, R. and Nickell, S. (1986) Unemployment in Britain. *Economica*, **53**(210):S121-S169.

Lazear, E. P., Shaw, K. L. and Stanton, C. (2013) Making do with less: Working harder during recessions. *NBER Working Paper*, 19328.

Leiderman, L. (1980) Macroeconometric testing of the rational expectations and structural neutrality hypotheses for the united states. *Journal of Monetary Economics*, **6**(1):69-82.

Leijonhufvud, A. (1987) 'IS-LM Analysis' in *The New Palgrave: Dictionary of Economics*, eds John Eatwell, Murray Milgate and Peter Newman. Macmillan and Stockton, London and New York.

Lindbeck, A. and Snower, D. J. (1986) Wage setting, unemployment, and insider-outsider relations. *The American Economic Review*, **76**(2):235-239.

Lipsey, R. G. and Carlaw, K. I. (2004) Total factor productivity and the measurement of technological change. *Canadian Journal of Economics/Revue Canadienne d'conomique*, **37**(4):1118-1150.

Loisel, O. (2008) Central bank reputation in a forward-looking model. *Journal of Economic Dynamics and Control*, **32**(11):3718-3742.

Long Jr, J. B. and Plosser, C. I. (1983) Real business cycles. *Journal of Political Economy*, **91**(1):39-69.

Lucas Jr, R. E. (1972) Expectations and the neutrality of money. *Journal of Economic Theory*, **4**(2):103-124.

Lucas Jr, R. E. (1973) Some international evidence on output-inflation tradeoffs. *The American Economic Review*, **63**(3):326-334.

Lucas Jr, R. E. (1975) An equilibrium model of the business cycle. *Journal of Political Economy*, **83**(6):1113-1144.

Lucas Jr, R. E. (1976) Econometric policy evaluation: A critique. *Carnegie-Rochester Conference Series on Public Policy*, **1**(0):19-46.

Lucas Jr, R. E. (1990) Supply-side economics: An analytical review. *Oxford Economic Papers*, **42**(2):293-316.

McCallum, B. T. (1976) Rational expectations and the natural rate hypothesis: Some consistent estimates. *Econometrica*, **44**(1):43-52.

MacKenzie, D. (2009) All those arrows. *London Review of Books*, **31**(12):20-22.

Maddison, A. (2006) *The World Economy, Volume 1: A Millenial Perspective and Volume 2: Historical Statistics*. OECD Publishing, Paris.

Maddison, A. (2007) *Contours of the World Economy 1-2030 AD: Essays in Macro-Economic History*. Oxford University Press, Oxford.

Mankiw, N. G. (2003) *Macroeconomics: Fifth edition*. Worth Publishers, New York.

Mankiw, N. G., Romer, D. and Weil, D. N. (1992) A contribution to the empirics of economic growth. *The Quarterly Journal of Economics*, **107**(2):407-437.

Mariger, R. P. (1986) *Consumption Behaviourand the Effects of Government Fiscal Policies*. Harvard University Press, Cambridge, MA.

Meghir, C. (2004) A retrospective on Friedman's theory of permanent income. *The Economic Journal*, **114**(496):F293-F306.

Melitz, J. and Zumer, F. (2002) Regional redistribution and stabilization by the center in Canada, France, the

UK and the US: A reassessment and new tests. *Journal of Public Economics*, **86**(2):263–286.

de Mello, L., Kongsrud, P. M. and Price, R. W. R. (2004) Saving behaviour and the effectiveness of fiscal policy. *OECD Economic Department Working Paper*, No. 397.

Mendoza, E. G. and Terrones, M. E. (2008) An anatomy of credit booms: Evidence from macro aggregates and micro data. *NBER Working Paper*, No. 14049.

Micco, A., Stein, E. and Ordoñez, G. (2003) The currency union effect on trade: early evidence from EMU. *Economic Policy*, **18**(37):315–356.

Miles, D. and Scott, A. *Macroeconomics: Understanding the Wealth of Nations*. John Wiley and Sons, Inc., New York.

Miles, D., Yang, J. and Marcheggiano, G. (2013) Optimal bank capital. *The Economic Journal*, **123**(567):1–37.

Minsky, H. P. (1982) *Can "It" Happen Again?: Essays on Instability and Finance*. M.E. Sharpe, Armonk, NY.

Mishkin, F. S. (1982) Does anticipated monetary policy matter? An econometric investigation. *Journal of Political Economy*, **90**(1):22–51.

Mishkin, F. S. (1999) International experiences with different monetary policy regimes. *Journal of Monetary Economics*, **43**(3):579–605.

Mishkin, F. S. (2011) Over the cliff: From the subprime to the global financial crisis. *The Journal of Economic Perspectives*, **25**(1):49–70.

Modigliani, F. and Brumberg, R. (1954) 'Utility Analysis and the Consumption Function: An Interpretation of Cross-Section Data' in *Post-Keynesian Economics*, pp. 383–436. Rutgers University Press, New Brunswick, NJ.

Modigliani, F. and Miller, M. H. (1958) The cost of capital, corporation finance and the theory of investment. *The American Economic Review*, **48**(3):261–297.

Mohanty, M. S., Cecchetti, S. G. and Zampolli, F. (2011) The real effects of debt. *BIS Working Papers*, 352.

Muellbauer, J. (2010) Household decisions, credit markets and the macroeconomy: Implications for the design of central bank models. *BIS Working Papers*, No. 306.

Muellbauer, J. and Nunziata, L. (2004) Forecasting (and explaining) US business cycles. *CEPR Discussion Paper*, No. 4584.

Muth, J. F. (1961) Rational expectations and the theory of price movements. *Econometrica*, **29**(3):315–335.

Nickell, S. (1997) Unemployment and labor market rigidities: Europe versus North America. *The Journal of Economic Perspectives*, **11**(3):55–74.

Nickell, S., Nunziata, L., Ochel, W. and Quintini, G. (2003) 'The Beveridge Curve, Unemployment and Wages in the OECD from the 1960s to the 1990s' in *Knowledge, Information and Expectations in Modern Macroeconomics*, eds P. Aghion et al. Princeton University Press, New Jersey.

Nickell, S. and van Ours, J. (2000a) The Netherlands and the United Kingdom: a European unemployment miracle? *Economic Policy*, **15**(30):135–180.

Nickell, S. and van Ours, J. (2000b) Why has unemployment in The Netherlands and the United Kingdom fallen so much? *Canadian Public Policy/Analyse de Politiques*, **26**:S201–S220.

Nijkamp, P. and Poot, J. (2005) The last word on the wage curve? *Journal of Economic Surveys*, **19**(3):421–450.

North, D. C. (1991) Institutions. *The Journal of Economic Perspectives*, **5**(1):97–112.

Obstfeld, M. (2001) International macroeconomics: Beyond the Mundell-Fleming model. *NBER Working Paper*, 8369.

Obstfeld, M. and Rogoff, K. (2000) New directions for stochastic open economy models. *Journal of International Economics*, **50**(1):117–153.

Obstfeld, M. and Rogoff, K. (2005) Global current account imbalances and exchange rate adjustments. *Brookings Paperson Economic Activity*, **2005**(1):67–123.

Obstfeld, M. and Rogoff, K. (2009) Global imbalances and the financial crisis: Products of common causes. *CEPR Discussion Paper No. 7606*.

OECD (1994) Jobs study. Technical report, OECD, Paris.

OECD (1999a) Employment protection and labour market performance employment outlook. Technical report, OECD, Paris.

OECD (1999b) Implementing the jobs study. Technical report, OECD, Paris.

OECD (2006) Employment outlook: Boosting jobs and income. Technical report, OECD, Paris.

Bank of England. (2012) The framework for the Bank of England's operations in the sterling money markets: Updated June 2012. Technical report, Bank of England, London.

Bank of England Monetary Policy Committee. (1999) The transmission mechanism of monetary policy. Technical report, Bank of England, London.

Orphanides, A. and Williams, J. C. (2005) 'Imperfect Knowledge, Inflation Expectations, and Monetary Policy' in *The Inflation-Targeting Debate*, eds Ben S. Bernanke and Michael Woodford. University of Chicago Press, Chicago.

Oswald, A. J. (1997) Happiness and economic performance. *The Economic Journal*, **107**(445):1815–1831.

Owyang, M. T., Ramey, V. A. and Zubairy, S. (2013) Are government spending multipliers greater during periods of slack? Evidence from twentieth-century historical data. *American Economic Review*, **103**(3):129–34.

Pavoni, N. (2008) Notes of dynamic methods in macroeconomics. *UCL lecture notes*.

Peach, E. K. and Stanley, T. (2009) Effciency wages, productivity and simultaneity: A meta-regression analysis. *Journal of Labor Research*, **30**:262–268.

Perotti, R. (2013) 'Fiscal Policy after the Financial Crisis' in *The 'Austerity Myth': Gain without Pain?*, pp. 307–354. University of Chicago Press, Chicago.

Phelps, E. S. (1967) Phillips curves, expectations of inflation and optimal unemployment over time. *Economica*, **34**(135):254–281.

Phillips, A. W. (1958) The relation between unemployment and the rate of change of money wage rates in the United Kingdom, 1861–1957. *Economica*, **25**(100):283–299.

Pindyck, R. S. (1991) Irreversibility, uncertainty, and investment. *Journal of Economic Literature*, **29**(3):1110–1148.

Pisani-Ferry, J. (2012) 'The Euro crisis and the new impossible trinity' http://www.bruegel.org/publications/publication-detail/publication/674-the-euro-crisis-and-the-new-impossible-trinity/

Pisani-Ferry, J. and Sapir, A. (2006) Last Exit to Lisbon. *Bruegel Policy Brief 2006/02*, March.

Pissarides, C. A. (1990) *Equilibrium Unemployment Theory: Second Edition*. MIT Press, Cambridge, MA.

Pissarides, C. A. (2001) Employment protection. *Labour Economics*, **8**(2):131–159.

Posen, A. (1998) Central bank independence and disinflationary credibility: a missing link? *Oxford Economic Papers*, **50**(3):335–359.

Posen, A. (2003) It takes more than a bubble to become Japan. *IIE Working Paper 03-9*.

Posen, A. and Ito, T. (2004) Inflation targeting and Japan: Why has the Bank of Japan not adopted inflation targeting? *NBER Working Paper No. 10818*.

Prescott, E. (1986) Theory ahead of business cycle measurement. *Federal Reserve Bank of Minneapolis Quarterly Review*, Fall:922.

Prescott, E. (1998) Business cycle research: Methods and problems. *Federal Reserve Bank of Minneapolis Working Paper 590*.

Raff, D. M. G. and Summers, L. H. (1987) Did Henry Ford pay efficiency wages? *Journal of Labor Economics*, **5**(4):S57–S86.

Rajan, R. (2010) *Fault lines*. HarperCollins Publishers, India.

Ranciere, R. and Kumhof, M. (2010) *Inequality, leverage and crises*. International Monetary Fund.

Ramey, V. A. (2011) Can government purchases stimulate the economy? *Journal of Economic Literature*, **49**(3):673–85.

Rau, N. (1985) Simplifying the theory of the government budget restraint. *Oxford Economic Papers*, **37**(2):210–229.

Read, D. and van Leeuwen, B. (1998) Predicting hunger: The effects of appetite and delay on choice. *Organizational Behavior and Human Decision Processes*, **76**(2):189–205.

Reinhart, C. M. and Rogoff, K. (2009a) *This Time is Different: Eight Centuries of Financial Folly*. Princeton University Press, Princeton, NJ.

Reinhart, C. M. and Rogoff, K. (2009b) The aftermath of financial crises. *The American Economic Review*, **99**(2):466–472.

Reinhart, C. M. and Rogoff, K. (2010) Growth in a time of debt. *The American Economic Review*, **100**(2):573–578.

Rogoff, K. (2002) Dornbusch's overshooting model after twenty-five years. *International Monetary Fund's Second Annual Research Conference Mundell-Fleming Lecture*.

Röhn, O. (2010) New evidence on the private saving offset and Ricardian equivalence. *OECD Economics Department Working Papers*, 762.

Romer, C. and Romer, D. (2010) The macroeconomic effects of tax changes: Estimates based on a new measure of fiscal shocks. *The American Economic Review*, **100**(june):763–801.

Romer, D. (2011) *Advanced Macroeconomics: 4th edition*. McGraw-Hill/Irwin, New York.

Romer, P. M. (1990) Endogenous technological change. *Journal of Political Economy*, **98**(5):S71–S102.

Rose, A. K. and Stanley, T. D. (2005) A Meta-Analysis of the Effect of Common Currencies on International Trade. *Journal of Economic Surveys*, **19**(3):347–365.

Rowthorn, R. and Coutts, K. (2004) De-industrialisation and the balance of payments in advanced economies. *Cambridge Journal of Economics*, **28**(5):767–790.

Rudd, J. and Whelan, K. (2007) Modeling inflation dynamics: A critical review of recent research. *Journal of Money, Credit and Banking*, **39**:155–170.

Ryan-Collins, J., Greenham, T., Werner, R. and Jackson, A. (2011) *Where Does Money Come From? A Guide to the UK Monetary and Banking System*, New Economics Foundation, London.

Sargent, T. (1976) 'Testing for neutrality and rationality' in *The Federal Reserve Bank of Minneapolis Studies in Monetary Policy: Rational Expectations and the Theory of Economic Policy: Arguments and Evidence*. The Federal Reserve Bank of Minneapolis.

Sargent, T. J. and Wallace, N. (1975) 'Rational' expectations, the optimal monetary instrument, and the optimal money supply rule. *Journal of Political Economy*, **83**(2):241–254.

Sauer, S. and Sturm, J.-E. (2007) Using Taylor rules to understand European Central Bank monetary policy. *German Economic Review*, **8**(3):375–398.

Schularick, M. and Taylor, A. M. (2012) Credit booms gone bust: Monetary policy, leverage cycles, and financial crises, 1870–2008. *American Economic Review*, **102**(2):1029–61.

Schumpeter, J. A. (1934) *The Theory of Economic Development: 1961 Edition*. OUP Galaxy, New York.

Schumpeter, J. A. (1942) *Capitalism, Socialism and Democracy: 2003 Edition*. George Allen and Unwin, London.

Seabright, P. (2010) *The Company of Strangers: A Natural History of Economic Life (Revised Edition)*. Princeton University Press, Princeton, NJ.

Seater, J. J. (1993) Ricardian equivalence. *Journal of Economic Literature*, **31**(1):142–190.

Shapiro, C. and Stiglitz, J. E. (1984) Equilibrium unemployment as a worker discipline device. *The American Economic Review*, **74**(3):433–444.

Sheets, N. and Sockin, R. (2012) Escaping the zero lower bound—are bulging central bank balance sheets a good substitute for rate cuts? *Citi group - Global Economics - Empirical and Thematic Perspectives*.

Shiller, R. J. (1997) 'Why Do People Dislike Inflation?' in *Reducing Inflation: Motivation and Strategy*, eds Christina D. Romer and David H. Romer. University of Chicago Press, Chicago.

Shin, H. S. (2009a) Discussion of the leverage cycle by John Geanakoplos. *NBER Macroeconomics Annual*, **24**:75–84.

Shin, H. S. (2009b) Reflections on Northern Rock: the bank run that heralded the global financial crisis. *The Journal of Economic Perspectives*, **23**(1):101–119.

Shin, H. S. (2010) Financial intermediation and the post-crisis financial system. *BIS*, 304.

Shin, H. S. (2010) *Risk and Liquidity: Clarendon Lectures in Finance*. Oxford University Press, Oxford.

Shin, H. S. (2012) Global banking glut and loan risk premium. *IMF Economic Review*, **60**(2).155–192.

Smets, F. and Wouters, R. (2003) An estimated dynamic stochastic general equilibrium model of the euro area. *Journal of the European Economic Association*, **1**(5):1123–1175.

Smets, F. and Wouters, R. (2007) Shocks and frictions in us business cycles: A Bayesian DSGE approach. *The American Economic Review*, **97**(3):586–606.

Sokoloff, K. L. and Engerman, S. L. (2000) History lessons: Institutions, factors endowments, and paths of development in the new world. *The Journal of Economic Perspectives*, **14**(3):217–232.

Solow, R. (1956) A contribution to the theory of economic growth. *The Quarterly Journal of Economics*, **70**(1):65–94.

Solow, R. (1979) Alternative approaches to macroeconomic theory: A partial view. The Canadian Journal of Economics/Revue Canadienne d'Economique, **12**(3):339–354.

Solow, R. (1998) *Monopolistic Competition and Macroeconomic Theory: Federico Caff Lectures*. Cambridge University Press, Cambridge.

Solow, R. (2000) *Growth Theory: An Exposition: 2nd Edition*. Oxford University Press, Oxford.

Song, Z., Storesletten, K. and Zilibotti, F. (2012) Rotten parents and disciplined children: A politico-economic theory of public expenditure and debt. *Econometrica*, **80**(6):2785–2804.

Soskice, D. (1990) Wage determination: The changing role of institutions in advanced industrialized countries. *Oxford Review of Economic Policy*, **6**(4):36–61.

Soskice, D. and Iversen, T (2000) The Non-Neutrality of Monetary Policy with Large Price or Wage Setters, *Quarterly Journal of Economics*, **115**(1):265–284.

Soyer, E. and Hogarth, R. M. (2012) The illusion of predictability: How regression statistics mislead experts. *International Journal of Forecasting*, **28**(3):695–711.

Stanley, T. D. (2004) Does unemployment hysteresis falsify the natural rate hypothesis? A meta-regression analysis. *Journal of Economic Surveys*, **18**(4):589–612.

Stehn, S. J., Hatzius, J., Wilson, D. and Carlson, S. (2011) The speed limit of fiscal consolidation. *Goldman Sachs: Global Economics Paper No. 207*.

Stiglitz, J. E. (2009) The global crisis, social protection and jobs. *International Labour Review*, **148**(1-2): 1–13.

Stockhammer, E. and Sturn, S. (2012) The impact of monetary policy on unemployment hysteresis. *Applied Economics*, **44**(21):2743–2756.

Stulz, R. M. (2010) Credit default swaps and the credit crisis. *The Journal of Economic Perspectives*, **24**(1):73–92.

Sturm, J.-E. and De Haan, J. (2011) Does central bank communication really lead to better forecasts of policy decisions? new evidence based on a Taylor rule model for the ECB. *Review of World Economics*, **147**(1):41–58.

Summers, L. H. (1986) Some skeptical observations on real business cycle theory. *Federal Reserve Bank of Minneapolis Quarterly Review*, **10**(4):23–27.

Svensson, L. E. O. (1997) Inflation forecast targeting: Implementing and monitoring inflation targets. *European Economic Review*, **41**(6):1111– 1146.

Svensson, L. E. O. (2003) Escaping from a liquidity trap and deflation: The foolproof way and others. *The Journal of Economic Perspectives*, **17**(4):145–166.

Swan, T. W. (1956) Economic growth and capital accumulation. *Economic Record*, **32**(2):334–361.

Taylor, J. B. (1993) Discretion versus policy rules in practice. *Carnegie-Rochester Conference Series on Public Policy*, **39**(0):195–214.

Taylor, J. B. (1997) The policy rule mix: A macroeconomic policy evaluation. *Prepared for the Robert A. Mundell Festschrift Conference*.

Taylor, J. B. (1999) 'A Historical Analysis of Monetary Policy Rules' in *Monetary Policy Rules*, pp. 319–348. National Bureau of Economic Research, 1999.

Taylor, J. B. (2006) Lessons from the recovery from the lost decade in Japan: The case of the great intervention and money injection. *Background paper for the International Conference of the Economic and Social Research Institute, Cabinet Office, Government of Japan*.

Tett, G. (2009) *Fool's Gold: How Unrestrained Greed Corrupted a Dream, Shattered Global Markets and Unleashed a Catastrophe*. Little, Brown, London.

Tobin, T. (1969) A general equilibrium approach to monetary theory. *Journal of Money, Credit and Banking*, **1**(1):15–29.

Tobin, T. and Brainard, W. C. (1977) 'Asset Market and the Cost of Capital' in *Economic Progress, Private Values and Public Policy: Essays in Honor of William Fellner*, eds Bela Balassa and Richard Nelson, pp. 235–62. North-Holland, New York.

Tobin, J., Phelps, E. S., Poole, W., Feldstein, M., Houthakker, H., Modigliani, F., Hendershott, P.,

Friedman, B., Perry, G., Duesenberry, J., Fellner, W., Gordon, R., Branson, W., Baily, M. and Nordhaus, W. (1980) Stabilization policy ten years after. *Brookings Papers on Economic Activity*, **1980**(1):19–89.

Tuckett, D. (2012) Financial markets are markets in stories: Some possible advantages of using interviews to supplement existing economic data sources. *Journal of Economic Dynamics and Control*, **36**(8):1077–1087.

Vickers, J. (1986) Signalling in a model of monetary policy with incomplete information. *Oxford Economic Papers*, **38**(3):443–455.

Vickers, J. (2012) Some economics of banking reform. *University of Oxford Department of Economics Discussion Paper Series*, No. 632.

de Vroey, M. (2004a) *Involuntary Unemployment: The Elusive Quest for a Theory*. Routledge, London.

de Vroey, M. (2004b) Involuntary unemployment: The elusive quest for a theory. *Université Catholique de Louvain Discussion Paper, Department of Economics 2005-04*.

Walsh, C. E. (2010) *Monetary Theory and Policy (3rd revised edition)*. MIT Press, Cambridge, MA.

Weber, A. (2012) Stock-flow adjustments and fiscal transparency: A cross-country comparison. *IMF Working Paper No. 12/39*.

Weil, D. N. (2012) *Economic Growth: International Edition: Third Edition*. Pearson Education, Harlow.

White, W. R. (2008) Globalisation and the determinants of domestic inflation. *BIS Working Paper*, No. 250.

Williamson, S. D. (2011) *Macroeconomics: Fourth Edition*. Pearson Education, Inc.

Winckler, A. (2011) The joint production of confidence: lessons from nineteenth-century US commercial banks for twenty-first-century Euro area governments, *Financial History Review*, **18**(03):249-276.

Woodford, M. (1999) 'Revolution and Evolution in Twentieth-Century Macroeconomics' [Presented at a conference, *Frontiers of the Mind in the Twenty-First Century*, US Library of Congress, Washington, DC, June 1999.]

Woodford, M. (2007) The case for forecast targeting as a monetary policy strategy. *The Journal of Economic Perspectives*, **21**(4):3–24.

Woodford, M. (2008) Forward guidance for monetary policy: Is it still possible? *Vox*, http://www.voxeu.org/

# Index